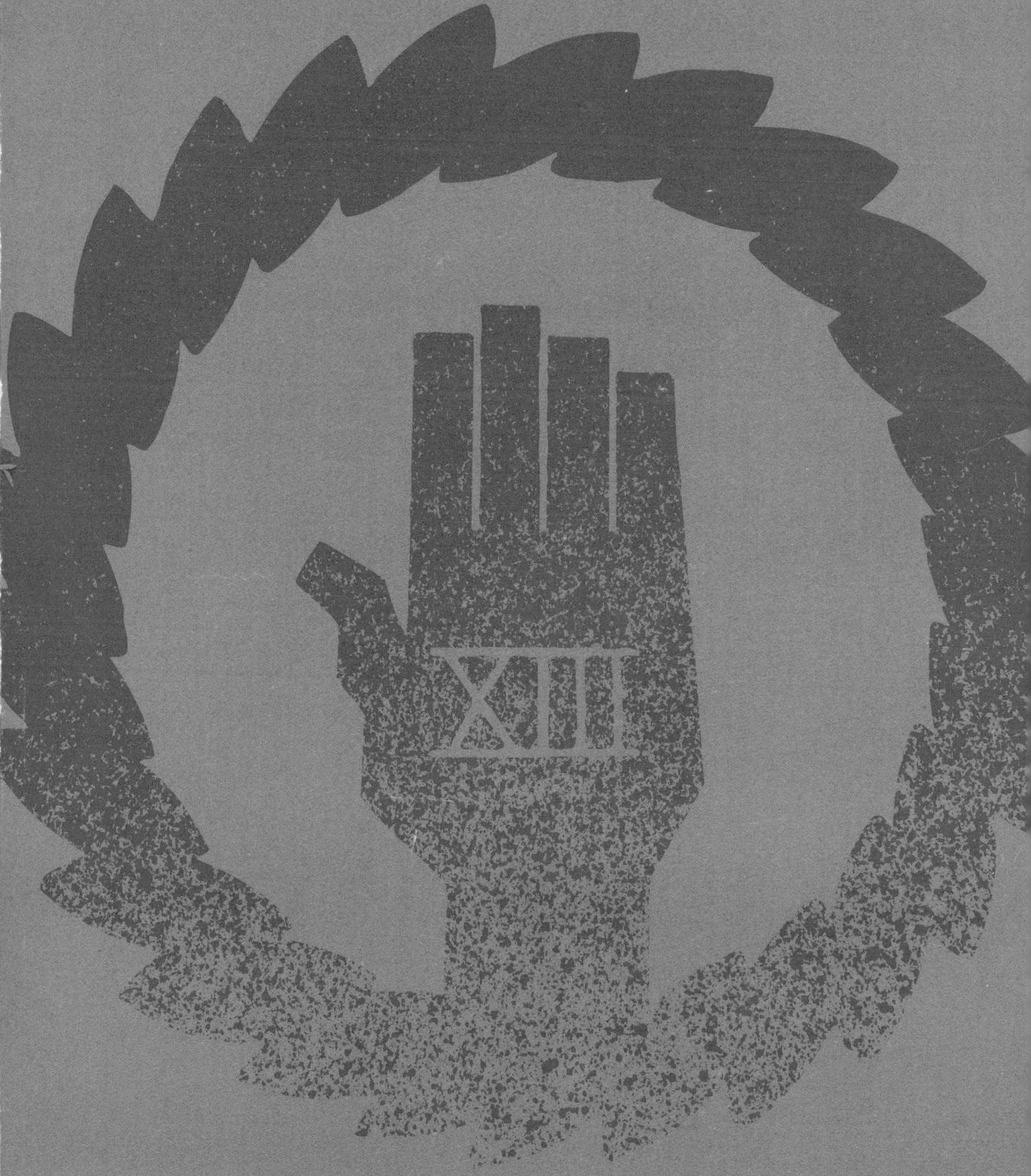
XIII

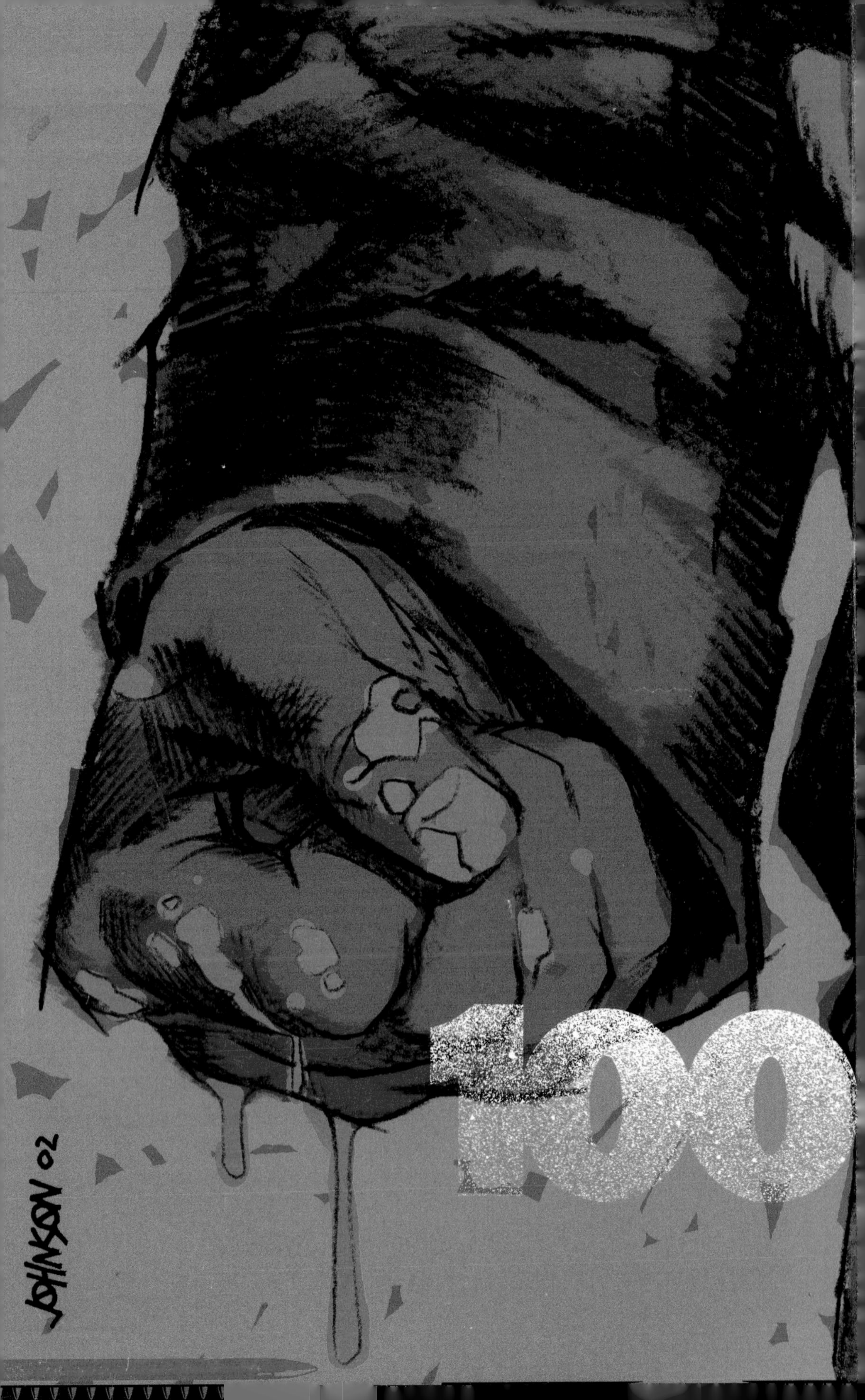
100
JOHNSON 02

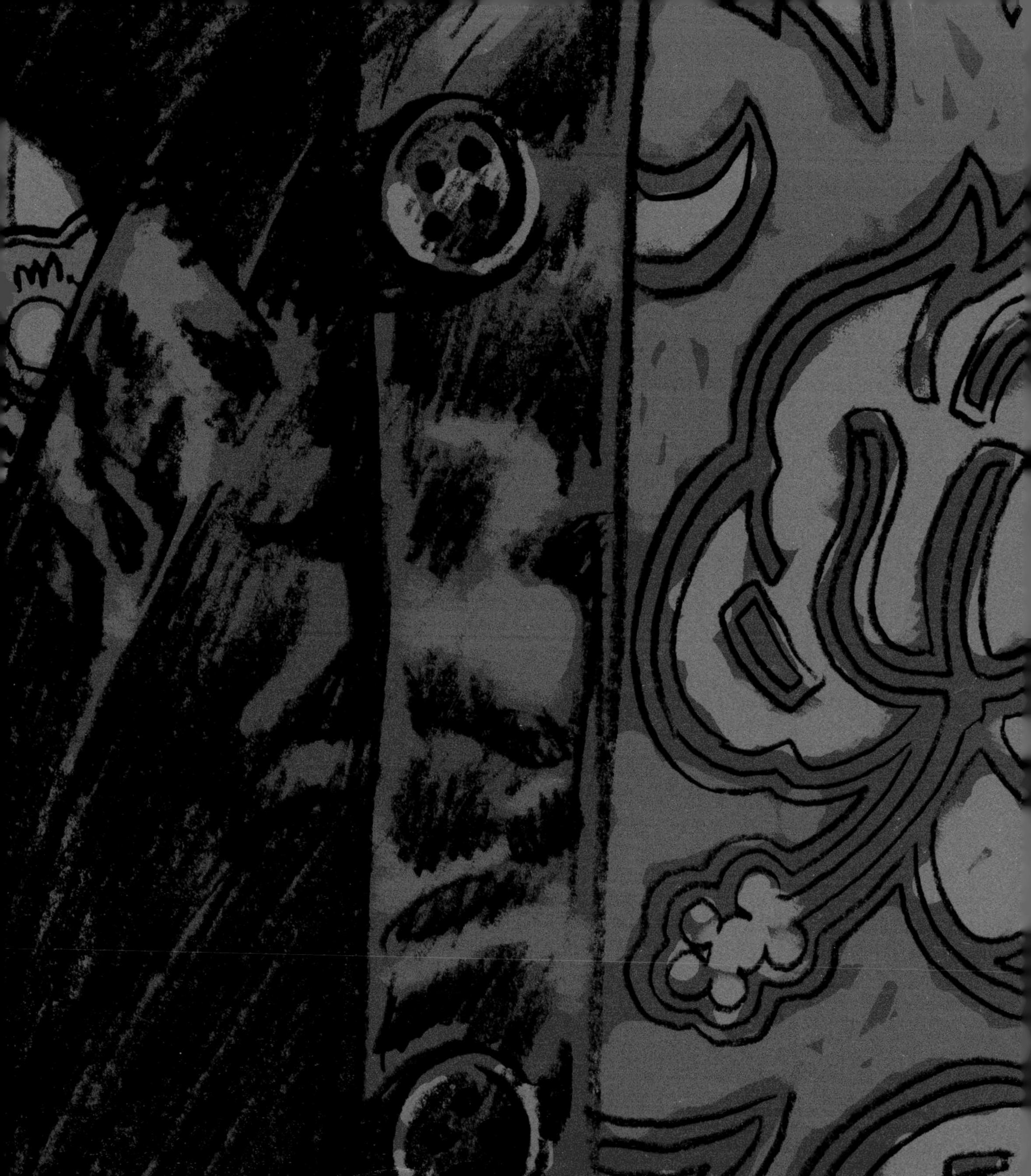

BULLETS

BOOK THREE

BRIAN AZZARELLO WRITER
EDUARDO RISSO ARTIST
PATRICIA MULVIHILL COLORIST
CLEM ROBINS LETTERER
DAVE JOHNSON COVER ART AND ORIGINAL SERIES COVERS
100 BULLETS CREATED BY **BRIAN AZZARELLO** AND **EDUARDO RISSO**

Will Dennis Editor – Original Series
Zachary Rau **Casey Seijas** Assistant Editors – Original Series
Scott Nybakken Editor
Robbin Brosterman Design Director – Books
Louis Prandi Publication Design

Shelly Bond VP and Executive Editor – Vertigo

Diane Nelson President
Dan DiDio and **Jim Lee** Co-Publishers
Geoff Johns Chief Creative Officer
Amit Desai Senior VP – Marketing and Global Franchise Management
Nairi Gardiner Senior VP – Finance
Sam Ades VP – Digital Marketing
Bobbie Chase VP – Talent Development
Mark Chiarello Senior VP – Art, Design and Collected Editions
John Cunningham VP – Content Strategy
Anne DePies VP – Strategy Planning and Reporting
Don Falletti VP – Manufacturing Operations
Lawrence Ganem VP – Editorial Administration and Talent Relations
Alison Gill Senior VP – Manufacturing and Operations
Hank Kanalz Senior VP – Editorial Strategy and Administration
Jay Kogan VP – Legal Affairs
Derek Maddalena Senior VP – Sales and Business Development
Dan Miron VP – Sales Planning and Trade Development
Nick Napolitano VP – Manufacturing Administration
Carol Roeder VP – Marketing
Eddie Scannell VP – Mass Account and Digital Sales
Susan Sheppard VP – Business Affairs
Courtney Simmons Senior VP – Publicity and Communications
Jim (Ski) Sokolowski VP – Comic Book Specialty and Newsstand Sales

Special thanks to Eduardo A. Santillan Marcus for his translating assistance.

SUSTAINABLE FORESTRY INITIATIVE

Certified Chain of Custody
20% Certified Forest Content,
80% Certified Sourcing
www.sfiprogram.org
SFI-01042
APPLIES TO TEXT STOCK ONLY

Library of Congress Cataloging-in-Publication Data

Azzarello, Brian.
  100 bullets Book three / Brian Azzarello, Eduardo Risso.
    p. cm.
  "Originally published in single magazine form in 100 Bullets 37-58."
  ISBN 978-1-4012-5795-8 (alk. paper)
  1. Crime—Comic books, strips, etc. 2. Graphic novels. I. Risso, Eduardo. II. Title.
  PN6728.A14A995 2012
  741.5'973—dc23
                                 2012021221

Table of Contents

XIII

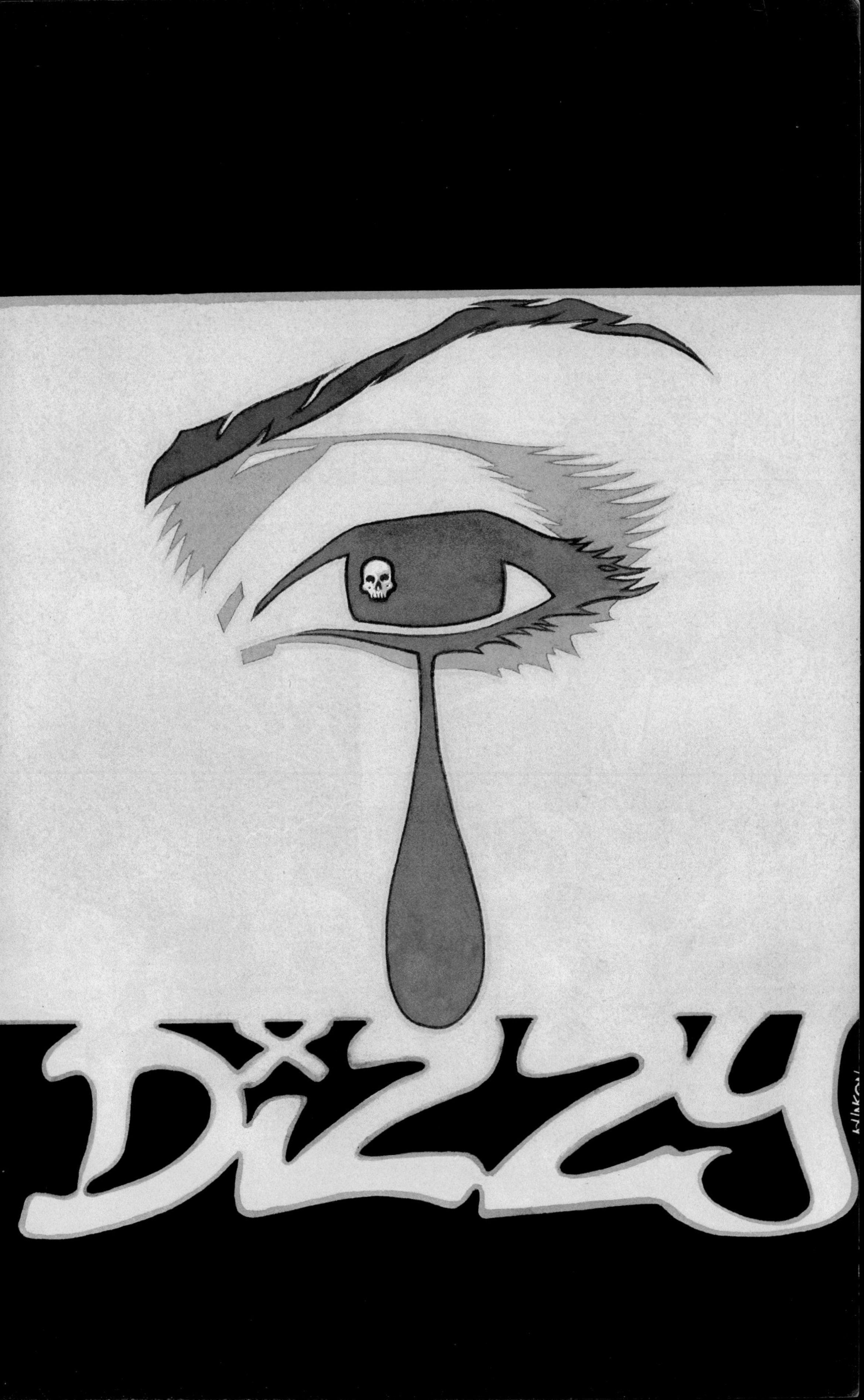
Dizzy

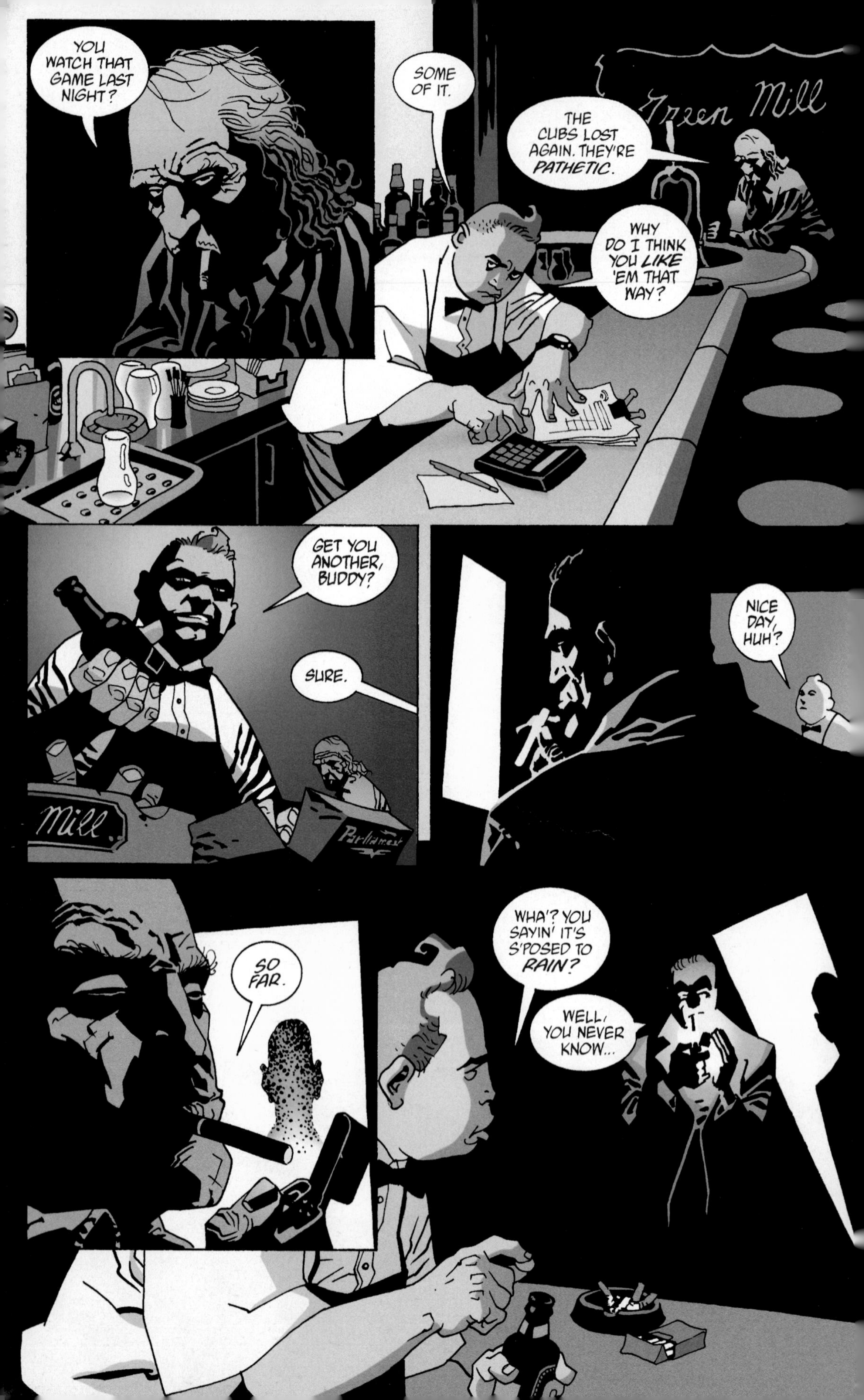
YOU WATCH THAT GAME LAST NIGHT?
SOME OF IT.
Green Mill
THE CUBS LOST AGAIN. THEY'RE PATHETIC.
WHY DO I THINK YOU LIKE 'EM THAT WAY?
GET YOU ANOTHER, BUDDY?
SURE.
Mill
Parliament
NICE DAY, HUH?
SO FAR.
WHA'? YOU SAYIN' IT'S S'POSED TO RAIN?
WELL, YOU NEVER KNOW...

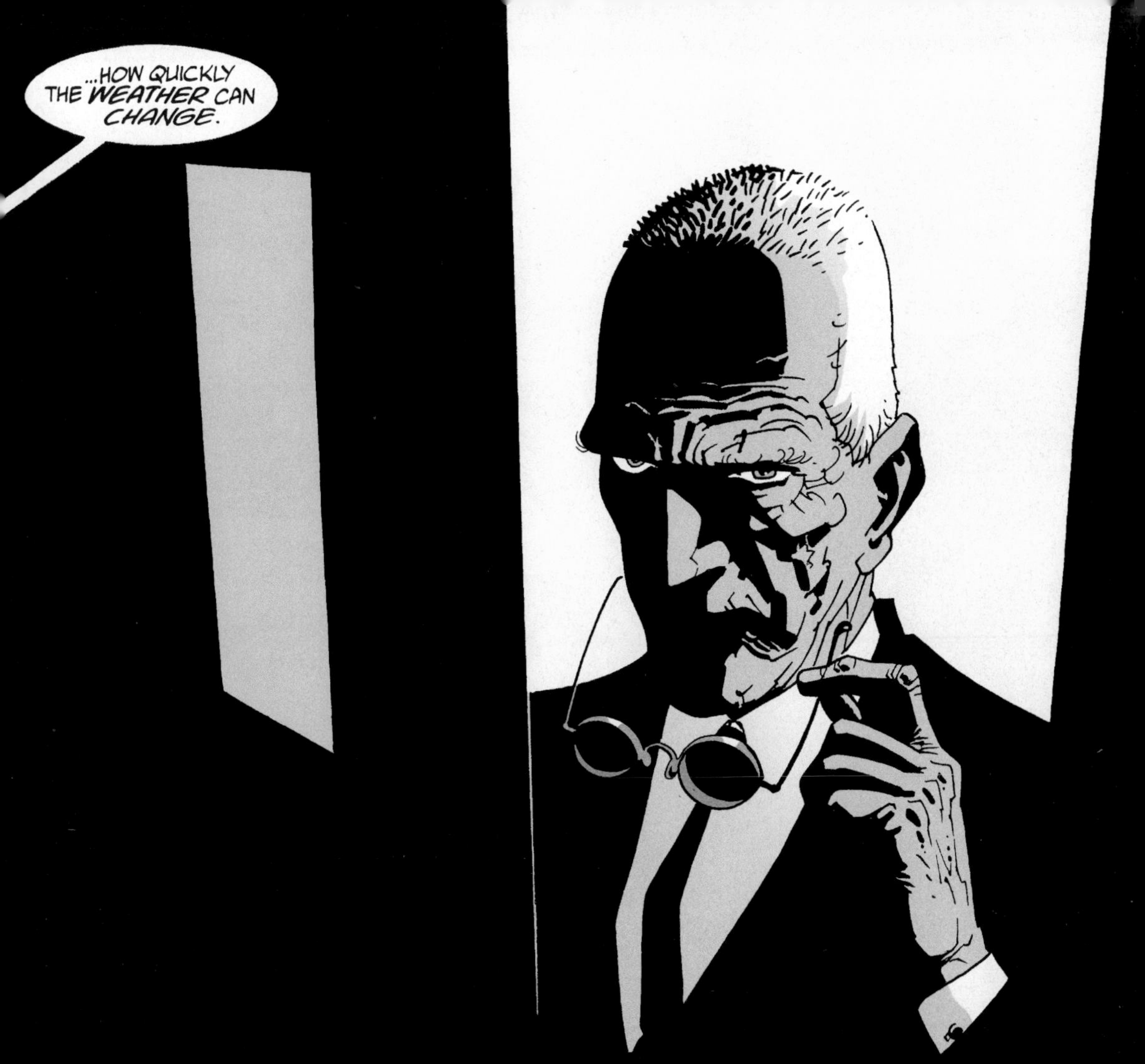
...HOW QUICKLY THE WEATHER CAN CHANGE.

ON ACCIDENTAL PURPOSE

BRIAN AZZARELLO, WRITER **EDUARDO RISSO**, ARTIST
PATRICIA MULVIHILL, COLORIST CLEM ROBINS, LETTERER
DIGITAL CHAMELEON, SEPARATIONS DAVE JOHNSON, COVER ARTIST
ZACHARY RAU, ASSISTANT EDITOR WILL DENNIS, EDITOR

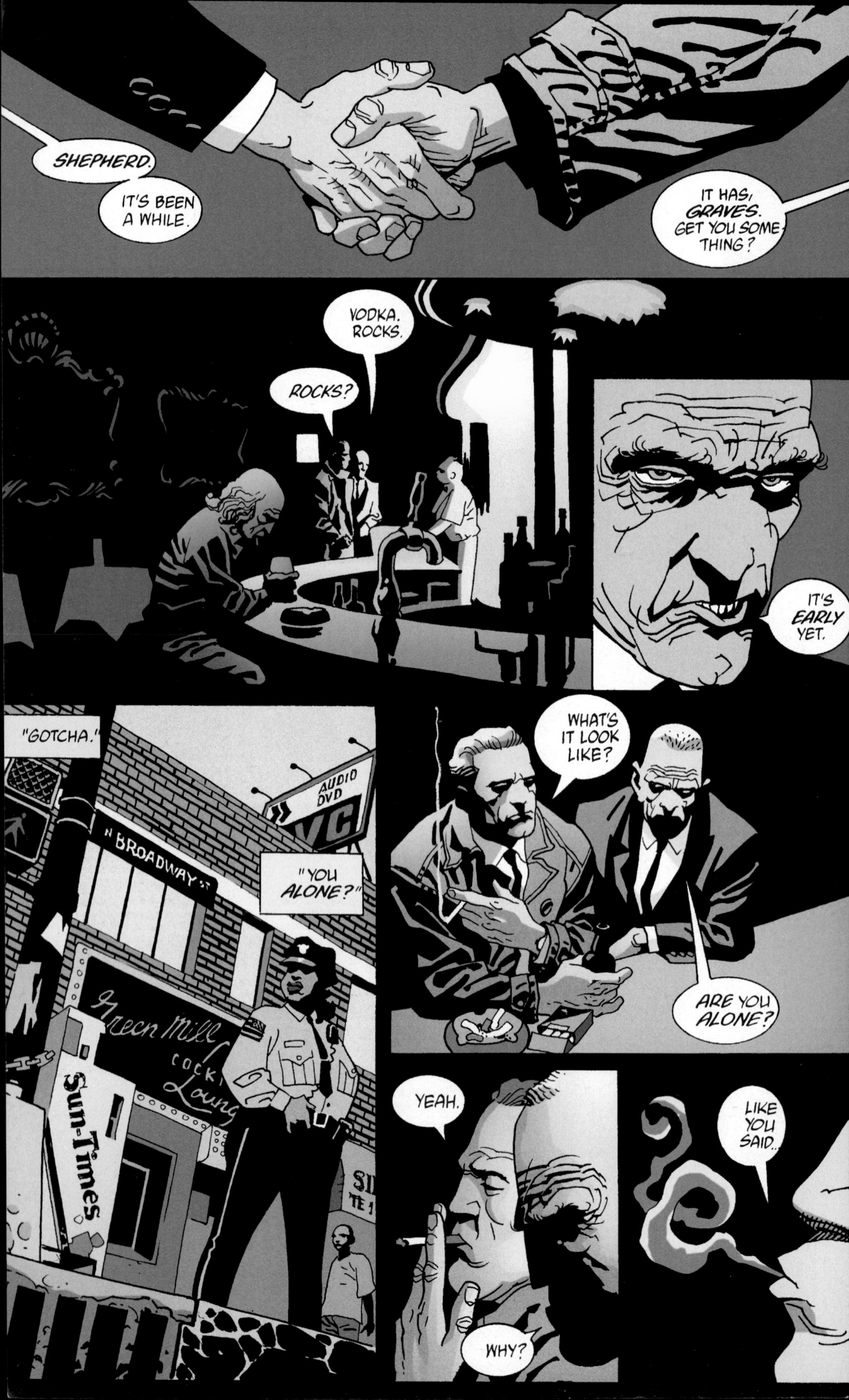
SHEPHERD.
IT'S BEEN A WHILE.
IT HAS, GRAVES. GET YOU SOMETHING?
VODKA. ROCKS.
ROCKS?
IT'S EARLY YET.
"GOTCHA."
AUDIO DVD
N BROADWAY ST
"YOU ALONE?"
Green Mill
Cocktail Lounge
Sun-Times
WHAT'S IT LOOK LIKE?
ARE YOU ALONE?
YEAH.
LIKE YOU SAID...
WHY?

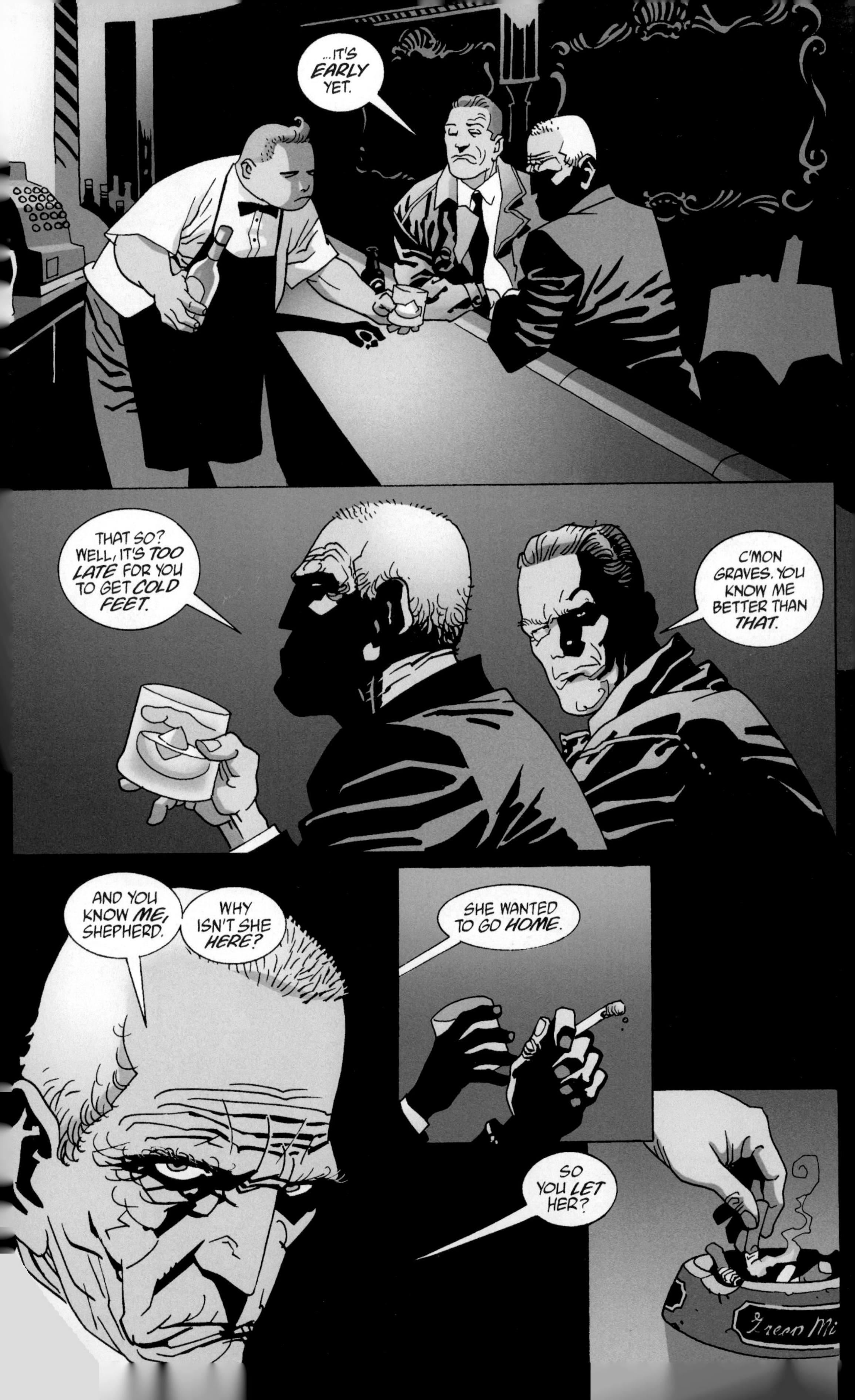
...IT'S EARLY YET.
THAT SO? WELL, IT'S TOO LATE FOR YOU TO GET COLD FEET.
C'MON GRAVES. YOU KNOW ME BETTER THAN THAT.
AND YOU KNOW ME, SHEPHERD.
WHY ISN'T SHE HERE?
SHE WANTED TO GO HOME.
SO YOU LET HER?

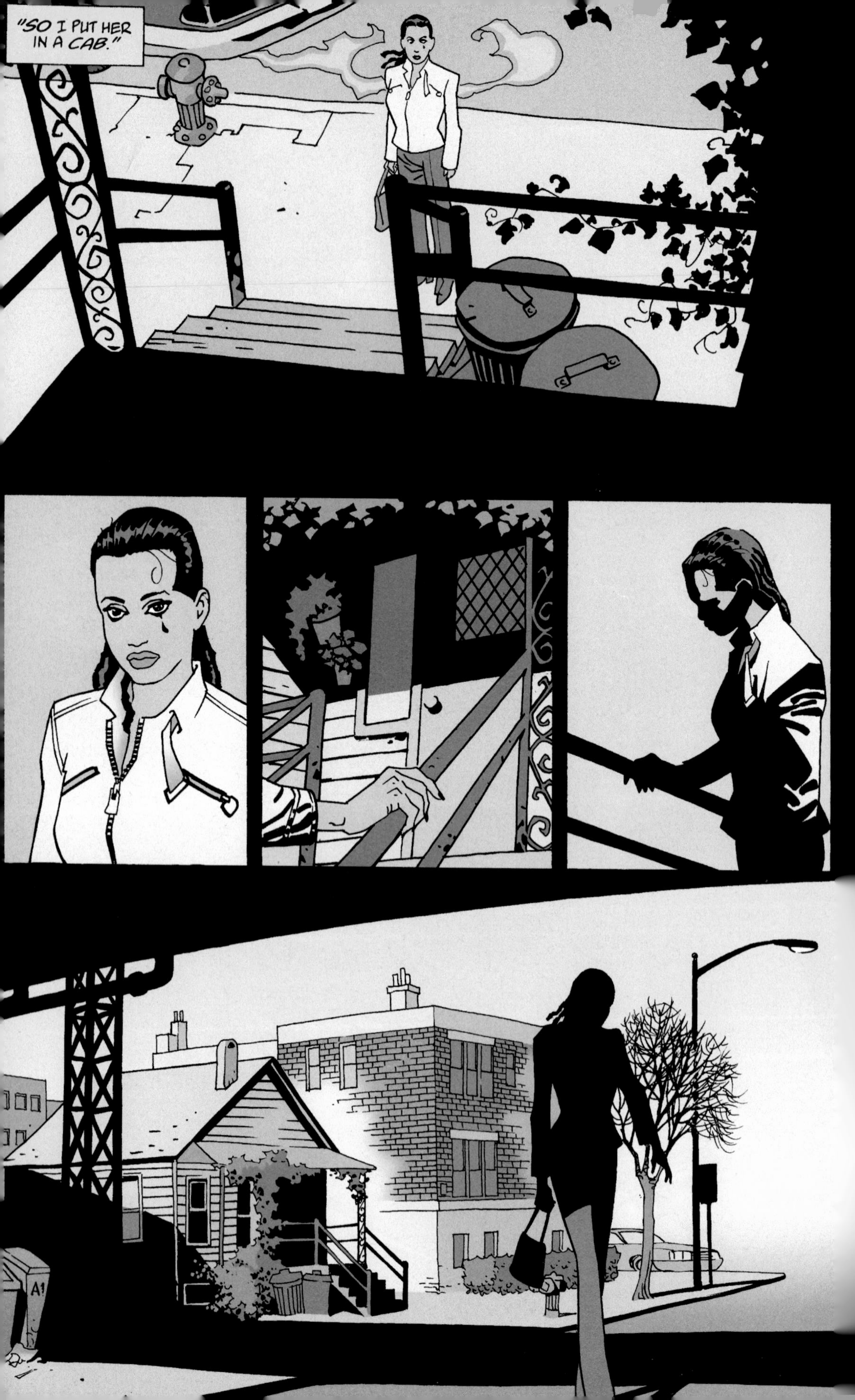
"SO I PUT HER IN A CAB."

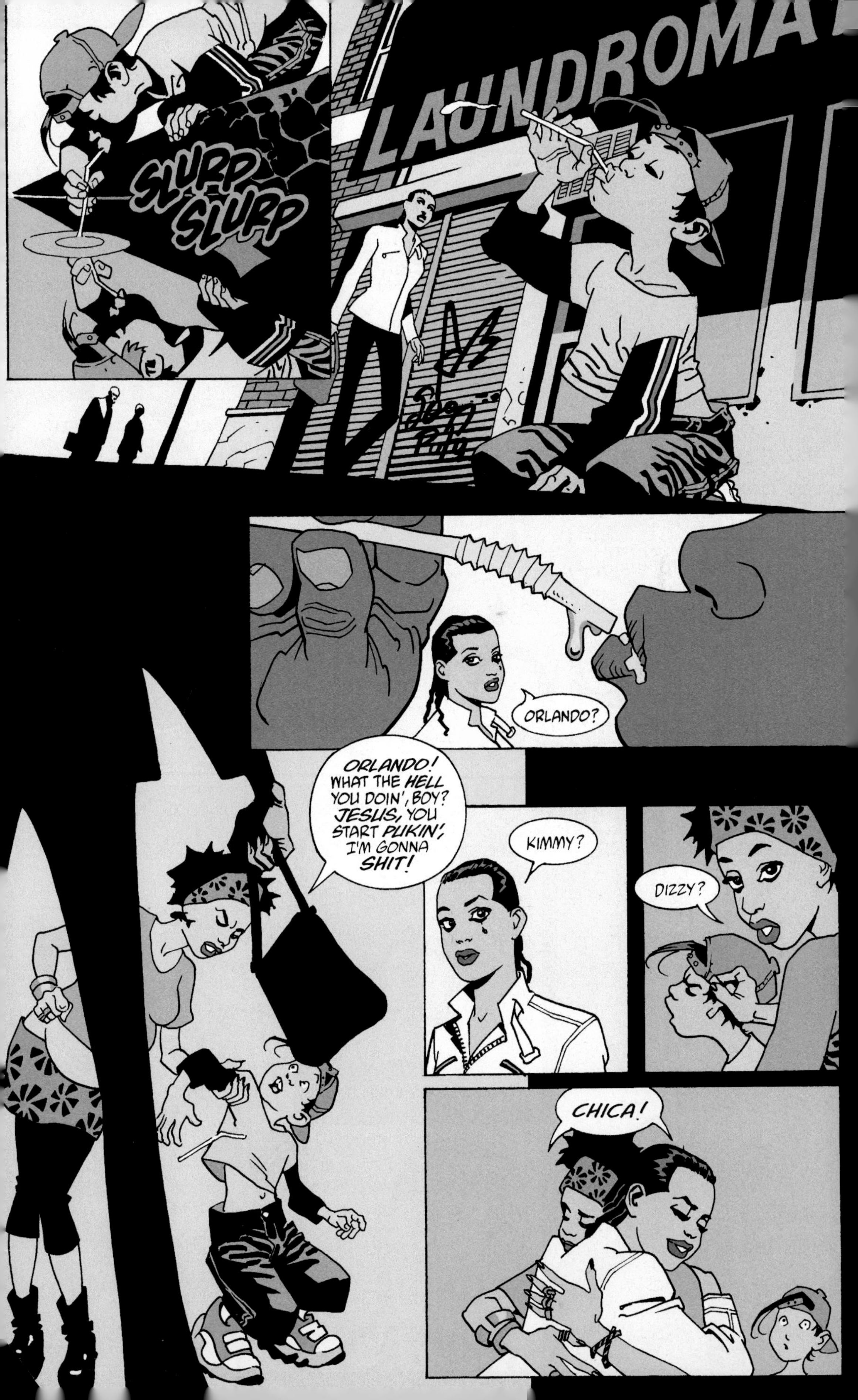
SLURP SLURP
LAUNDROMA
ORLANDO?
ORLANDO! WHAT THE HELL YOU DOIN', BOY? JESUS, YOU START PUKIN', I'M GONNA SHIT!
KIMMY?
DIZZY?
CHICA!

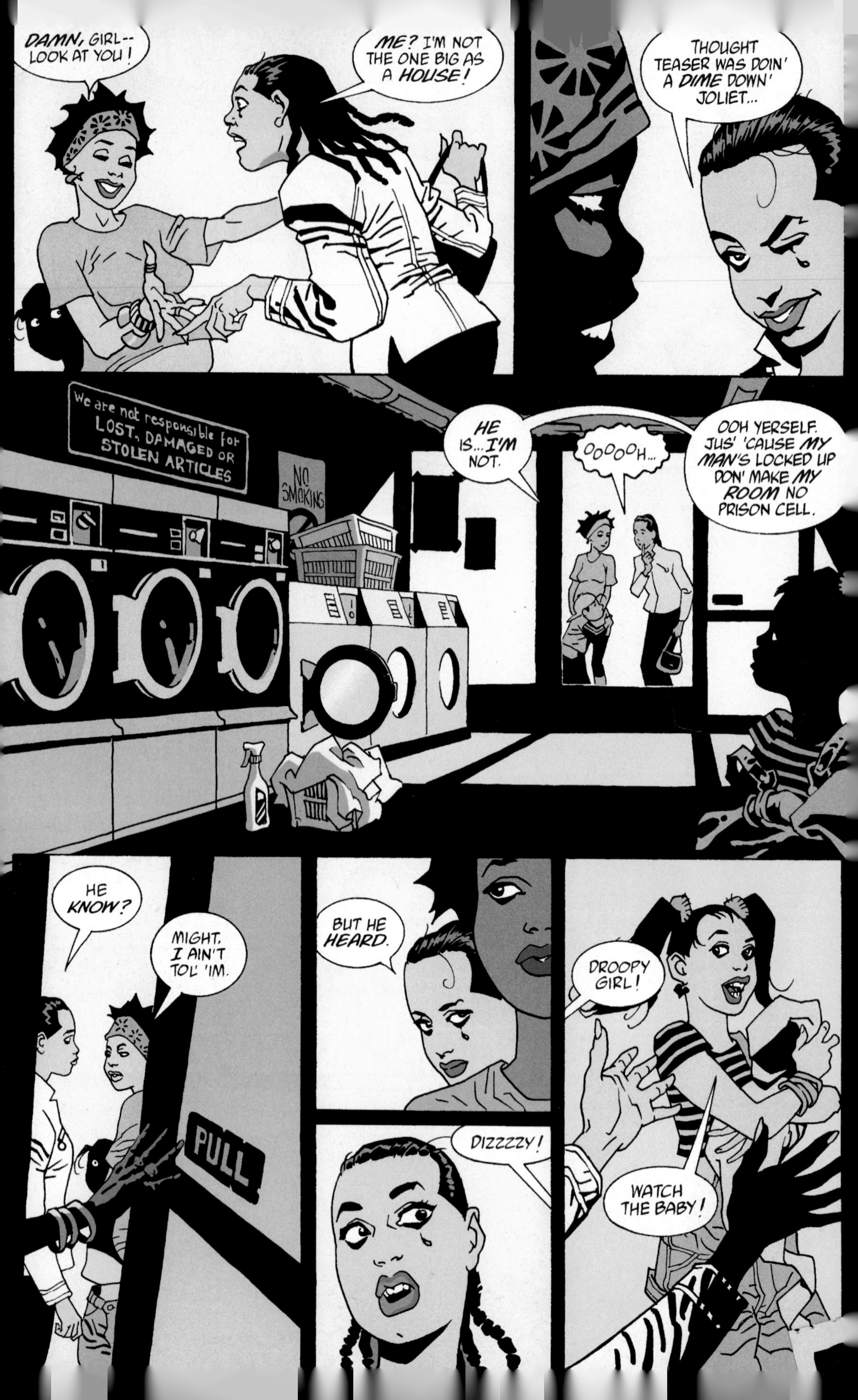
DAMN, GIRL-- LOOK AT YOU!
ME? I'M NOT THE ONE BIG AS A HOUSE!
THOUGHT TEASER WAS DOIN' A DIME DOWN' JOLIET...
We are not responsible for LOST, DAMAGED OR STOLEN ARTICLES
NO SMOKING
HE IS... I'M NOT.
OOOOOH...
OOH YERSELF. JUS' 'CAUSE MY MAN'S LOCKED UP DON' MAKE MY ROOM NO PRISON CELL.
HE KNOW?
MIGHT. I AIN'T TOL' 'IM.
PULL
BUT HE HEARD.
DROOPY GIRL!
DIZZZZY!
WATCH THE BABY!

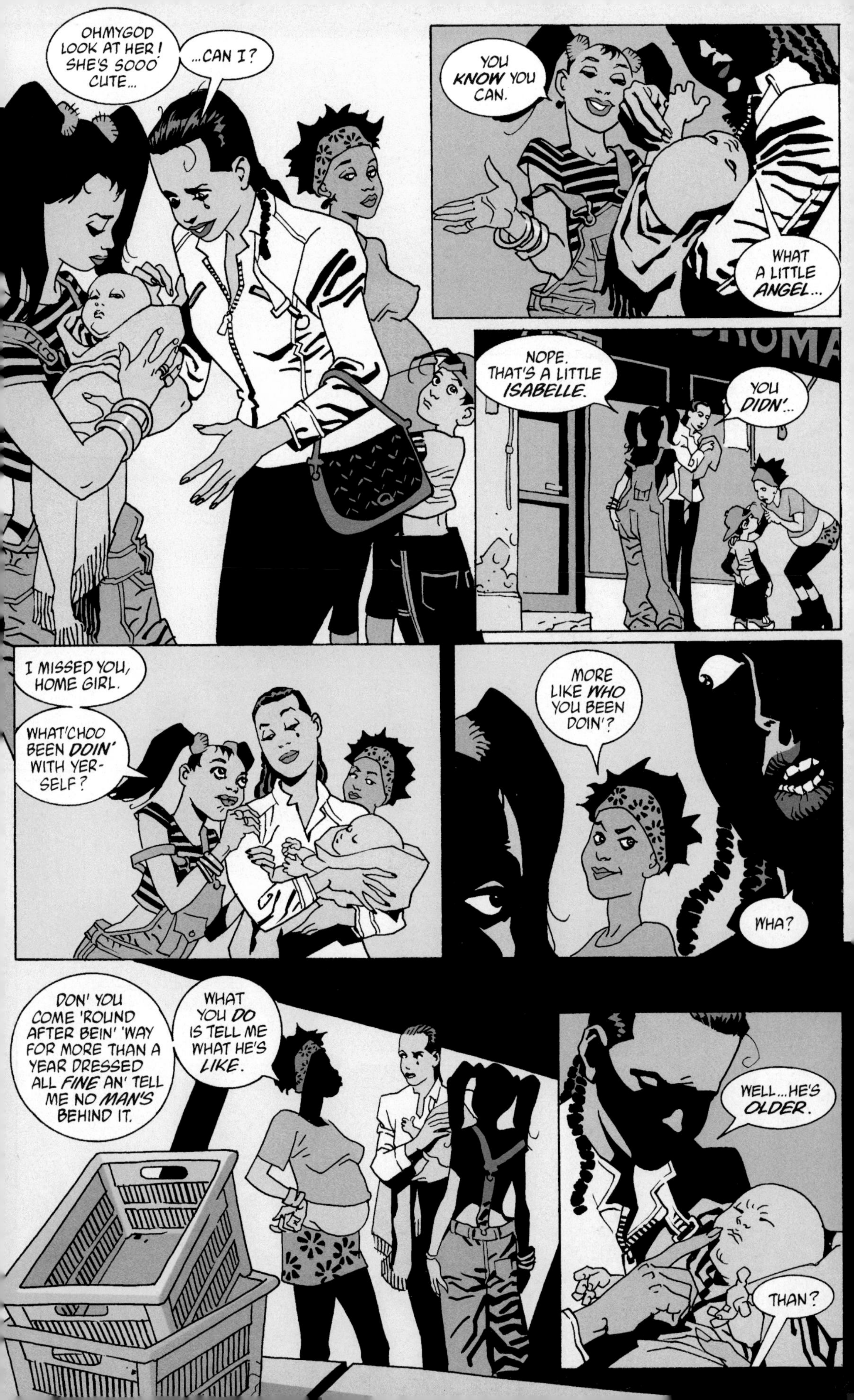

OHMYGOD LOOK AT HER! SHE'S SOOO CUTE...
...CAN I?
YOU KNOW YOU CAN.
WHAT A LITTLE ANGEL...
NOPE. THAT'S A LITTLE ISABELLE.
YOU DIDN'...
I MISSED YOU, HOME GIRL.
WHAT'CHOO BEEN DOIN' WITH YER-SELF?
MORE LIKE WHO YOU BEEN DOIN'?
WHA?
DON' YOU COME 'ROUND AFTER BEIN' 'WAY FOR MORE THAN A YEAR DRESSED ALL FINE AN' TELL ME NO MAN'S BEHIND IT.
WHAT YOU DO IS TELL ME WHAT HE'S LIKE.
WELL...HE'S OLDER.
THAN?

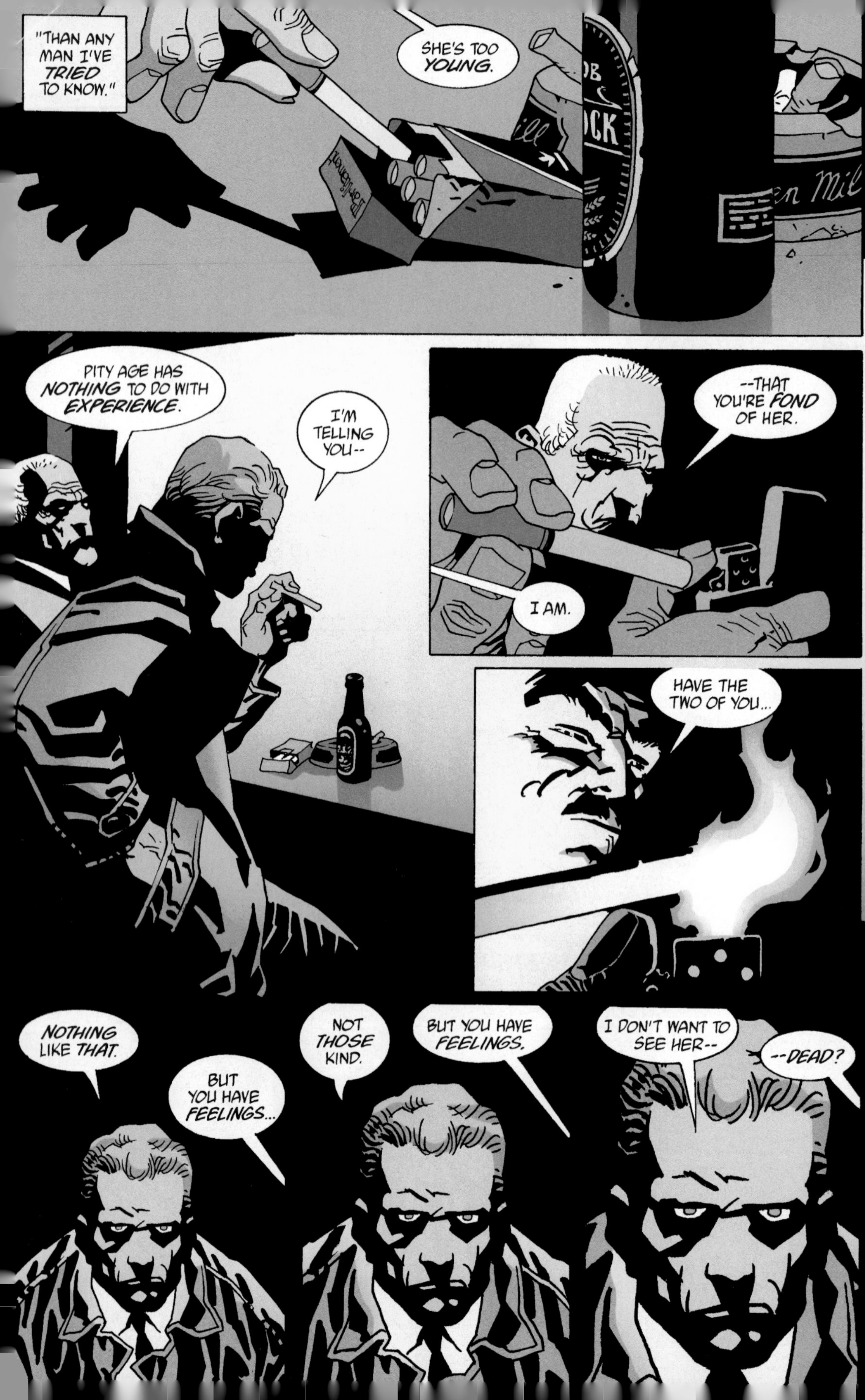
"THAN ANY MAN I'VE TRIED TO KNOW."
SHE'S TOO YOUNG.
PITY AGE HAS NOTHING TO DO WITH EXPERIENCE.
I'M TELLING YOU--
--THAT YOU'RE FOND OF HER.
I AM.
HAVE THE TWO OF YOU...
NOTHING LIKE THAT.
BUT YOU HAVE FEELINGS...
NOT THOSE KIND.
BUT YOU HAVE FEELINGS.
I DON'T WANT TO SEE HER--
--DEAD?

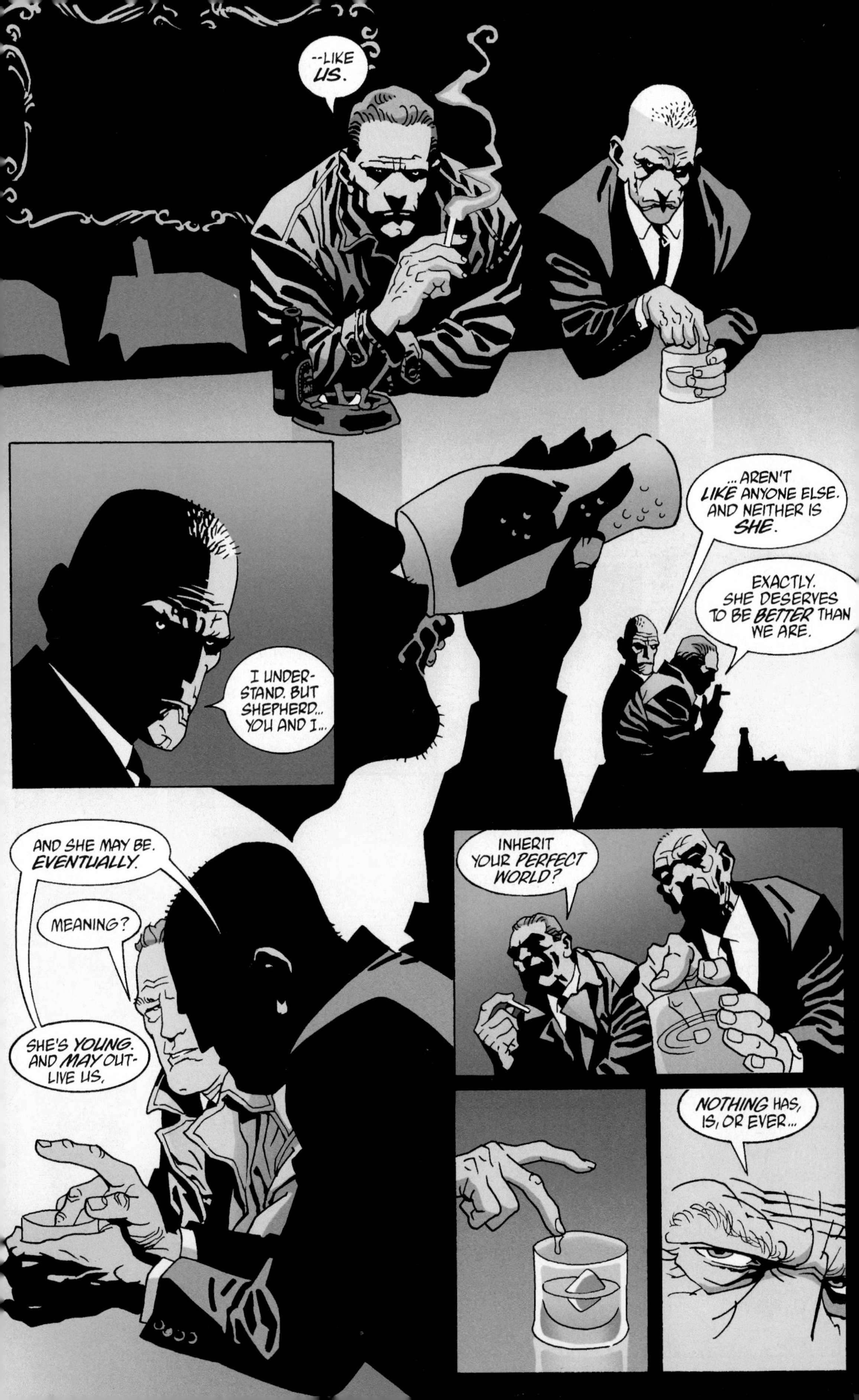
--LIKE US.
I UNDERSTAND. BUT SHEPHERD... YOU AND I...
... AREN'T LIKE ANYONE ELSE. AND NEITHER IS SHE.
EXACTLY. SHE DESERVES TO BE BETTER THAN WE ARE.
AND SHE MAY BE. EVENTUALLY.
MEANING?
SHE'S YOUNG. AND MAY OUTLIVE US.
INHERIT YOUR PERFECT WORLD?
NOTHING HAS, IS, OR EVER...

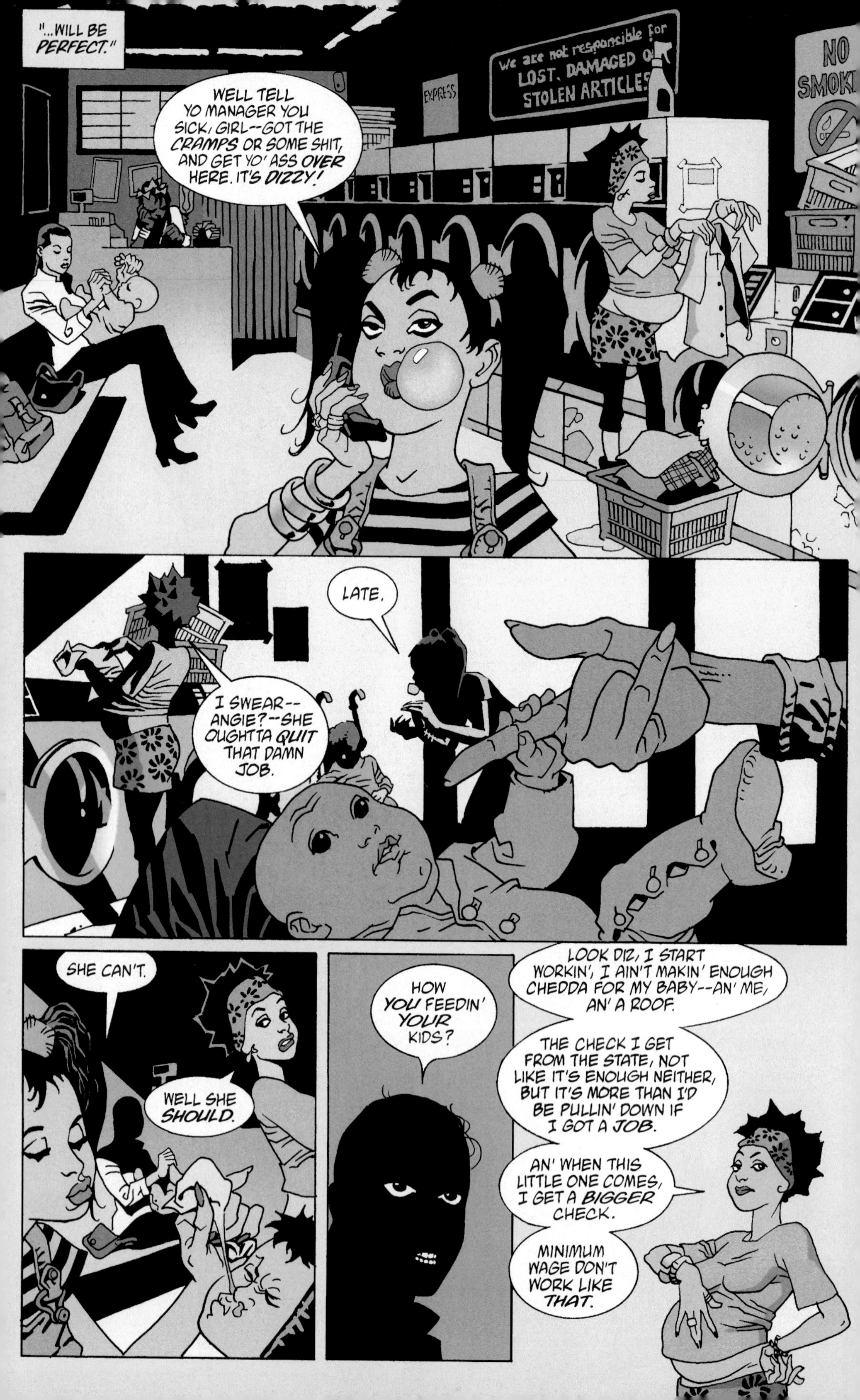
"...WILL BE PERFECT."
We are not responsible for LOST, DAMAGED OR STOLEN ARTICLES
EXPRESS
NO SMOK
WELL TELL YO MANAGER YOU SICK, GIRL--GOT THE CRAMPS OR SOME SHIT, AND GET YO' ASS OVER HERE. IT'S DIZZY!
LATE.
I SWEAR-- ANGIE?--SHE OUGHTTA QUIT THAT DAMN JOB.
SHE CAN'T.
WELL SHE SHOULD.
HOW YOU FEEDIN' YOUR KIDS?
LOOK DIZ, I START WORKIN', I AIN'T MAKIN' ENOUGH CHEDDA FOR MY BABY--AN' ME, AN' A ROOF.
THE CHECK I GET FROM THE STATE, NOT LIKE IT'S ENOUGH NEITHER, BUT IT'S MORE THAN I'D BE PULLIN' DOWN IF I GOT A JOB.
AN' WHEN THIS LITTLE ONE COMES, I GET A BIGGER CHECK.
MINIMUM WAGE DON'T WORK LIKE THAT.

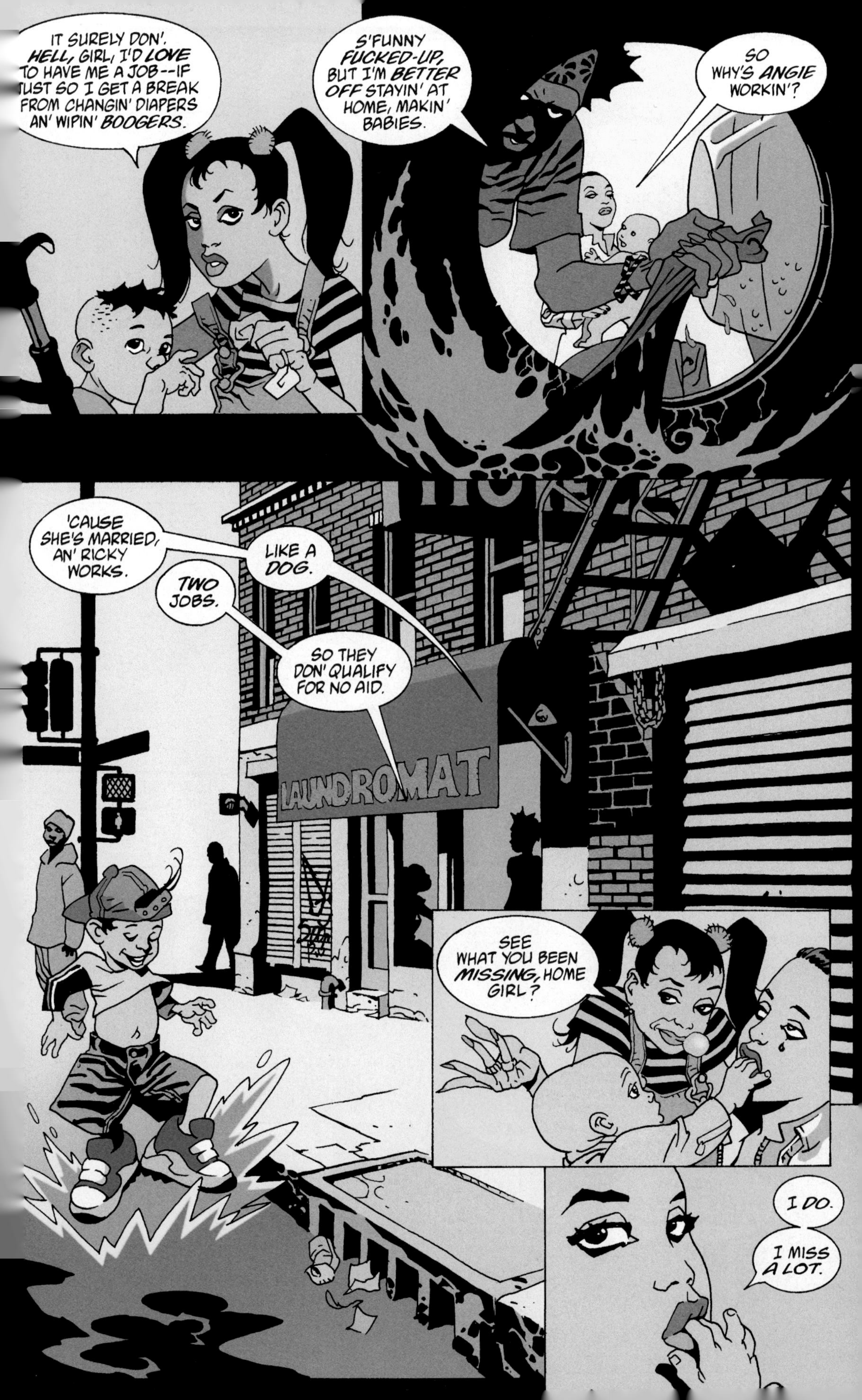

IT SURELY DON'. HELL, GIRL, I'D LOVE TO HAVE ME A JOB--IF JUST SO I GET A BREAK FROM CHANGIN' DIAPERS AN' WIPIN' BOOGERS.
S'FUNNY FUCKED-UP, BUT I'M BETTER OFF STAYIN' AT HOME, MAKIN' BABIES.
SO WHY'S ANGIE WORKIN'?
'CAUSE SHE'S MARRIED, AN' RICKY WORKS.
LIKE A DOG.
TWO JOBS.
SO THEY DON' QUALIFY FOR NO AID.
LAUNDROMAT
SEE WHAT YOU BEEN MISSING, HOME GIRL?
I DO.
I MISS A LOT.

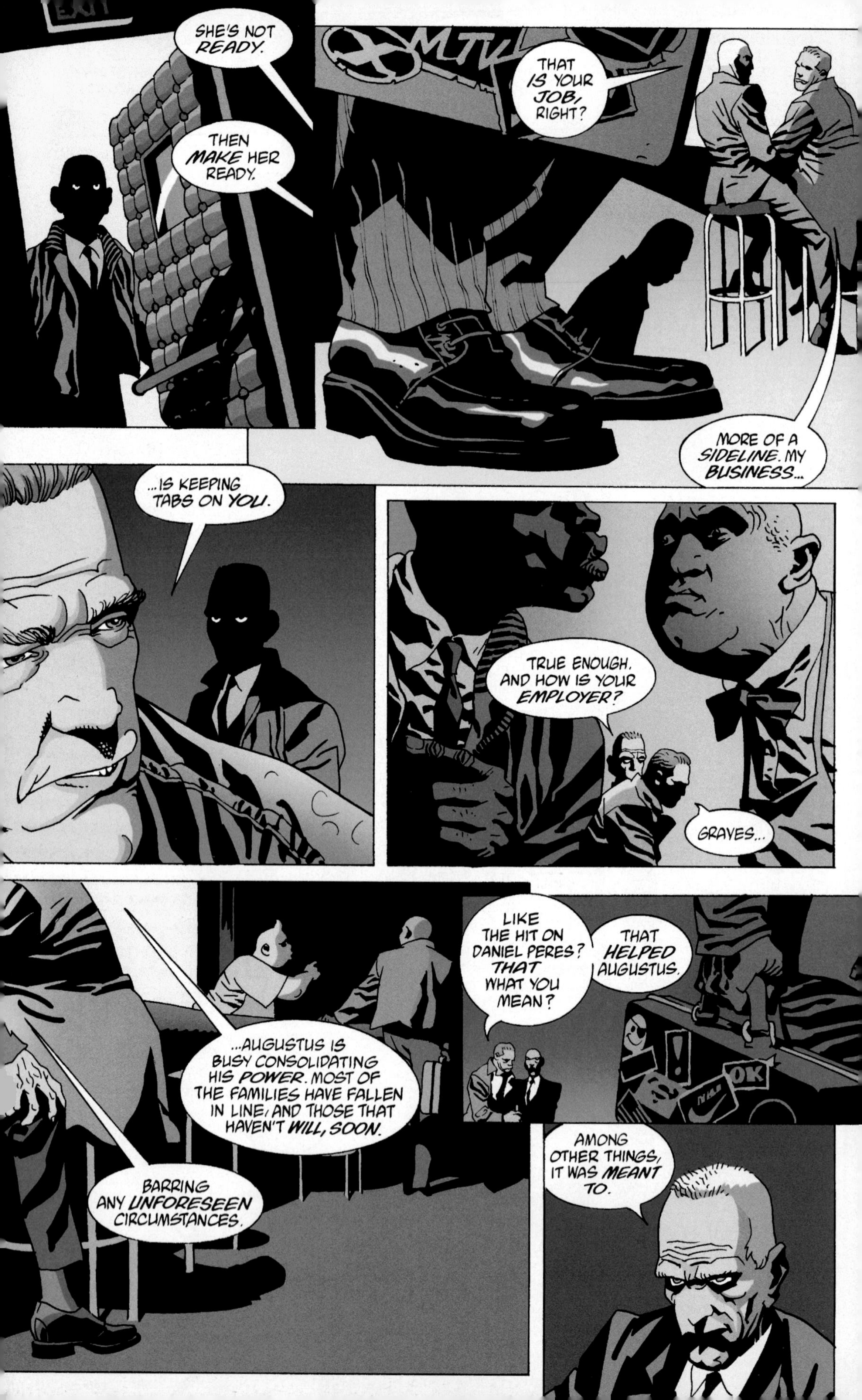
EXIT
SHE'S NOT READY.
THEN MAKE HER READY.
MTV
THAT IS YOUR JOB, RIGHT?
MORE OF A SIDELINE. MY BUSINESS...
...IS KEEPING TABS ON YOU.
TRUE ENOUGH. AND HOW IS YOUR EMPLOYER?
GRAVES...
...AUGUSTUS IS BUSY CONSOLIDATING HIS POWER. MOST OF THE FAMILIES HAVE FALLEN IN LINE, AND THOSE THAT HAVEN'T WILL, SOON.
BARRING ANY UNFORESEEN CIRCUMSTANCES.
LIKE THE HIT ON DANIEL PERES? THAT WHAT YOU MEAN?
THAT HELPED AUGUSTUS.
OK
AMONG OTHER THINGS, IT WAS MEANT TO.

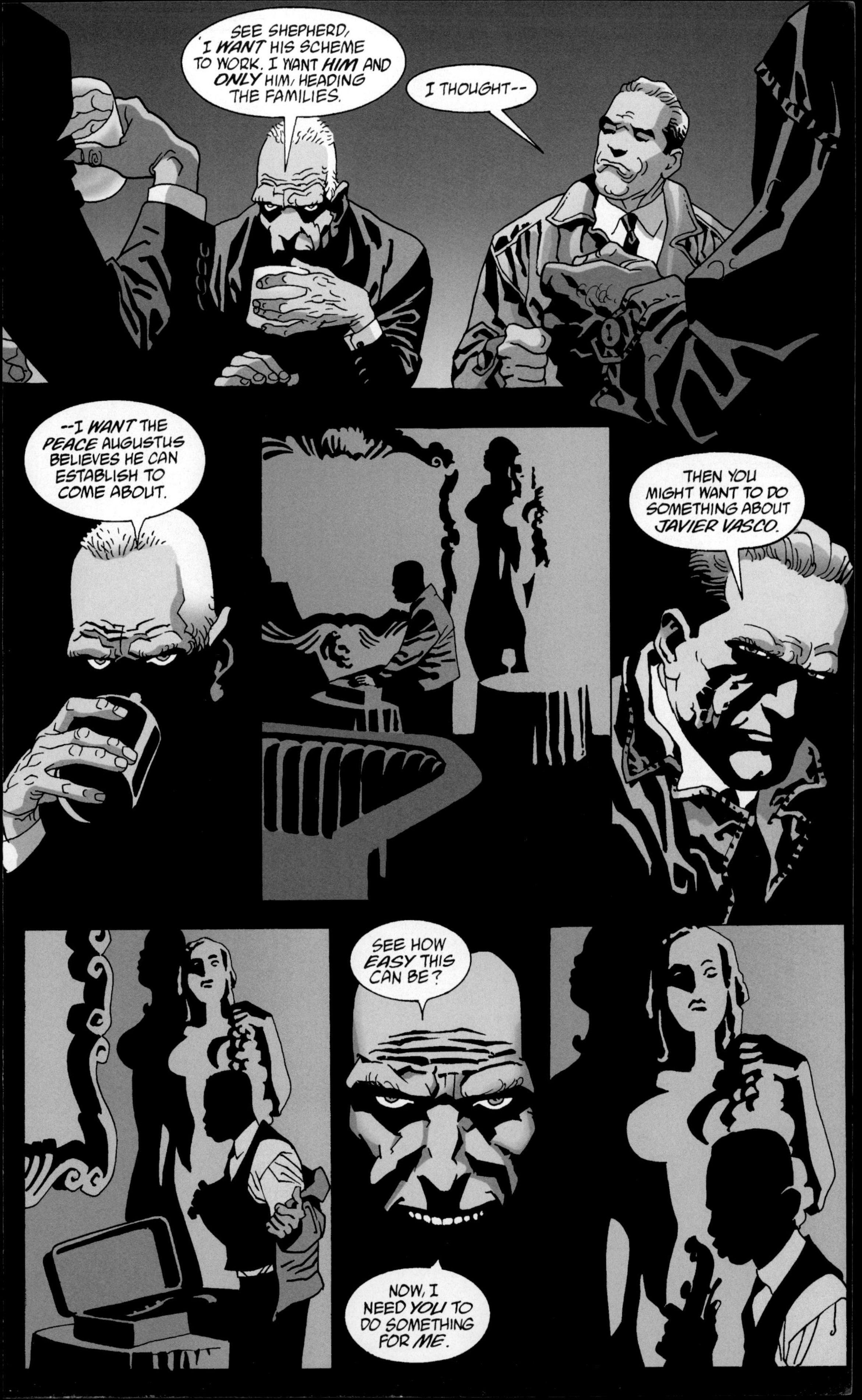
SEE SHEPHERD, I WANT HIS SCHEME TO WORK. I WANT HIM AND ONLY HIM, HEADING THE FAMILIES.
I THOUGHT--
--I WANT THE PEACE AUGUSTUS BELIEVES HE CAN ESTABLISH TO COME ABOUT.
THEN YOU MIGHT WANT TO DO SOMETHING ABOUT JAVIER VASCO.
SEE HOW EASY THIS CAN BE?
NOW, I NEED YOU TO DO SOMETHING FOR ME.

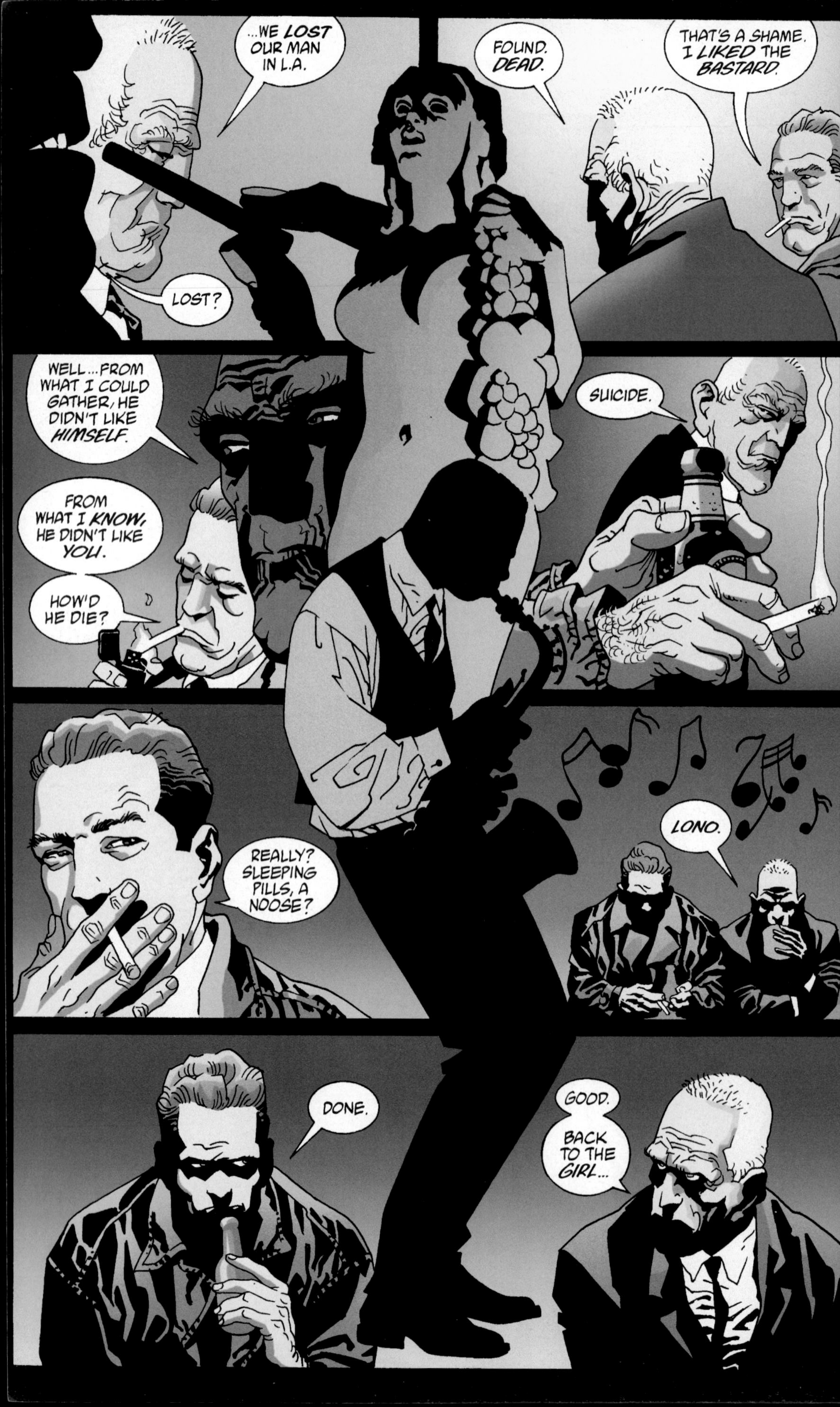
...WE LOST OUR MAN IN L.A.
LOST?
FOUND. DEAD.
THAT'S A SHAME. I LIKED THE BASTARD.
WELL...FROM WHAT I COULD GATHER, HE DIDN'T LIKE HIMSELF.
SUICIDE.
FROM WHAT I KNOW, HE DIDN'T LIKE YOU.
HOW'D HE DIE?
REALLY? SLEEPING PILLS, A NOOSE?
LONO.
DONE.
GOOD.
BACK TO THE GIRL...

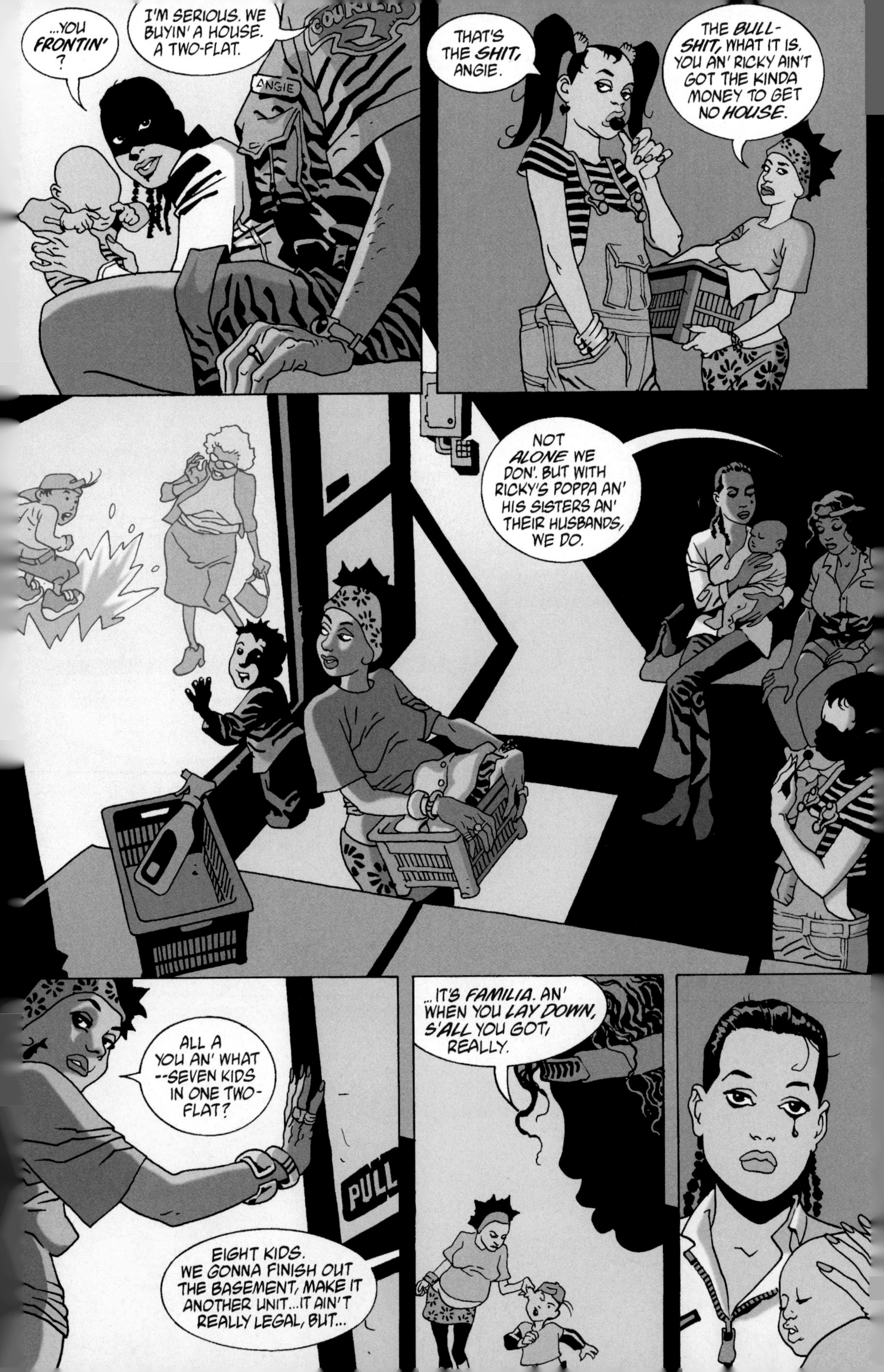
...YOU FRONTIN'?
I'M SERIOUS. WE BUYIN' A HOUSE. A TWO-FLAT.
ANGIE
THAT'S THE SHIT, ANGIE.
THE BULL-SHIT, WHAT IT IS. YOU AN' RICKY AIN'T GOT THE KINDA MONEY TO GET NO HOUSE.
NOT ALONE WE DON'. BUT WITH RICKY'S POPPA AN' HIS SISTERS AN' THEIR HUSBANDS, WE DO.
ALL A YOU AN' WHAT --SEVEN KIDS IN ONE TWO-FLAT?
EIGHT KIDS. WE GONNA FINISH OUT THE BASEMENT, MAKE IT ANOTHER UNIT...IT AIN'T REALLY LEGAL, BUT...
PULL
...IT'S FAMILIA. AN' WHEN YOU LAY DOWN, S'ALL YOU GOT, REALLY.

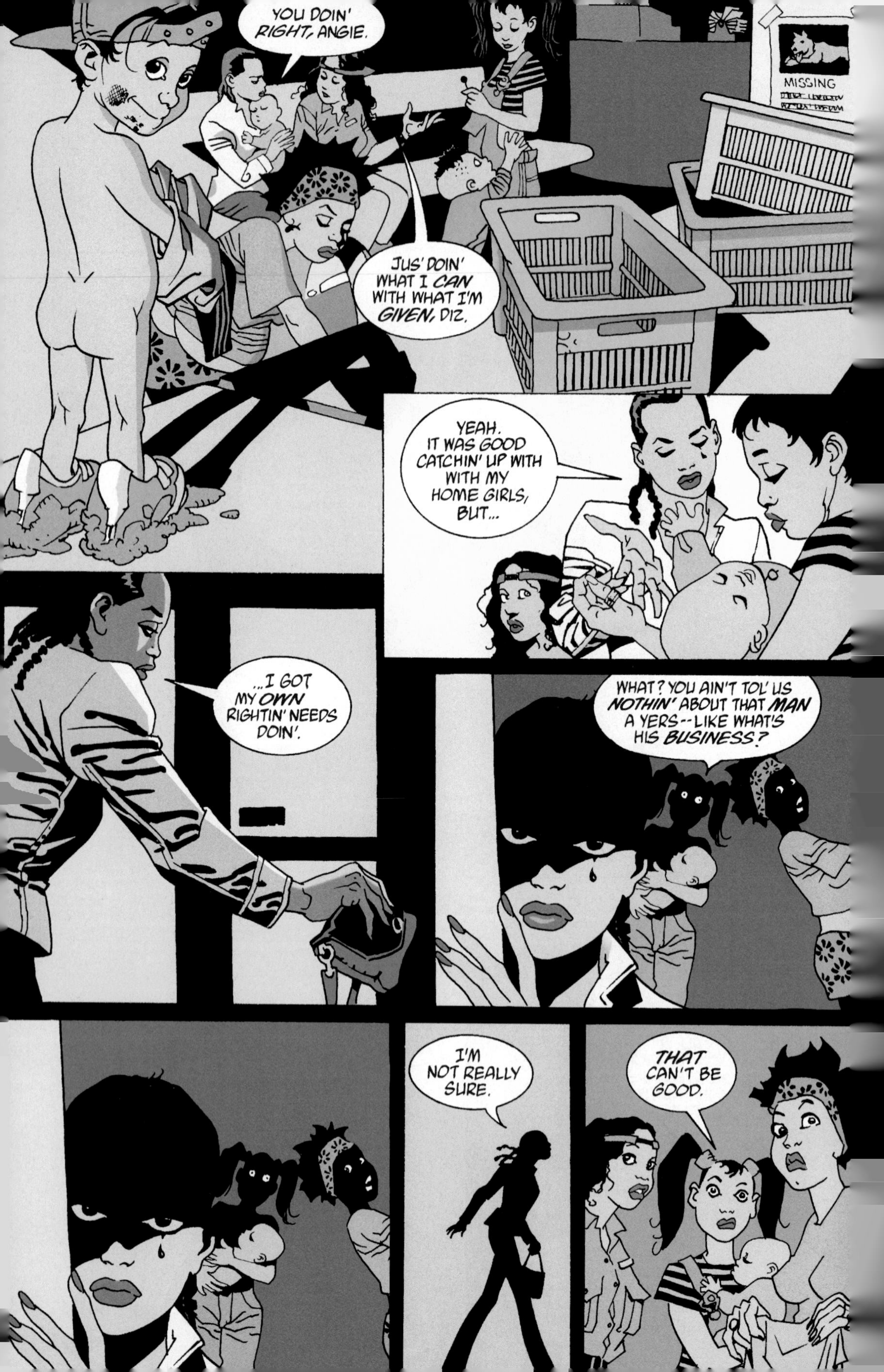

YOU DOIN' RIGHT, ANGIE.
MISSING
JUS' DOIN' WHAT I CAN WITH WHAT I'M GIVEN, DIZ.
YEAH. IT WAS GOOD CATCHIN' UP WITH WITH MY HOME GIRLS, BUT...
...I GOT MY OWN RIGHTIN' NEEDS DOIN'.
WHAT? YOU AIN'T TOL' US NOTHIN' ABOUT THAT MAN A YERS--LIKE WHAT'S HIS BUSINESS?
I'M NOT REALLY SURE.
THAT CAN'T BE GOOD.

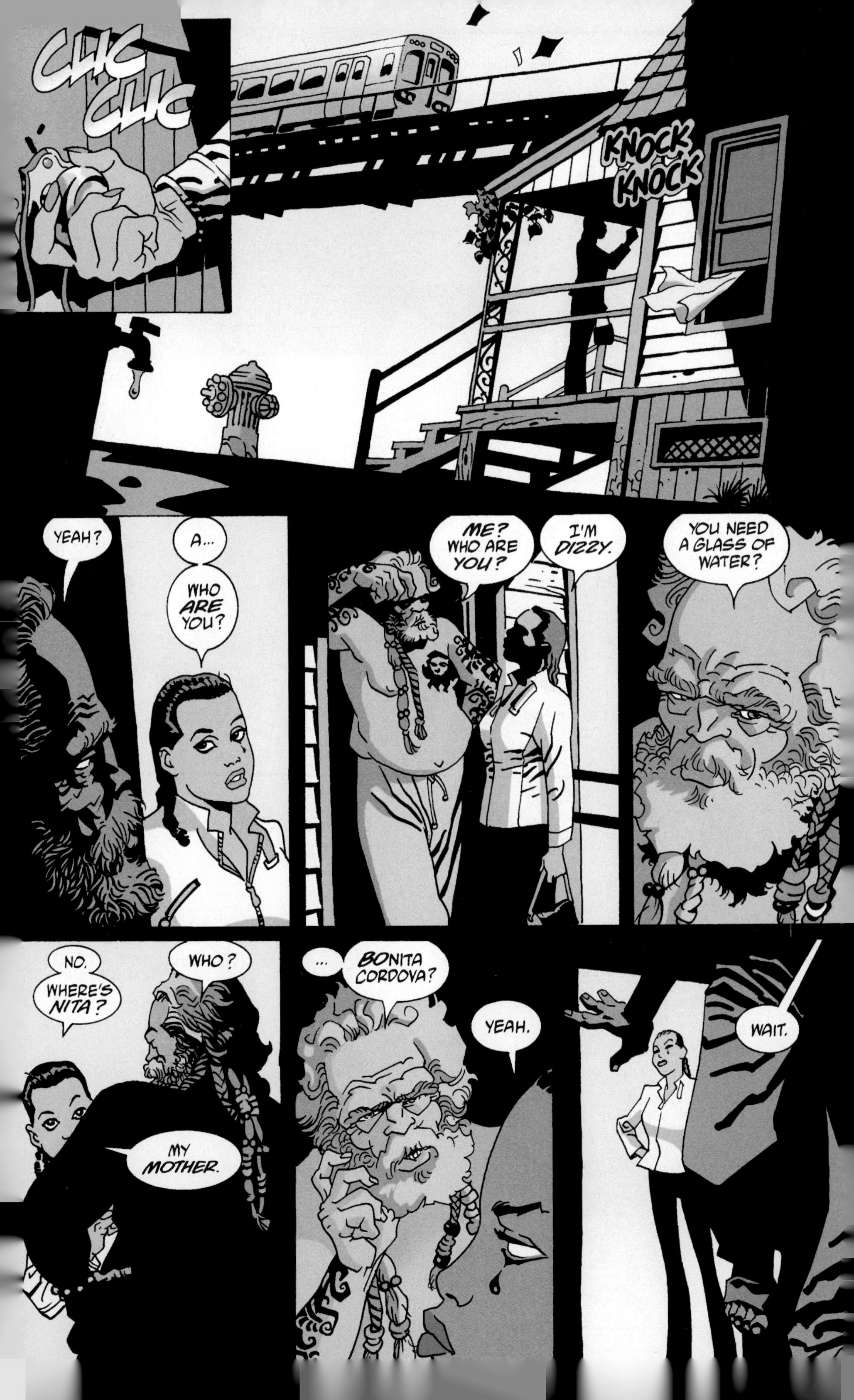
CLIC
CLIC
KNOCK
KNOCK
YEAH?
A...
WHO ARE YOU?
ME? WHO ARE YOU?
I'M DIZZY.
YOU NEED A GLASS OF WATER?
NO. WHERE'S NITA?
WHO?
MY MOTHER.
...
BONITA CORDOVA?
YEAH.
WAIT.

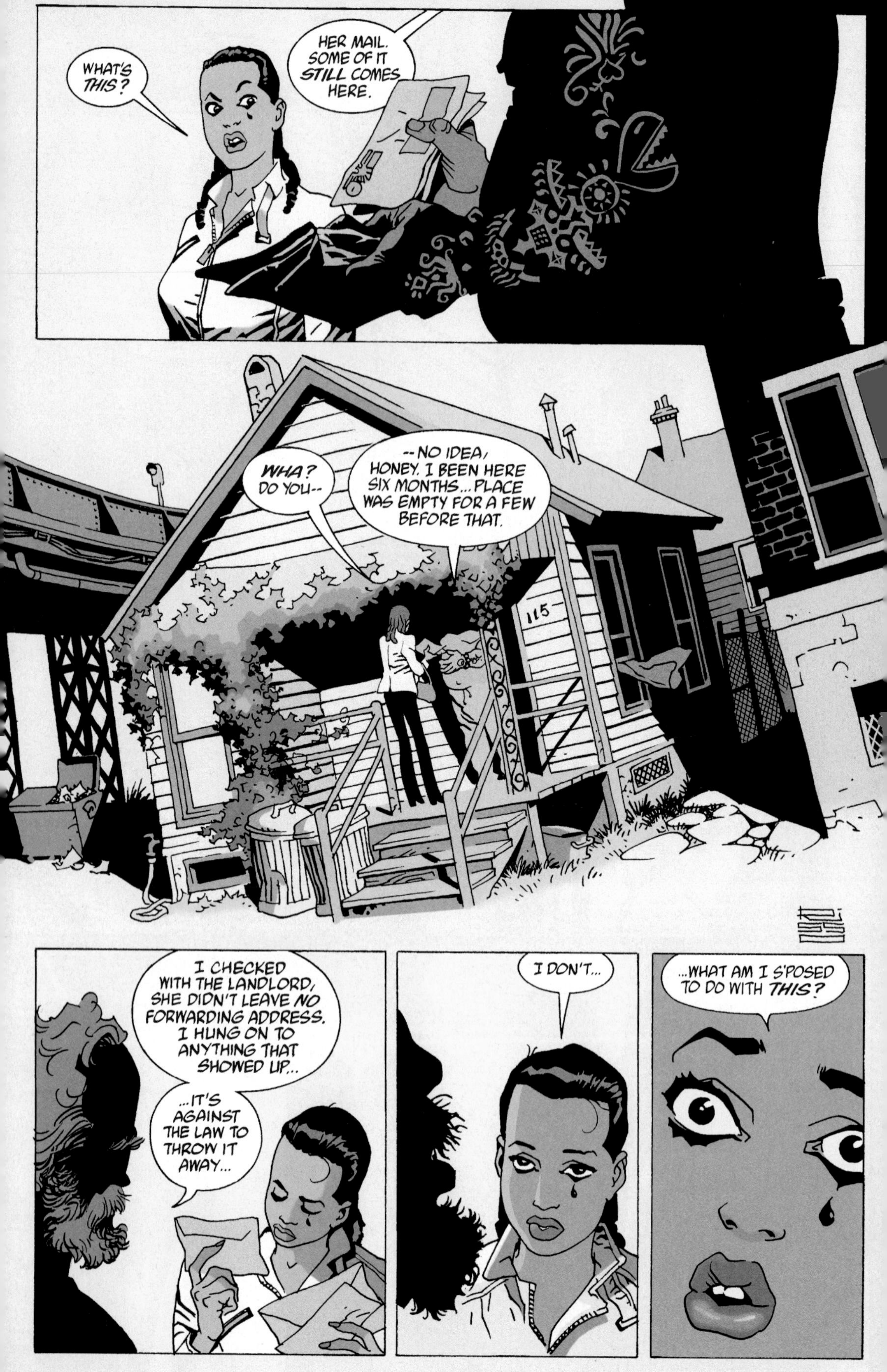
WHAT'S THIS?
HER MAIL. SOME OF IT STILL COMES HERE.
WHA? DO YOU--
--NO IDEA, HONEY. I BEEN HERE SIX MONTHS... PLACE WAS EMPTY FOR A FEW BEFORE THAT.
115
I CHECKED WITH THE LANDLORD, SHE DIDN'T LEAVE NO FORWARDING ADDRESS. I HUNG ON TO ANYTHING THAT SHOWED UP...
...IT'S AGAINST THE LAW TO THROW IT AWAY...
I DON'T...
...WHAT AM I S'POSED TO DO WITH THIS?

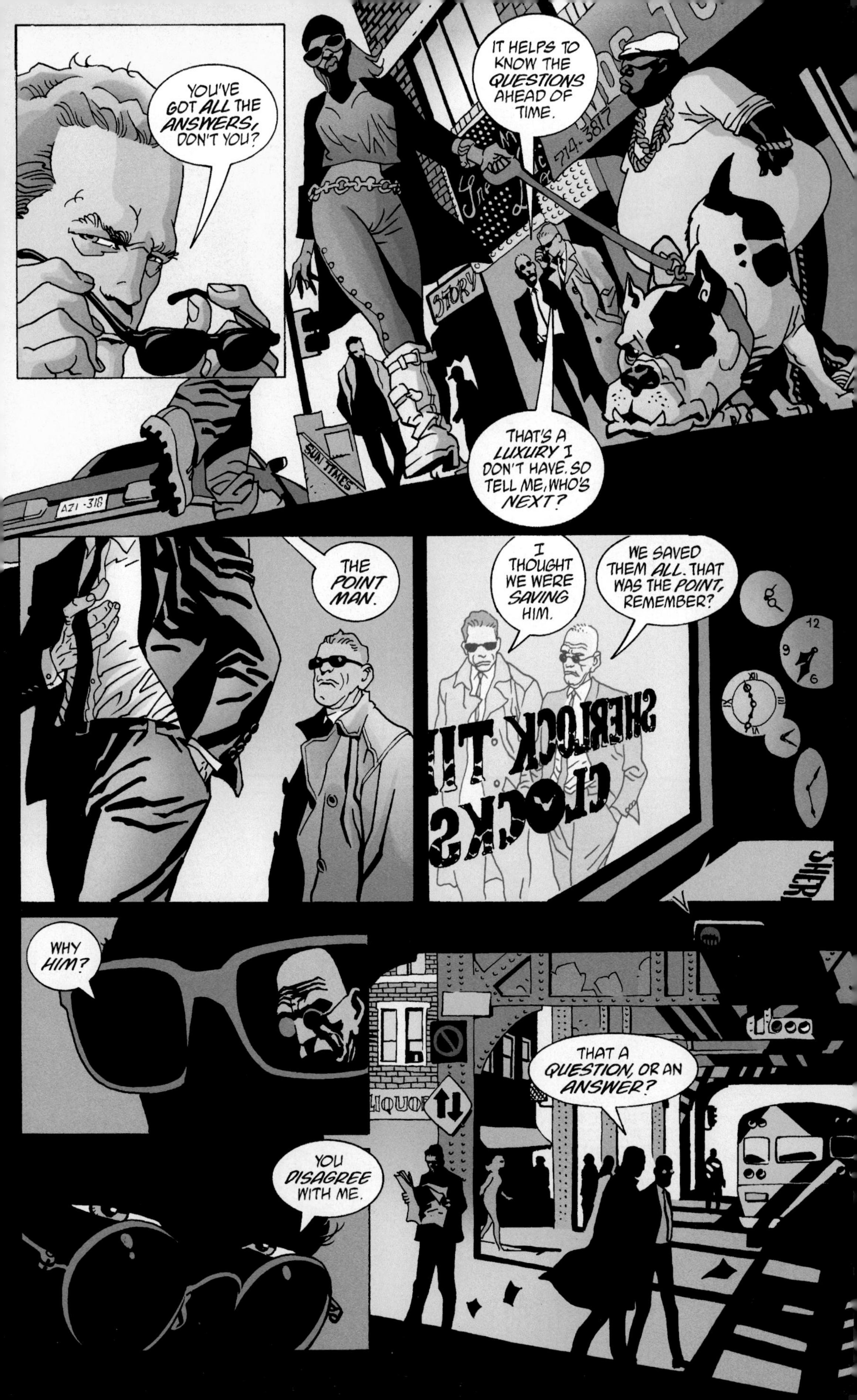
YOU'VE GOT ALL THE ANSWERS, DON'T YOU?
IT HELPS TO KNOW THE QUESTIONS AHEAD OF TIME.
THAT'S A LUXURY I DON'T HAVE. SO TELL ME, WHO'S NEXT?
THE POINT MAN.
I THOUGHT WE WERE SAVING HIM.
WE SAVED THEM ALL. THAT WAS THE POINT, REMEMBER?
WHY HIM?
THAT A QUESTION, OR AN ANSWER?
YOU DISAGREE WITH ME.

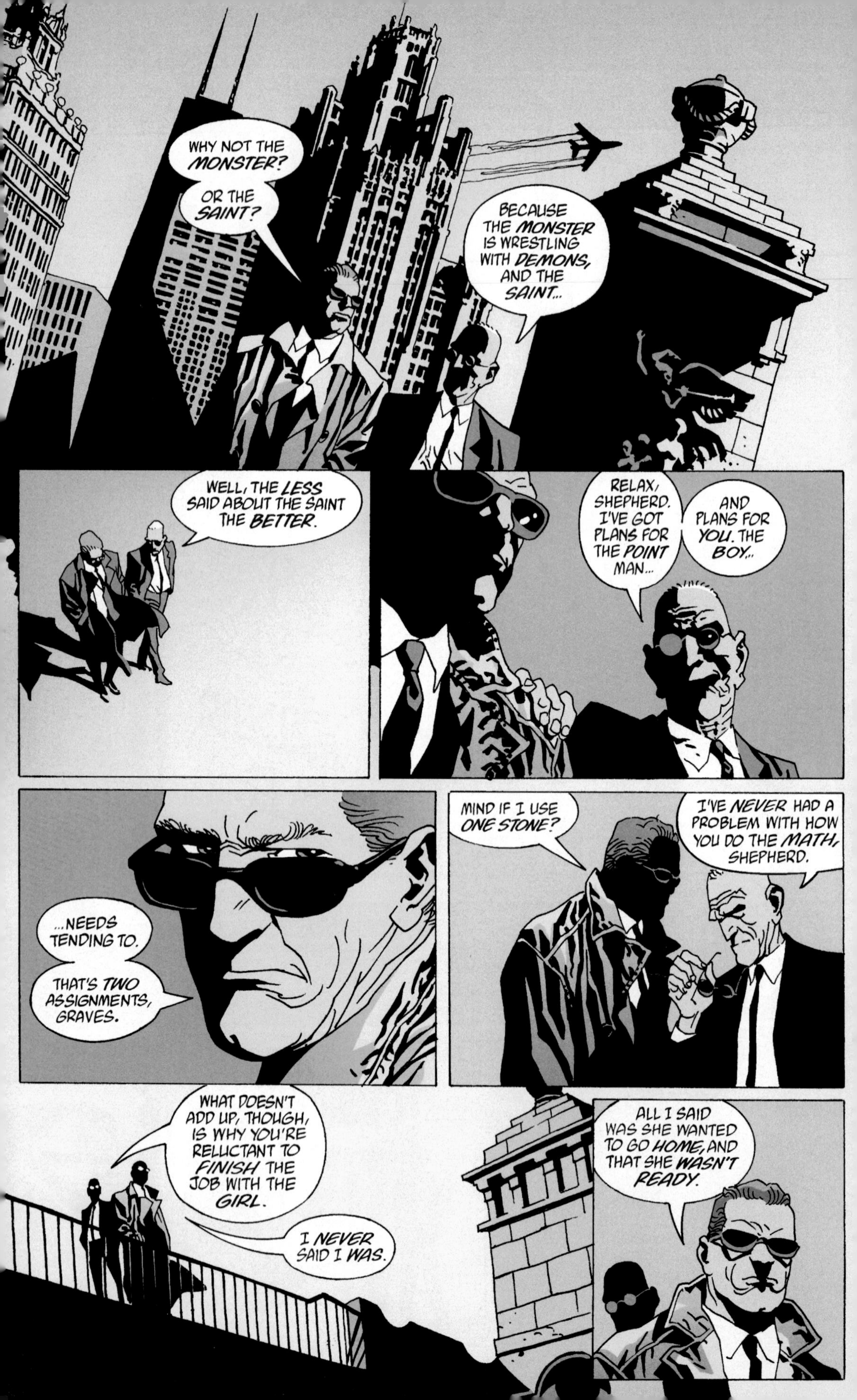
WHY NOT THE MONSTER?
OR THE SAINT?
BECAUSE THE MONSTER IS WRESTLING WITH DEMONS, AND THE SAINT...
WELL, THE LESS SAID ABOUT THE SAINT THE BETTER.
RELAX, SHEPHERD. I'VE GOT PLANS FOR THE POINT MAN...
AND PLANS FOR YOU. THE BOY...
...NEEDS TENDING TO.
THAT'S TWO ASSIGNMENTS, GRAVES.
MIND IF I USE ONE STONE?
I'VE NEVER HAD A PROBLEM WITH HOW YOU DO THE MATH, SHEPHERD.
WHAT DOESN'T ADD UP, THOUGH, IS WHY YOU'RE RELUCTANT TO FINISH THE JOB WITH THE GIRL.
I NEVER SAID I WAS.
ALL I SAID WAS SHE WANTED TO GO HOME, AND THAT SHE WASN'T READY.

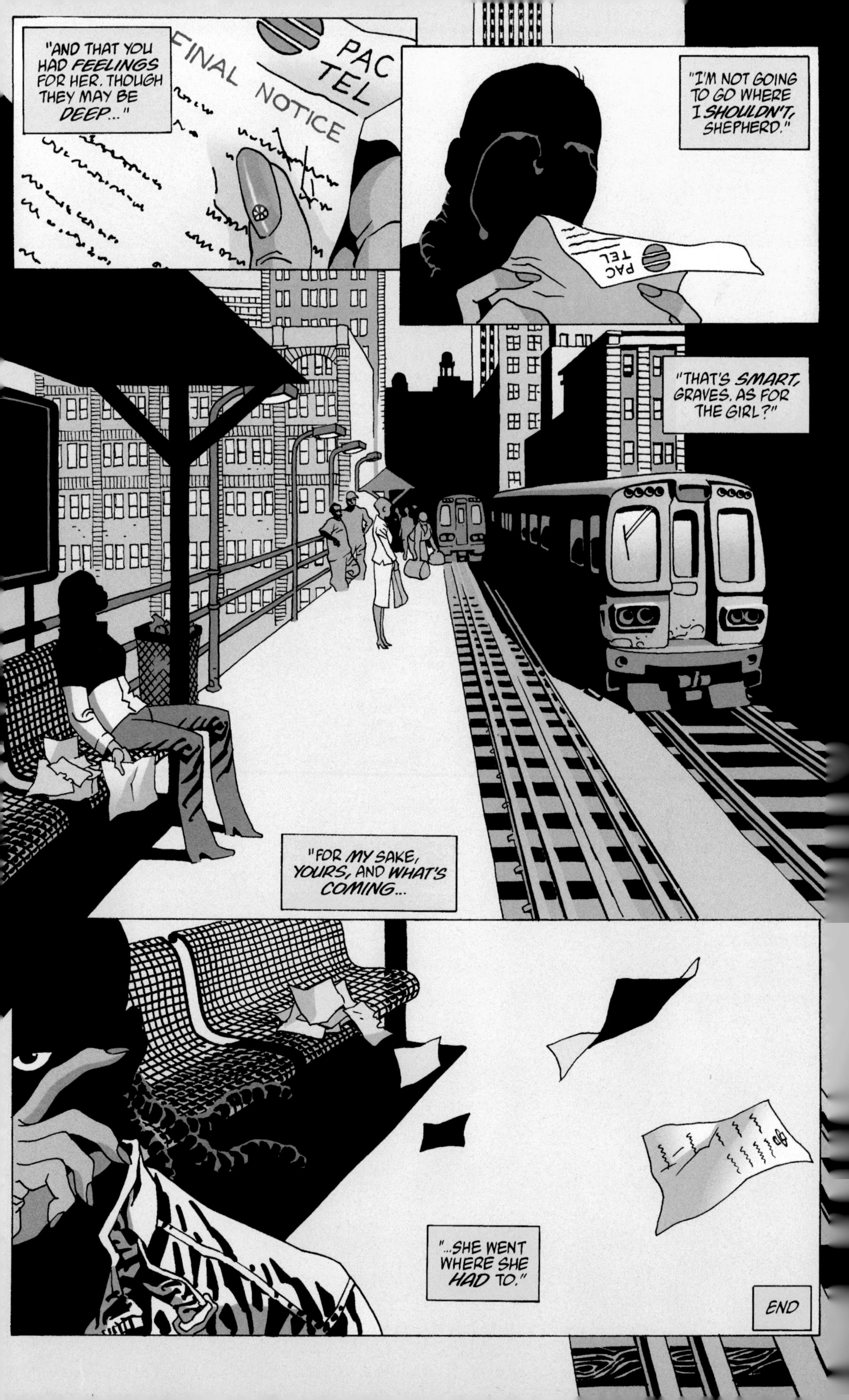
"AND THAT YOU HAD FEELINGS FOR HER. THOUGH THEY MAY BE DEEP..."
PAC TEL
FINAL NOTICE
"I'M NOT GOING TO GO WHERE I SHOULDN'T, SHEPHERD."
PAC TEL
"THAT'S SMART, GRAVES. AS FOR THE GIRL?"
"FOR MY SAKE, YOURS, AND WHAT'S COMING...
"...SHE WENT WHERE SHE HAD TO."
END

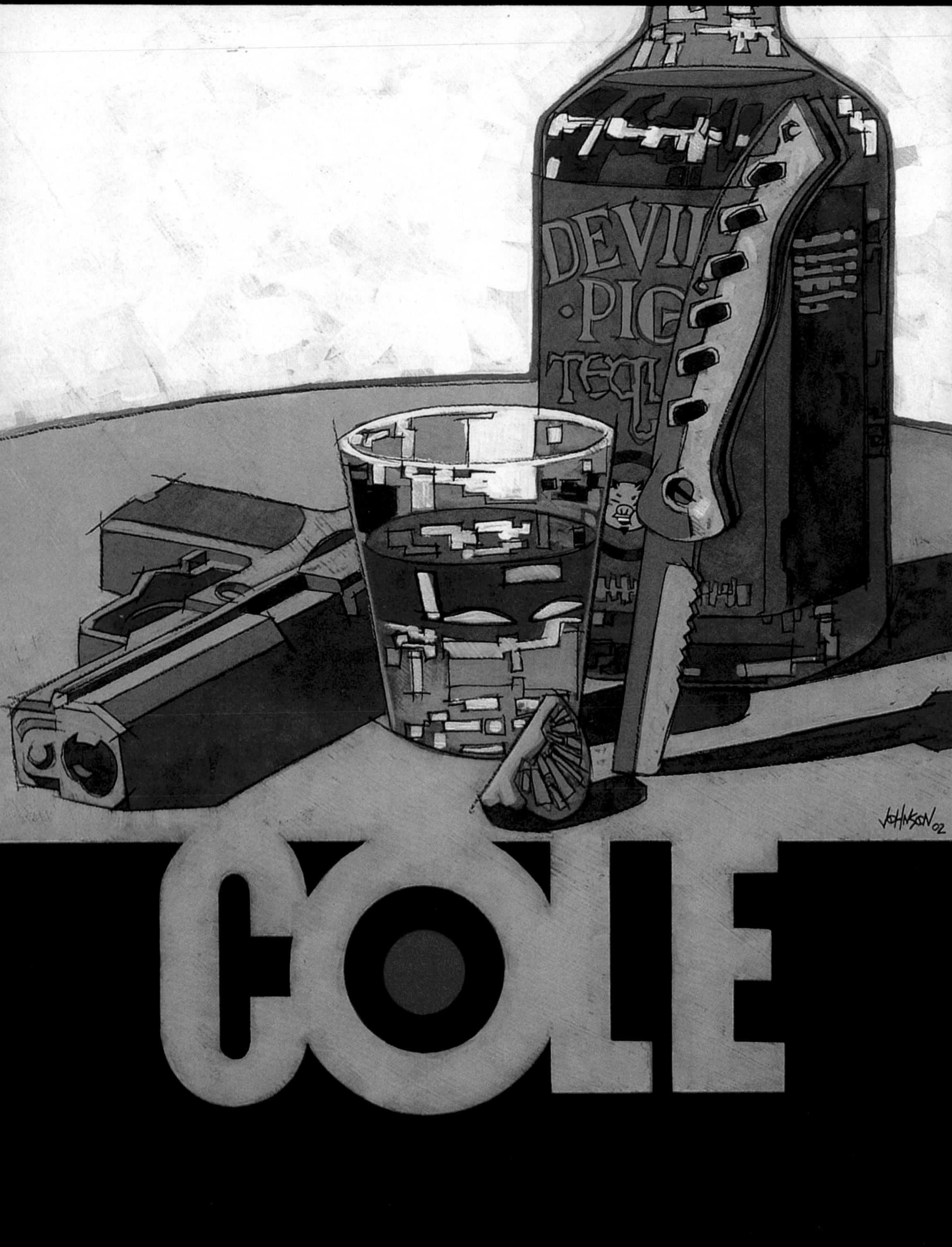
JOHNSON 02
COLE

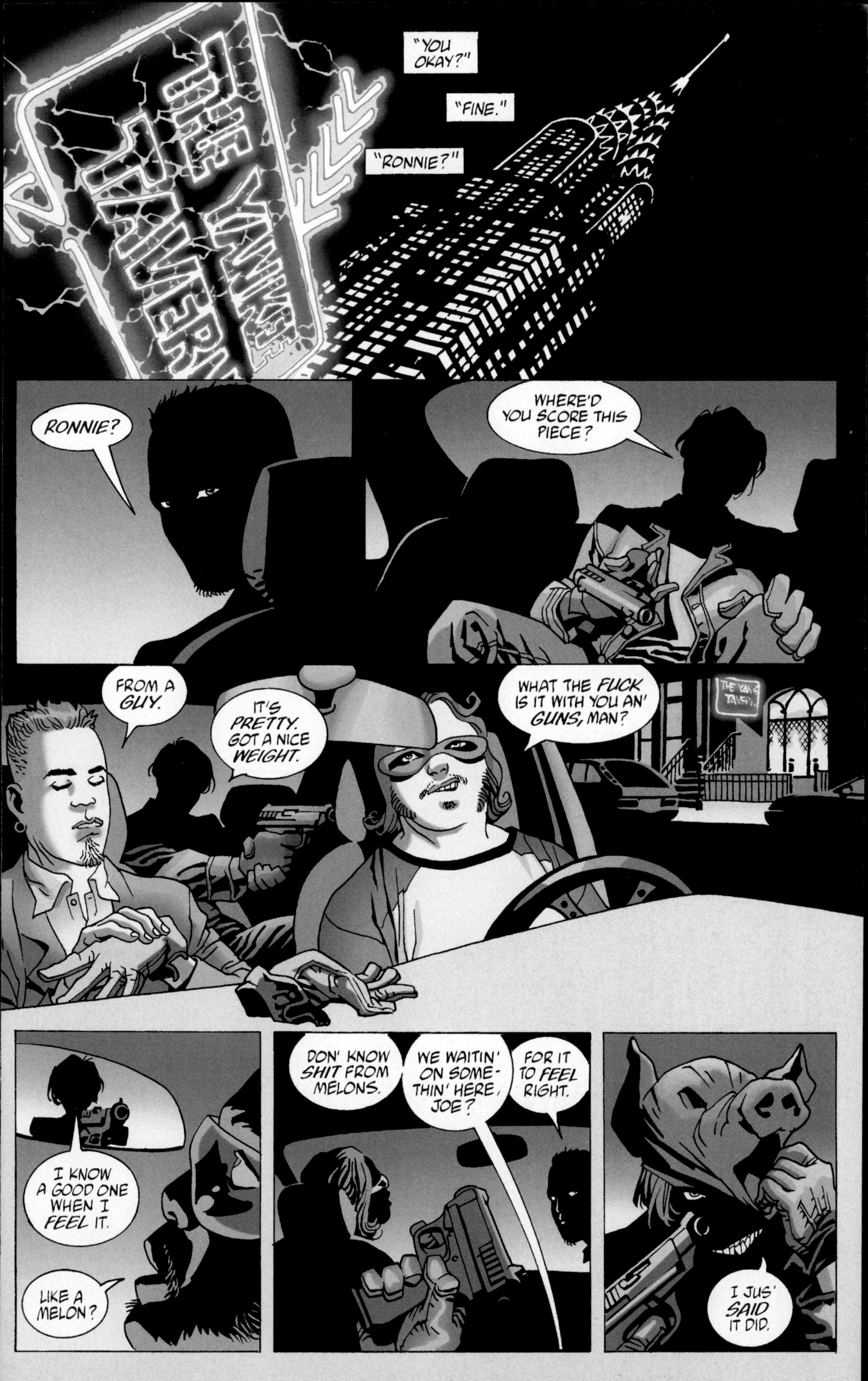

THE YANKS TAVERN
"YOU OKAY?"
"FINE."
"RONNIE?"
RONNIE?
WHERE'D YOU SCORE THIS PIECE?
FROM A GUY.
IT'S PRETTY. GOT A NICE WEIGHT.
WHAT THE FUCK IS IT WITH YOU AN' GUNS, MAN?
I KNOW A GOOD ONE WHEN I FEEL IT.
LIKE A MELON?
DON' KNOW SHIT FROM MELONS.
WE WAITIN' ON SOME-THIN' HERE, JOE?
FOR IT TO FEEL RIGHT.
I JUS' SAID IT DID.

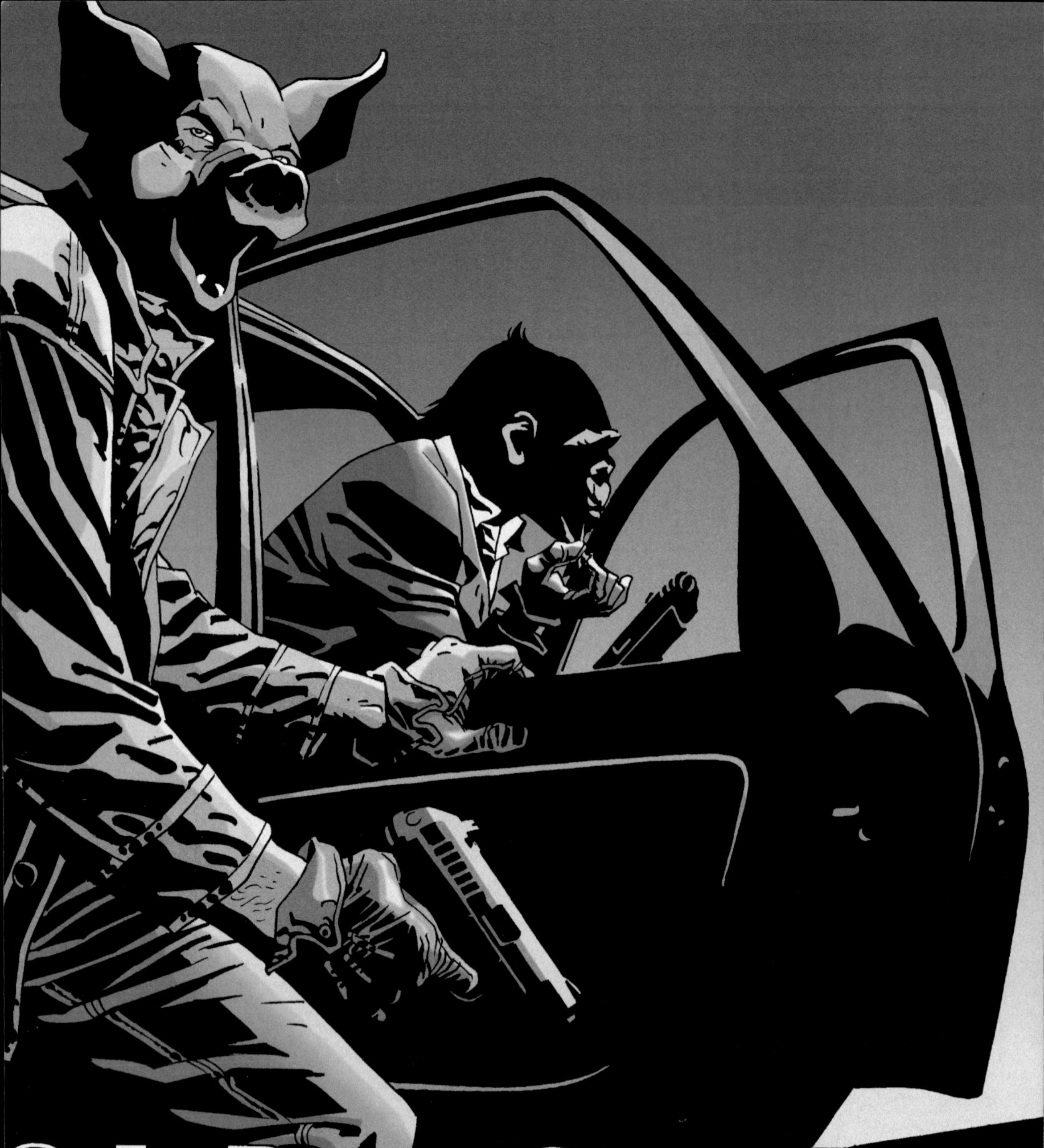

Cole Burns Slow Hand

BRIAN AZZARELLO, writer
PATRICIA MULVIHILL, colorist
DIGITAL CHAMELEON, separations
ZACHARY RAU, assistant editor

EDUARDO RISSO, artist
CLEM ROBINS, letterer
DAVE JOHNSON, cover artist
WILL DENNIS, editor

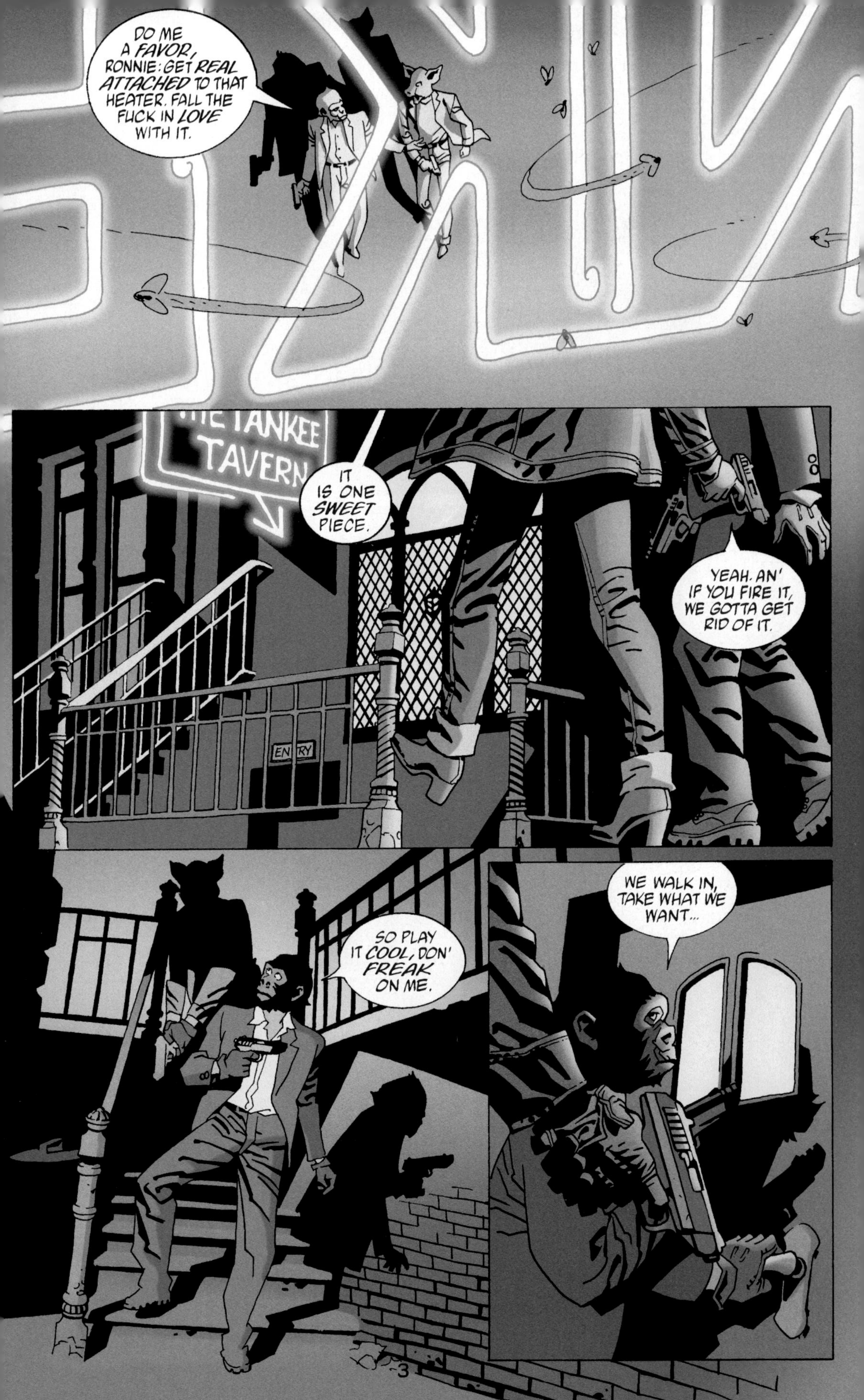
DO ME A *FAVOR*, RONNIE: GET *REAL ATTACHED* TO THAT HEATER. FALL THE FUCK IN *LOVE* WITH IT.
THE TANKEE TAVERN
IT IS ONE *SWEET* PIECE.
YEAH. AN' IF YOU FIRE IT, WE GOTTA GET RID OF IT.
ENTRY
SO PLAY IT *COOL*, DON' *FREAK* ON ME.
WE WALK IN, TAKE WHAT WE WANT...

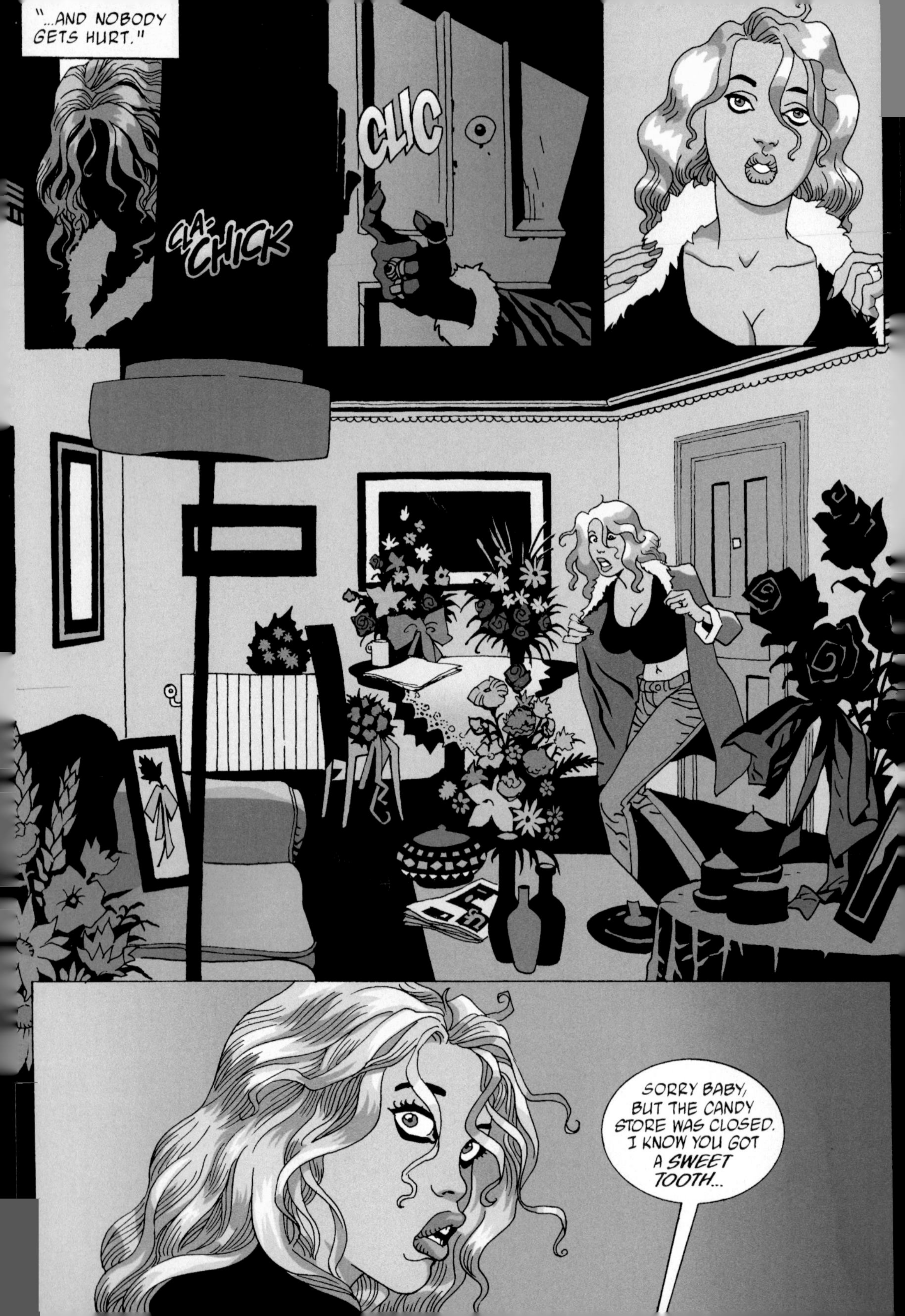
"...AND NOBODY GETS HURT."
CLA-CHICK
CLIC
SORRY BABY, BUT THE CANDY STORE WAS CLOSED. I KNOW YOU GOT A SWEET TOOTH...

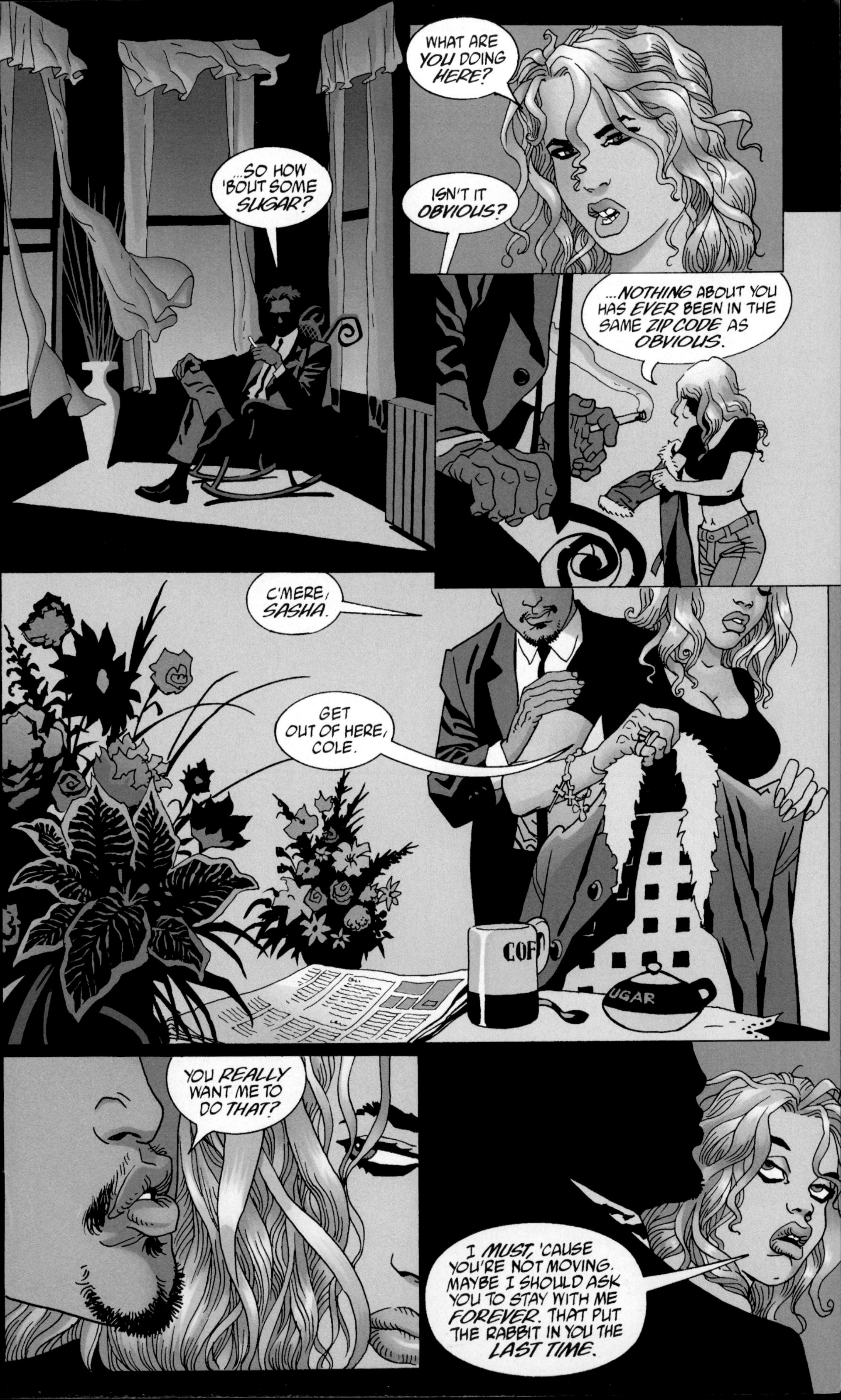

...SO HOW 'BOUT SOME SUGAR?
WHAT ARE YOU DOING HERE?
ISN'T IT OBVIOUS?
...NOTHING ABOUT YOU HAS EVER BEEN IN THE SAME ZIP CODE AS OBVIOUS.
C'MERE, SASHA.
GET OUT OF HERE, COLE.
COF
UGAR
YOU REALLY WANT ME TO DO THAT?
I MUST, 'CAUSE YOU'RE NOT MOVING. MAYBE I SHOULD ASK YOU TO STAY WITH ME FOREVER. THAT PUT THE RABBIT IN YOU THE LAST TIME.

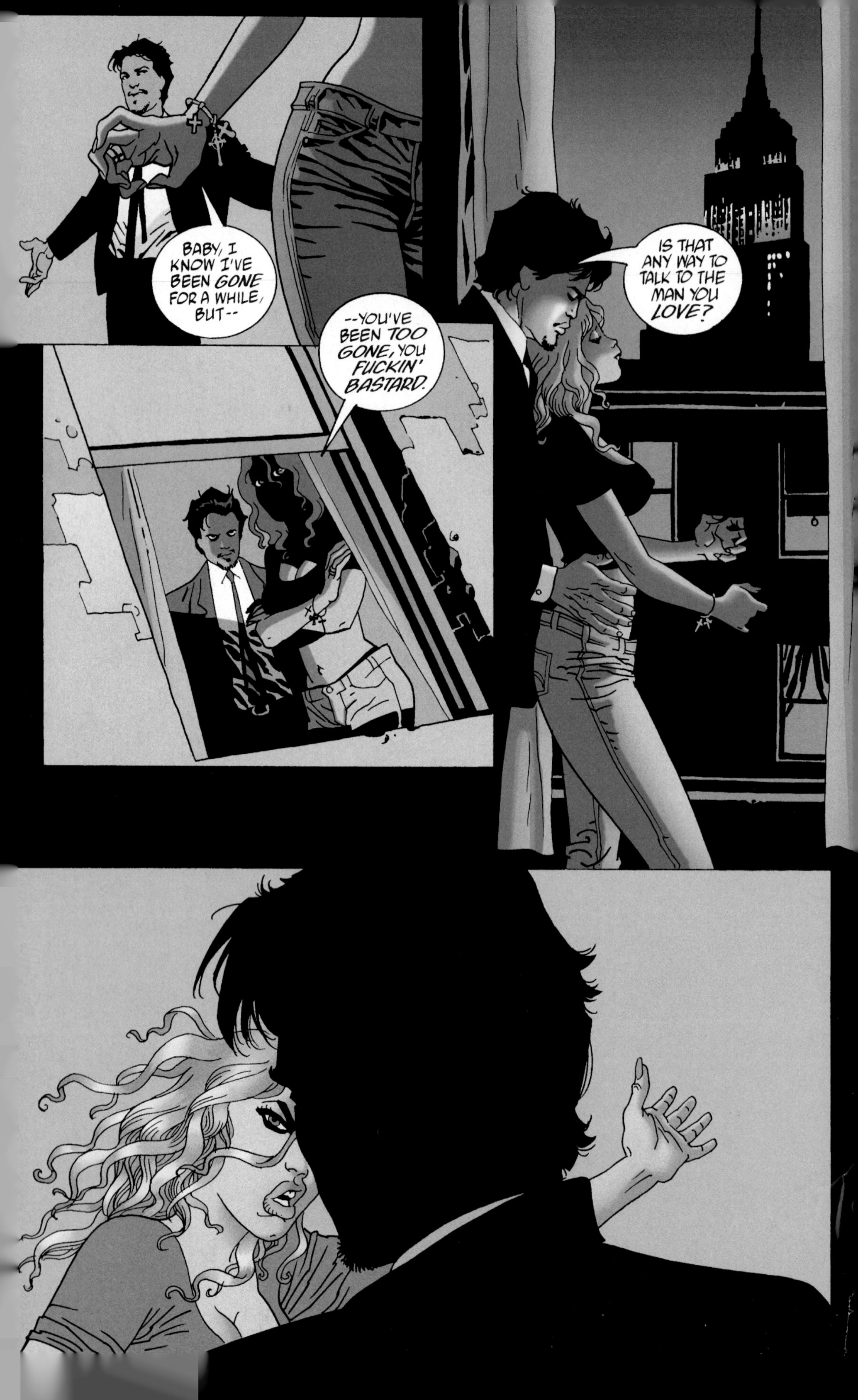
BABY, I KNOW I'VE BEEN GONE FOR A WHILE, BUT--
--YOU'VE BEEN TOO GONE, YOU FUCKIN' BASTARD.
IS THAT ANY WAY TO TALK TO THE MAN YOU LOVE?

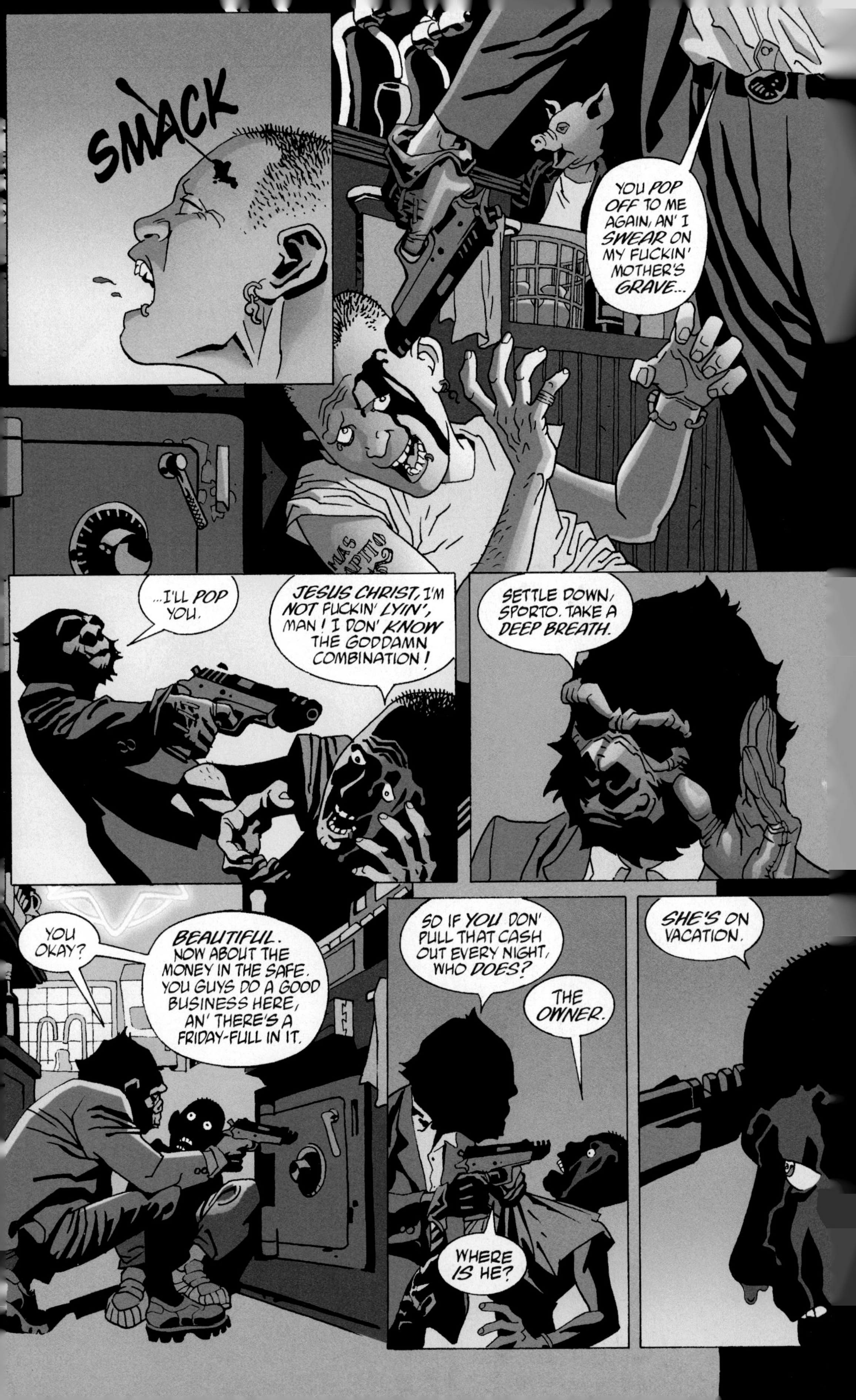
SMACK
YOU POP OFF TO ME AGAIN, AN' I SWEAR ON MY FUCKIN' MOTHER'S GRAVE...
...I'LL POP YOU.
JESUS CHRIST, I'M NOT FUCKIN' LYIN', MAN! I DON' KNOW THE GODDAMN COMBINATION!
SETTLE DOWN, SPORTO. TAKE A DEEP BREATH.
YOU OKAY?
BEAUTIFUL. NOW ABOUT THE MONEY IN THE SAFE. YOU GUYS DO A GOOD BUSINESS HERE, AN' THERE'S A FRIDAY-FULL IN IT.
SO IF YOU DON' PULL THAT CASH OUT EVERY NIGHT, WHO DOES?
THE OWNER.
WHERE IS HE?
SHE'S ON VACATION.

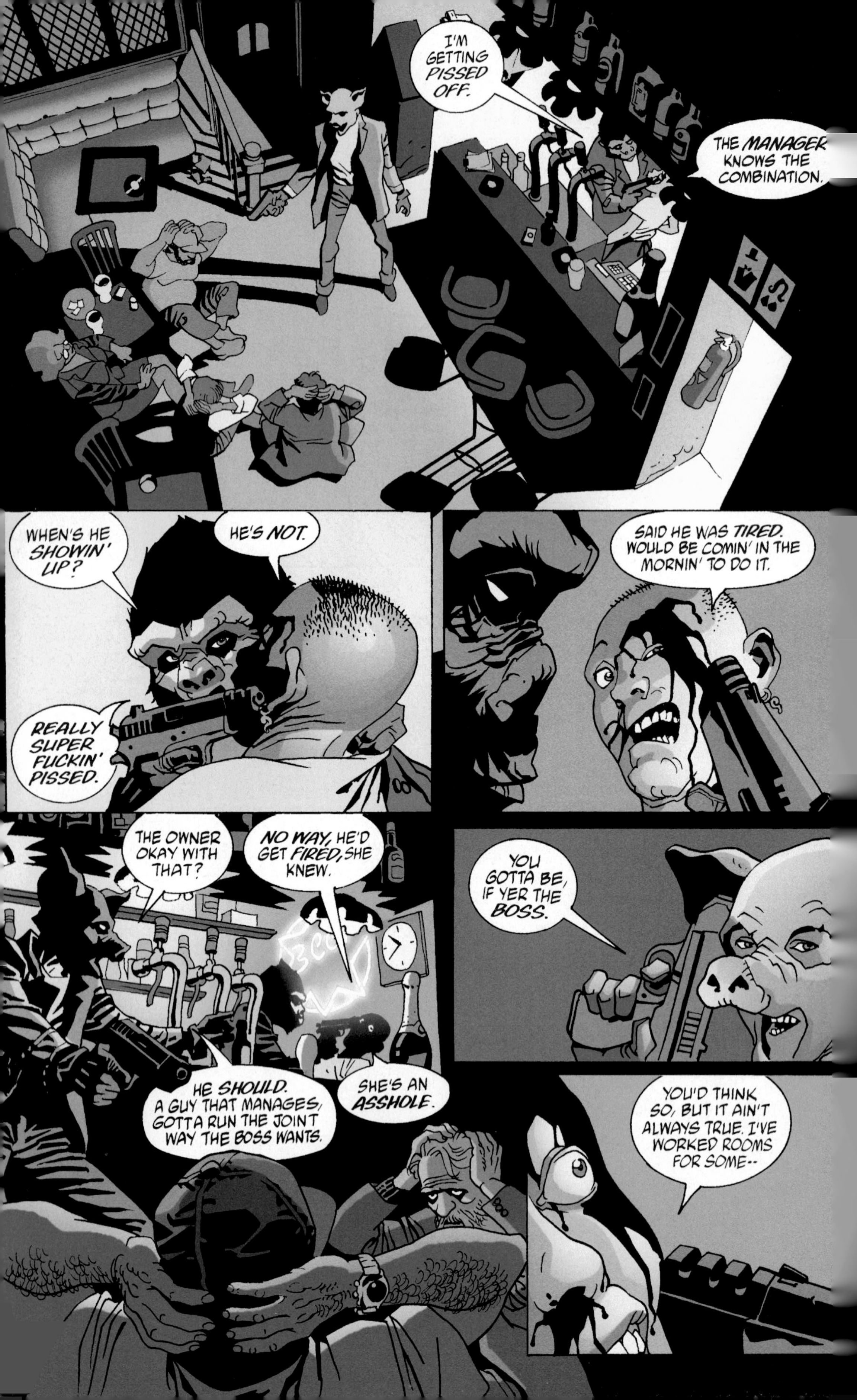
I'M GETTING PISSED OFF.
THE MANAGER KNOWS THE COMBINATION.
WHEN'S HE SHOWIN' UP?
HE'S NOT.
REALLY SUPER FUCKIN' PISSED.
SAID HE WAS TIRED. WOULD BE COMIN' IN THE MORNIN' TO DO IT.
THE OWNER OKAY WITH THAT?
NO WAY, HE'D GET FIRED, SHE KNEW.
HE SHOULD. A GUY THAT MANAGES, GOTTA RUN THE JOINT WAY THE BOSS WANTS.
SHE'S AN ASSHOLE.
YOU GOTTA BE, IF YER THE BOSS.
YOU'D THINK SO, BUT IT AIN'T ALWAYS TRUE. I'VE WORKED ROOMS FOR SOME--

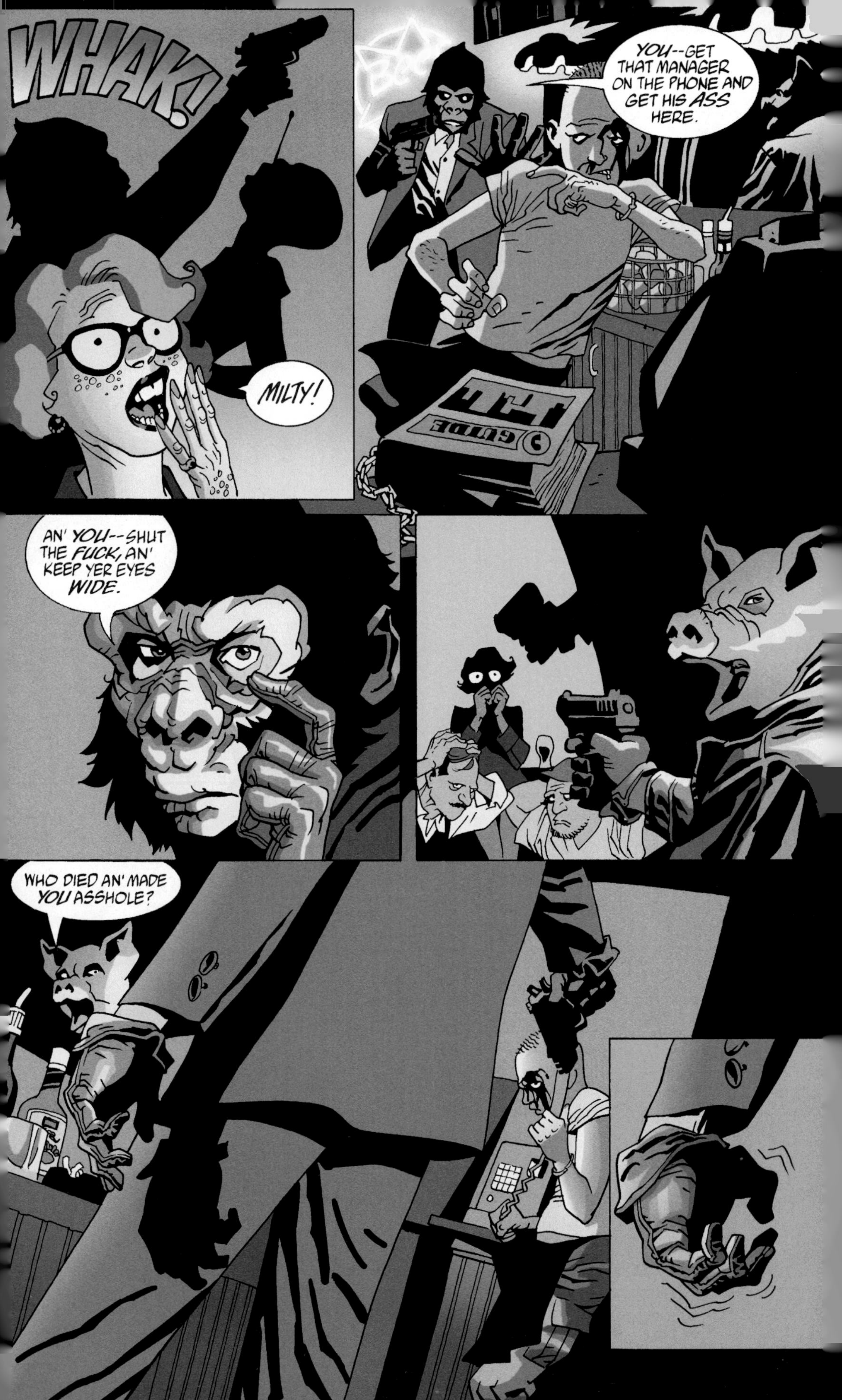
WHAK!
MILTY!
YOU--GET THAT MANAGER ON THE PHONE AND GET HIS ASS HERE.
GUIDE
AN' YOU--SHUT THE FUCK, AN' KEEP YER EYES WIDE.
WHO DIED AN' MADE YOU ASSHOLE?

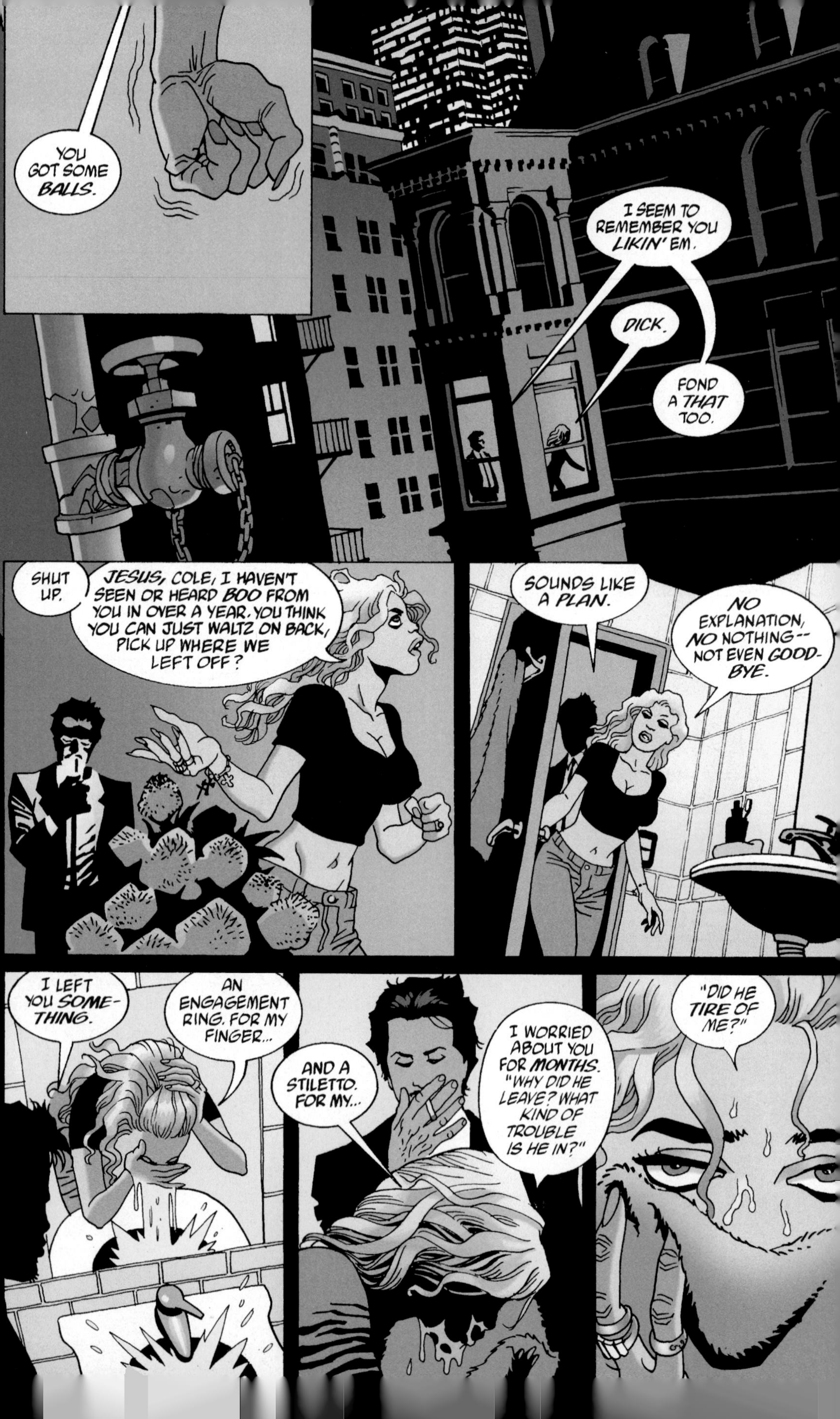
YOU GOT SOME BALLS.
I SEEM TO REMEMBER YOU LIKIN' EM.
DICK.
FOND A THAT TOO.
SHUT UP.
JESUS, COLE, I HAVEN'T SEEN OR HEARD BOO FROM YOU IN OVER A YEAR. YOU THINK YOU CAN JUST WALTZ ON BACK, PICK UP WHERE WE LEFT OFF?
SOUNDS LIKE A PLAN.
NO EXPLANATION, NO NOTHING-- NOT EVEN GOOD-BYE.
I LEFT YOU SOME-THING.
AN ENGAGEMENT RING. FOR MY FINGER...
AND A STILETTO. FOR MY...
I WORRIED ABOUT YOU FOR MONTHS. "WHY DID HE LEAVE? WHAT KIND OF TROUBLE IS HE IN?"
"DID HE TIRE OF ME?"

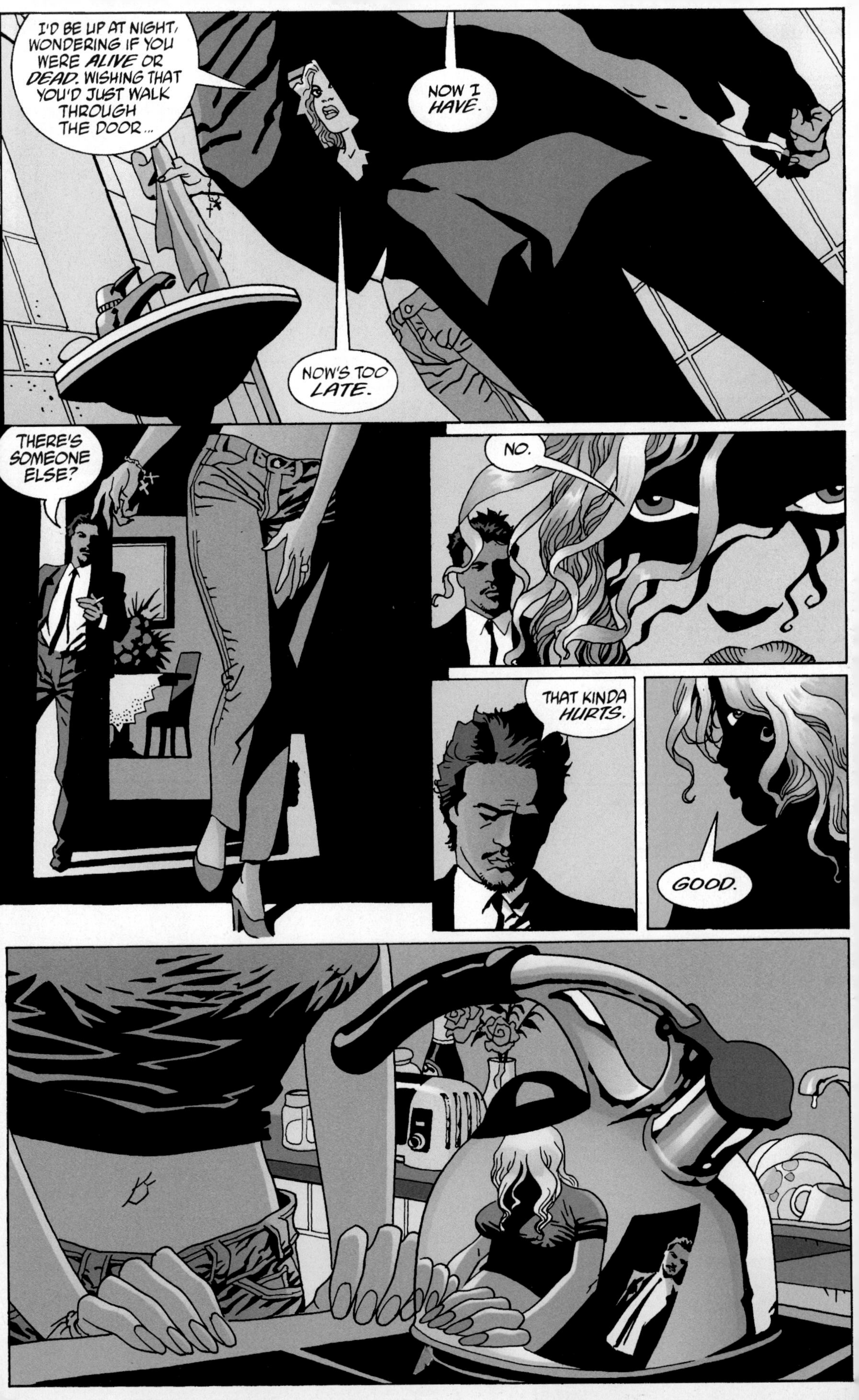
I'D BE UP AT NIGHT, WONDERING IF YOU WERE ALIVE OR DEAD. WISHING THAT YOU'D JUST WALK THROUGH THE DOOR...
NOW I HAVE.
NOW'S TOO LATE.
THERE'S SOMEONE ELSE?
NO.
THAT KINDA HURTS.
GOOD.

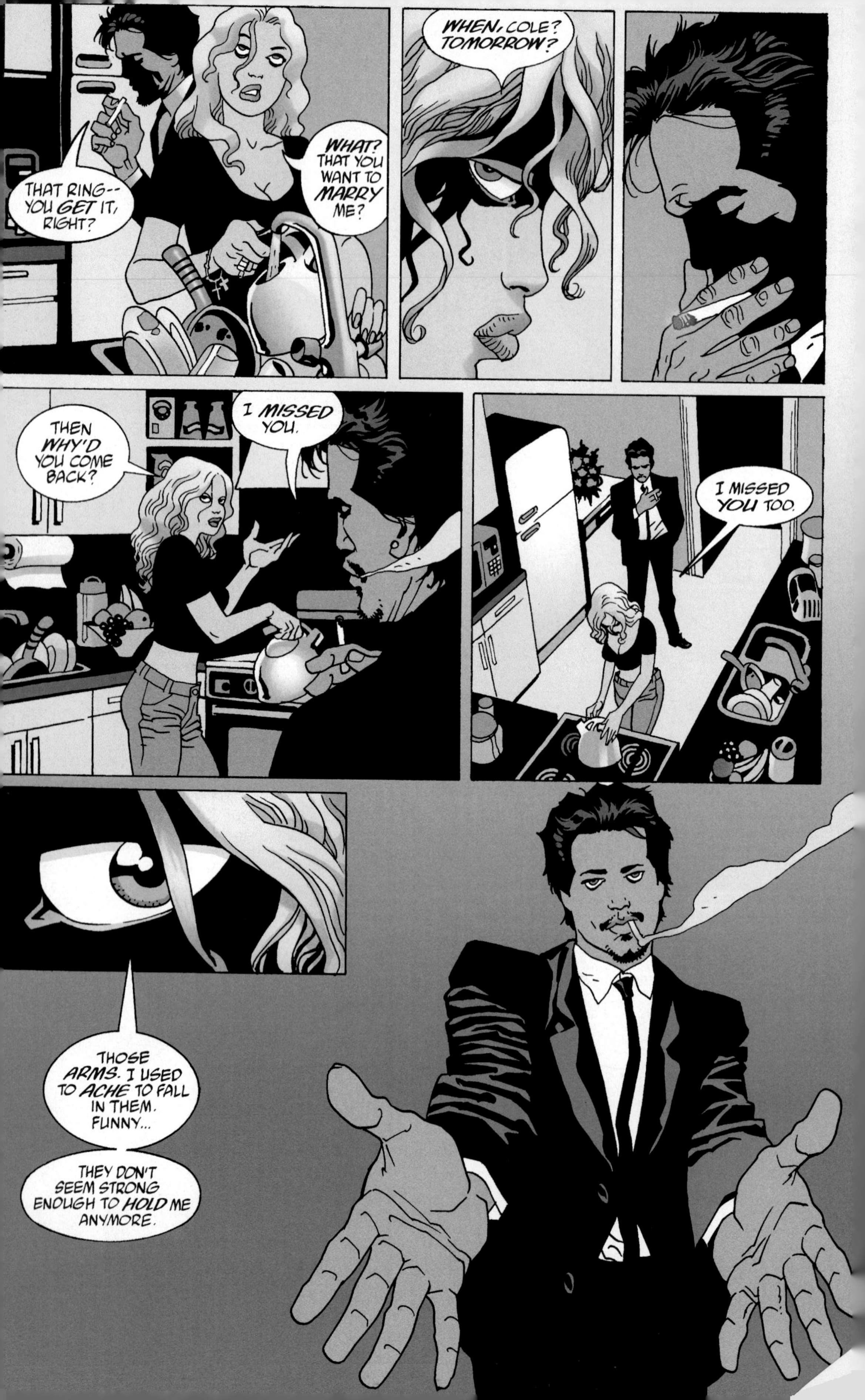
THAT RING-- YOU GET IT, RIGHT?
WHAT? THAT YOU WANT TO MARRY ME?
WHEN, COLE? TOMORROW?
THEN WHY'D YOU COME BACK?
I MISSED YOU.
I MISSED YOU TOO.
THOSE ARMS. I USED TO ACHE TO FALL IN THEM. FUNNY...
THEY DON'T SEEM STRONG ENOUGH TO HOLD ME ANYMORE.

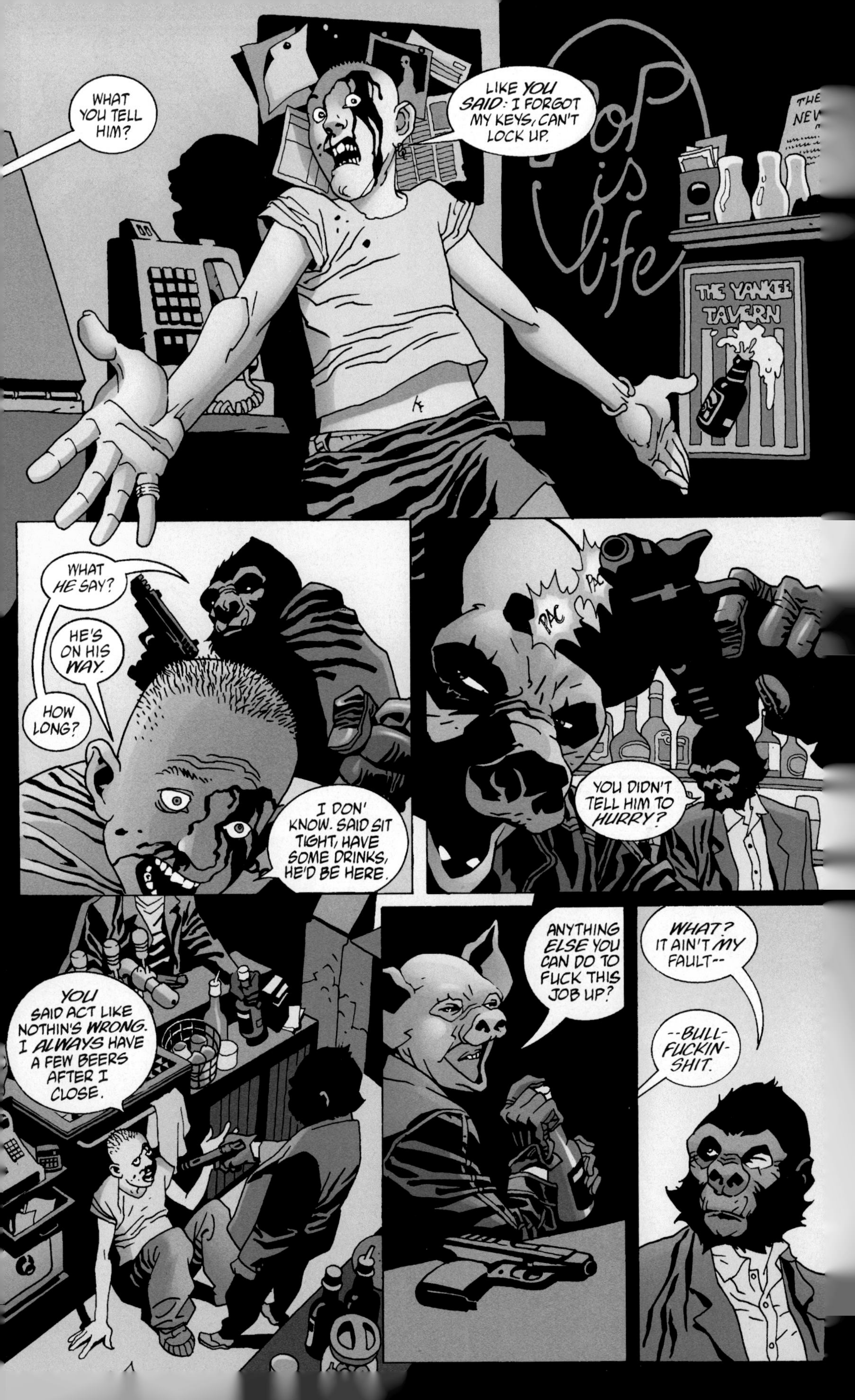
WHAT YOU TELL HIM?
LIKE YOU SAID: I FORGOT MY KEYS, CAN'T LOCK UP.
POP is life
THE YANKEE TAVERN
WHAT HE SAY?
HE'S ON HIS WAY.
HOW LONG?
I DON' KNOW. SAID SIT TIGHT, HAVE SOME DRINKS, HE'D BE HERE.
PAC
PAC
YOU DIDN'T TELL HIM TO HURRY?
YOU SAID ACT LIKE NOTHIN'S WRONG. I ALWAYS HAVE A FEW BEERS AFTER I CLOSE.
ANYTHING ELSE YOU CAN DO TO FUCK THIS JOB UP?
WHAT? IT AIN'T MY FAULT--
--BULL-FUCKIN-SHIT.

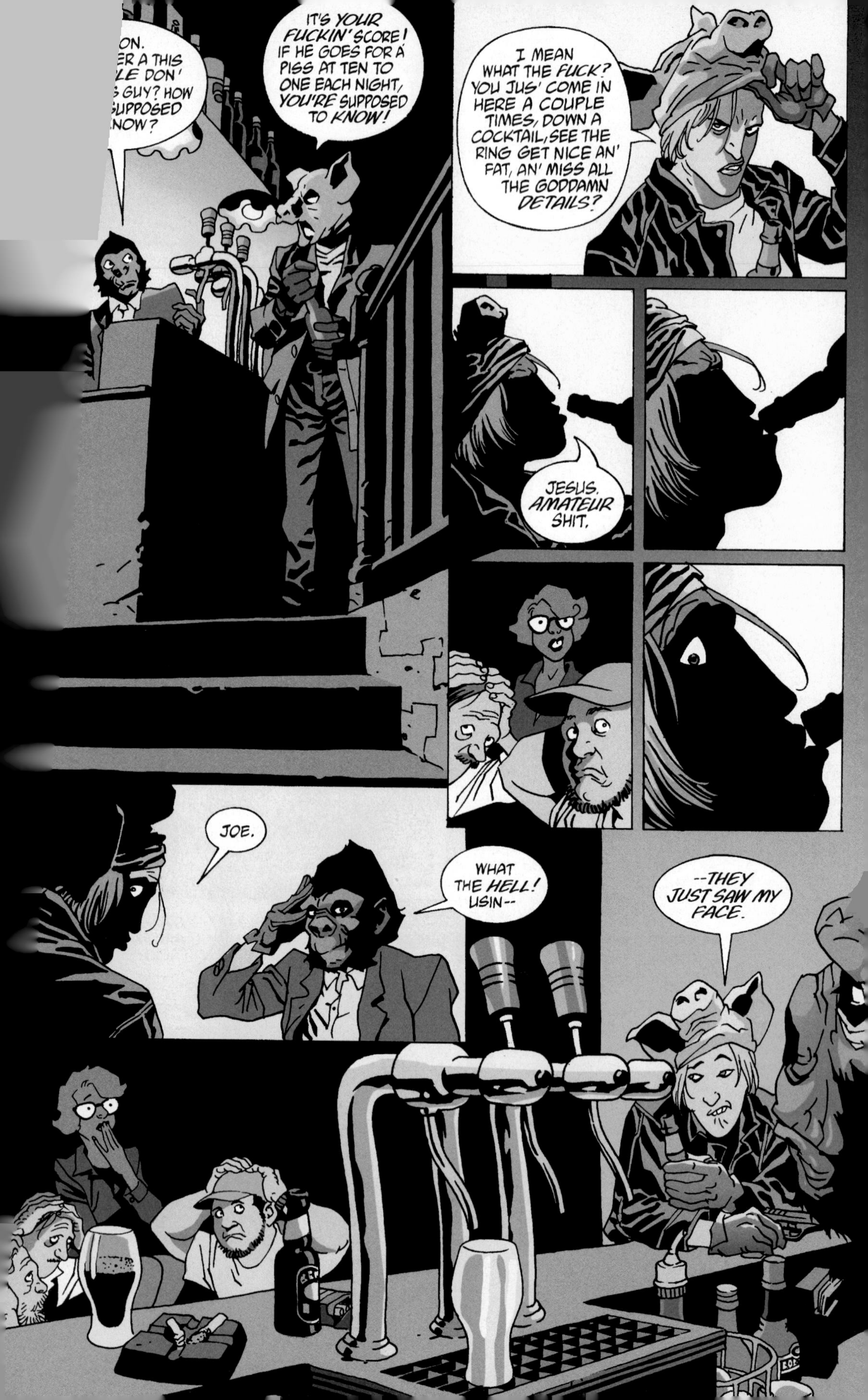

ON. ER A THIS LE DON' GUY? HOW SUPPOSED NOW?
IT'S YOUR FUCKIN' SCORE! IF HE GOES FOR A PISS AT TEN TO ONE EACH NIGHT, YOU'RE SUPPOSED TO KNOW!
I MEAN WHAT THE FUCK? YOU JUS' COME IN HERE A COUPLE TIMES, DOWN A COCKTAIL, SEE THE RING GET NICE AN' FAT, AN' MISS ALL THE GODDAMN DETAILS?
JESUS. AMATEUR SHIT.
JOE.
WHAT THE HELL! USIN--
--THEY JUST SAW MY FACE.

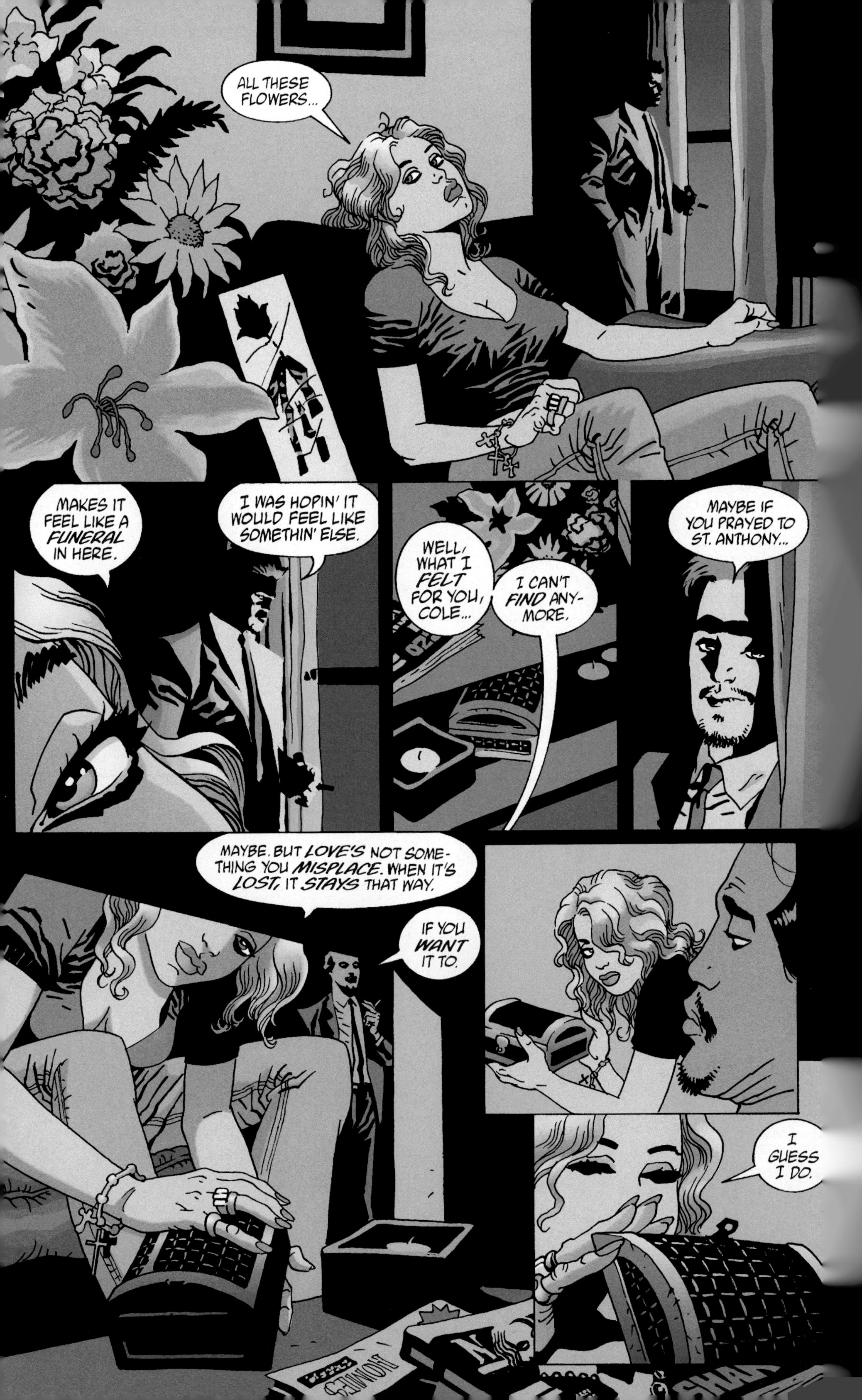
ALL THESE FLOWERS...
MAKES IT FEEL LIKE A *FUNERAL* IN HERE.
I WAS HOPIN' IT WOULD FEEL LIKE SOMETHIN' ELSE.
WELL, WHAT I *FELT* FOR YOU, COLE...
I CAN'T *FIND* ANY-MORE.
MAYBE IF YOU PRAYED TO ST. ANTHONY...
MAYBE. BUT *LOVE'S* NOT SOME-THING YOU *MISPLACE*. WHEN IT'S *LOST*, IT *STAYS* THAT WAY.
IF YOU *WANT* IT TO.
I GUESS I DO.

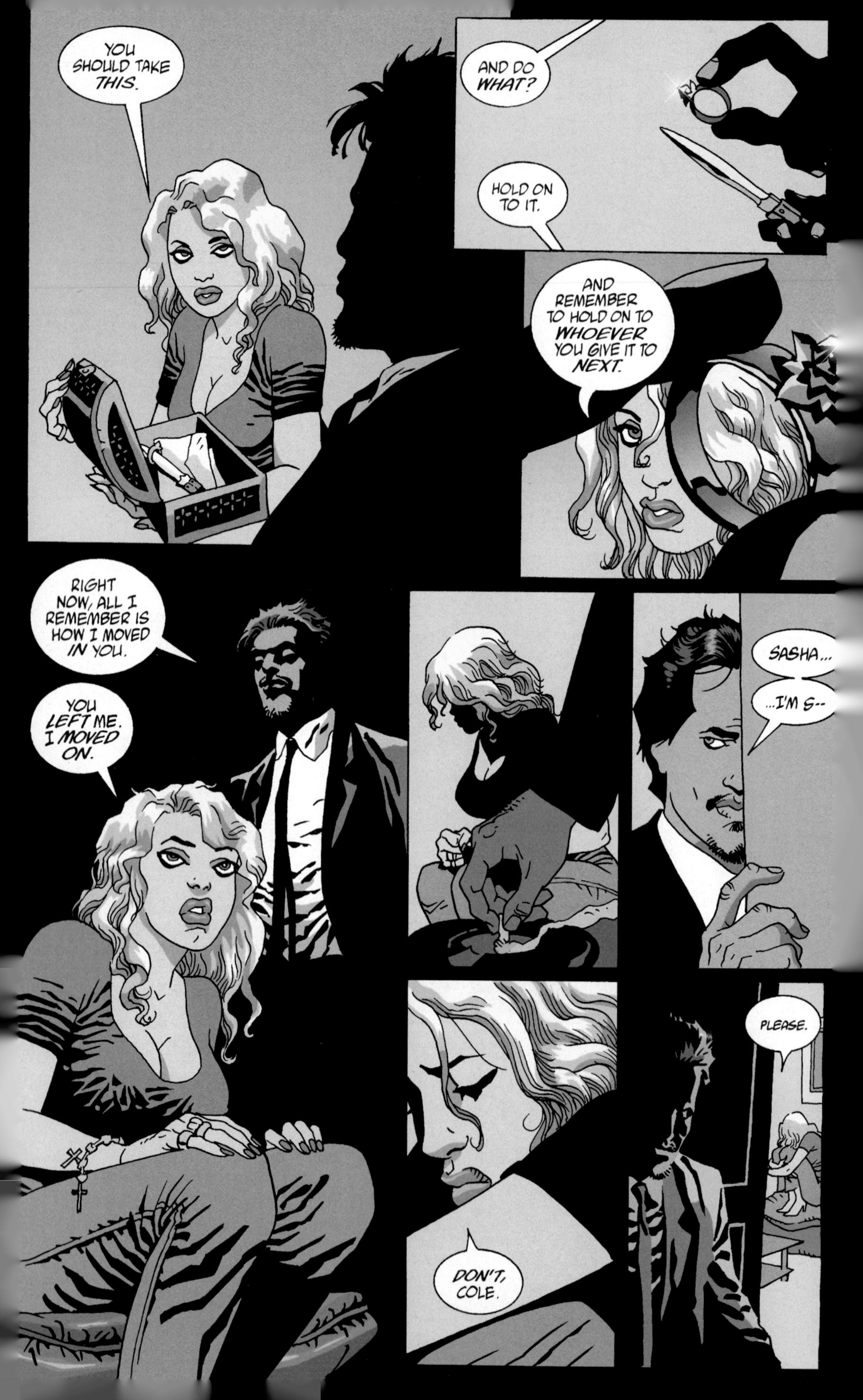
YOU SHOULD TAKE THIS.
AND DO WHAT?
HOLD ON TO IT.
AND REMEMBER TO HOLD ON TO WHOEVER YOU GIVE IT TO NEXT.
RIGHT NOW, ALL I REMEMBER IS HOW I MOVED IN YOU.
YOU LEFT ME. I MOVED ON.
SASHA...
...I'M S--
DON'T, COLE.
PLEASE.

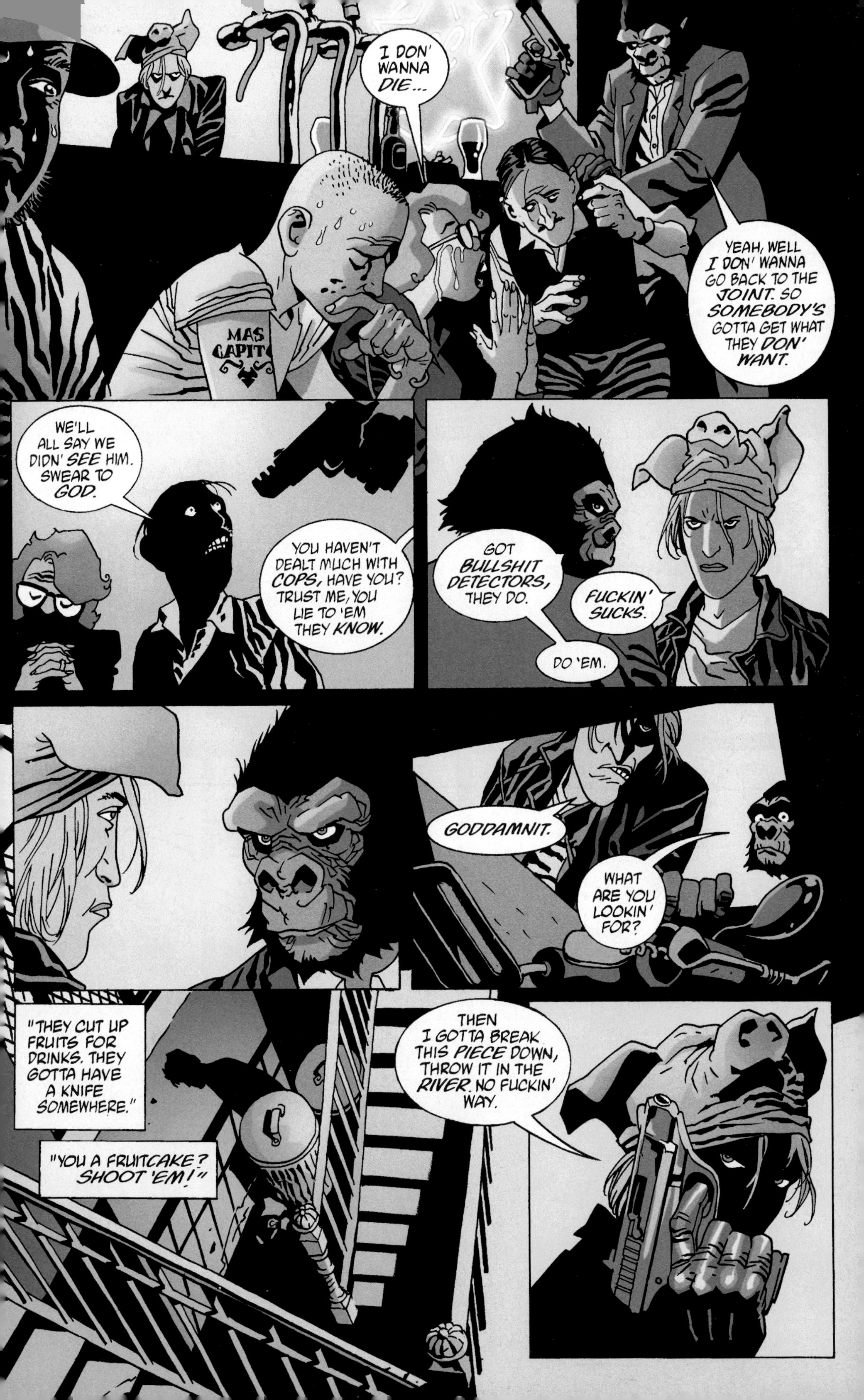
I DON' WANNA DIE...
YEAH, WELL I DON' WANNA GO BACK TO THE JOINT. SO SOMEBODY'S GOTTA GET WHAT THEY DON' WANT.
MAS CAPIT
WE'LL ALL SAY WE DIDN' SEE HIM. SWEAR TO GOD.
YOU HAVEN'T DEALT MUCH WITH COPS, HAVE YOU? TRUST ME, YOU LIE TO 'EM THEY KNOW.
GOT BULLSHIT DETECTORS, THEY DO.
FUCKIN' SUCKS.
DO 'EM.
GODDAMNIT.
WHAT ARE YOU LOOKIN' FOR?
"THEY CUT UP FRUITS FOR DRINKS. THEY GOTTA HAVE A KNIFE SOMEWHERE."
"YOU A FRUITCAKE? SHOOT 'EM!"
THEN I GOTTA BREAK THIS PIECE DOWN, THROW IT IN THE RIVER. NO FUCKIN' WAY.

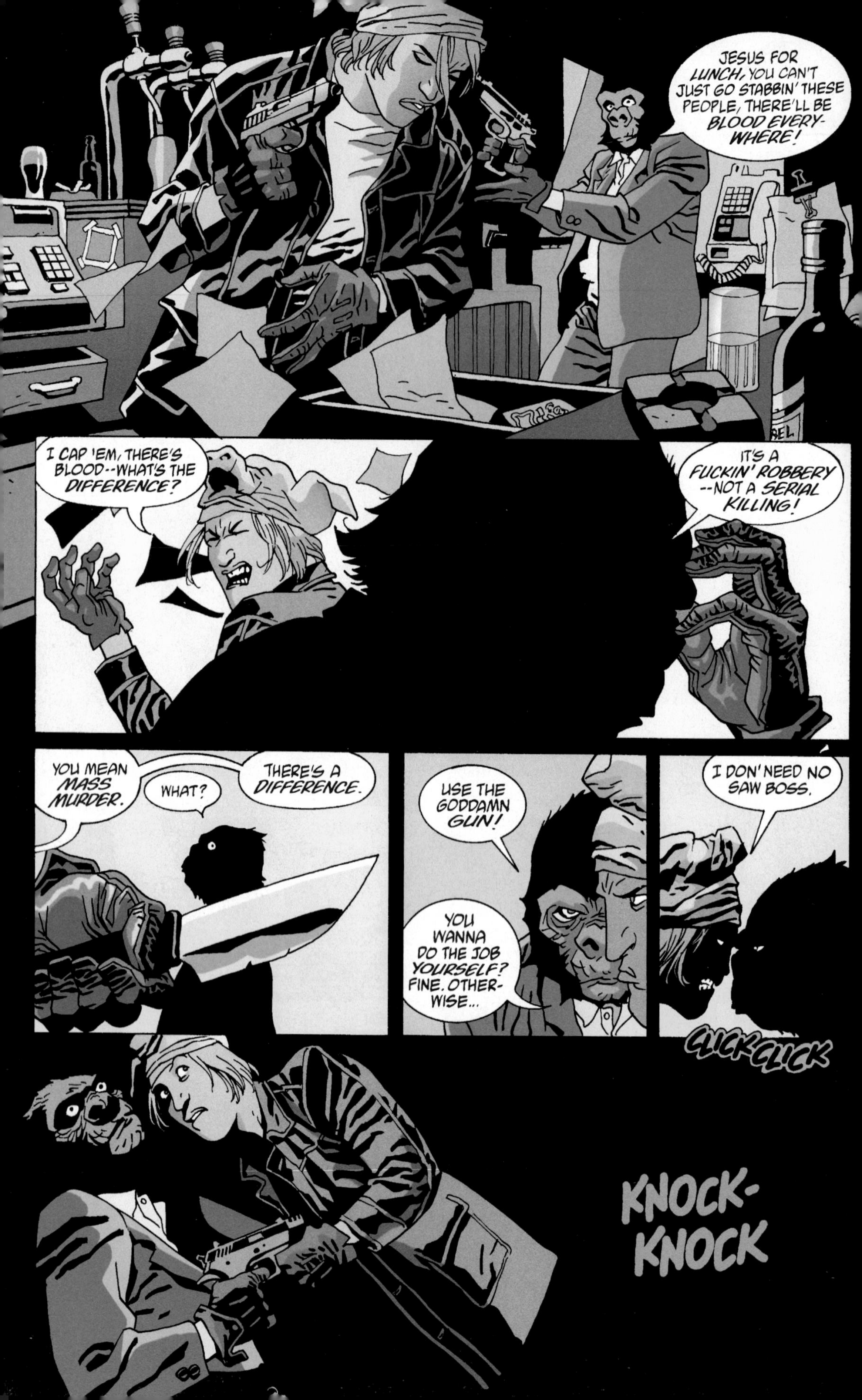
JESUS FOR LUNCH, YOU CAN'T JUST GO STABBIN' THESE PEOPLE, THERE'LL BE BLOOD EVERY-WHERE!
I CAP 'EM, THERE'S BLOOD--WHAT'S THE DIFFERENCE?
IT'S A FUCKIN' ROBBERY --NOT A SERIAL KILLING!
YOU MEAN MASS MURDER.
WHAT?
THERE'S A DIFFERENCE.
USE THE GODDAMN GUN!
YOU WANNA DO THE JOB YOURSELF? FINE. OTHER-WISE...
I DON' NEED NO SAW BOSS.
CLICK CLICK
KNOCK-KNOCK

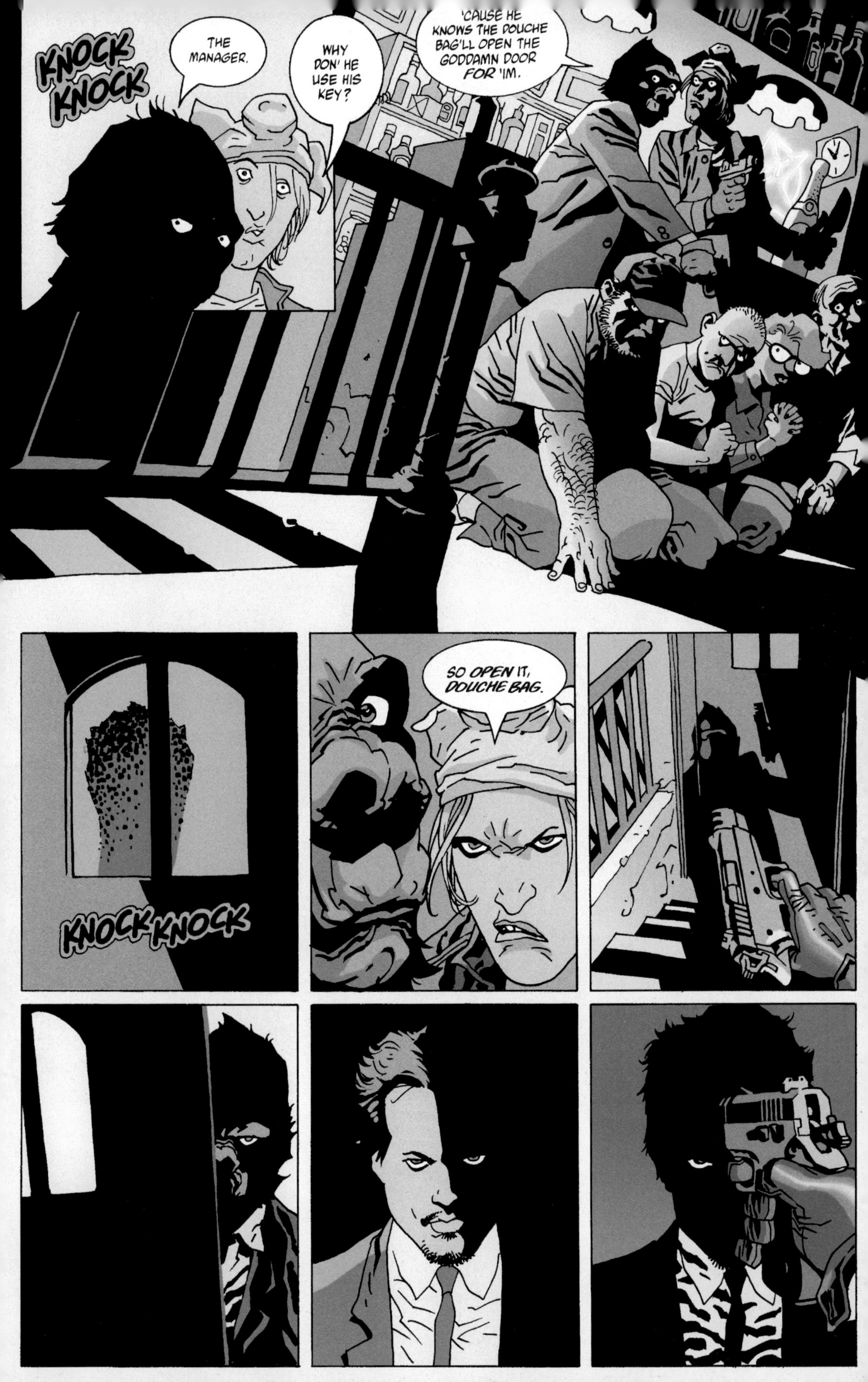
KNOCK KNOCK
THE MANAGER.
WHY DON' HE USE HIS KEY?
'CAUSE HE KNOWS THE DOUCHE BAG'LL OPEN THE GODDAMN DOOR FOR 'IM.
KNOCK KNOCK
SO OPEN IT, DOUCHE BAG.

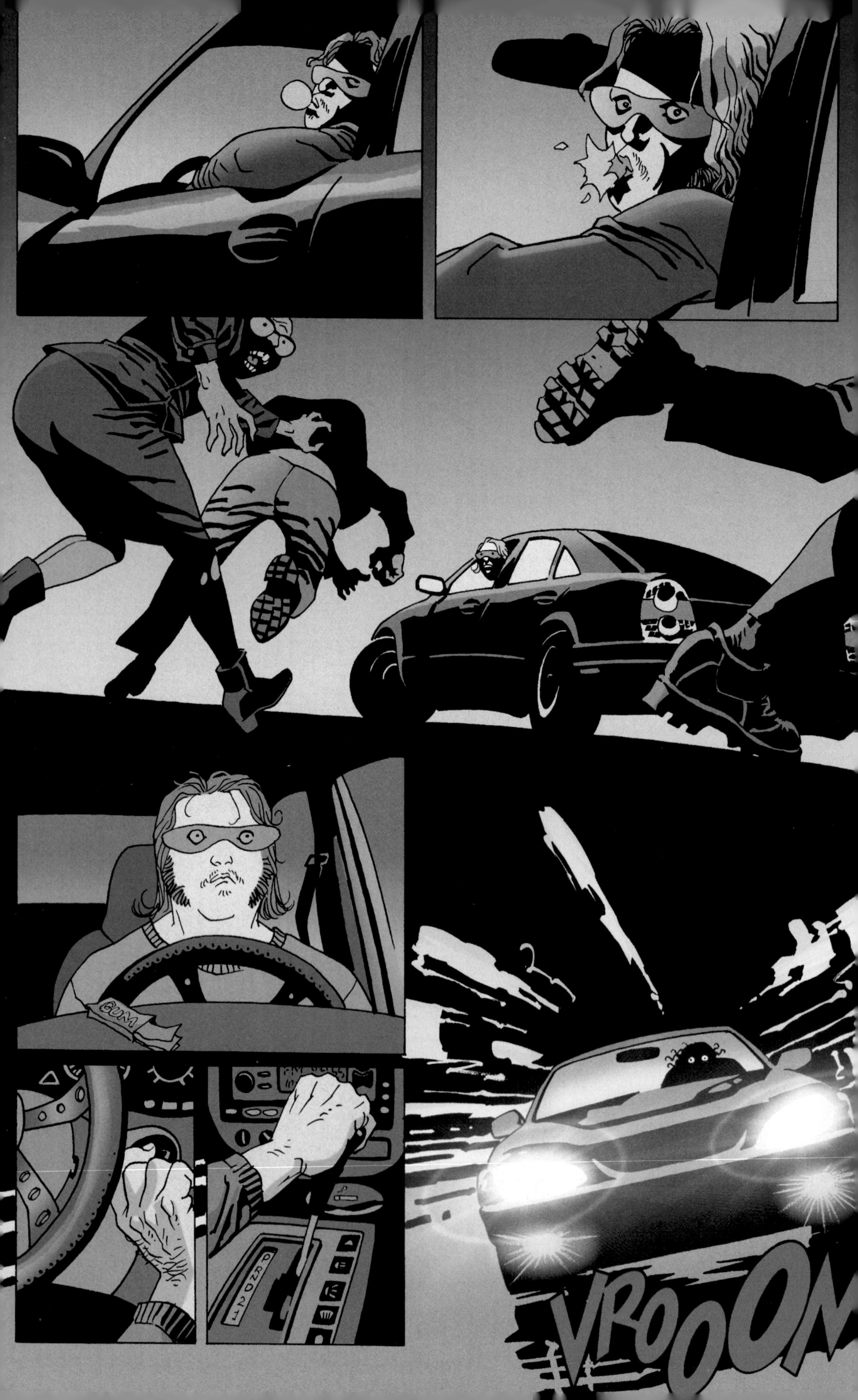
GUM
PRND21
VROOOM

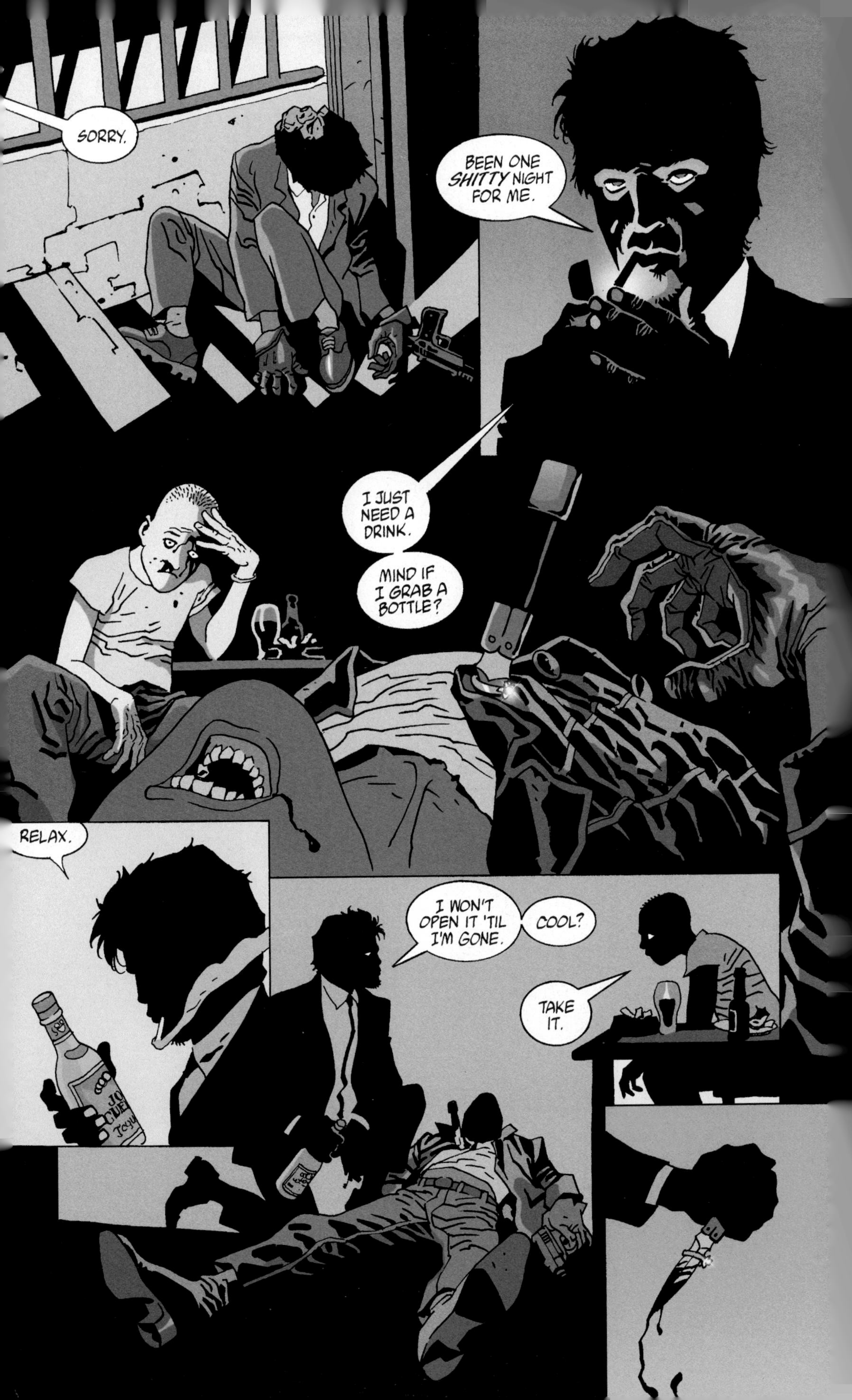
SORRY.
BEEN ONE SHITTY NIGHT FOR ME.
I JUST NEED A DRINK.
MIND IF I GRAB A BOTTLE?
RELAX.
I WON'T OPEN IT 'TIL I'M GONE.
COOL?
TAKE IT.

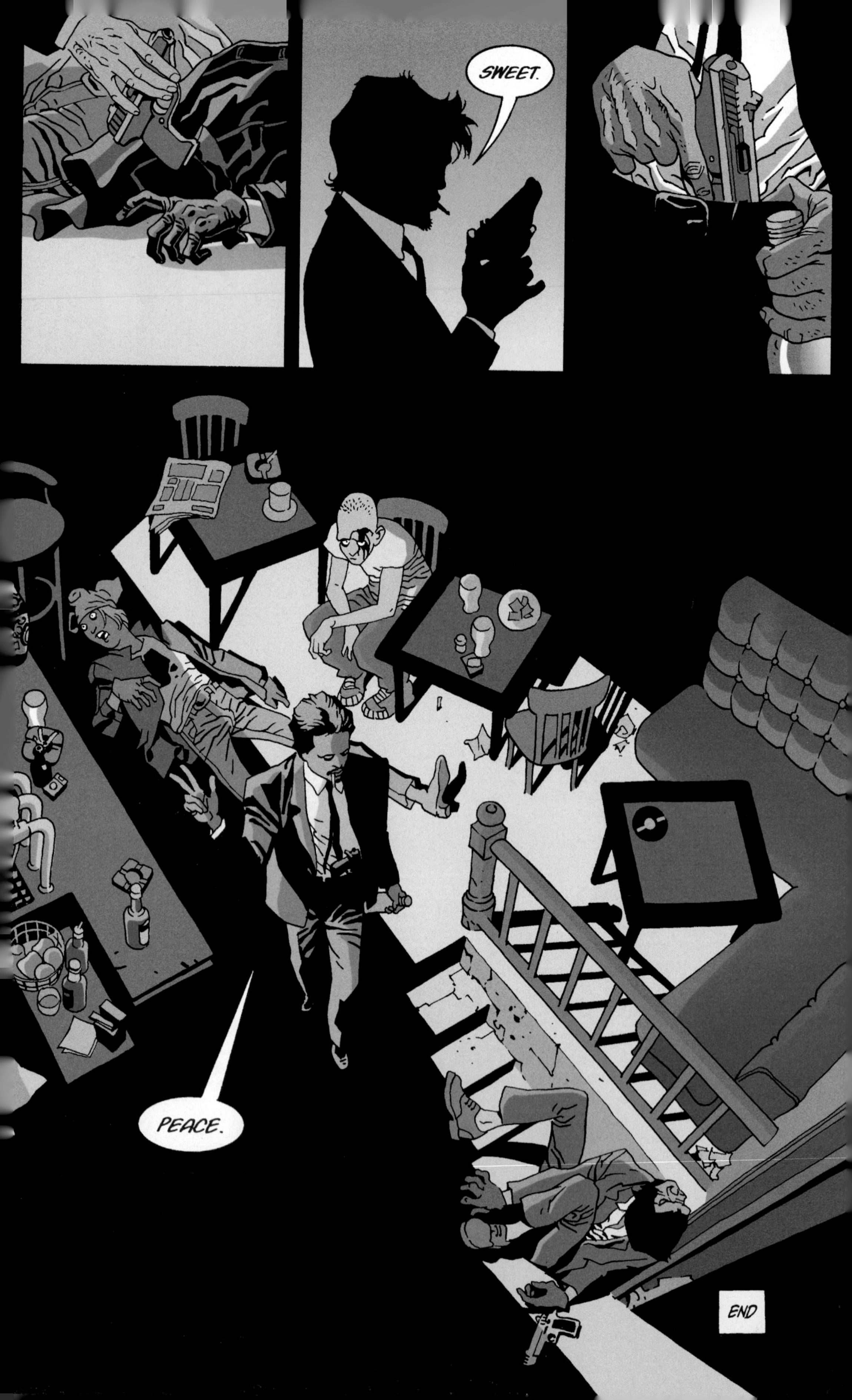
SWEET.
PEACE.
END

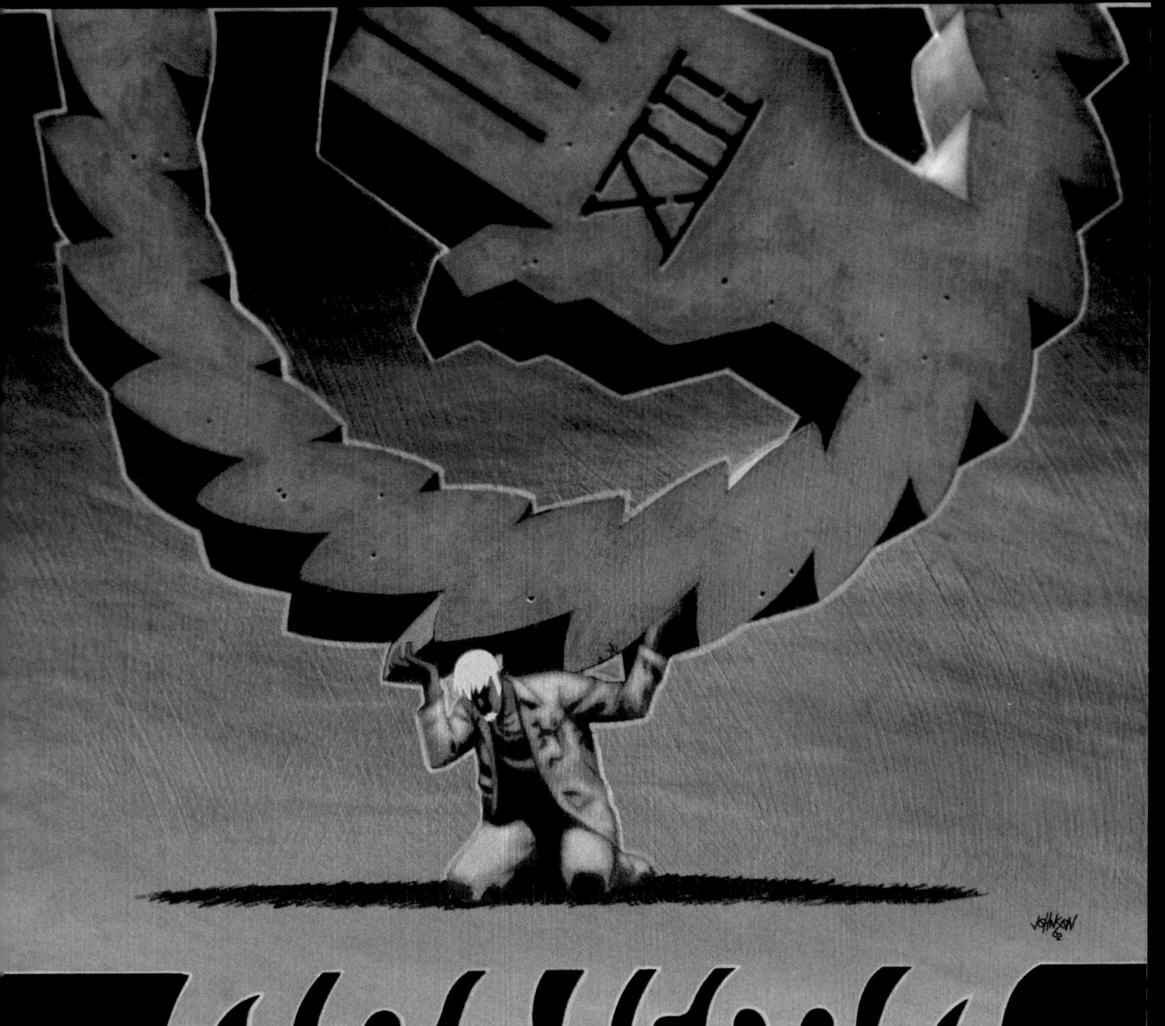
BENITO

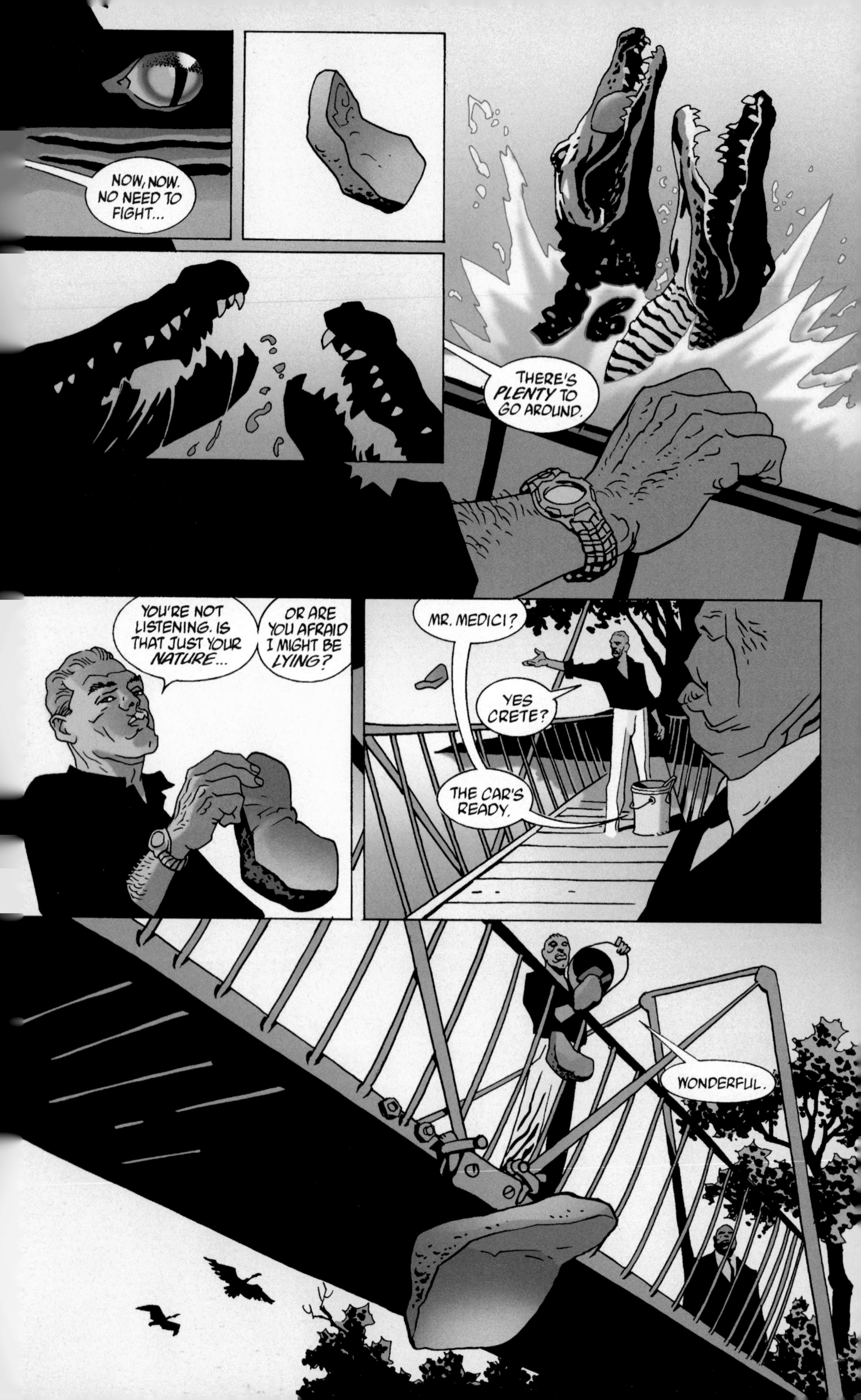
NOW, NOW. NO NEED TO FIGHT...
THERE'S PLENTY TO GO AROUND.
YOU'RE NOT LISTENING. IS THAT JUST YOUR NATURE...
OR ARE YOU AFRAID I MIGHT BE LYING?
MR. MEDICI?
YES CRETE?
THE CAR'S READY.
WONDERFUL.

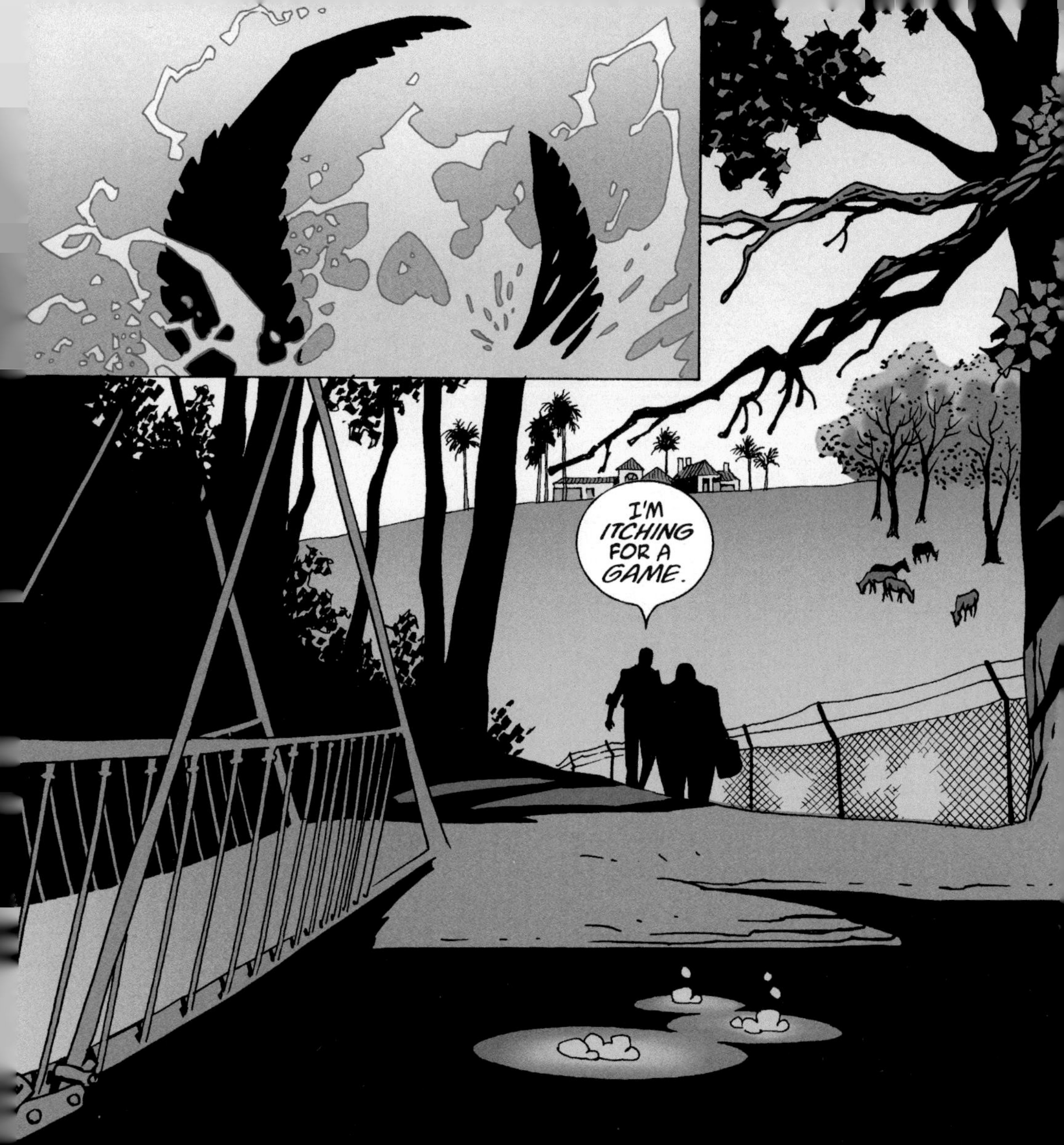
I'M ITCHING FOR A GAME.

Ambition's Audition

Written by **Brian Azzarello** *Illustrated by* **Eduardo Risso**

Patricia Mulvihill **Clem Robins** **Digital Chameleon** **Dave Johnson** **Zachary Rau** **Will Denn**

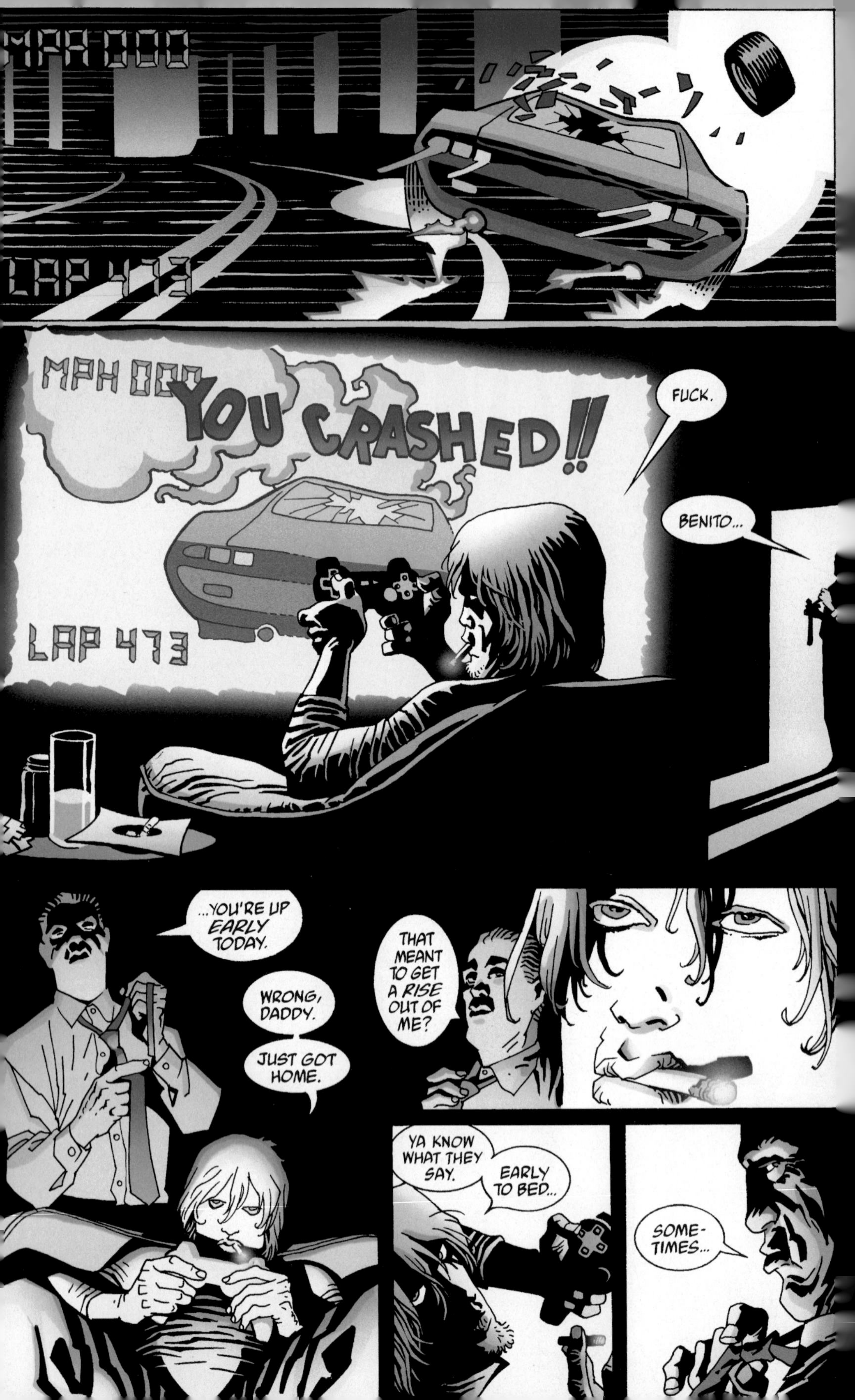
MPH 000
LAP 473
MPH 000
YOU CRASHED!!
LAP 473
FUCK.
BENITO...
...YOU'RE UP EARLY TODAY.
WRONG, DADDY.
JUST GOT HOME.
THAT MEANT TO GET A RISE OUT OF ME?
YA KNOW WHAT THEY SAY.
EARLY TO BED...
SOME-TIMES...

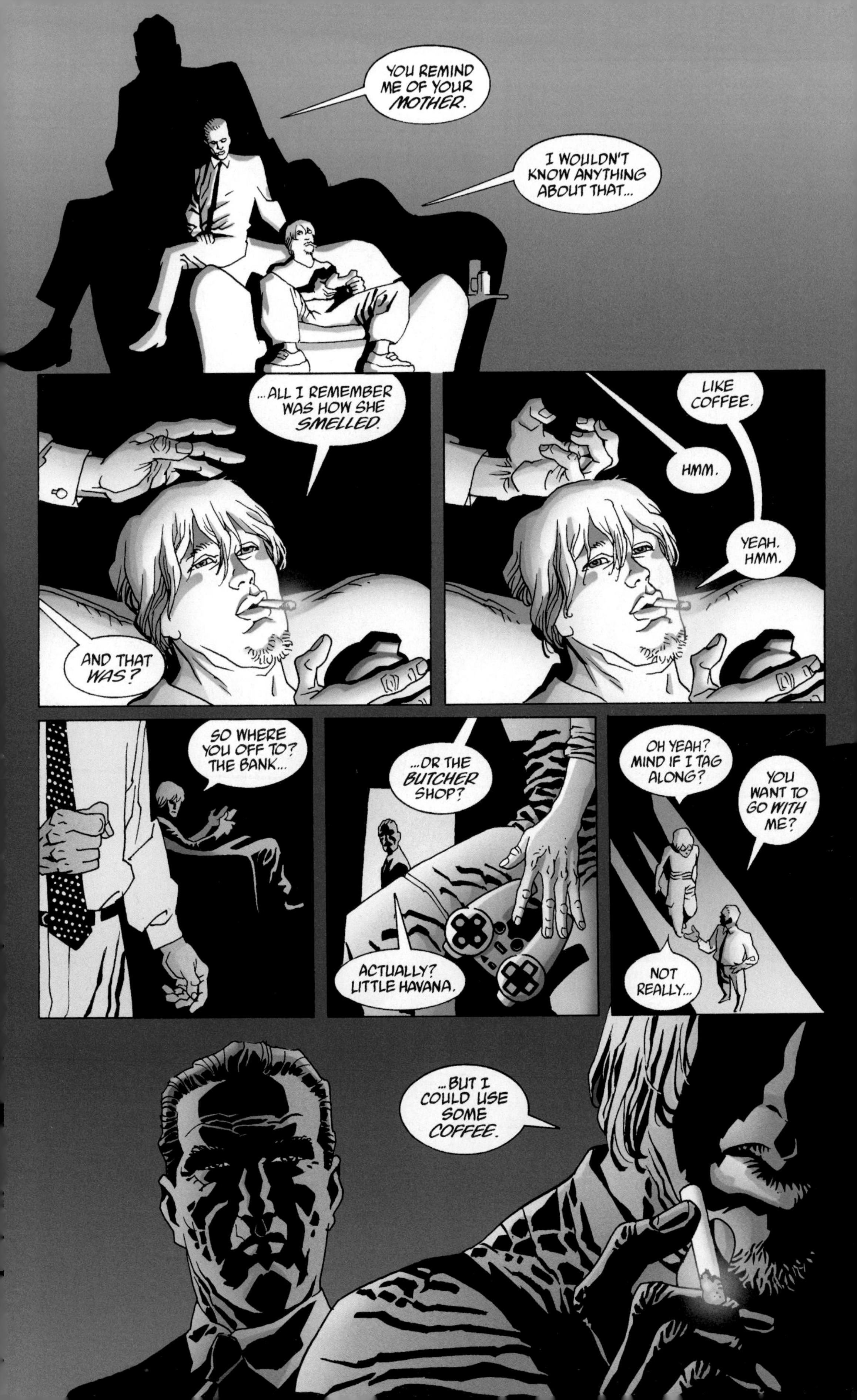
YOU REMIND ME OF YOUR MOTHER.
I WOULDN'T KNOW ANYTHING ABOUT THAT...
...ALL I REMEMBER WAS HOW SHE SMELLED.
AND THAT WAS?
LIKE COFFEE.
HMM.
YEAH. HMM.
SO WHERE YOU OFF TO? THE BANK...
...OR THE BUTCHER SHOP?
ACTUALLY? LITTLE HAVANA.
OH YEAH? MIND IF I TAG ALONG?
YOU WANT TO GO WITH ME?
NOT REALLY...
...BUT I COULD USE SOME COFFEE.

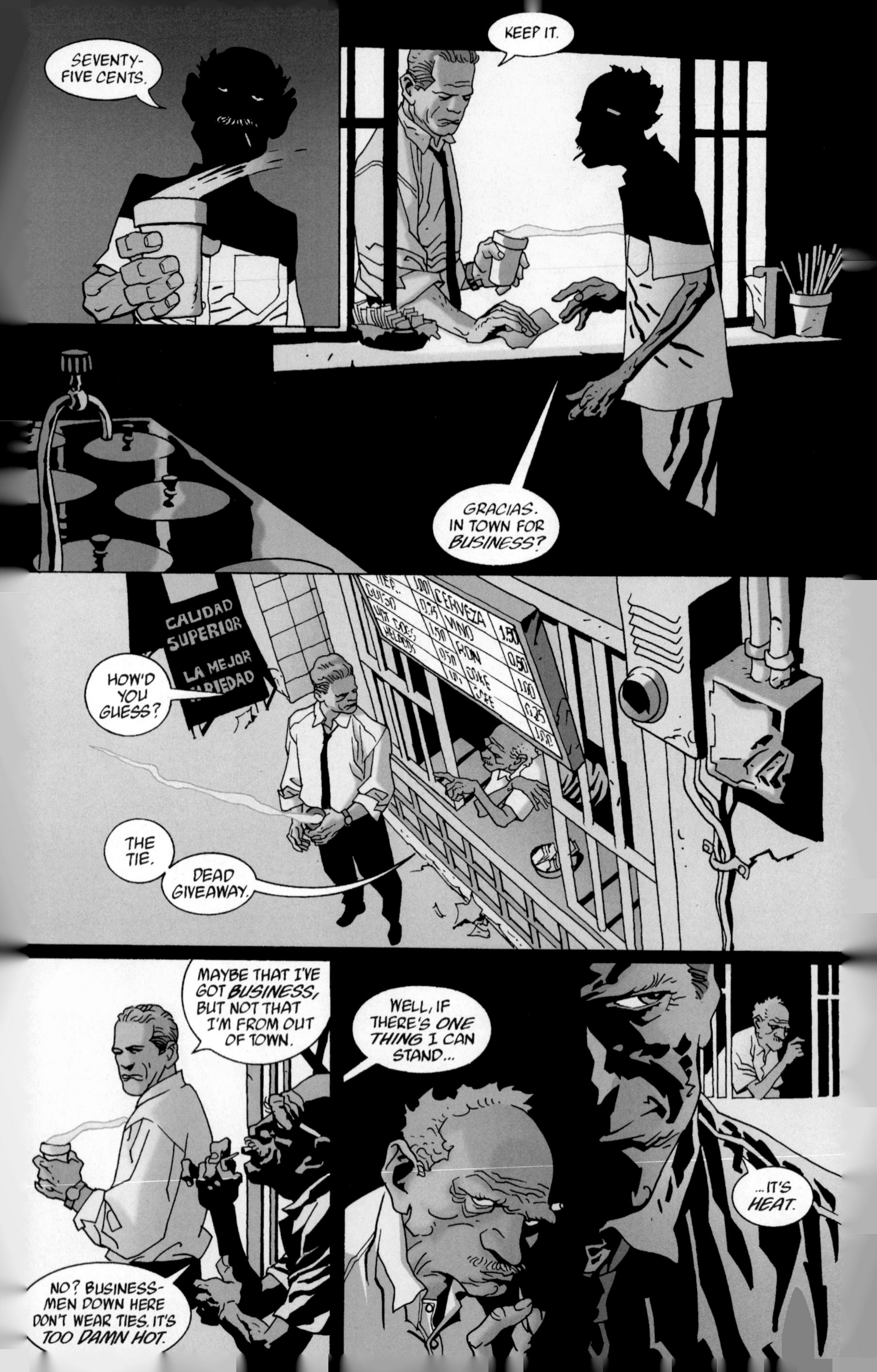
SEVENTY-FIVE CENTS.
KEEP IT.
GRACIAS. IN TOWN FOR BUSINESS?
CALIDAD SUPERIOR
LA MEJOR
HOW'D YOU GUESS?
THE TIE.
DEAD GIVEAWAY.
MAYBE THAT I'VE GOT BUSINESS, BUT NOT THAT I'M FROM OUT OF TOWN.
NO? BUSINESSMEN DOWN HERE DON'T WEAR TIES. IT'S TOO DAMN HOT.
WELL, IF THERE'S ONE THING I CAN STAND...
...IT'S HEAT.

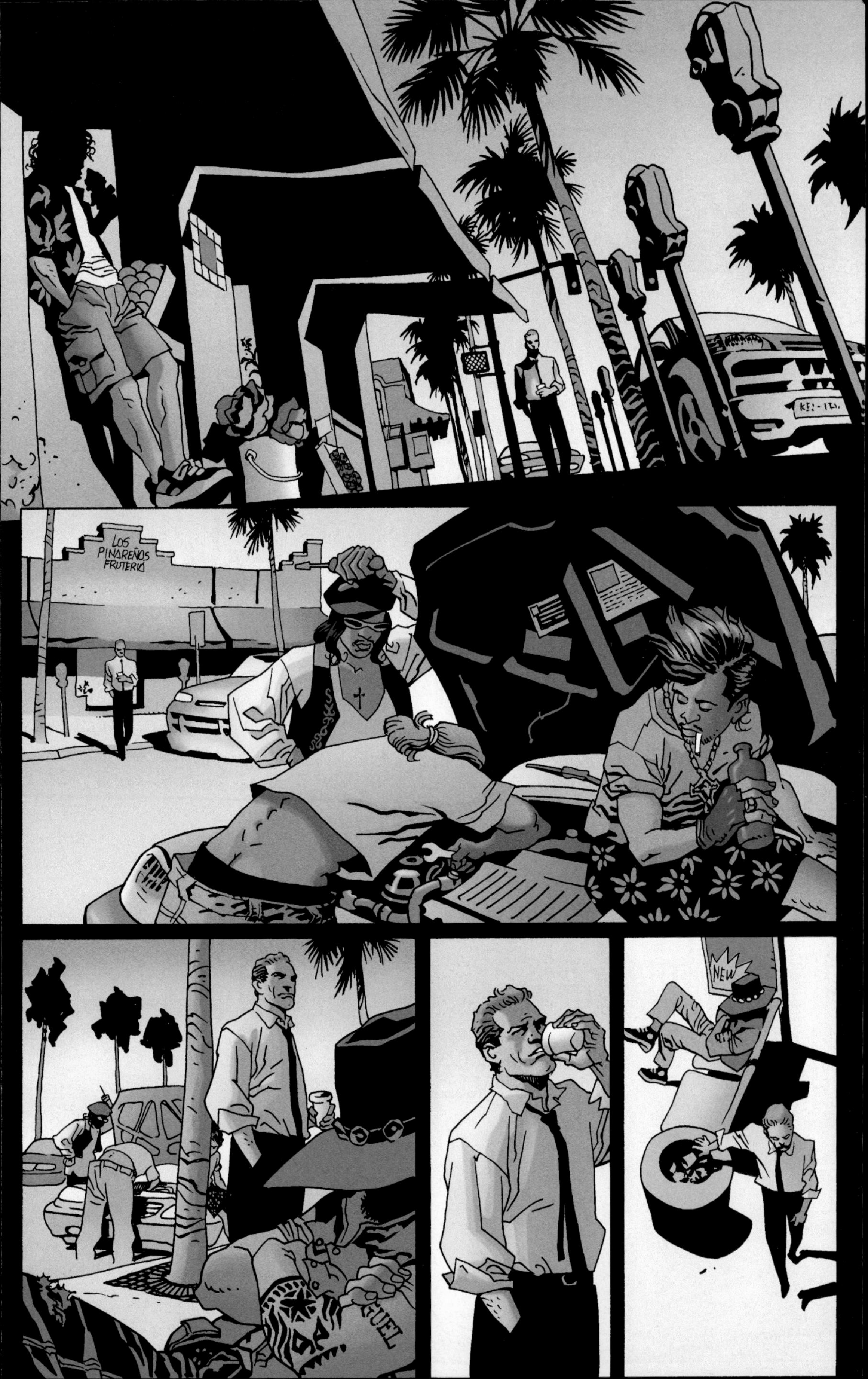
LOS PINAREÑOS FRUTERIA
NEW

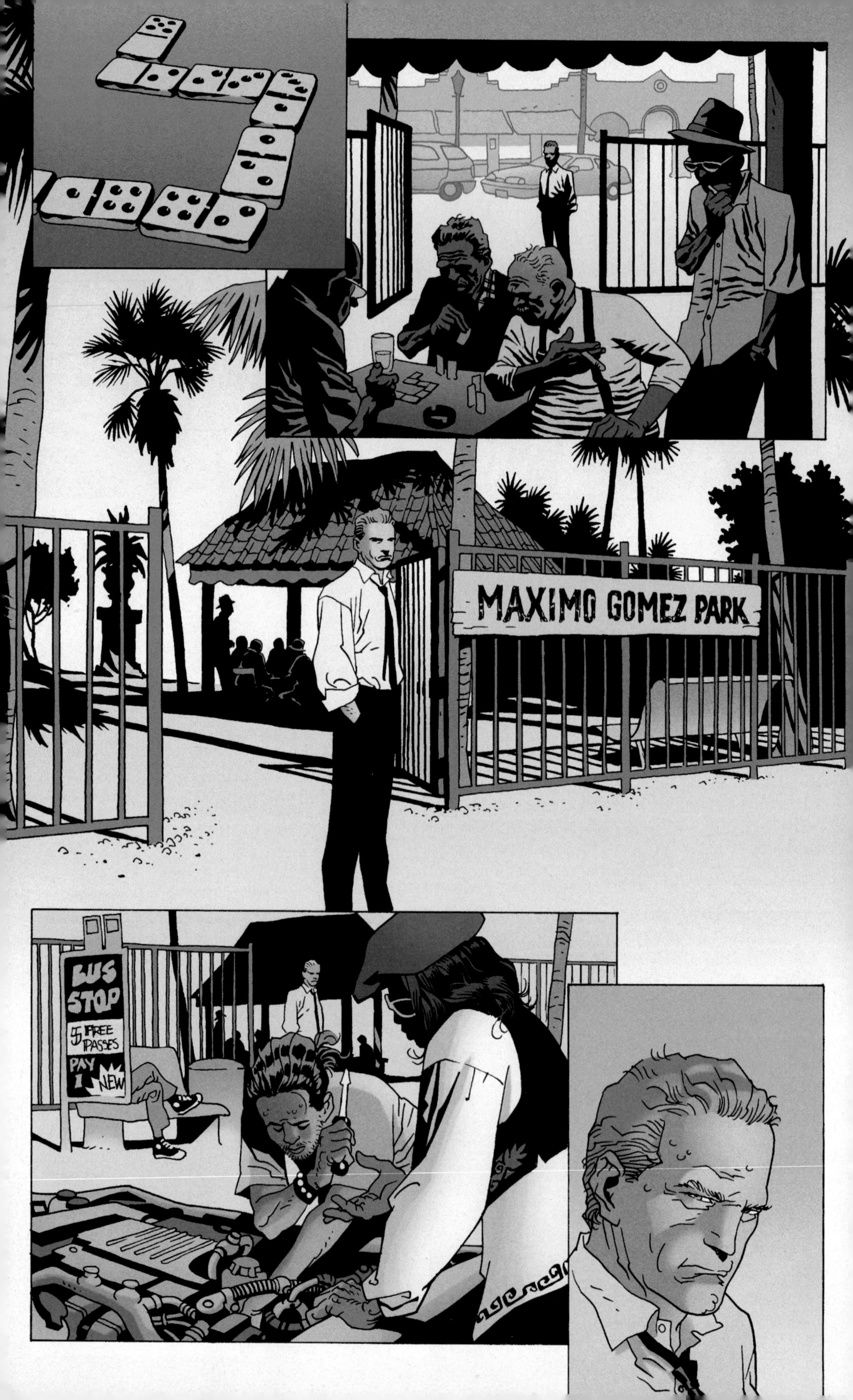
MAXIMO GOMEZ PARK
BUS STOP
5 FREE PASSES
PAY 1
NEW

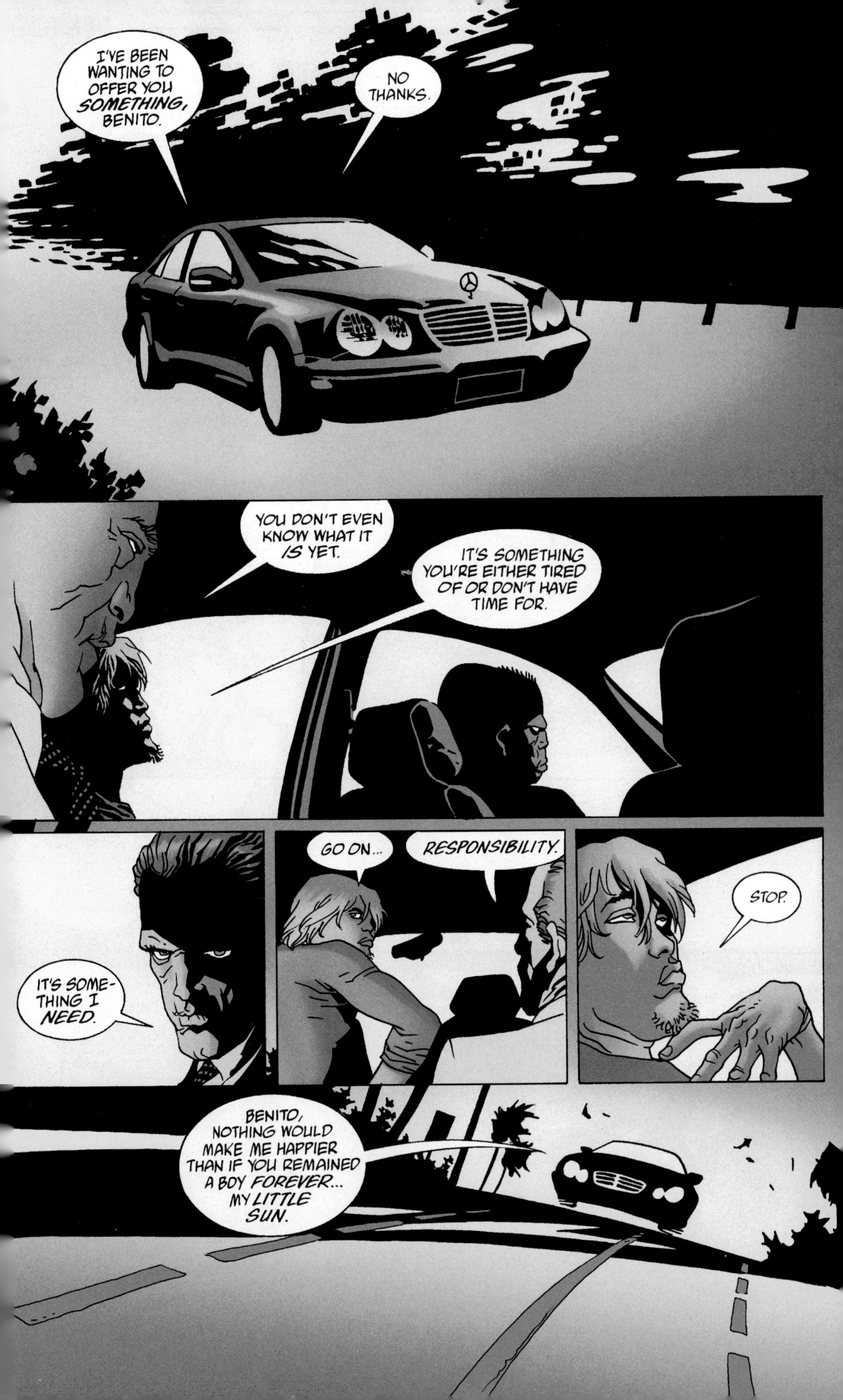
I'VE BEEN WANTING TO OFFER YOU SOMETHING, BENITO.
NO THANKS.
YOU DON'T EVEN KNOW WHAT IT IS YET.
IT'S SOMETHING YOU'RE EITHER TIRED OF OR DON'T HAVE TIME FOR.
IT'S SOME-THING I NEED.
GO ON...
RESPONSIBILITY.
STOP.
BENITO, NOTHING WOULD MAKE ME HAPPIER THAN IF YOU REMAINED A BOY FOREVER... MY LITTLE SUN.

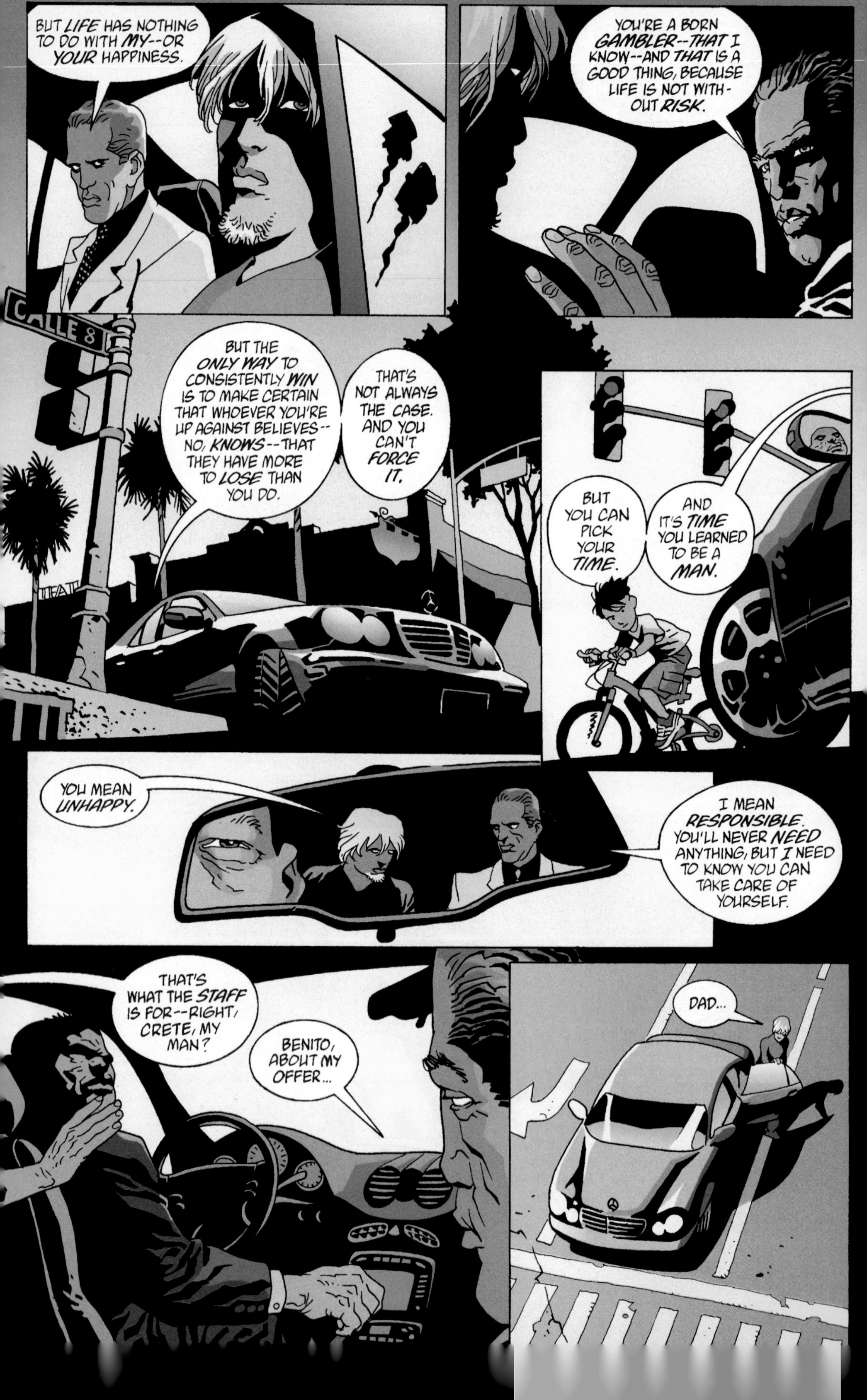
BUT LIFE HAS NOTHING TO DO WITH MY--OR YOUR HAPPINESS.
YOU'RE A BORN GAMBLER--THAT I KNOW--AND THAT IS A GOOD THING, BECAUSE LIFE IS NOT WITHOUT RISK.
CALLE 8
BUT THE ONLY WAY TO CONSISTENTLY WIN IS TO MAKE CERTAIN THAT WHOEVER YOU'RE UP AGAINST BELIEVES--NO, KNOWS--THAT THEY HAVE MORE TO LOSE THAN YOU DO.
THAT'S NOT ALWAYS THE CASE. AND YOU CAN'T FORCE IT.
BUT YOU CAN PICK YOUR TIME.
AND IT'S TIME YOU LEARNED TO BE A MAN.
YOU MEAN UNHAPPY.
I MEAN RESPONSIBLE. YOU'LL NEVER NEED ANYTHING, BUT I NEED TO KNOW YOU CAN TAKE CARE OF YOURSELF.
THAT'S WHAT THE STAFF IS FOR--RIGHT, CRETE, MY MAN?
BENITO, ABOUT MY OFFER...
DAD...

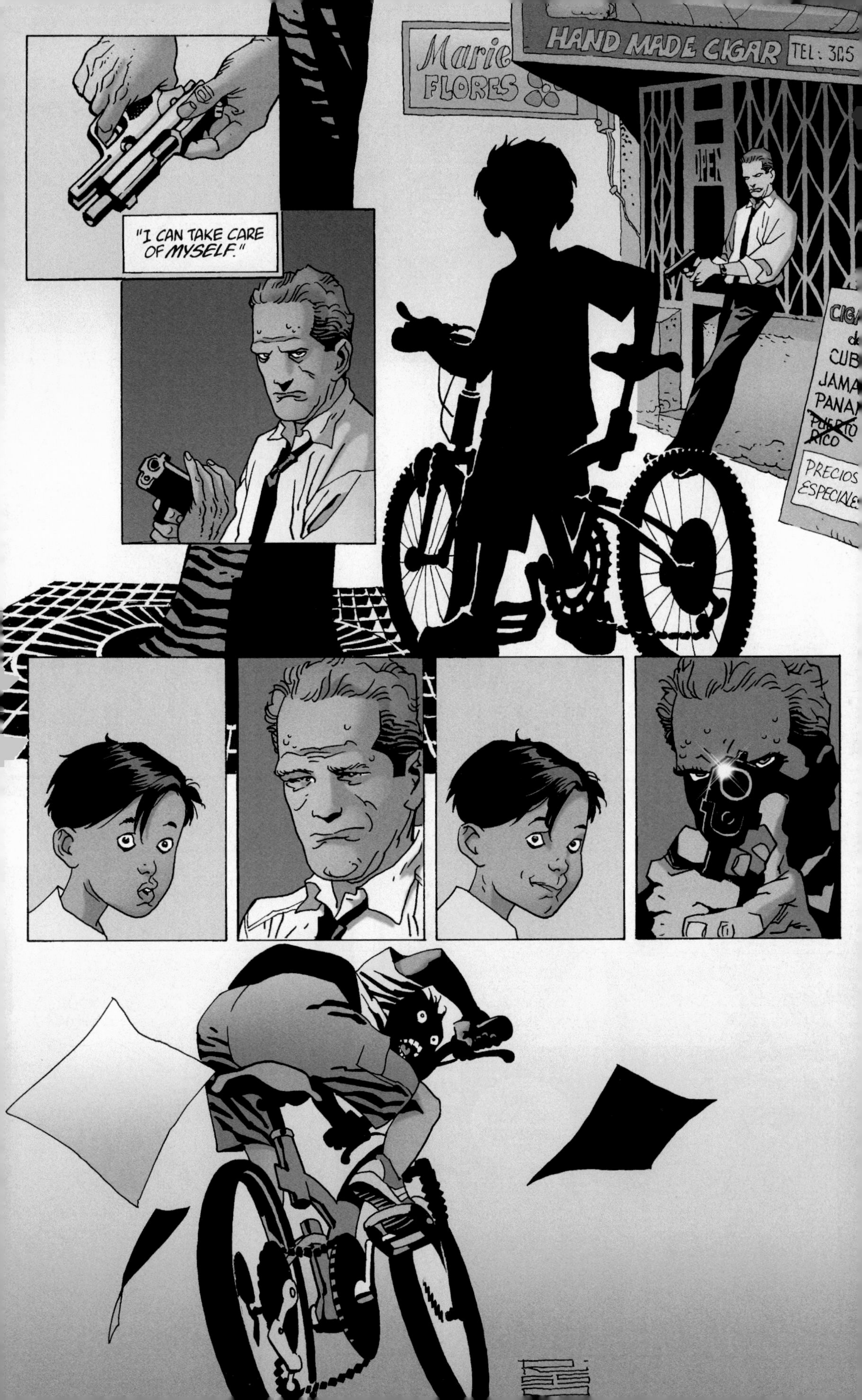

Marie
FLORES
HAND MADE CIGAR
TEL: 305
"I CAN TAKE CARE OF MYSELF."
PRECIOS ESPECIALES

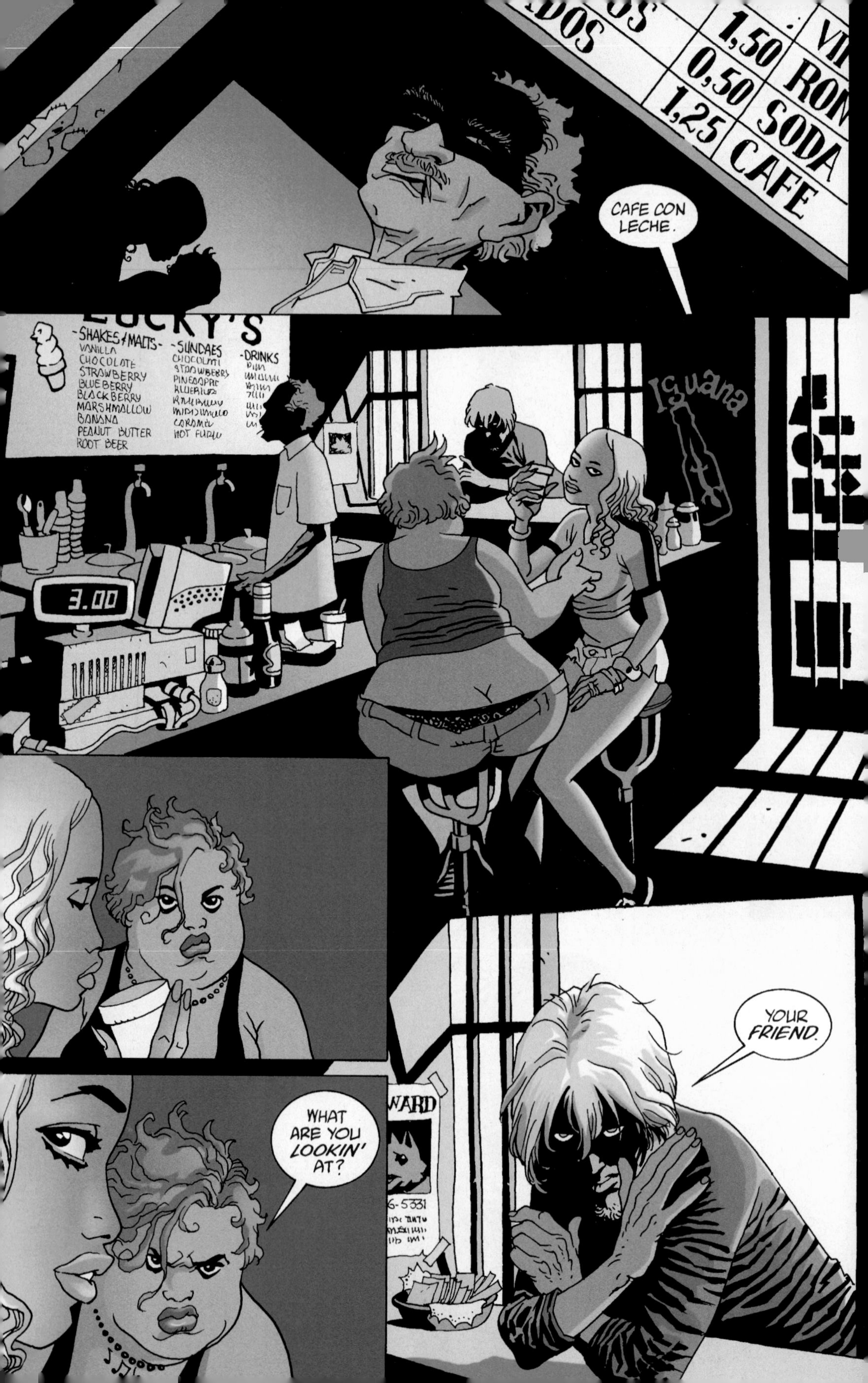

1,50 RON
0,50 SODA
1,25 CAFE
CAFE CON LECHE.
SHAKES & MALTS
VANILLA
CHOCOLATE
STRAWBERRY
BLUEBERRY
BLACKBERRY
MARSHMALLOW
BANANA
PEANUT BUTTER
ROOT BEER
SUNDAES
DRINKS
Iguana
3.00
WHAT ARE YOU LOOKIN' AT?
YOUR FRIEND.

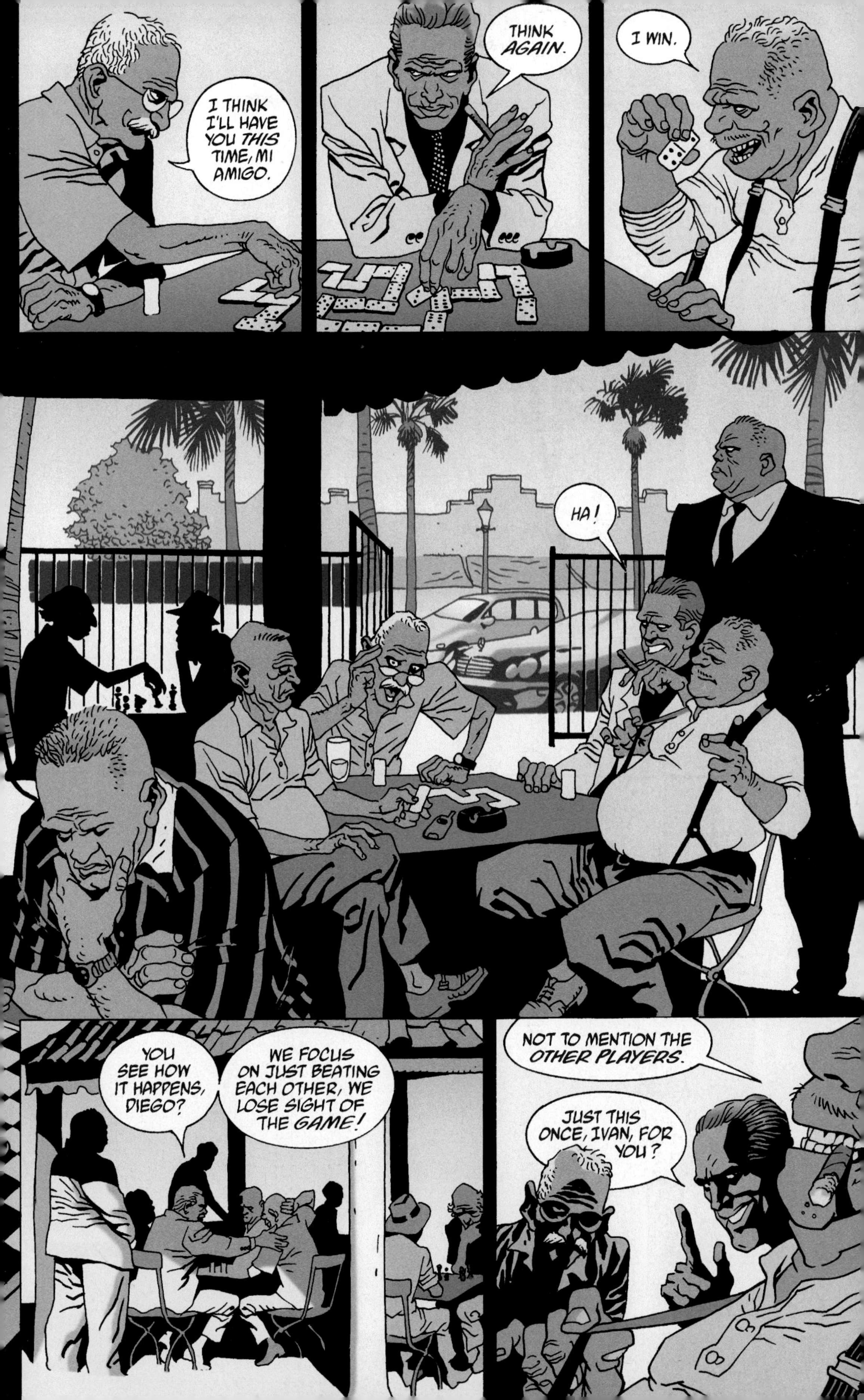
I THINK I'LL HAVE YOU THIS TIME, MI AMIGO.
THINK AGAIN.
I WIN.
HA!
YOU SEE HOW IT HAPPENS, DIEGO?
WE FOCUS ON JUST BEATING EACH OTHER, WE LOSE SIGHT OF THE GAME!
NOT TO MENTION THE OTHER PLAYERS.
JUST THIS ONCE, IVAN, FOR YOU?

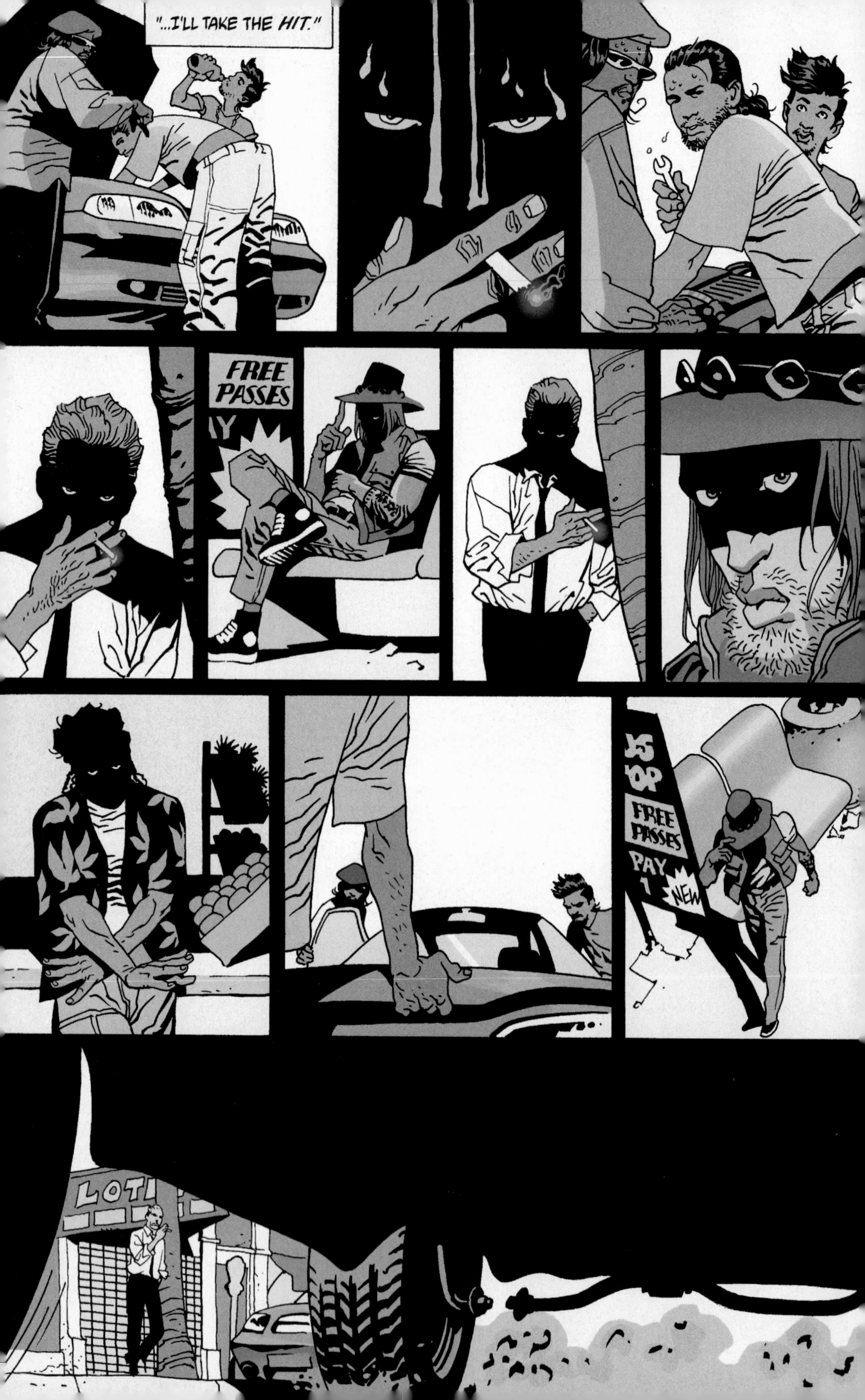
"...I'LL TAKE THE HIT."
FREE PASSES
FREE PASSES
PAY 1
NEW
LOT

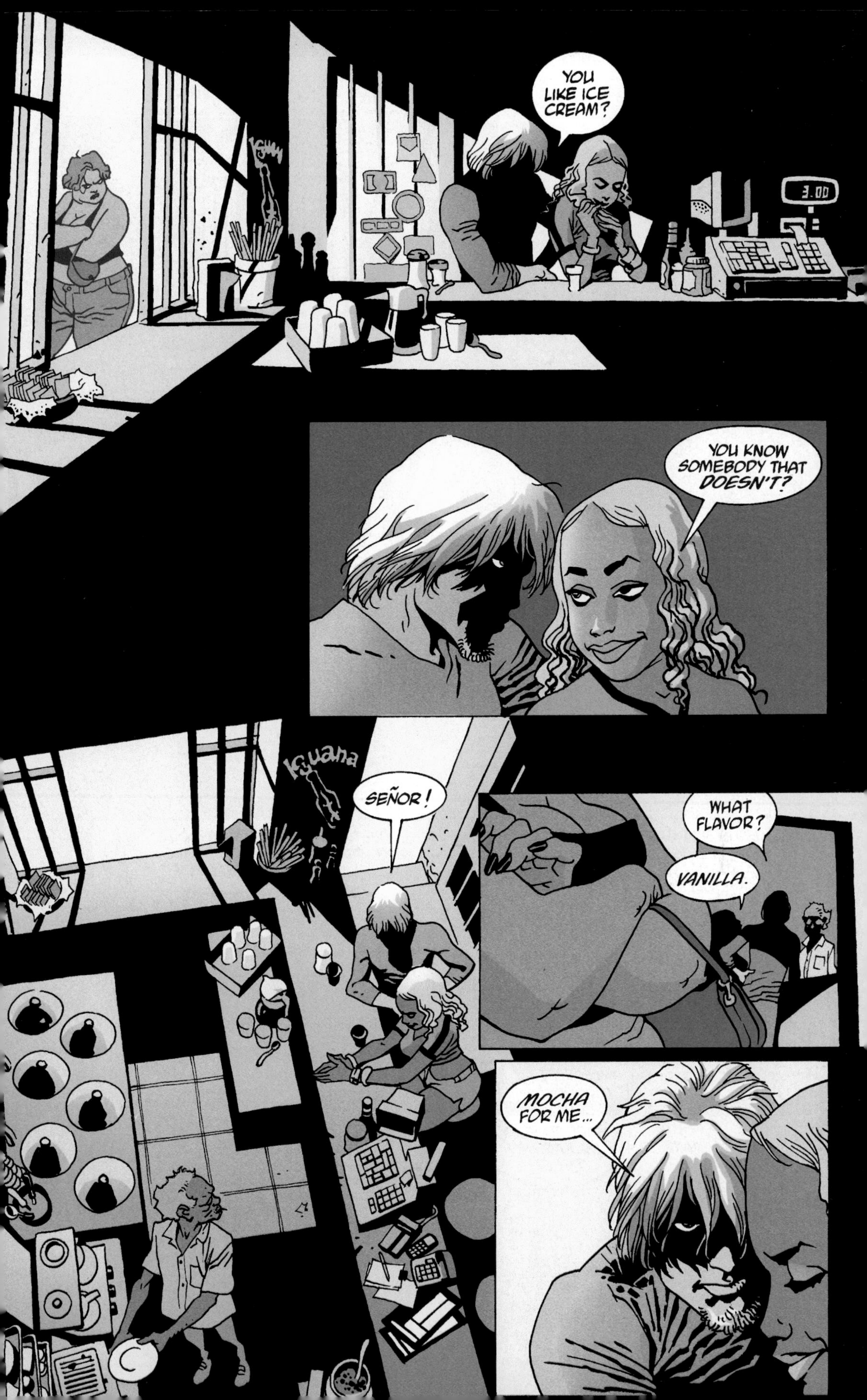
YOU LIKE ICE CREAM?
3.00
YOU KNOW SOMEBODY THAT DOESN'T?
Iguana
SEÑOR!
WHAT FLAVOR?
VANILLA.
MOCHA FOR ME...

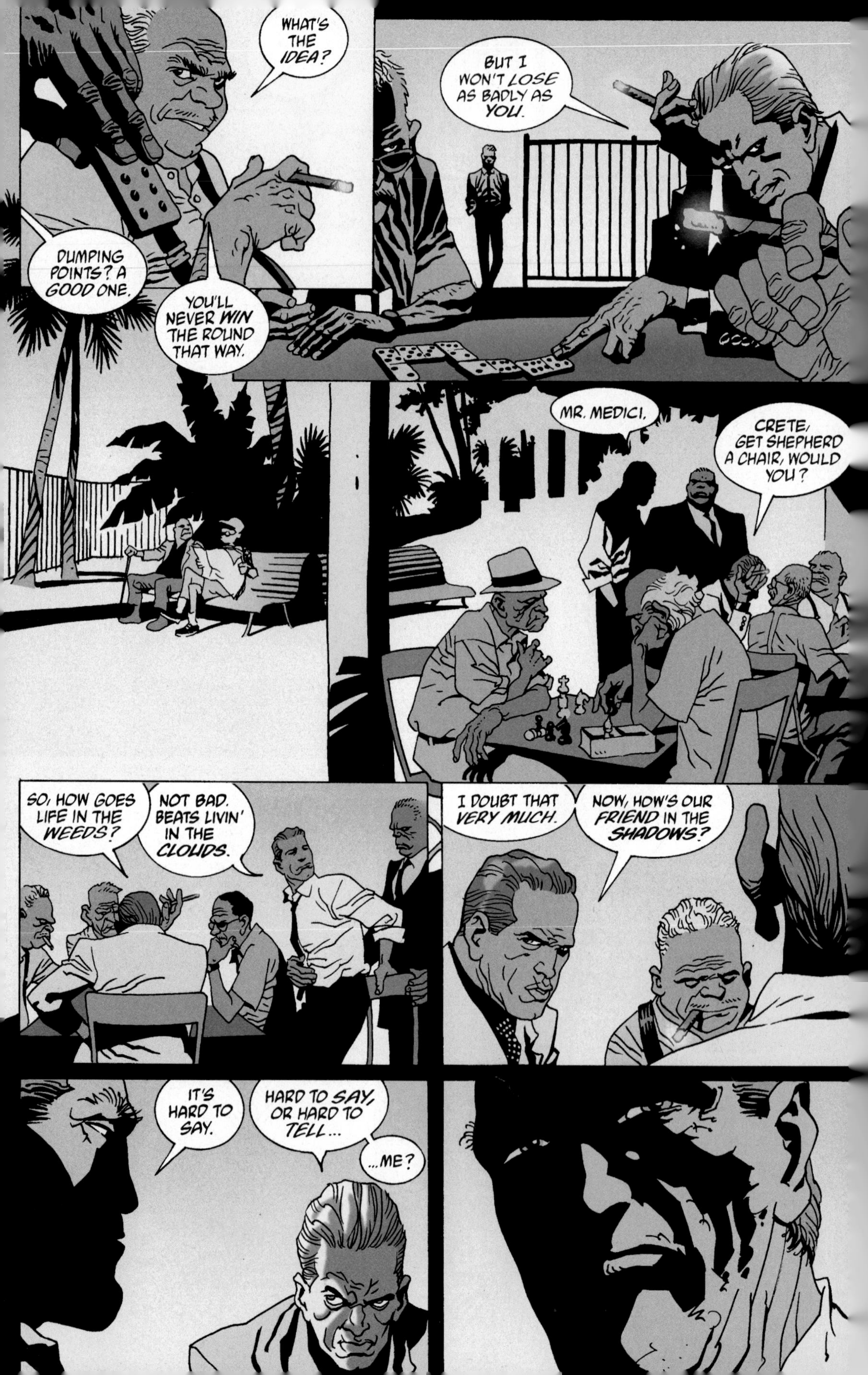
WHAT'S THE IDEA?
BUT I WON'T LOSE AS BADLY AS YOU.
DUMPING POINTS? A GOOD ONE.
YOU'LL NEVER WIN THE ROUND THAT WAY.
MR. MEDICI.
CRETE, GET SHEPHERD A CHAIR, WOULD YOU?
SO, HOW GOES LIFE IN THE WEEDS?
NOT BAD. BEATS LIVIN' IN THE CLOUDS.
I DOUBT THAT VERY MUCH.
NOW, HOW'S OUR FRIEND IN THE SHADOWS?
IT'S HARD TO SAY.
HARD TO SAY, OR HARD TO TELL...
...ME?

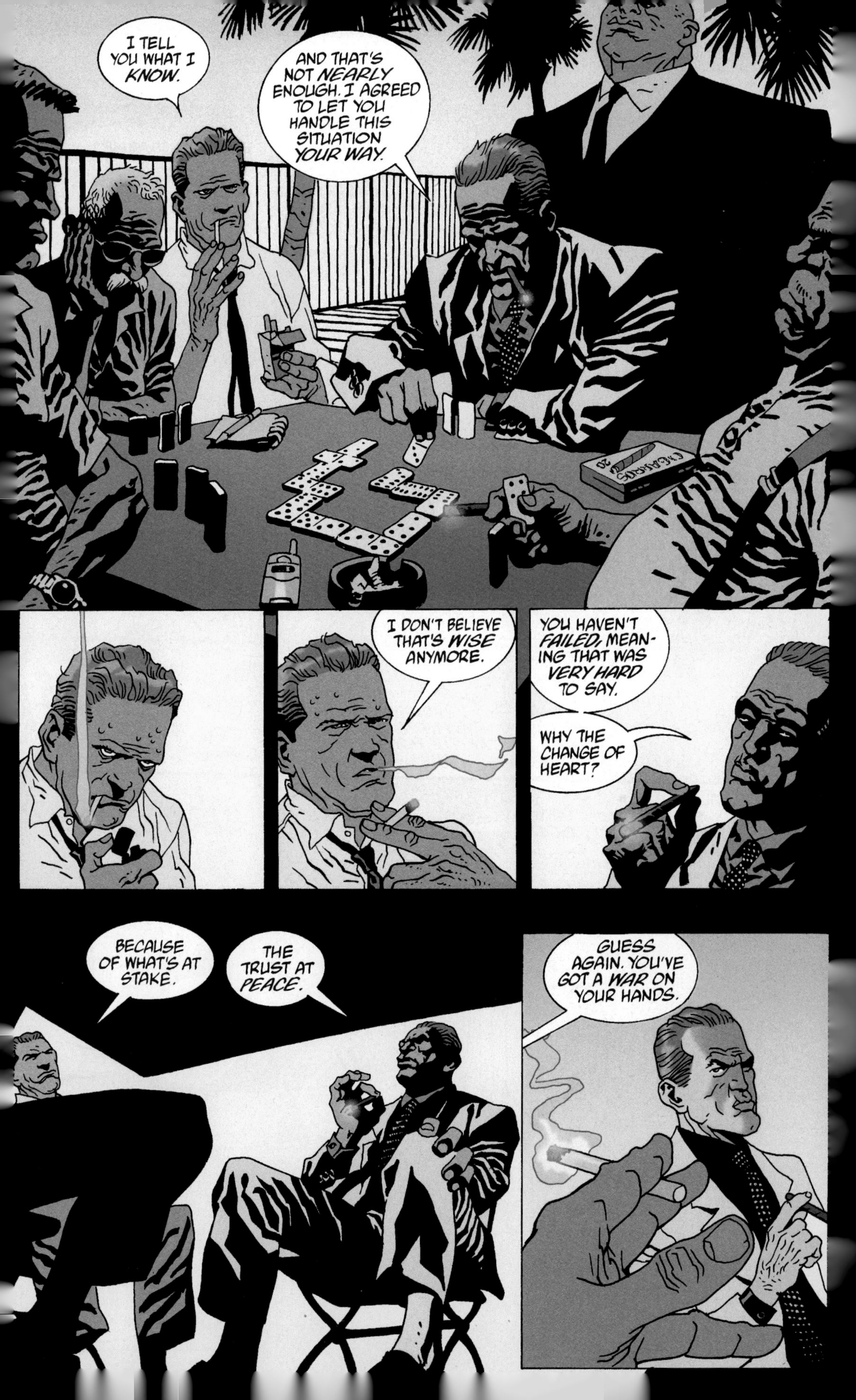
I TELL YOU WHAT I KNOW.
AND THAT'S NOT NEARLY ENOUGH. I AGREED TO LET YOU HANDLE THIS SITUATION YOUR WAY.
I DON'T BELIEVE THAT'S WISE ANYMORE.
YOU HAVEN'T FAILED, MEANING THAT WAS VERY HARD TO SAY.
WHY THE CHANGE OF HEART?
BECAUSE OF WHAT'S AT STAKE.
THE TRUST AT PEACE.
GUESS AGAIN. YOU'VE GOT A WAR ON YOUR HANDS.

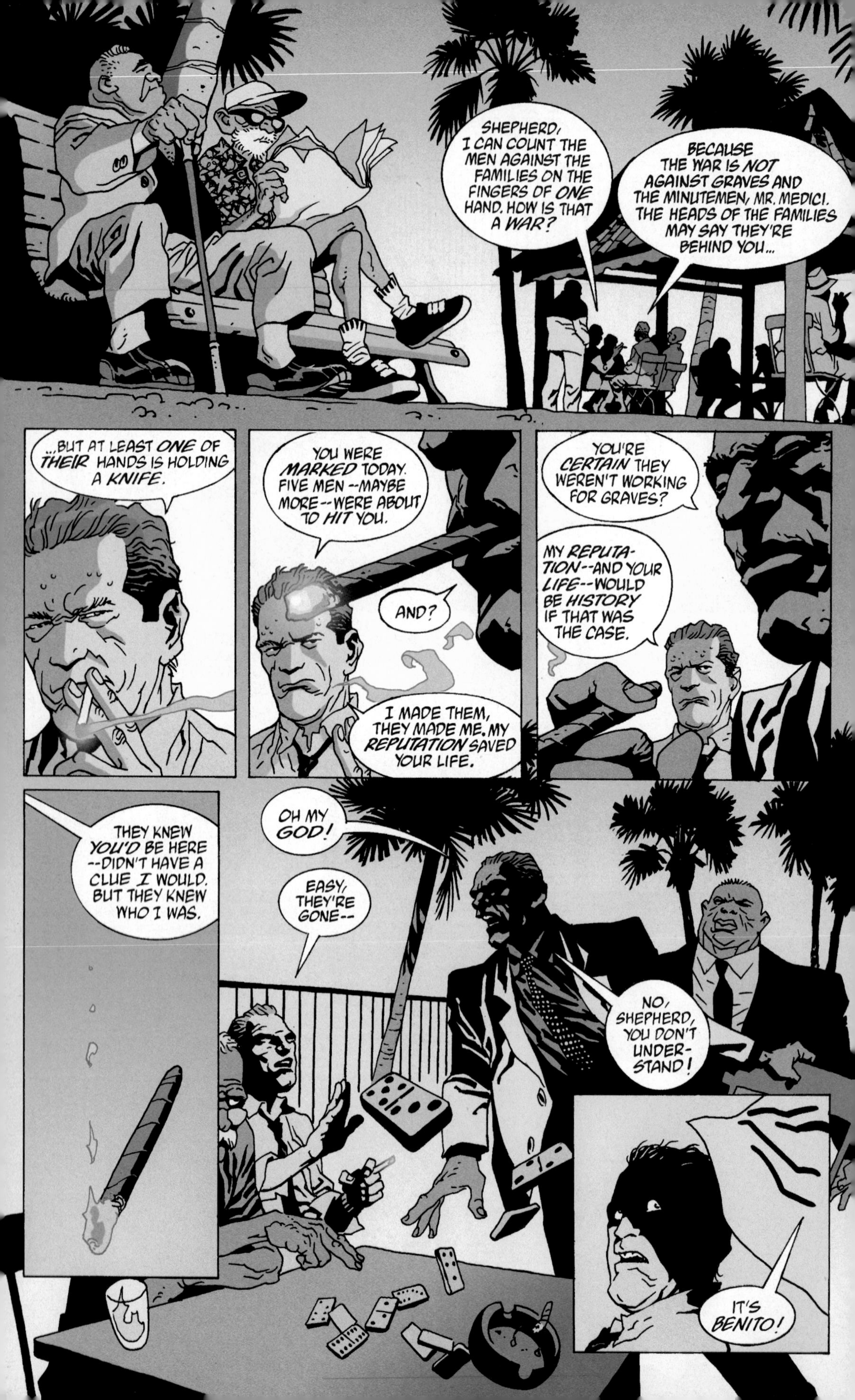
SHEPHERD, I CAN COUNT THE MEN AGAINST THE FAMILIES ON THE FINGERS OF ONE HAND. HOW IS THAT A WAR?
BECAUSE THE WAR IS NOT AGAINST GRAVES AND THE MINUTEMEN, MR. MEDICI. THE HEADS OF THE FAMILIES MAY SAY THEY'RE BEHIND YOU...
...BUT AT LEAST ONE OF THEIR HANDS IS HOLDING A KNIFE.
YOU WERE MARKED TODAY. FIVE MEN --MAYBE MORE-- WERE ABOUT TO HIT YOU.
AND?
I MADE THEM, THEY MADE ME. MY REPUTATION SAVED YOUR LIFE.
YOU'RE CERTAIN THEY WEREN'T WORKING FOR GRAVES?
MY REPUTATION--AND YOUR LIFE--WOULD BE HISTORY IF THAT WAS THE CASE.
THEY KNEW YOU'D BE HERE --DIDN'T HAVE A CLUE I WOULD. BUT THEY KNEW WHO I WAS.
OH MY GOD!
EASY, THEY'RE GONE--
NO, SHEPHERD, YOU DON'T UNDER-STAND!
IT'S BENITO!

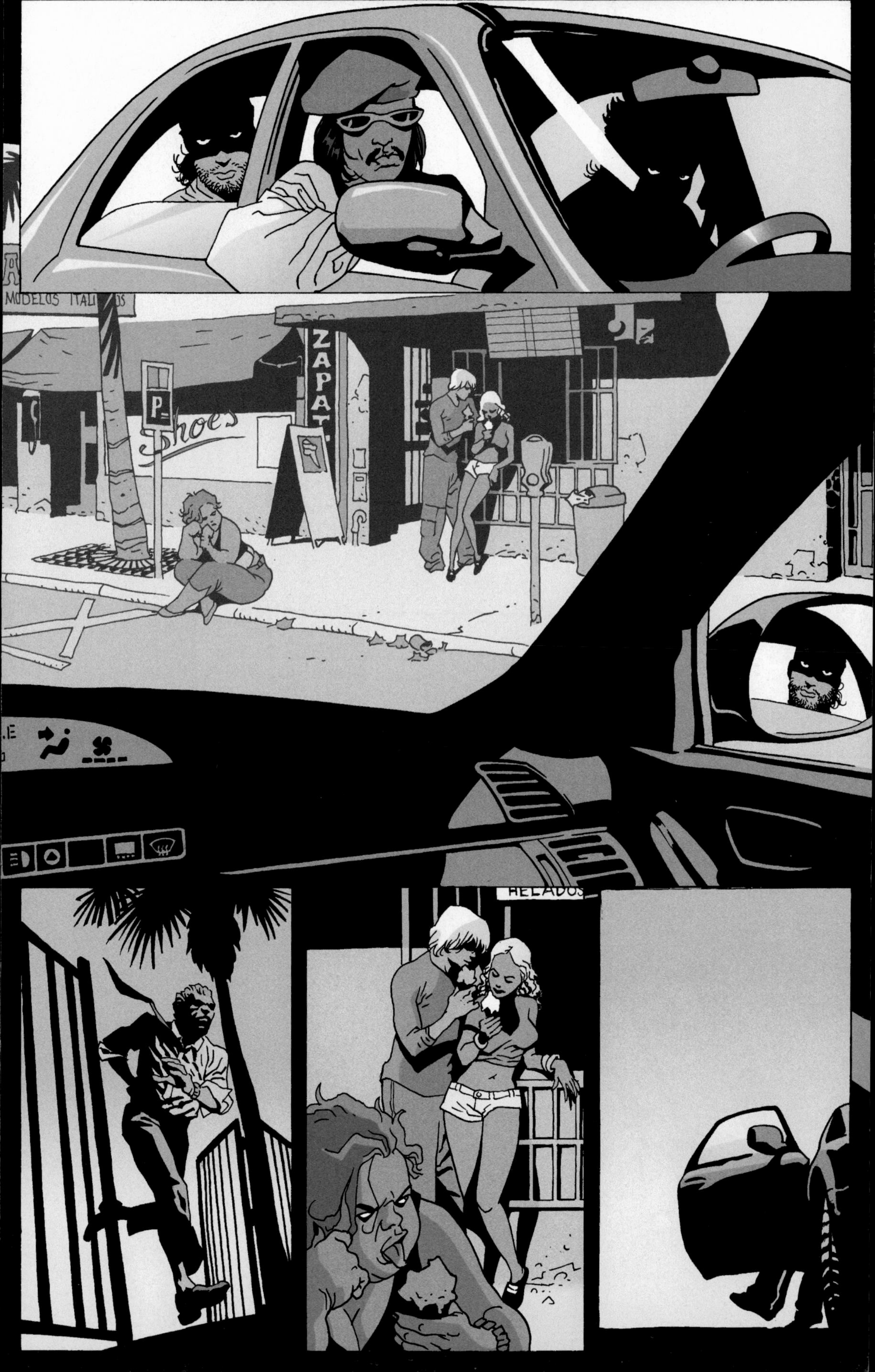

MODELOS ITALI
ZAPAT
P
Shoes
HELADOS

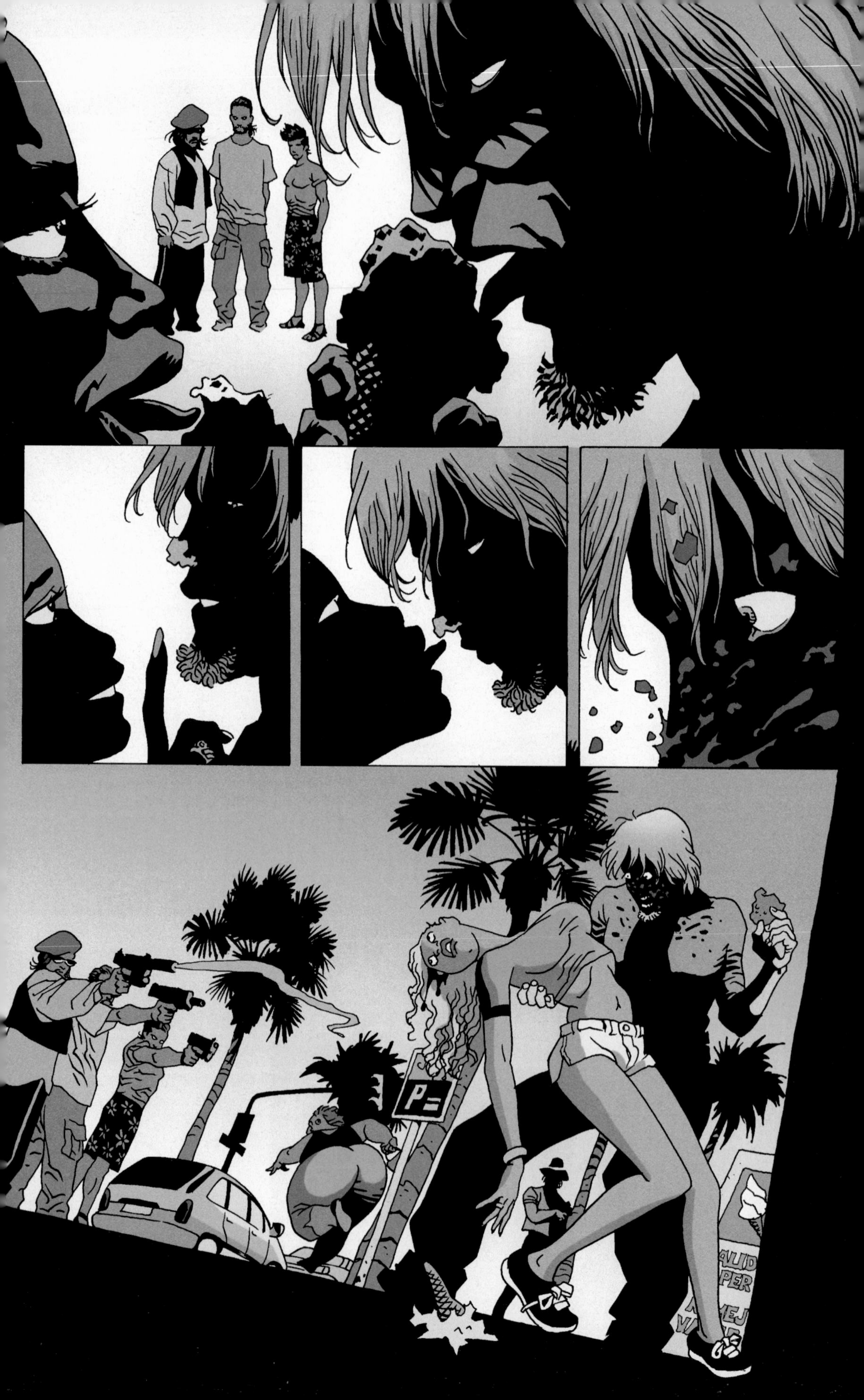

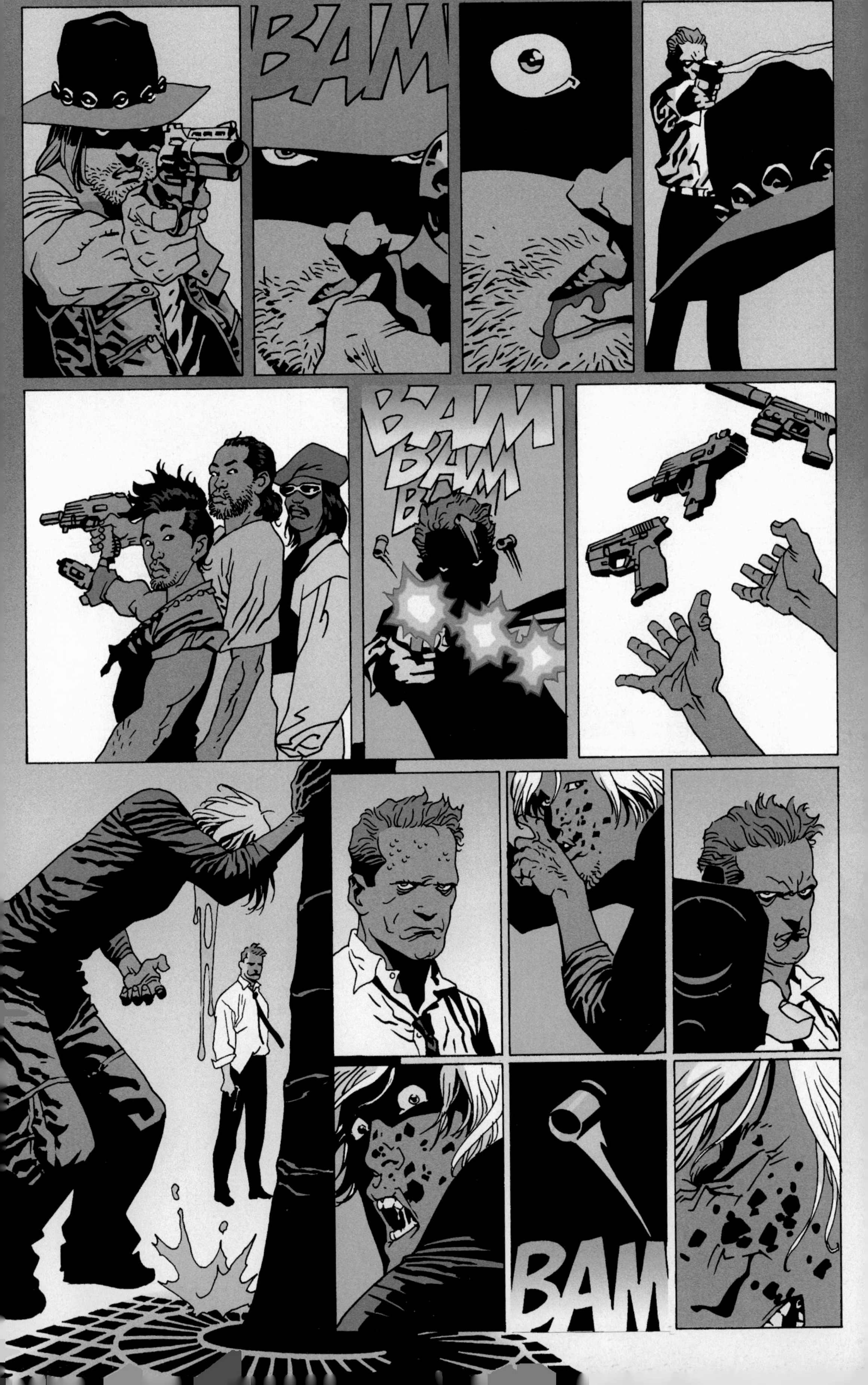
BAM
BAM
BAM
BAM
BAM

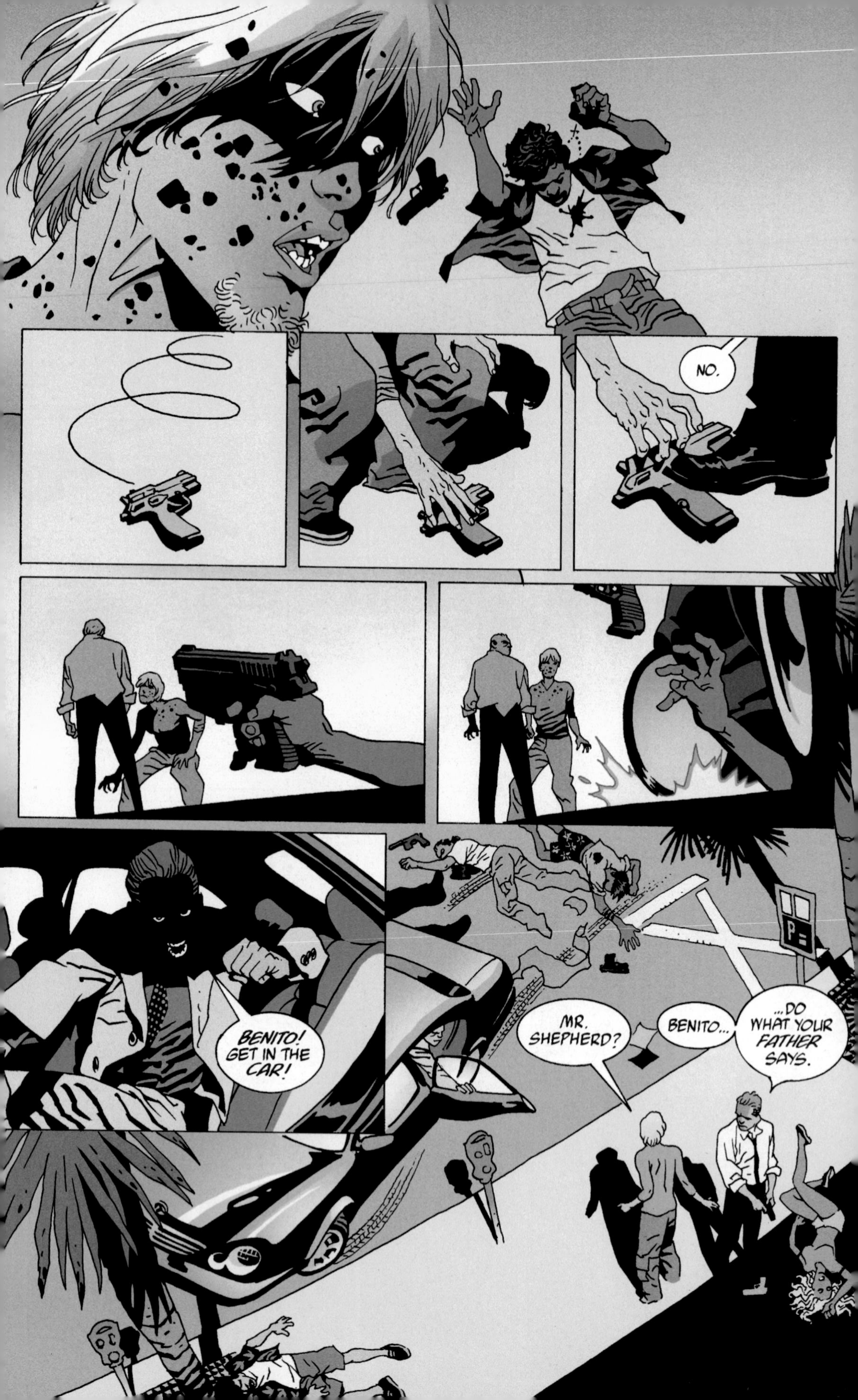
NO.
BENITO! GET IN THE CAR!
MR. SHEPHERD?
BENITO...
...DO WHAT YOUR FATHER SAYS.

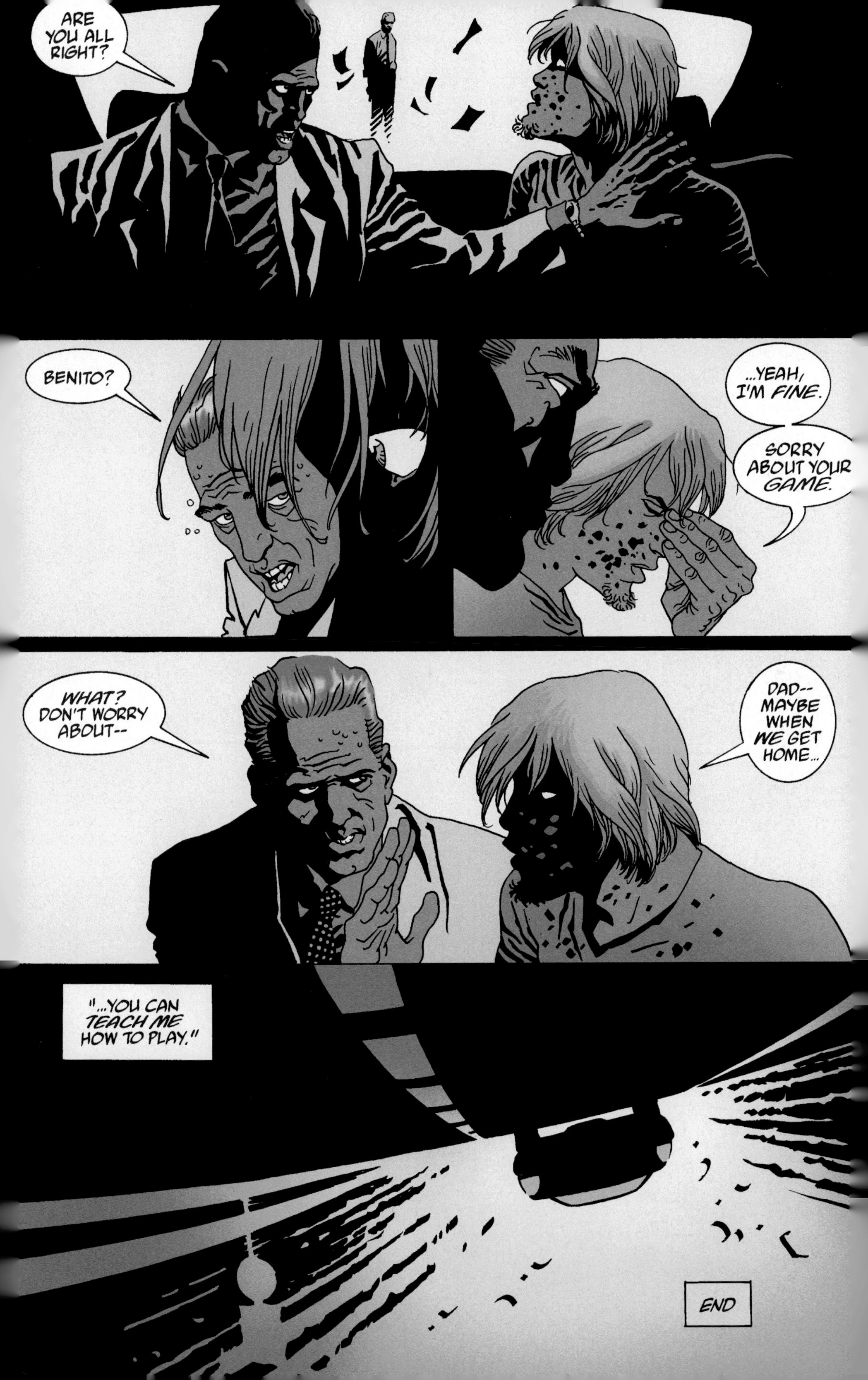
ARE YOU ALL RIGHT?
BENITO?
...YEAH, I'M *FINE*.
SORRY ABOUT YOUR *GAME*.
WHAT? DON'T WORRY ABOUT--
DAD-- MAYBE WHEN *WE* GET HOME...
"...YOU CAN *TEACH ME* HOW TO PLAY."
END

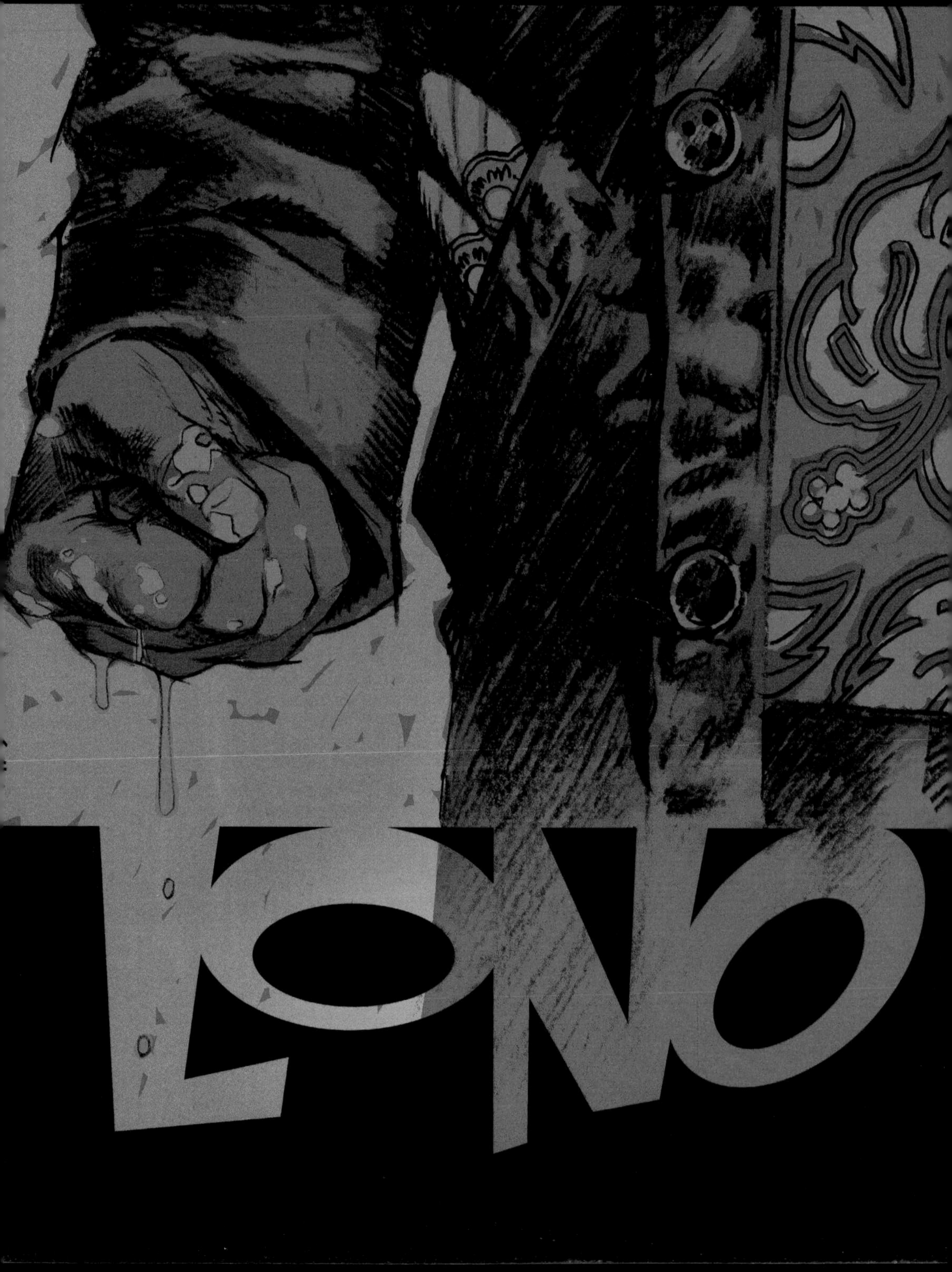
LONO

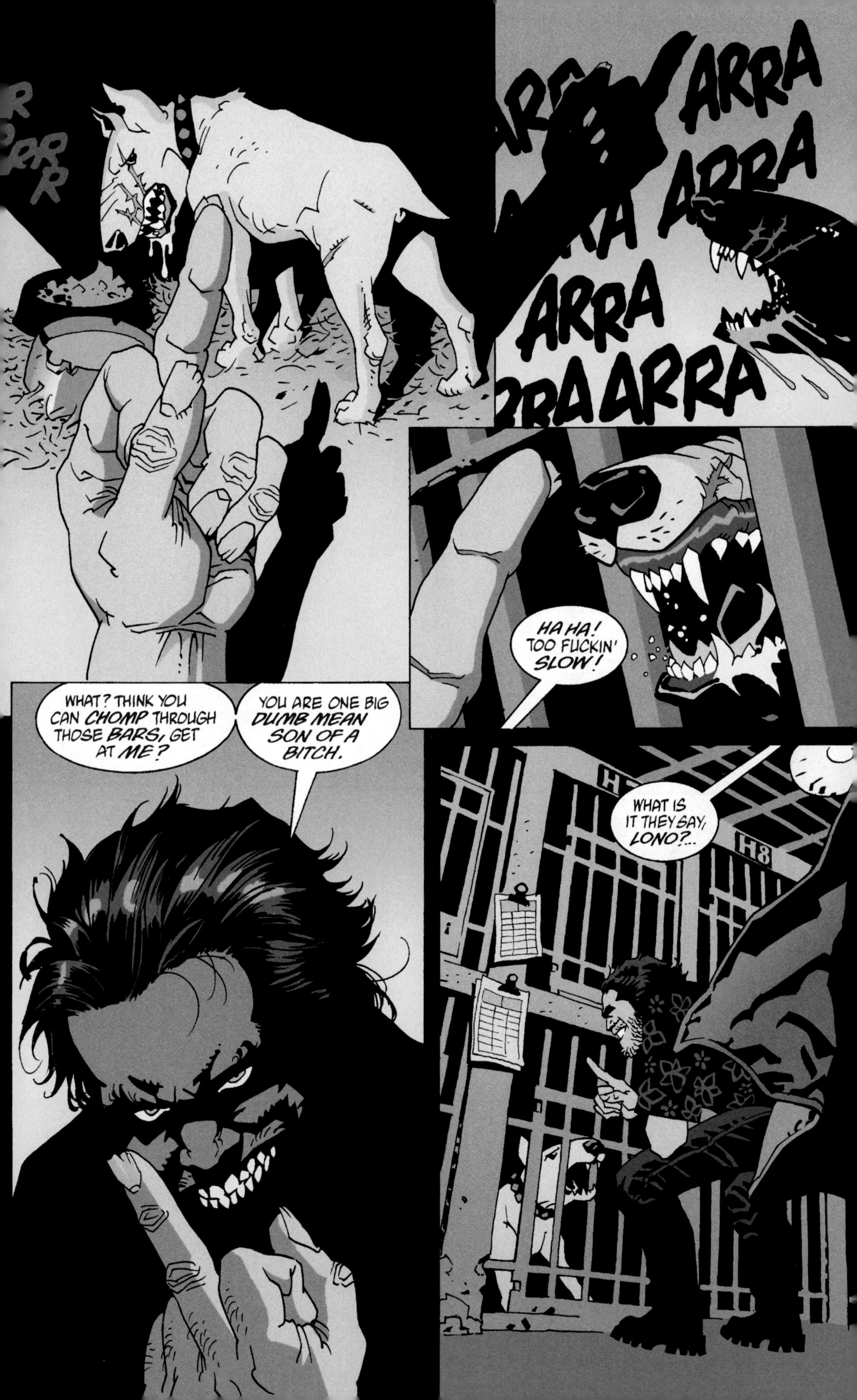
RRRRR
ARRA ARRA ARRA ARRA ARRA ARRA RRA ARRA
HA HA! TOO FUCKIN' SLOW!
WHAT? THINK YOU CAN CHOMP THROUGH THOSE BARS, GET AT ME?
YOU ARE ONE BIG DUMB MEAN SON OF A BITCH.
WHAT IS IT THEY SAY, LONO?...
H8

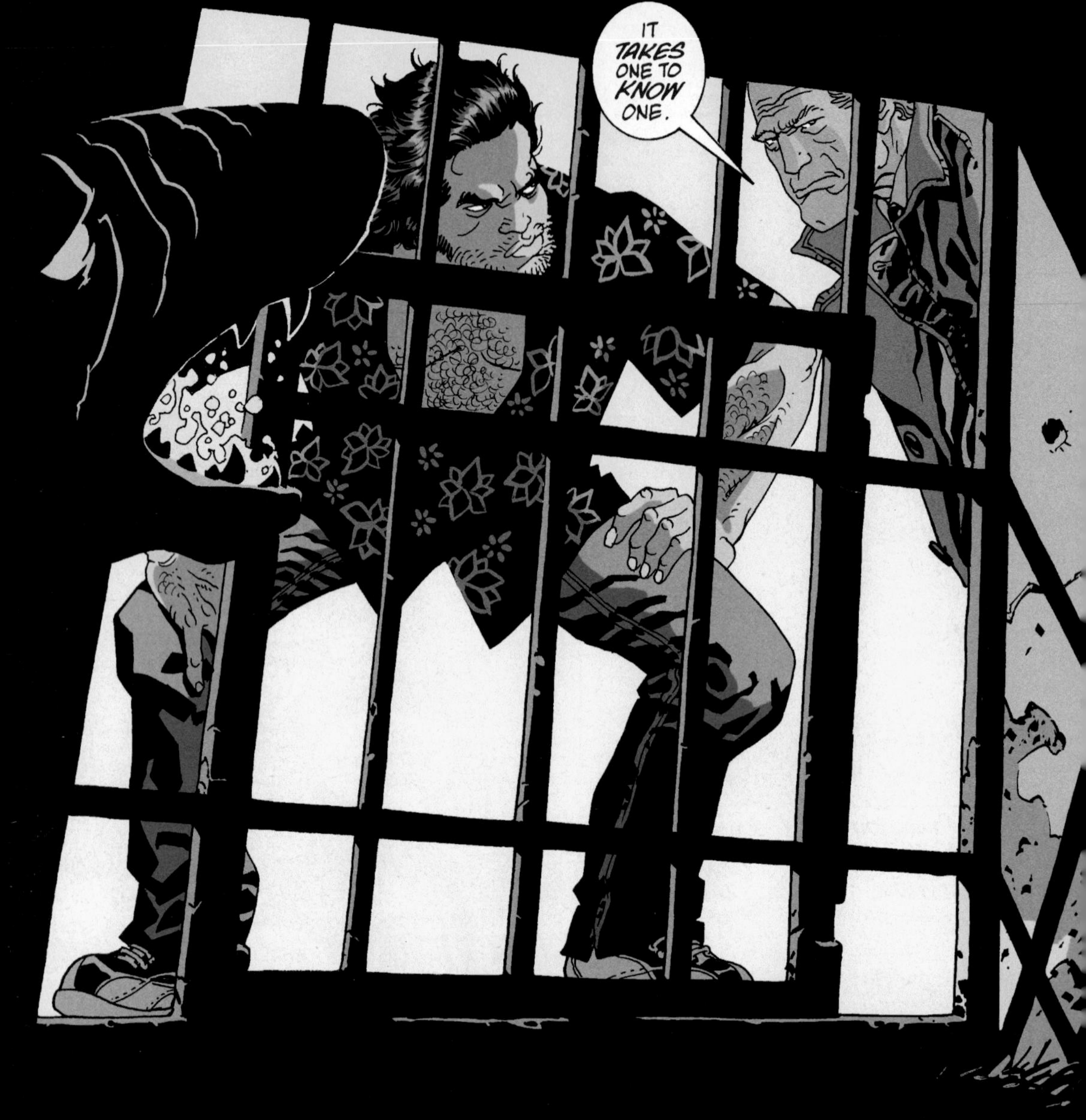
IT TAKES ONE TO KNOW ONE.

NIGHT of the PAYDAY

BRIAN AZZARELLO *writer*
EDUARDO RISSO *artist*
PATRICIA MULVIHILL *colorist*
CLEM ROBINS *letterer*
DIGITAL CHAMELEON *separations*
DAVE JOHNSON *cover*
ZACHARY RAU *ass't ed*
WILL DENNIS *editor*

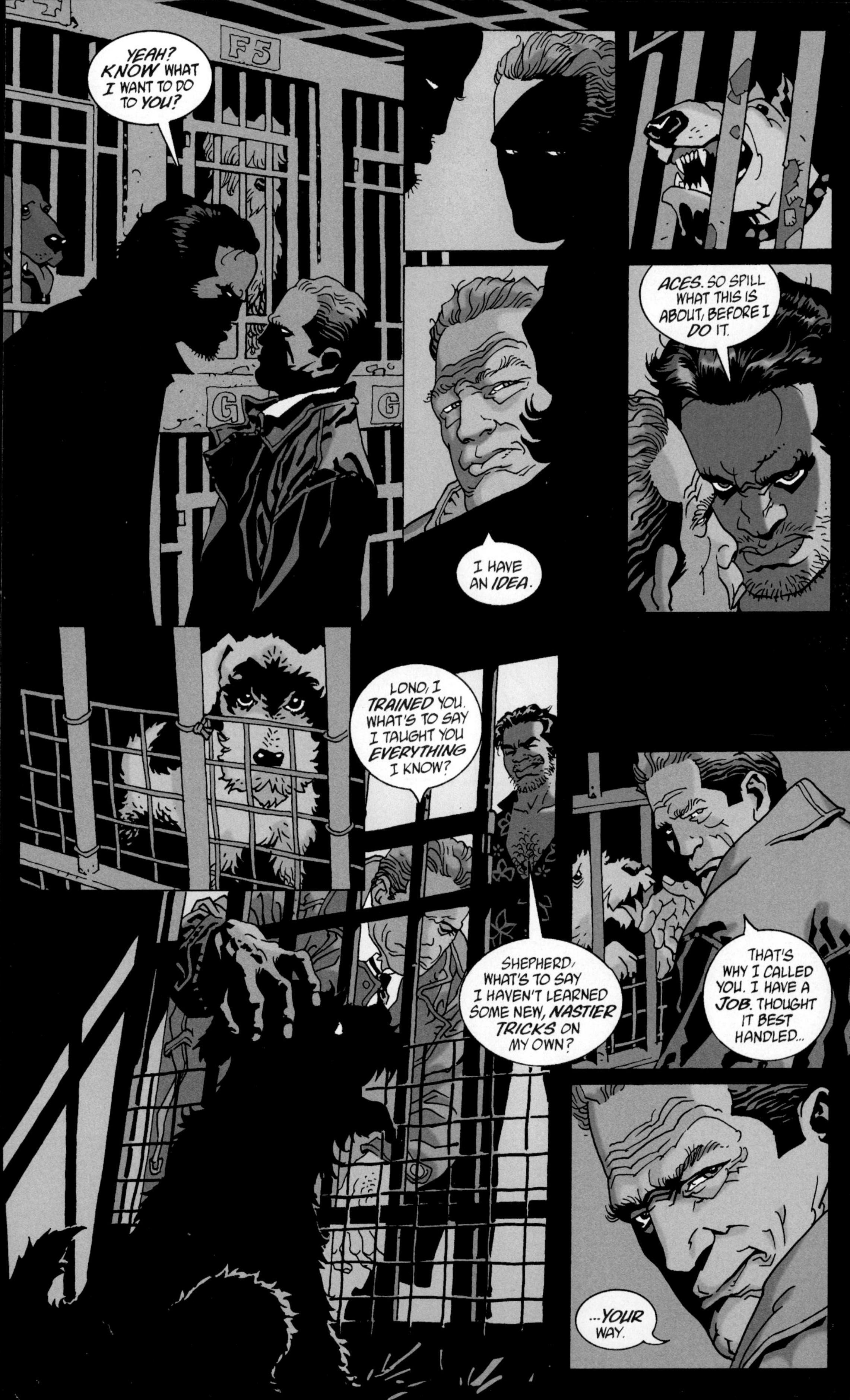
F5
YEAH? KNOW WHAT I WANT TO DO TO YOU?
G
G
I HAVE AN IDEA.
ACES. SO SPILL WHAT THIS IS ABOUT, BEFORE I DO IT.
LONO, I TRAINED YOU. WHAT'S TO SAY I TAUGHT YOU EVERYTHING I KNOW?
SHEPHERD, WHAT'S TO SAY I HAVEN'T LEARNED SOME NEW, NASTIER TRICKS ON MY OWN?
THAT'S WHY I CALLED YOU. I HAVE A JOB. THOUGHT IT BEST HANDLED...
...YOUR WAY.

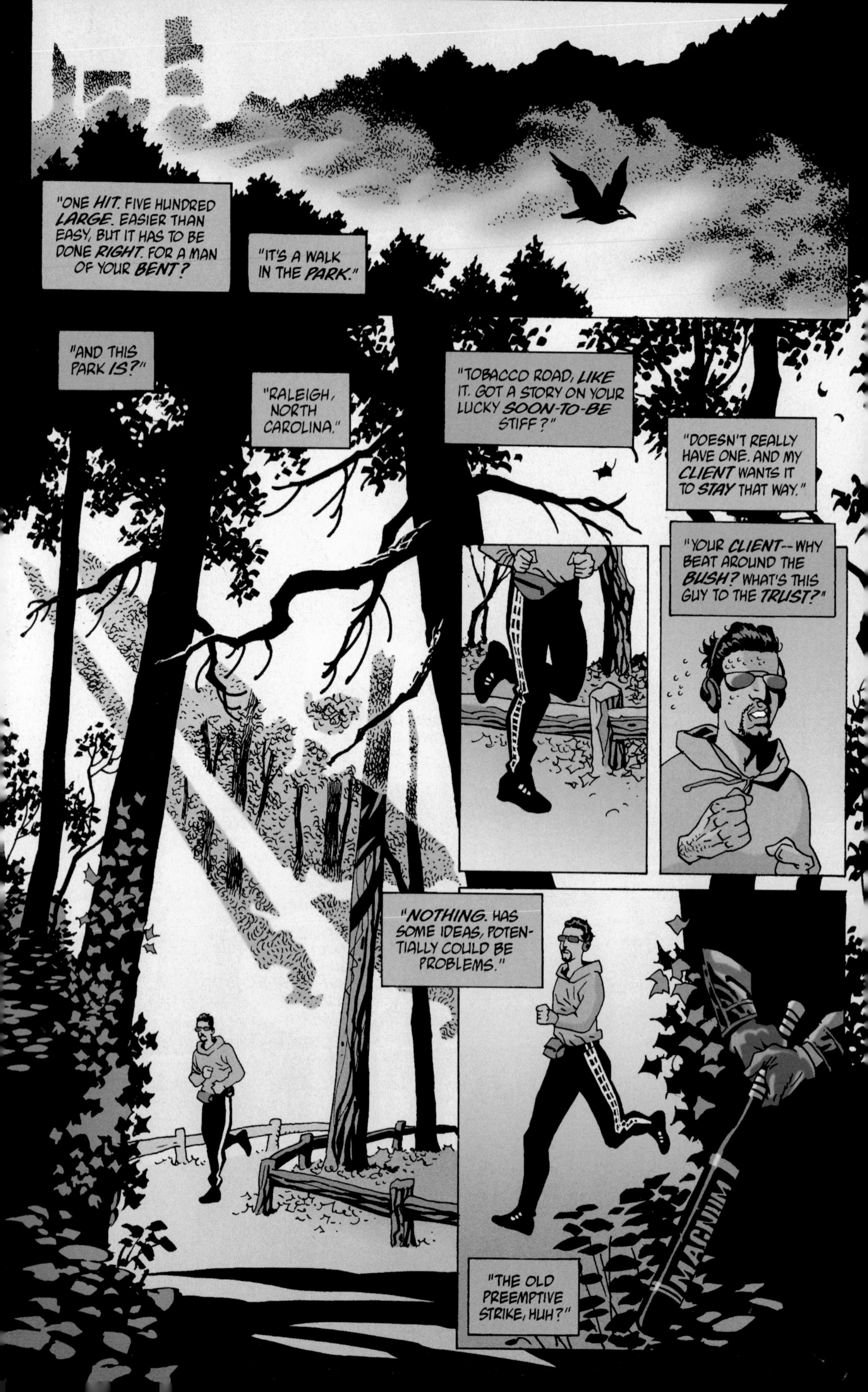
"ONE HIT. FIVE HUNDRED LARGE. EASIER THAN EASY, BUT IT HAS TO BE DONE RIGHT. FOR A MAN OF YOUR BENT?
"IT'S A WALK IN THE PARK."
"AND THIS PARK IS?"
"RALEIGH, NORTH CAROLINA."
"TOBACCO ROAD, LIKE IT. GOT A STORY ON YOUR LUCKY SOON-TO-BE STIFF?"
"DOESN'T REALLY HAVE ONE. AND MY CLIENT WANTS IT TO STAY THAT WAY."
"YOUR CLIENT--WHY BEAT AROUND THE BUSH? WHAT'S THIS GUY TO THE TRUST?"
"NOTHING. HAS SOME IDEAS, POTENTIALLY COULD BE PROBLEMS."
"THE OLD PREEMPTIVE STRIKE, HUH?"
MAGNUM

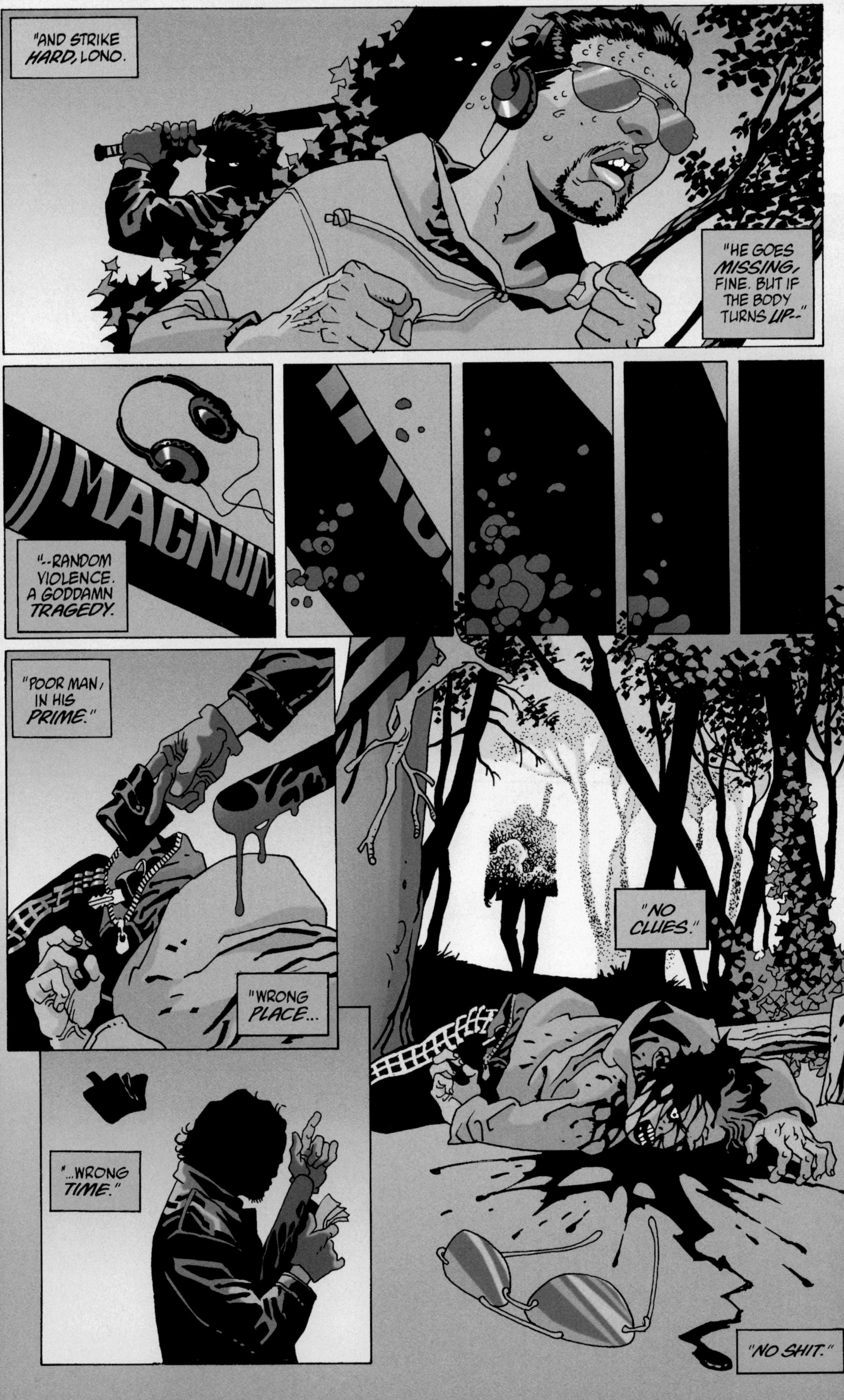
"AND STRIKE HARD, LONO.
"HE GOES MISSING, FINE. BUT IF THE BODY TURNS UP--"
MAGNUM
"--RANDOM VIOLENCE. A GODDAMN TRAGEDY.
"POOR MAN, IN HIS PRIME."
"WRONG PLACE...
"...WRONG TIME."
"NO CLUES."
"NO SHIT."

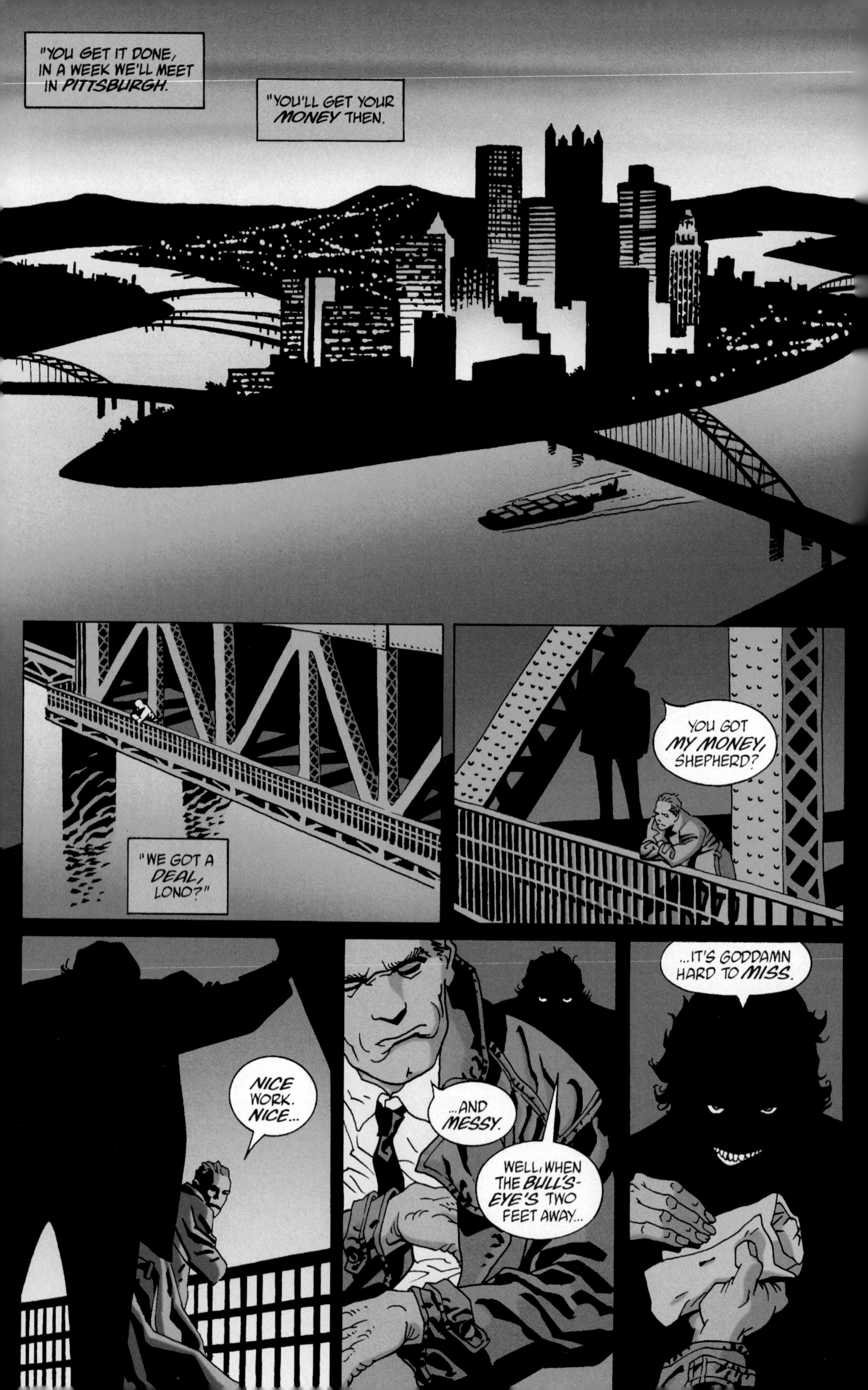
"YOU GET IT DONE, IN A WEEK WE'LL MEET IN PITTSBURGH.
"YOU'LL GET YOUR MONEY THEN.
"WE GOT A DEAL, LONO?"
YOU GOT MY MONEY, SHEPHERD?
NICE WORK. NICE...
...AND MESSY.
WELL, WHEN THE BULL'S-EYE'S TWO FEET AWAY...
...IT'S GODDAMN HARD TO MISS.

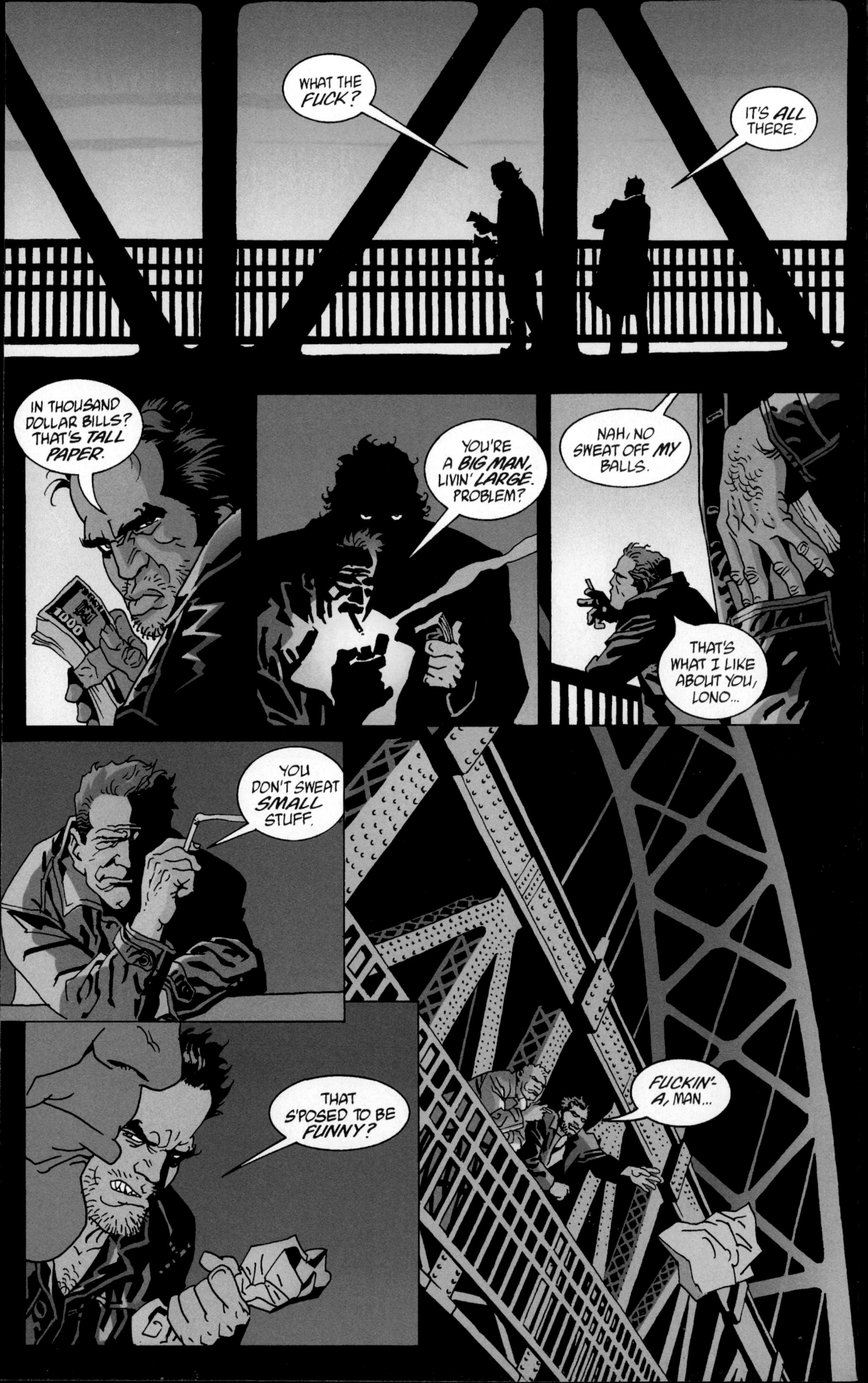
WHAT THE FUCK?
IT'S ALL THERE.
IN THOUSAND DOLLAR BILLS? THAT'S TALL PAPER.
YOU'RE A BIG MAN, LIVIN' LARGE. PROBLEM?
NAH, NO SWEAT OFF MY BALLS.
THAT'S WHAT I LIKE ABOUT YOU, LONO...
YOU DON'T SWEAT SMALL STUFF.
THAT S'POSED TO BE FUNNY?
FUCKIN'-A, MAN...

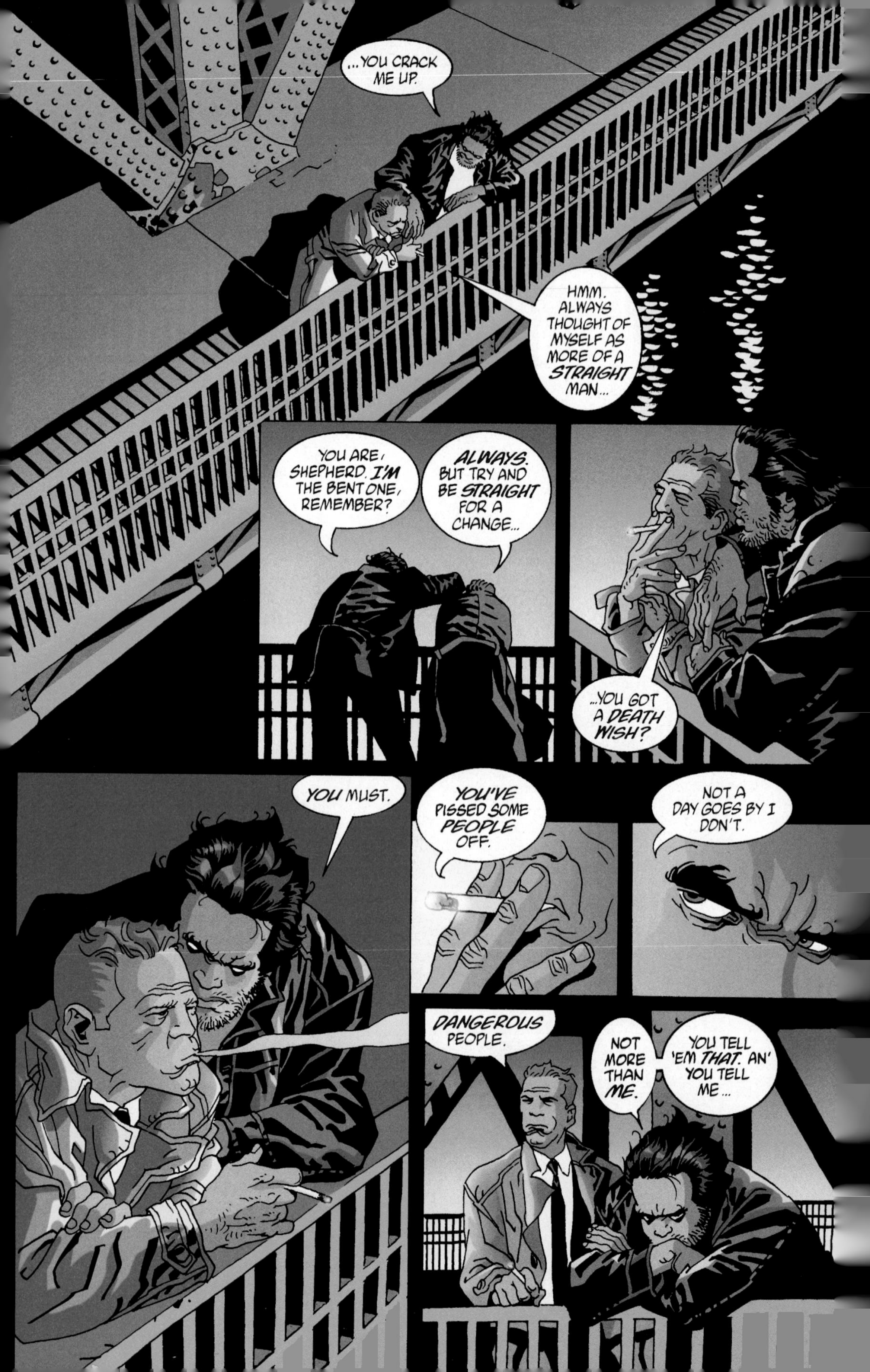
...YOU CRACK ME UP.
HMM. ALWAYS THOUGHT OF MYSELF AS MORE OF A STRAIGHT MAN...
YOU ARE, SHEPHERD. I'M THE BENT ONE, REMEMBER?
ALWAYS. BUT TRY AND BE STRAIGHT FOR A CHANGE...
...YOU GOT A DEATH WISH?
YOU MUST.
YOU'VE PISSED SOME PEOPLE OFF.
NOT A DAY GOES BY I DON'T.
DANGEROUS PEOPLE.
NOT MORE THAN ME.
YOU TELL 'EM THAT. AN' YOU TELL ME ...

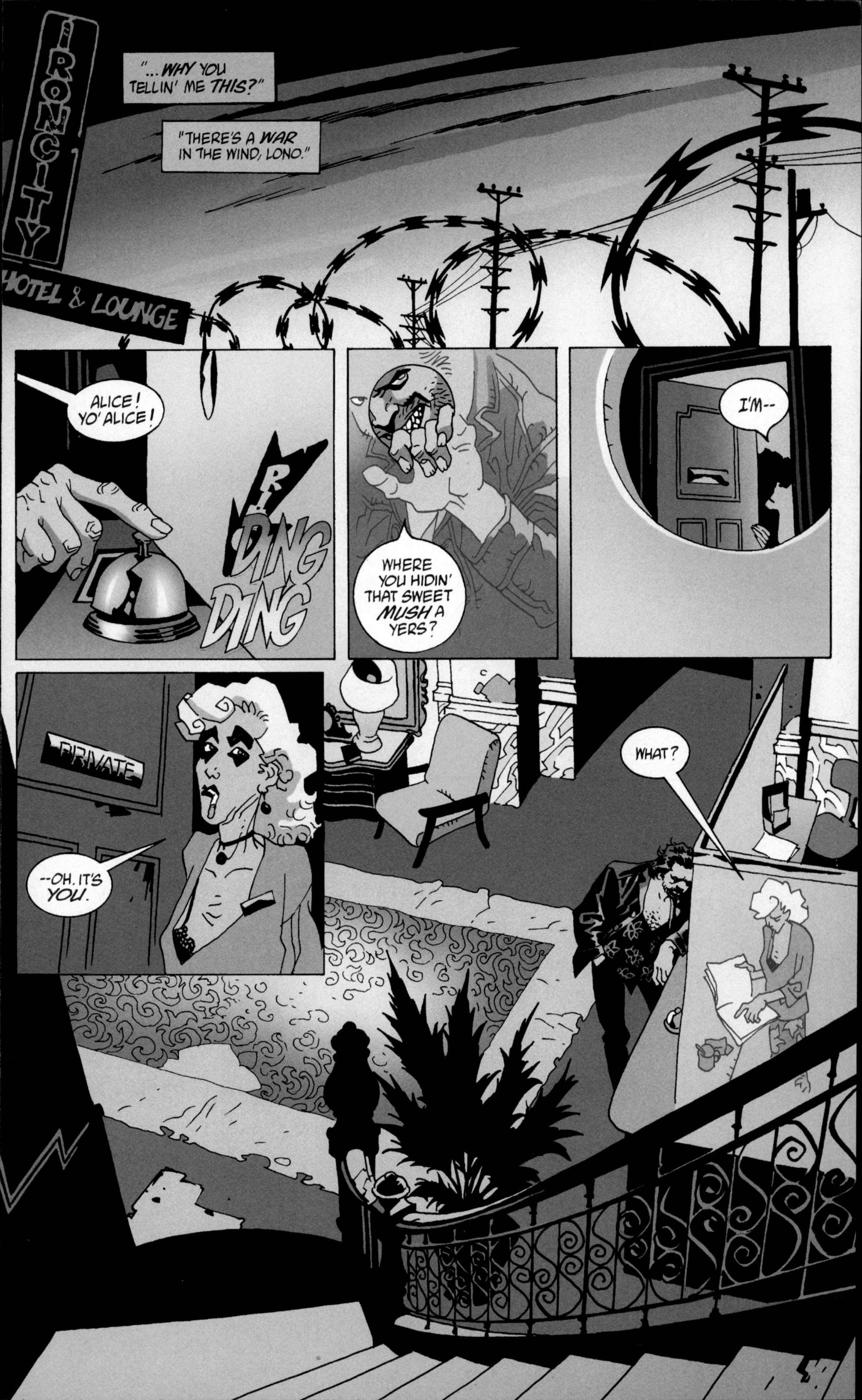
IRONCITY
HOTEL & LOUNGE
"...WHY YOU TELLIN' ME THIS?"
"THERE'S A WAR IN THE WIND, LONO."
ALICE! YO' ALICE!
RI..
DING DING
WHERE YOU HIDIN' THAT SWEET MUSH A YERS?
I'M--
PRIVATE
--OH. IT'S YOU.
WHAT?

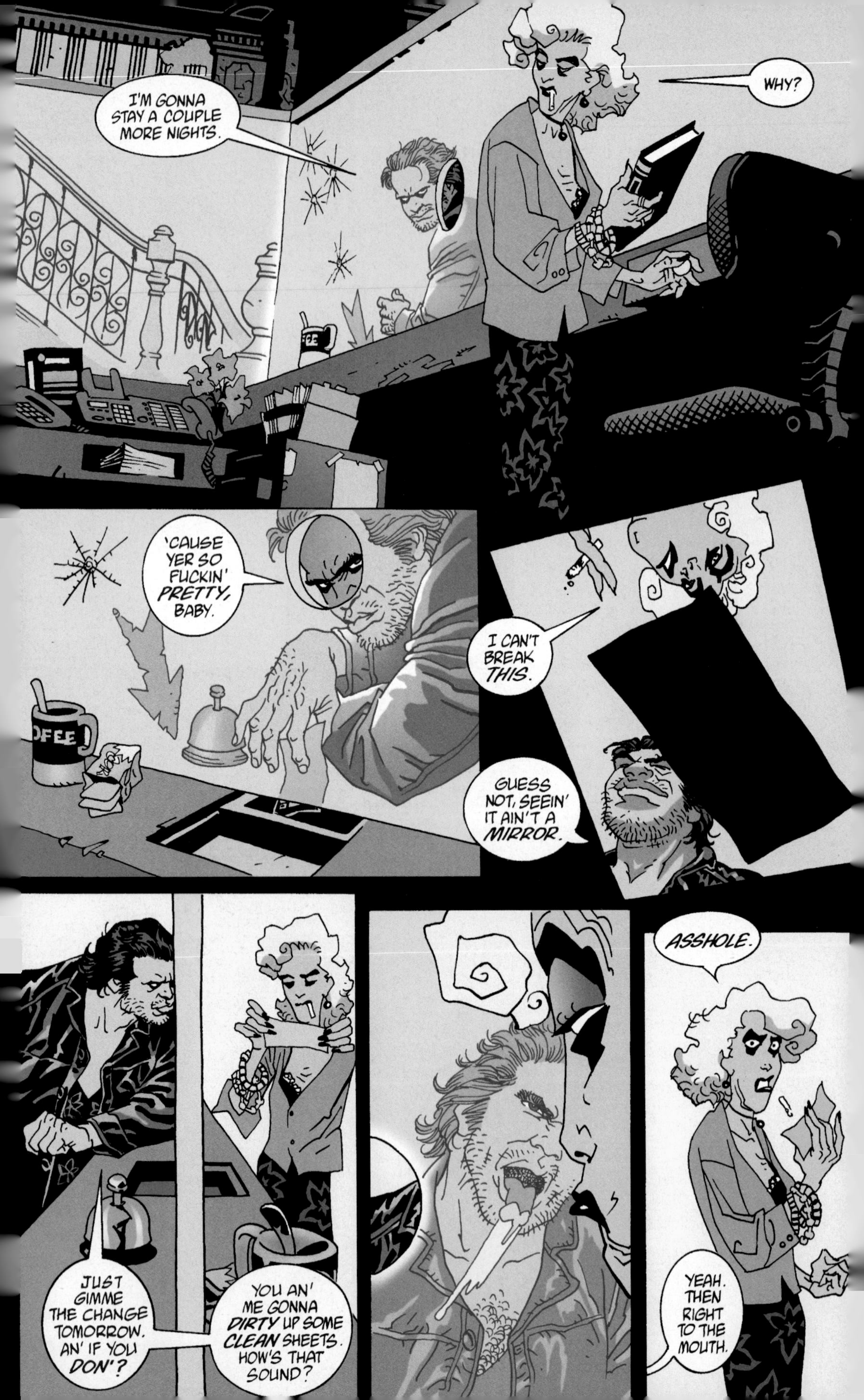
I'M GONNA STAY A COUPLE MORE NIGHTS.
WHY?
'CAUSE YER SO FUCKIN' PRETTY, BABY.
I CAN'T BREAK THIS.
GUESS NOT, SEEIN' IT AIN'T A MIRROR.
JUST GIMME THE CHANGE TOMORROW.
YOU AN' ME GONNA DIRTY UP SOME CLEAN SHEETS. HOW'S THAT SOUND?
AN' IF YOU DON'?
ASSHOLE.
YEAH. THEN RIGHT TO THE MOUTH.

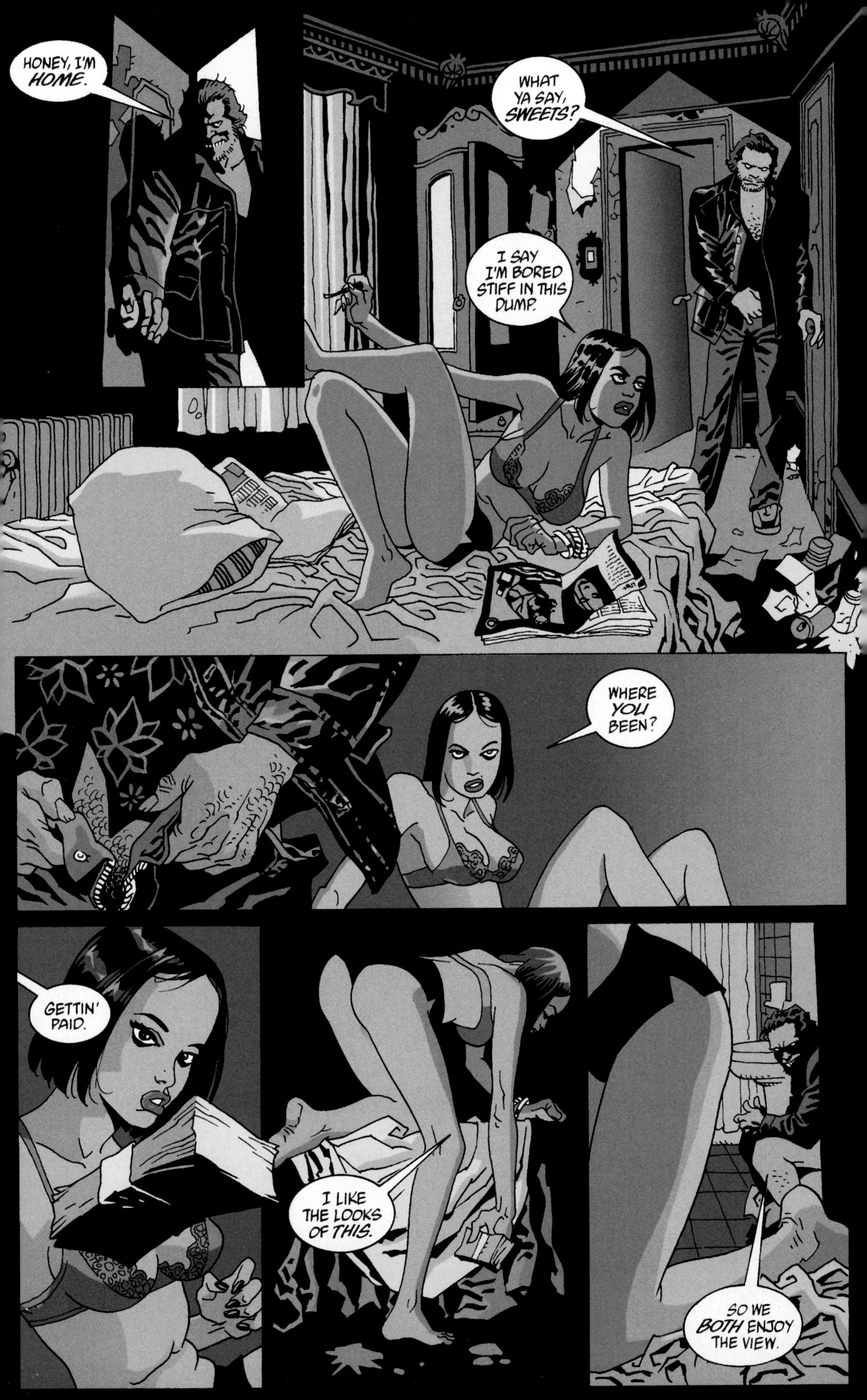
HONEY, I'M *HOME*.
WHAT YA SAY, *SWEETS*?
I SAY I'M BORED STIFF IN THIS DUMP.
WHERE *YOU* BEEN?
GETTIN' PAID.
I LIKE THE LOOKS OF *THIS*.
SO WE *BOTH* ENJOY THE VIEW.

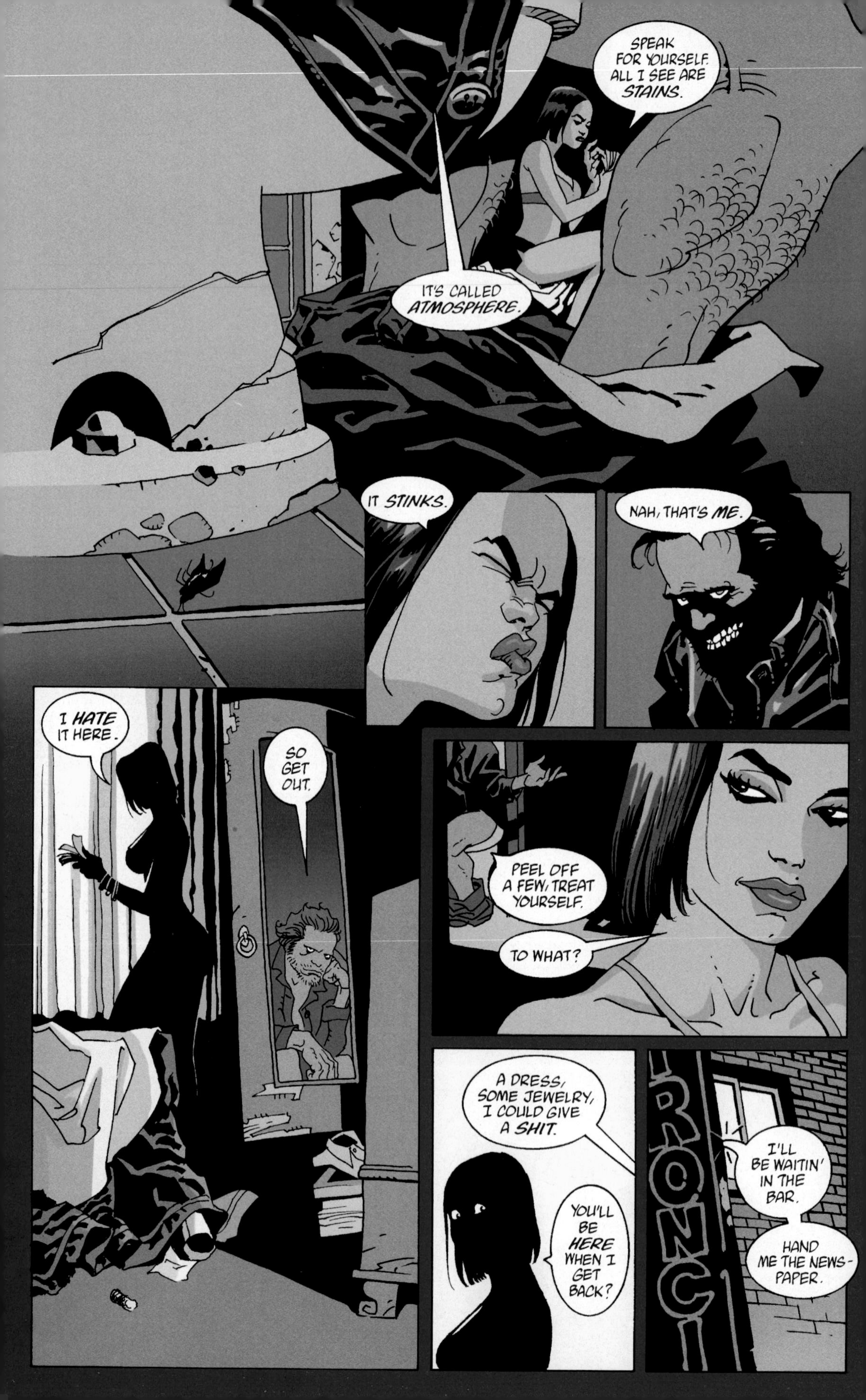
SPEAK FOR YOURSELF. ALL I SEE ARE STAINS.
IT'S CALLED ATMOSPHERE.
IT STINKS.
NAH, THAT'S ME.
I HATE IT HERE.
SO GET OUT.
PEEL OFF A FEW, TREAT YOURSELF.
TO WHAT?
A DRESS, SOME JEWELRY, I COULD GIVE A SHIT.
YOU'LL BE HERE WHEN I GET BACK?
I'LL BE WAITIN' IN THE BAR.
HAND ME THE NEWS-PAPER.
RONC

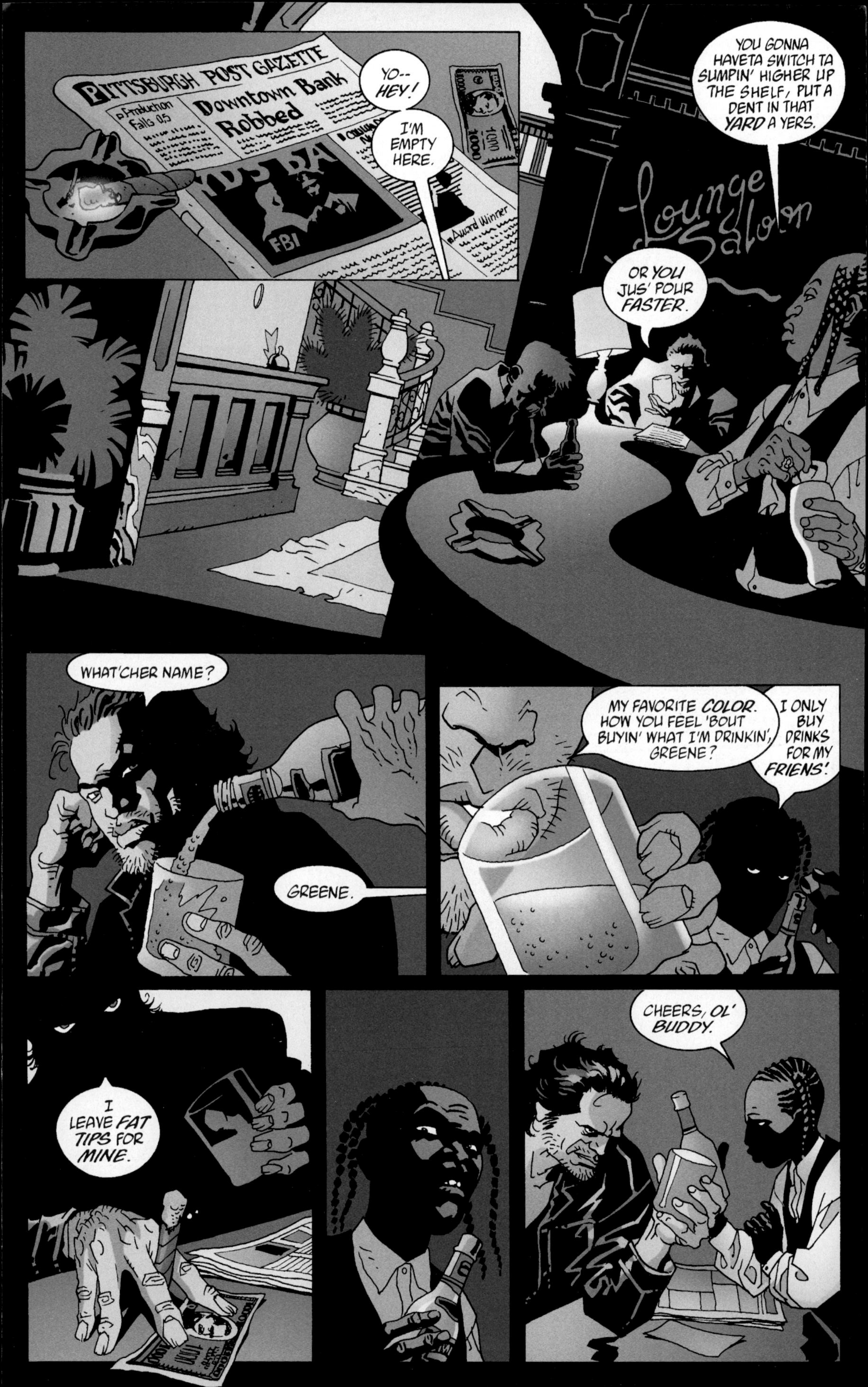
PITTSBURGH POST GAZETTE
Downtown Bank Robbed
Production Falls 0.5
FBI
Award Winner
YO-- HEY!
I'M EMPTY HERE.
YOU GONNA HAVETA SWITCH TA SUMPIN' HIGHER UP THE SHELF, PUT A DENT IN THAT YARD A YERS.
Lounge Saloon
OR YOU JUS' POUR FASTER.
WHAT'CHER NAME?
GREENE.
MY FAVORITE COLOR. HOW YOU FEEL 'BOUT BUYIN' WHAT I'M DRINKIN', GREENE?
I ONLY BUY DRINKS FOR MY FRIENS!
I LEAVE FAT TIPS FOR MINE.
CHEERS, OL' BUDDY.

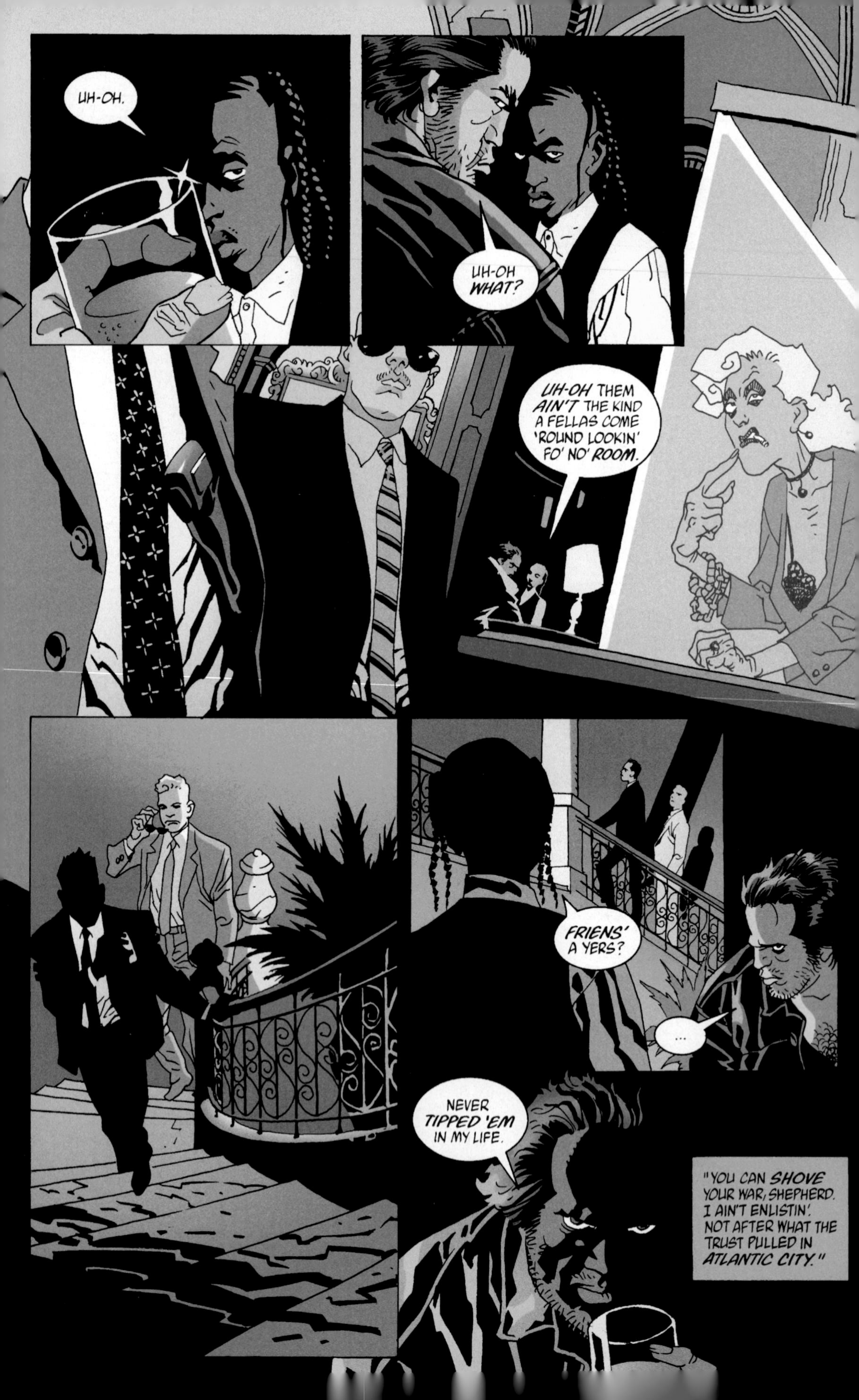
UH-OH.
UH-OH WHAT?
UH-OH THEM AIN'T THE KIND A FELLAS COME 'ROUND LOOKIN' FO' NO' ROOM.
FRIENS' A YERS?
...
NEVER TIPPED 'EM IN MY LIFE.
"YOU CAN SHOVE YOUR WAR, SHEPHERD. I AIN'T ENLISTIN'. NOT AFTER WHAT THE TRUST PULLED IN ATLANTIC CITY."

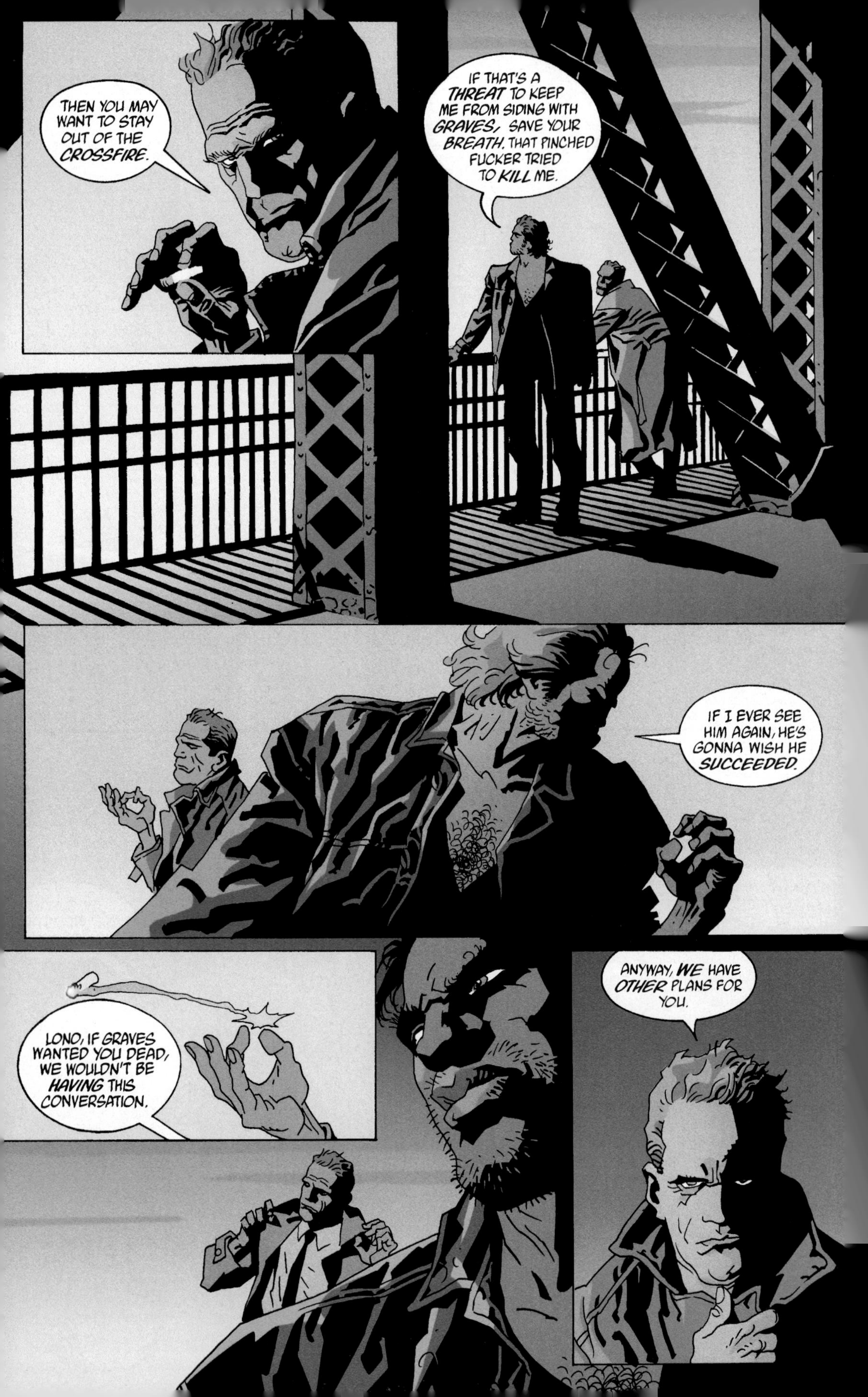

THEN YOU MAY WANT TO STAY OUT OF THE CROSSFIRE.
IF THAT'S A THREAT TO KEEP ME FROM SIDING WITH GRAVES, SAVE YOUR BREATH. THAT PINCHED FUCKER TRIED TO KILL ME.
IF I EVER SEE HIM AGAIN, HE'S GONNA WISH HE SUCCEEDED.
LONO, IF GRAVES WANTED YOU DEAD, WE WOULDN'T BE HAVING THIS CONVERSATION.
ANYWAY, WE HAVE OTHER PLANS FOR YOU.

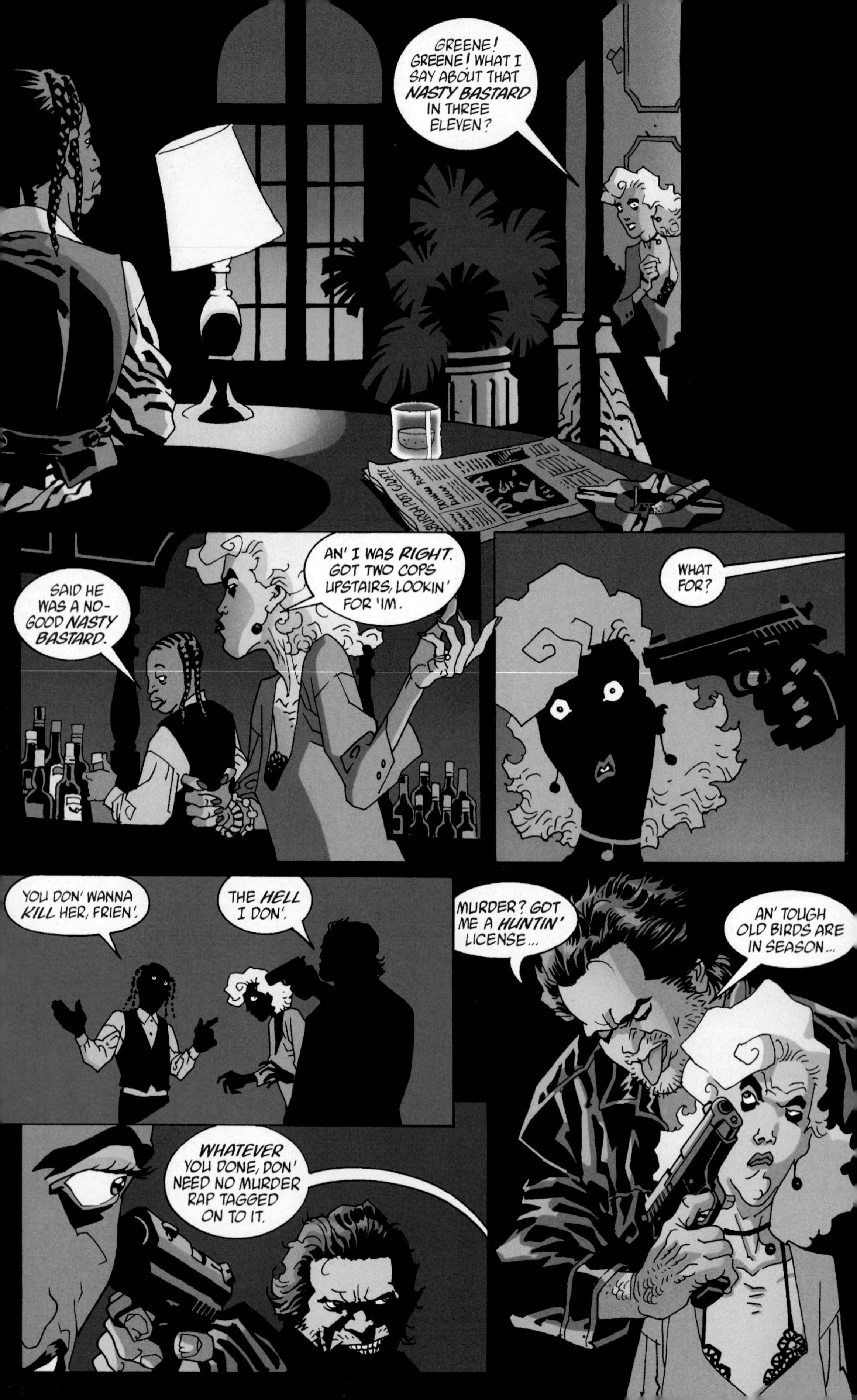
GREENE! GREENE! WHAT I SAY ABOUT THAT NASTY BASTARD IN THREE ELEVEN?
SAID HE WAS A NO-GOOD NASTY BASTARD.
AN' I WAS RIGHT. GOT TWO COPS UPSTAIRS, LOOKIN' FOR 'IM.
WHAT FOR?
YOU DON' WANNA KILL HER, FRIEN'.
THE HELL I DON'.
MURDER? GOT ME A HUNTIN' LICENSE...
AN' TOUGH OLD BIRDS ARE IN SEASON...
WHATEVER YOU DONE, DON' NEED NO MURDER RAP TAGGED ON TO IT.

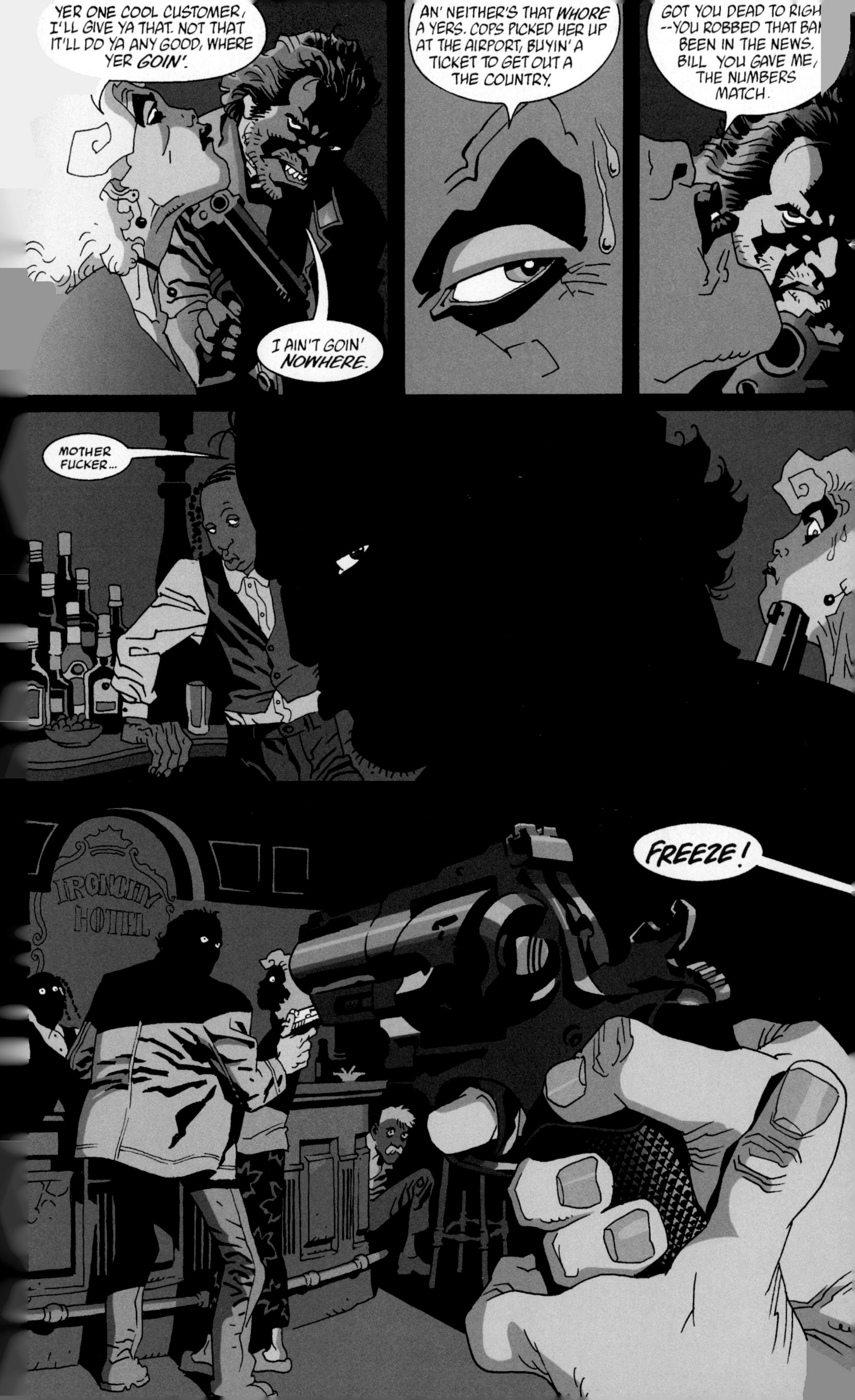
YER ONE COOL CUSTOMER, I'LL GIVE YA THAT. NOT THAT IT'LL DO YA ANY GOOD, WHERE YER GOIN'.
I AIN'T GOIN' NOWHERE.
AN' NEITHER'S THAT WHORE A YERS. COPS PICKED HER UP AT THE AIRPORT, BUYIN' A TICKET TO GET OUT A THE COUNTRY.
GOT YOU DEAD TO RIGH --YOU ROBBED THAT BA BEEN IN THE NEWS. BILL YOU GAVE ME, THE NUMBERS MATCH.
MOTHER FUCKER...
IRON CITY HOTEL
FREEZE!

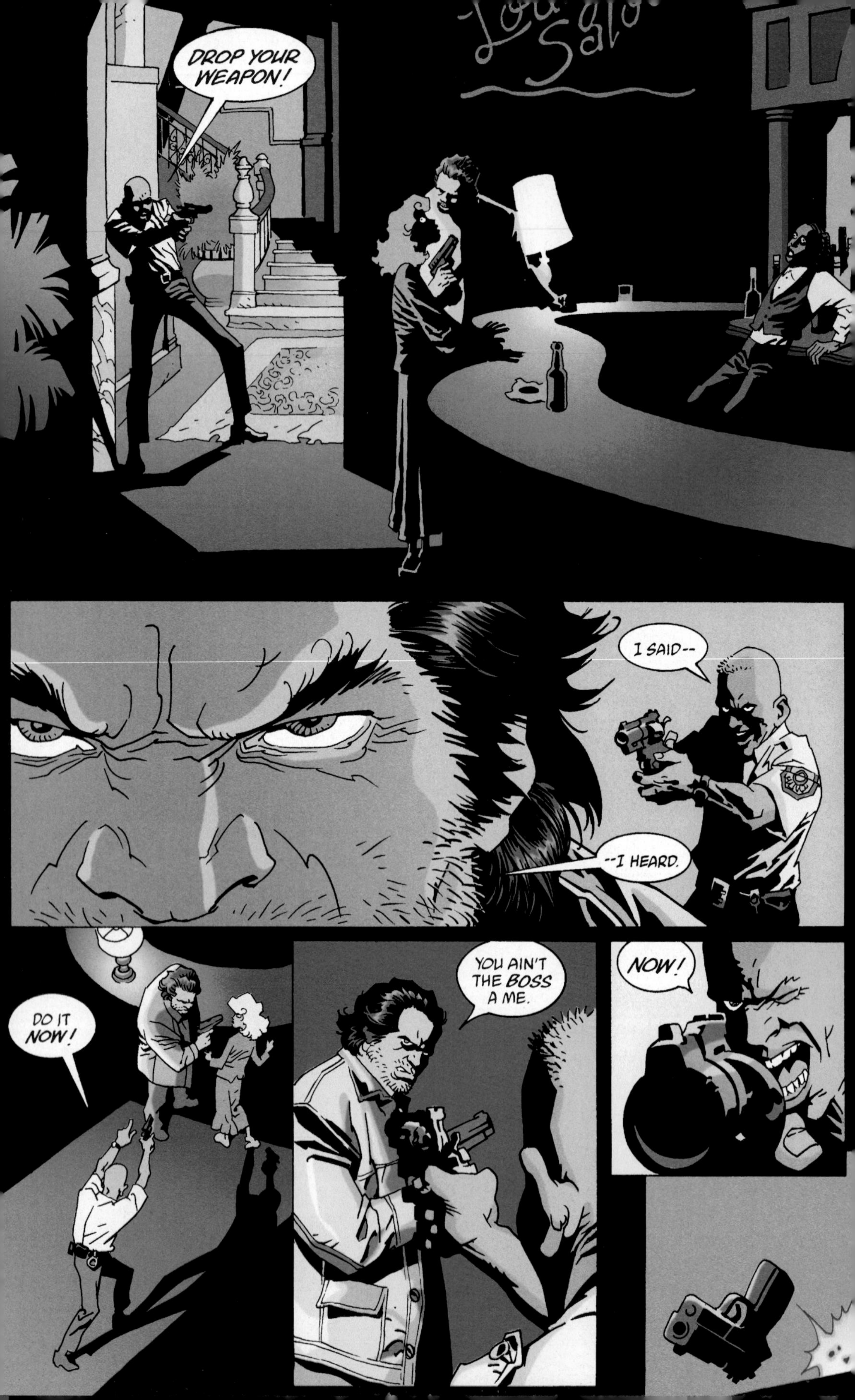
DROP YOUR WEAPON!
I SAID--
--I HEARD.
DO IT NOW!
YOU AIN'T THE BOSS A ME.
NOW!

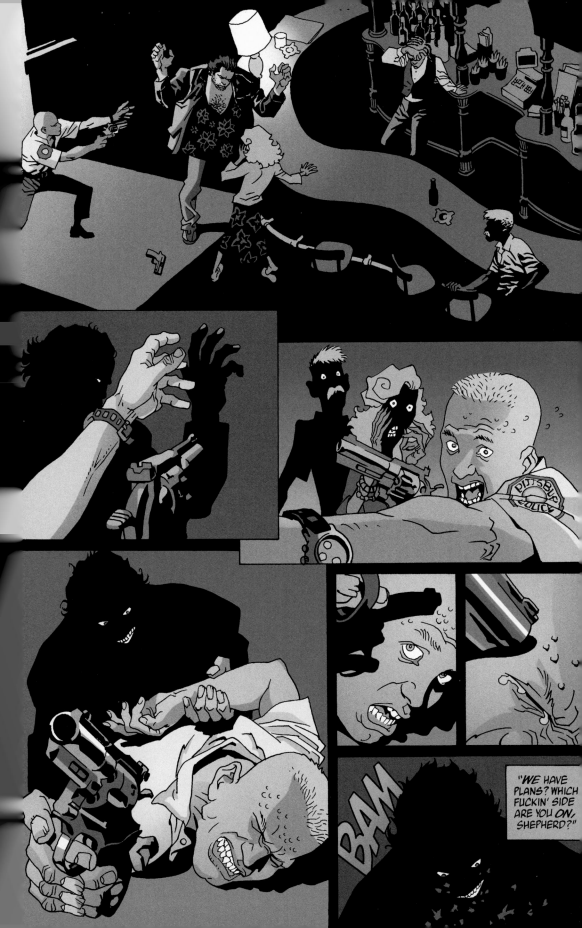

BAM

"WE HAVE PLANS? WHICH FUCKIN' SIDE ARE YOU ON, SHEPERD?"

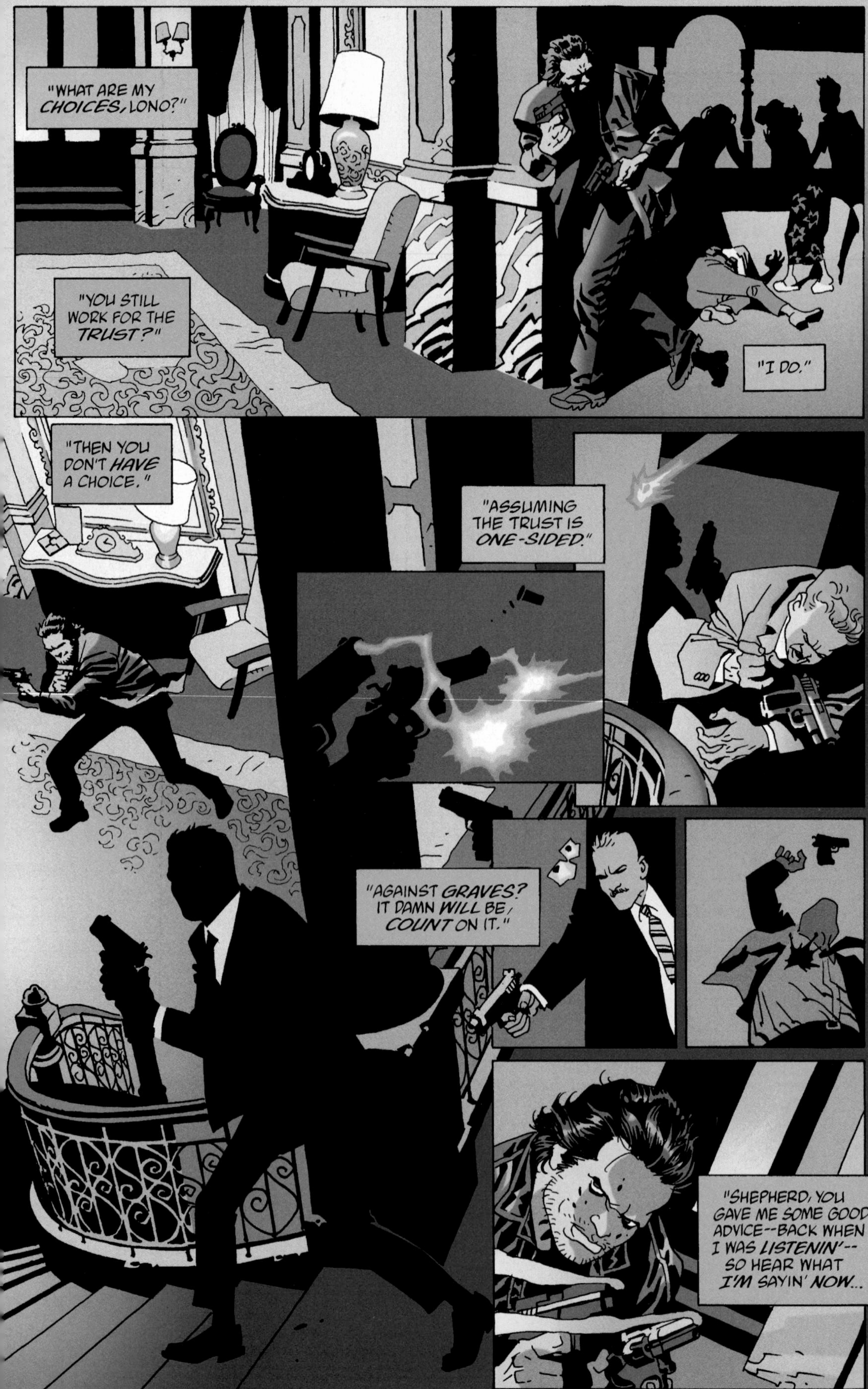
"WHAT ARE MY CHOICES, LONO?"
"YOU STILL WORK FOR THE TRUST?"
"I DO."
"THEN YOU DON'T HAVE A CHOICE."
"ASSUMING THE TRUST IS ONE-SIDED."
"AGAINST GRAVES? IT DAMN WILL BE, COUNT ON IT."
"SHEPHERD, YOU GAVE ME SOME GOOD ADVICE--BACK WHEN I WAS LISTENIN'-- SO HEAR WHAT I'M SAYIN' NOW...

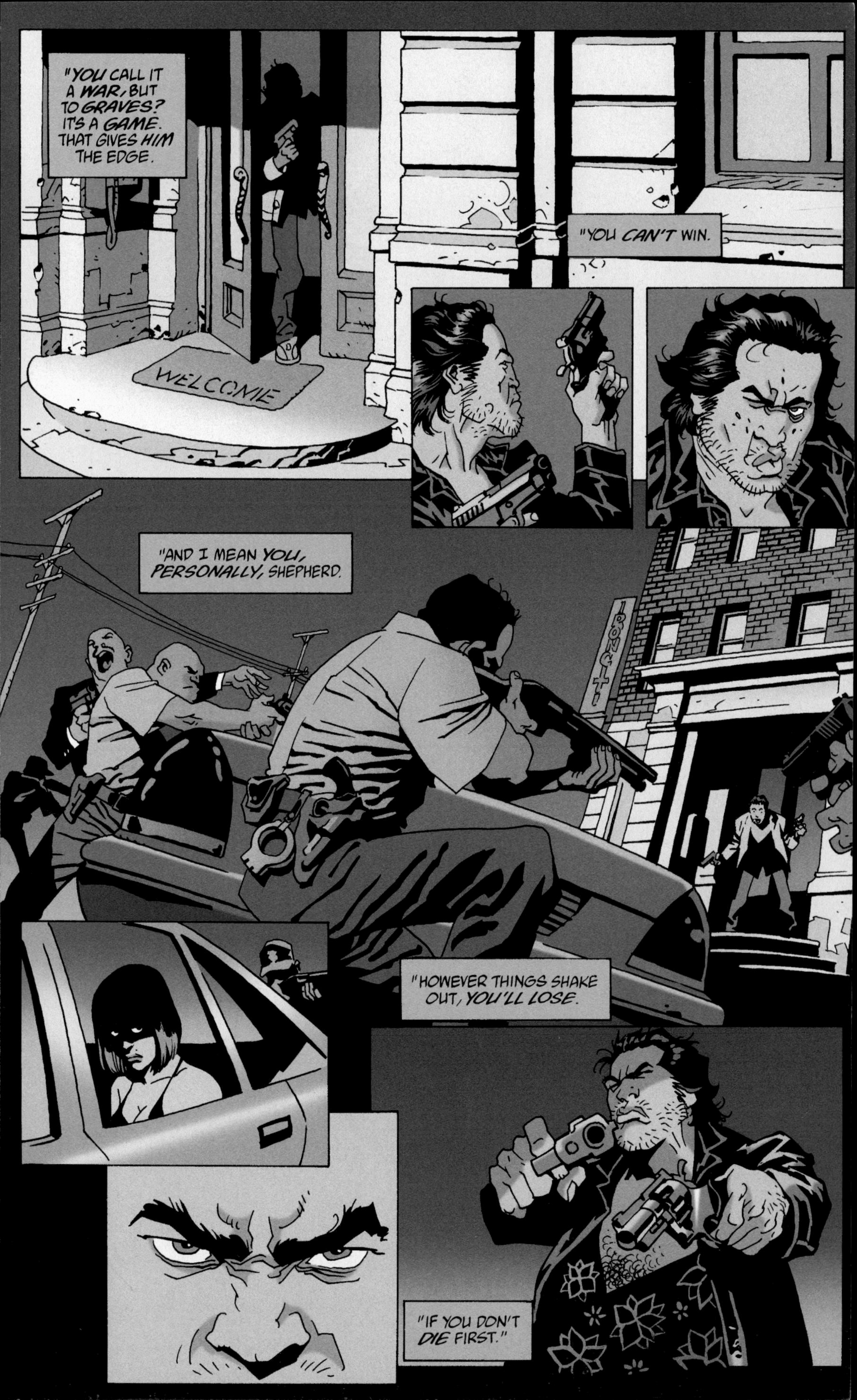
"YOU CALL IT A WAR, BUT TO GRAVES? IT'S A GAME. THAT GIVES HIM THE EDGE.
WELCOME
"YOU CAN'T WIN.
"AND I MEAN YOU, PERSONALLY, SHEPHERD.
IRONGATE
"HOWEVER THINGS SHAKE OUT, YOU'LL LOSE.
"IF YOU DON'T DIE FIRST."

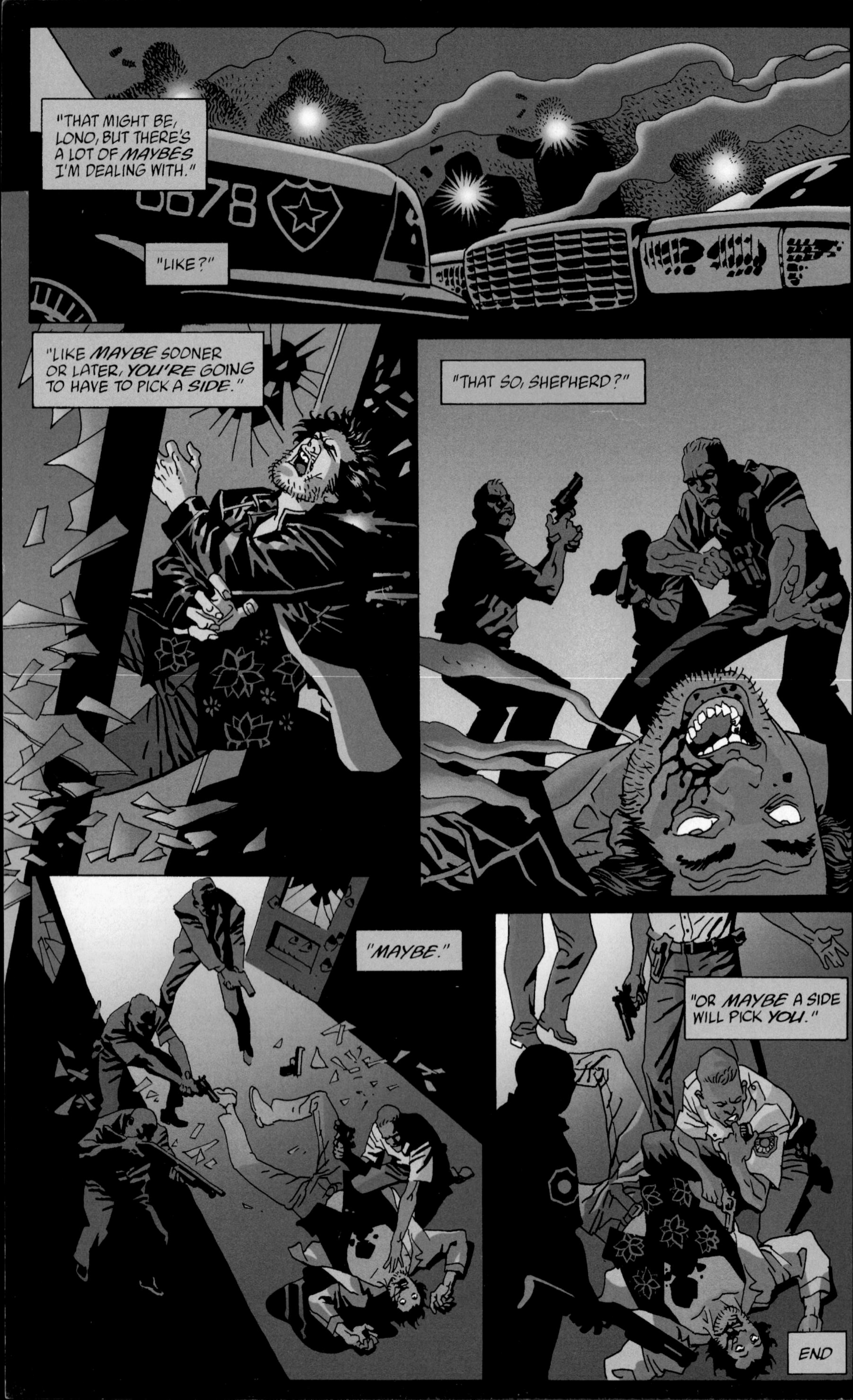

"THAT MIGHT BE, LONO, BUT THERE'S A LOT OF MAYBES I'M DEALING WITH."
"LIKE?"
"LIKE MAYBE SOONER OR LATER, YOU'RE GOING TO HAVE TO PICK A SIDE."
"THAT SO, SHEPHERD?"
"MAYBE."
"OR MAYBE A SIDE WILL PICK YOU."
END

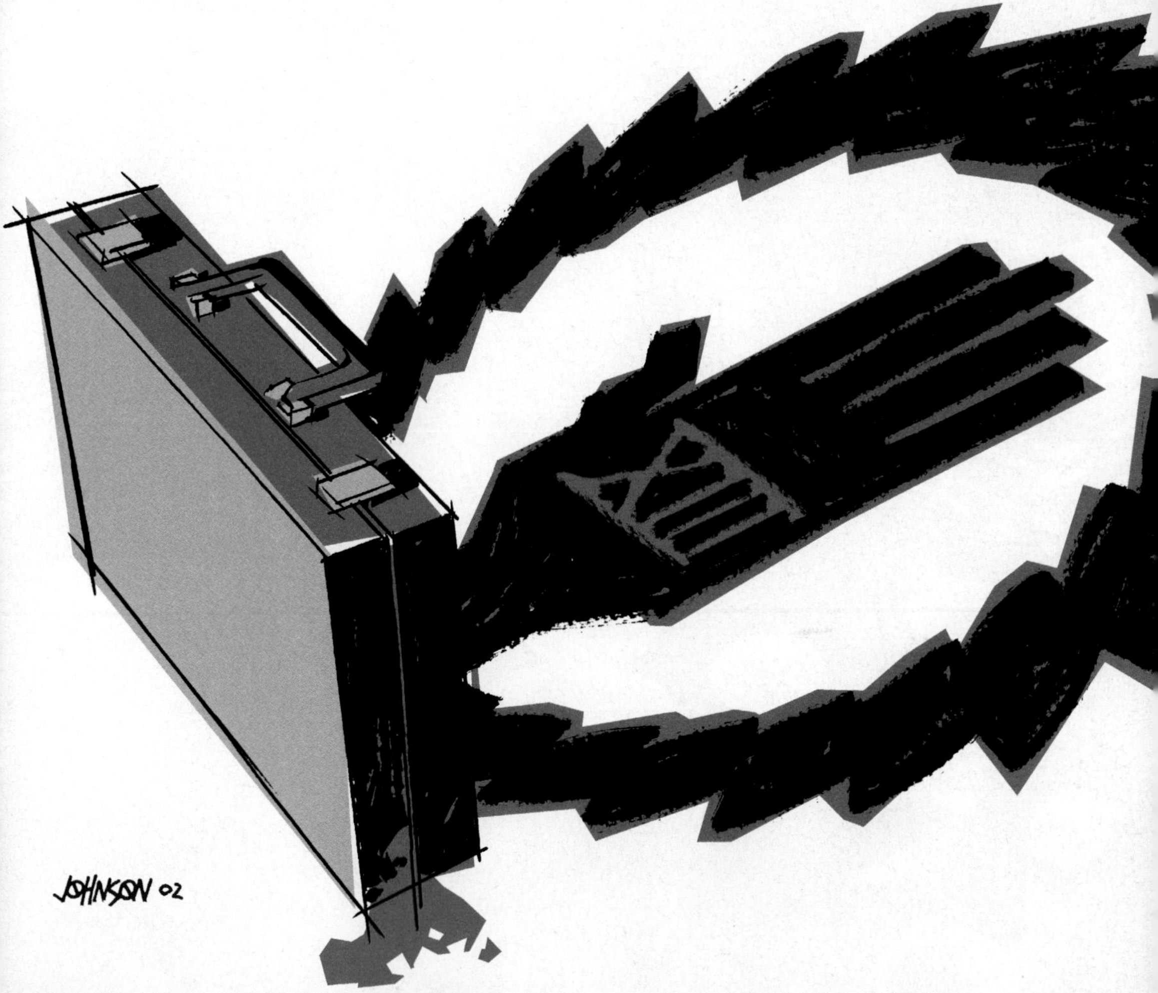
JOHNSON 02

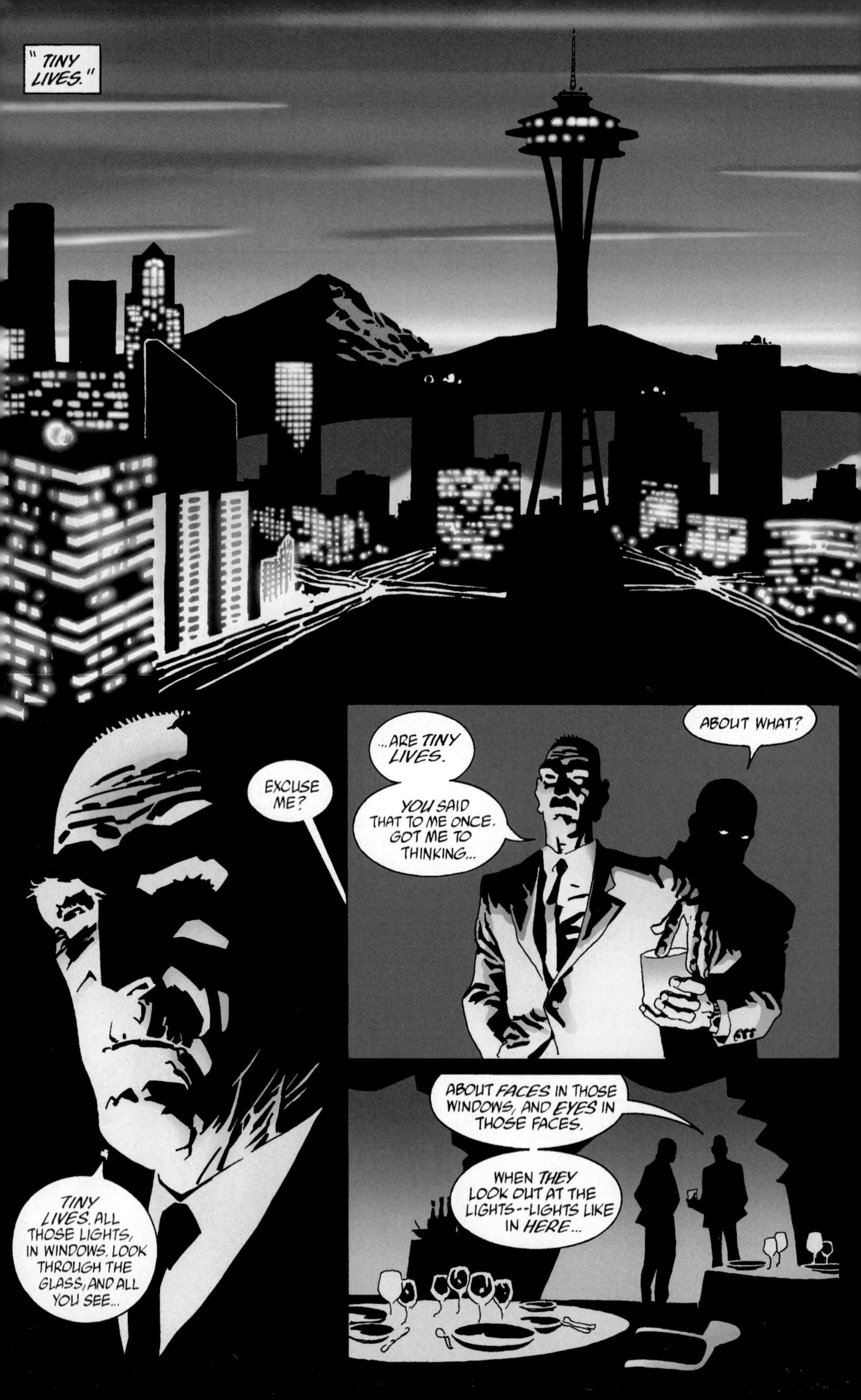
"TINY LIVES."
EXCUSE ME?
...ARE TINY LIVES.
YOU SAID THAT TO ME ONCE. GOT ME TO THINKING...
ABOUT WHAT?
TINY LIVES. ALL THOSE LIGHTS, IN WINDOWS. LOOK THROUGH THE GLASS, AND ALL YOU SEE...
ABOUT FACES IN THOSE WINDOWS, AND EYES IN THOSE FACES.
WHEN THEY LOOK OUT AT THE LIGHTS--LIGHTS LIKE IN HERE...

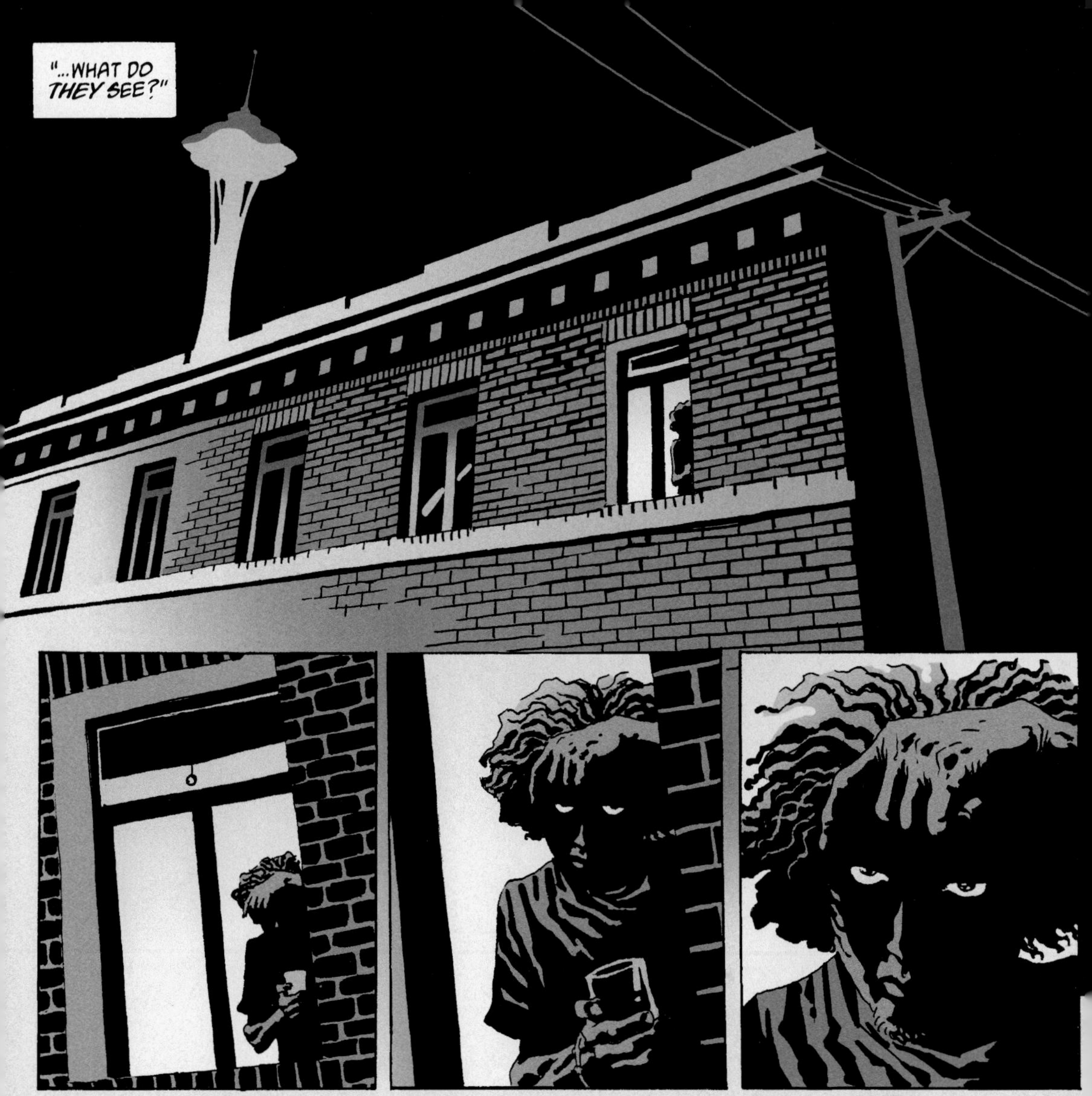
"...WHAT DO THEY SEE?"

a crash

BRIAN AZZARELLO writer

EDUARDO RISSO artist

PATRICIA MULVIHILL colorist

CLEM ROBINS letterer

DIGITAL CHAMELEON separations

DAVE JOHNSON cover

ZACHARY RAU ass't ed

WILL DENNIS editor

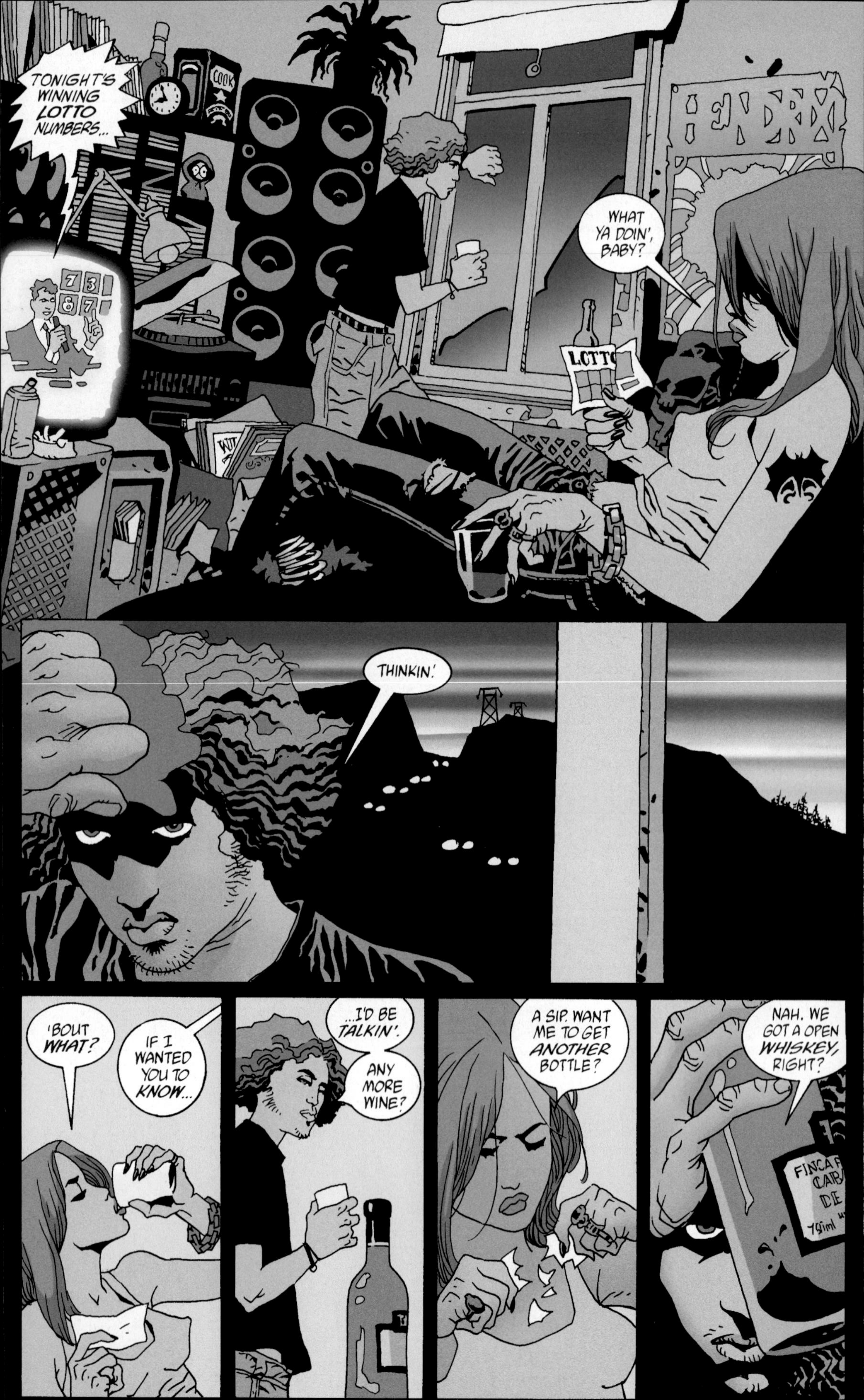

TONIGHT'S WINNING LOTTO NUMBERS...
WHAT YA DOIN', BABY?
LOTTO
THINKIN'.
'BOUT WHAT?
IF I WANTED YOU TO KNOW...
...I'D BE TALKIN'.
ANY MORE WINE?
A SIP. WANT ME TO GET ANOTHER BOTTLE?
NAH. WE GOT A OPEN WHISKEY, RIGHT?

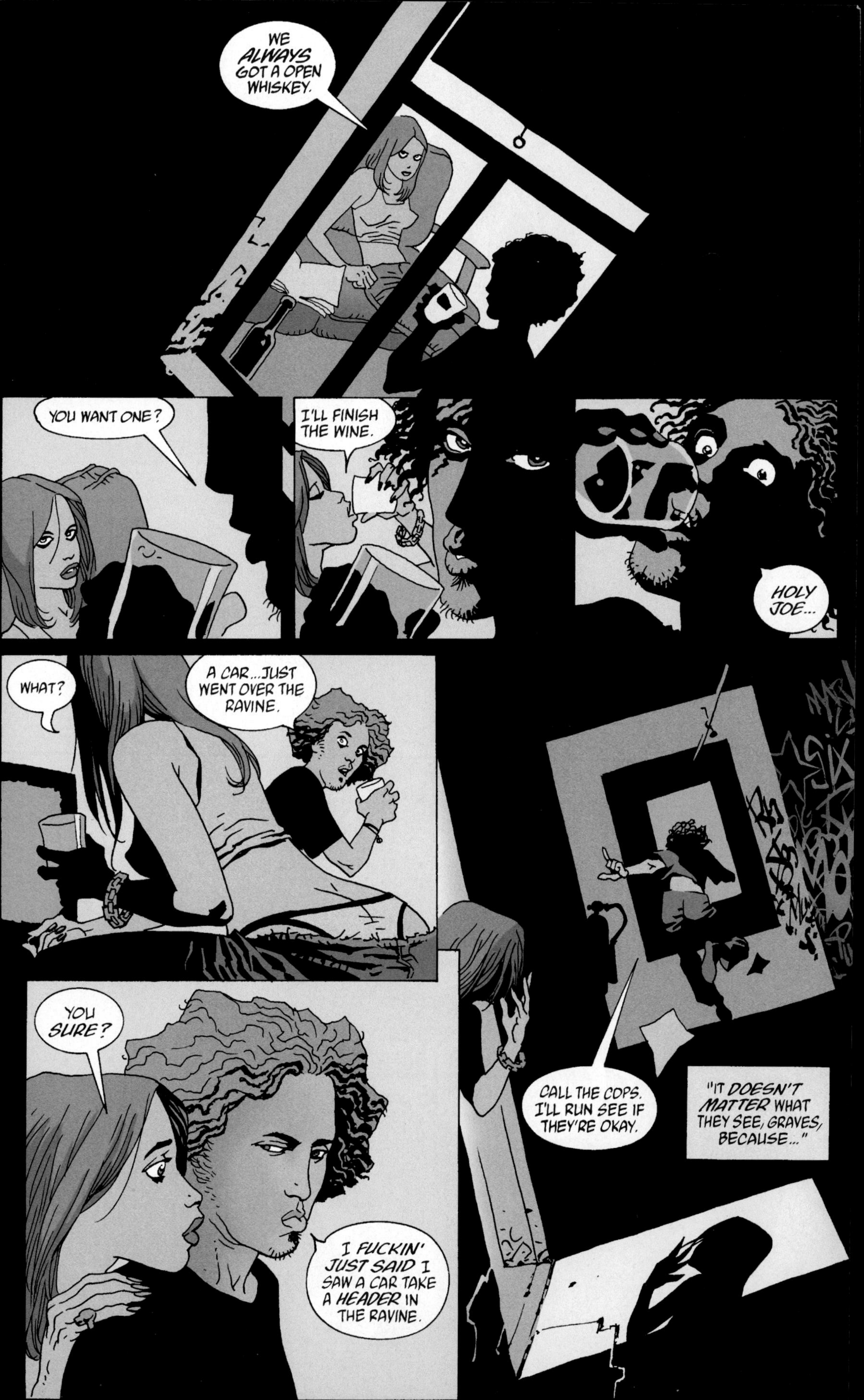
WE ALWAYS GOT A OPEN WHISKEY.
YOU WANT ONE?
I'LL FINISH THE WINE.
HOLY JOE...
WHAT?
A CAR...JUST WENT OVER THE RAVINE.
YOU SURE?
I FUCKIN' JUST SAID I SAW A CAR TAKE A HEADER IN THE RAVINE.
CALL THE COPS. I'LL RUN SEE IF THEY'RE OKAY.
"IT DOESN'T MATTER WHAT THEY SEE, GRAVES, BECAUSE..."

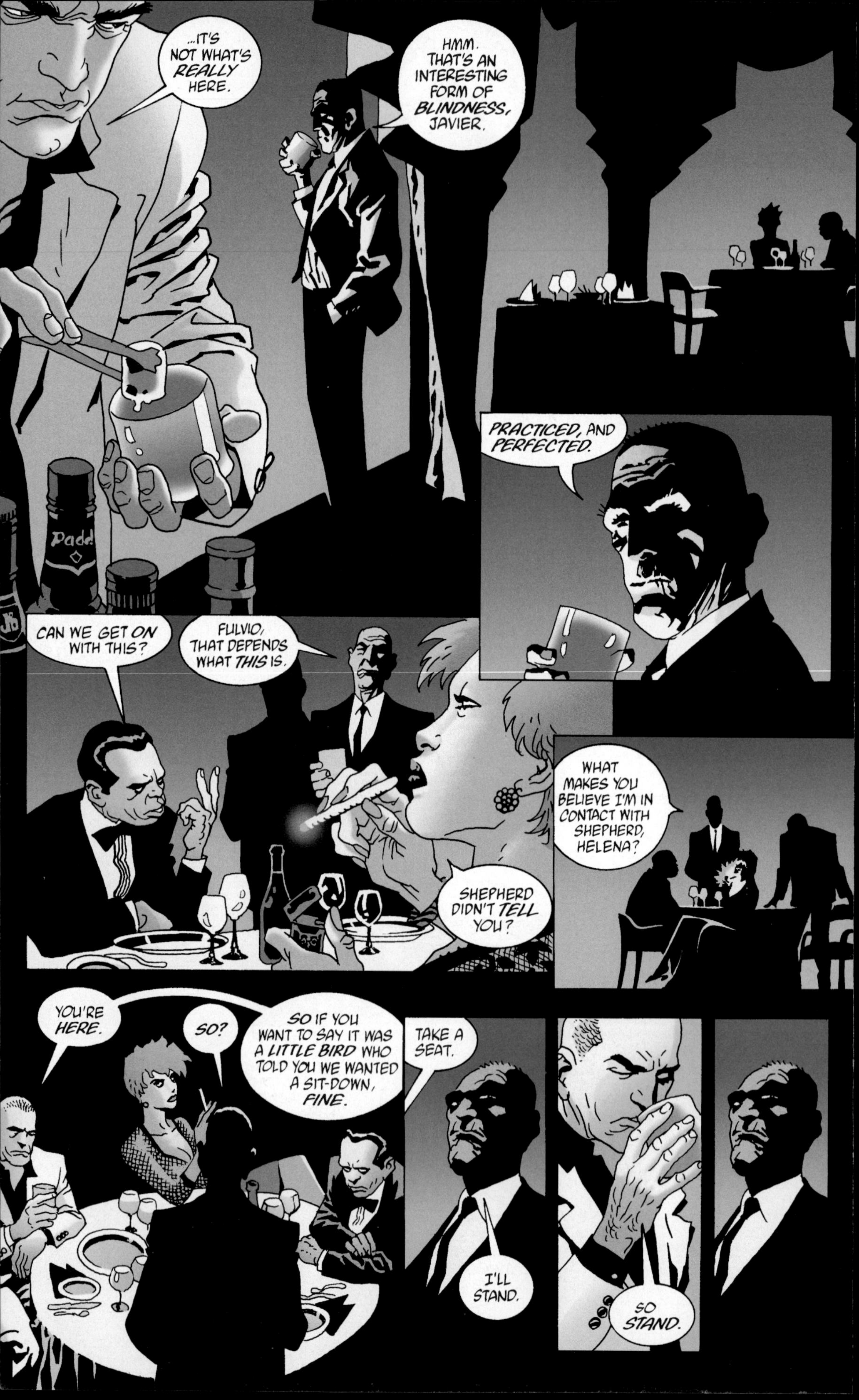
...IT'S NOT WHAT'S REALLY HERE.
HMM. THAT'S AN INTERESTING FORM OF BLINDNESS, JAVIER.
PRACTICED, AND PERFECTED.
CAN WE GET ON WITH THIS?
FULVIO, THAT DEPENDS WHAT THIS IS.
SHEPHERD DIDN'T TELL YOU?
WHAT MAKES YOU BELIEVE I'M IN CONTACT WITH SHEPHERD, HELENA?
YOU'RE HERE.
SO?
SO IF YOU WANT TO SAY IT WAS A LITTLE BIRD WHO TOLD YOU WE WANTED A SIT-DOWN, FINE.
TAKE A SEAT.
I'LL STAND.
SO STAND.

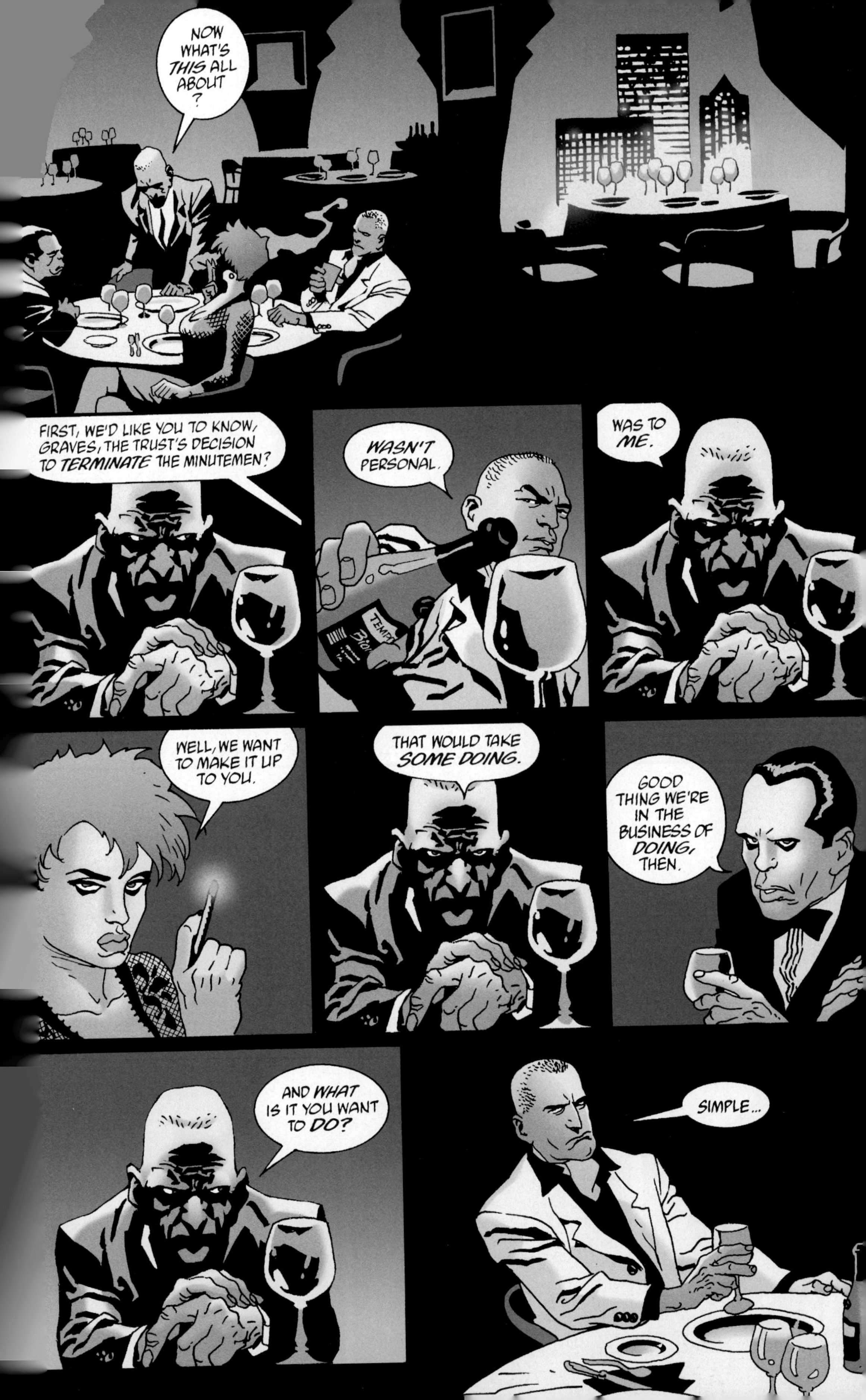
NOW WHAT'S THIS ALL ABOUT ?
FIRST, WE'D LIKE YOU TO KNOW, GRAVES, THE TRUST'S DECISION TO TERMINATE THE MINUTEMEN?
WASN'T PERSONAL.
WAS TO ME.
WELL, WE WANT TO MAKE IT UP TO YOU.
THAT WOULD TAKE SOME DOING.
GOOD THING WE'RE IN THE BUSINESS OF DOING, THEN.
AND WHAT IS IT YOU WANT TO DO?
SIMPLE...

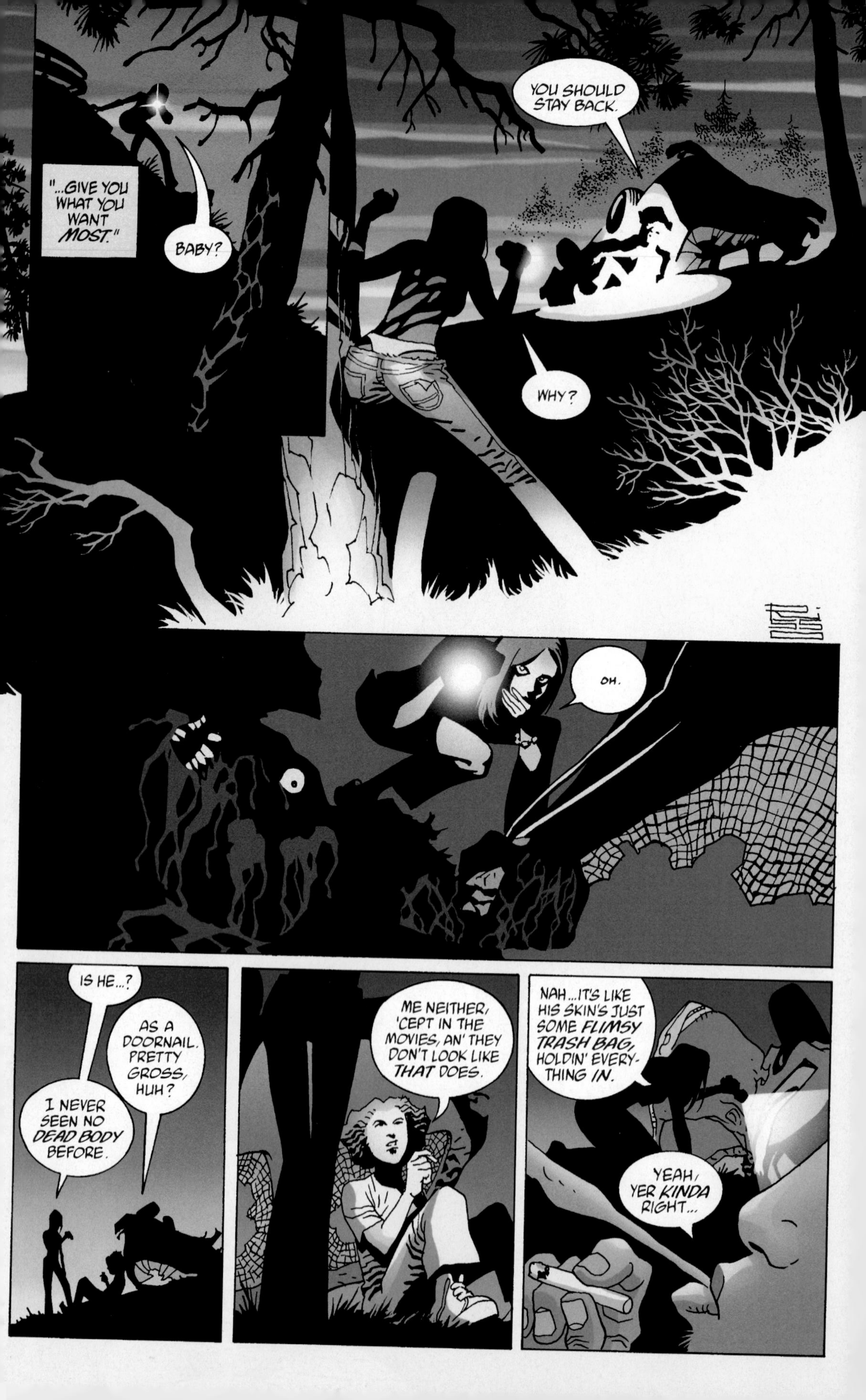
"...GIVE YOU WHAT YOU WANT MOST."
BABY?
YOU SHOULD STAY BACK.
WHY?
OH.
IS HE...?
AS A DOORNAIL. PRETTY GROSS, HUH?
I NEVER SEEN NO DEAD BODY BEFORE.
ME NEITHER, 'CEPT IN THE MOVIES, AN' THEY DON'T LOOK LIKE THAT DOES.
NAH...IT'S LIKE HIS SKIN'S JUST SOME FLIMSY TRASH BAG, HOLDIN' EVERYTHING IN.
YEAH, YER KINDA RIGHT...

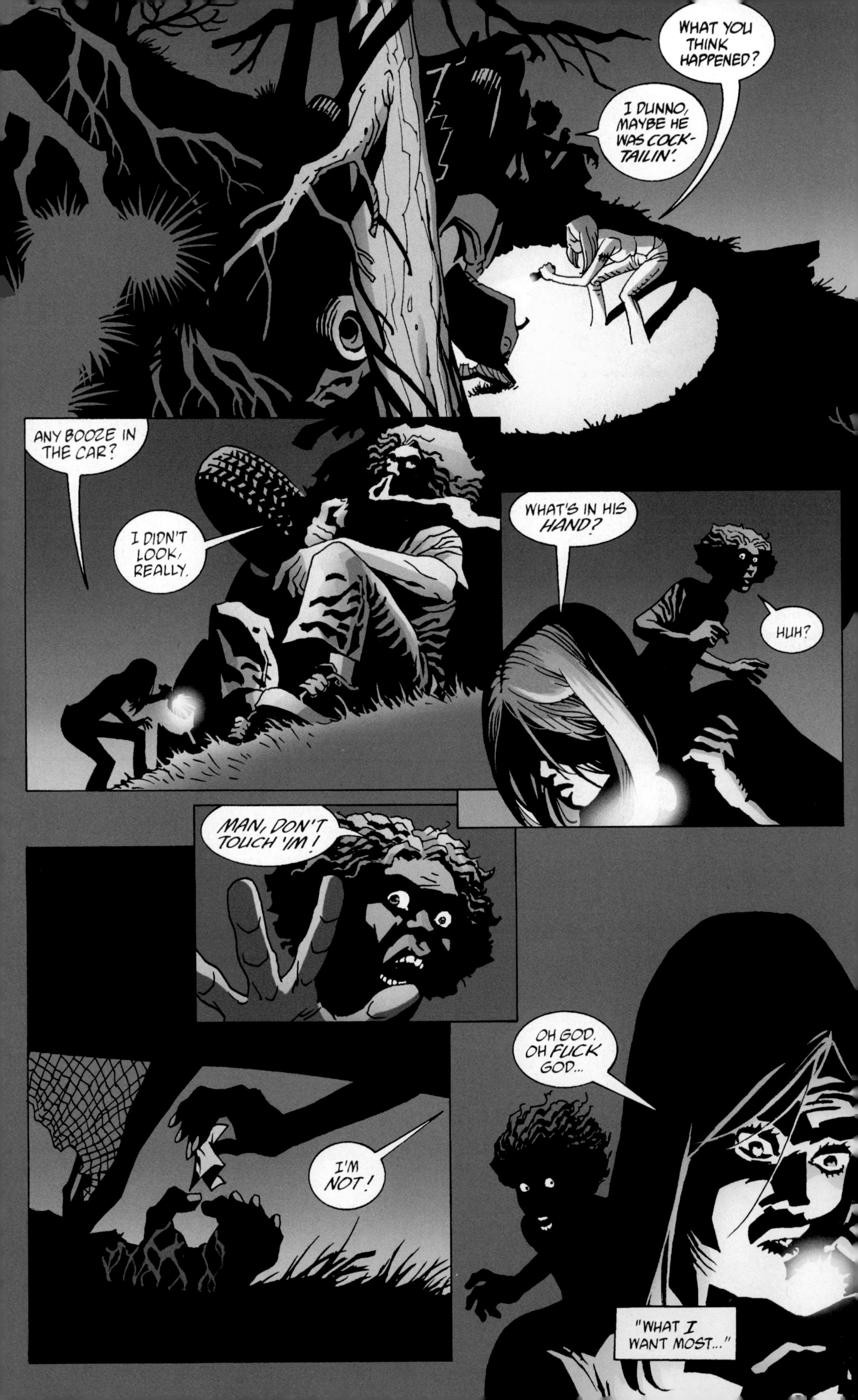
WHAT YOU THINK HAPPENED?
I DUNNO, MAYBE HE WAS COCK-TAILIN'.
ANY BOOZE IN THE CAR?
I DIDN'T LOOK, REALLY.
WHAT'S IN HIS HAND?
HUH?
MAN, DON'T TOUCH 'IM!
I'M NOT!
OH GOD, OH FUCK GOD...
"WHAT I WANT MOST..."

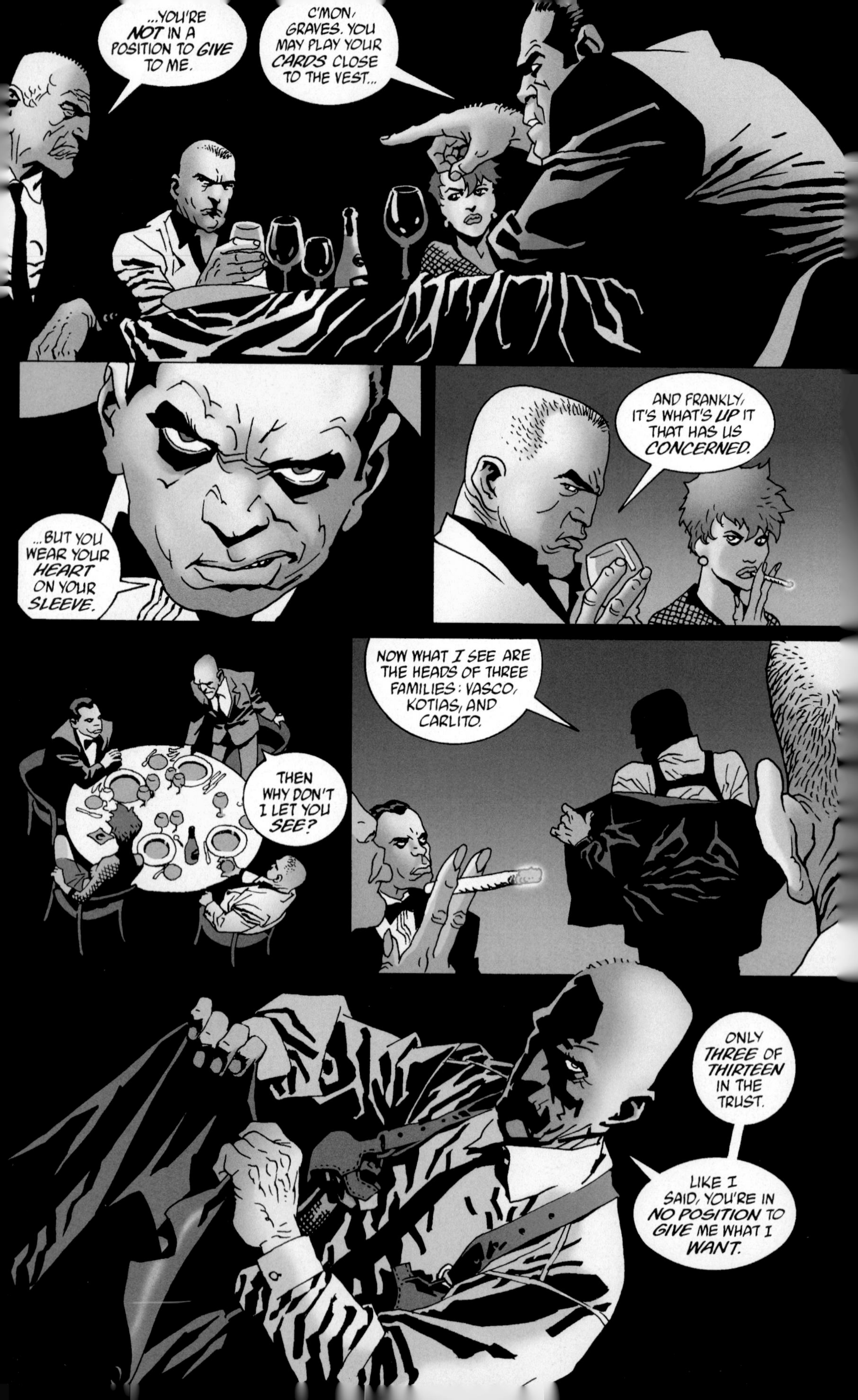
...YOU'RE NOT IN A POSITION TO GIVE TO ME.
C'MON, GRAVES. YOU MAY PLAY YOUR CARDS CLOSE TO THE VEST...
...BUT YOU WEAR YOUR HEART ON YOUR SLEEVE.
AND FRANKLY, IT'S WHAT'S UP IT THAT HAS US CONCERNED.
THEN WHY DON'T I LET YOU SEE?
NOW WHAT I SEE ARE THE HEADS OF THREE FAMILIES: VASCO, KOTIAS, AND CARLITO.
ONLY THREE OF THIRTEEN IN THE TRUST.
LIKE I SAID, YOU'RE IN NO POSITION TO GIVE ME WHAT I WANT.

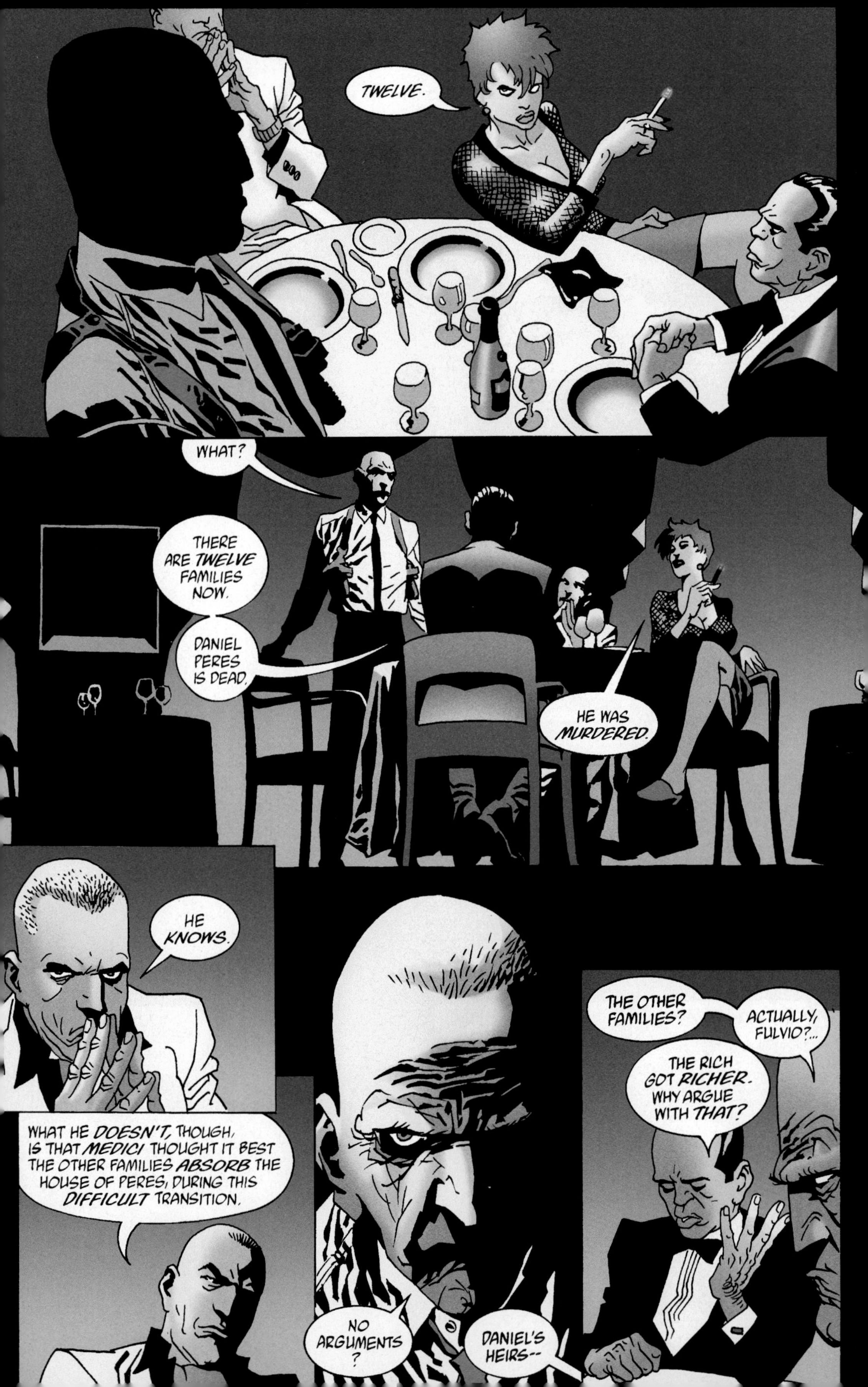

TWELVE.
WHAT?
THERE ARE TWELVE FAMILIES NOW.
DANIEL PERES IS DEAD.
HE WAS MURDERED.
HE KNOWS.
WHAT HE DOESN'T, THOUGH, IS THAT MEDICI THOUGHT IT BEST THE OTHER FAMILIES ABSORB THE HOUSE OF PERES, DURING THIS DIFFICULT TRANSITION.
NO ARGUMENTS?
DANIEL'S HEIRS--
THE OTHER FAMILIES?
ACTUALLY, FULVIO?...
THE RICH GOT RICHER. WHY ARGUE WITH THAT?

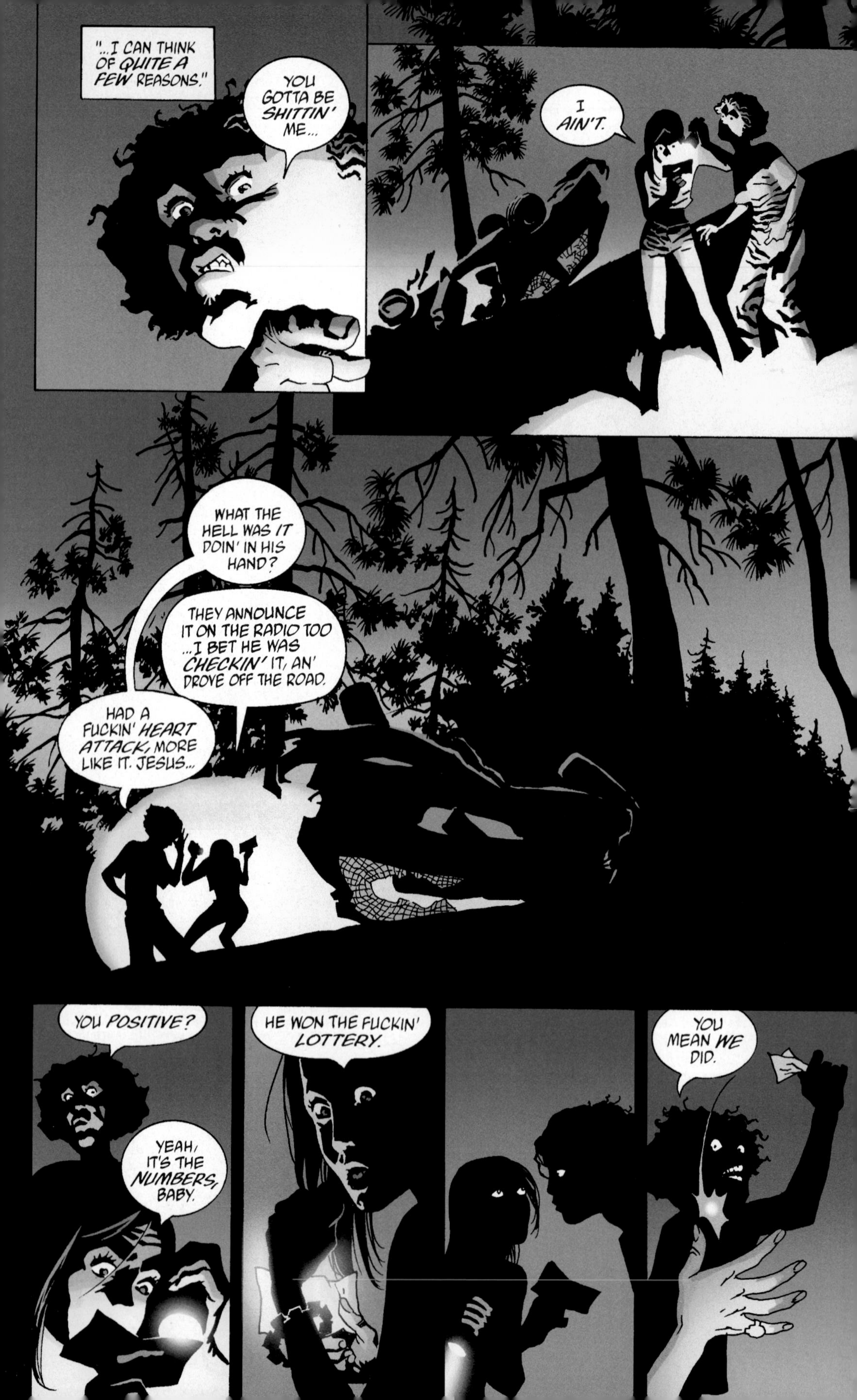
"...I CAN THINK OF QUITE A FEW REASONS."
YOU GOTTA BE SHITTIN' ME...
I AIN'T.
WHAT THE HELL WAS IT DOIN' IN HIS HAND?
THEY ANNOUNCE IT ON THE RADIO TOO ...I BET HE WAS CHECKIN' IT, AN' DROVE OFF THE ROAD.
HAD A FUCKIN' HEART ATTACK, MORE LIKE IT. JESUS...
YOU POSITIVE?
YEAH, IT'S THE NUMBERS, BABY.
HE WON THE FUCKIN' LOTTERY.
YOU MEAN WE DID.

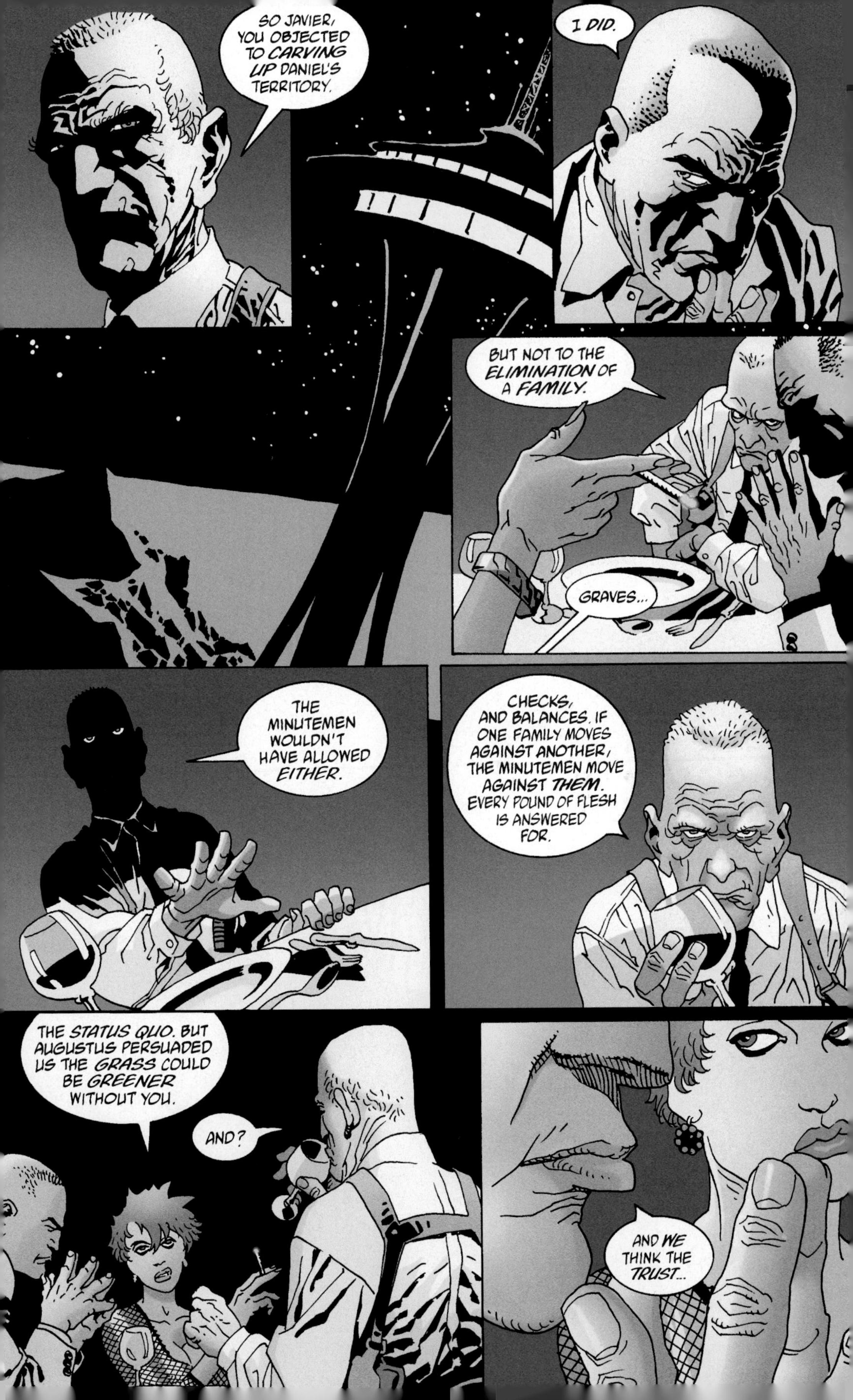
SO JAVIER, YOU OBJECTED TO CARVING UP DANIEL'S TERRITORY.
I DID.
BUT NOT TO THE ELIMINATION OF A FAMILY.
GRAVES...
THE MINUTEMEN WOULDN'T HAVE ALLOWED EITHER.
CHECKS, AND BALANCES. IF ONE FAMILY MOVES AGAINST ANOTHER, THE MINUTEMEN MOVE AGAINST THEM. EVERY POUND OF FLESH IS ANSWERED FOR.
THE STATUS QUO. BUT AUGUSTUS PERSUADED US THE GRASS COULD BE GREENER WITHOUT YOU.
AND?
AND WE THINK THE TRUST...

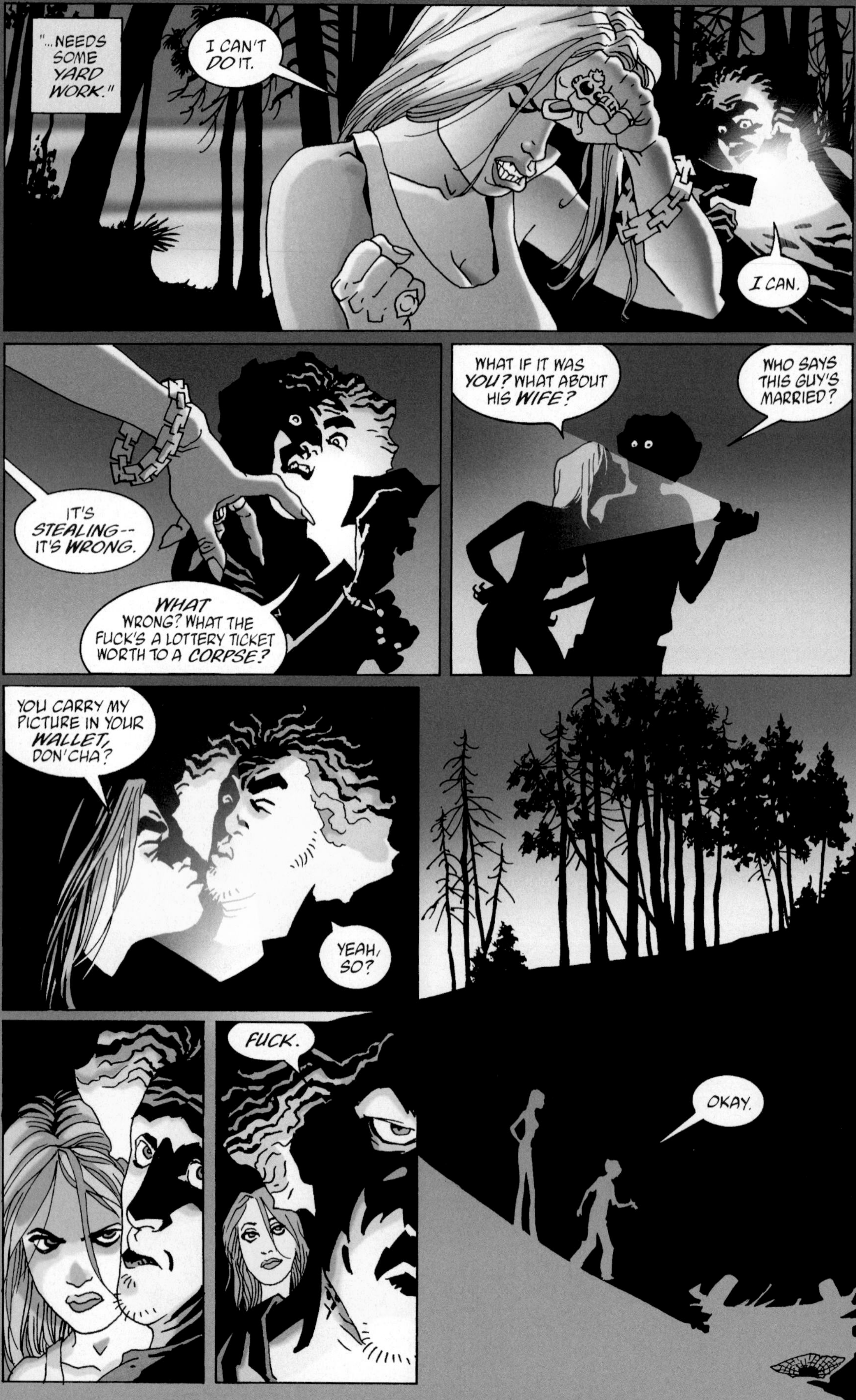
"...NEEDS SOME YARD WORK."
I CAN'T DO IT.
I CAN.
IT'S STEALING-- IT'S WRONG.
WHAT WRONG? WHAT THE FUCK'S A LOTTERY TICKET WORTH TO A CORPSE?
WHAT IF IT WAS YOU? WHAT ABOUT HIS WIFE?
WHO SAYS THIS GUY'S MARRIED?
YOU CARRY MY PICTURE IN YOUR WALLET, DON'CHA?
YEAH, SO?
FUCK.
OKAY.

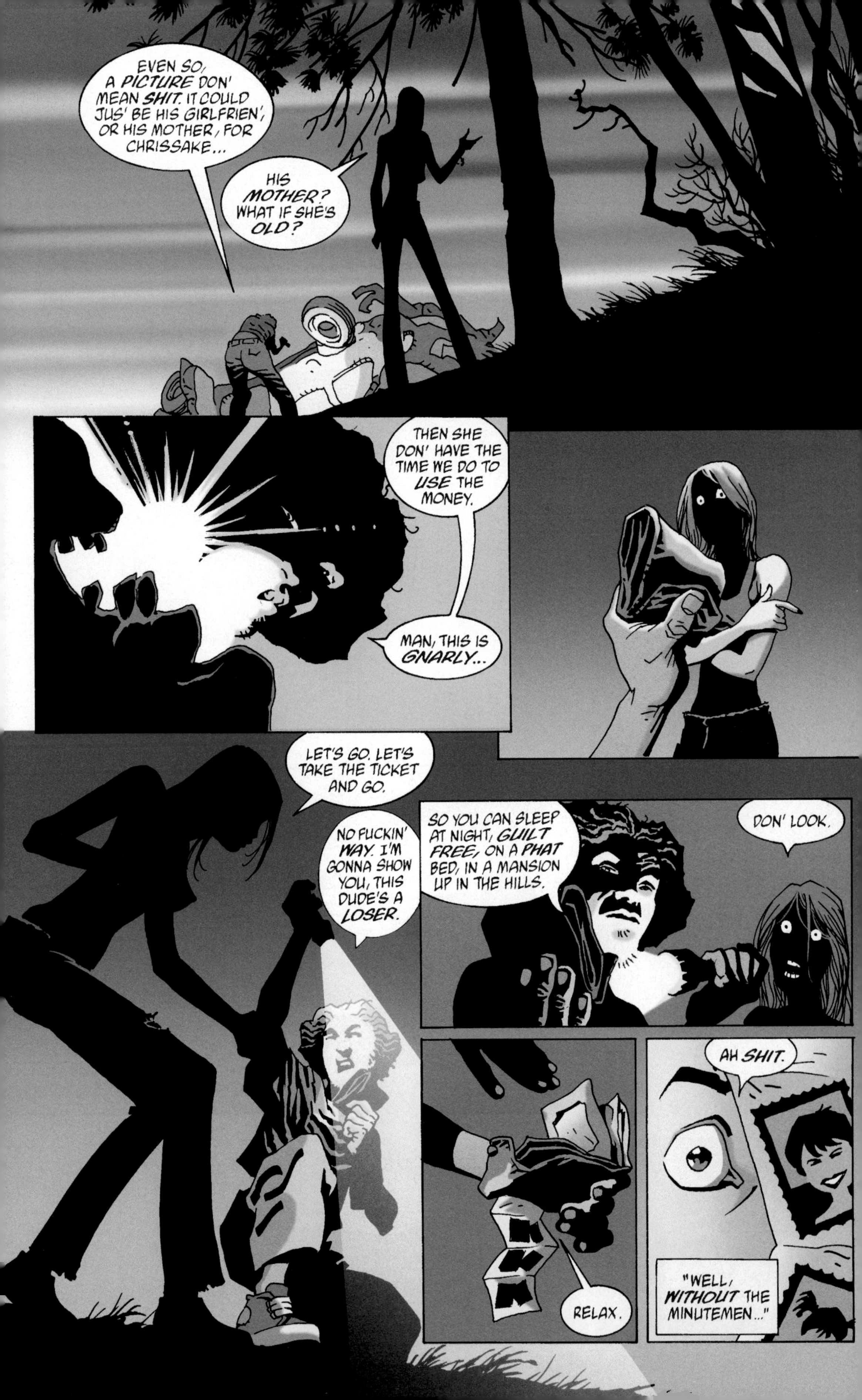
EVEN SO, A *PICTURE* DON' MEAN *SHIT.* IT COULD JUS' BE HIS GIRLFRIEN', OR HIS MOTHER, FOR CHRISSAKE...
HIS *MOTHER?* WHAT IF SHE'S *OLD?*
THEN SHE DON' HAVE THE TIME WE DO TO *USE* THE MONEY.
MAN, THIS IS *GNARLY...*
LET'S GO. LET'S TAKE THE TICKET AND GO.
NO FUCKIN' *WAY.* I'M GONNA SHOW YOU, THIS DUDE'S A *LOSER.*
SO YOU CAN SLEEP AT NIGHT, *GUILT FREE,* ON A *PHAT* BED, IN A MANSION UP IN THE HILLS.
DON' LOOK.
RELAX.
AH *SHIT.*
"WELL, *WITHOUT* THE MINUTEMEN..."

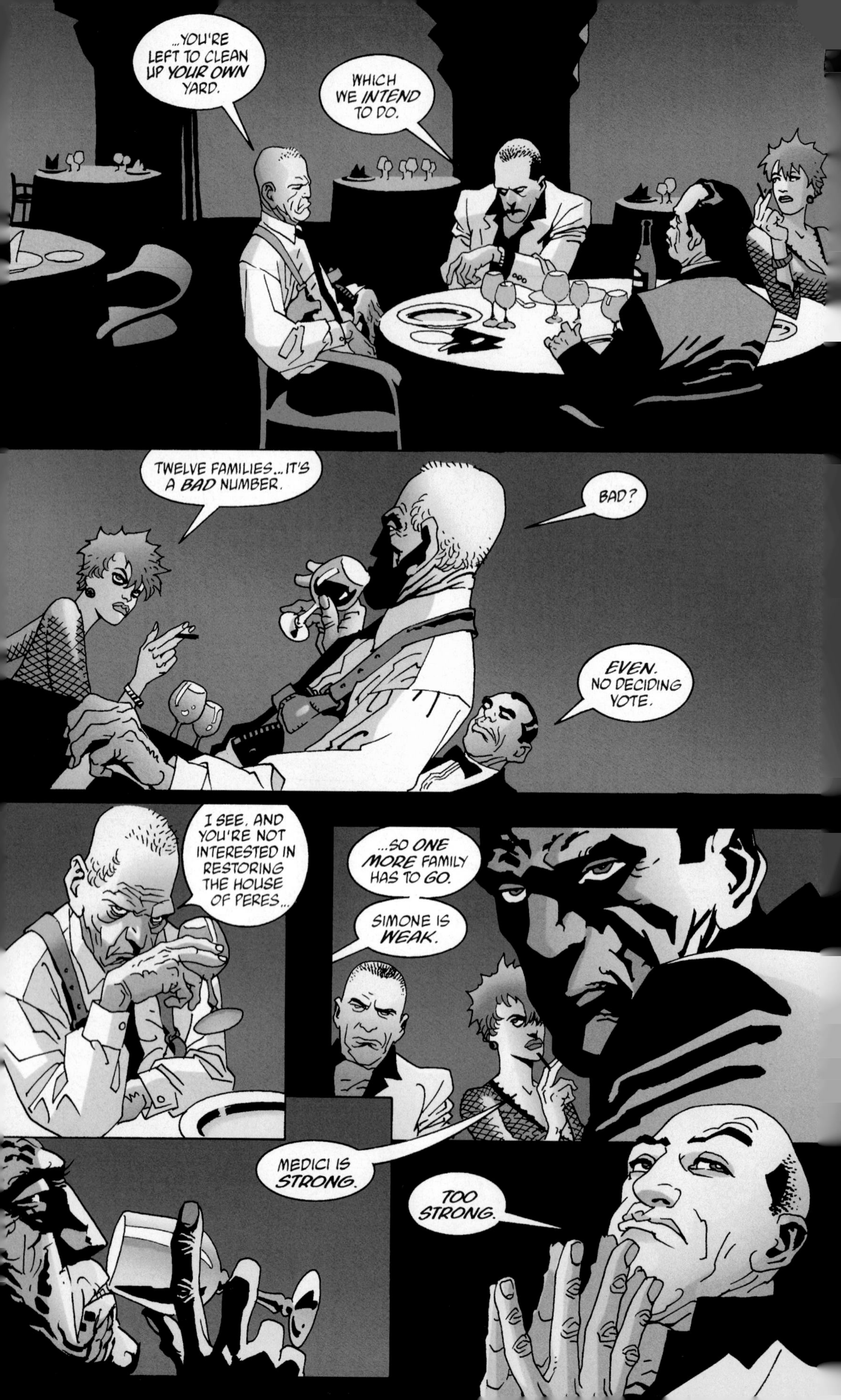
...YOU'RE LEFT TO CLEAN UP YOUR OWN YARD.
WHICH WE INTEND TO DO.
TWELVE FAMILIES... IT'S A BAD NUMBER.
BAD?
EVEN. NO DECIDING VOTE.
I SEE. AND YOU'RE NOT INTERESTED IN RESTORING THE HOUSE OF PERES...
...SO ONE MORE FAMILY HAS TO GO.
SIMONE IS WEAK.
MEDICI IS STRONG.
TOO STRONG.

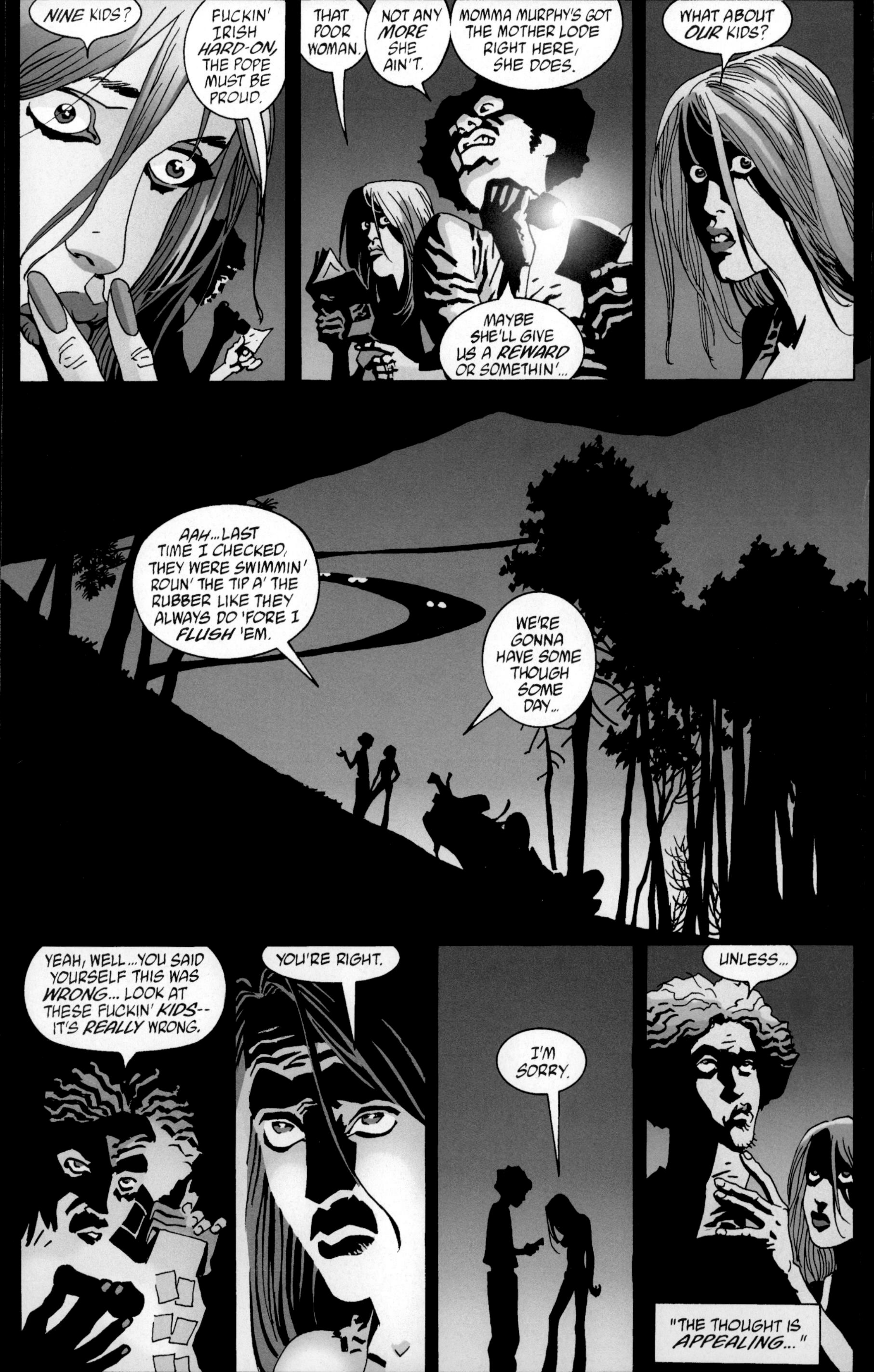
NINE KIDS?
FUCKIN' IRISH HARD-ON, THE POPE MUST BE PROUD.
THAT POOR WOMAN.
NOT ANY MORE SHE AIN'T.
MOMMA MURPHY'S GOT THE MOTHER LODE RIGHT HERE, SHE DOES.
MAYBE SHE'LL GIVE US A REWARD OR SOMETHIN'...
WHAT ABOUT OUR KIDS?
AAH...LAST TIME I CHECKED, THEY WERE SWIMMIN' ROUN' THE TIP A' THE RUBBER LIKE THEY ALWAYS DO 'FORE I FLUSH 'EM.
WE'RE GONNA HAVE SOME THOUGH SOME DAY...
YEAH, WELL...YOU SAID YOURSELF THIS WAS WRONG... LOOK AT THESE FUCKIN' KIDS-- IT'S REALLY WRONG.
YOU'RE RIGHT.
I'M SORRY.
UNLESS...
"THE THOUGHT IS APPEALING..."

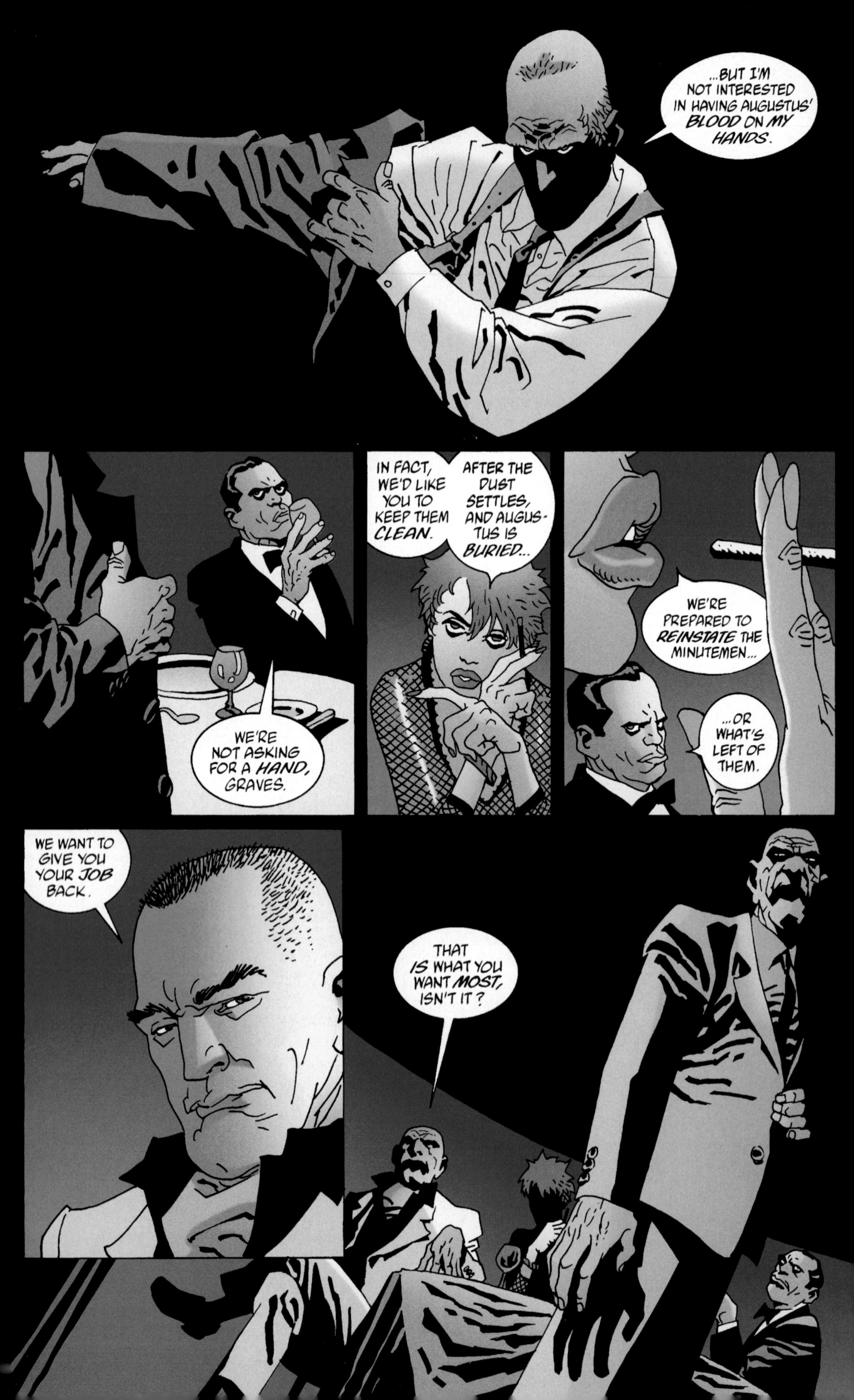
...BUT I'M NOT INTERESTED IN HAVING AUGUSTUS' BLOOD ON MY HANDS.
WE'RE NOT ASKING FOR A HAND, GRAVES.
IN FACT, WE'D LIKE YOU TO KEEP THEM CLEAN.
AFTER THE DUST SETTLES, AND AUGUS-TUS IS BURIED...
WE'RE PREPARED TO REINSTATE THE MINUTEMEN...
...OR WHAT'S LEFT OF THEM.
WE WANT TO GIVE YOU YOUR JOB BACK.
THAT IS WHAT YOU WANT MOST, ISN'T IT?

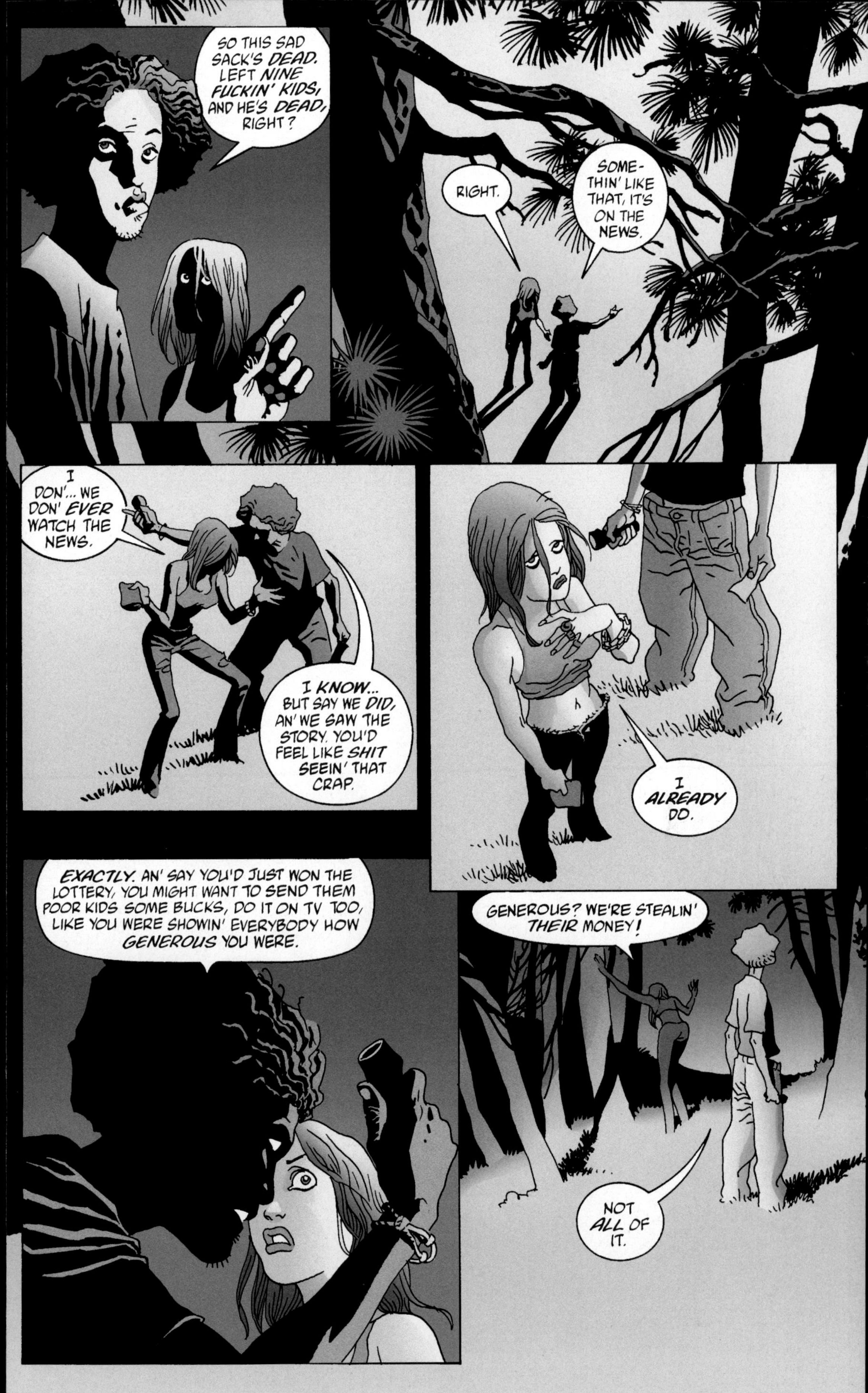
SO THIS SAD SACK'S DEAD. LEFT NINE FUCKIN' KIDS, AND HE'S DEAD, RIGHT?
RIGHT.
SOME-THIN' LIKE THAT, IT'S ON THE NEWS.
I DON'... WE DON' EVER WATCH THE NEWS.
I KNOW... BUT SAY WE DID, AN' WE SAW THE STORY. YOU'D FEEL LIKE SHIT SEEIN' THAT CRAP.
I ALREADY DO.
EXACTLY. AN' SAY YOU'D JUST WON THE LOTTERY, YOU MIGHT WANT TO SEND THEM POOR KIDS SOME BUCKS, DO IT ON TV TOO, LIKE YOU WERE SHOWIN' EVERYBODY HOW GENEROUS YOU WERE.
GENEROUS? WE'RE STEALIN' THEIR MONEY!
NOT ALL OF IT.

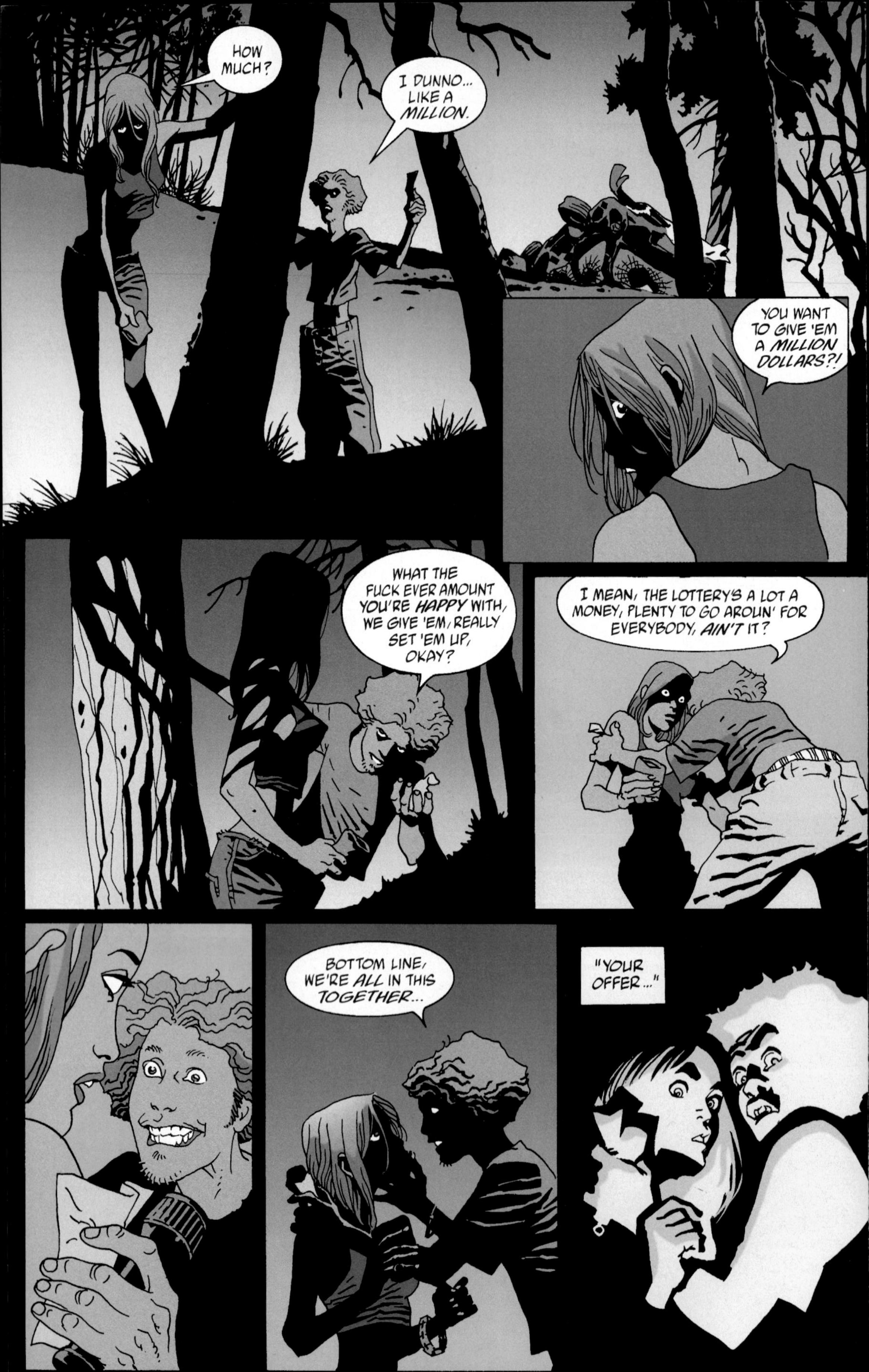
HOW MUCH?
I DUNNO... LIKE A *MILLION*.
YOU WANT TO GIVE 'EM A *MILLION DOLLARS?!*
WHAT THE FUCK EVER AMOUNT YOU'RE *HAPPY* WITH, WE GIVE 'EM, REALLY SET 'EM UP, OKAY?
I MEAN, THE LOTTERY'S A LOT A MONEY, PLENTY TO GO AROUN' FOR EVERYBODY, *AIN'T* IT?
BOTTOM LINE, WE'RE *ALL* IN THIS *TOGETHER*...
"YOUR OFFER..."

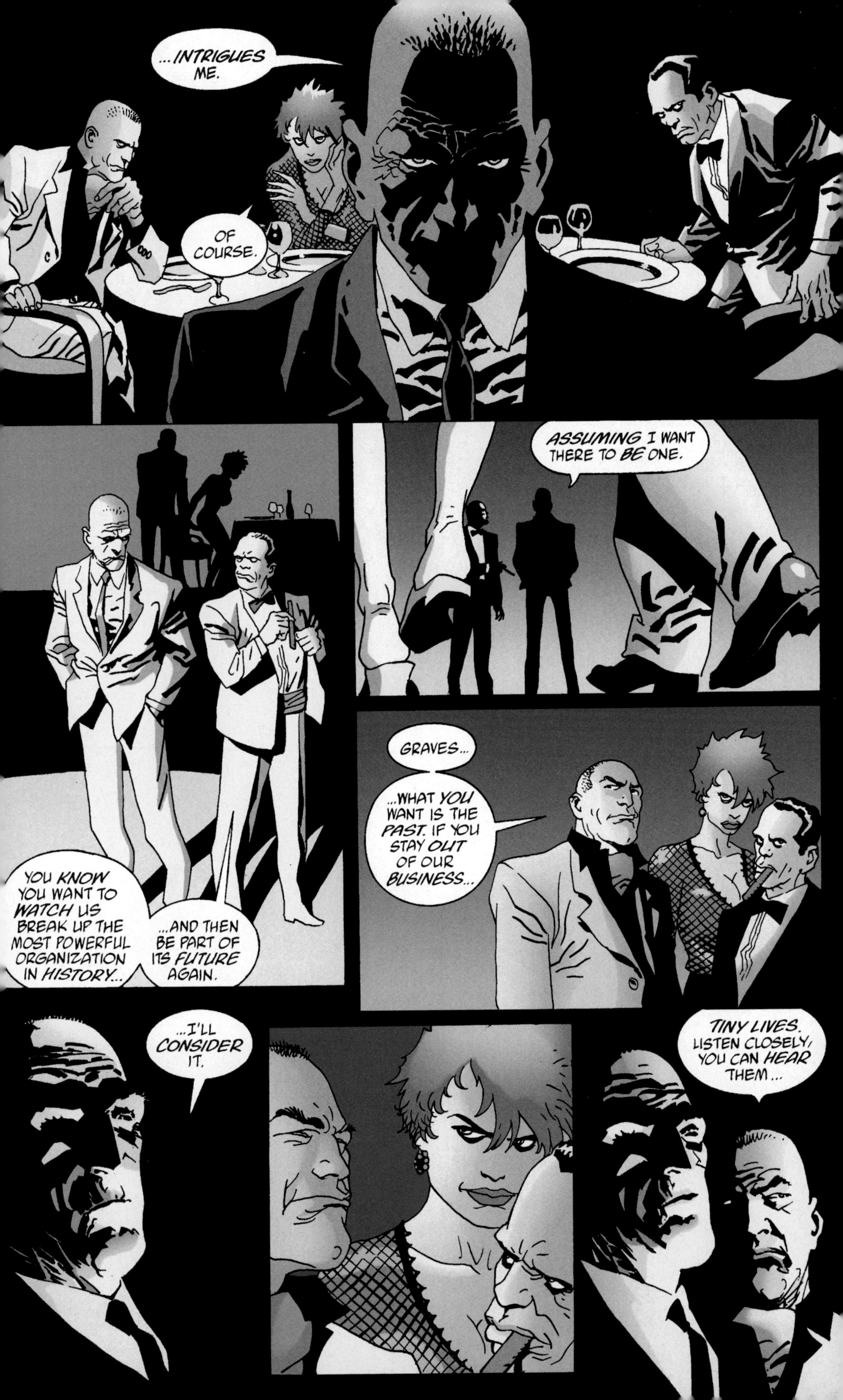

...INTRIGUES ME.
OF COURSE.
YOU KNOW YOU WANT TO WATCH US BREAK UP THE MOST POWERFUL ORGANIZATION IN HISTORY...
...AND THEN BE PART OF ITS FUTURE AGAIN.
ASSUMING I WANT THERE TO BE ONE.
GRAVES...
...WHAT YOU WANT IS THE PAST. IF YOU STAY OUT OF OUR BUSINESS...
...I'LL CONSIDER IT.
TINY LIVES. LISTEN CLOSELY, YOU CAN HEAR THEM...

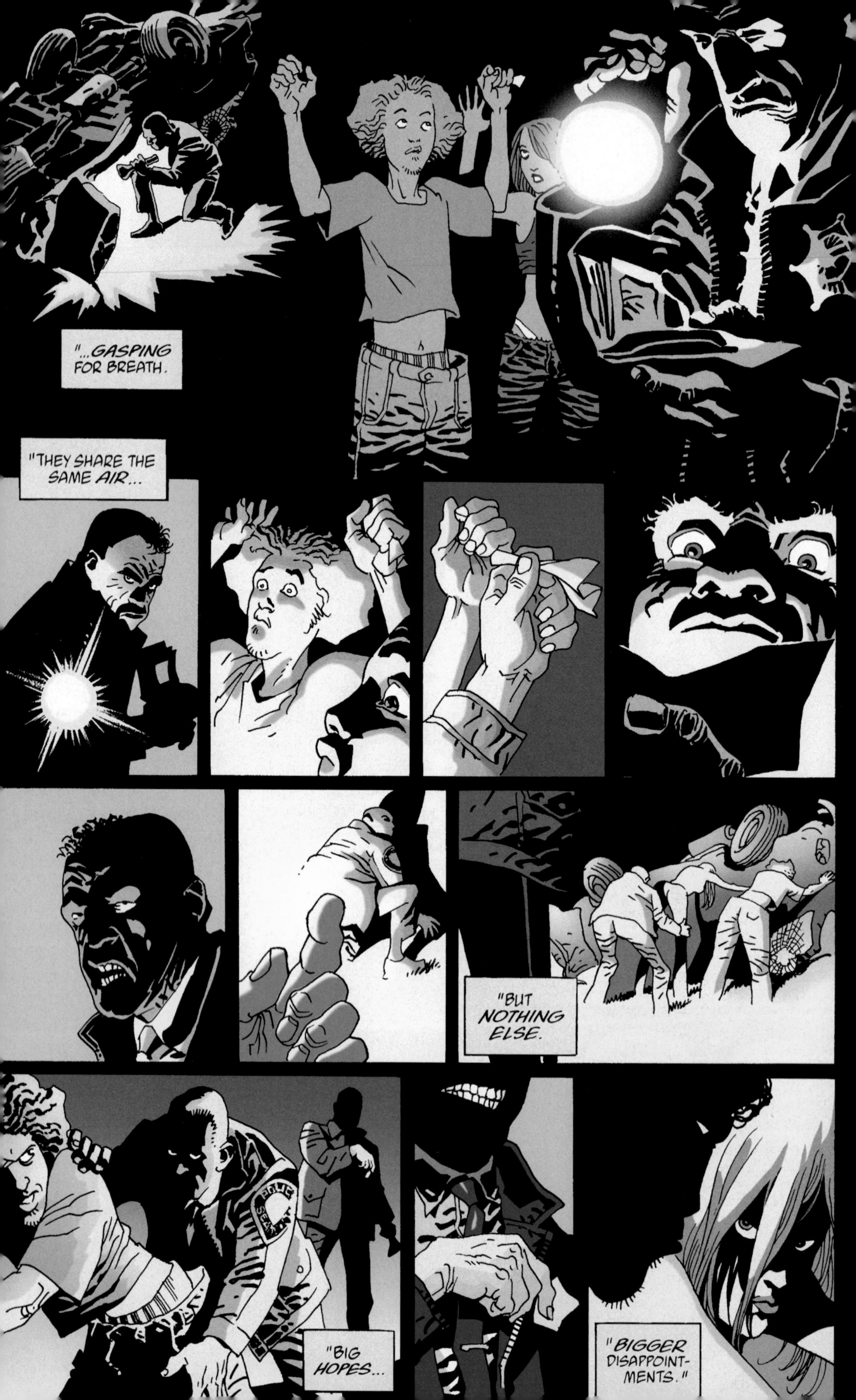
"...GASPING FOR BREATH.
"THEY SHARE THE SAME AIR...
"BUT NOTHING ELSE.
"BIG HOPES...
"BIGGER DISAPPOINT-MENTS."

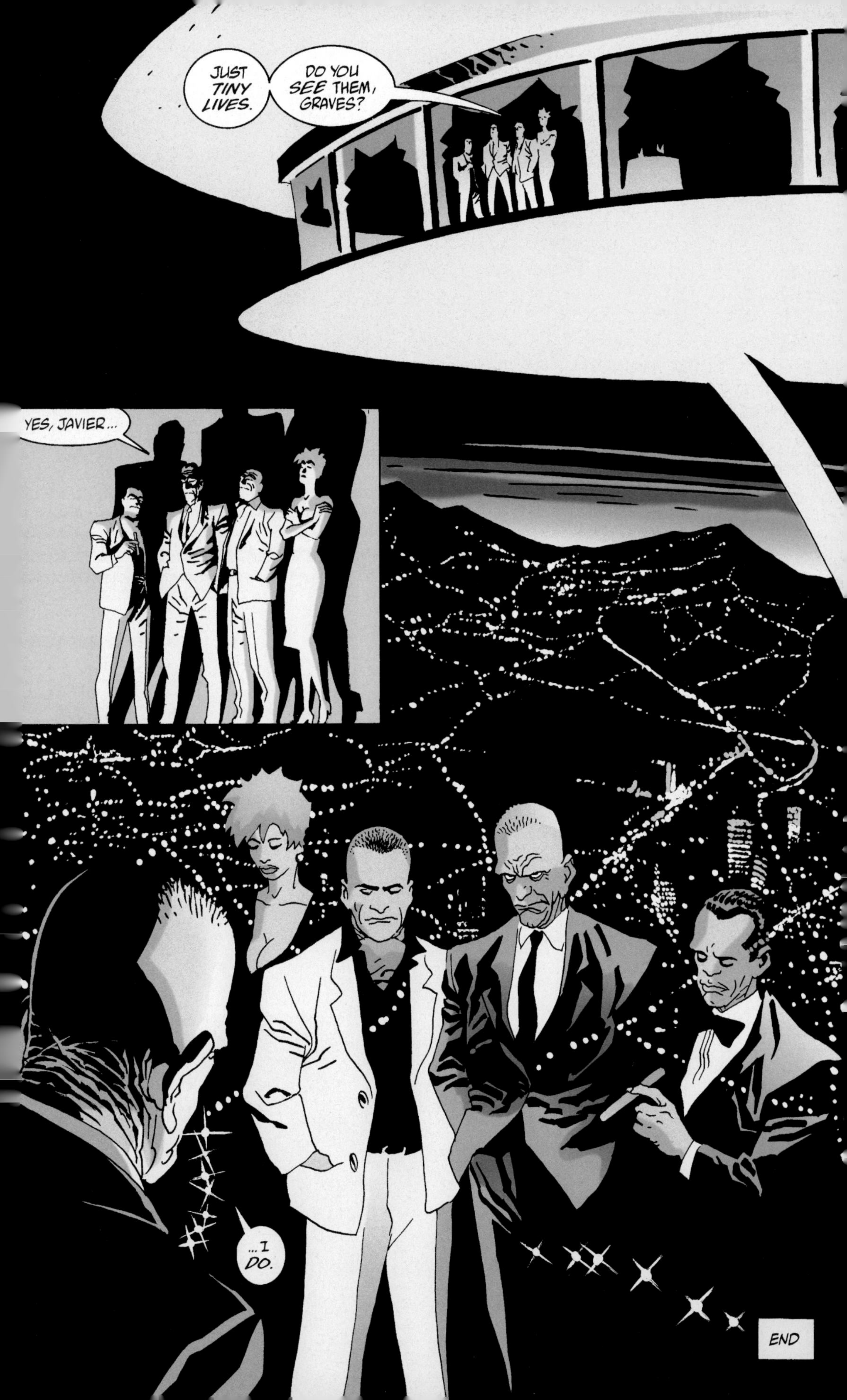
JUST TINY LIVES.
DO YOU SEE THEM, GRAVES?
YES, JAVIER...
...I DO.
END

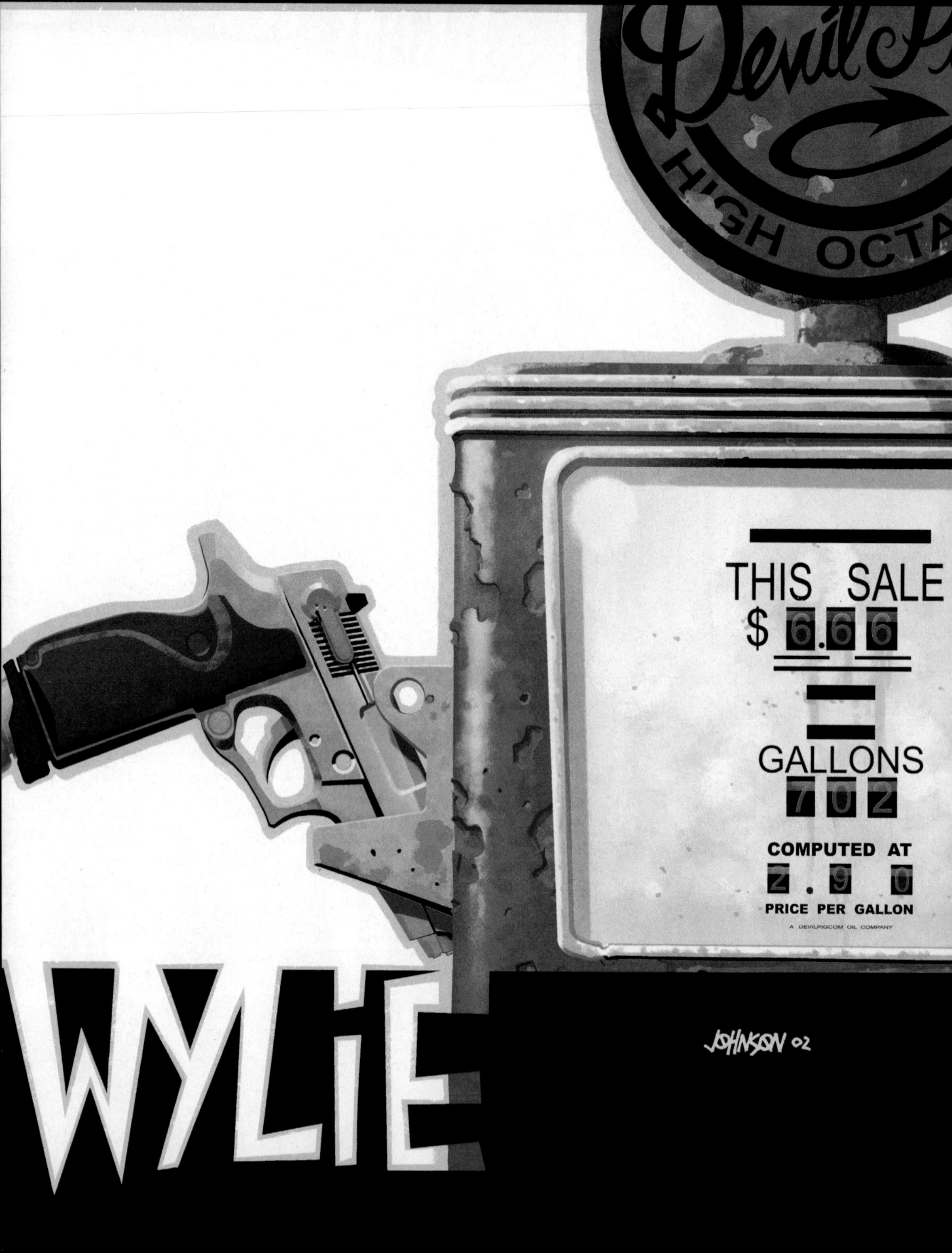
THIS SALE
$ 6.66
GALLONS
702
COMPUTED AT
2.90
PRICE PER GALLON
A DEVILPIGCOM OIL COMPANY
WYLIE
JOHNSON 02

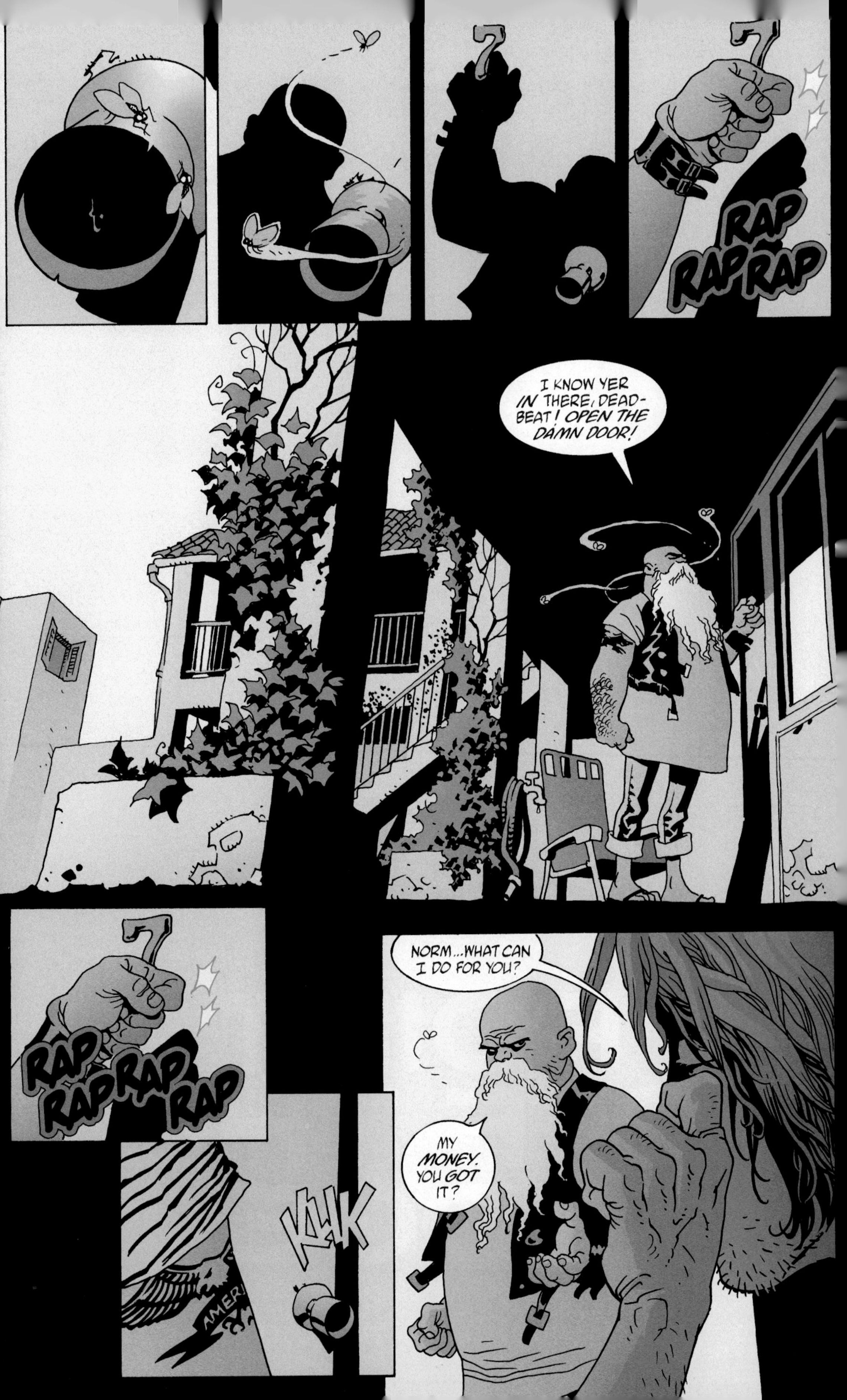
RAP
RAP RAP
I KNOW YER IN THERE, DEAD-BEAT! OPEN THE DAMN DOOR!
RAP RAP RAP RAP
KLIK
AMER
NORM...WHAT CAN I DO FOR YOU?
MY MONEY. YOU GOT IT?

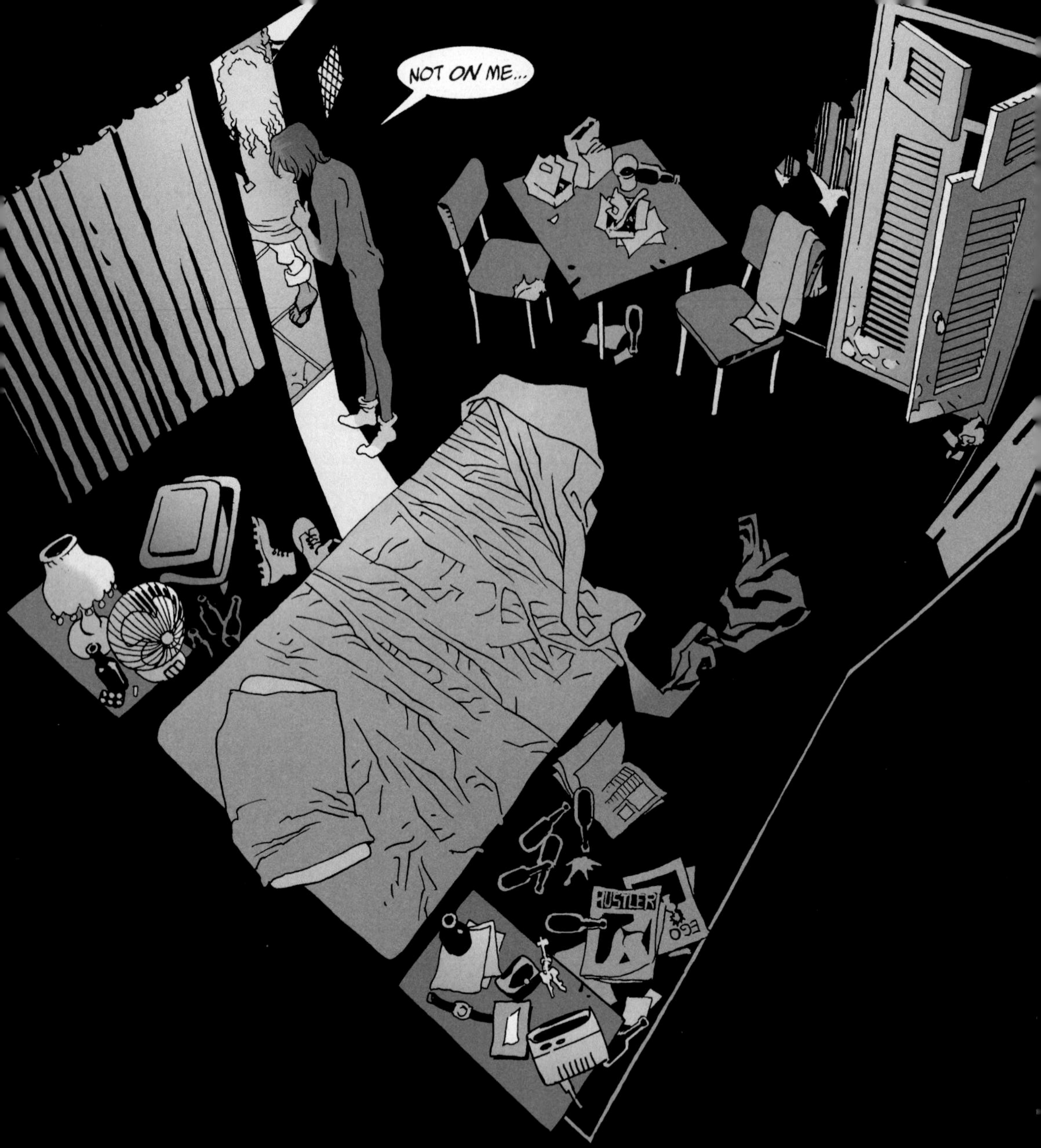
NOT ON ME...
HUSTLER
EGO

POINT OFF THE EDGE

BRIAN AZZARELLO	EDUARDO RISSO	PATRICIA MULVIHILL	CLEM ROBINS	ZYLONOL	DAVE JOHNSON	ZACHARY RAU	WILL DENNIS
WRITER	ARTIST	COLORIST	LETTERER	SEPARATIONS	COVER	ASS'T ED	EDITOR

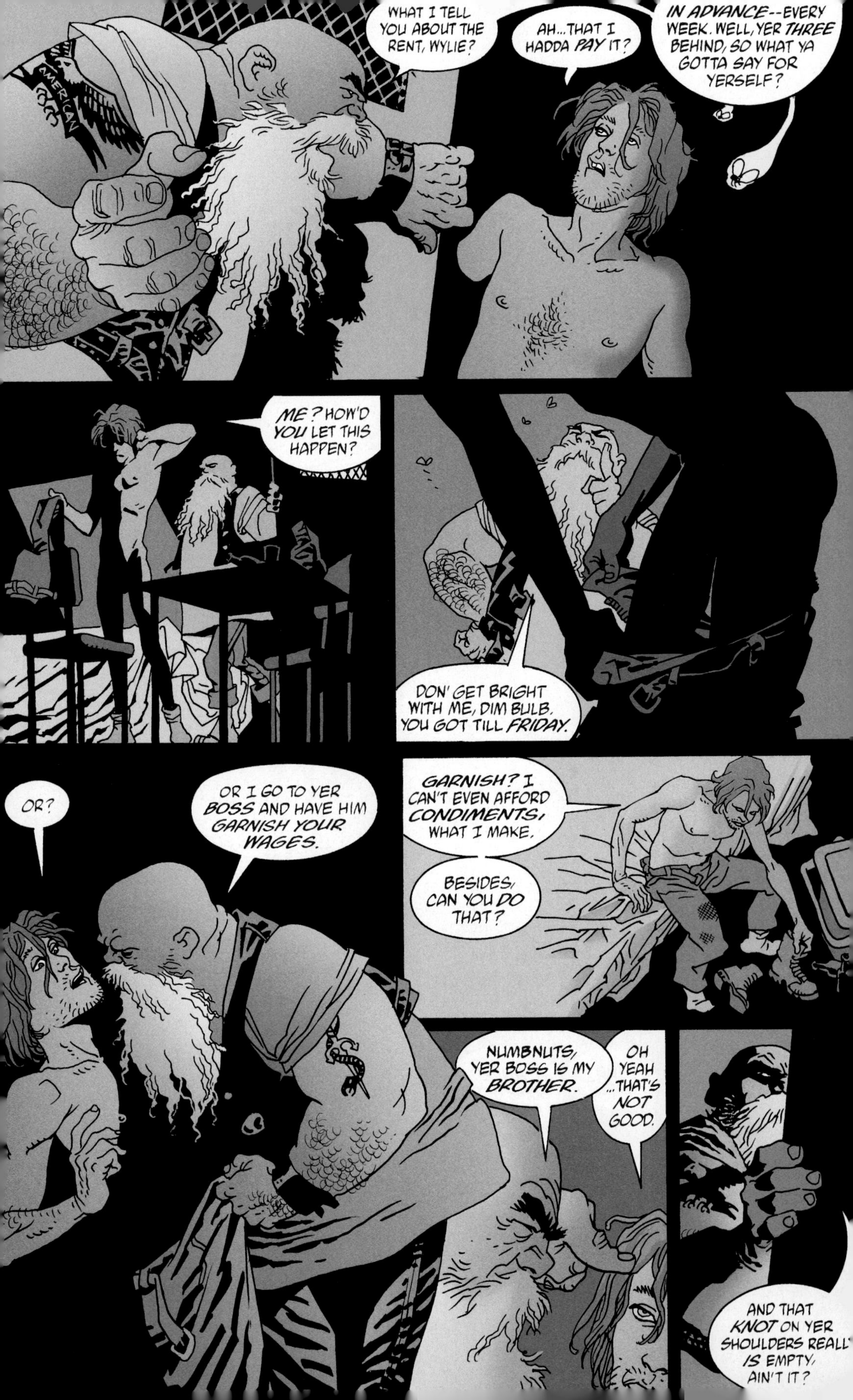
AMERICAN
WHAT I TELL YOU ABOUT THE RENT, WYLIE?
AH...THAT I HADDA PAY IT?
IN ADVANCE--EVERY WEEK. WELL, YER THREE BEHIND, SO WHAT YA GOTTA SAY FOR YERSELF?
ME? HOW'D YOU LET THIS HAPPEN?
DON' GET BRIGHT WITH ME, DIM BULB. YOU GOT TILL FRIDAY.
OR?
OR I GO TO YER BOSS AND HAVE HIM GARNISH YOUR WAGES.
GARNISH? I CAN'T EVEN AFFORD CONDIMENTS, WHAT I MAKE.
BESIDES, CAN YOU DO THAT?
NUMBNUTS, YER BOSS IS MY BROTHER.
OH YEAH ...THAT'S NOT GOOD.
AND THAT KNOT ON YER SHOULDERS REALL IS EMPTY, AIN'T IT?

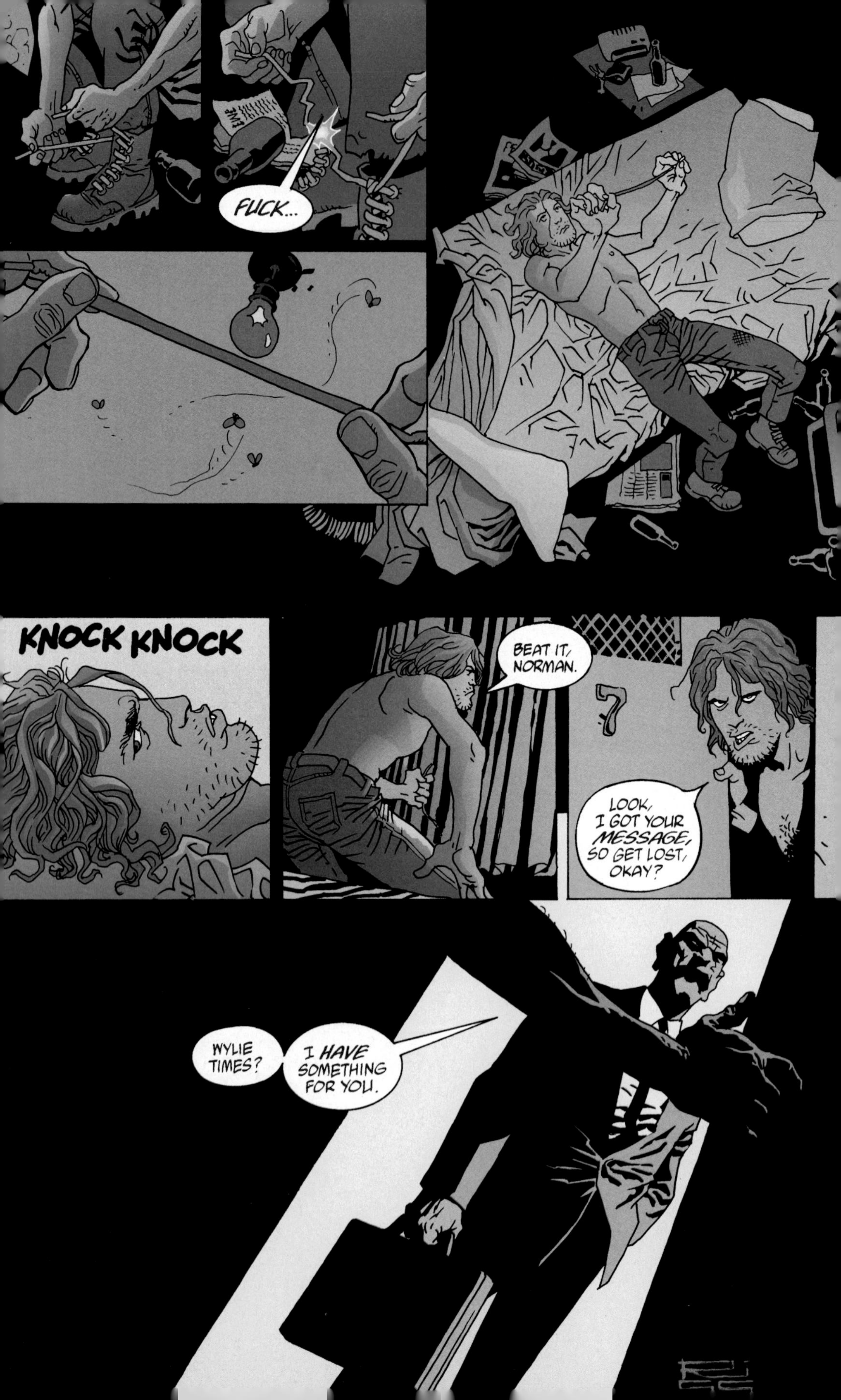
FUCK...
KNOCK KNOCK
BEAT IT, NORMAN.
LOOK, I GOT YOUR MESSAGE, SO GET LOST, OKAY?
WYLIE TIMES?
I HAVE SOMETHING FOR YOU.

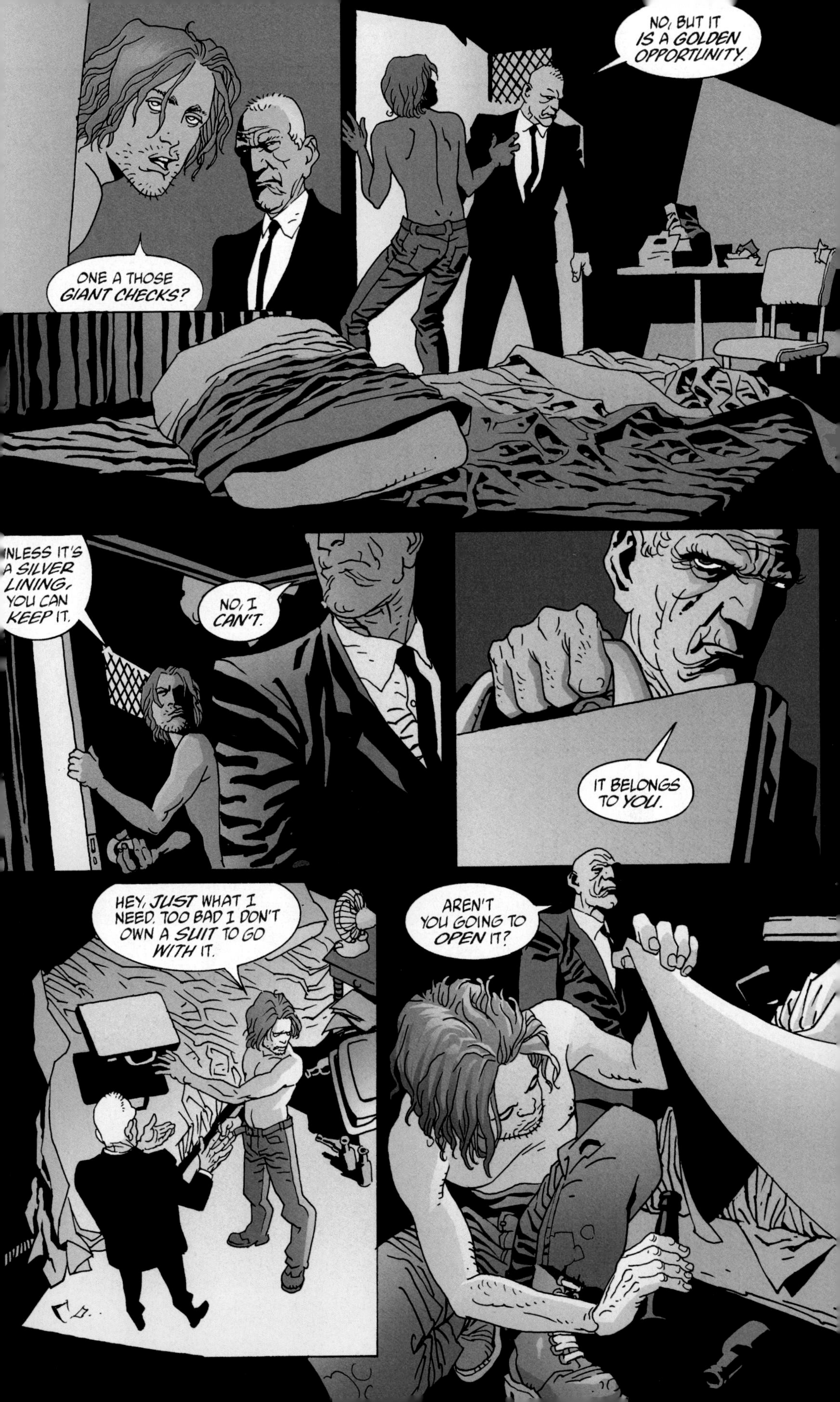

ONE A THOSE GIANT CHECKS?
NO, BUT IT IS A GOLDEN OPPORTUNITY.
NLESS IT'S A SILVER LINING, YOU CAN KEEP IT.
NO, I CAN'T.
IT BELONGS TO YOU.
HEY, JUST WHAT I NEED. TOO BAD I DON'T OWN A SUIT TO GO WITH IT.
AREN'T YOU GOING TO OPEN IT?

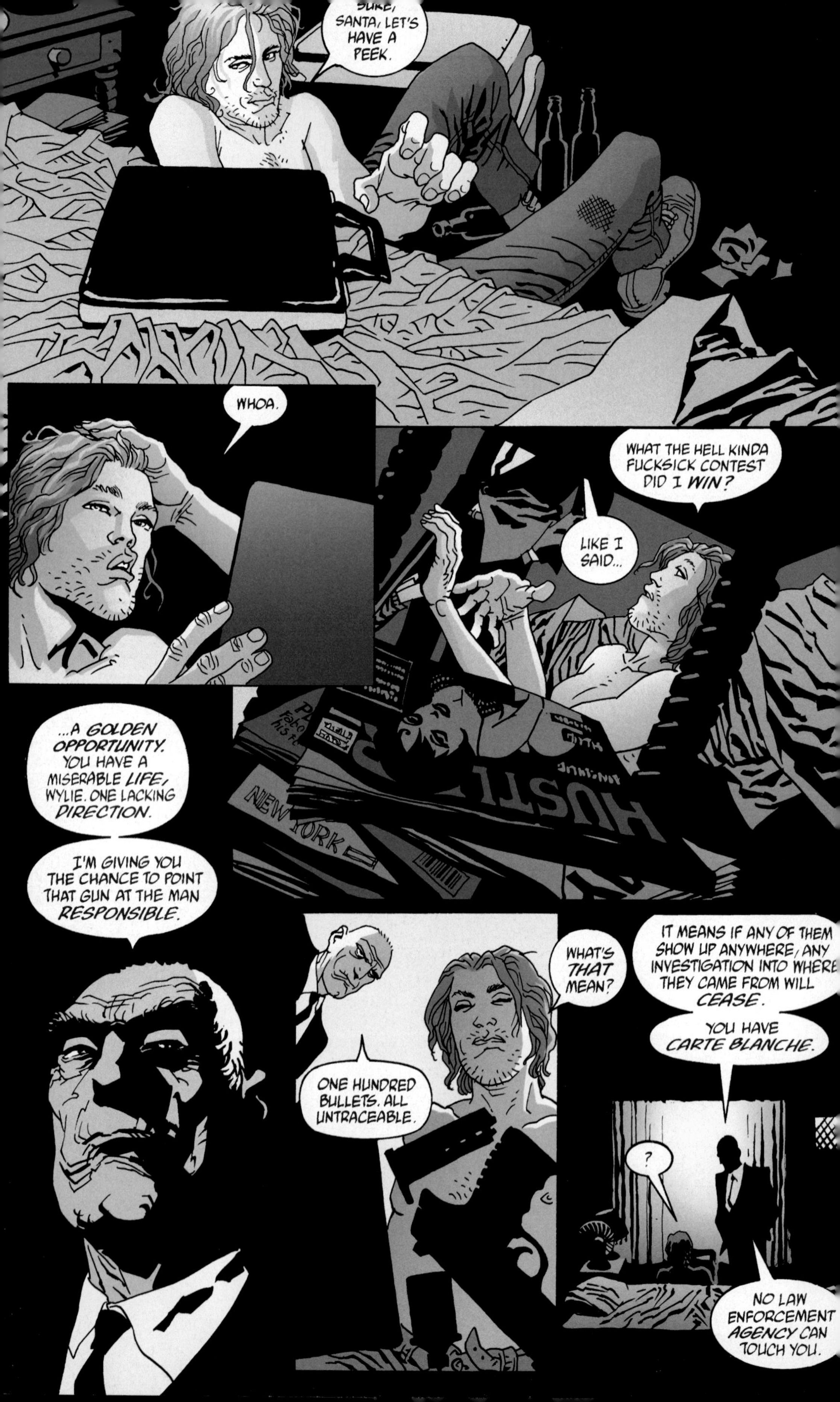
SURE, SANTA, LET'S HAVE A PEEK.
WHOA.
WHAT THE HELL KINDA FUCKSICK CONTEST DID I WIN?
LIKE I SAID...
...A GOLDEN OPPORTUNITY. YOU HAVE A MISERABLE LIFE, WYLIE. ONE LACKING DIRECTION.
I'M GIVING YOU THE CHANCE TO POINT THAT GUN AT THE MAN RESPONSIBLE.
ONE HUNDRED BULLETS. ALL UNTRACEABLE.
WHAT'S THAT MEAN?
IT MEANS IF ANY OF THEM SHOW UP ANYWHERE, ANY INVESTIGATION INTO WHERE THEY CAME FROM WILL CEASE.
YOU HAVE CARTE BLANCHE.
?
NO LAW ENFORCEMENT AGENCY CAN TOUCH YOU.

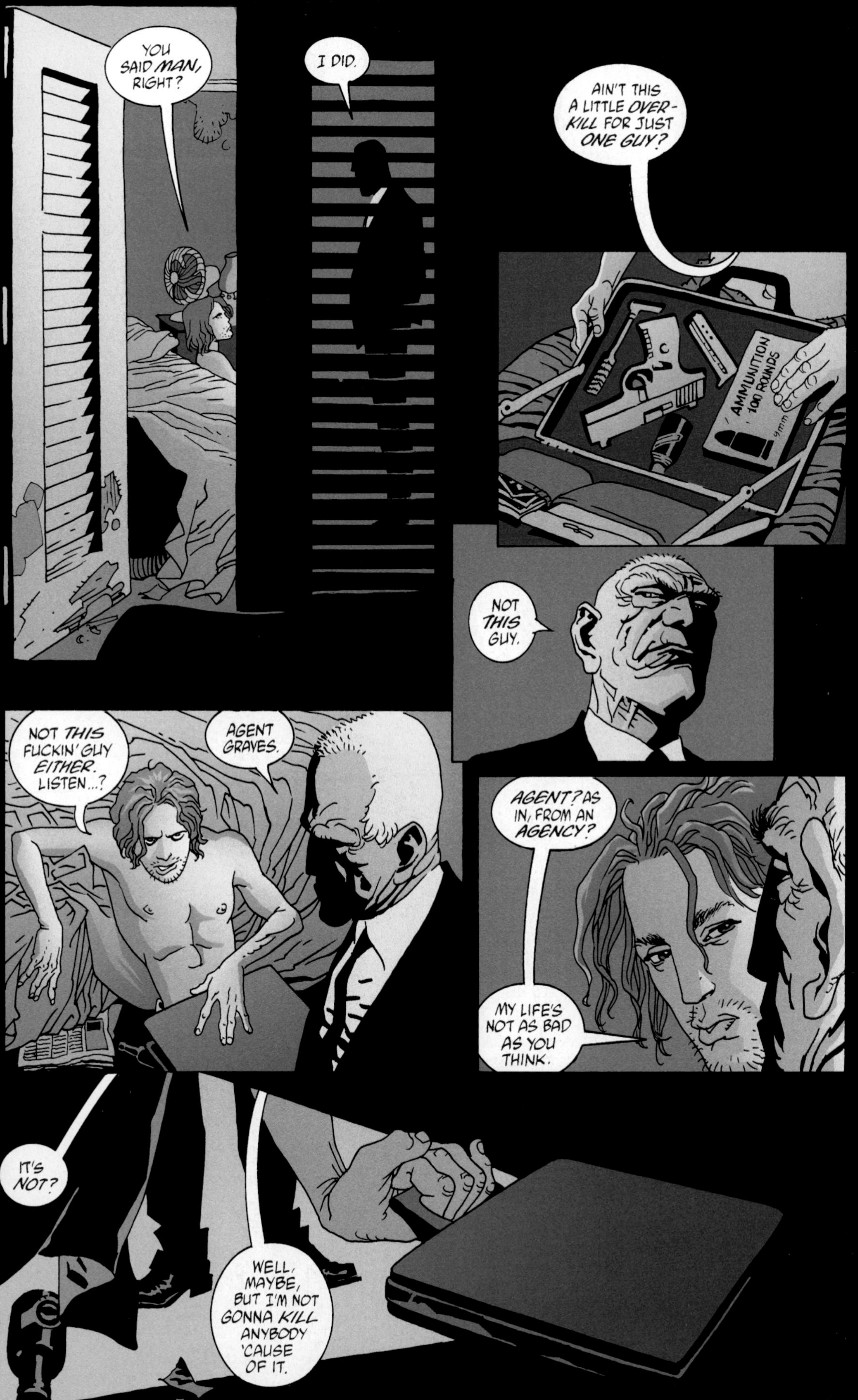
YOU SAID *MAN,* RIGHT?
I DID.
AIN'T THIS A LITTLE *OVER-KILL* FOR JUST *ONE GUY?*
AMMUNITION 100 ROUNDS
9mm
NOT *THIS* GUY.
NOT *THIS* FUCKIN' GUY *EITHER.* LISTEN...?
AGENT GRAVES.
AGENT? AS IN, FROM AN *AGENCY?*
MY LIFE'S NOT AS BAD AS YOU THINK.
IT'S *NOT?*
WELL, MAYBE, BUT I'M NOT GONNA *KILL* ANYBODY 'CAUSE OF IT.

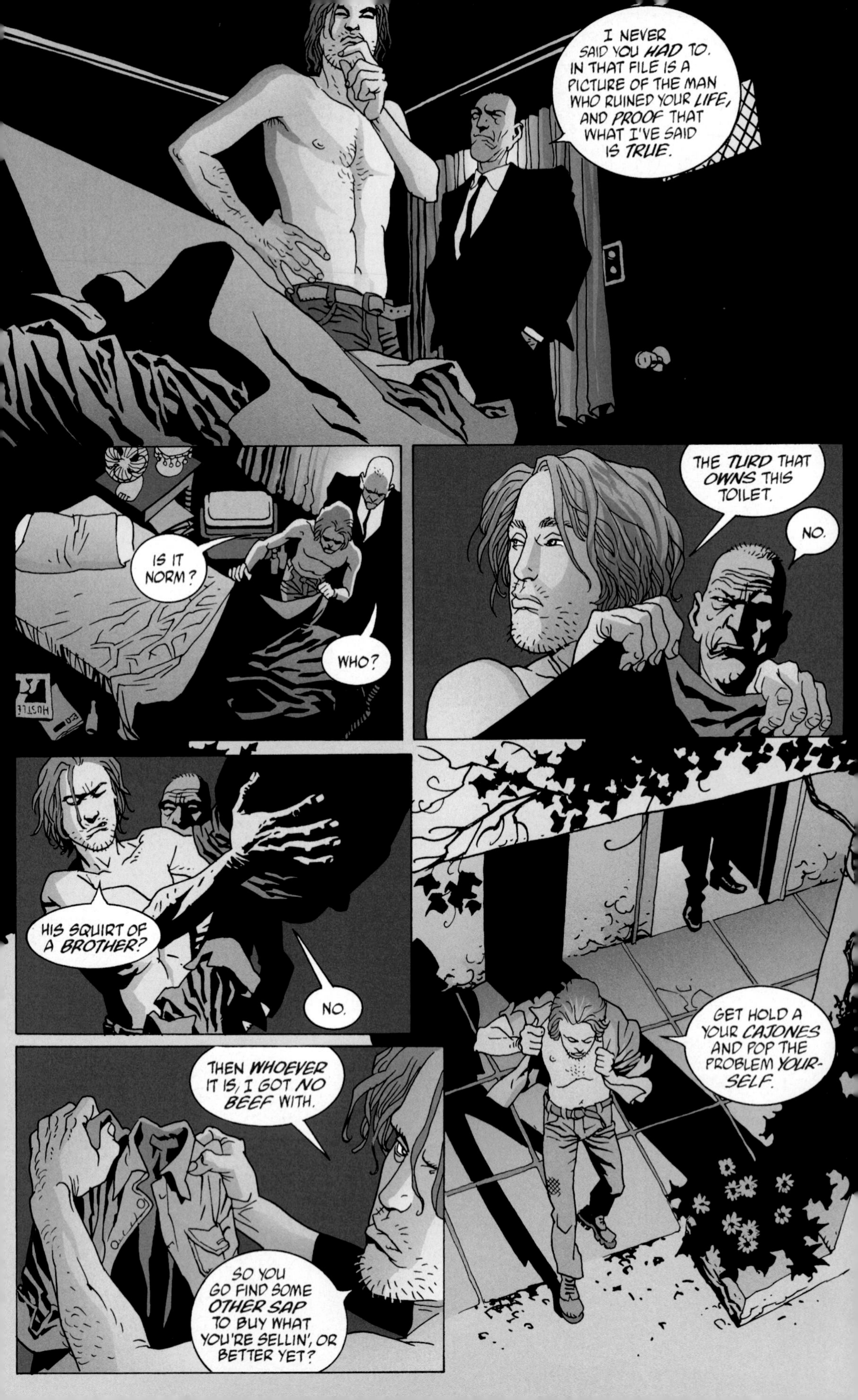
I NEVER SAID YOU *HAD* TO. IN THAT FILE IS A PICTURE OF THE MAN WHO RUINED YOUR *LIFE*, AND *PROOF* THAT WHAT I'VE SAID IS *TRUE*.
IS IT NORM?
WHO?
THE *TURD* THAT *OWNS* THIS TOILET.
NO.
HIS SQUIRT OF A *BROTHER*?
NO.
THEN *WHOEVER* IT IS, I GOT *NO BEEF* WITH.
SO YOU GO FIND SOME *OTHER SAP* TO BUY WHAT YOU'RE SELLIN', OR BETTER YET?
GET HOLD A YOUR *CAJONES* AND POP THE PROBLEM *YOURSELF*.

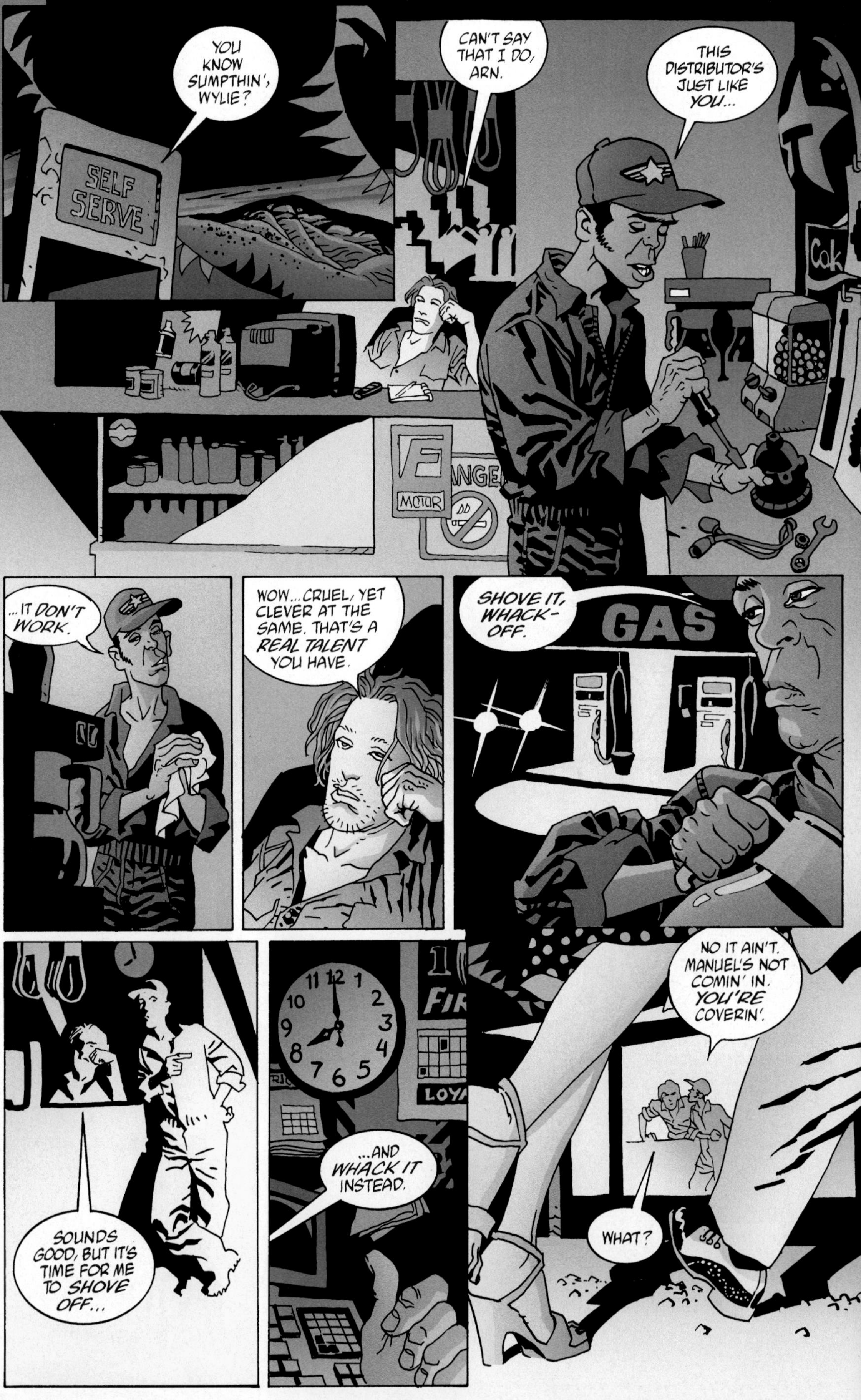
YOU KNOW SUMPTHIN', WYLIE?
SELF SERVE
CAN'T SAY THAT I DO, ARN.
THIS DISTRIBUTOR'S JUST LIKE YOU...
...IT DON'T WORK.
WOW...CRUEL, YET CLEVER AT THE SAME. THAT'S A REAL TALENT YOU HAVE.
SHOVE IT, WHACK-OFF.
GAS
SOUNDS GOOD, BUT IT'S TIME FOR ME TO SHOVE OFF...
...AND WHACK IT INSTEAD.
NO IT AIN'T. MANUEL'S NOT COMIN' IN. YOU'RE COVERIN'.
WHAT?

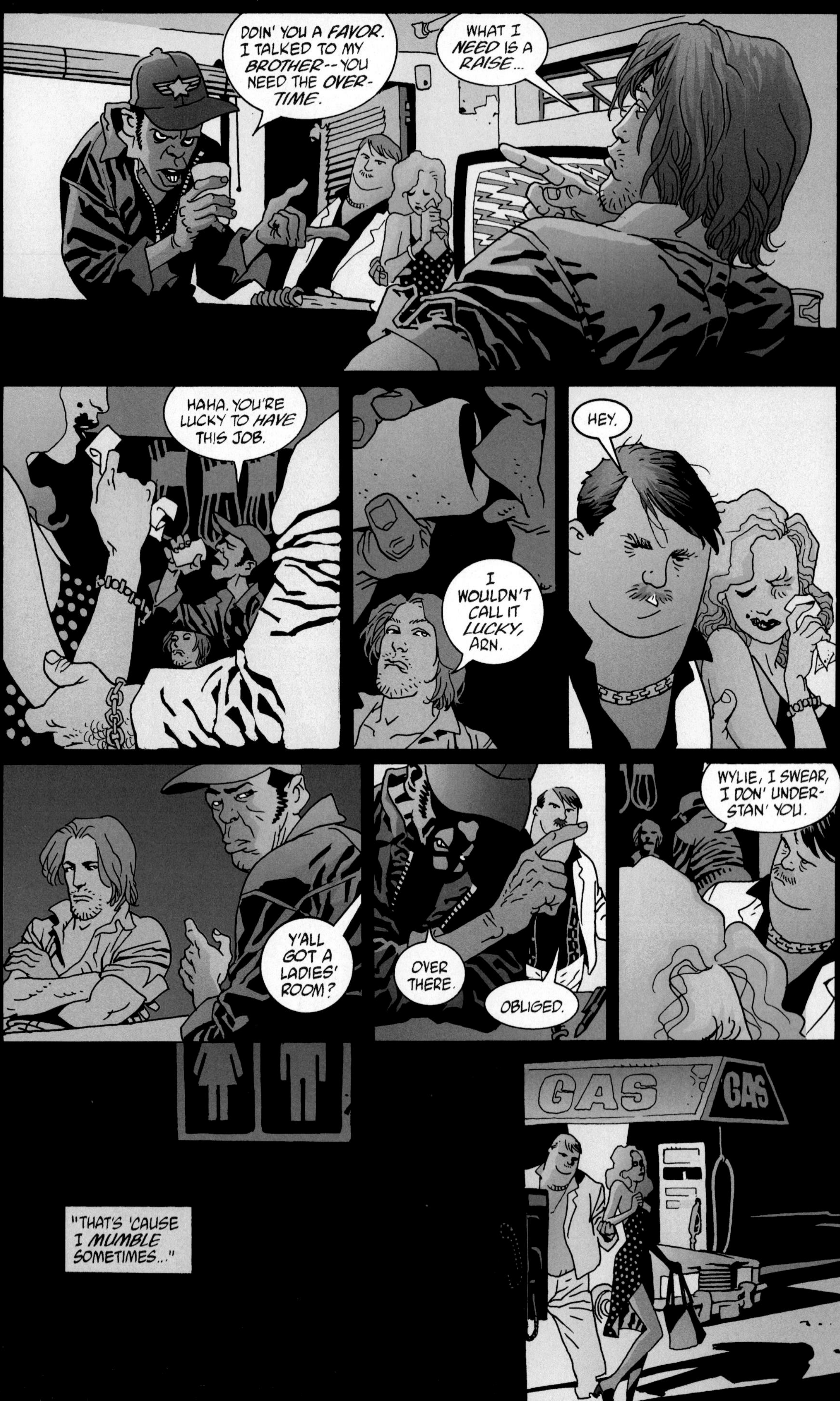
DOIN' YOU A FAVOR. I TALKED TO MY BROTHER--YOU NEED THE OVER-TIME.
WHAT I NEED IS A RAISE...
HAHA. YOU'RE LUCKY TO HAVE THIS JOB.
I WOULDN'T CALL IT LUCKY, ARN.
HEY.
Y'ALL GOT A LADIES' ROOM?
OVER THERE.
OBLIGED.
WYLIE, I SWEAR, I DON' UNDER-STAN' YOU.
GAS
GAS
"THAT'S 'CAUSE I MUMBLE SOMETIMES..."

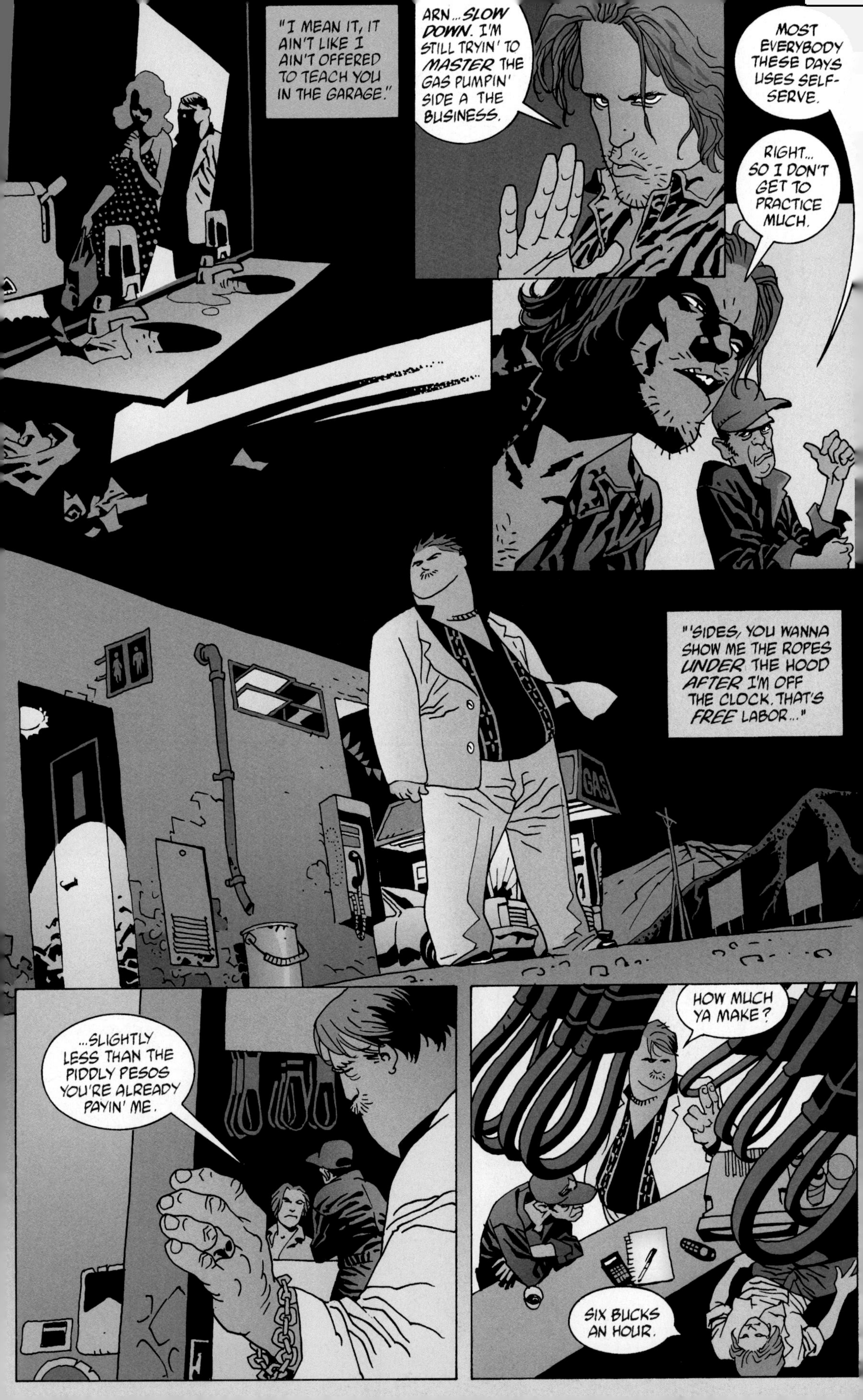
"I MEAN IT, IT AIN'T LIKE I AIN'T OFFERED TO TEACH YOU IN THE GARAGE."
ARN... SLOW DOWN. I'M STILL TRYIN' TO MASTER THE GAS PUMPIN' SIDE A THE BUSINESS.
MOST EVERYBODY THESE DAYS USES SELF-SERVE.
RIGHT... SO I DON'T GET TO PRACTICE MUCH.
"'SIDES, YOU WANNA SHOW ME THE ROPES UNDER THE HOOD AFTER I'M OFF THE CLOCK, THAT'S FREE LABOR..."
GAS
...SLIGHTLY LESS THAN THE PIDDLY PESOS YOU'RE ALREADY PAYIN' ME.
HOW MUCH YA MAKE?
SIX BUCKS AN HOUR.

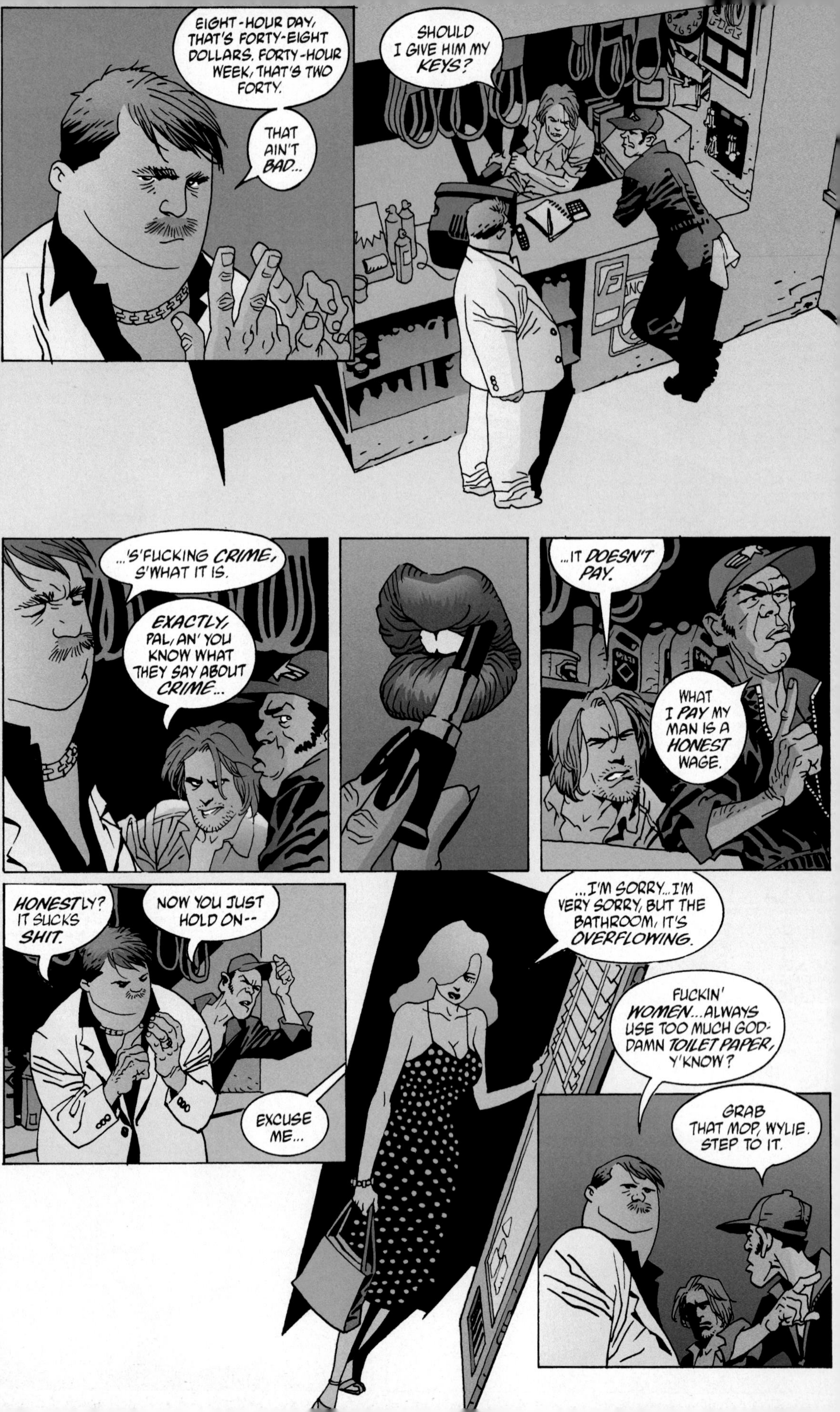
EIGHT-HOUR DAY, THAT'S FORTY-EIGHT DOLLARS. FORTY-HOUR WEEK, THAT'S TWO FORTY.
THAT AIN'T BAD...
SHOULD I GIVE HIM MY KEYS?
...'S'FUCKING CRIME, S'WHAT IT IS.
EXACTLY, PAL, AN' YOU KNOW WHAT THEY SAY ABOUT CRIME...
...IT DOESN'T PAY.
WHAT I PAY MY MAN IS A HONEST WAGE.
HONESTLY? IT SUCKS SHIT.
NOW YOU JUST HOLD ON--
EXCUSE ME...
...I'M SORRY...I'M VERY SORRY, BUT THE BATHROOM, IT'S OVERFLOWING.
FUCKIN' WOMEN...ALWAYS USE TOO MUCH GOD-DAMN TOILET PAPER, Y'KNOW?
GRAB THAT MOP, WYLIE. STEP TO IT.

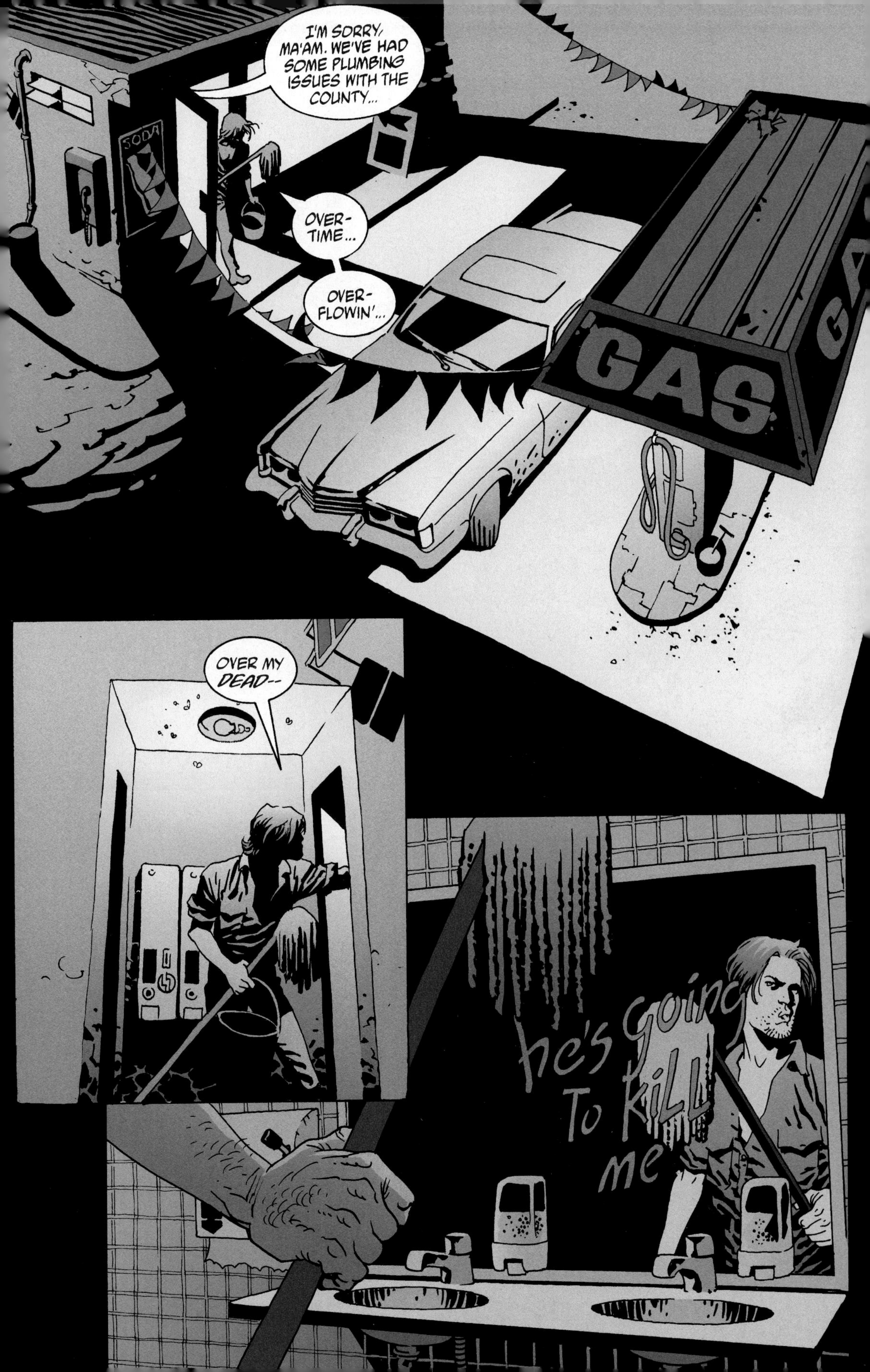
I'M SORRY, MA'AM. WE'VE HAD SOME PLUMBING ISSUES WITH THE COUNTY...
SODA
OVER-TIME...
OVER-FLOWIN'...
GAS
OVER MY DEAD--
he's going To KiLL me

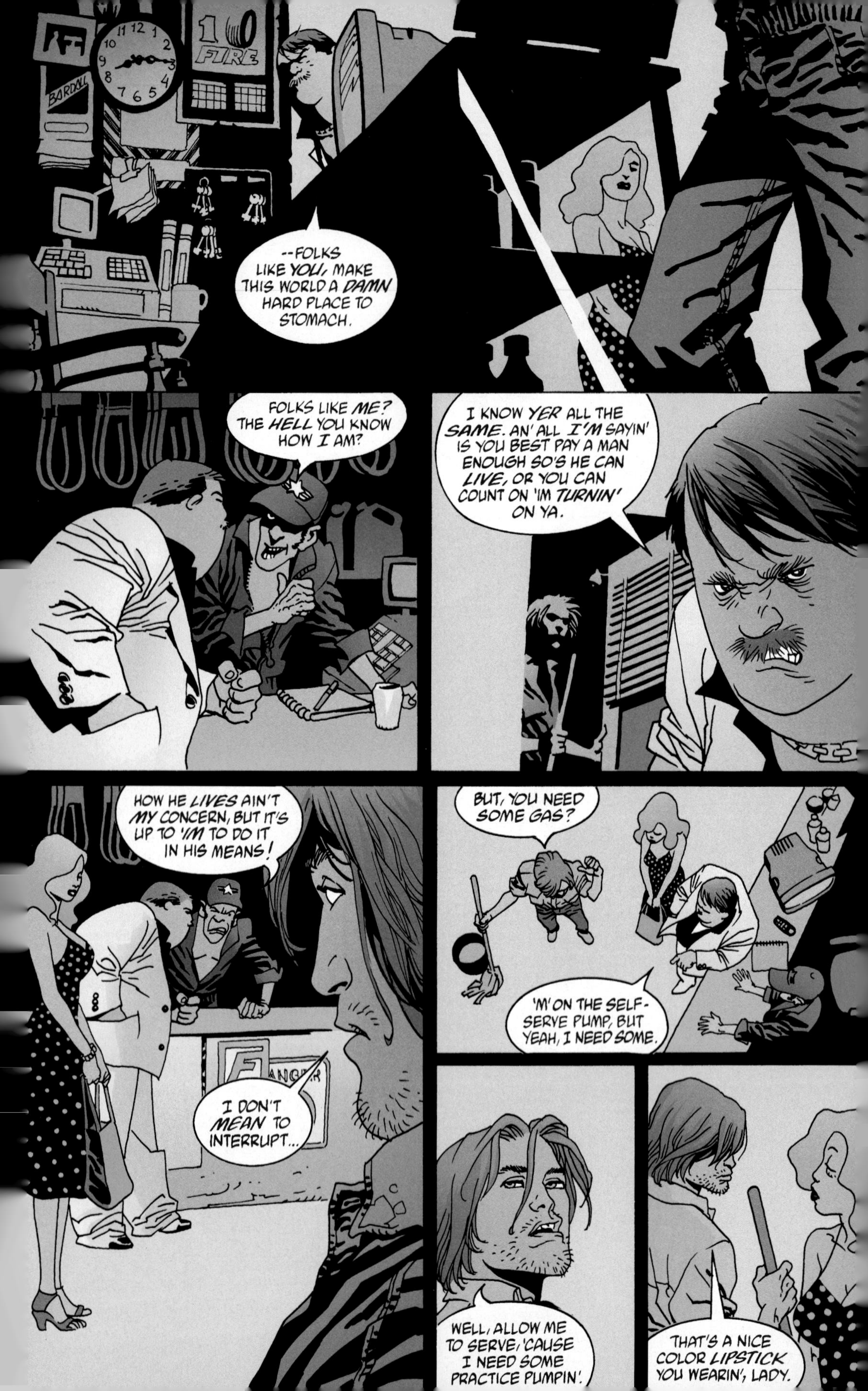
--FOLKS LIKE YOU, MAKE THIS WORLD A DAMN HARD PLACE TO STOMACH.
FOLKS LIKE ME? THE HELL YOU KNOW HOW I AM?
I KNOW YER ALL THE SAME. AN' ALL I'M SAYIN' IS YOU BEST PAY A MAN ENOUGH SO'S HE CAN LIVE, OR YOU CAN COUNT ON 'IM TURNIN' ON YA.
HOW HE LIVES AIN'T MY CONCERN, BUT IT'S UP TO 'IM TO DO IT IN HIS MEANS!
I DON'T MEAN TO INTERRUPT...
BUT, YOU NEED SOME GAS?
'M' ON THE SELF-SERVE PUMP, BUT YEAH, I NEED SOME.
WELL, ALLOW ME TO SERVE, 'CAUSE I NEED SOME PRACTICE PUMPIN'.
THAT'S A NICE COLOR LIPSTICK YOU WEARIN', LADY.

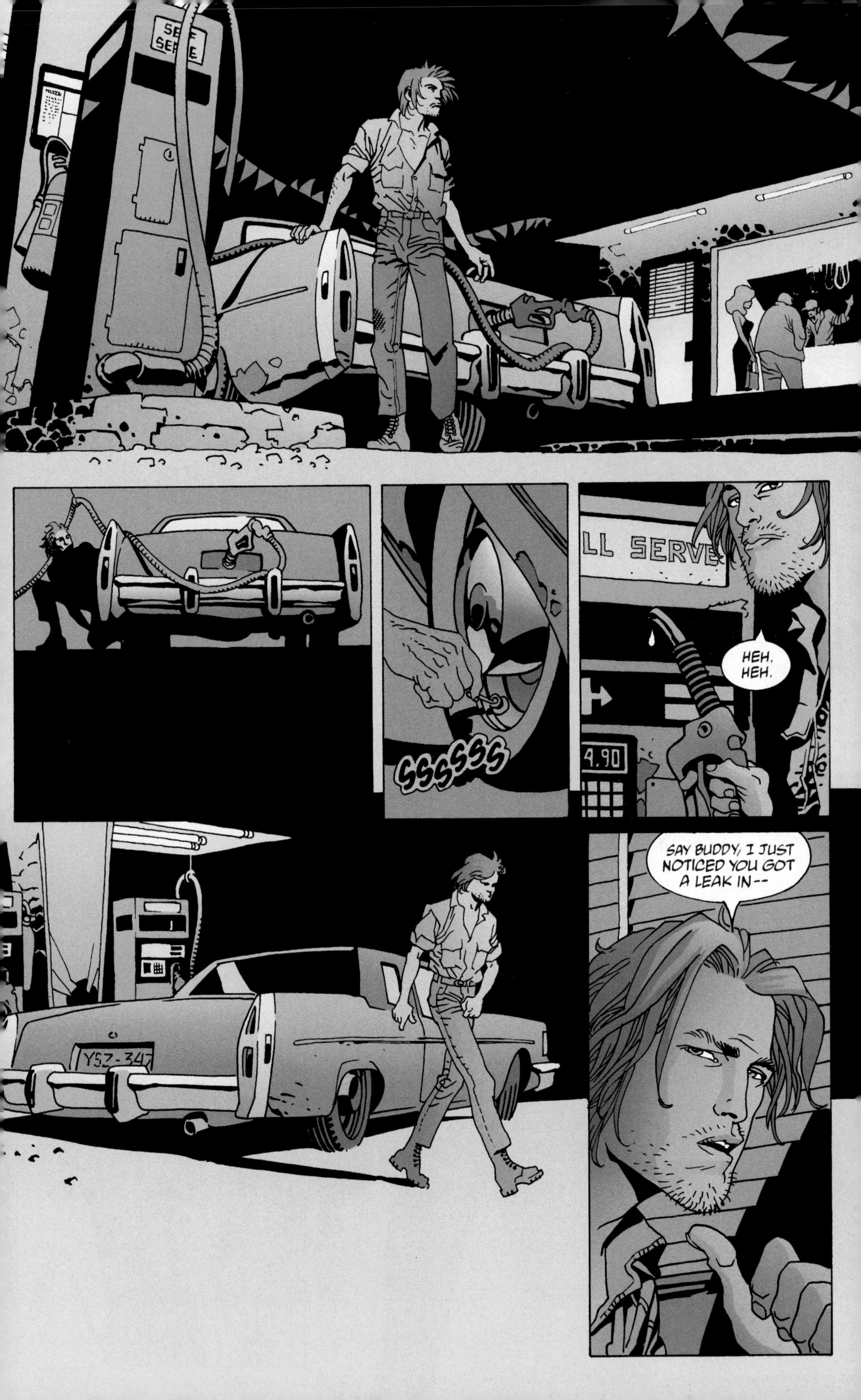
SELF SERVE
LL SERVE
SSSSSS
4.90
HEH. HEH.
YSZ-347
SAY BUDDY, I JUST NOTICED YOU GOT A LEAK IN--

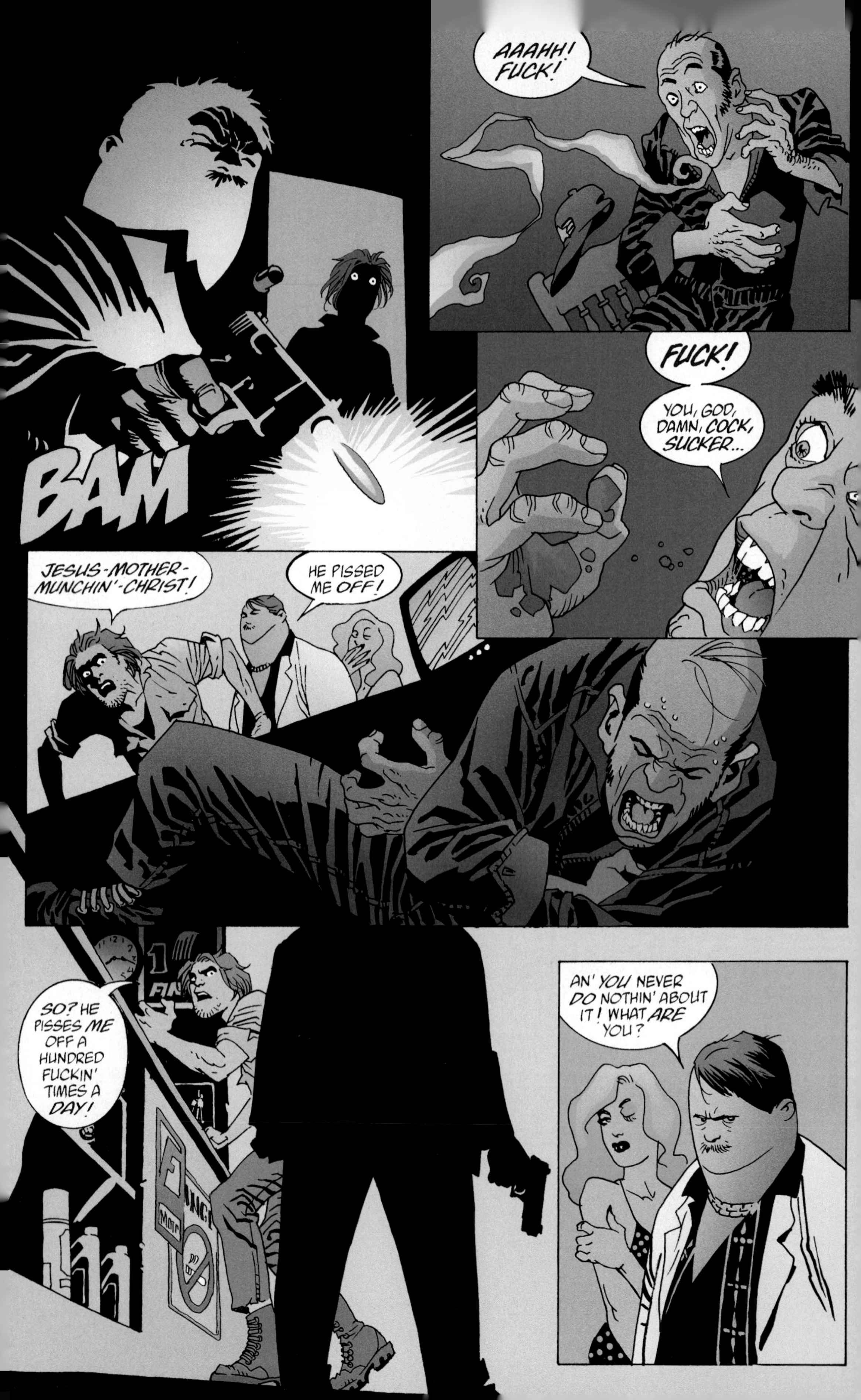
BAM
AAAHH! FUCK!
FUCK!
YOU, GOD, DAMN, COCK, SUCKER...
JESUS-MOTHER-MUNCHIN'-CHRIST!
HE PISSED ME OFF!
SO? HE PISSES ME OFF A HUNDRED FUCKIN' TIMES A DAY!
AN' YOU NEVER DO NOTHIN' ABOUT IT! WHAT ARE YOU?

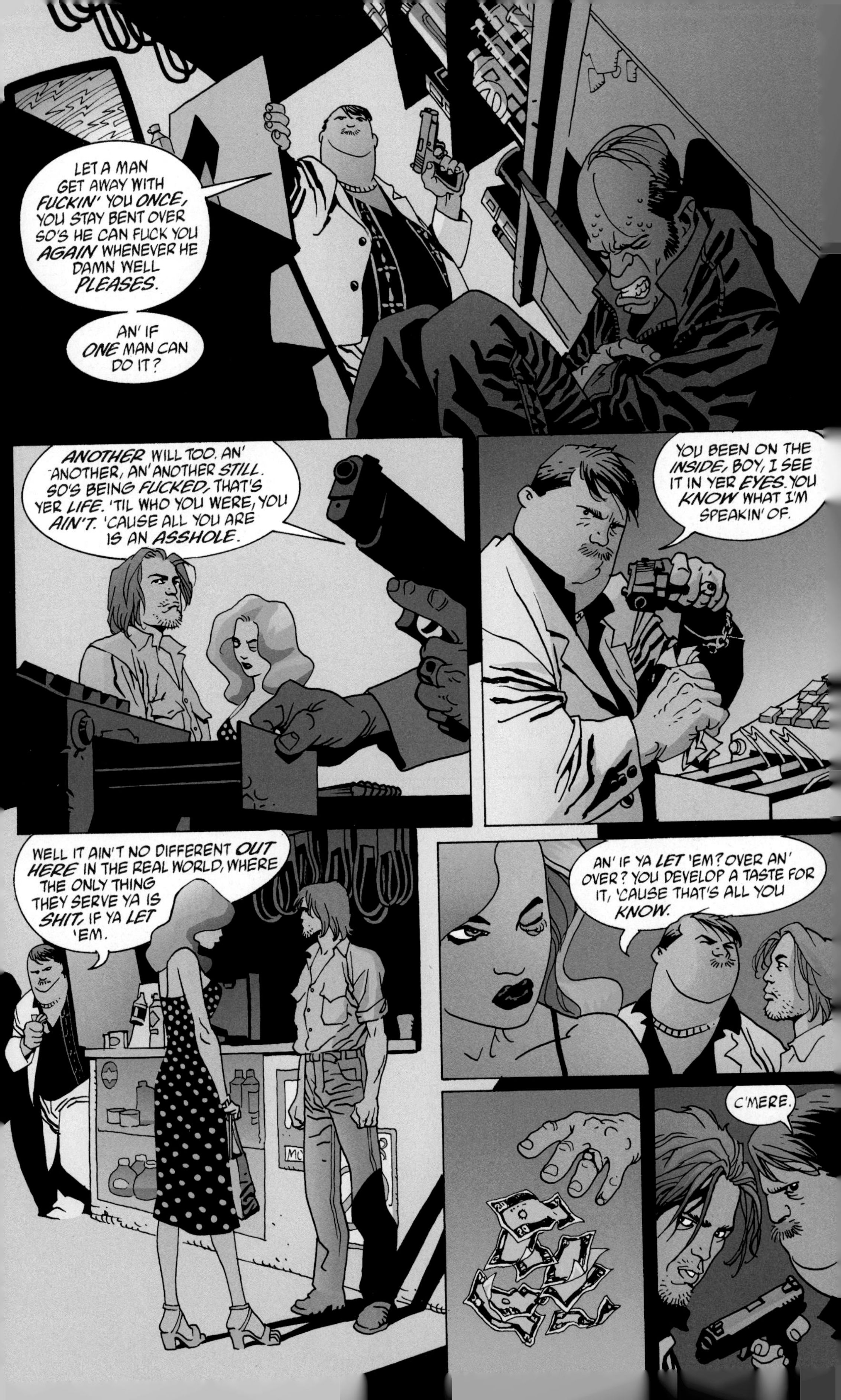
LET A MAN GET AWAY WITH FUCKIN' YOU ONCE, YOU STAY BENT OVER SO'S HE CAN FUCK YOU AGAIN WHENEVER HE DAMN WELL PLEASES.
AN' IF ONE MAN CAN DO IT?
ANOTHER WILL TOO. AN' ANOTHER, AN' ANOTHER STILL. SO'S BEING FUCKED, THAT'S YER LIFE. 'TIL WHO YOU WERE, YOU AIN'T. 'CAUSE ALL YOU ARE IS AN ASSHOLE.
YOU BEEN ON THE INSIDE, BOY, I SEE IT IN YER EYES. YOU KNOW WHAT I'M SPEAKIN' OF.
WELL IT AIN'T NO DIFFERENT OUT HERE IN THE REAL WORLD, WHERE THE ONLY THING THEY SERVE YA IS SHIT, IF YA LET 'EM.
AN' IF YA LET 'EM? OVER AN' OVER? YOU DEVELOP A TASTE FOR IT, 'CAUSE THAT'S ALL YOU KNOW.
C'MERE.

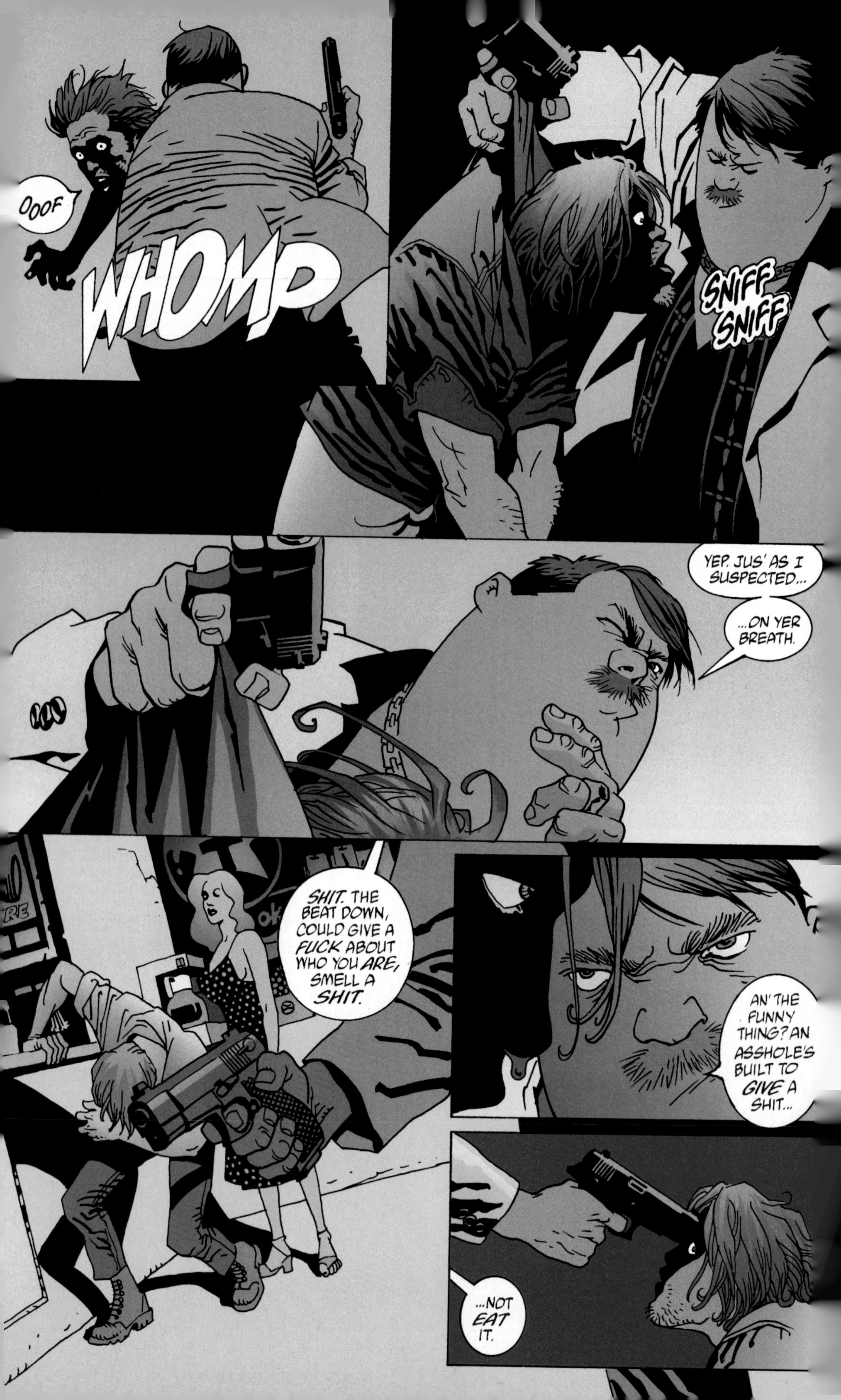
OOOF
WHOMP
SNIFF SNIFF
YEP. JUS' AS I SUSPECTED...
...ON YER BREATH.
SHIT. THE BEAT DOWN, COULD GIVE A FUCK ABOUT WHO YOU ARE, SMELL A SHIT.
AN' THE FUNNY THING? AN ASSHOLE'S BUILT TO GIVE A SHIT...
...NOT EAT IT.

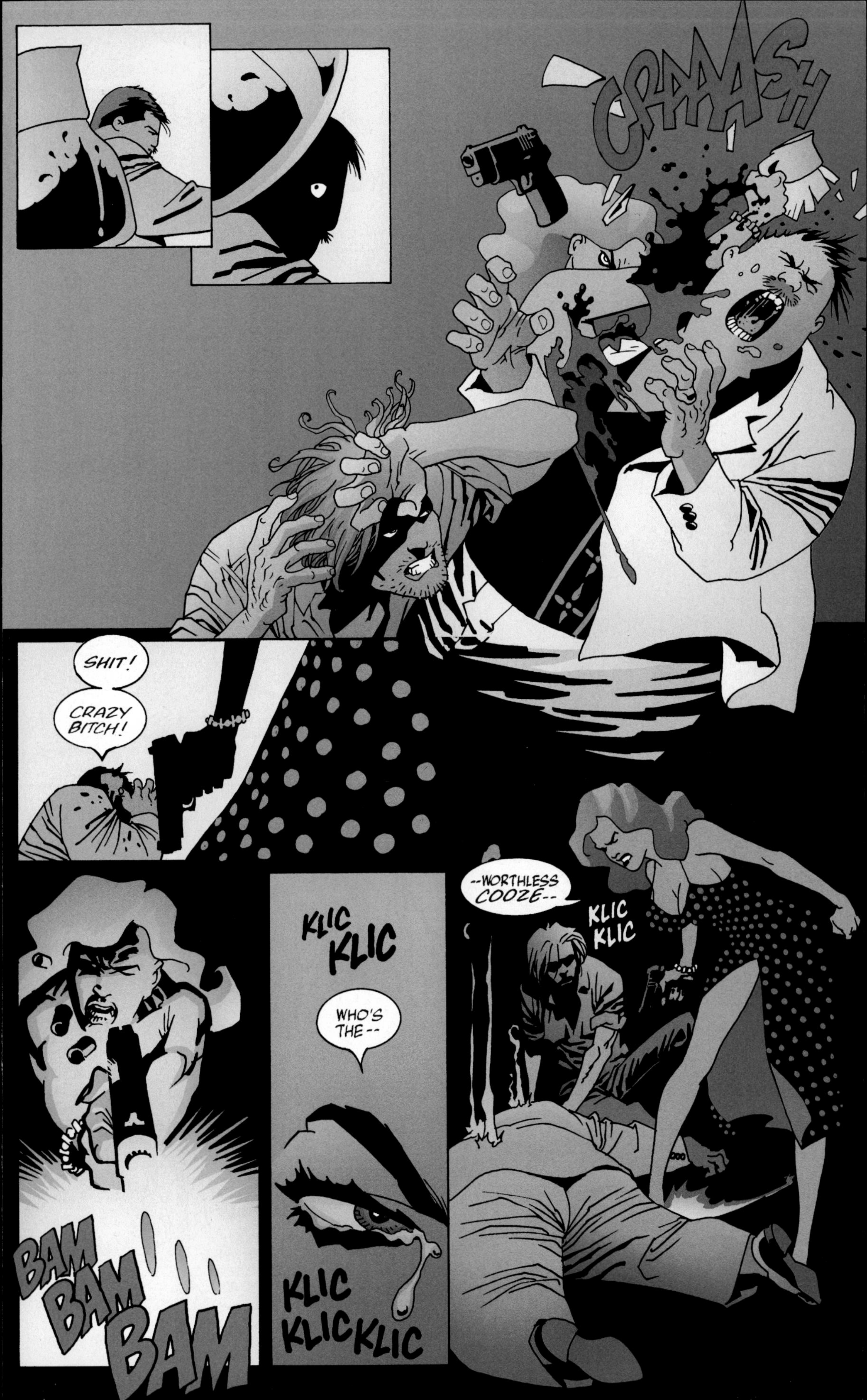
CRAAASH
SHIT!
CRAZY BITCH!
BAM
BAM
BAM
KLIC
KLIC
WHO'S THE--
KLIC
KLIC KLIC
--WORTHLESS COOZE--
KLIC
KLIC

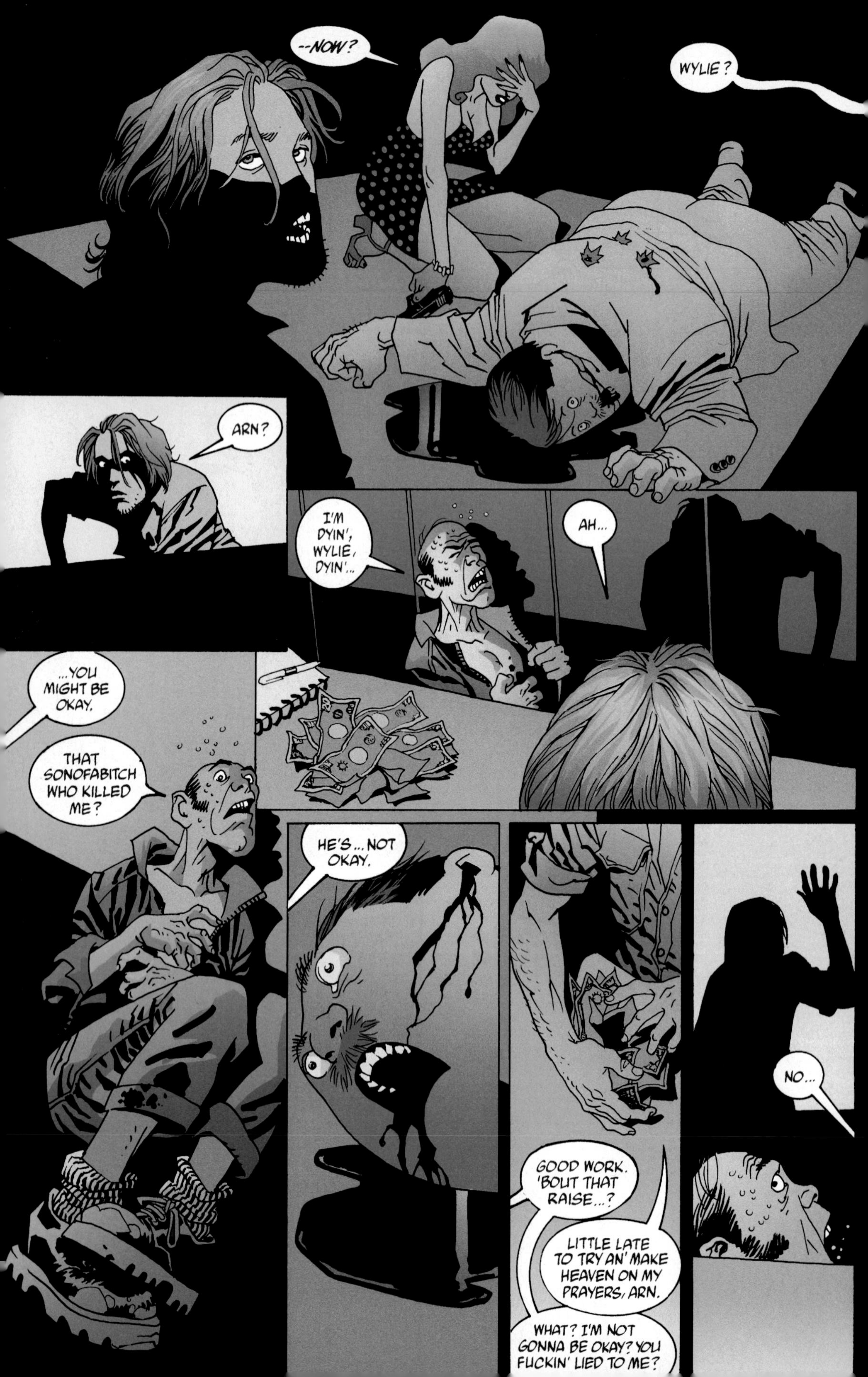
--NOW?
WYLIE?
ARN?
I'M DYIN', WYLIE, DYIN'...
AH...
...YOU MIGHT BE OKAY.
THAT SONOFABITCH WHO KILLED ME?
HE'S... NOT OKAY.
GOOD WORK. 'BOUT THAT RAISE...?
LITTLE LATE TO TRY AN' MAKE HEAVEN ON MY PRAYERS, ARN.
WHAT? I'M NOT GONNA BE OKAY? YOU FUCKIN' LIED TO ME?
NO...

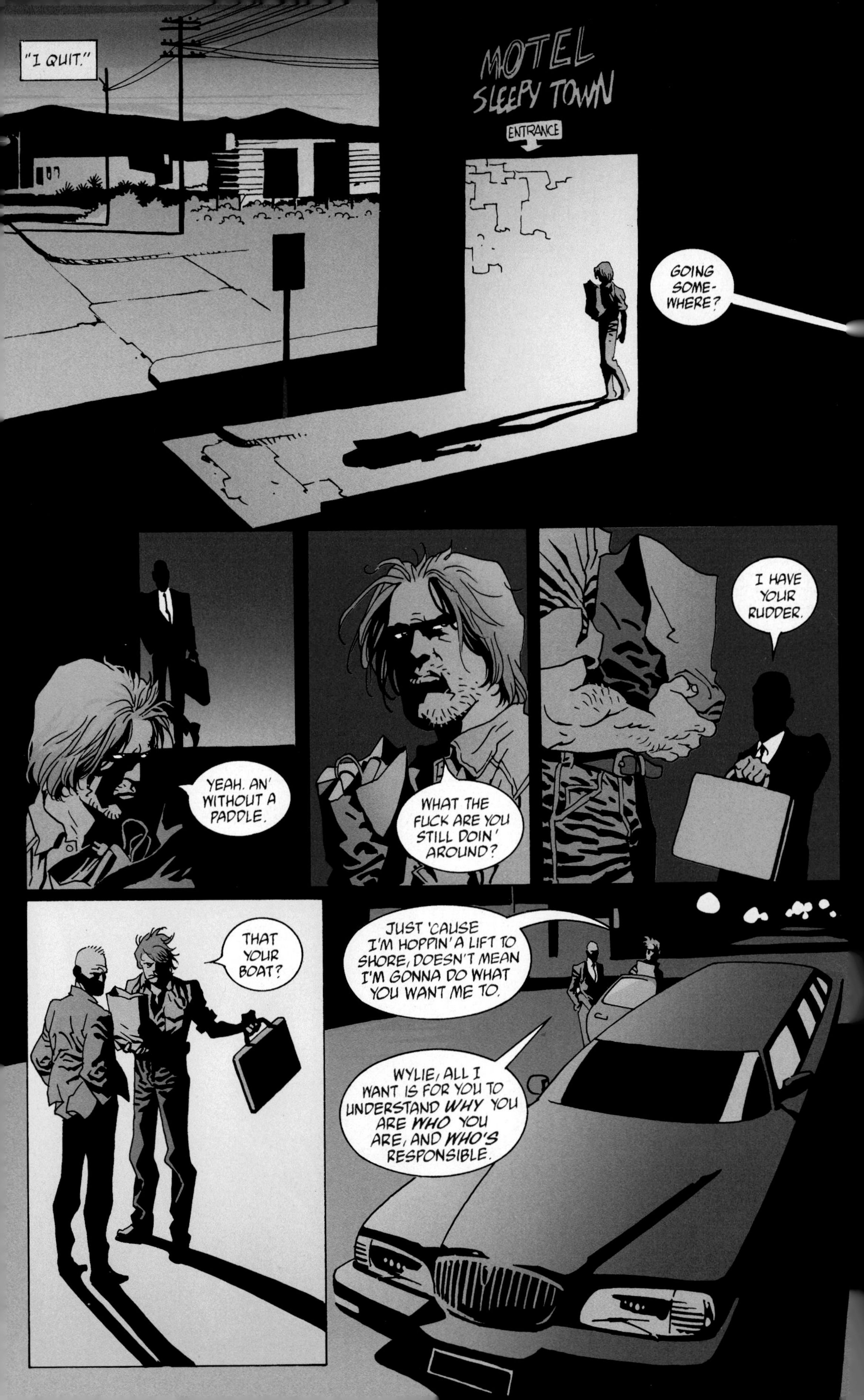
"I QUIT."
MOTEL
SLEEPY TOWN
ENTRANCE
GOING SOME-WHERE?
YEAH. AN' WITHOUT A PADDLE.
WHAT THE FUCK ARE YOU STILL DOIN' AROUND?
I HAVE YOUR RUDDER.
THAT YOUR BOAT?
JUST 'CAUSE I'M HOPPIN' A LIFT TO SHORE, DOESN'T MEAN I'M GONNA DO WHAT YOU WANT ME TO.
WYLIE, ALL I WANT IS FOR YOU TO UNDERSTAND *WHY* YOU ARE *WHO* YOU ARE, AND *WHO'S* RESPONSIBLE.

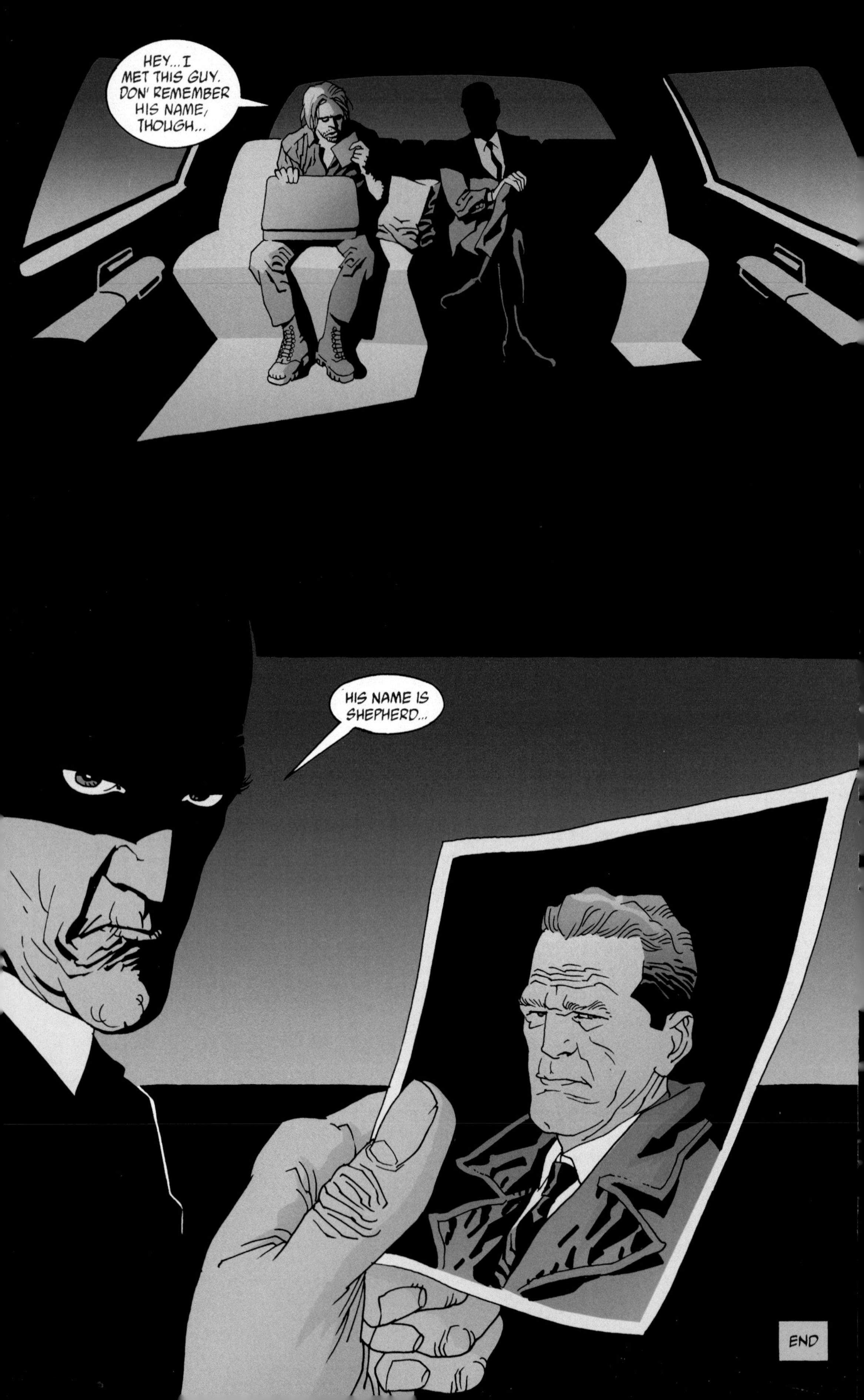
HEY... I MET THIS GUY. DON' REMEMBER HIS NAME, THOUGH...
HIS NAME IS SHEPHERD...
END

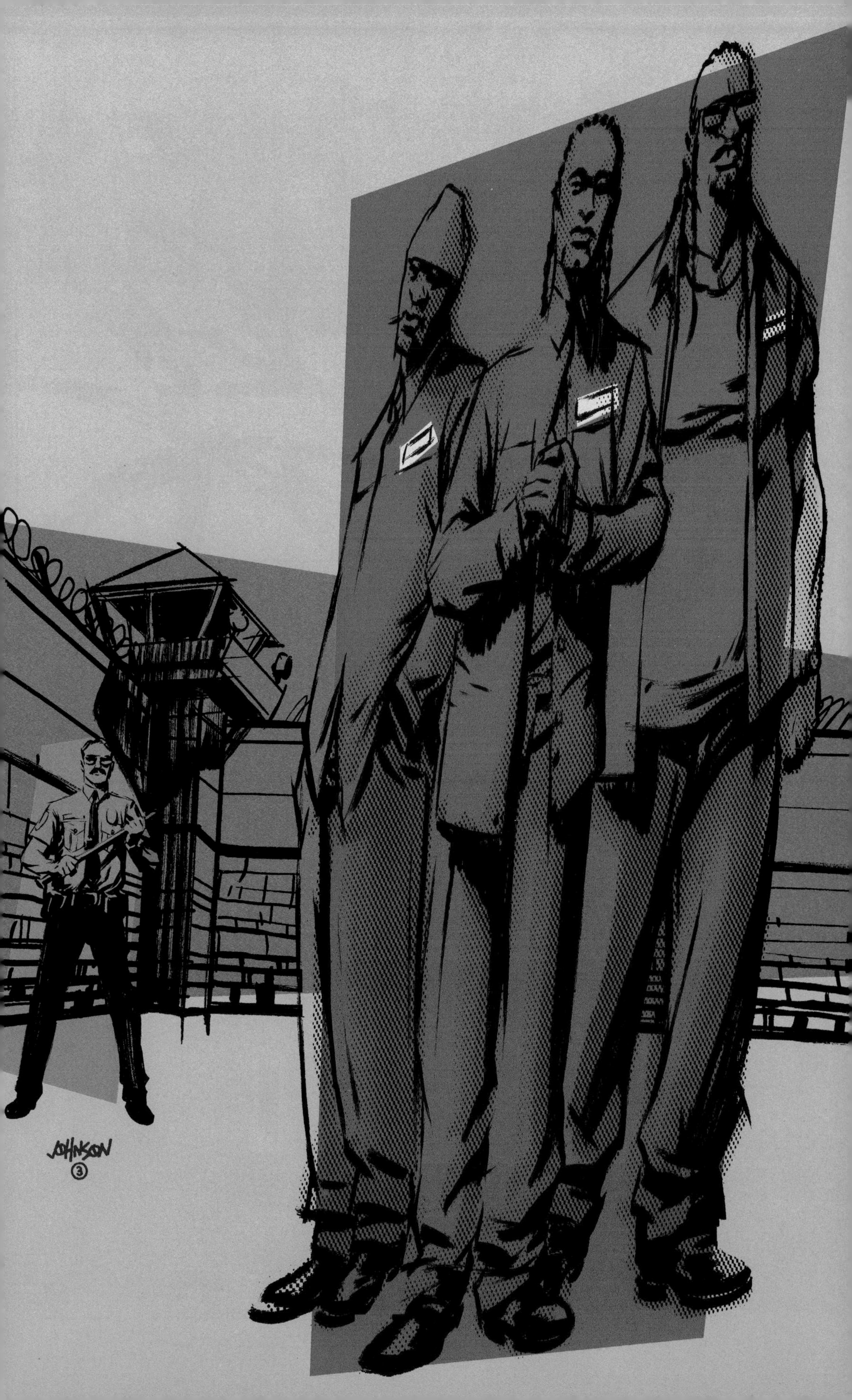
JOHNSON
3

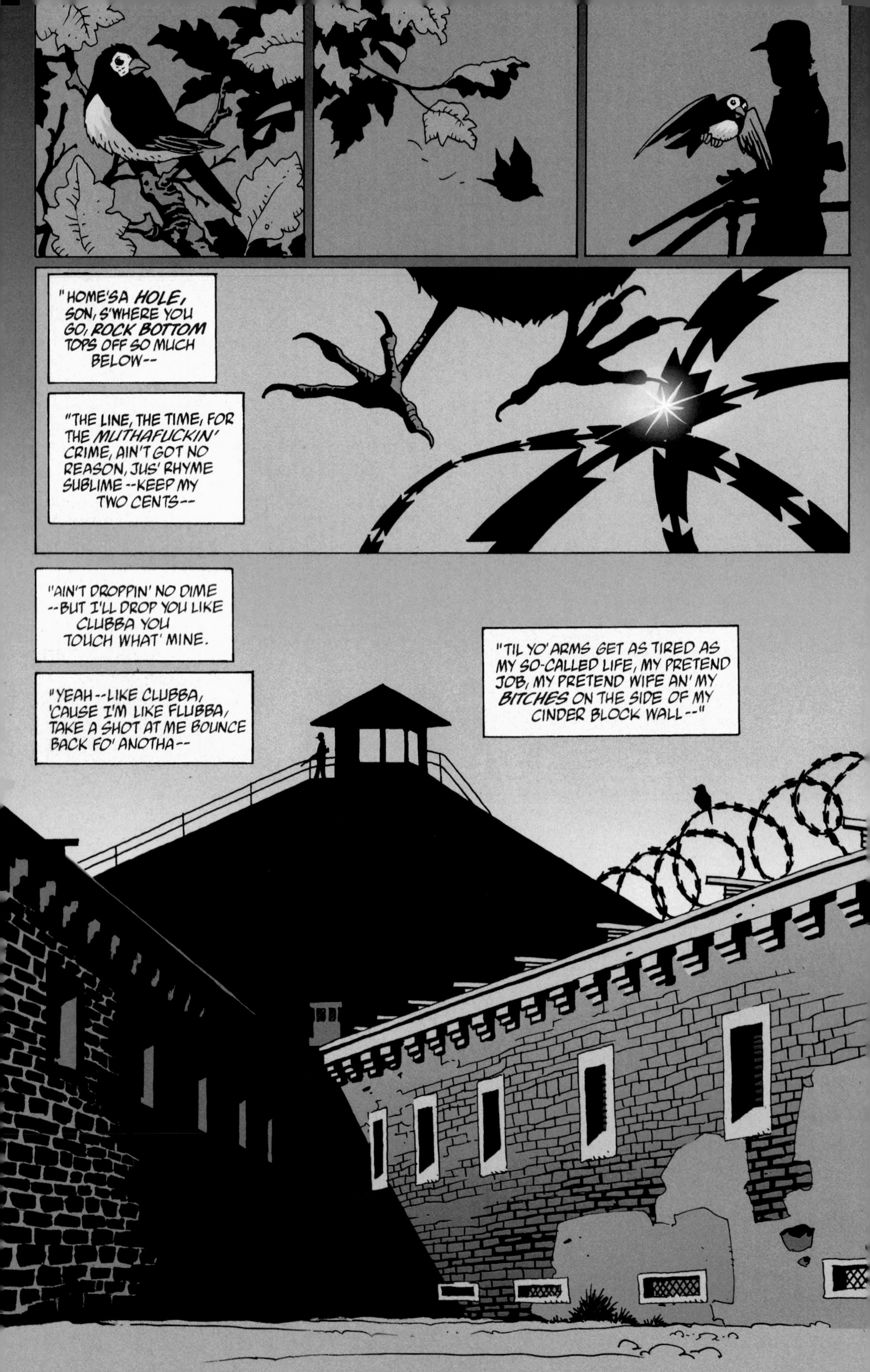
"HOME'SA HOLE, SON, S'WHERE YOU GO, ROCK BOTTOM TOPS OFF SO MUCH BELOW--
"THE LINE, THE TIME, FOR THE MUTHAFUCKIN' CRIME, AIN'T GOT NO REASON, JUS' RHYME SUBLIME --KEEP MY TWO CENTS--
"AIN'T DROPPIN' NO DIME --BUT I'LL DROP YOU LIKE CLUBBA YOU TOUCH WHAT' MINE.
"YEAH --LIKE CLUBBA, 'CAUSE I'M LIKE FLUBBA, TAKE A SHOT AT ME BOUNCE BACK FO' ANOTHA--
"TIL YO' ARMS GET AS TIRED AS MY SO-CALLED LIFE, MY PRETEND JOB, MY PRETEND WIFE AN' MY BITCHES ON THE SIDE OF MY CINDER BLOCK WALL--"

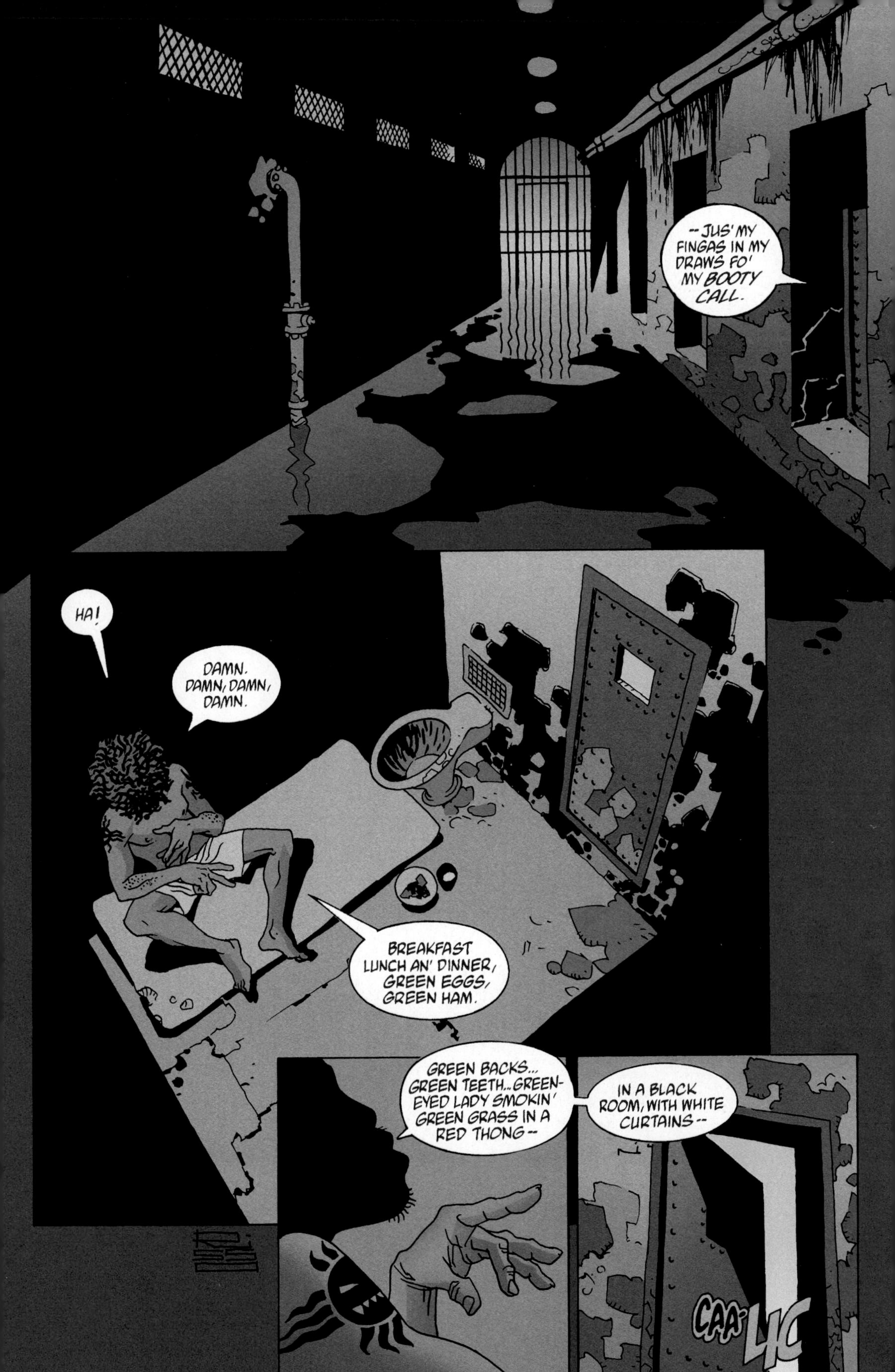
--JUS' MY FINGAS IN MY DRAWS FO' MY BOOTY CALL.
HA!
DAMN. DAMN, DAMN, DAMN.
BREAKFAST LUNCH AN' DINNER, GREEN EGGS, GREEN HAM.
GREEN BACKS... GREEN TEETH... GREEN-EYED LADY SMOKIN' GREEN GRASS IN A RED THONG--
IN A BLACK ROOM, WITH WHITE CURTAINS--
CAA-LIC

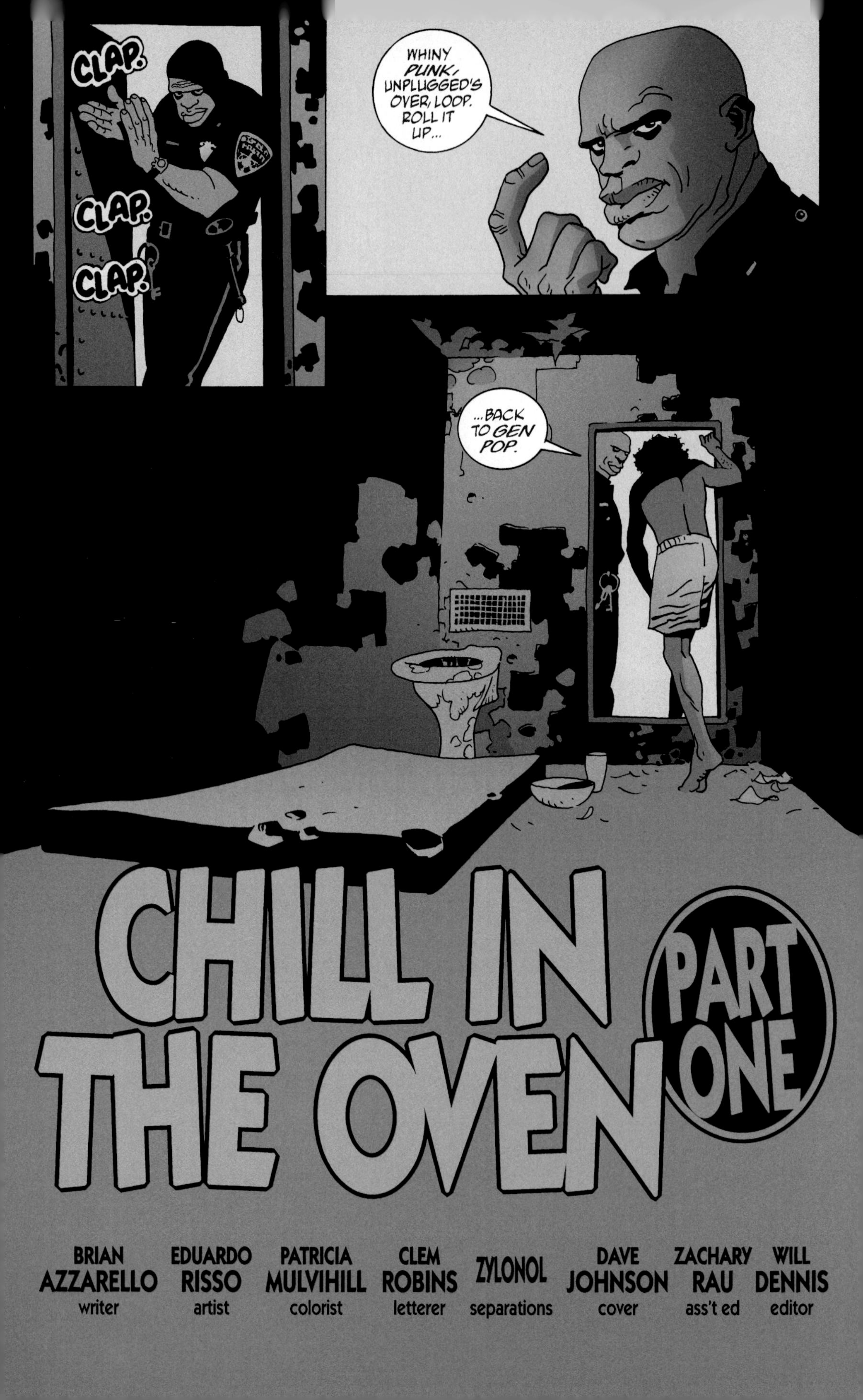
CLAP.
CLAP.
CLAP.
WHINY PUNK, UNPLUGGED'S OVER, LOOP. ROLL IT UP...
...BACK TO GEN POP.
CHILL IN THE OVEN
PART ONE
BRIAN AZZARELLO writer
EDUARDO RISSO artist
PATRICIA MULVIHILL colorist
CLEM ROBINS letterer
ZYLONOL separations
DAVE JOHNSON cover
ZACHARY RAU ass't ed
WILL DENNIS editor

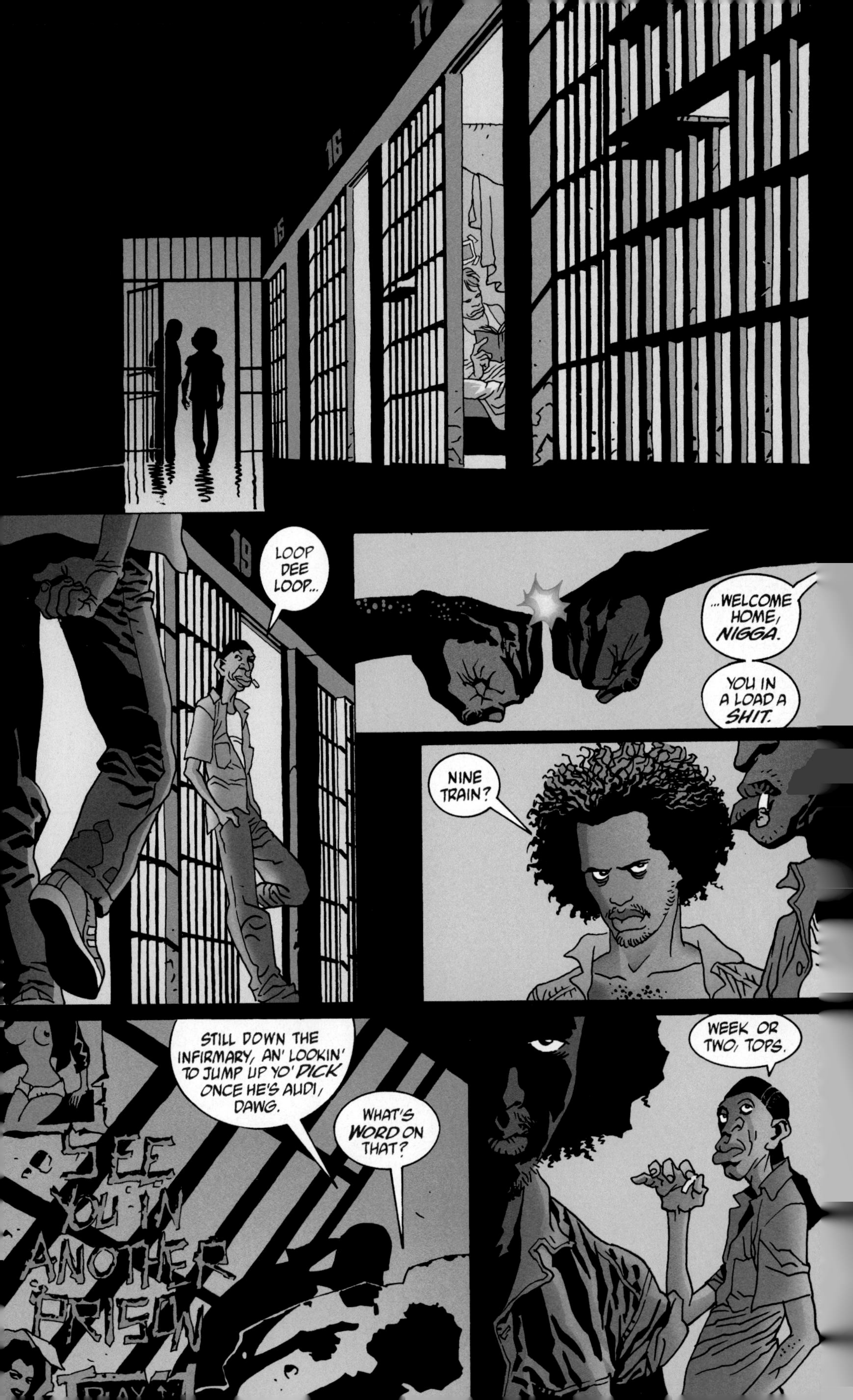
LOOP DEE LOOP...
...WELCOME HOME, NIGGA.
YOU IN A LOAD A SHIT.
NINE TRAIN?
STILL DOWN THE INFIRMARY, AN' LOOKIN' TO JUMP UP YO' DICK ONCE HE'S AUDI, DAWG.
WHAT'S WORD ON THAT?
WEEK OR TWO, TOPS.
SEE YOU IN ANOTHER PRISON

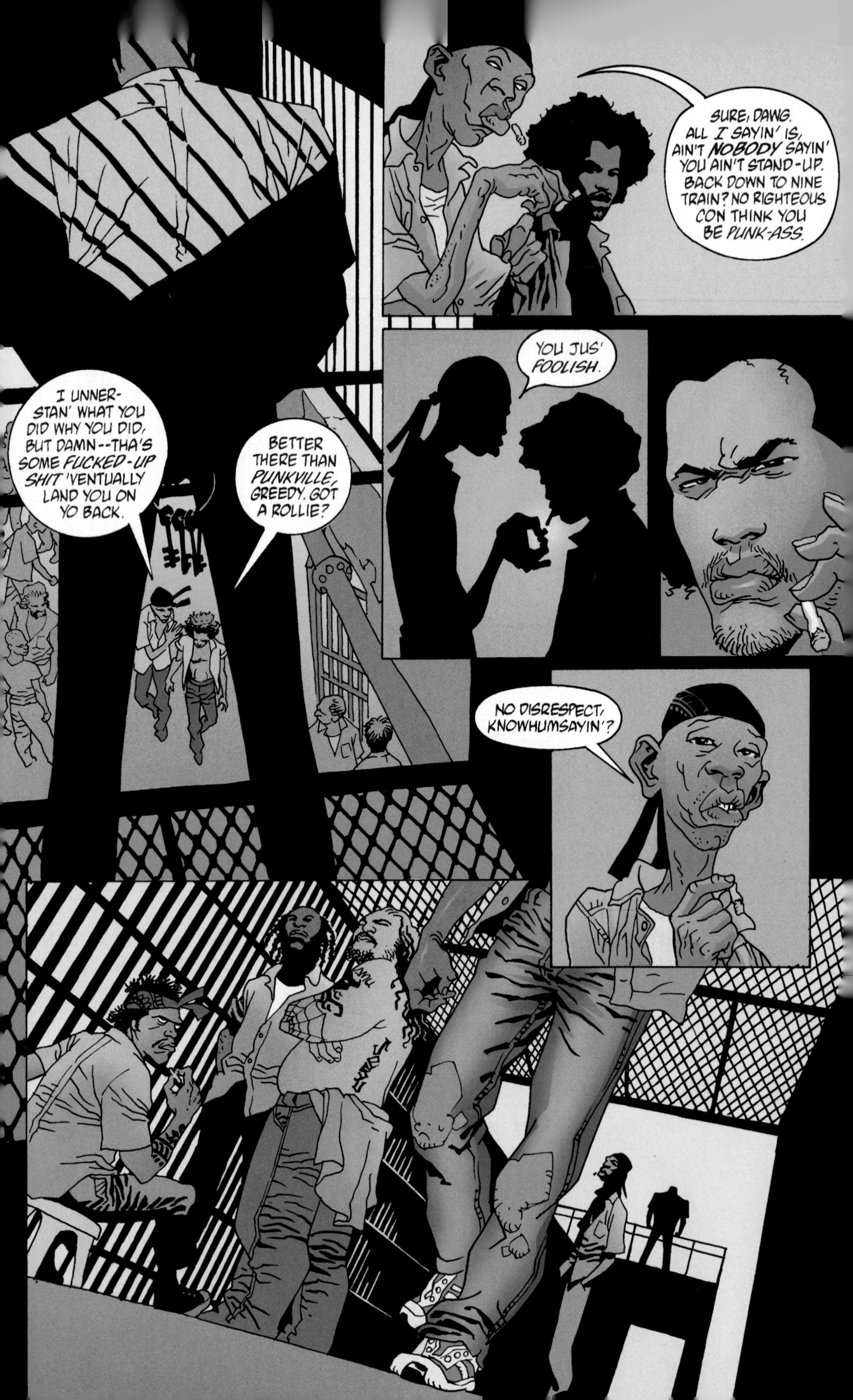
SURE, DAWG. ALL *I* SAYIN' IS, AIN'T ***NOBODY*** SAYIN' YOU AIN'T STAND-UP. BACK DOWN TO NINE TRAIN? NO RIGHTEOUS CON THINK YOU BE *PUNK-ASS*.
I UNNER-STAN' WHAT YOU DID WHY YOU DID, BUT DAMN--THA'S SOME *FUCKED-UP SHIT* 'VENTUALLY LAND YOU ON YO BACK.
BETTER THERE THAN *PUNKVILLE*, GREEDY. GOT A ROLLIE?
YOU JUS' *FOOLISH*.
NO DISRESPECT, KNOWHUMSAYIN'?

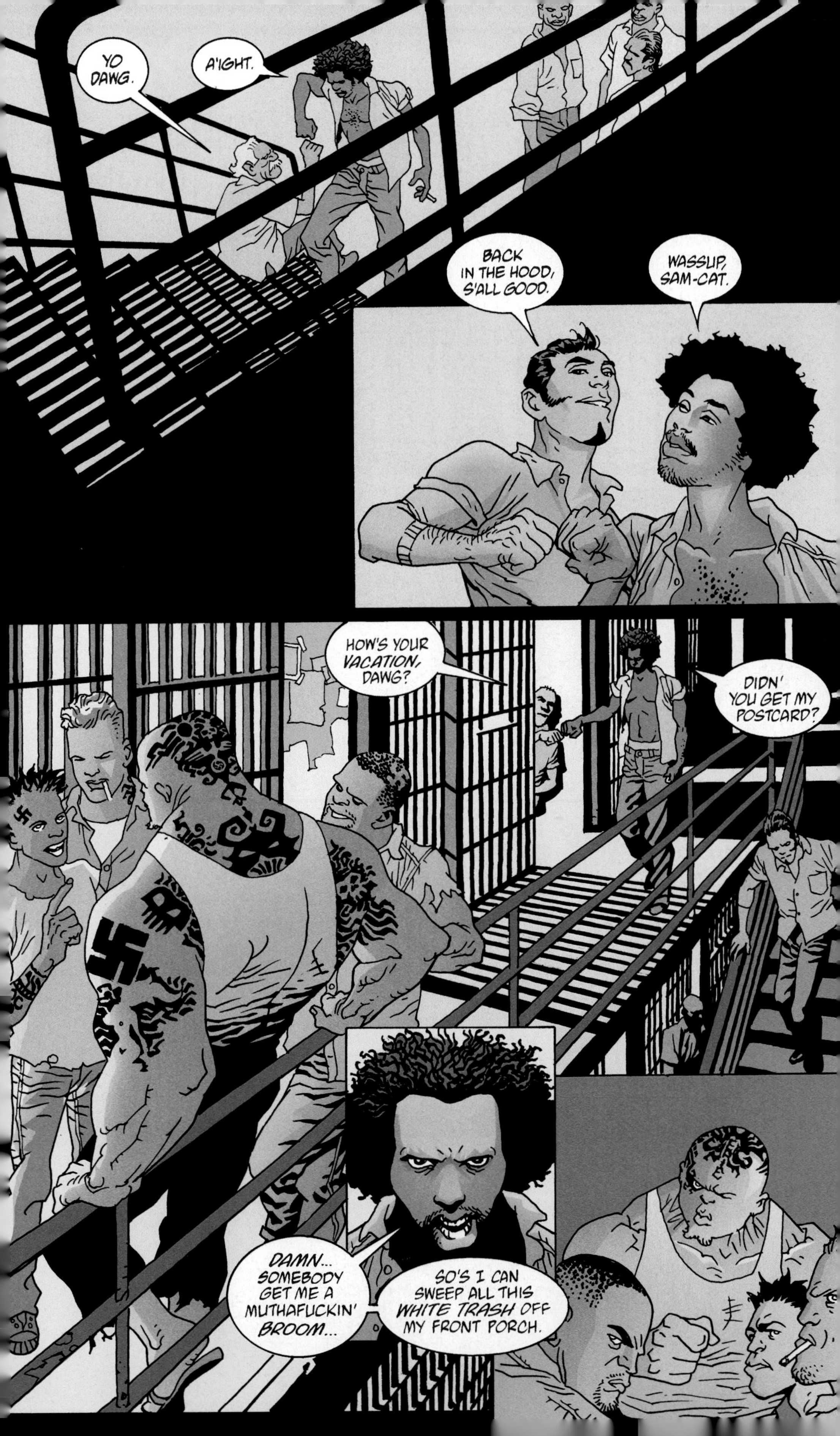

YO DAWG.
A'IGHT.
BACK IN THE HOOD, S'ALL GOOD.
WASSUP, SAM-CAT.
HOW'S YOUR *VACATION,* DAWG?
DIDN' YOU GET MY POSTCARD?
DAMN... SOMEBODY GET ME A MUTHAFUCKIN' *BROOM*...
SO'S I CAN SWEEP ALL THIS *WHITE TRASH* OFF MY FRONT PORCH.

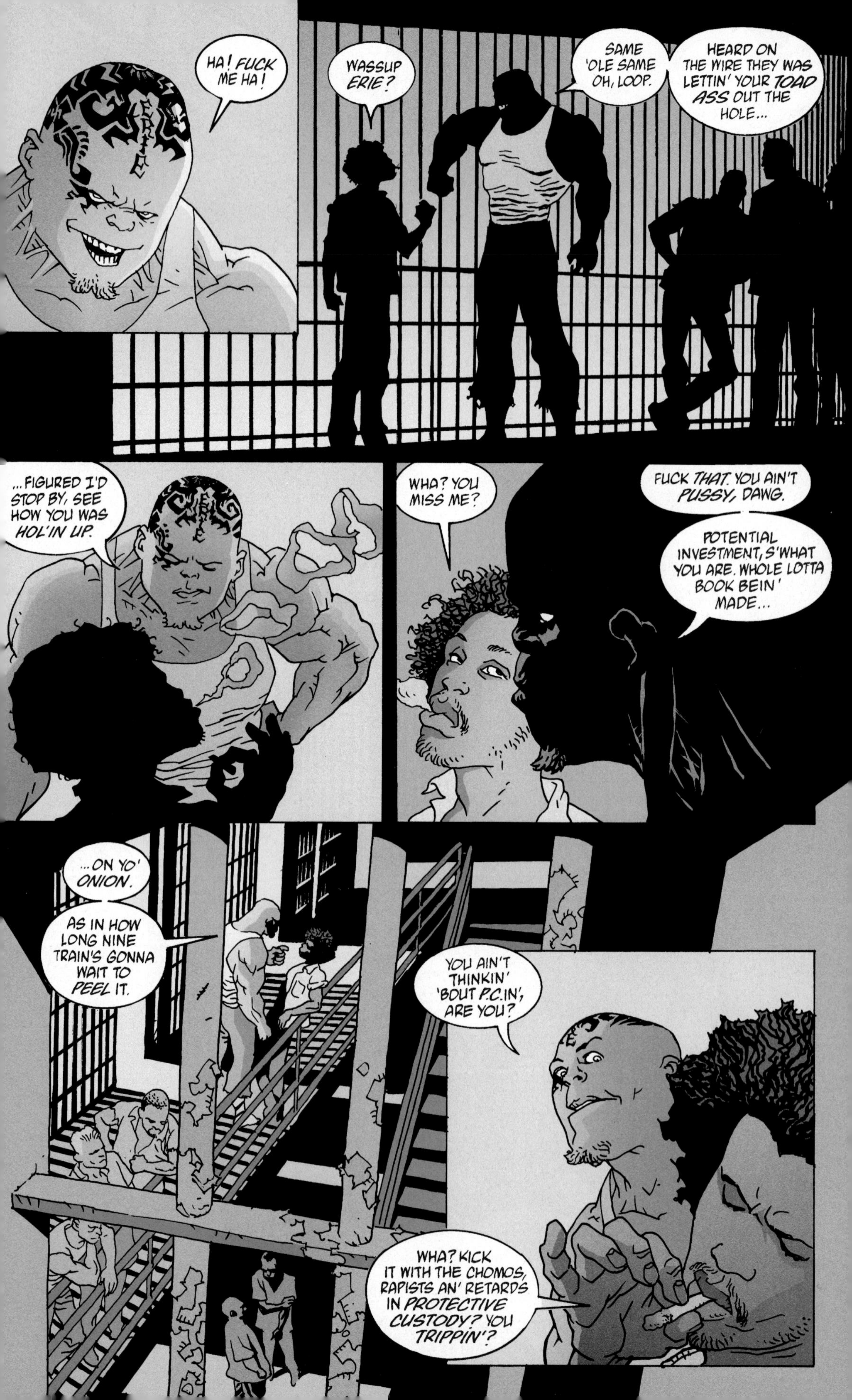
HA! FUCK ME HA!
WASSUP ERIE?
SAME 'OLE SAME OH, LOOP.
HEARD ON THE WIRE THEY WAS LETTIN' YOUR TOAD ASS OUT THE HOLE...
...FIGURED I'D STOP BY, SEE HOW YOU WAS HOL'IN UP.
WHA? YOU MISS ME?
FUCK THAT. YOU AIN'T PUSSY, DAWG.
POTENTIAL INVESTMENT, S'WHAT YOU ARE. WHOLE LOTTA BOOK BEIN' MADE...
...ON YO' ONION.
AS IN HOW LONG NINE TRAIN'S GONNA WAIT TO PEEL IT.
YOU AIN'T THINKIN' 'BOUT P.C.IN', ARE YOU?
WHA? KICK IT WITH THE CHOMOS, RAPISTS AN' RETARDS IN PROTECTIVE CUSTODY? YOU TRIPPIN'?

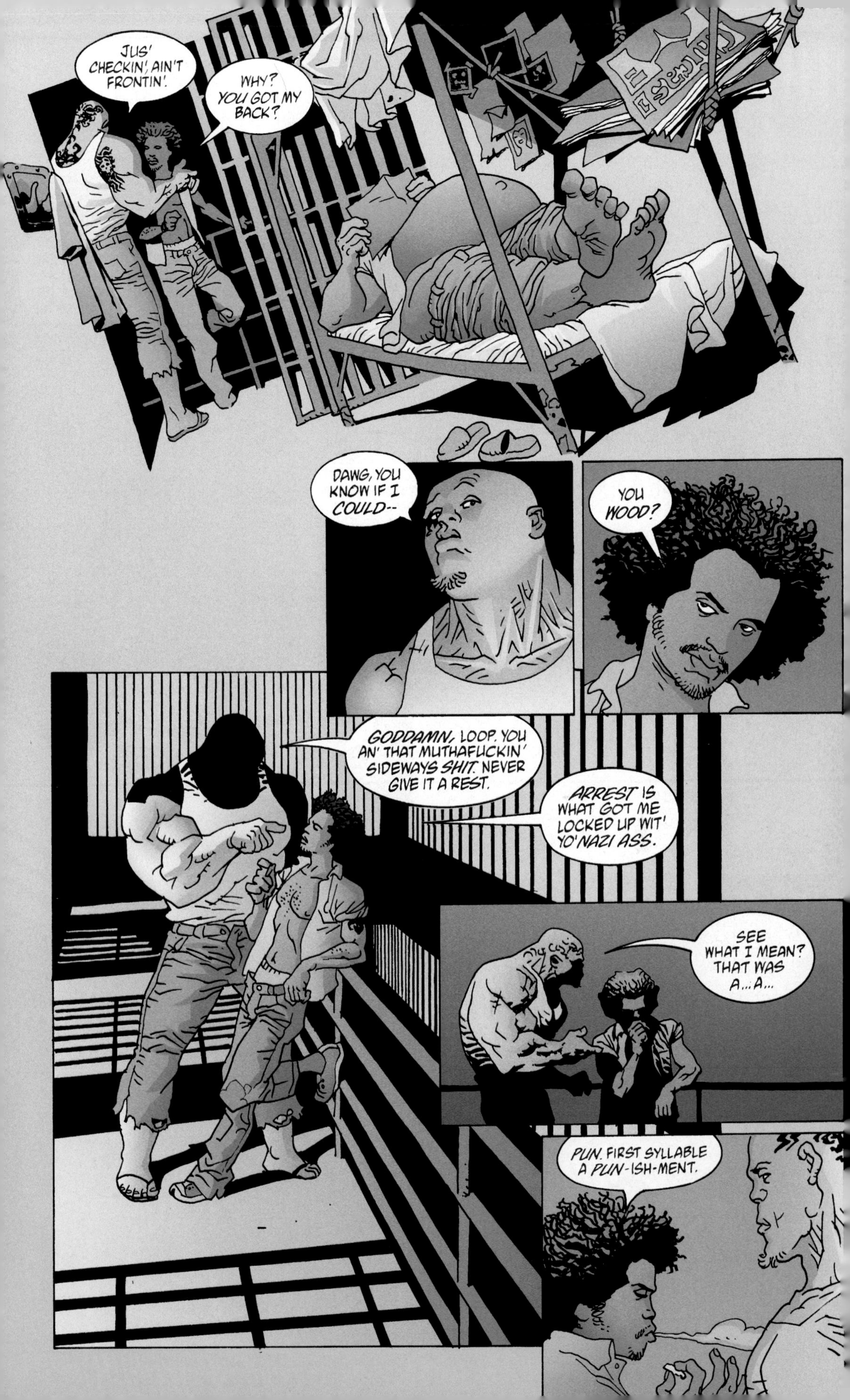
JUS' CHECKIN', AIN'T FRONTIN'.
WHY? YOU GOT MY BACK?
DAWG, YOU KNOW IF I COULD--
YOU WOOD?
GODDAMN, LOOP. YOU AN' THAT MUTHAFUCKIN' SIDEWAYS SHIT. NEVER GIVE IT A REST.
ARREST IS WHAT GOT ME LOCKED UP WIT' YO' NAZI ASS.
SEE WHAT I MEAN? THAT WAS A... A...
PUN. FIRST SYLLABLE A PUN-ISH-MENT.

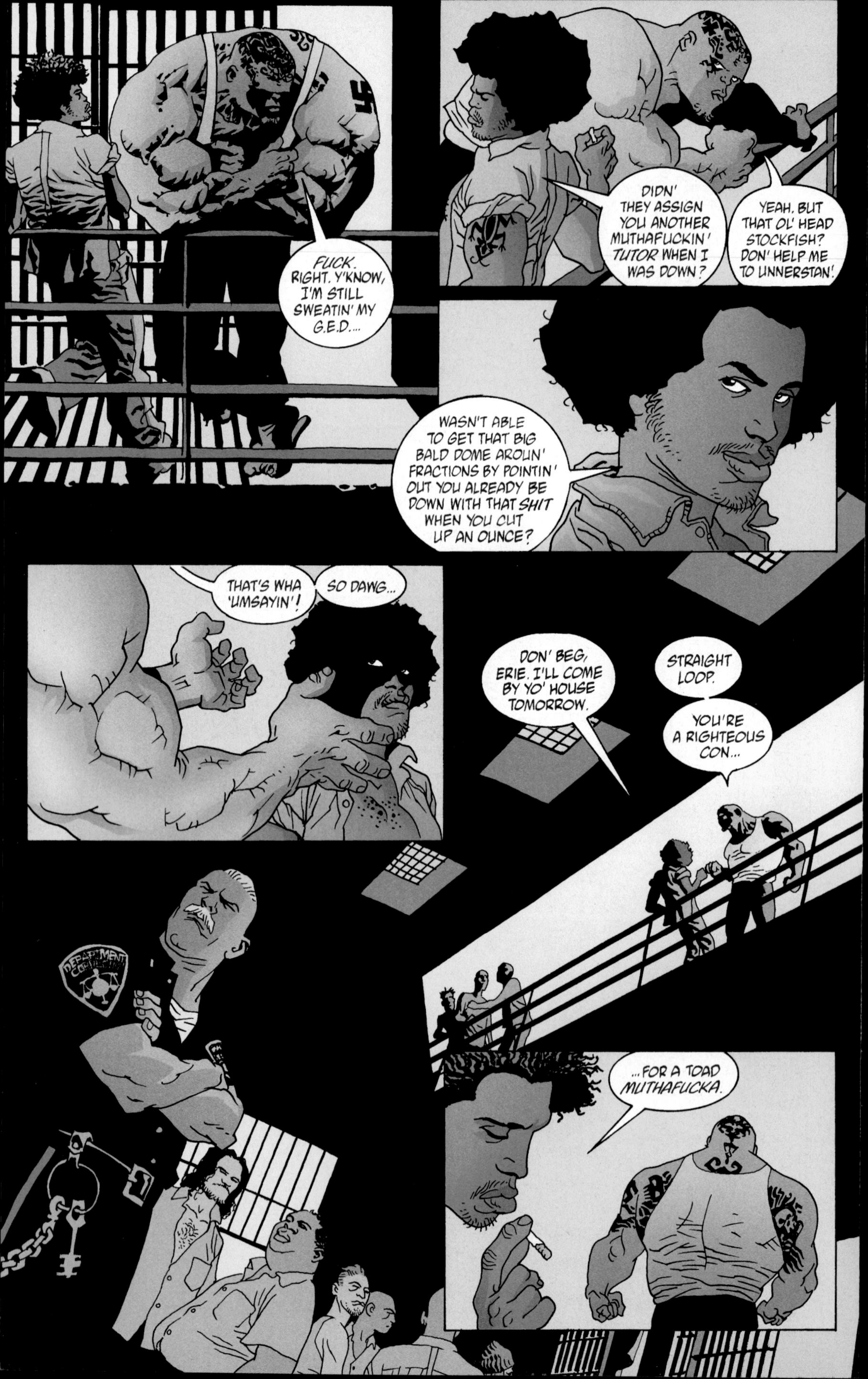
FUCK. RIGHT. Y'KNOW, I'M STILL SWEATIN' MY G.E.D....
DIDN' THEY ASSIGN YOU ANOTHER MUTHAFUCKIN' TUTOR WHEN I WAS DOWN?
YEAH. BUT THAT OL' HEAD STOCKFISH? DON' HELP ME TO UNNERSTAN'!
WASN'T ABLE TO GET THAT BIG BALD DOME AROUN' FRACTIONS BY POINTIN' OUT YOU ALREADY BE DOWN WITH THAT SHIT WHEN YOU CUT UP AN OUNCE?
THAT'S WHA 'UMSAYIN'!
SO DAWG...
DON' BEG, ERIE. I'LL COME BY YO' HOUSE TOMORROW.
STRAIGHT LOOP.
YOU'RE A RIGHTEOUS CON...
...FOR A TOAD MUTHAFUCKA.

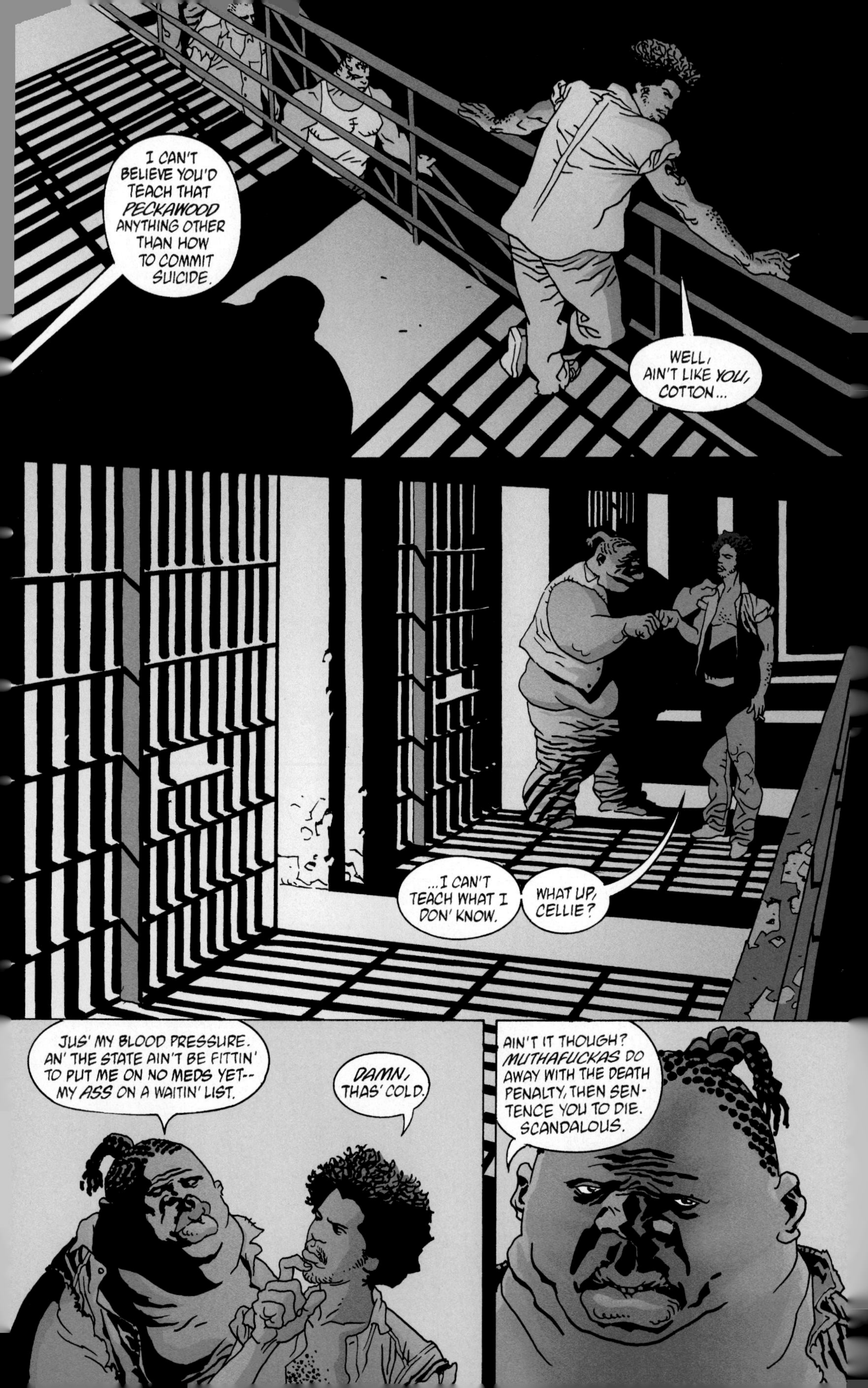
I CAN'T BELIEVE YOU'D TEACH THAT *PECKAWOOD* ANYTHING OTHER THAN HOW TO COMMIT SUICIDE.
WELL, AIN'T LIKE *YOU*, COTTON...
...I CAN'T TEACH WHAT I DON' KNOW.
WHAT UP, CELLIE?
JUS' MY BLOOD PRESSURE. AN' THE STATE AIN'T BE FITTIN' TO PUT ME ON NO MEDS YET-- MY *ASS* ON A WAITIN' LIST.
DAMN, THAS' COLD.
AIN'T IT THOUGH? *MUTHAFUCKAS* DO AWAY WITH THE DEATH PENALTY, THEN SENTENCE YOU TO DIE. SCANDALOUS.

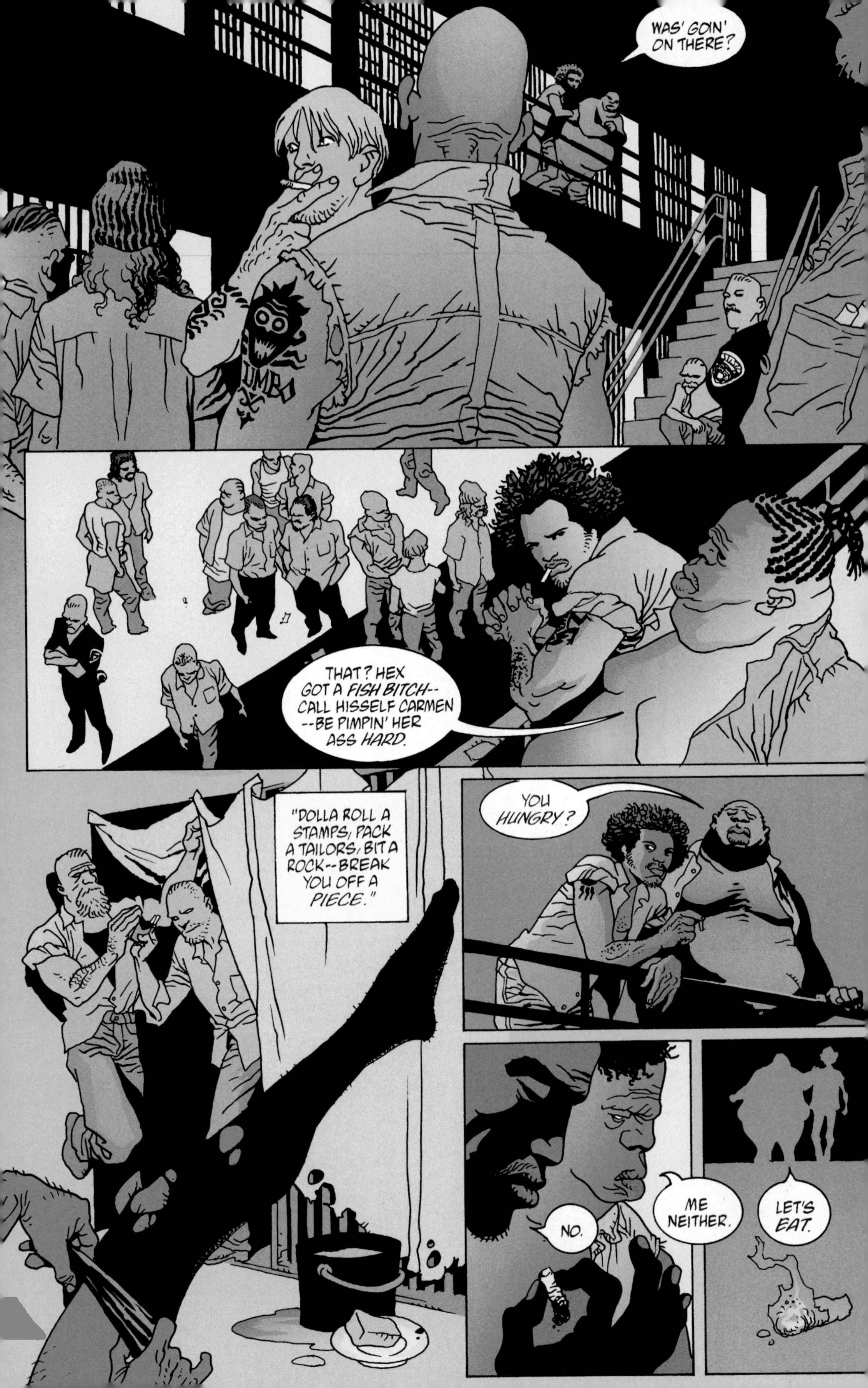
WAS' GOIN' ON THERE?
UMBO
THAT? HEX GOT A FISH BITCH-- CALL HISSELF CARMEN --BE PIMPIN' HER ASS HARD.
"DOLLA ROLL A STAMPS, PACK A TAILORS, BIT A ROCK--BREAK YOU OFF A PIECE."
YOU HUNGRY?
NO.
ME NEITHER.
LET'S EAT.

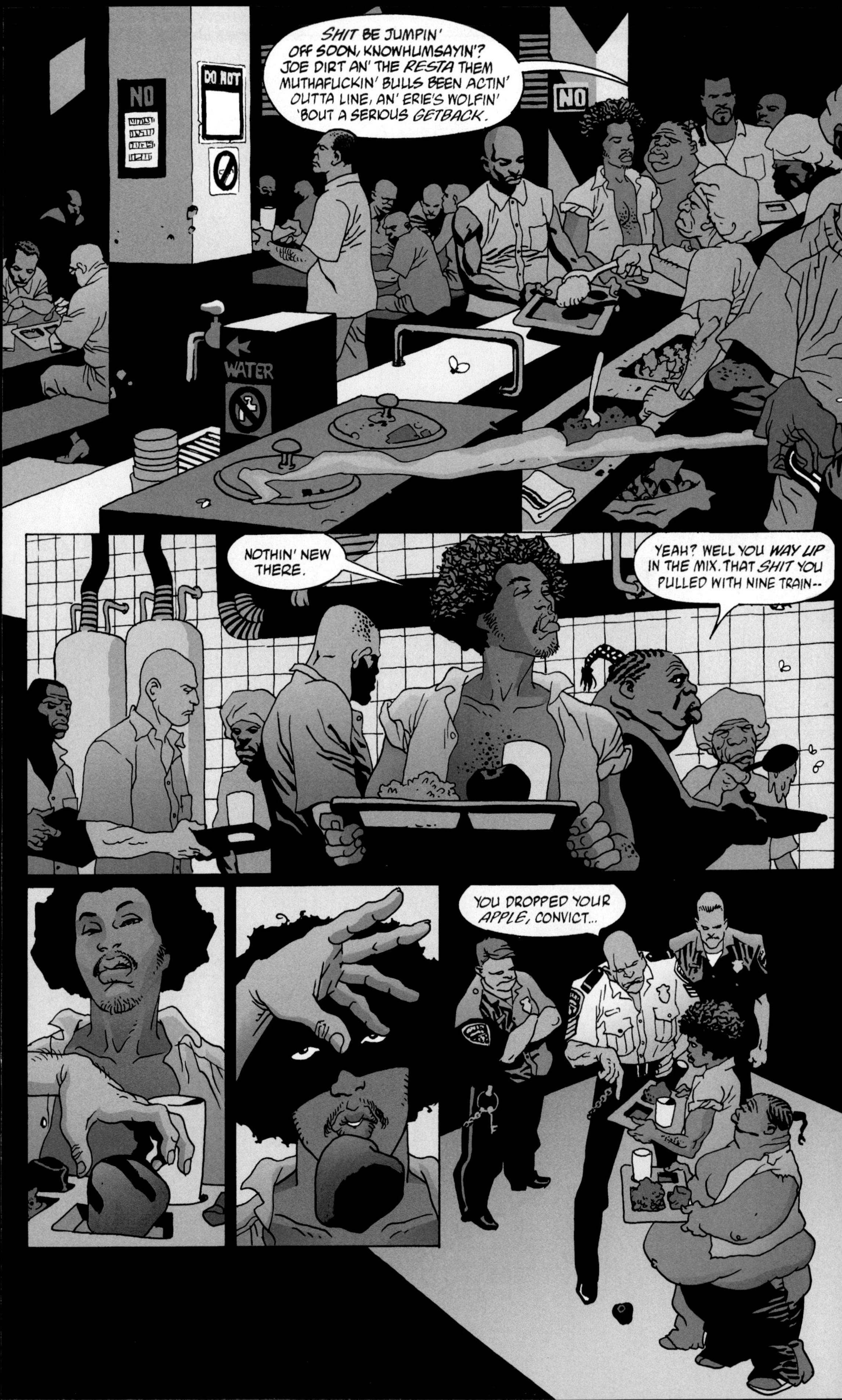
SHIT BE JUMPIN' OFF SOON, KNOWHUMSAYIN'? JOE DIRT AN' THE RESTA THEM MUTHAFUCKIN' BULLS BEEN ACTIN' OUTTA LINE, AN' ERIE'S WOLFIN' 'BOUT A SERIOUS GETBACK.
DO NOT
NO
NO
WATER
NOTHIN' NEW THERE.
YEAH? WELL YOU WAY UP IN THE MIX. THAT SHIT YOU PULLED WITH NINE TRAIN--
YOU DROPPED YOUR APPLE, CONVICT...

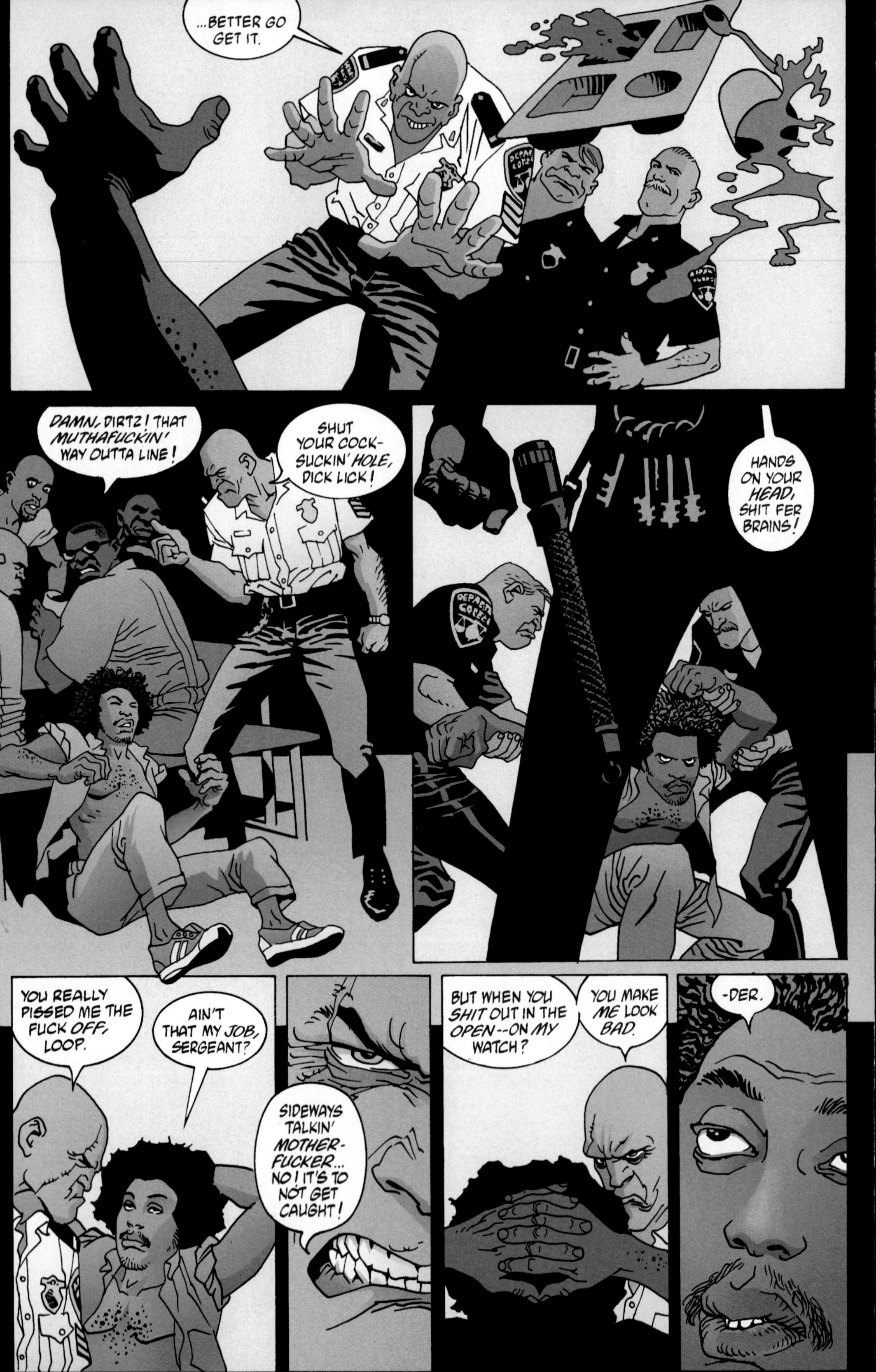
...BETTER GO GET IT.
DAMN, DIRTZ! THAT MUTHAFUCKIN' WAY OUTTA LINE!
SHUT YOUR COCK-SUCKIN' HOLE, DICK LICK!
HANDS ON YOUR HEAD, SHIT FER BRAINS!
YOU REALLY PISSED ME THE FUCK OFF, LOOP.
AIN'T THAT MY JOB, SERGEANT?
SIDEWAYS TALKIN' MOTHER-FUCKER... NO! IT'S TO NOT GET CAUGHT!
BUT WHEN YOU SHIT OUT IN THE OPEN--ON MY WATCH?
YOU MAKE ME LOOK BAD.
-DER.

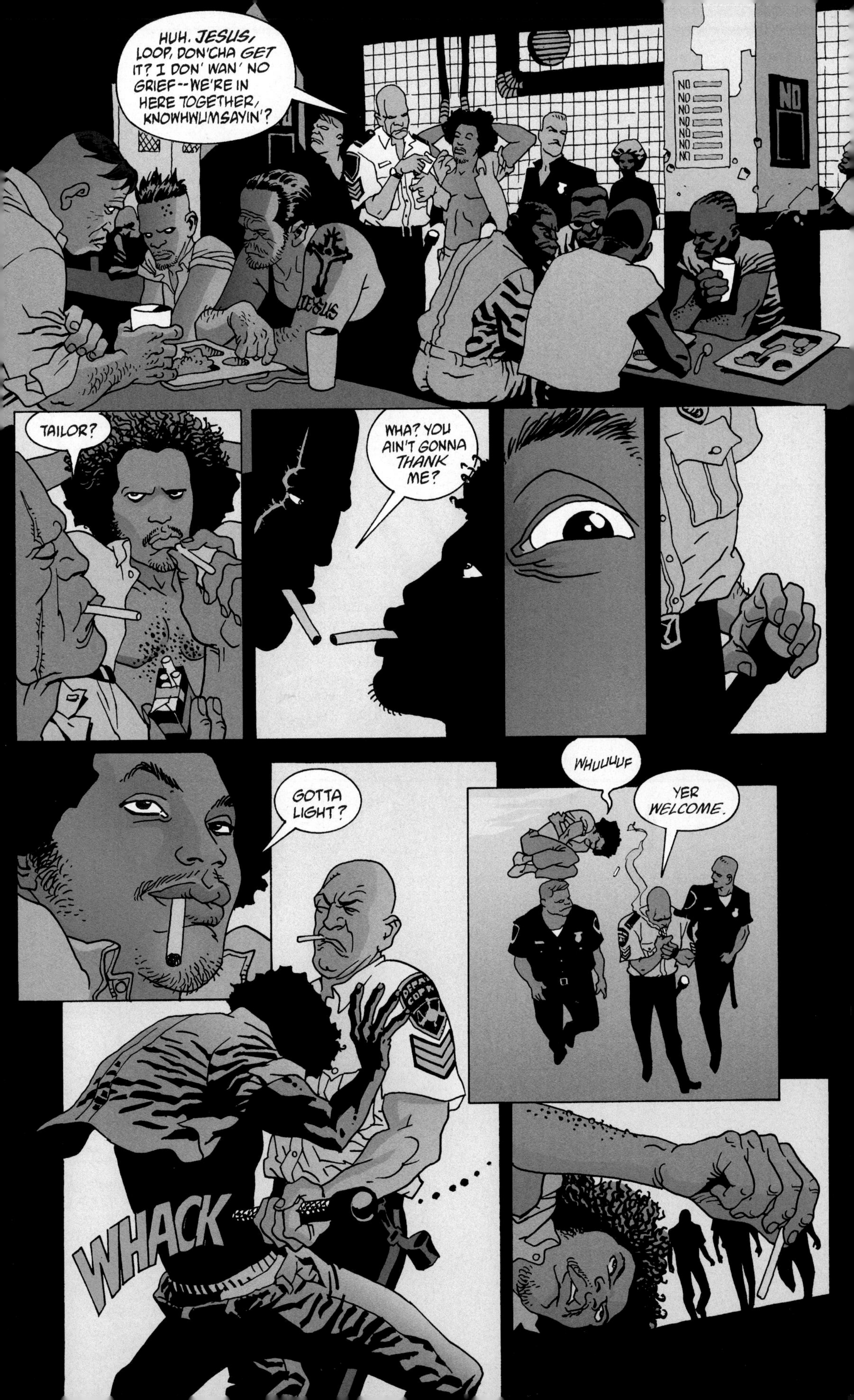
HUH. JESUS, LOOP, DON'CHA GET IT? I DON' WAN' NO GRIEF--WE'RE IN HERE TOGETHER, KNOWHWUMSAYIN'?
NO
NO
NO
NO
NO
NO
NO
NO
JESUS
TAILOR?
WHA? YOU AIN'T GONNA THANK ME?
GOTTA LIGHT?
WHACK
WHUUUUF
YER WELCOME.

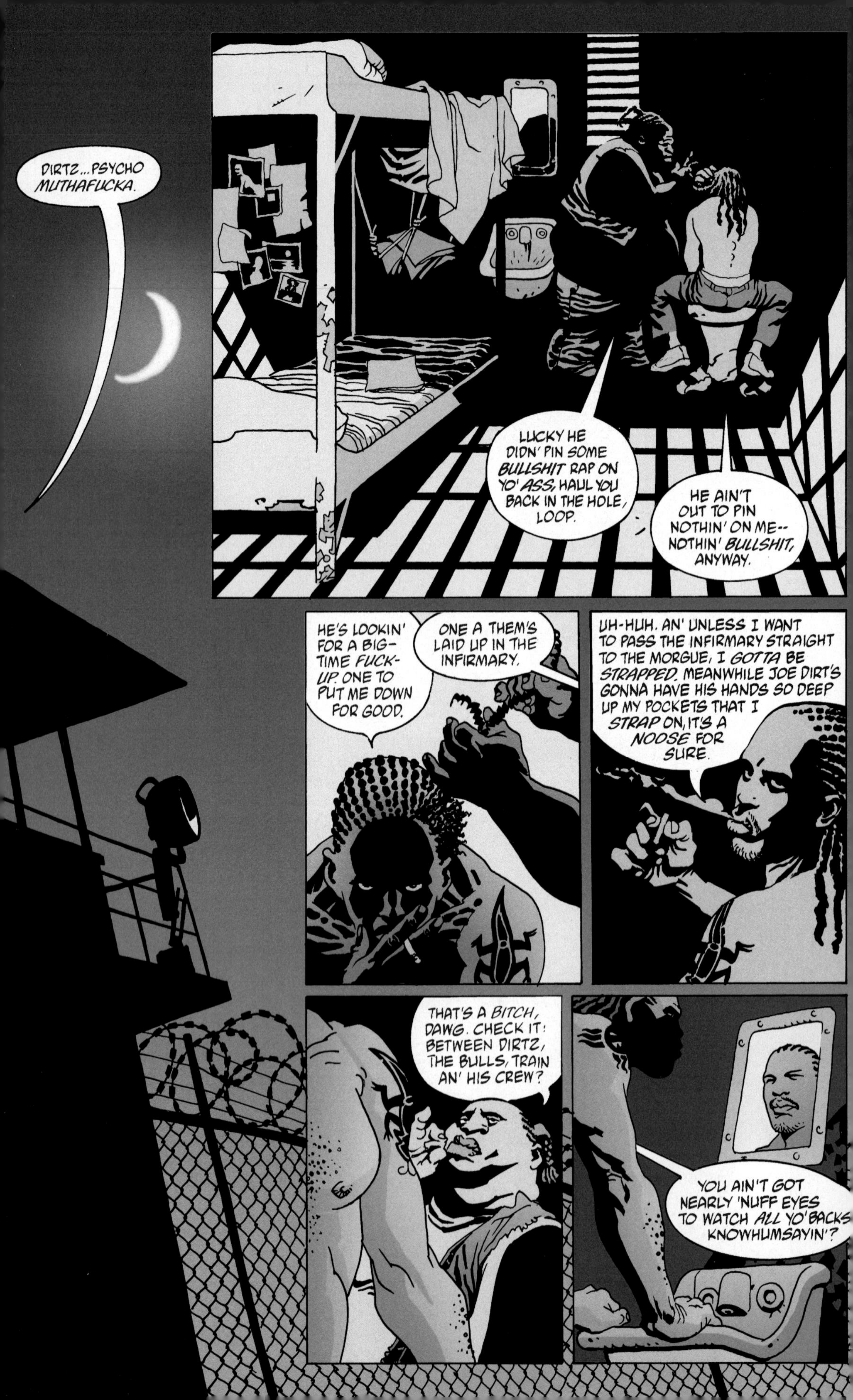
DIRTZ... PSYCHO MUTHAFUCKA.
LUCKY HE DIDN' PIN SOME BULLSHIT RAP ON YO' ASS, HAUL YOU BACK IN THE HOLE, LOOP.
HE AIN'T OUT TO PIN NOTHIN' ON ME-- NOTHIN' BULLSHIT, ANYWAY.
HE'S LOOKIN' FOR A BIG-TIME FUCK-UP. ONE TO PUT ME DOWN FOR GOOD.
ONE A THEM'S LAID UP IN THE INFIRMARY.
UH-HUH. AN' UNLESS I WANT TO PASS THE INFIRMARY STRAIGHT TO THE MORGUE, I GOTTA BE STRAPPED. MEANWHILE JOE DIRT'S GONNA HAVE HIS HANDS SO DEEP UP MY POCKETS THAT I STRAP ON, IT'S A NOOSE FOR SURE.
THAT'S A BITCH, DAWG. CHECK IT: BETWEEN DIRTZ, THE BULLS, TRAIN AN' HIS CREW?
YOU AIN'T GOT NEARLY 'NUFF EYES TO WATCH ALL YO' BACKS KNOWHUMSAYIN'?

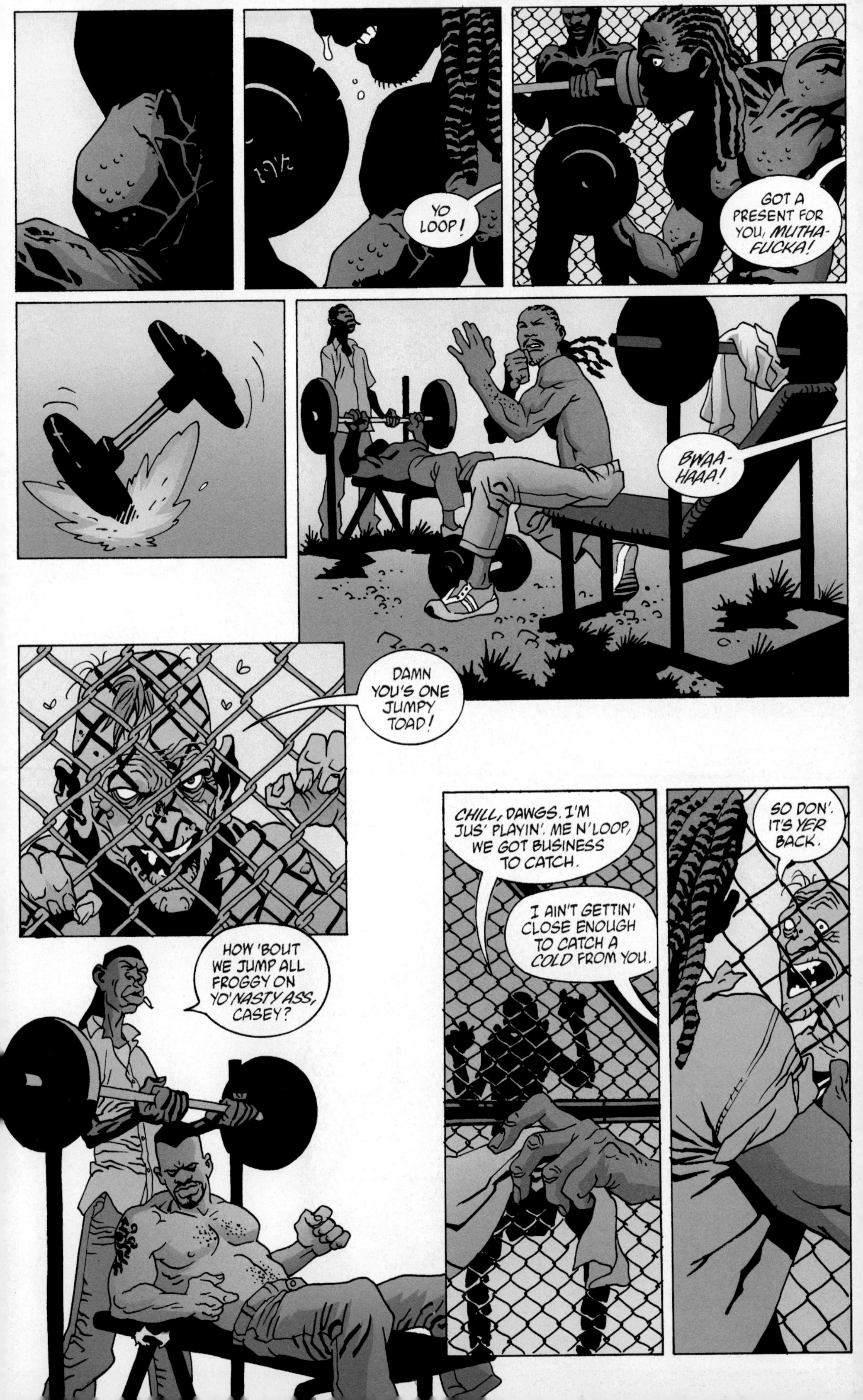
YO LOOP!
GOT A PRESENT FOR YOU, MUTHA-FUCKA!
BWAA-HAAA!
DAMN YOU'S ONE JUMPY TOAD!
HOW 'BOUT WE JUMP ALL FROGGY ON YO' NASTY ASS, CASEY?
CHILL, DAWGS. I'M JUS' PLAYIN'. ME N' LOOP, WE GOT BUSINESS TO CATCH.
I AIN'T GETTIN' CLOSE ENOUGH TO CATCH A COLD FROM YOU.
SO DON'. IT'S YER BACK.

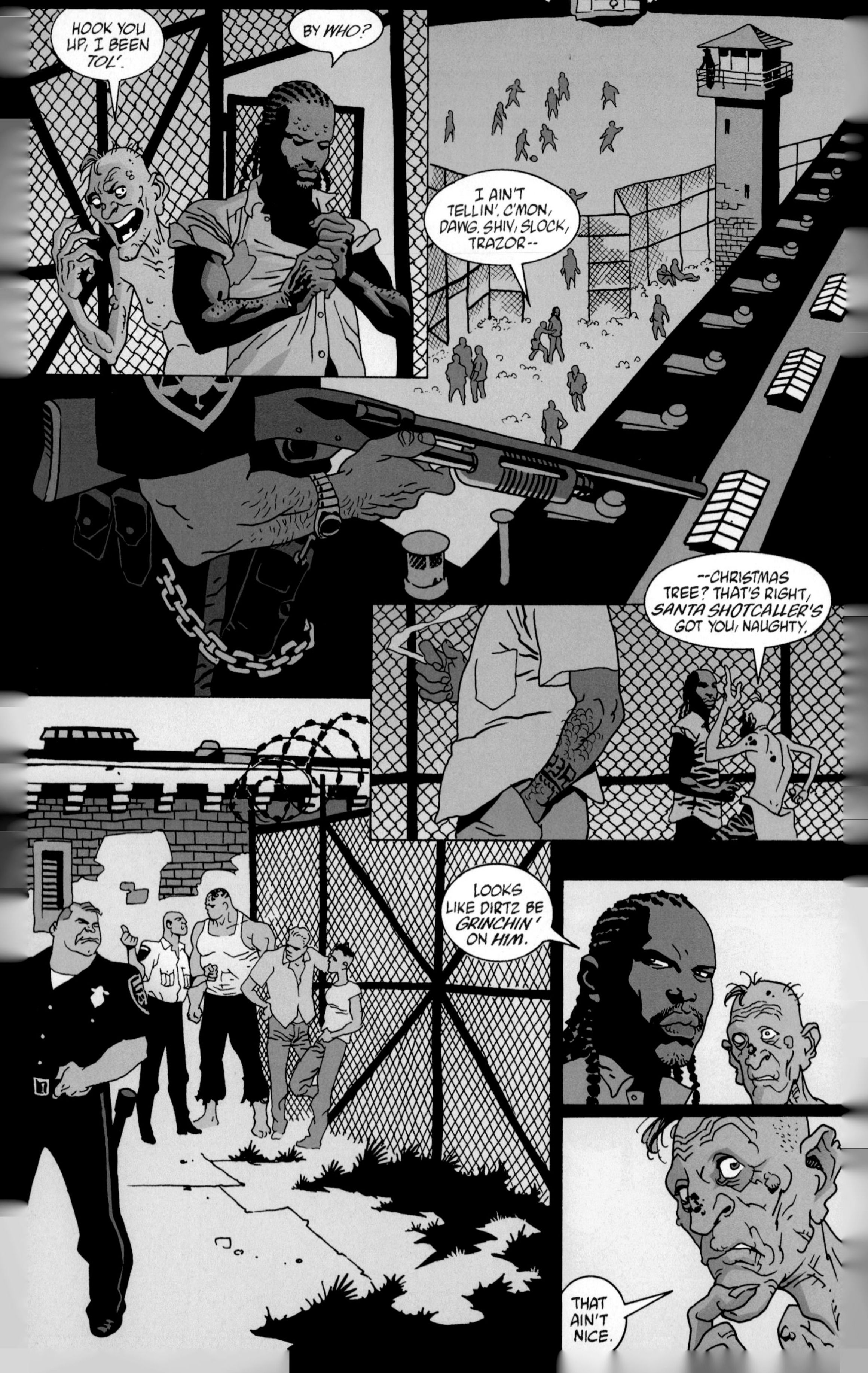
HOOK YOU UP, I BEEN TOL'.
BY WHO?
I AIN'T TELLIN', C'MON, DAWG. SHIV, SLOCK, TRAZOR--
--CHRISTMAS TREE? THAT'S RIGHT, SANTA SHOTCALLER'S GOT YOU, NAUGHTY.
LOOKS LIKE DIRTZ BE GRINCHIN' ON HIM.
THAT AIN'T NICE.

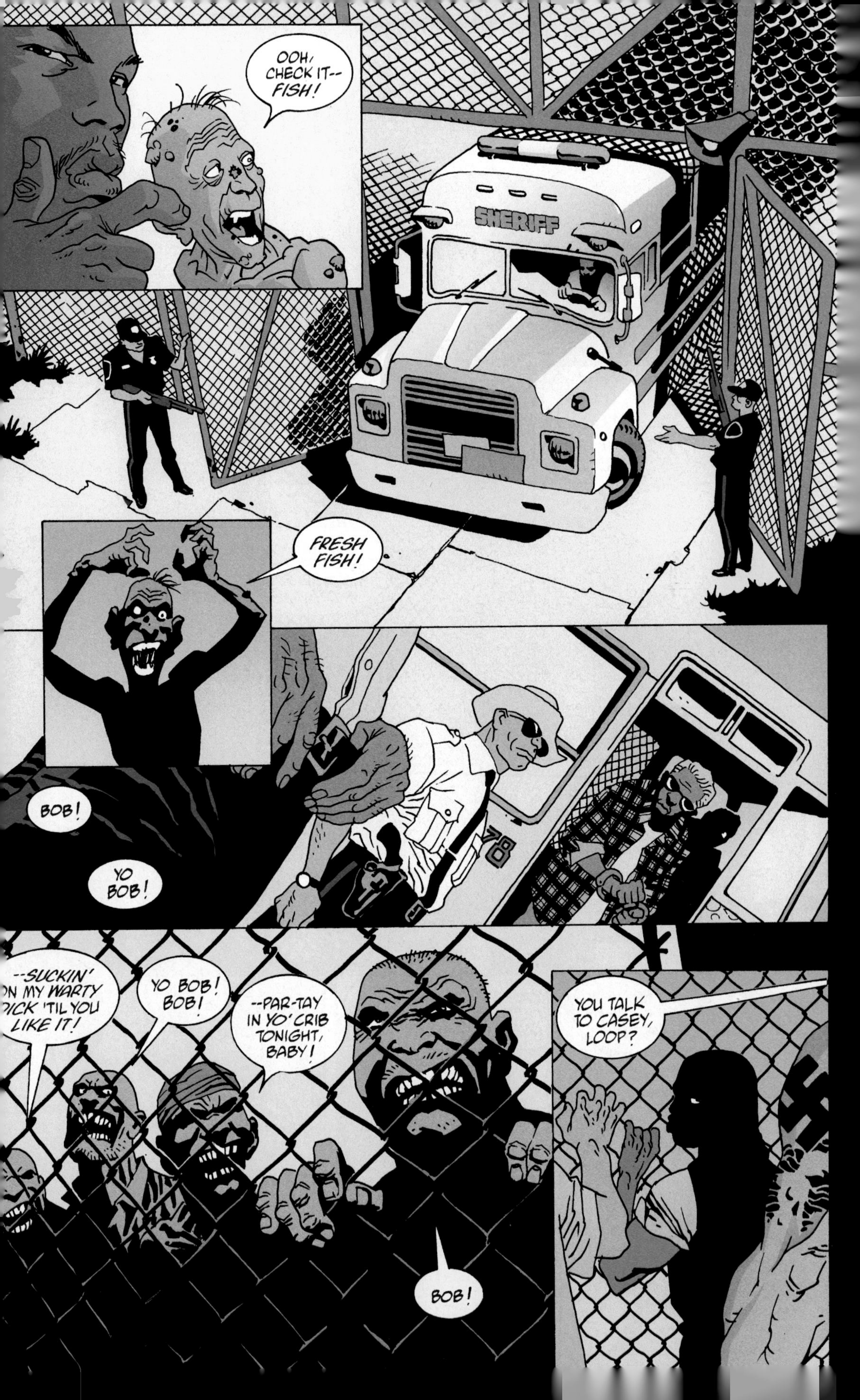
OOH, CHECK IT-- FISH!
FRESH FISH!
BOB!
YO BOB!
--SUCKIN' ON MY WARTY DICK 'TIL YOU LIKE IT!
YO BOB! BOB!
--PAR-TAY IN YO' CRIB TONIGHT, BABY!
BOB!
YOU TALK TO CASEY, LOOP?

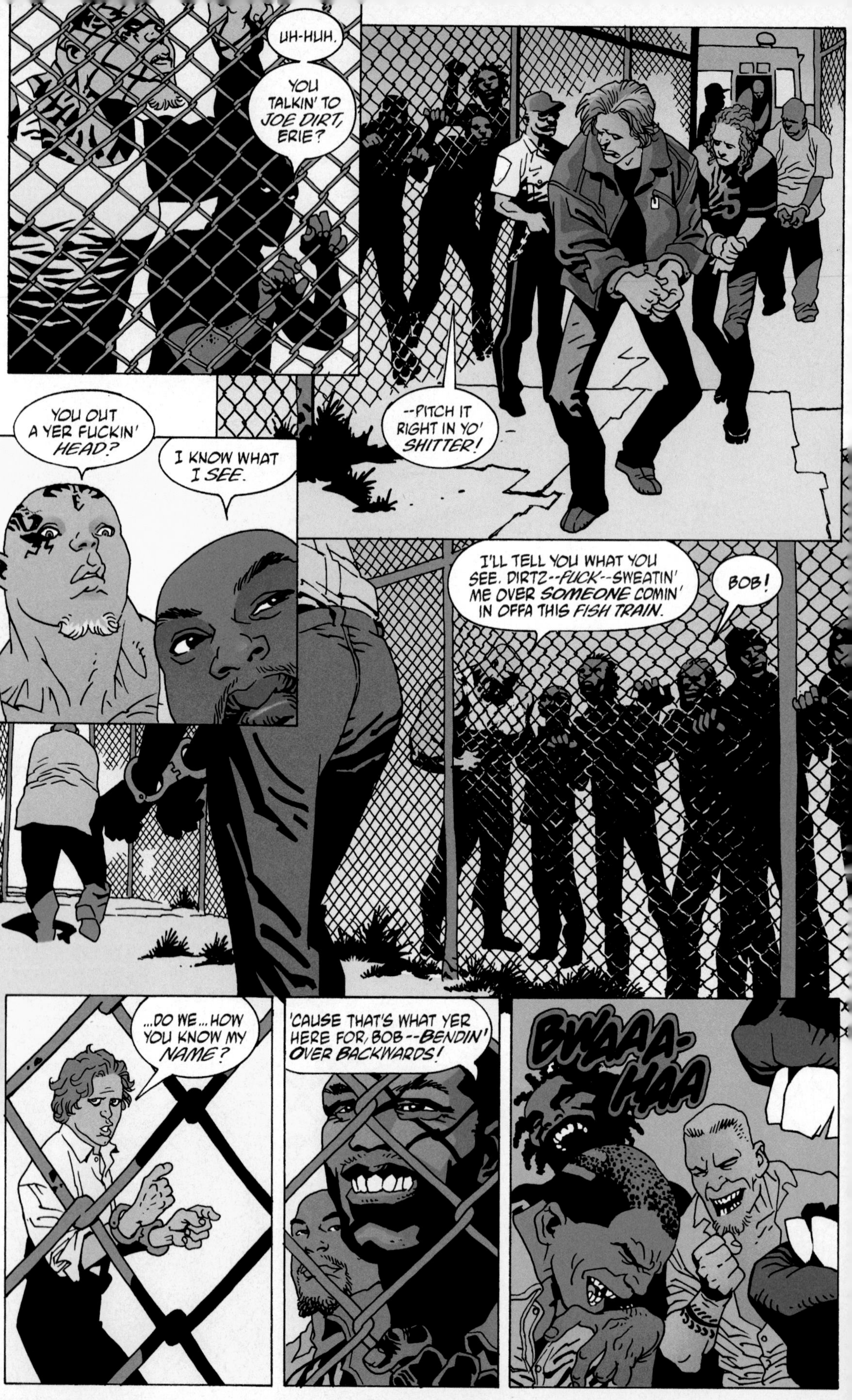
UH-HUH.
YOU TALKIN' TO JOE DIRT, ERIE?
--PITCH IT RIGHT IN YO' SHITTER!
YOU OUT A YER FUCKIN' HEAD?
I KNOW WHAT I SEE.
I'LL TELL YOU WHAT YOU SEE. DIRTZ--FUCK--SWEATIN' ME OVER SOMEONE COMIN' IN OFFA THIS FISH TRAIN.
BOB!
...DO WE... HOW YOU KNOW MY NAME?
'CAUSE THAT'S WHAT YER HERE FOR, BOB--BENDIN' OVER BACKWARDS!
BWAAA-HAA

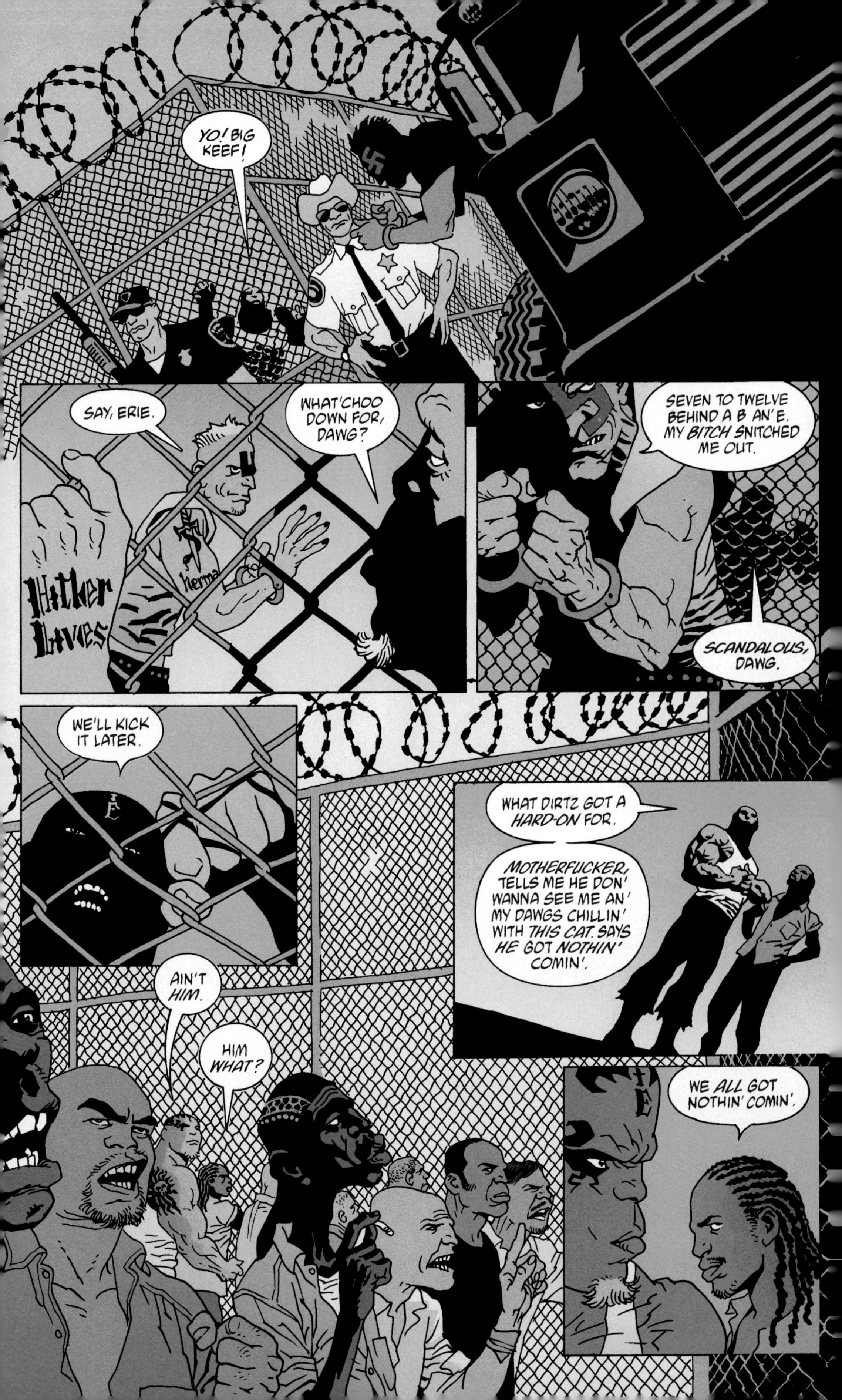
YO! BIG KEEF!
SAY, ERIE.
WHAT'CHOO DOWN FOR, DAWG?
SEVEN TO TWELVE BEHIND A B AN' E. MY BITCH SNITCHED ME OUT.
SCANDALOUS, DAWG.
Hitler Lives
WE'LL KICK IT LATER.
WHAT DIRTZ GOT A HARD-ON FOR.
MOTHERFUCKER, TELLS ME HE DON' WANNA SEE ME AN' MY DAWGS CHILLIN' WITH THIS CAT. SAYS HE GOT NOTHIN' COMIN'.
AIN'T HIM.
HIM WHAT?
WE ALL GOT NOTHIN' COMIN'.

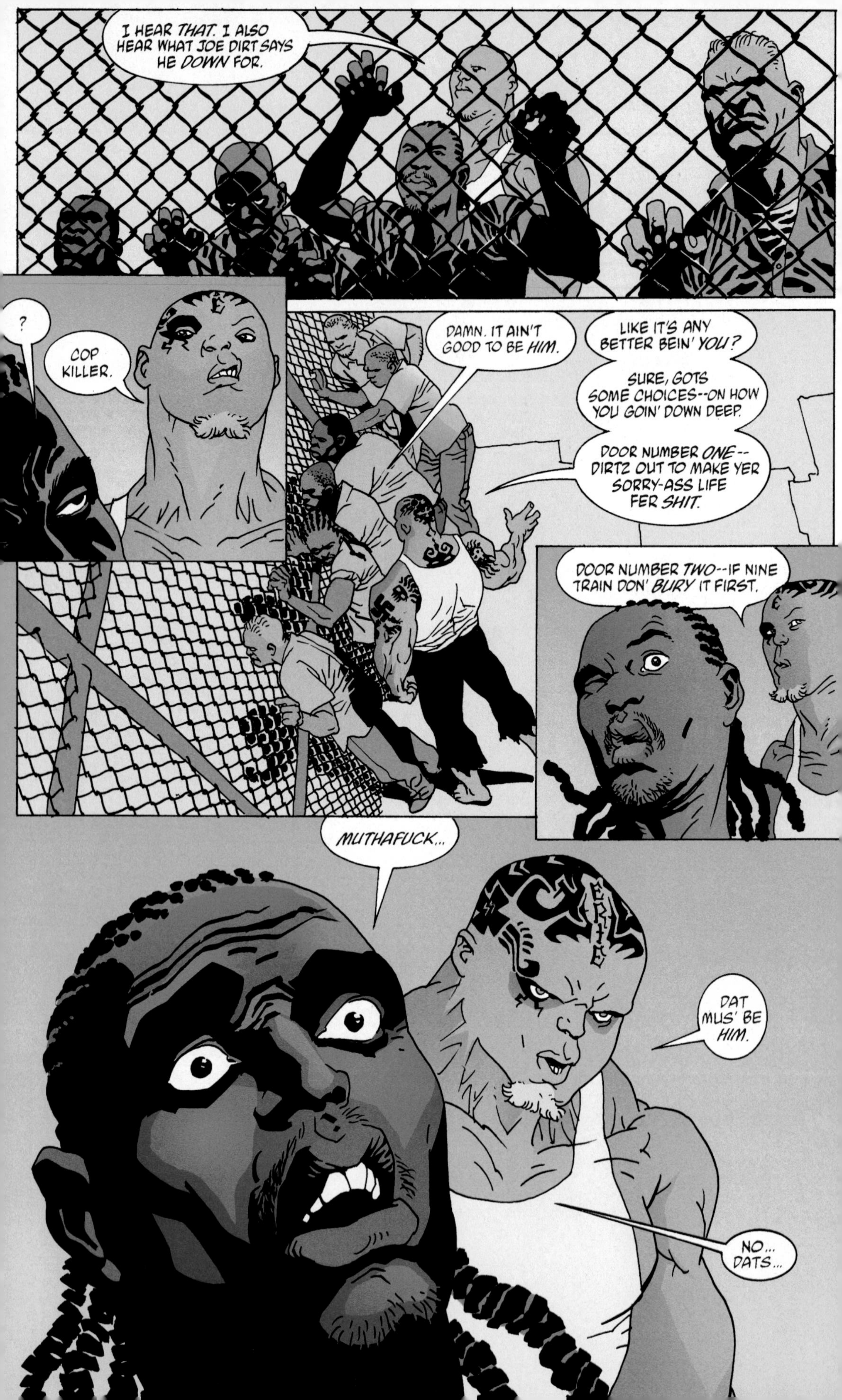
I HEAR *THAT.* I ALSO HEAR WHAT JOE DIRT SAYS HE *DOWN* FOR.
?
COP KILLER.
DAMN. IT AIN'T GOOD TO BE *HIM.*
LIKE IT'S ANY BETTER BEIN' *YOU?*
SURE, GOTS SOME CHOICES--ON HOW YOU GOIN' DOWN DEEP.
DOOR NUMBER *ONE*-- DIRTZ OUT TO MAKE YER SORRY-ASS LIFE FER *SHIT.*
DOOR NUMBER *TWO*--IF NINE TRAIN DON' *BURY* IT FIRST.
MUTHAFUCK...
DAT MUS' BE *HIM.*
NO... DATS...

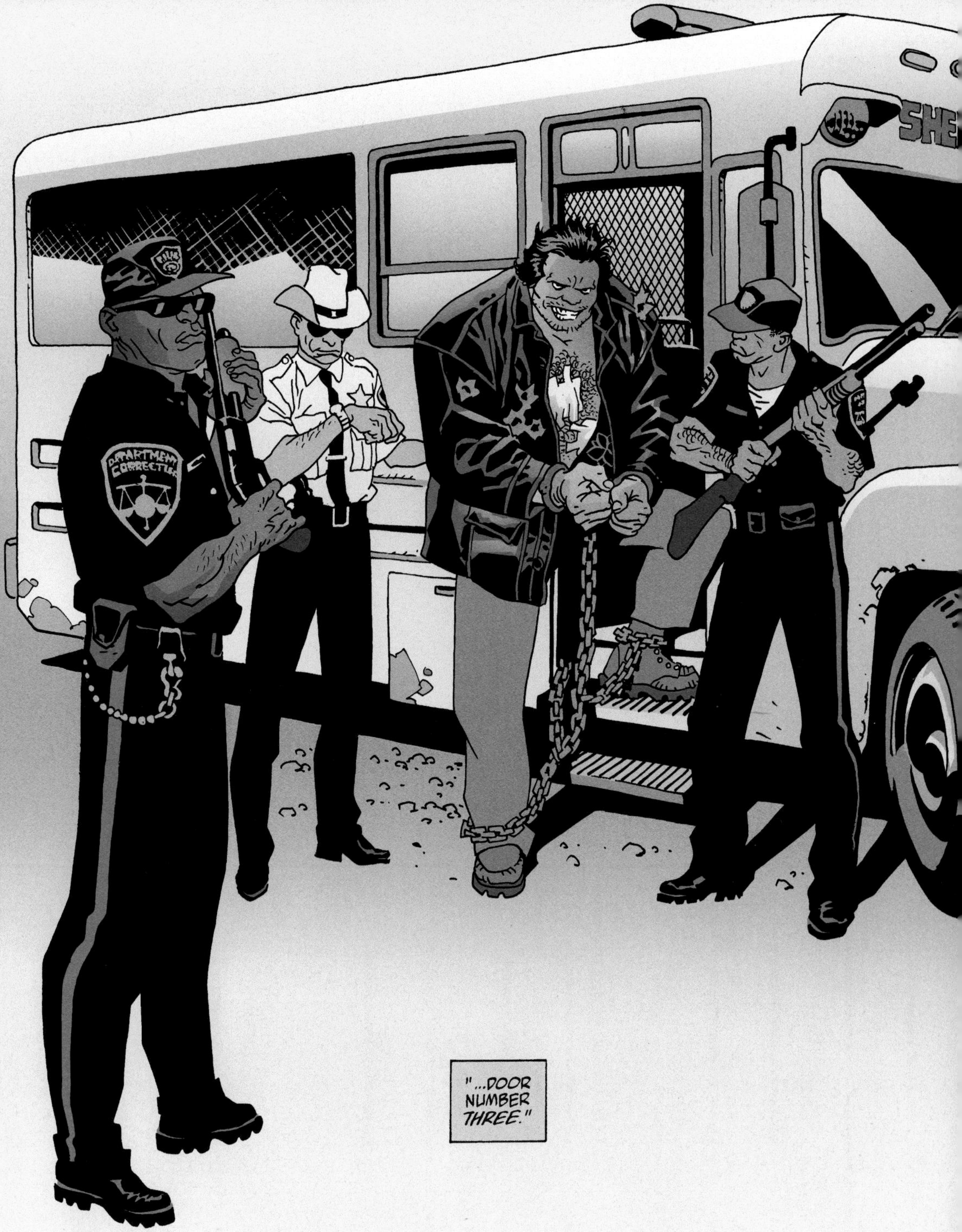
"...DOOR NUMBER THREE."

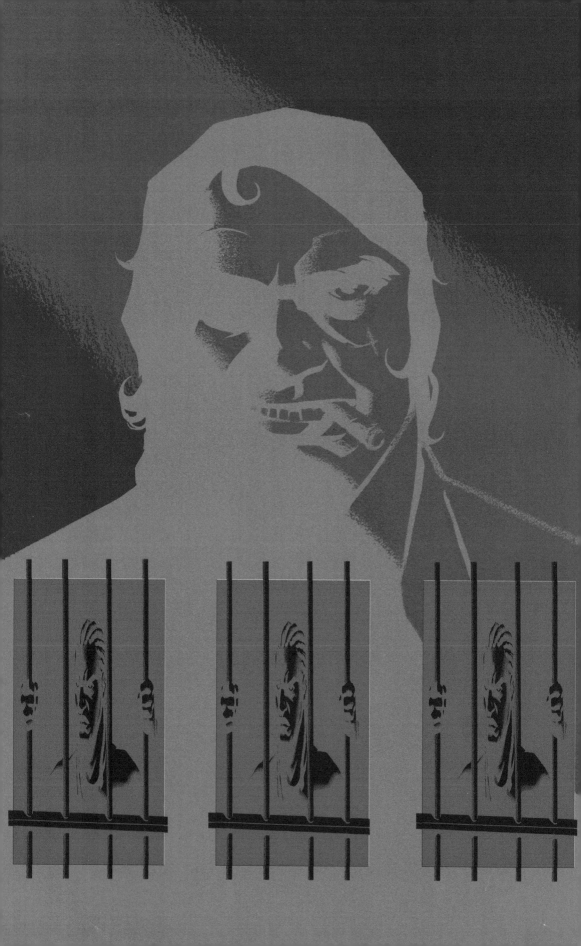

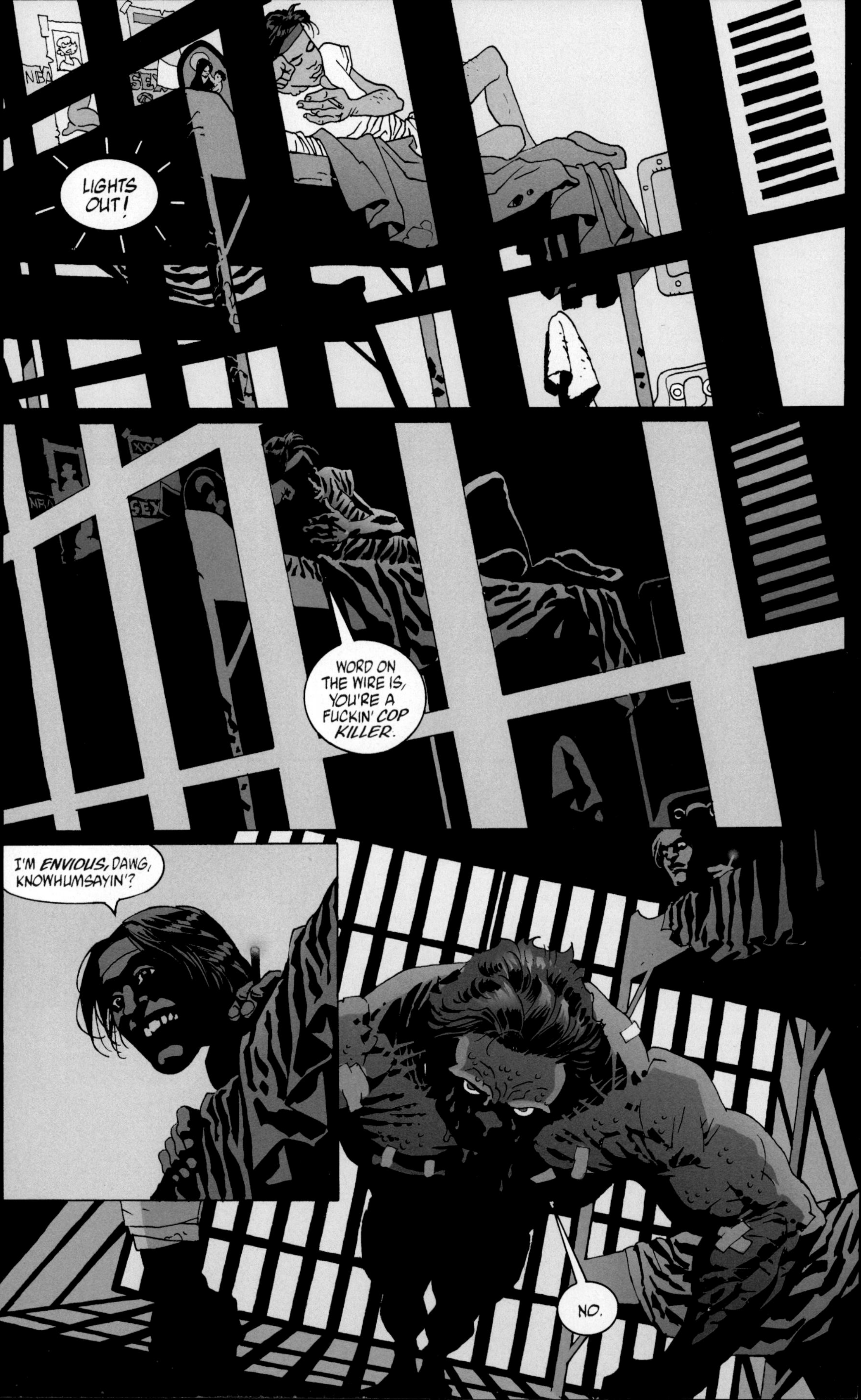
LIGHTS OUT!
WORD ON THE WIRE IS, YOU'RE A FUCKIN' COP KILLER.
I'M ENVIOUS, DAWG, KNOWHUMSAYIN'?
NO.

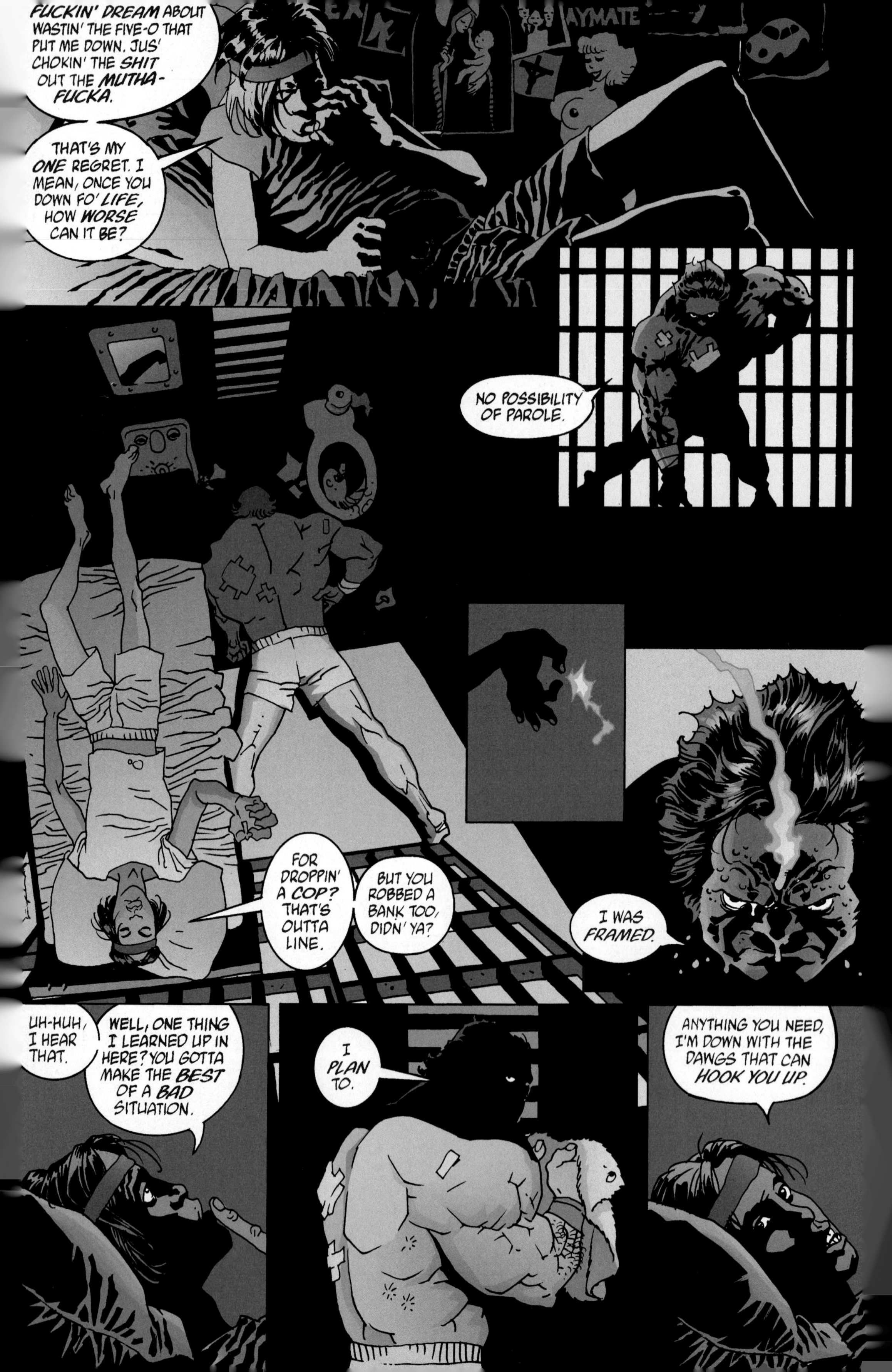

FUCKIN' DREAM ABOUT WASTIN' THE FIVE-O THAT PUT ME DOWN. JUS' CHOKIN' THE SHIT OUT THE MUTHA-FUCKA.
THAT'S MY ONE REGRET. I MEAN, ONCE YOU DOWN FO' LIFE, HOW WORSE CAN IT BE?
AYMATE
NO POSSIBILITY OF PAROLE.
FOR DROPPIN' A COP? THAT'S OUTTA LINE.
BUT YOU ROBBED A BANK TOO, DIDN' YA?
I WAS FRAMED.
UH-HUH, I HEAR THAT.
WELL, ONE THING I LEARNED UP IN HERE? YOU GOTTA MAKE THE BEST OF A BAD SITUATION.
I PLAN TO.
ANYTHING YOU NEED, I'M DOWN WITH THE DAWGS THAT CAN HOOK YOU UP.

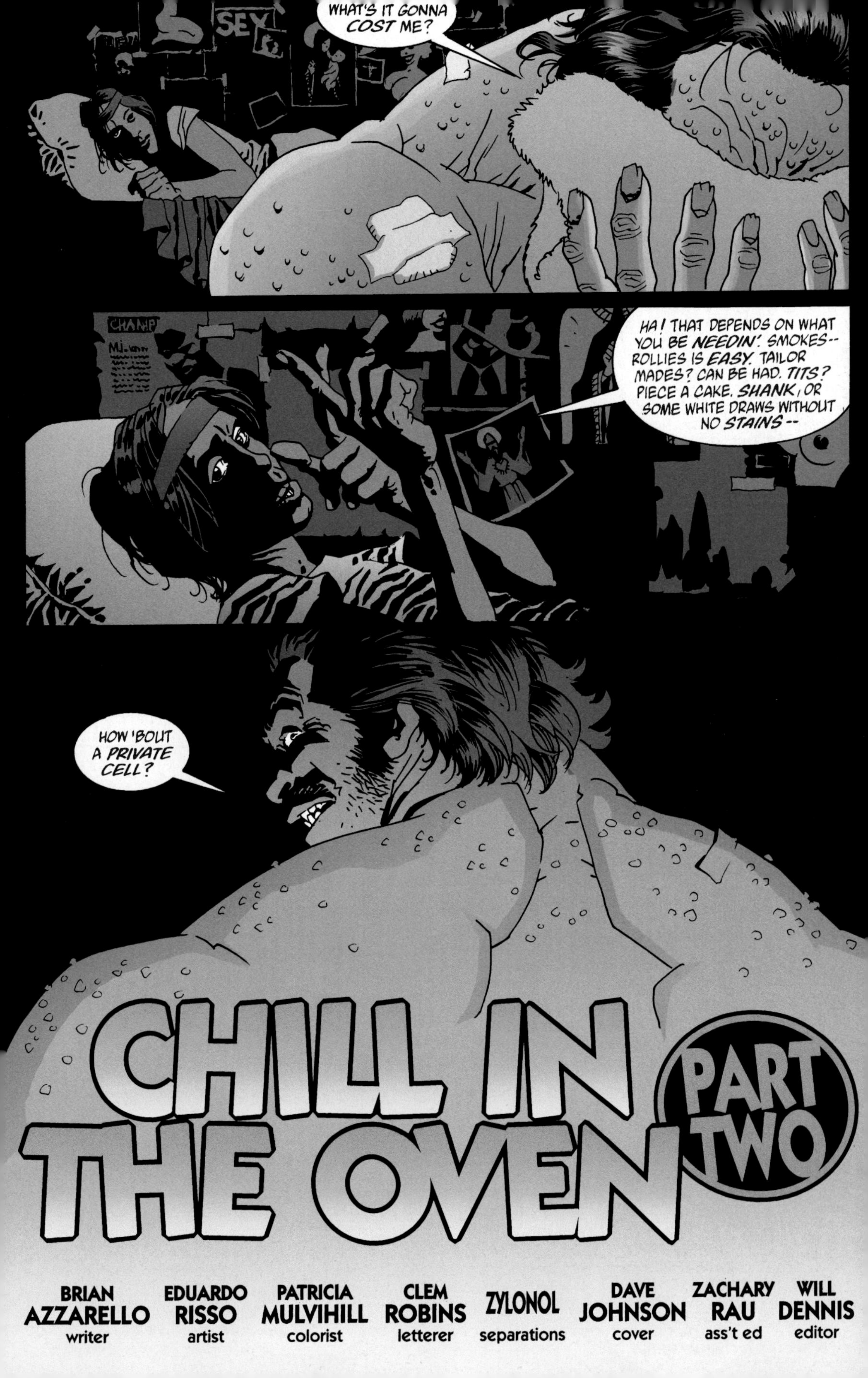
WHAT'S IT GONNA COST ME?
HA! THAT DEPENDS ON WHAT YOU BE NEEDIN'. SMOKES--ROLLIES IS EASY. TAILOR MADES? CAN BE HAD. TITS? PIECE A CAKE. SHANK, OR SOME WHITE DRAWS WITHOUT NO STAINS--
HOW 'BOUT A PRIVATE CELL?
CHILL IN THE OVEN
PART TWO
BRIAN AZZARELLO writer
EDUARDO RISSO artist
PATRICIA MULVIHILL colorist
CLEM ROBINS letterer
ZYLONOL separations
DAVE JOHNSON cover
ZACHARY RAU ass't ed
WILL DENNIS editor

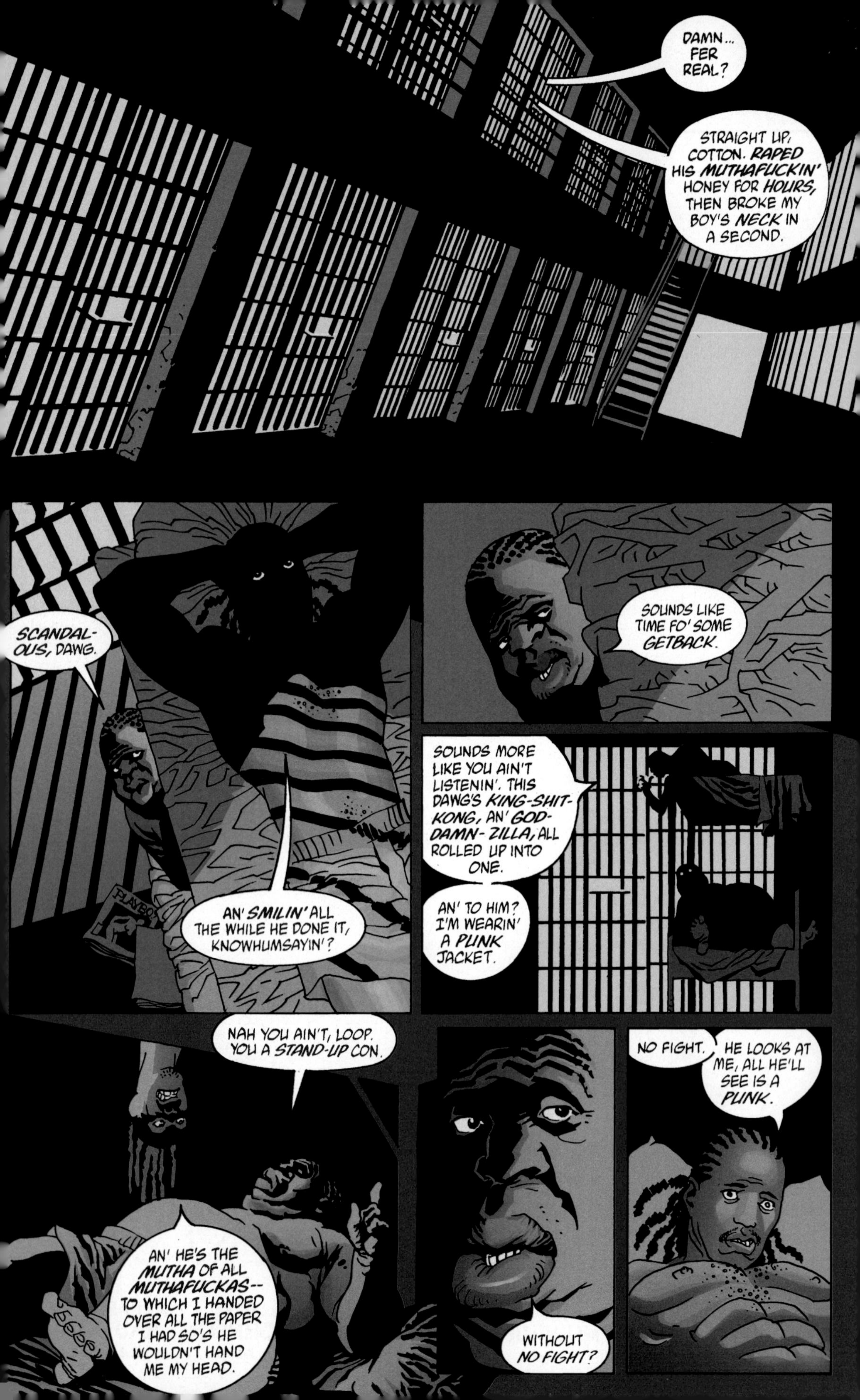
DAMN... FER REAL?
STRAIGHT UP, COTTON. RAPED HIS MUTHAFUCKIN' HONEY FOR HOURS, THEN BROKE MY BOY'S NECK IN A SECOND.
SCANDAL-OUS, DAWG.
AN' SMILIN' ALL THE WHILE HE DONE IT, KNOWHUMSAYIN'?
PLAYBOY
SOUNDS LIKE TIME FO' SOME GETBACK.
SOUNDS MORE LIKE YOU AIN'T LISTENIN'. THIS DAWG'S KING-SHIT-KONG, AN' GOD-DAMN-ZILLA, ALL ROLLED UP INTO ONE.
AN' TO HIM? I'M WEARIN' A PUNK JACKET.
NAH YOU AIN'T, LOOP. YOU A STAND-UP CON.
AN' HE'S THE MUTHA OF ALL MUTHAFUCKAS-- TO WHICH I HANDED OVER ALL THE PAPER I HAD SO'S HE WOULDN'T HAND ME MY HEAD.
WITHOUT NO FIGHT?
NO FIGHT.
HE LOOKS AT ME, ALL HE'LL SEE IS A PUNK.

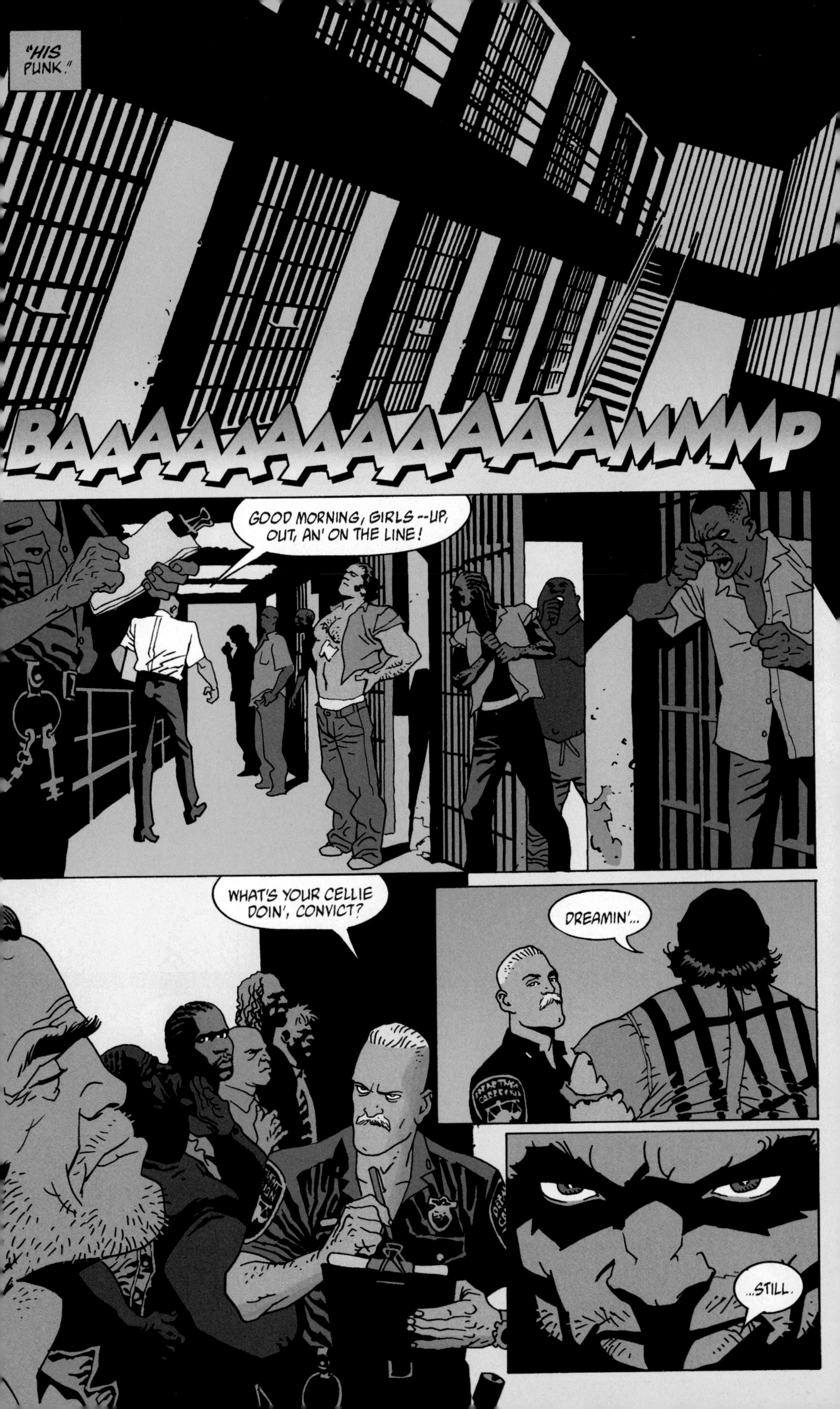
"HIS PUNK."
BAAAAAAAAAAAAAAMMMP
GOOD MORNING, GIRLS --UP, OUT, AN' ON THE LINE!
WHAT'S YOUR CELLIE DOIN', CONVICT?
DREAMIN'...
...STILL.

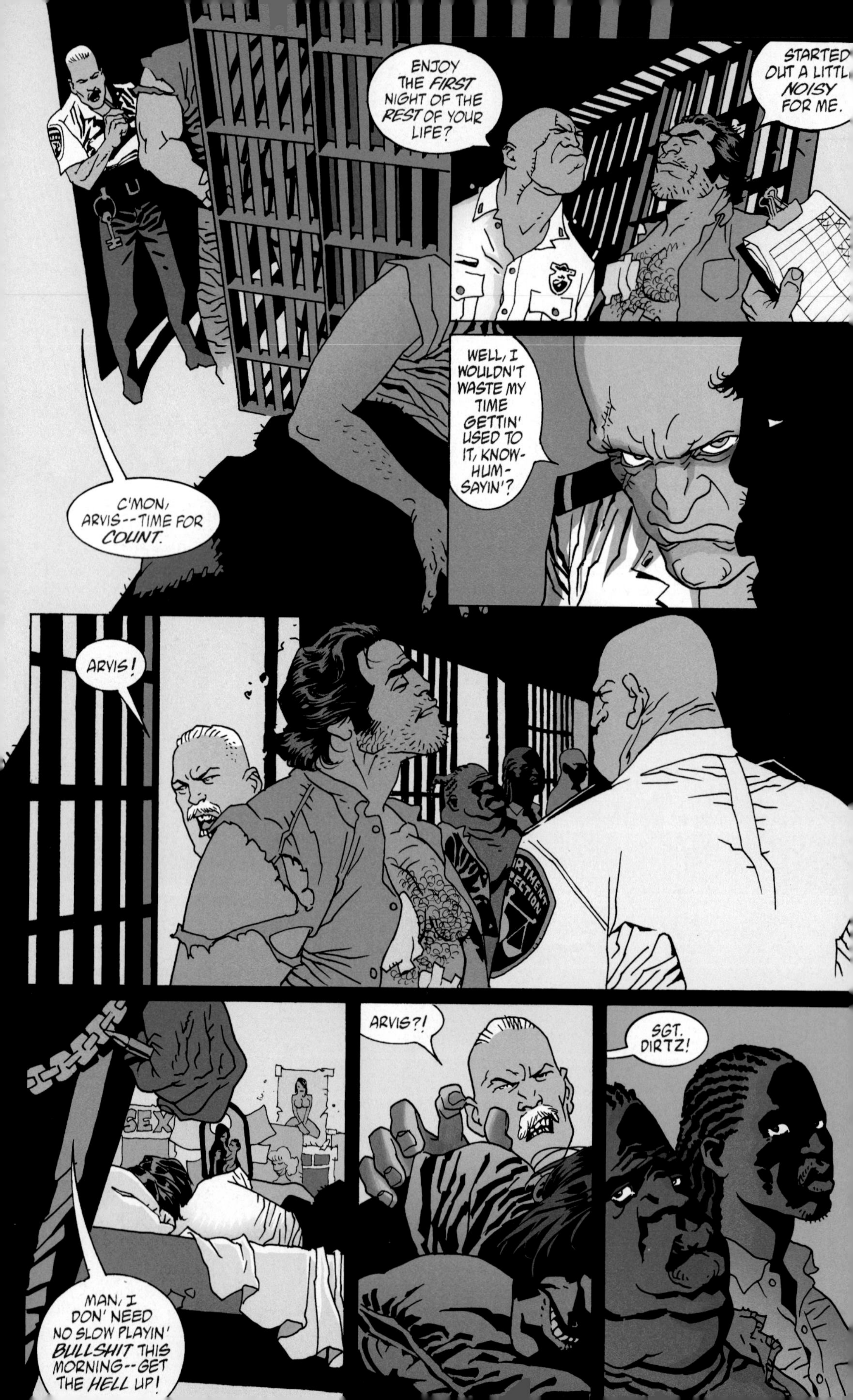

ENJOY THE FIRST NIGHT OF THE REST OF YOUR LIFE?
STARTED OUT A LITTL NOISY FOR ME.
WELL, I WOULDN'T WASTE MY TIME GETTIN' USED TO IT, KNOW-HUM-SAYIN'?
C'MON, ARVIS--TIME FOR COUNT.
ARVIS!
SEX
ARVIS?!
SGT. DIRTZ!
MAN, I DON' NEED NO SLOW PLAYIN' BULLSHIT THIS MORNING--GET THE HELL UP!

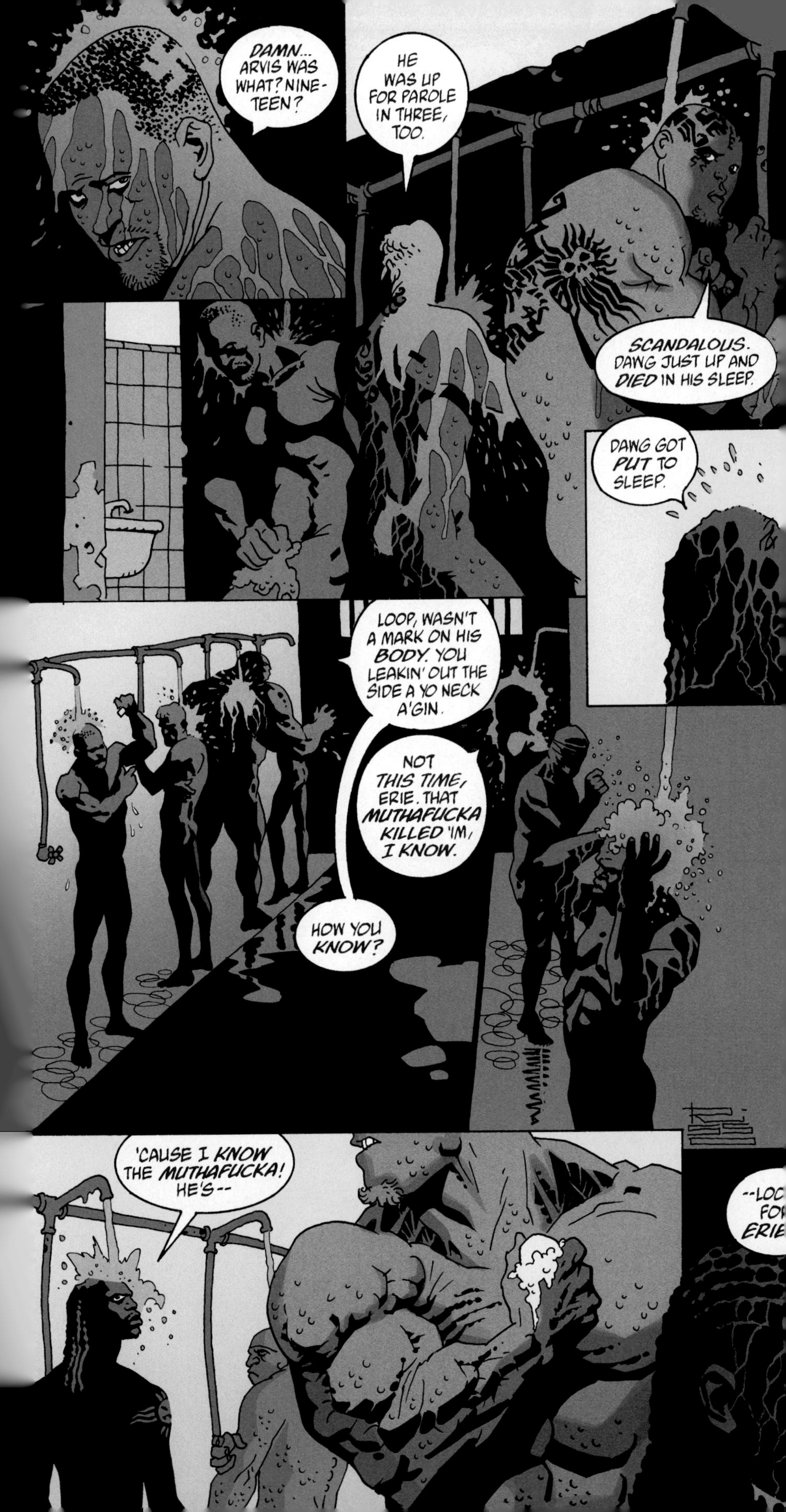
DAMN... ARVIS WAS WHAT? NINE-TEEN?
HE WAS UP FOR PAROLE IN THREE, TOO.
SCANDALOUS. DAWG JUST UP AND DIED IN HIS SLEEP.
DAWG GOT PUT TO SLEEP.
LOOP, WASN'T A MARK ON HIS BODY. YOU LEAKIN' OUT THE SIDE A YO NECK A'GIN.
NOT THIS TIME, ERIE. THAT MUTHAFUCKA KILLED 'IM, I KNOW.
HOW YOU KNOW?
'CAUSE I KNOW THE MUTHAFUCKA! HE'S--
--LOO FOR ERIE

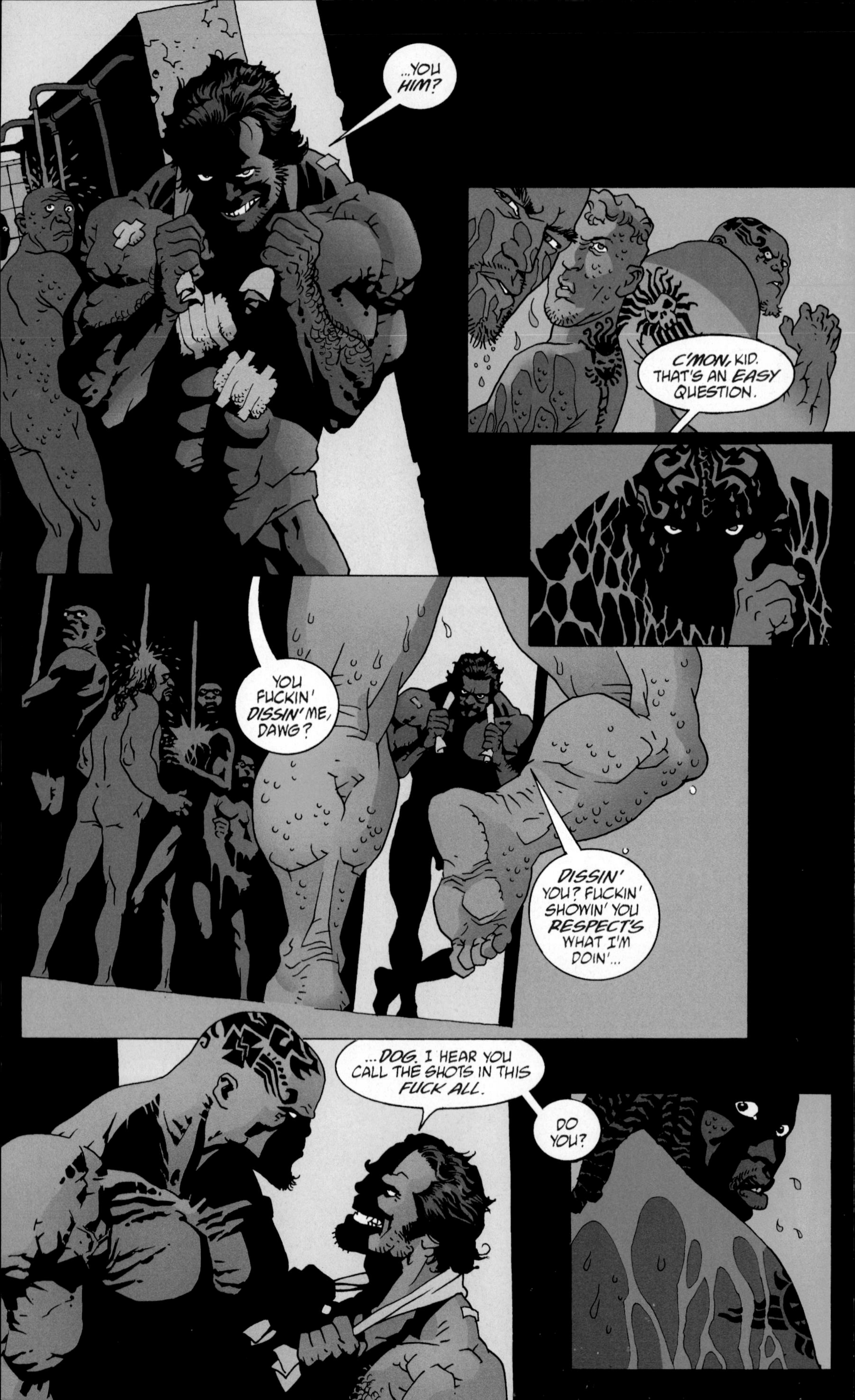
...YOU HIM?
C'MON, KID. THAT'S AN EASY QUESTION.
YOU FUCKIN' DISSIN' ME, DAWG?
DISSIN' YOU? FUCKIN' SHOWIN' YOU RESPECT'S WHAT I'M DOIN'...
...DOG. I HEAR YOU CALL THE SHOTS IN THIS FUCK ALL.
DO YOU?

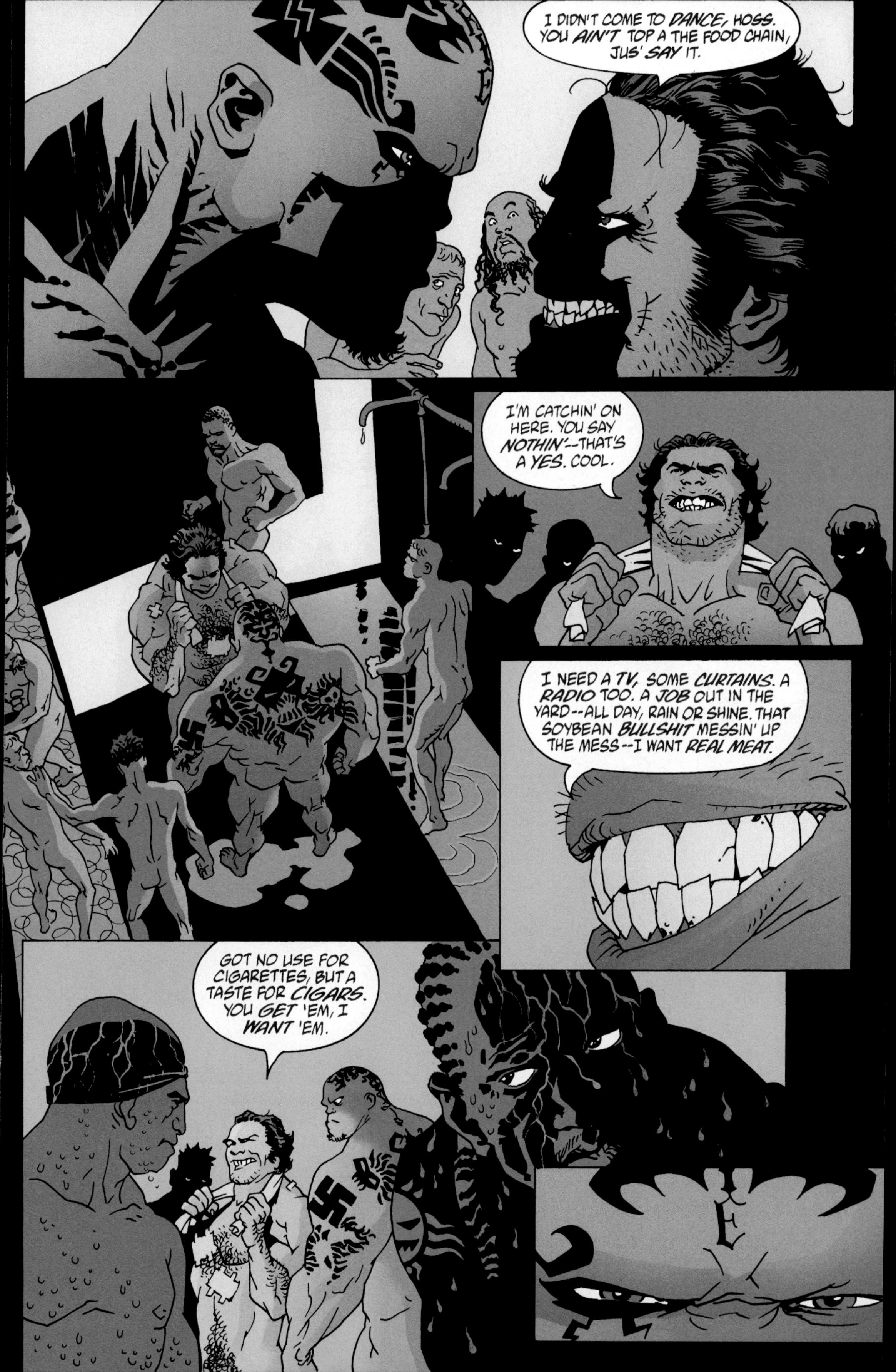
I DIDN'T COME TO DANCE, HOSS. YOU AIN'T TOP A THE FOOD CHAIN, JUS' SAY IT.
I'M CATCHIN' ON HERE. YOU SAY NOTHIN'--THAT'S A YES. COOL.
I NEED A TV, SOME CURTAINS. A RADIO TOO. A JOB OUT IN THE YARD--ALL DAY, RAIN OR SHINE. THAT SOYBEAN BULLSHIT MESSIN' UP THE MESS--I WANT REAL MEAT.
GOT NO USE FOR CIGARETTES, BUT A TASTE FOR CIGARS. YOU GET 'EM, I WANT 'EM.

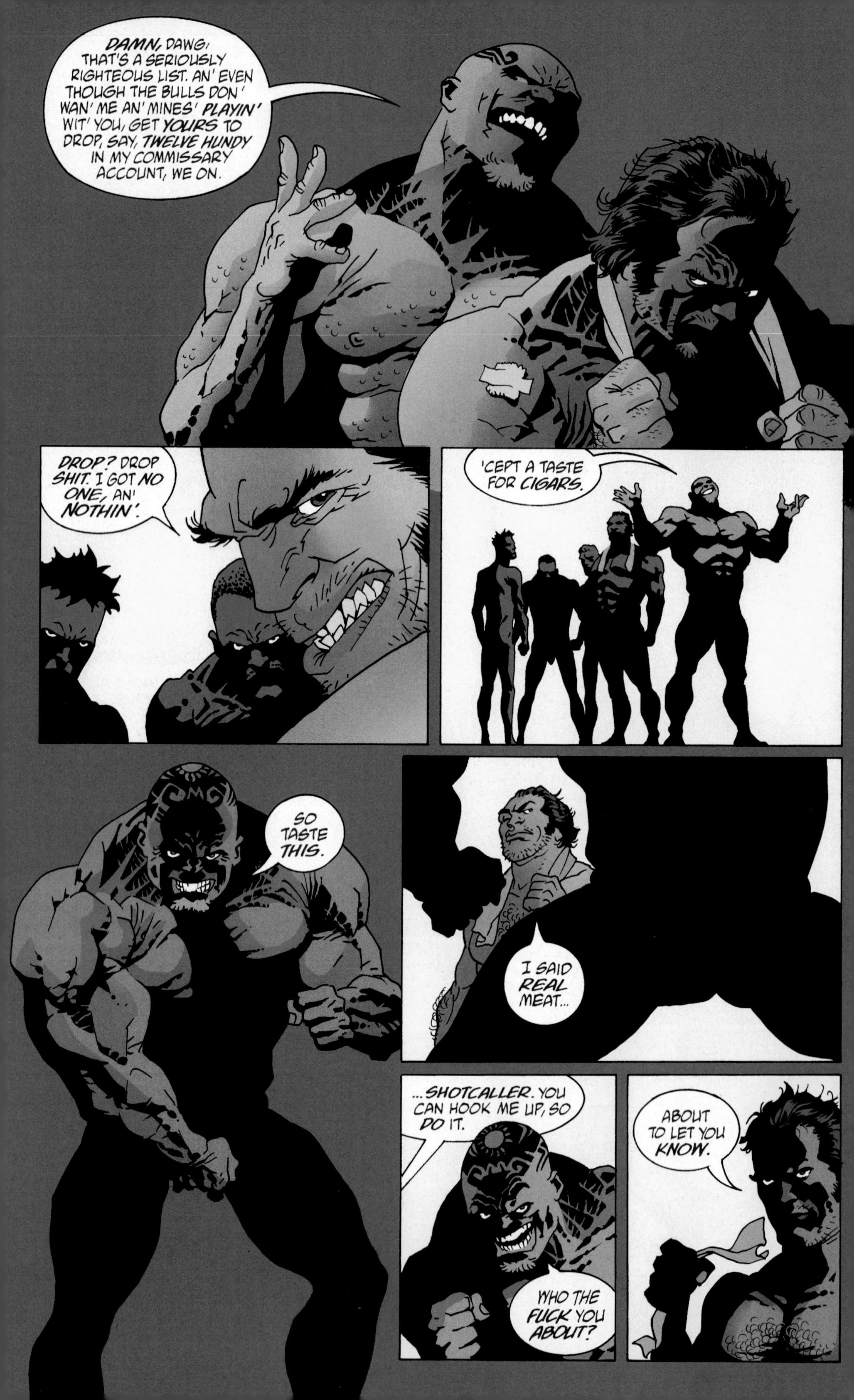
DAMN, DAWG, THAT'S A SERIOUSLY RIGHTEOUS LIST. AN' EVEN THOUGH THE BULLS DON' WAN' ME AN' MINES' PLAYIN' WIT' YOU, GET YOURS TO DROP, SAY, TWELVE HUNDY IN MY COMMISSARY ACCOUNT, WE ON.
DROP? DROP SHIT. I GOT NO ONE, AN' NOTHIN'.
'CEPT A TASTE FOR CIGARS.
SO TASTE THIS.
I SAID REAL MEAT...
...SHOTCALLER. YOU CAN HOOK ME UP, SO DO IT.
WHO THE FUCK YOU ABOUT?
ABOUT TO LET YOU KNOW.

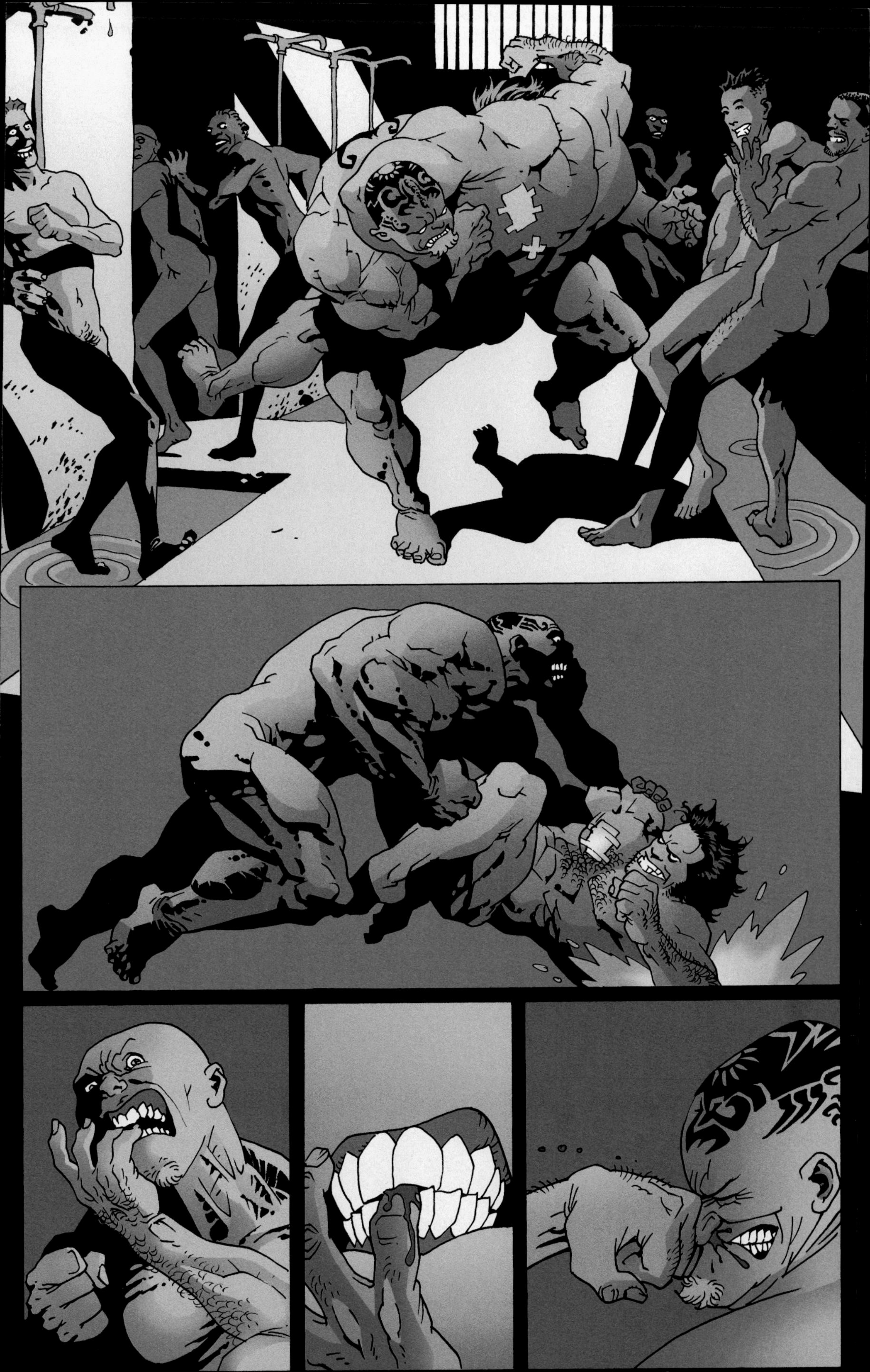

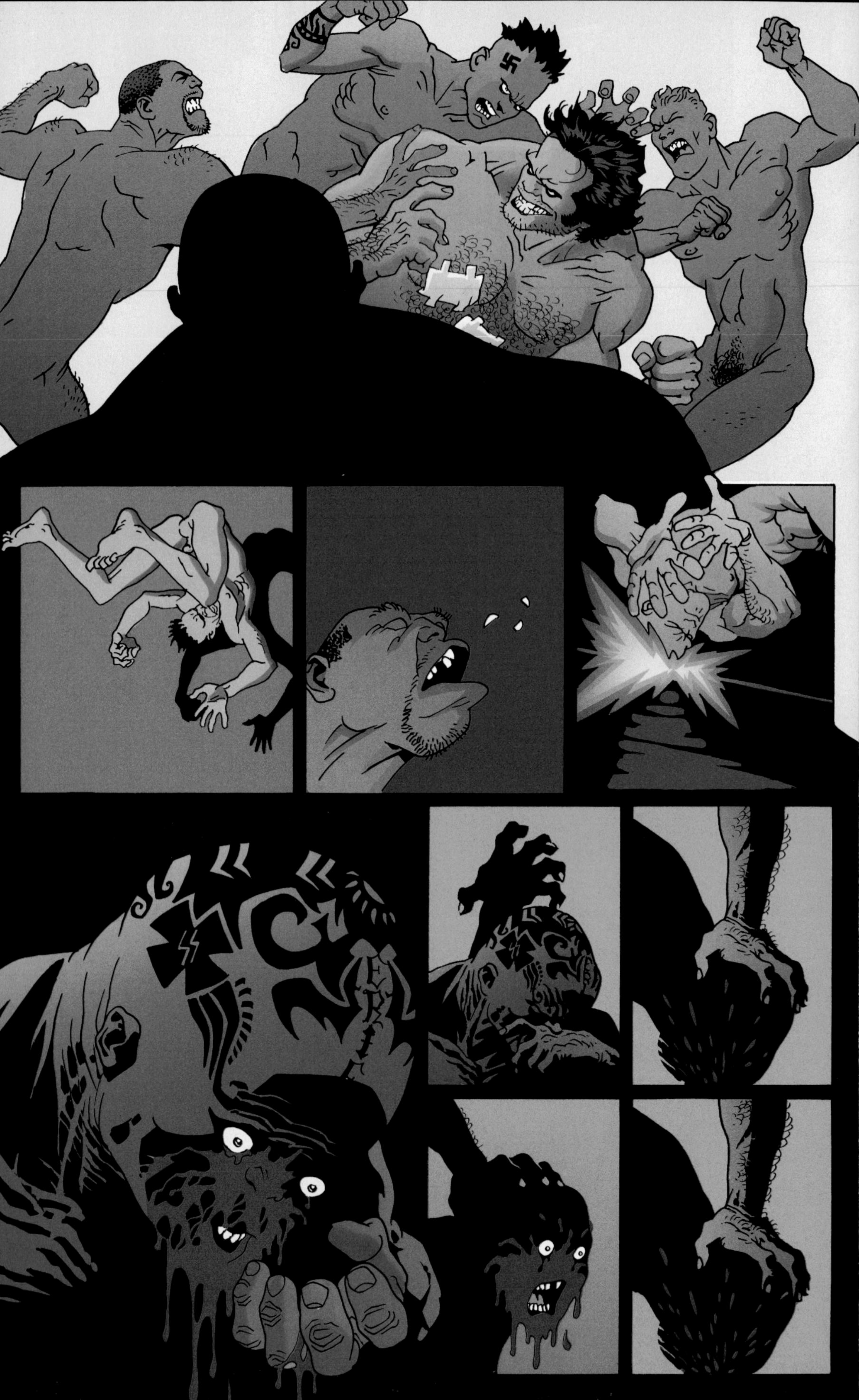

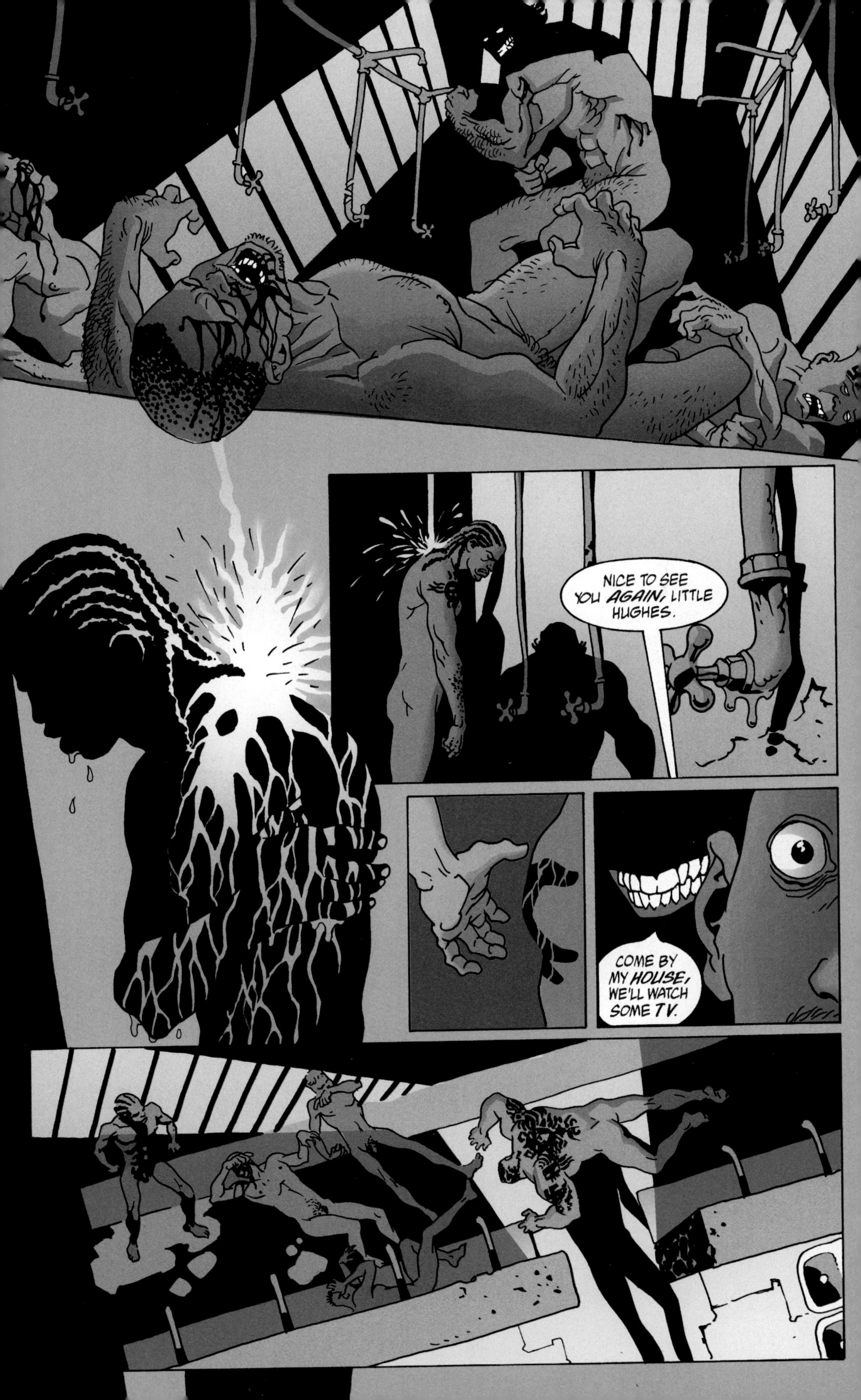
NICE TO SEE YOU AGAIN, LITTLE HUGHES.
COME BY MY HOUSE, WE'LL WATCH SOME TV.

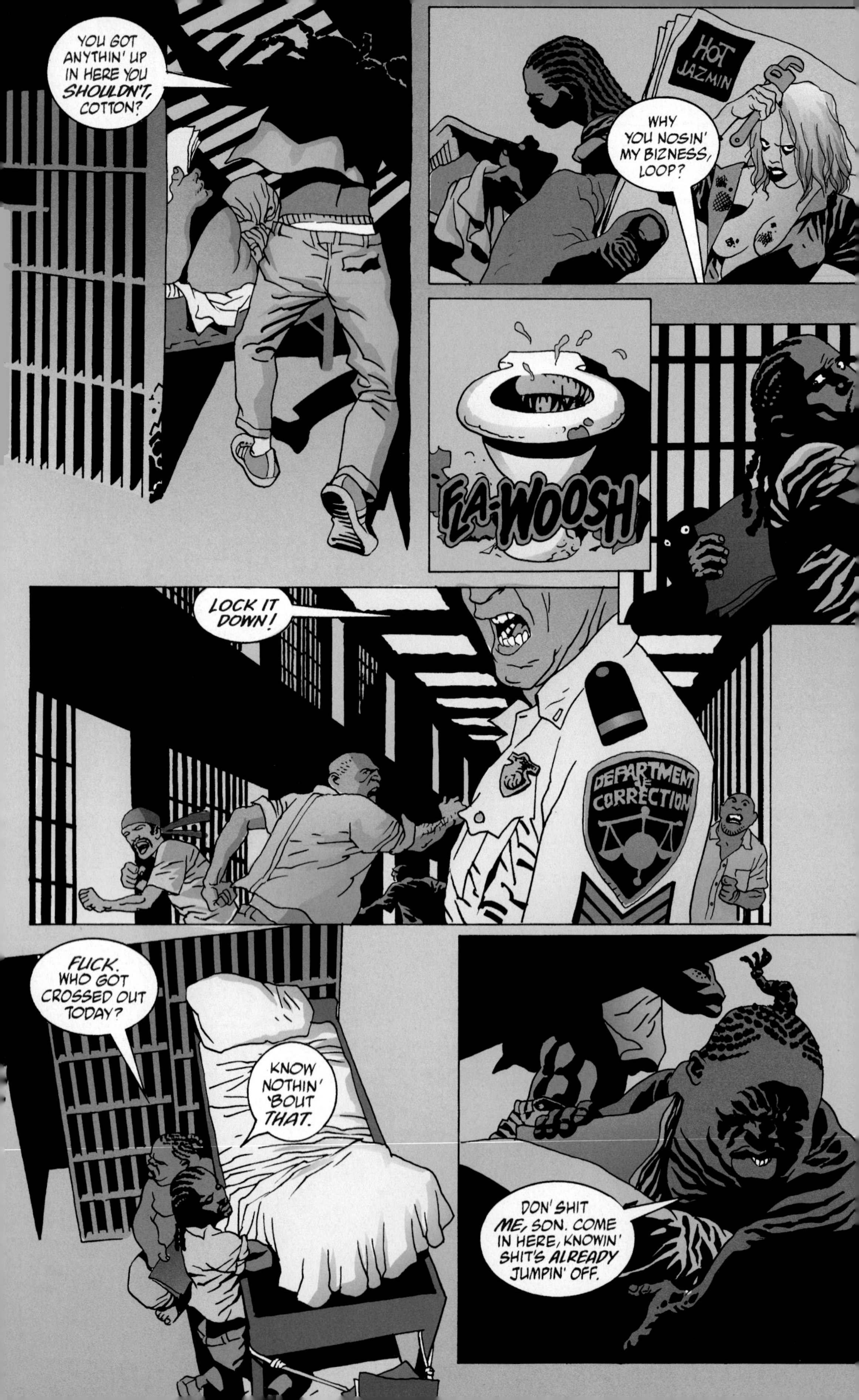
YOU GOT ANYTHIN' UP IN HERE YOU SHOULDN'T, COTTON?
HOT JAZMIN
WHY YOU NOSIN' MY BIZNESS, LOOP?
FLA-WOOSH
LOCK IT DOWN!
DEPARTMENT OF CORRECTION
FUCK. WHO GOT CROSSED OUT TODAY?
KNOW NOTHIN' 'BOUT THAT.
DON' SHIT ME, SON. COME IN HERE, KNOWIN' SHIT'S ALREADY JUMPIN' OFF.

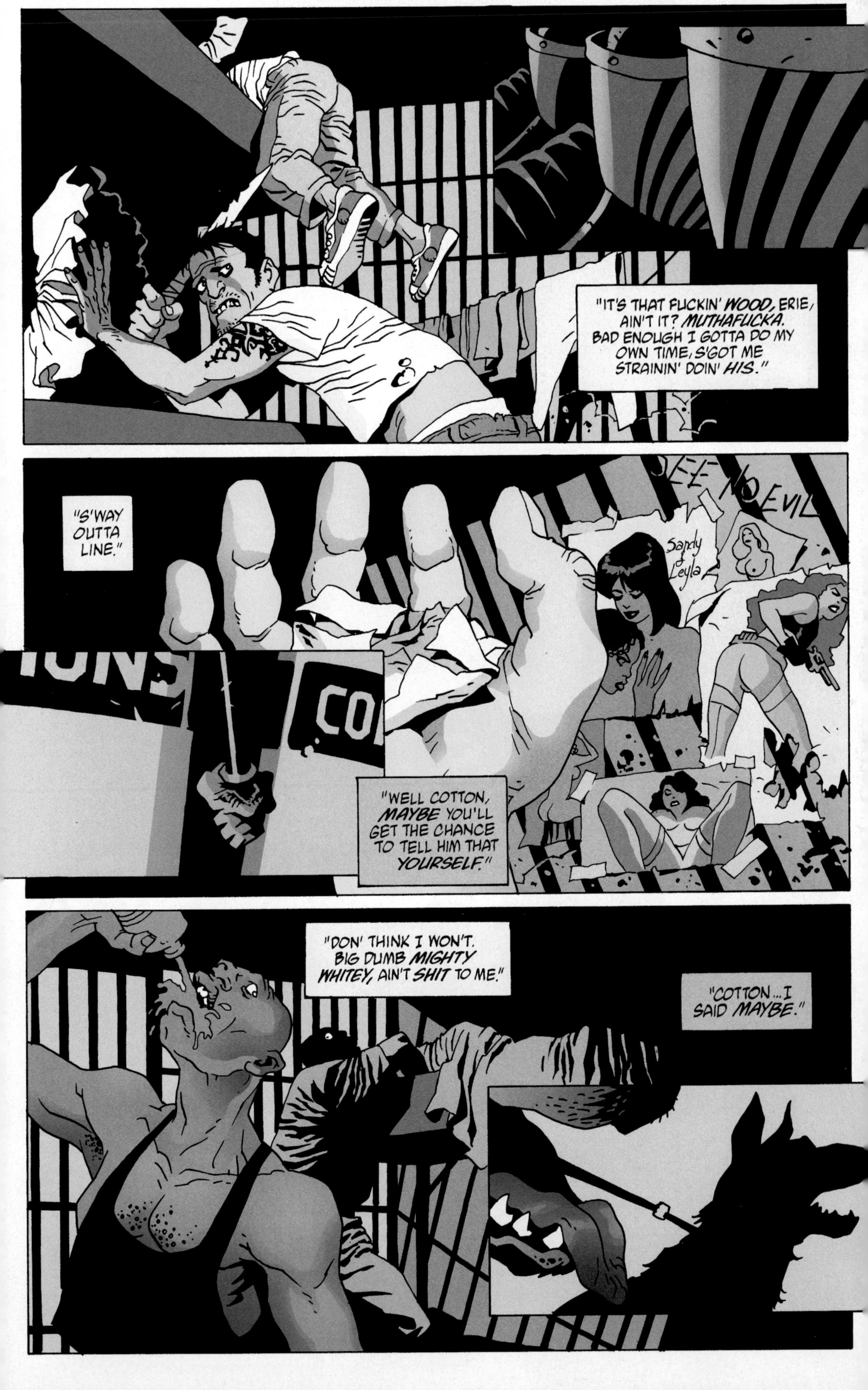
"IT'S THAT FUCKIN' WOOD, ERIE, AIN'T IT? MUTHAFUCKA. BAD ENOUGH I GOTTA DO MY OWN TIME, S'GOT ME STRAININ' DOIN' HIS."
"S'WAY OUTTA LINE."
SEE NO EVIL
Sandy
Leyla
"WELL COTTON, MAYBE YOU'LL GET THE CHANCE TO TELL HIM THAT YOURSELF."
"DON' THINK I WON'T. BIG DUMB MIGHTY WHITEY, AIN'T SHIT TO ME."
"COTTON...I SAID MAYBE."

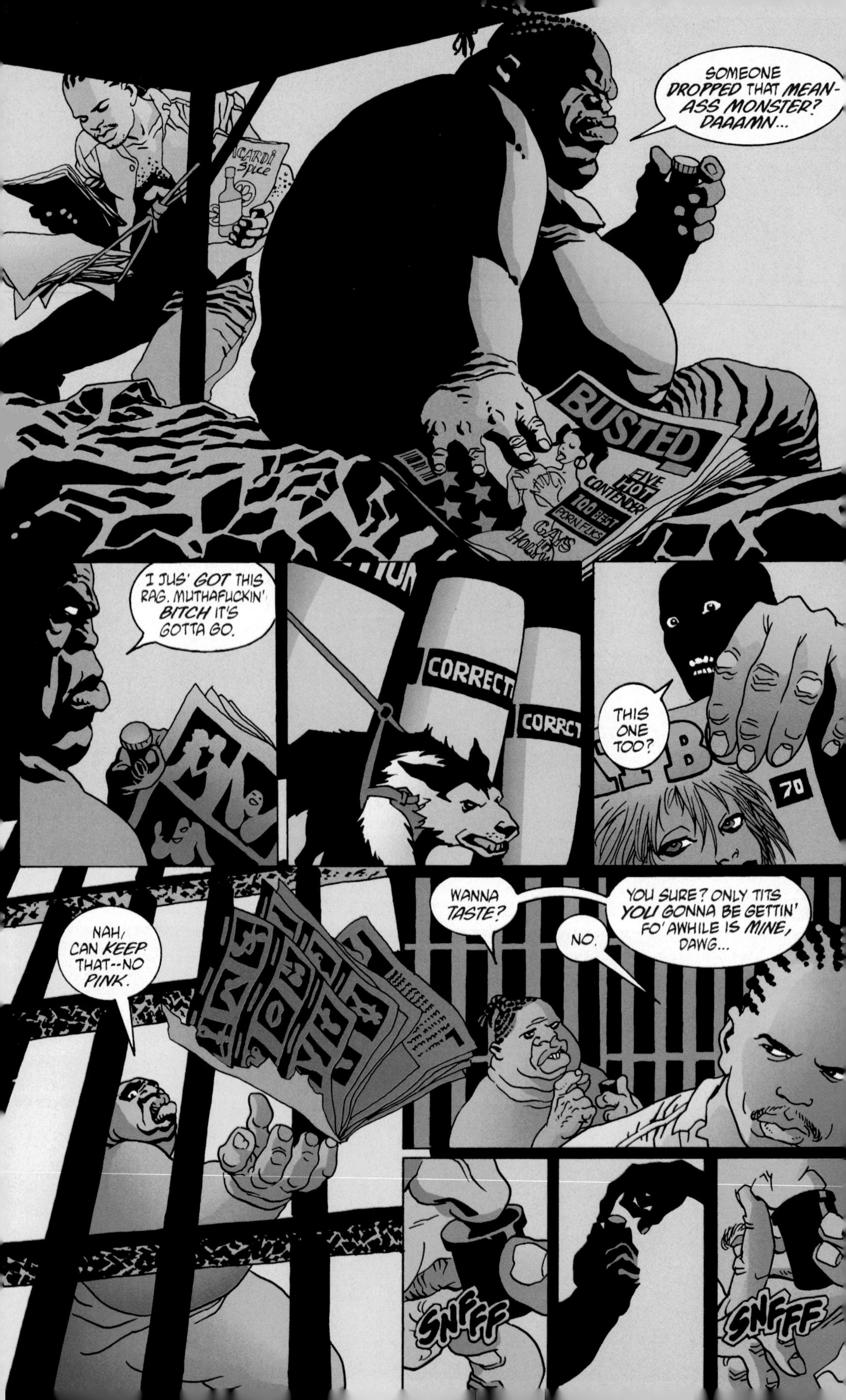
SOMEONE DROPPED THAT MEAN-ASS MONSTER? DAAAMN...
BUSTED
FIVE HOT CONTENDER
100 BEST PORN FUKS
I JUS' GOT THIS RAG. MUTHAFUCKIN' BITCH IT'S GOTTA GO.
CORRECT
CORRCT
THIS ONE TOO?
70
NAH, CAN KEEP THAT--NO PINK.
WANNA TASTE?
NO.
YOU SURE? ONLY TITS YOU GONNA BE GETTIN' FO' AWHILE IS MINE, DAWG...
SNFFF
SNFFF

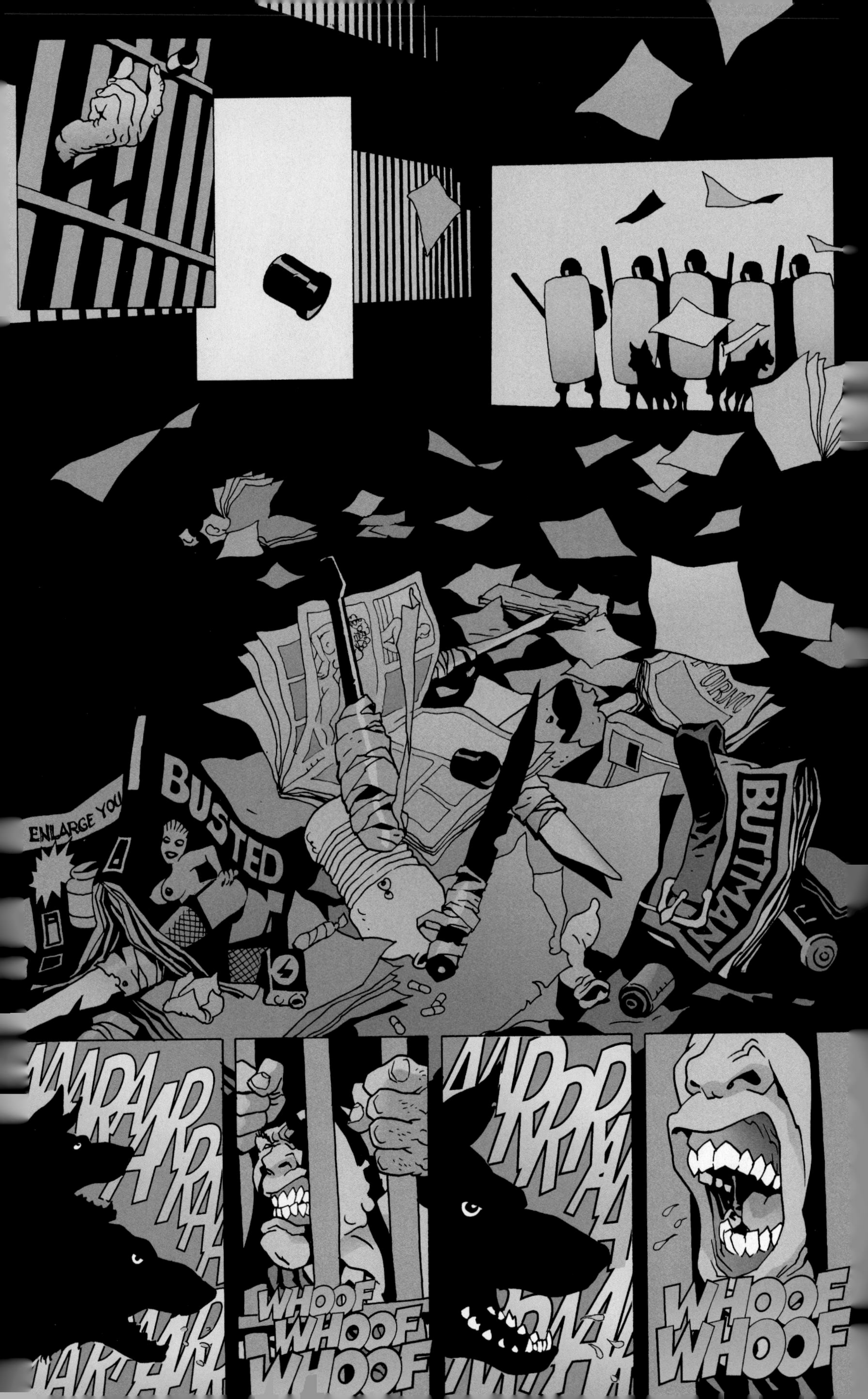

ENLARGE YOU
BUSTED
BUTTMAN
WHOOF
WHOOF
WHOOF
WHOOF
WHOOF

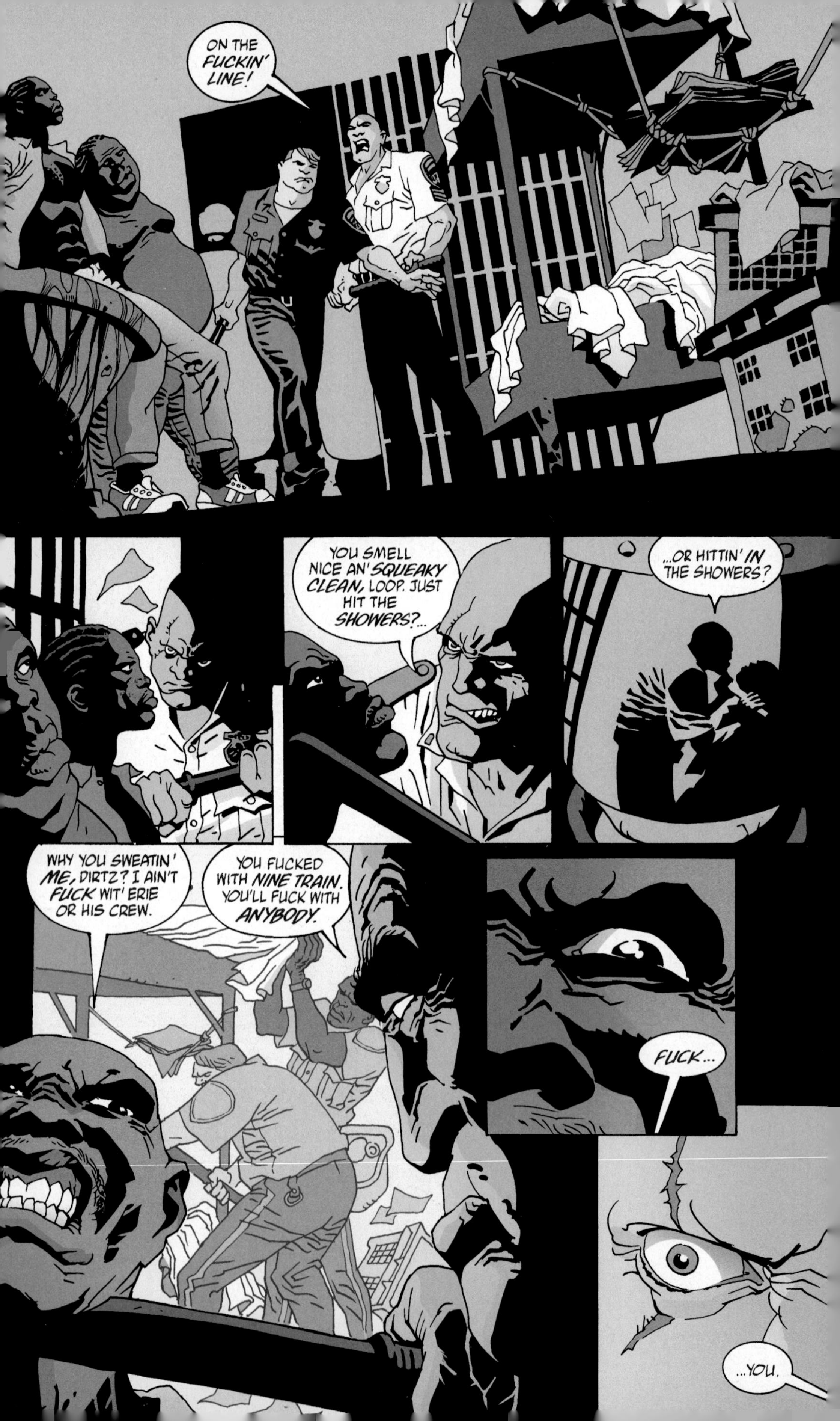
ON THE FUCKIN' LINE!
YOU SMELL NICE AN' SQUEAKY CLEAN, LOOP. JUST HIT THE SHOWERS?...
...OR HITTIN' IN THE SHOWERS?
WHY YOU SWEATIN' ME, DIRTZ? I AIN'T FUCK WIT' ERIE OR HIS CREW.
YOU FUCKED WITH NINE TRAIN. YOU'LL FUCK WITH ANYBODY.
FUCK...
...YOU.

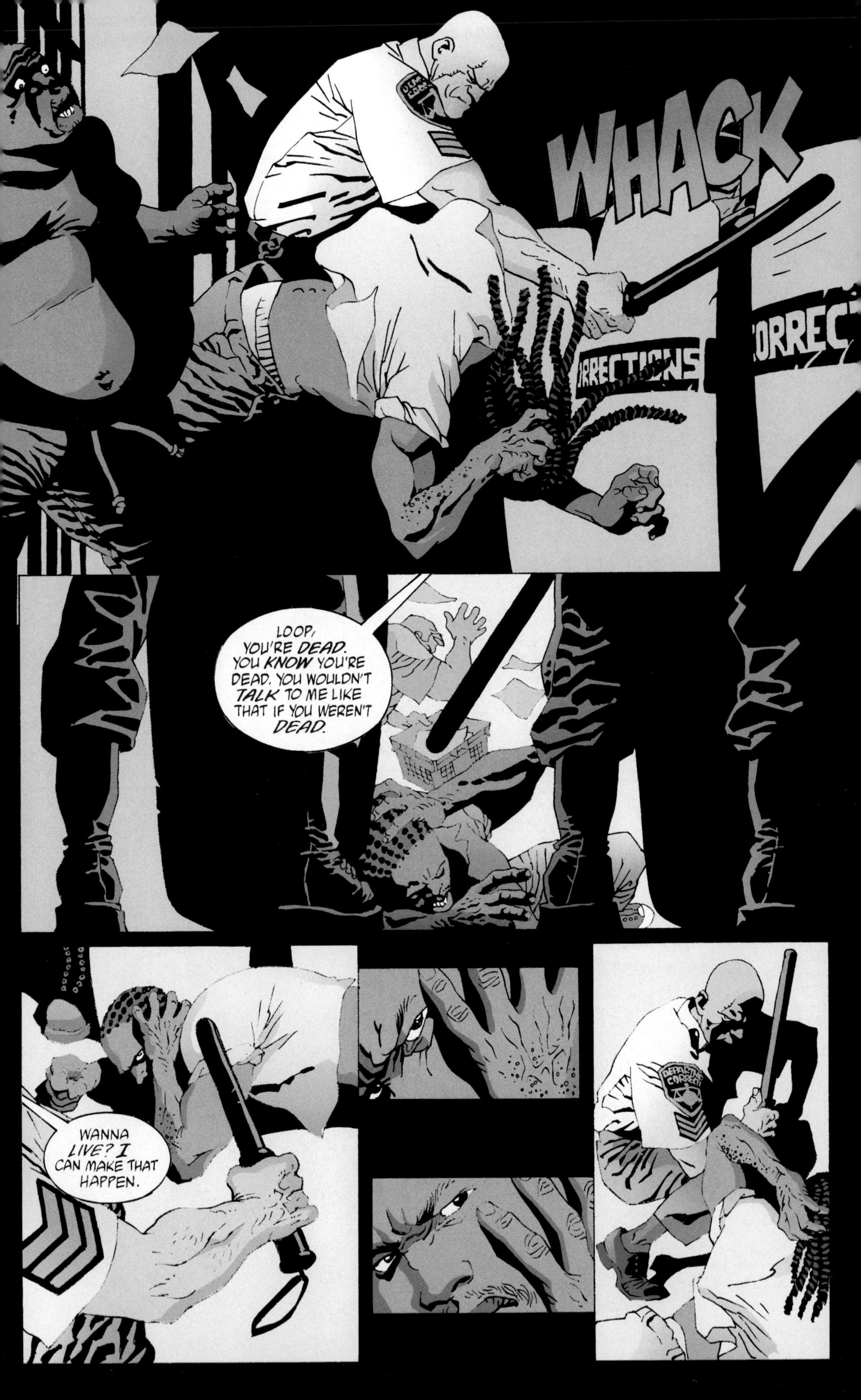
WHACK
RRECTIONS
CORRECT
LOOP, YOU'RE DEAD. YOU KNOW YOU'RE DEAD. YOU WOULDN'T TALK TO ME LIKE THAT IF YOU WEREN'T DEAD.
WANNA LIVE? I CAN MAKE THAT HAPPEN.

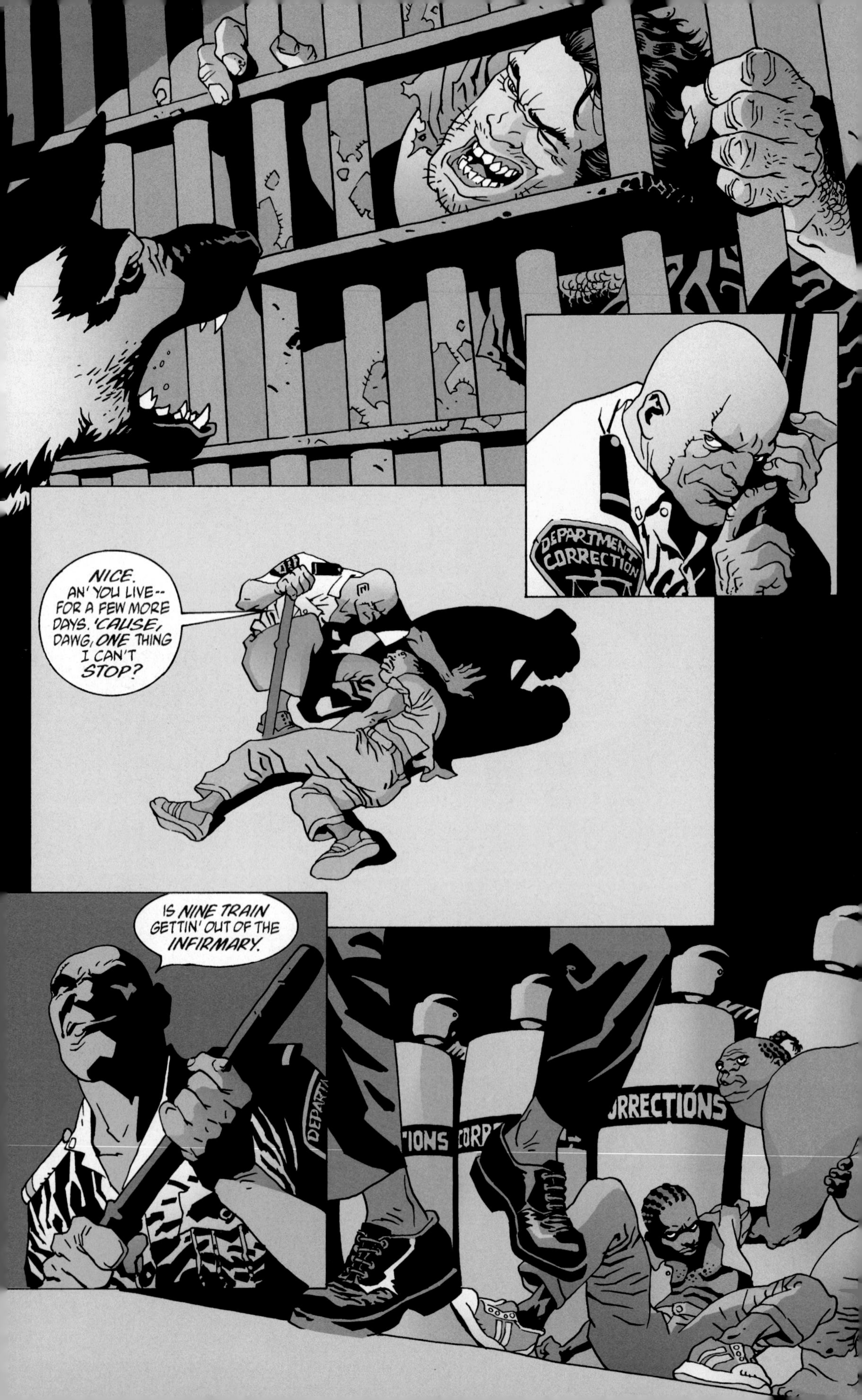
DEPARTMENT CORRECTION
NICE. AN' YOU LIVE-- FOR A FEW MORE DAYS. 'CAUSE, DAWG, ONE THING I CAN'T STOP?
IS NINE TRAIN GETTIN' OUT OF THE INFIRMARY.
CORRECTIONS

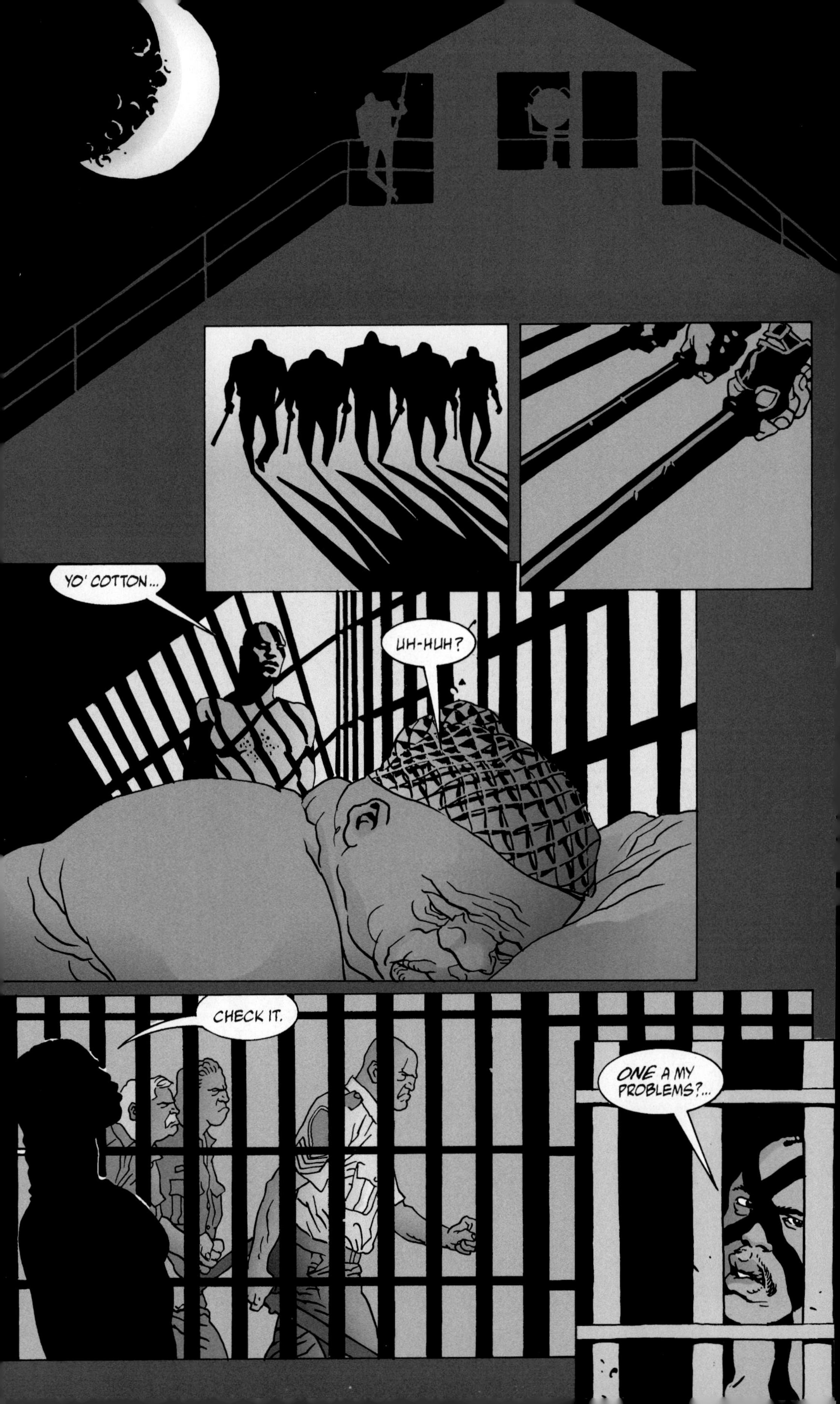
YO' COTTON...
UH-HUH?
CHECK IT.
ONE A MY PROBLEMS?...

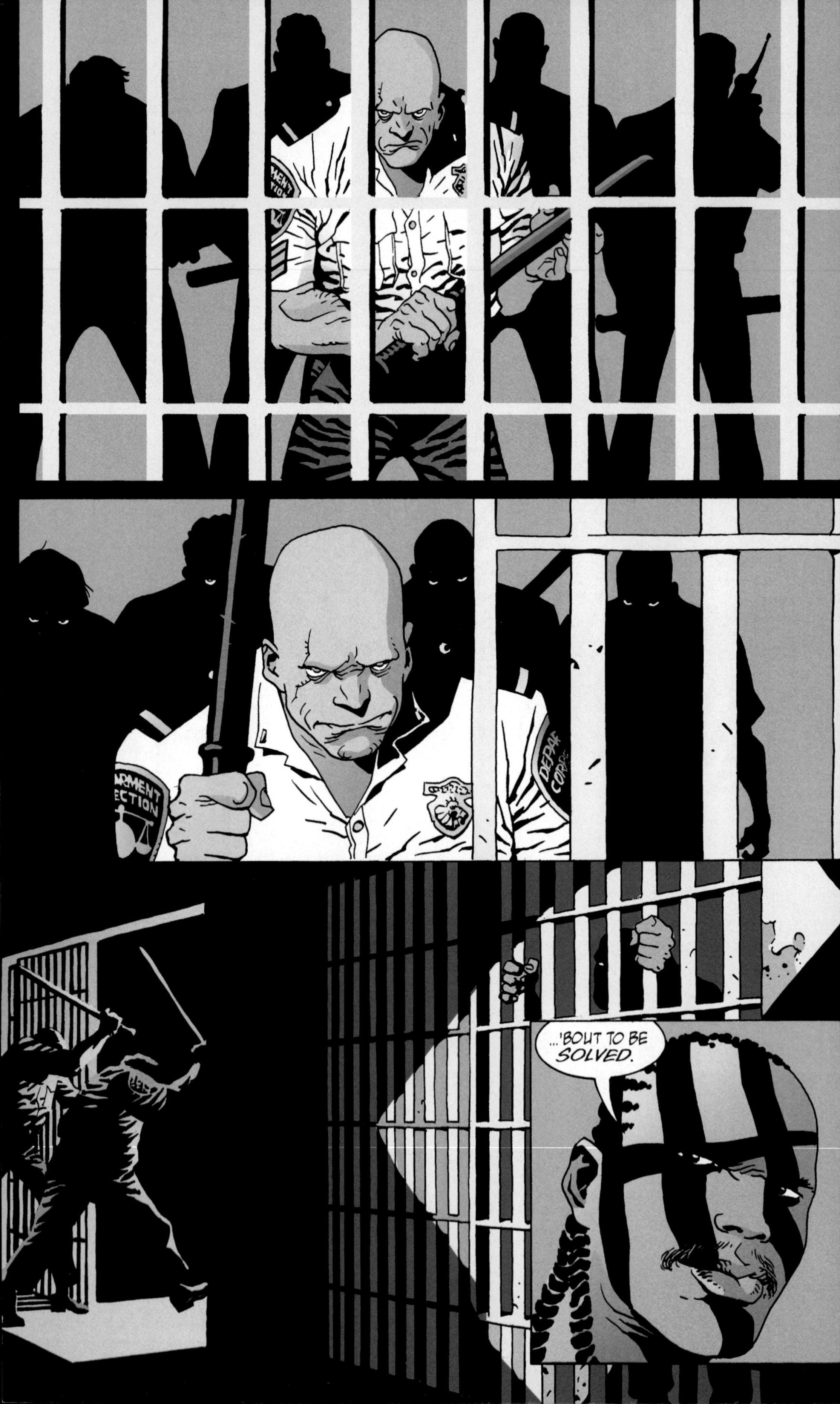
...'BOUT TO BE SOLVED.

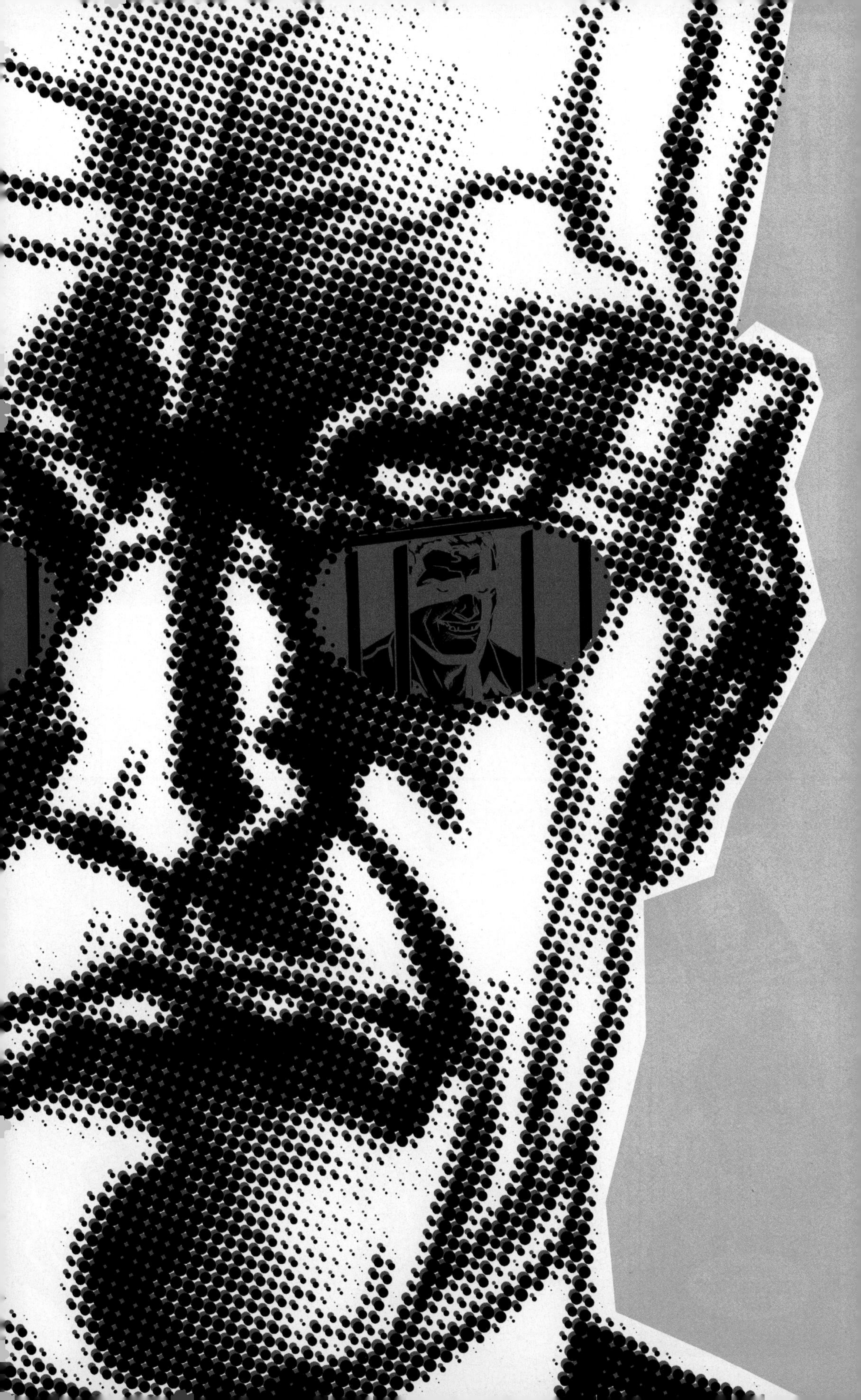

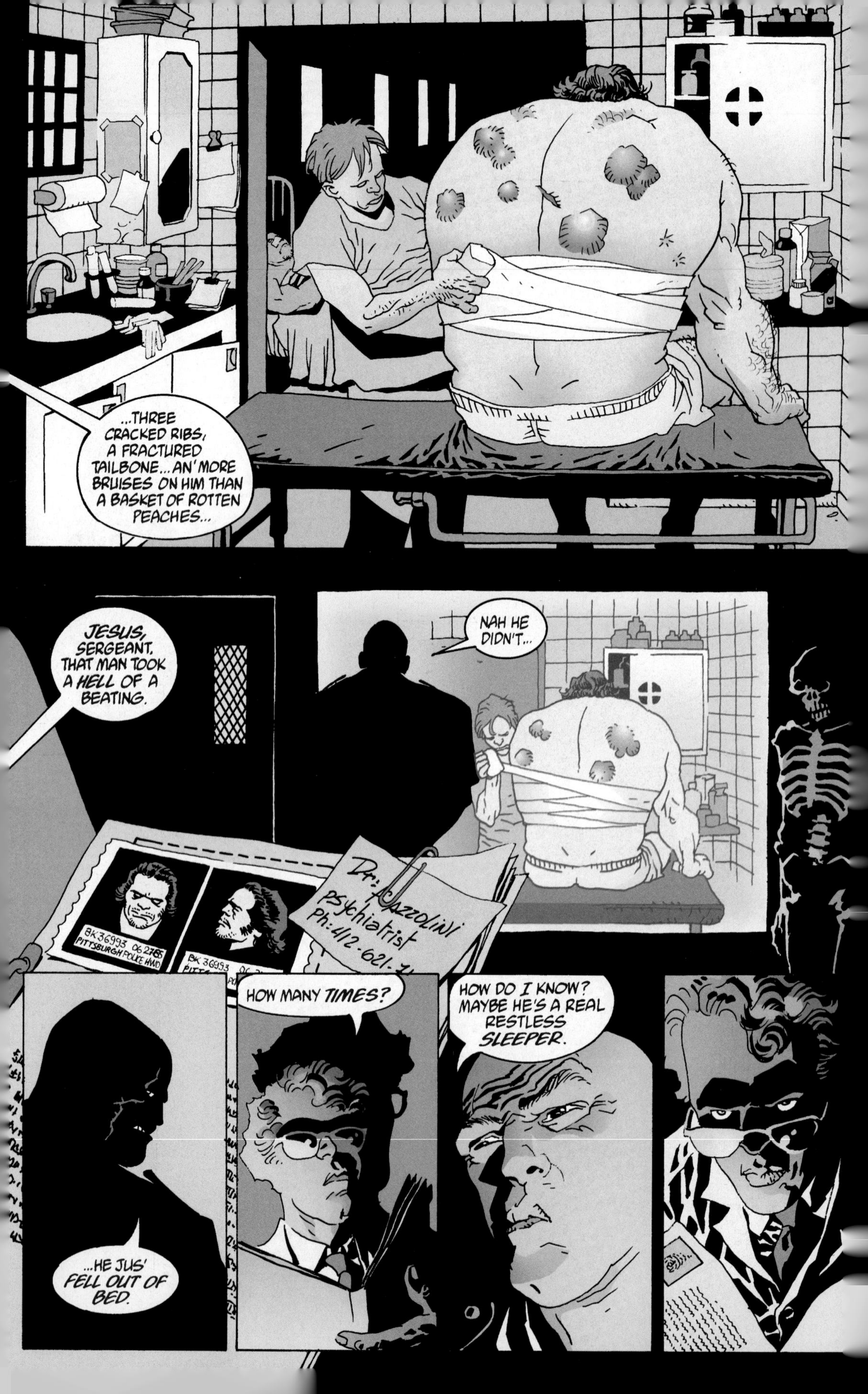
...THREE CRACKED RIBS, A FRACTURED TAILBONE... AN' MORE BRUISES ON HIM THAN A BASKET OF ROTTEN PEACHES...
JESUS, SERGEANT. THAT MAN TOOK A HELL OF A BEATING.
NAH HE DIDN'T...
BK 36993 06 27 85
PITTSBURGH POLICE HWD
Dr. Pazzolini
psychiatrist
Ph: 412-621-
...HE JUS' FELL OUT OF BED.
HOW MANY TIMES?
HOW DO I KNOW? MAYBE HE'S A REAL RESTLESS SLEEPER.

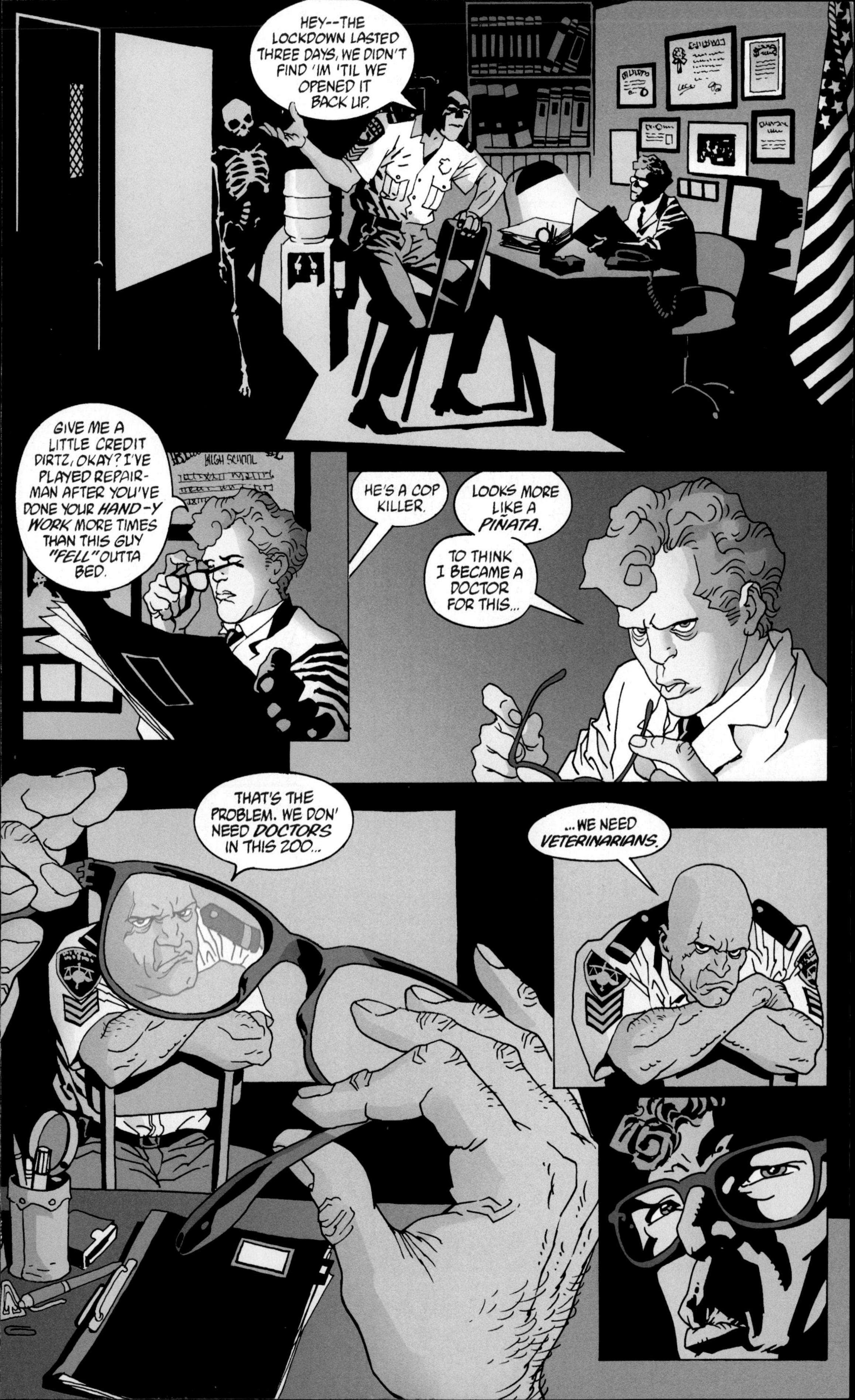
HEY--THE LOCKDOWN LASTED THREE DAYS, WE DIDN'T FIND 'IM 'TIL WE OPENED IT BACK UP.
GIVE ME A LITTLE CREDIT DIRTZ, OKAY? I'VE PLAYED REPAIR-MAN AFTER YOU'VE DONE YOUR HAND-Y WORK MORE TIMES THAN THIS GUY "FELL" OUTTA BED.
HIGH SCHOOL
HE'S A COP KILLER.
LOOKS MORE LIKE A PIÑATA.
TO THINK I BECAME A DOCTOR FOR THIS...
THAT'S THE PROBLEM. WE DON' NEED DOCTORS IN THIS ZOO...
...WE NEED VETERINARIANS.

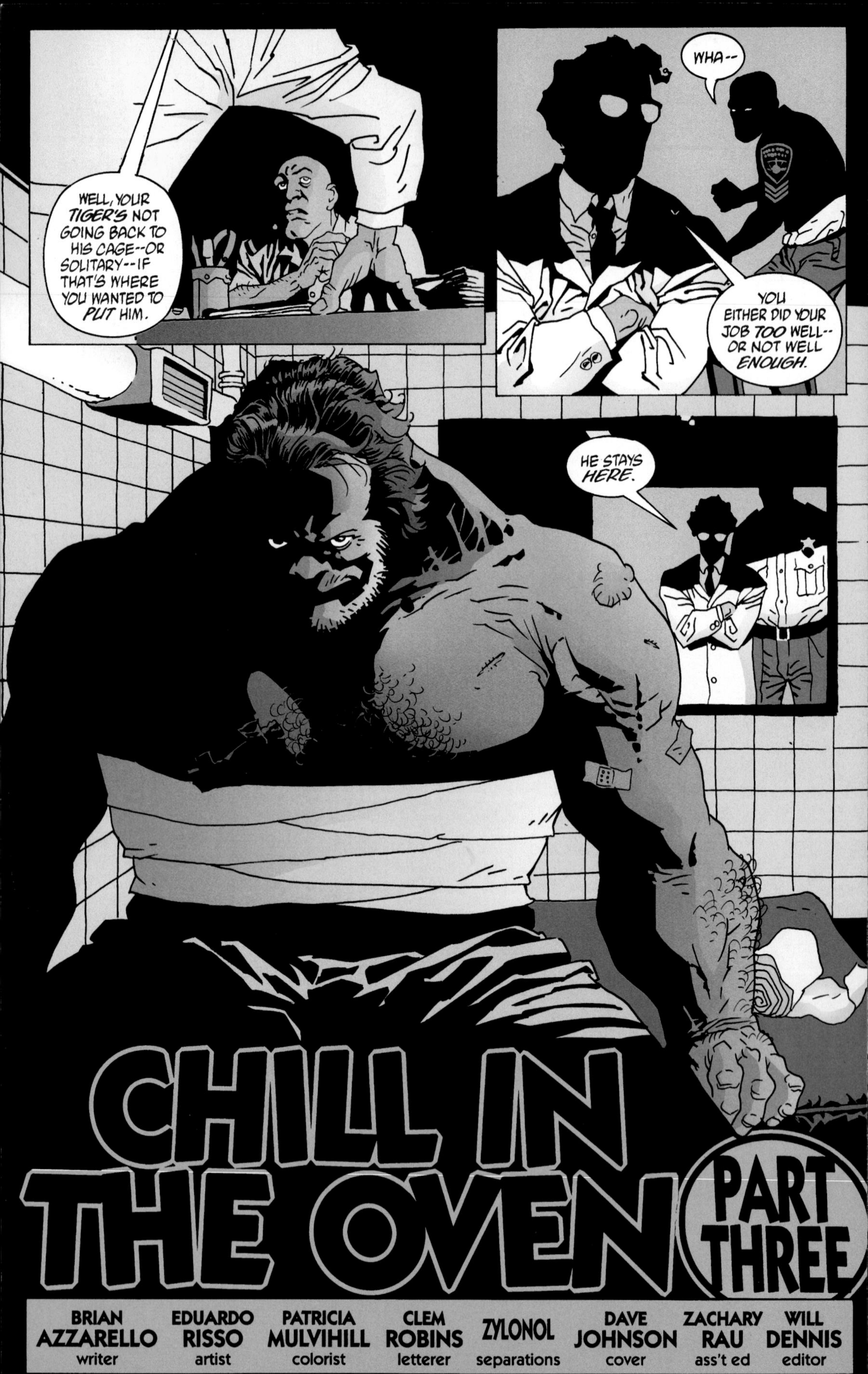
WELL, YOUR TIGER'S NOT GOING BACK TO HIS CAGE--OR SOLITARY--IF THAT'S WHERE YOU WANTED TO PUT HIM.
WHA--
YOU EITHER DID YOUR JOB TOO WELL--OR NOT WELL ENOUGH.
HE STAYS HERE.
CHILL IN THE OVEN
PART THREE
BRIAN AZZARELLO writer
EDUARDO RISSO artist
PATRICIA MULVIHILL colorist
CLEM ROBINS letterer
ZYLONOL separations
DAVE JOHNSON cover
ZACHARY RAU ass't ed
WILL DENNIS editor

NICE MOVE, YOUNG BLOOD. YOU BEEN LEARNIN' SOMETHIN' *FINALLY.*

UH-HUH. I BEEN STUDYIN' YO' *ASS,* OLD HEAD. HOW MANY GAMES WE PLAY?

HUN'RED.

AN' HOW MANY I *WON?*

YOU *AIN'T.*

SO MAYBE IT'S TIME I GOT *LUCKY.*

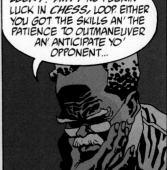

LUCKY? AIN'T NO FUCKIN' LUCK IN *CHESS,* LOOP. EITHER YOU GOT THE SKILLS AN' THE PATIENCE TO OUTMANEUVER AN' ANTICIPATE YO' OPPONENT...

...OR YOU *AIN'T.* CHECKMATE.

ONE-OH-ONE TO NONE.

YO' LOOPY LOOP...

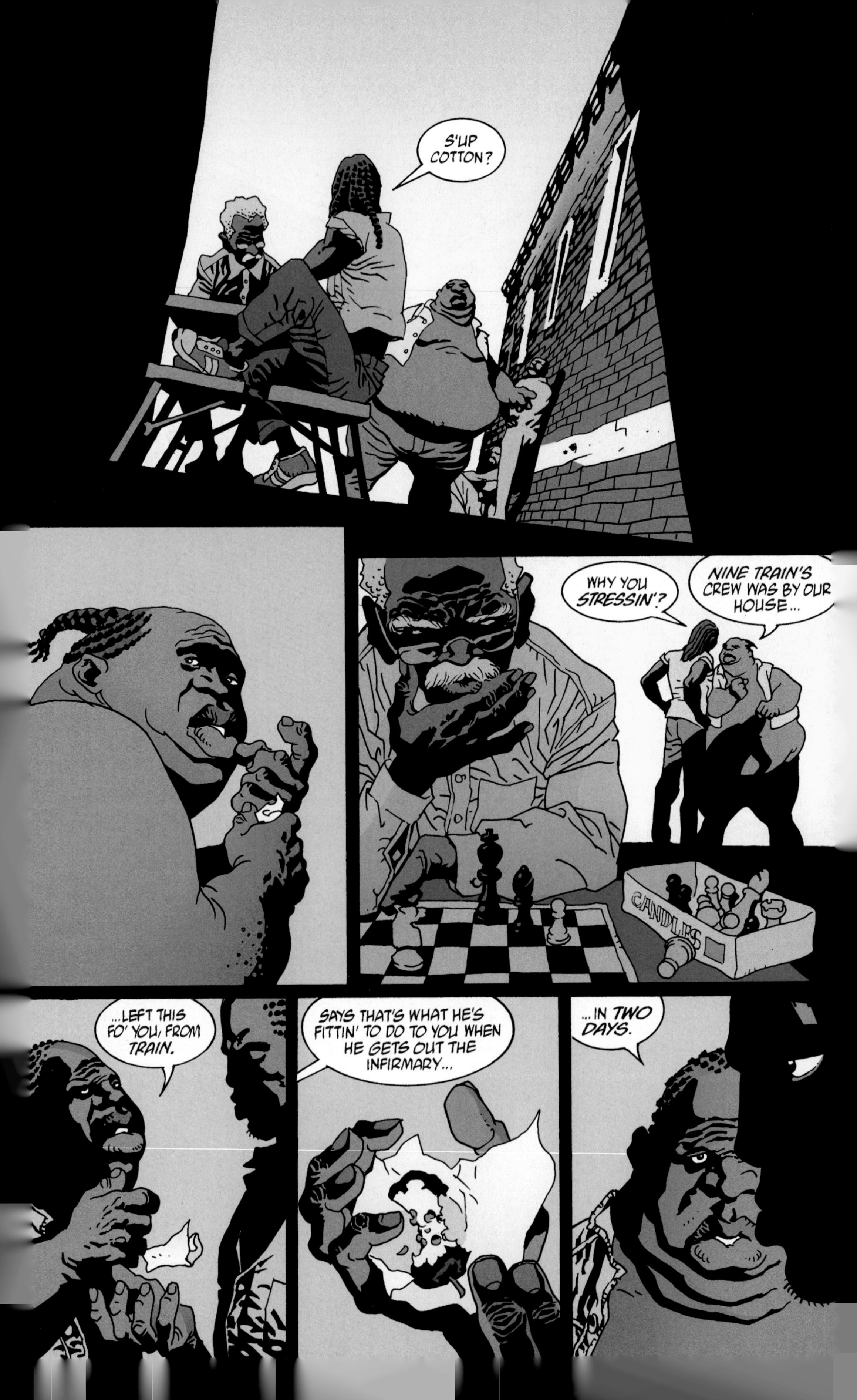
S'UP COTTON?
WHY YOU STRESSIN'?
NINE TRAIN'S CREW WAS BY OUR HOUSE...
CANDLES
...LEFT THIS FO' YOU, FROM TRAIN.
SAYS THAT'S WHAT HE'S FITTIN' TO DO TO YOU WHEN HE GETS OUT THE INFIRMARY...
...IN TWO DAYS.

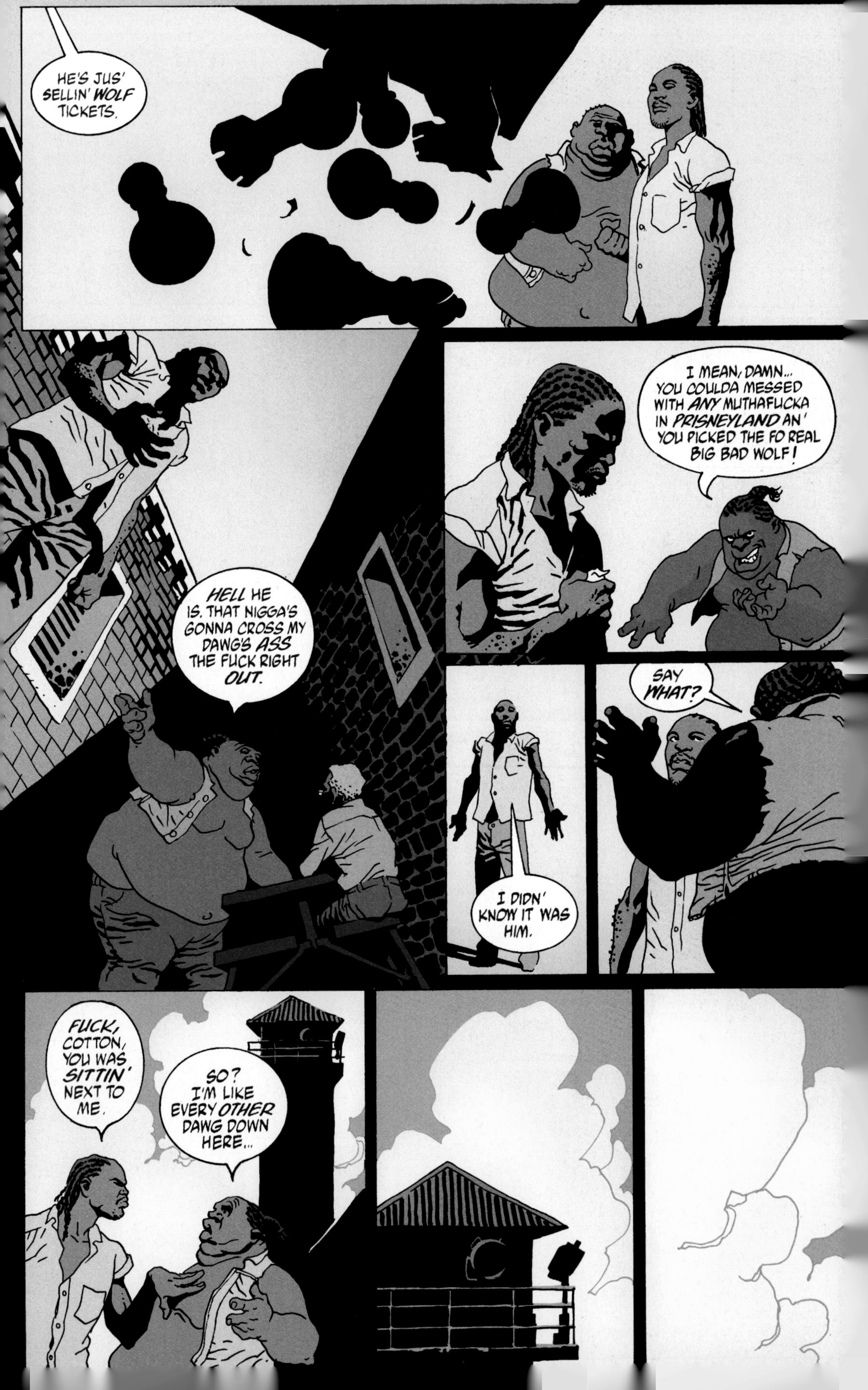
HE'S JUS' SELLIN' WOLF TICKETS.
HELL HE IS. THAT NIGGA'S GONNA CROSS MY DAWG'S ASS THE FUCK RIGHT OUT.
I MEAN, DAMN... YOU COULDA MESSED WITH ANY MUTHAFUCKA IN PRISNEYLAND AN' YOU PICKED THE FO REAL BIG BAD WOLF!
I DIDN' KNOW IT WAS HIM.
SAY WHAT?
FUCK, COTTON, YOU WAS SITTIN' NEXT TO ME.
SO? I'M LIKE EVERY OTHER DAWG DOWN HERE...

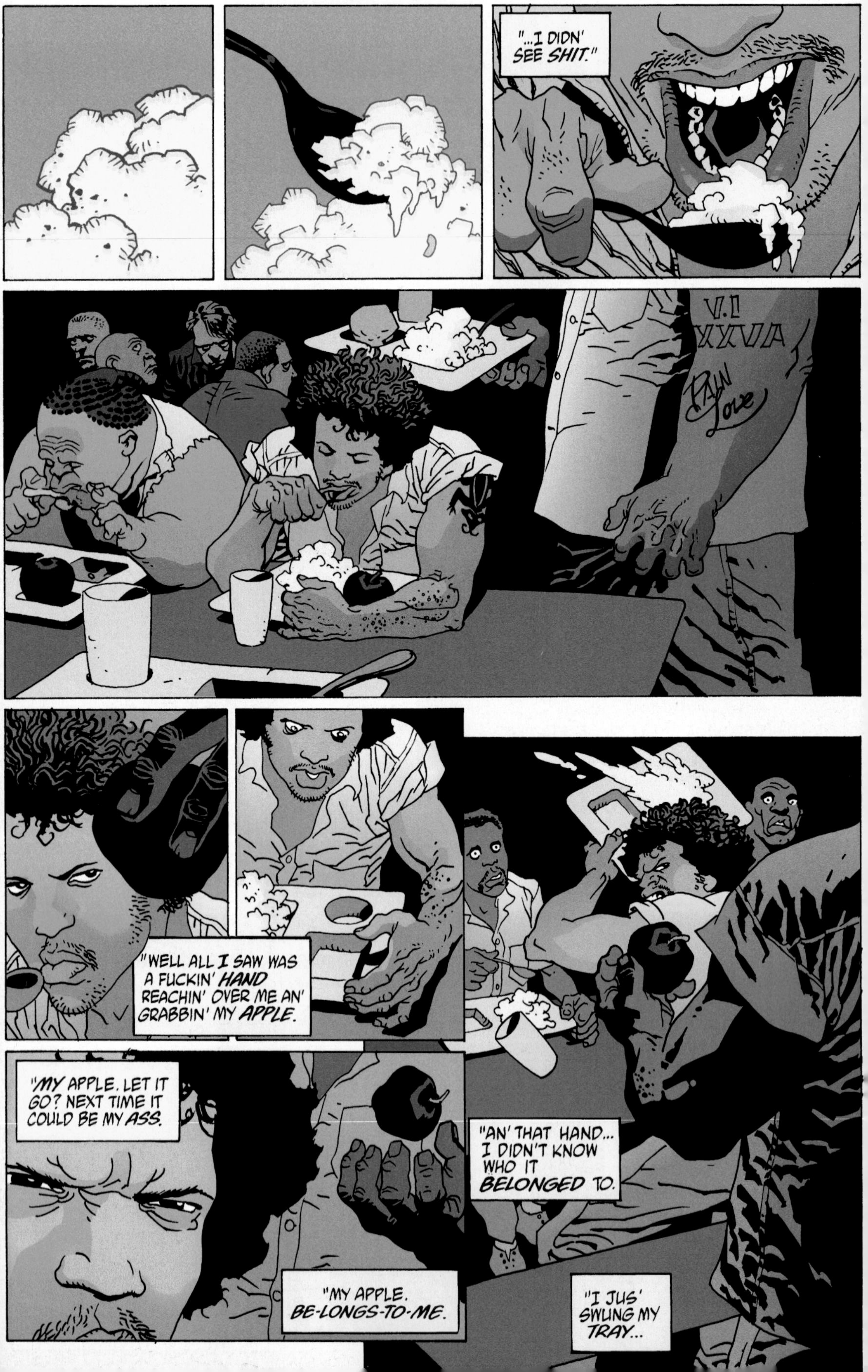
"...I DIDN' SEE SHIT."
V.I
XYVA
PAIN
LOVE
"WELL ALL I SAW WAS A FUCKIN' HAND REACHIN' OVER ME AN' GRABBIN' MY APPLE.
"MY APPLE. LET IT GO? NEXT TIME IT COULD BE MY ASS.
"MY APPLE. BE-LONGS-TO-ME.
"AN' THAT HAND... I DIDN'T KNOW WHO IT BELONGED TO.
"I JUS' SWUNG MY TRAY...

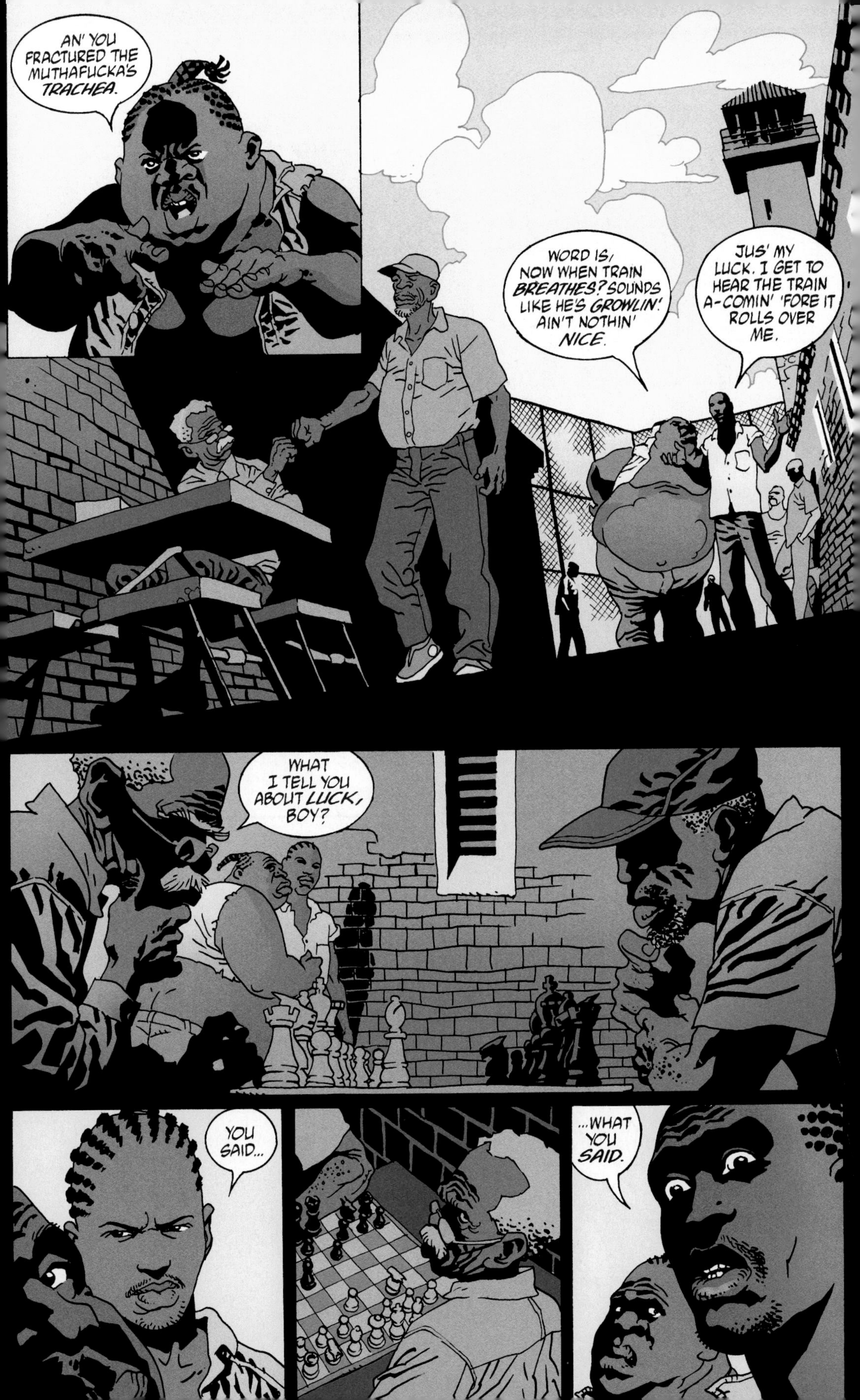
AN' YOU FRACTURED THE MUTHAFUCKA'S TRACHEA.
WORD IS, NOW WHEN TRAIN BREATHES? SOUNDS LIKE HE'S GROWLIN'. AIN'T NOTHIN' NICE.
JUS' MY LUCK. I GET TO HEAR THE TRAIN A-COMIN' 'FORE IT ROLLS OVER ME.
WHAT I TELL YOU ABOUT LUCK, BOY?
YOU SAID...
...WHAT YOU SAID.

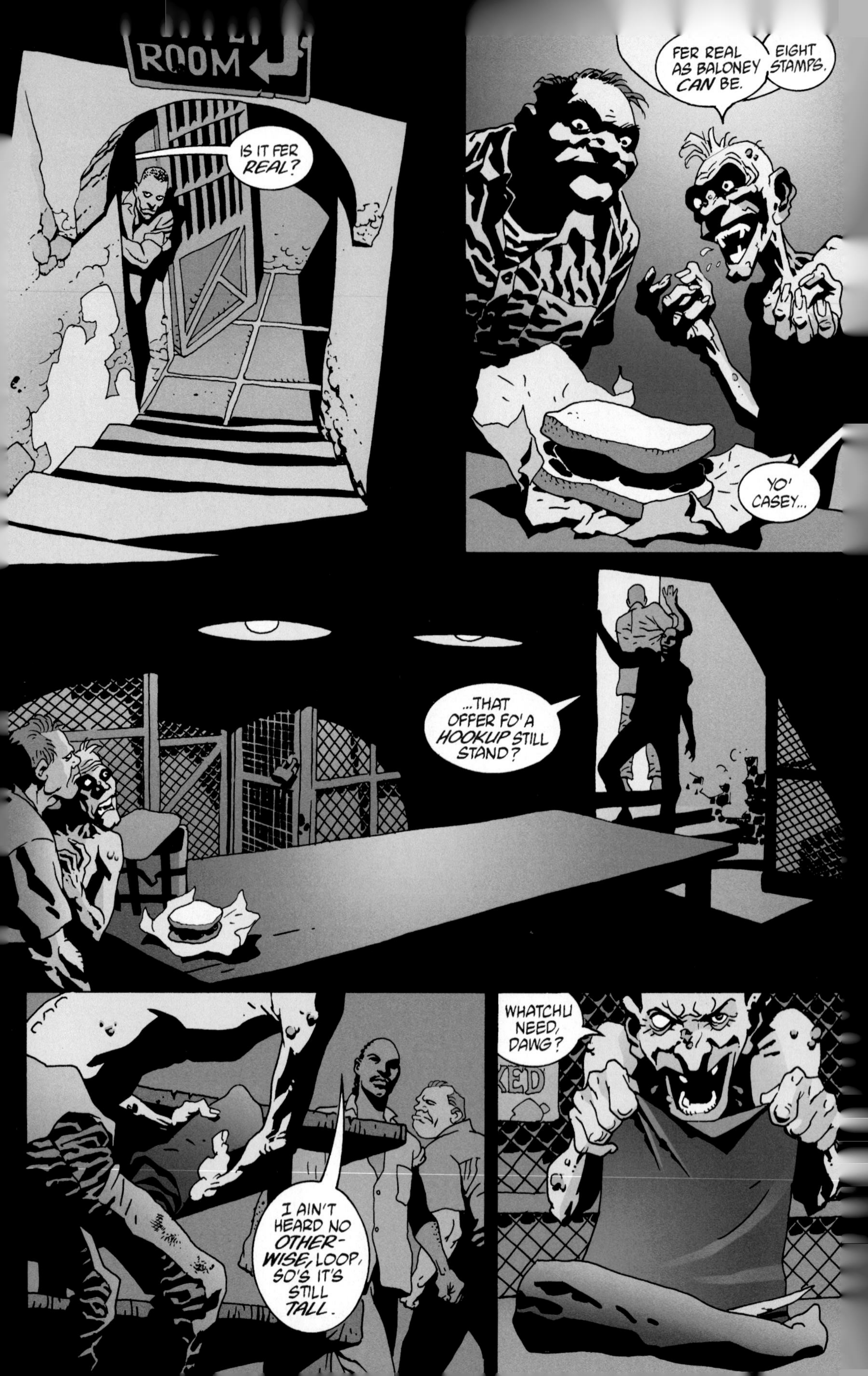
ROOM
IS IT FER REAL?
FER REAL AS BALONEY CAN BE.
EIGHT STAMPS.
YO' CASEY...
...THAT OFFER FO'A HOOKUP STILL STAND?
I AIN'T HEARD NO OTHER-WISE, LOOP, SO'S IT'S STILL TALL.
WHATCHU NEED, DAWG?

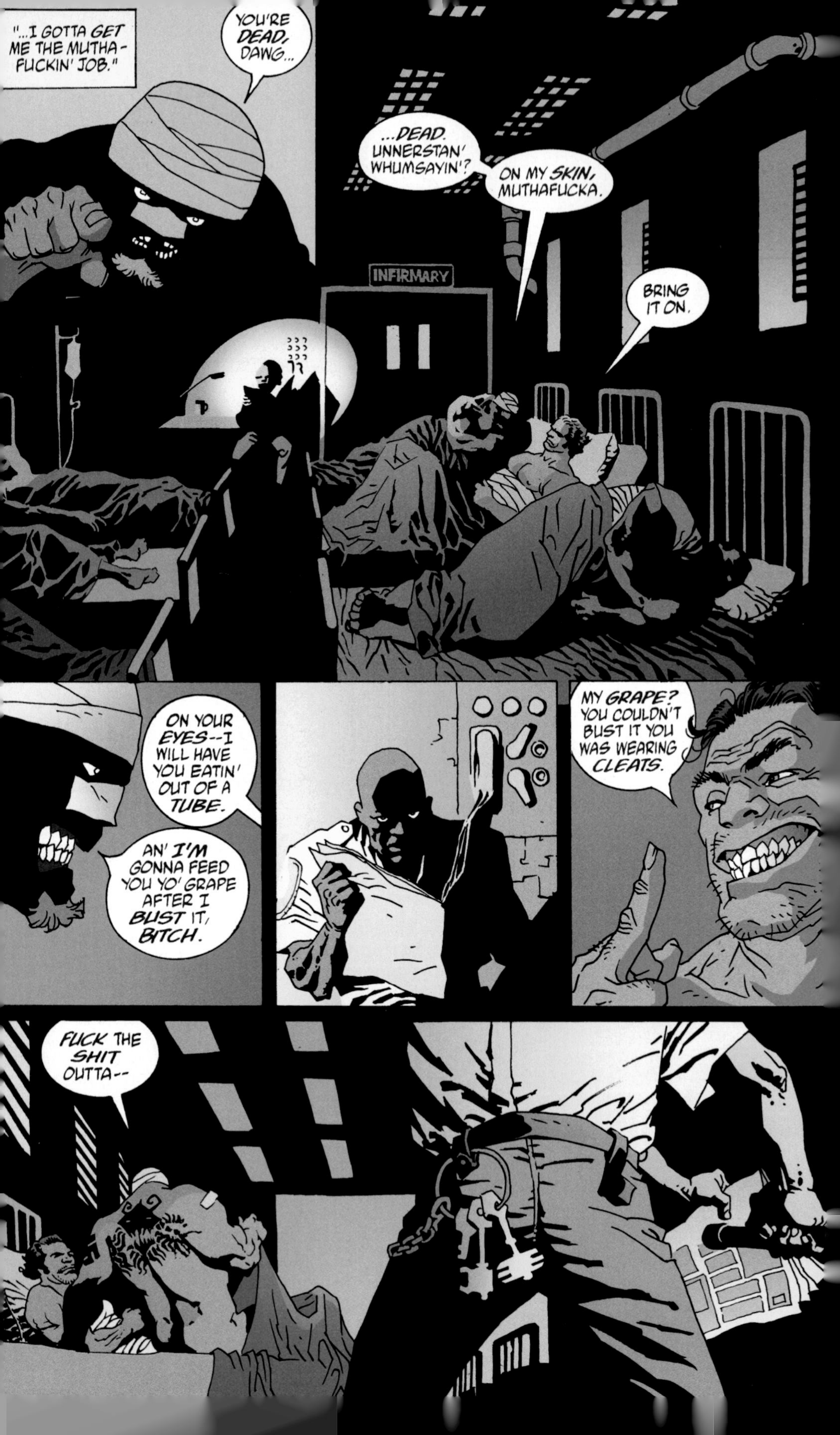
"...I GOTTA GET ME THE MUTHA-FUCKIN' JOB."
YOU'RE DEAD, DAWG...
...DEAD. UNNERSTAN' WHUMSAYIN'?
ON MY SKIN, MUTHAFUCKA.
INFIRMARY
BRING IT ON.
ON YOUR EYES--I WILL HAVE YOU EATIN' OUT OF A TUBE.
AN' I'M GONNA FEED YOU YO' GRAPE AFTER I BUST IT, BITCH.
MY GRAPE? YOU COULDN'T BUST IT YOU WAS WEARING CLEATS.
FUCK THE SHIT OUTTA--

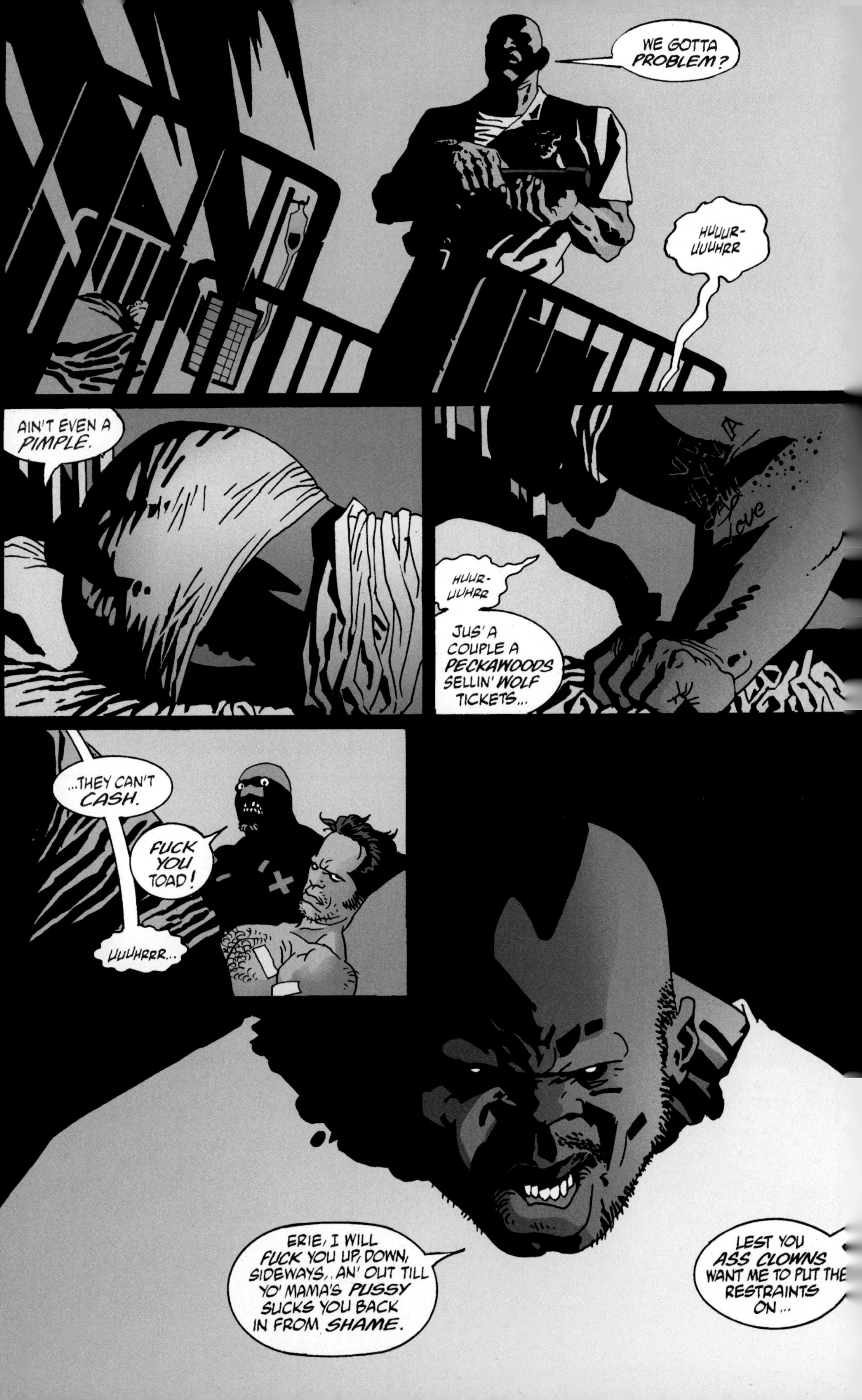
WE GOTTA PROBLEM?
HUUUR-UUUHRR
AIN'T EVEN A PIMPLE.
HUUR-UUHRR
JUS' A COUPLE A PECKAWOODS SELLIN' WOLF TICKETS...
...THEY CAN'T CASH.
FUCK YOU TOAD!
UUUHRRR...
ERIE, I WILL FUCK YOU UP, DOWN, SIDEWAYS, AN' OUT TILL YO' MAMA'S PUSSY SUCKS YOU BACK IN FROM SHAME.
LEST YOU ASS CLOWNS WANT ME TO PUT THE RESTRAINTS ON...

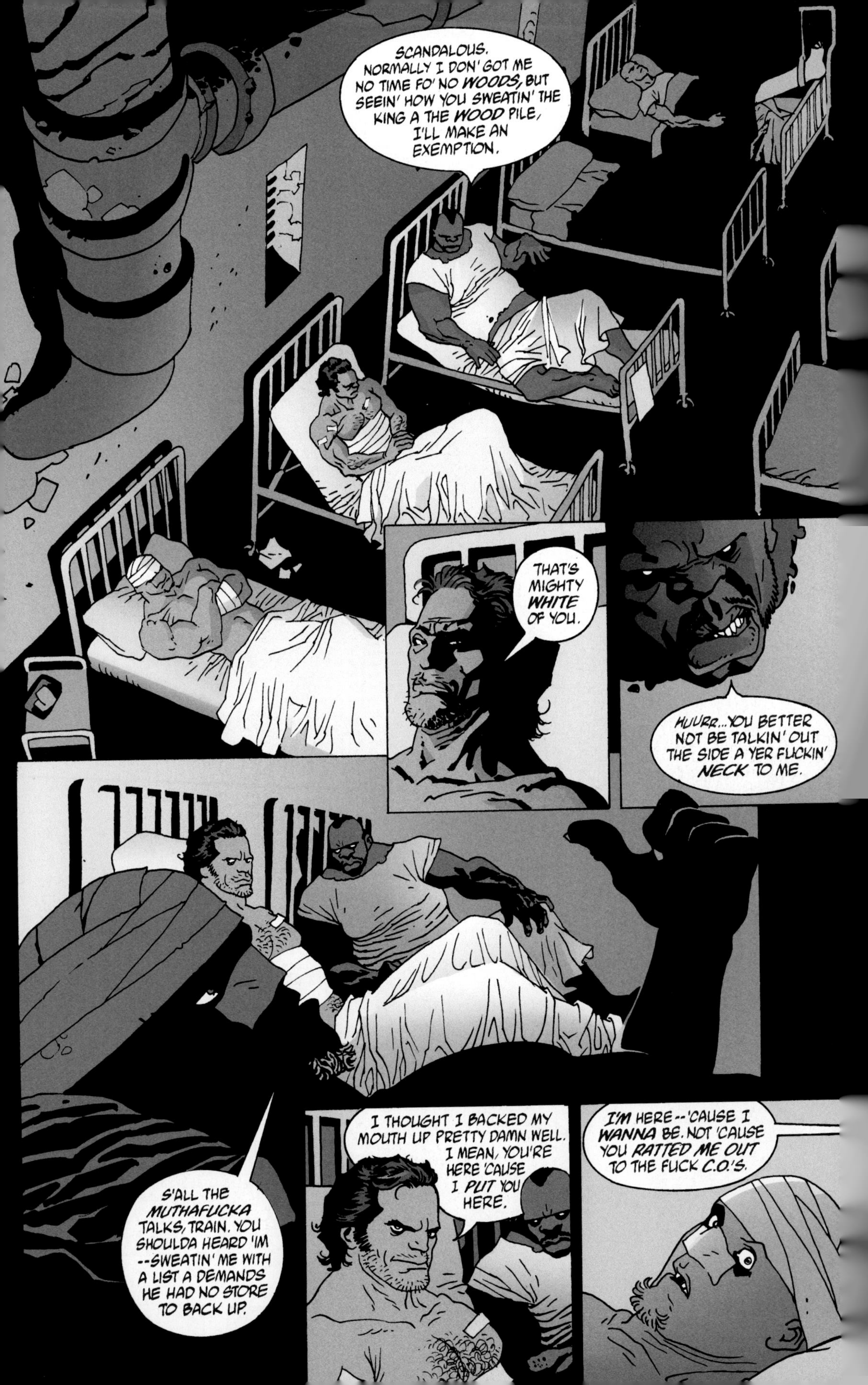
SCANDALOUS. NORMALLY I DON' GOT ME NO TIME FO' NO WOODS, BUT SEEIN' HOW YOU SWEATIN' THE KING A THE WOOD PILE, I'LL MAKE AN EXEMPTION.
THAT'S MIGHTY WHITE OF YOU.
HUURR... YOU BETTER NOT BE TALKIN' OUT THE SIDE A YER FUCKIN' NECK TO ME.
S'ALL THE MUTHAFUCKA TALKS, TRAIN. YOU SHOULDA HEARD 'IM --SWEATIN' ME WITH A LIST A DEMANDS HE HAD NO STORE TO BACK UP.
I THOUGHT I BACKED MY MOUTH UP PRETTY DAMN WELL. I MEAN, YOU'RE HERE 'CAUSE I PUT YOU HERE.
I'M HERE-- 'CAUSE I WANNA BE. NOT 'CAUSE YOU RATTED ME OUT TO THE FUCK C.O.'S.

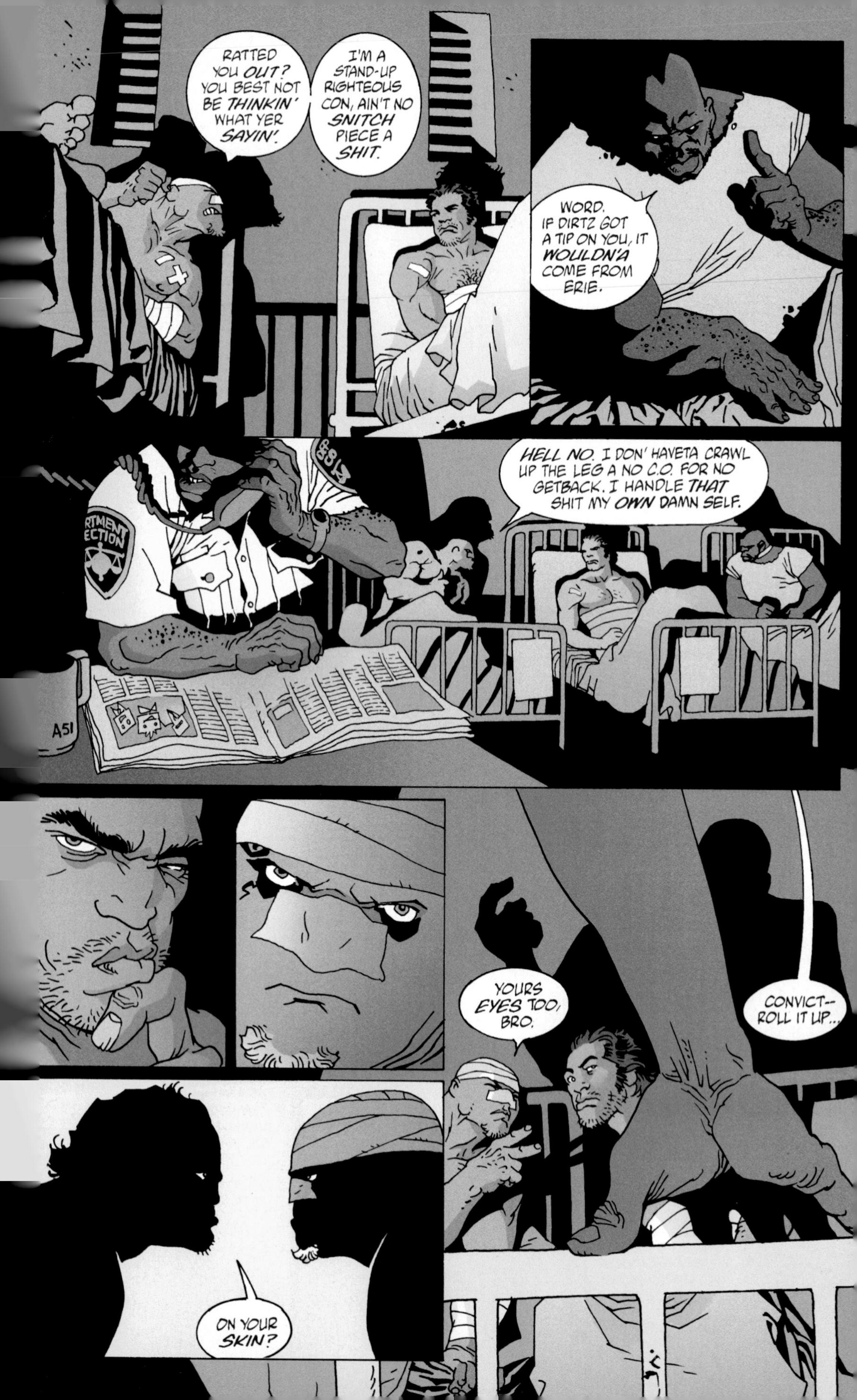

RATTED YOU OUT? YOU BEST NOT BE THINKIN' WHAT YER SAYIN'.
I'M A STAND-UP RIGHTEOUS CON, AIN'T NO SNITCH PIECE A SHIT.
WORD. IF DIRTZ GOT A TIP ON YOU, IT WOULDN'A COME FROM ERIE.
HELL NO. I DON' HAVETA CRAWL UP THE LEG A NO C.O. FOR NO GETBACK. I HANDLE THAT SHIT MY OWN DAMN SELF.
A51
YOURS EYES TOO, BRO.
CONVICT-- ROLL IT UP...
ON YOUR SKIN?

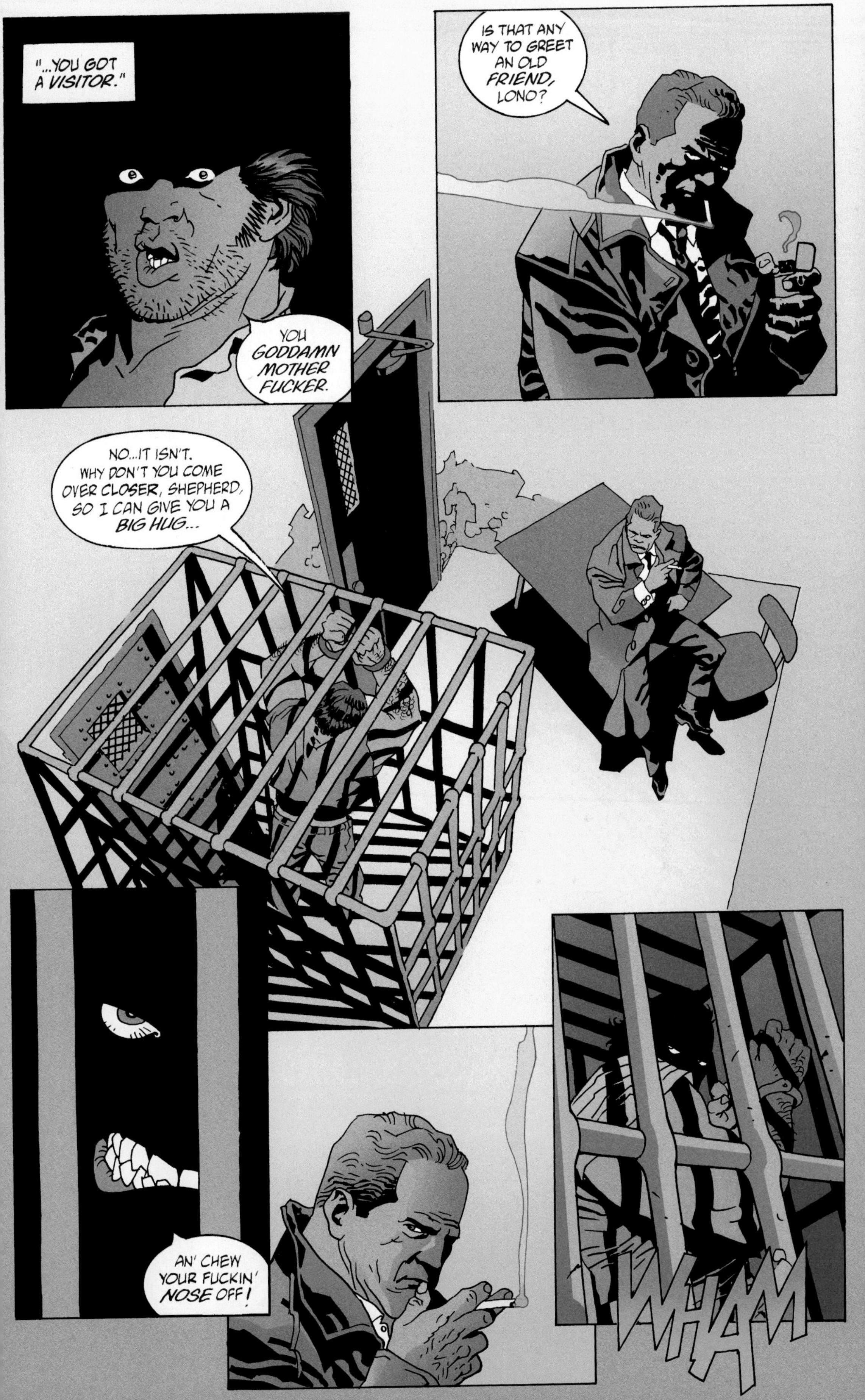
"...YOU GOT A VISITOR."
YOU GODDAMN MOTHER FUCKER.
IS THAT ANY WAY TO GREET AN OLD FRIEND, LONO?
NO...IT ISN'T. WHY DON'T YOU COME OVER CLOSER, SHEPHERD, SO I CAN GIVE YOU A BIG HUG...
AN' CHEW YOUR FUCKIN' NOSE OFF!
WHAM

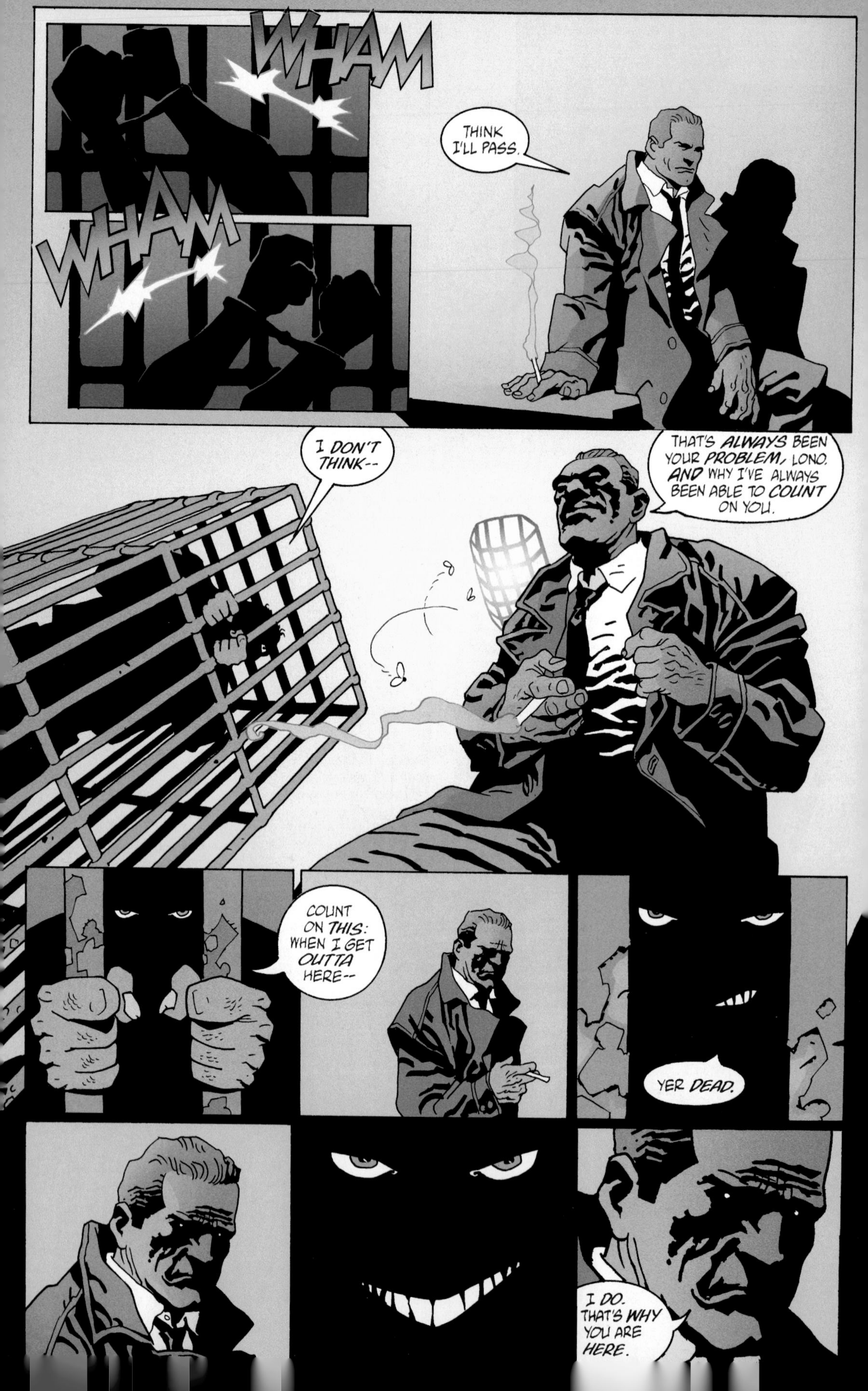
WHAM
WHAM
THINK I'LL PASS.
I DON'T THINK--
THAT'S ALWAYS BEEN YOUR PROBLEM, LONO. AND WHY I'VE ALWAYS BEEN ABLE TO COUNT ON YOU.
COUNT ON THIS: WHEN I GET OUTTA HERE--
YER DEAD.
I DO. THAT'S WHY YOU ARE HERE.

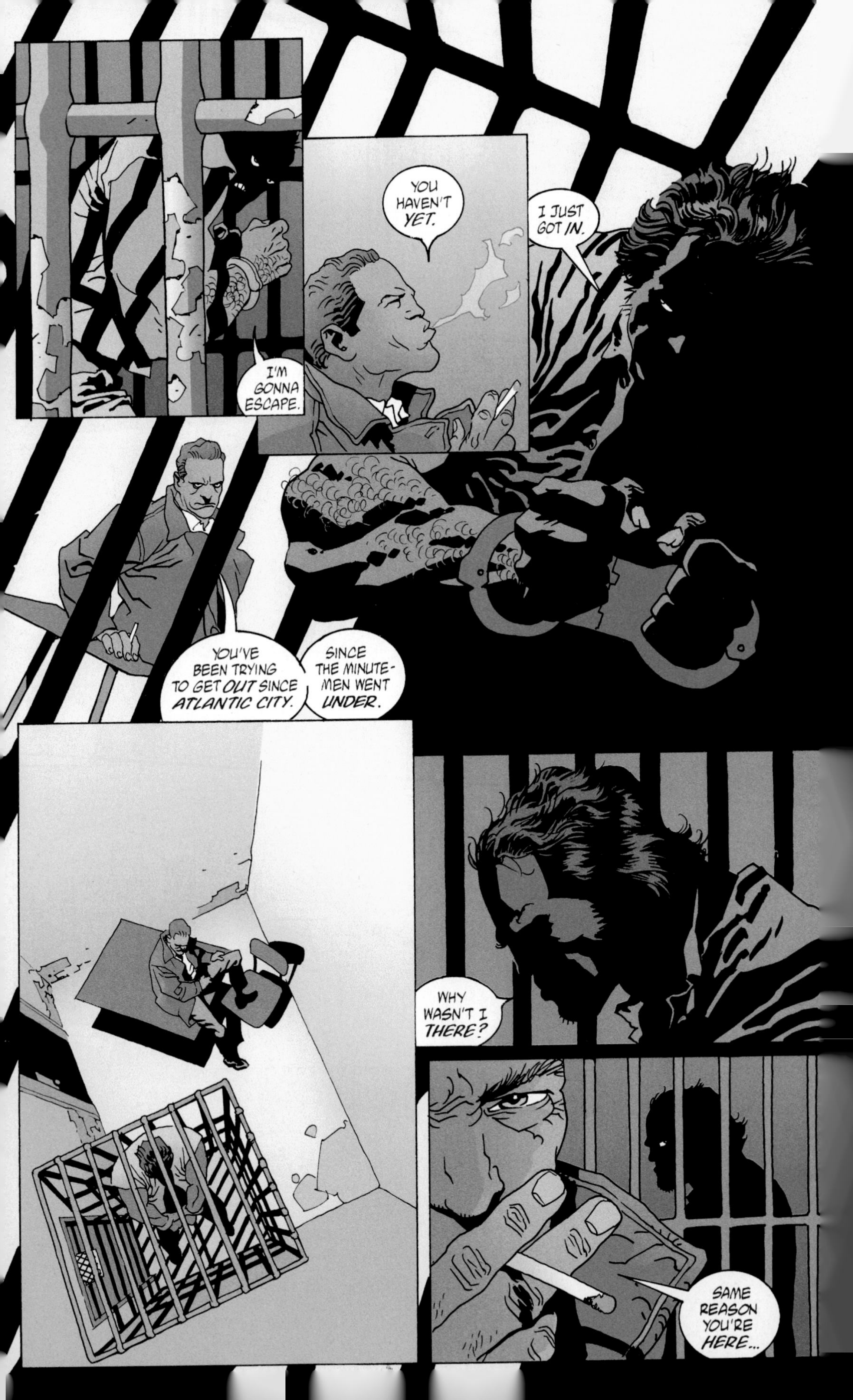
I'M GONNA ESCAPE.
YOU HAVEN'T YET.
I JUST GOT IN.
YOU'VE BEEN TRYING TO GET OUT SINCE ATLANTIC CITY.
SINCE THE MINUTE-MEN WENT UNDER.
WHY WASN'T I THERE?
SAME REASON YOU'RE HERE...

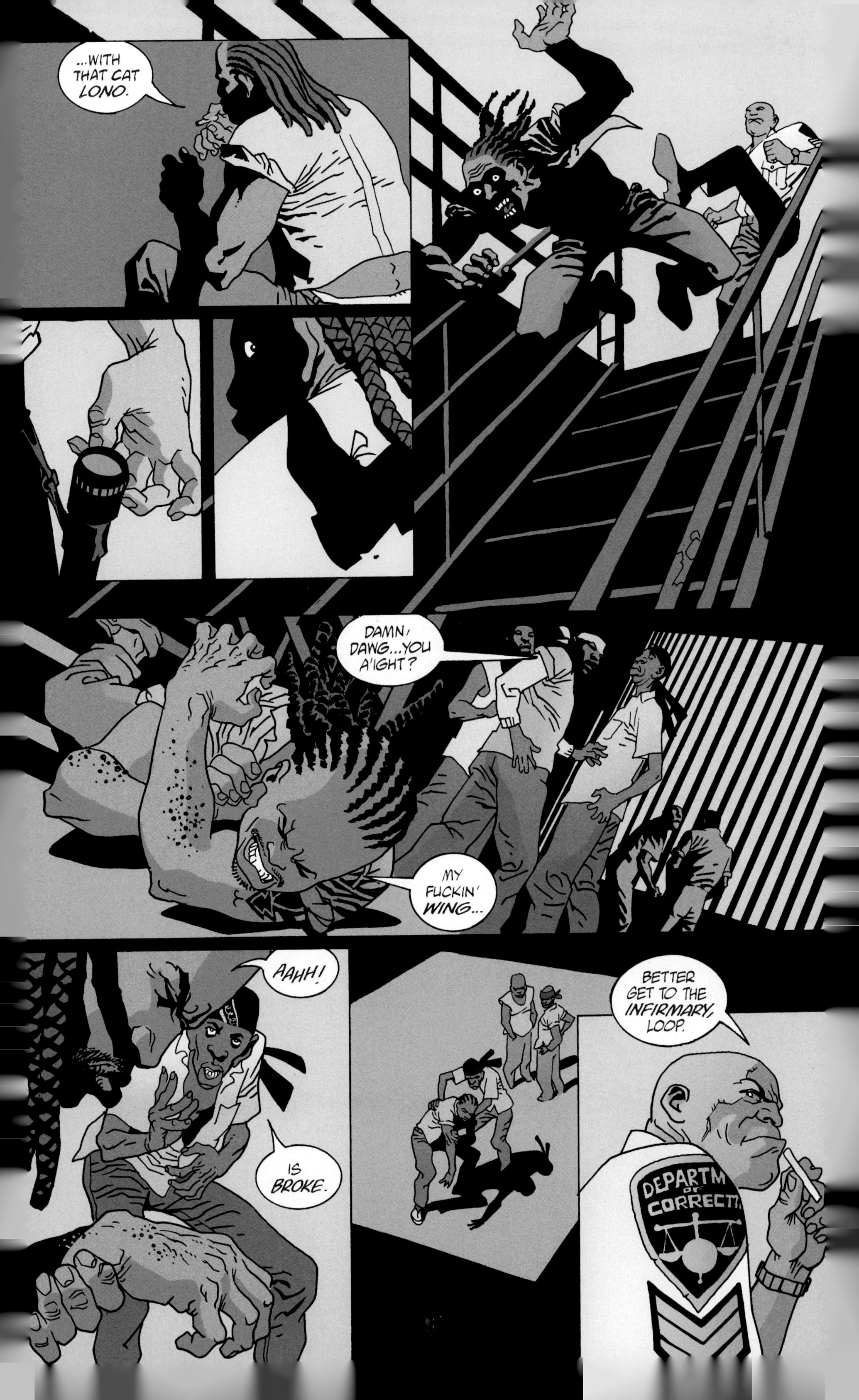
...WITH THAT CAT LONO.
DAMN, DAWG...YOU A'IGHT?
MY FUCKIN' WING...
AAHH!
IS BROKE.
BETTER GET TO THE INFIRMARY, LOOP.
DEPARTM OF CORRECTI

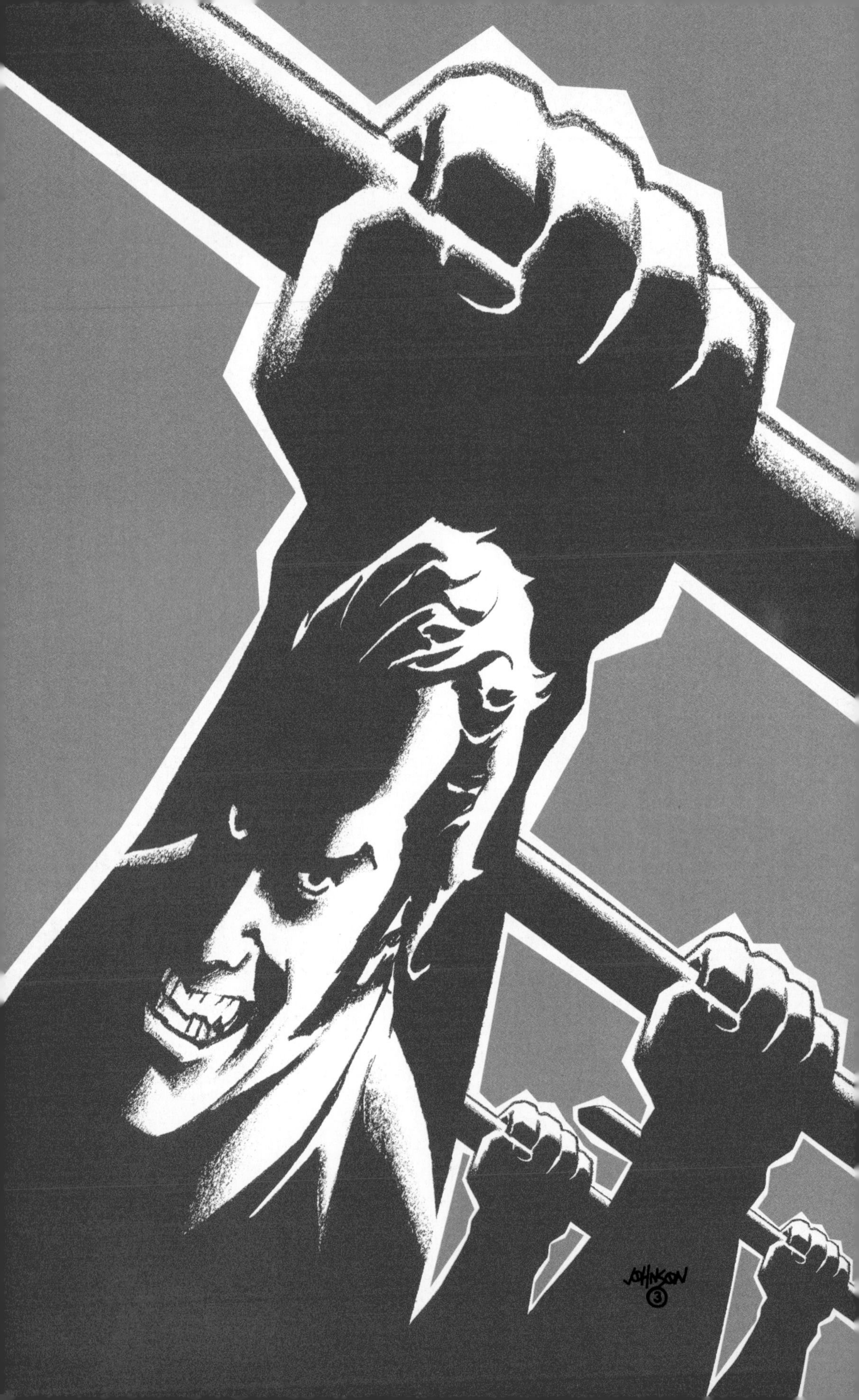
JOHNSON

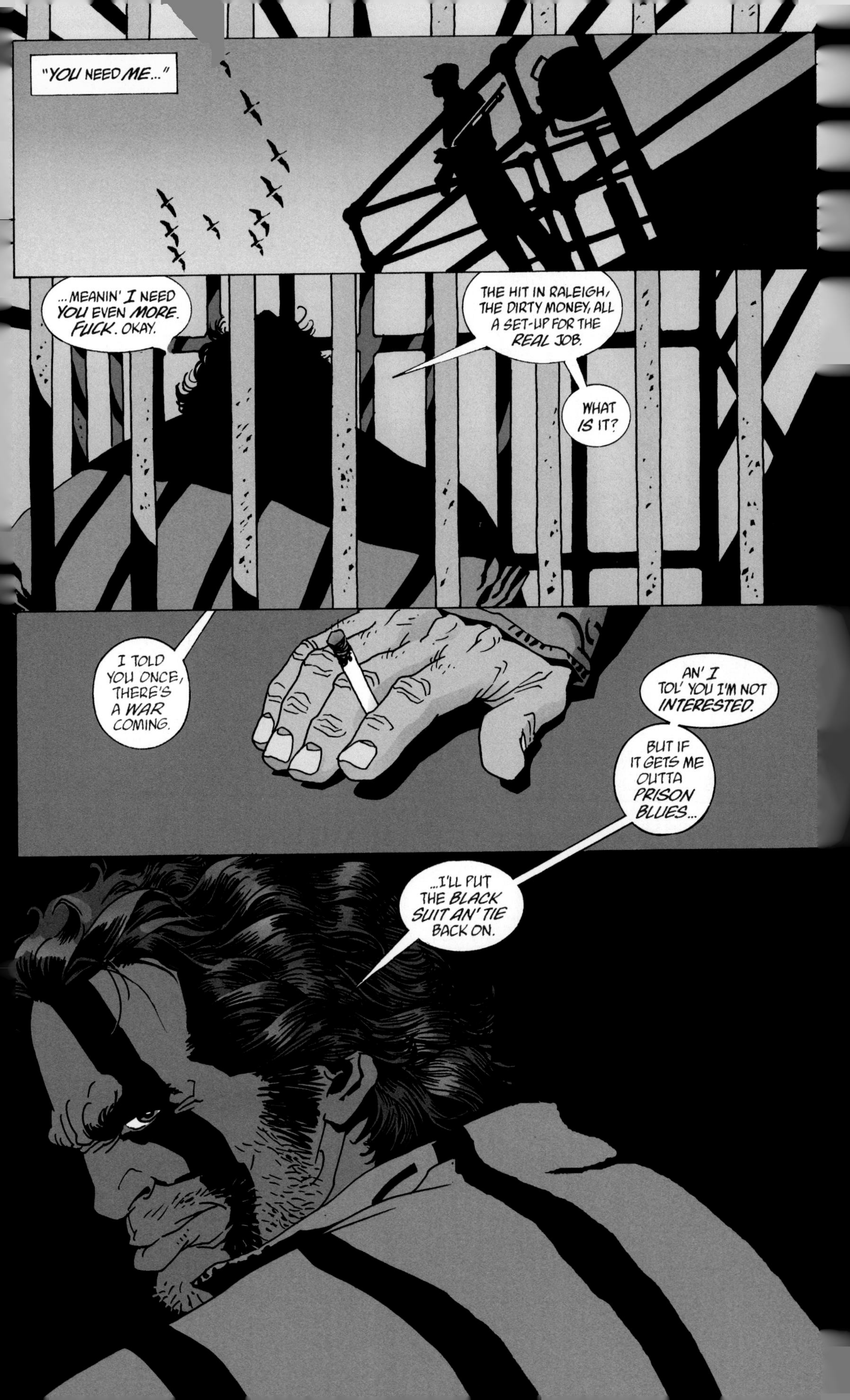
"YOU NEED ME..."
...MEANIN' I NEED YOU EVEN MORE. FUCK. OKAY.
THE HIT IN RALEIGH, THE DIRTY MONEY, ALL A SET-UP FOR THE REAL JOB.
WHAT IS IT?
I TOLD YOU ONCE, THERE'S A WAR COMING.
AN' I TOL' YOU I'M NOT INTERESTED.
BUT IF IT GETS ME OUTTA PRISON BLUES...
...I'LL PUT THE BLACK SUIT AN' TIE BACK ON.

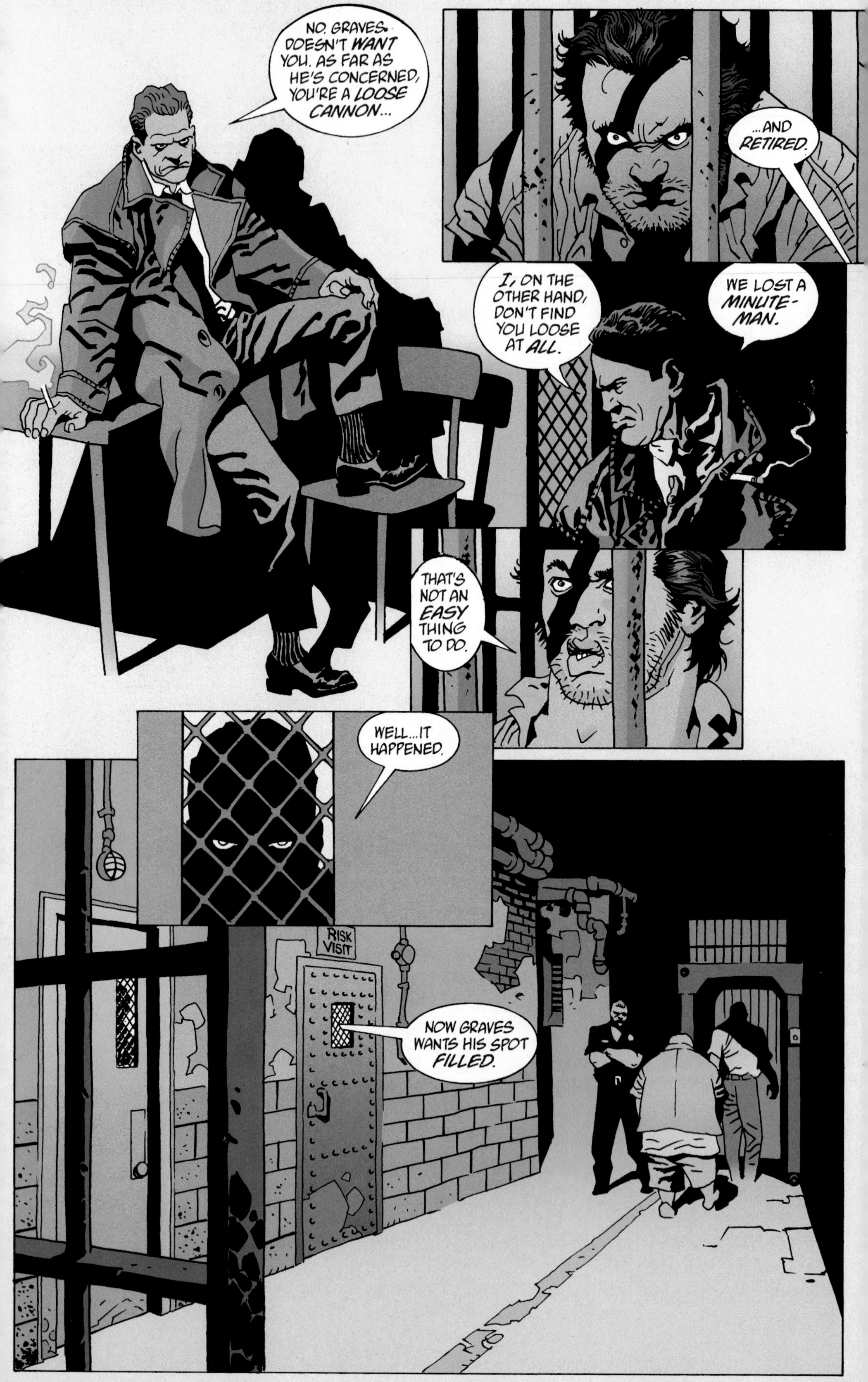
NO. GRAVES DOESN'T WANT YOU. AS FAR AS HE'S CONCERNED, YOU'RE A LOOSE CANNON...
...AND RETIRED.
I, ON THE OTHER HAND, DON'T FIND YOU LOOSE AT ALL.
WE LOST A MINUTE-MAN.
THAT'S NOT AN EASY THING TO DO.
WELL...IT HAPPENED.
RISK VISIT
NOW GRAVES WANTS HIS SPOT FILLED.

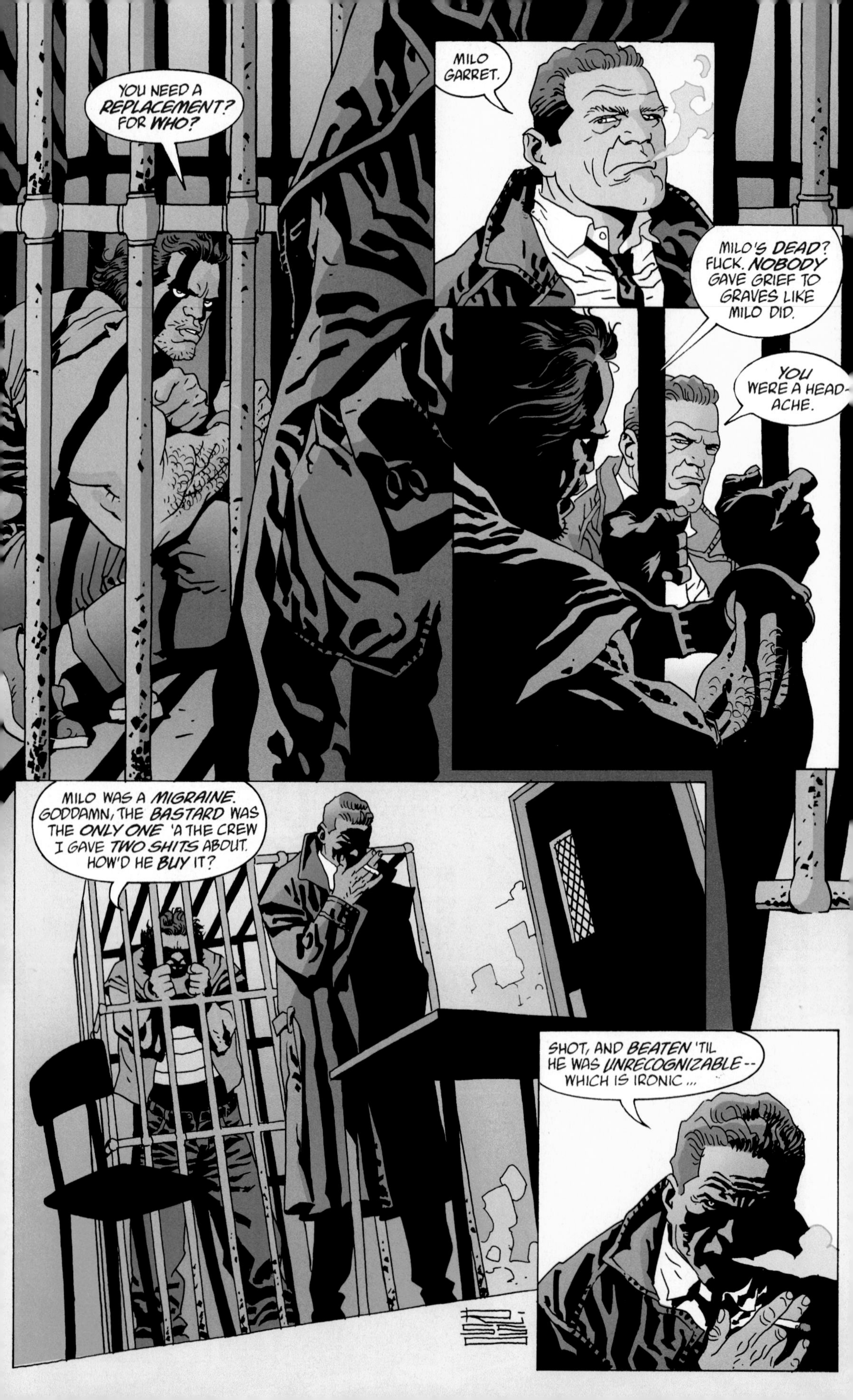
YOU NEED A REPLACEMENT? FOR WHO?
MILO GARRET.
MILO'S DEAD? FUCK. NOBODY GAVE GRIEF TO GRAVES LIKE MILO DID.
YOU WERE A HEAD-ACHE.
MILO WAS A MIGRAINE. GODDAMN, THE BASTARD WAS THE ONLY ONE 'A THE CREW I GAVE TWO SHITS ABOUT. HOW'D HE BUY IT?
SHOT, AND BEATEN 'TIL HE WAS UNRECOGNIZABLE -- WHICH IS IRONIC ...

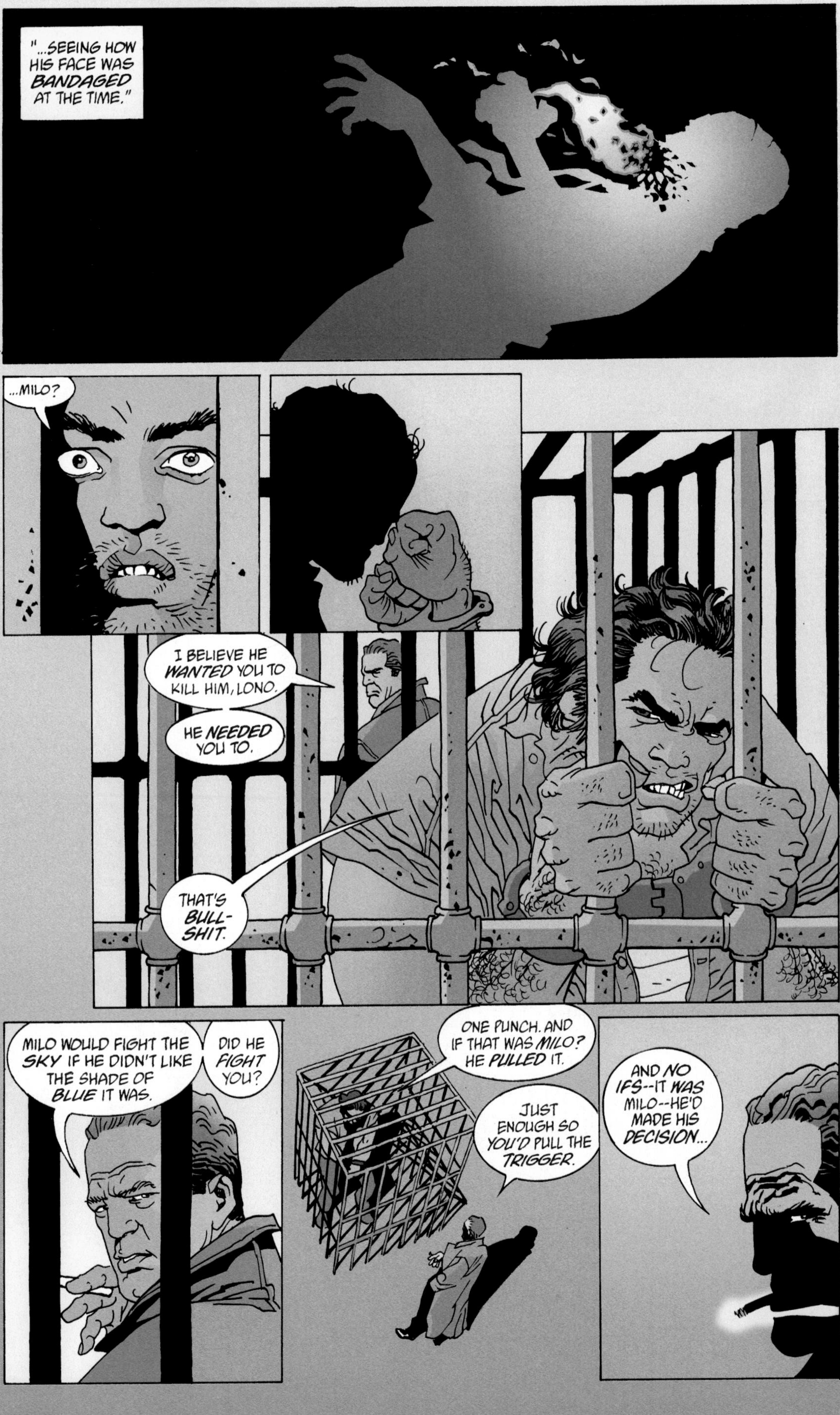
"...SEEING HOW HIS FACE WAS BANDAGED AT THE TIME."
...MILO?
I BELIEVE HE WANTED YOU TO KILL HIM, LONO.
HE NEEDED YOU TO.
THAT'S BULL-SHIT.
MILO WOULD FIGHT THE SKY IF HE DIDN'T LIKE THE SHADE OF BLUE IT WAS.
DID HE FIGHT YOU?
ONE PUNCH. AND IF THAT WAS MILO? HE PULLED IT.
JUST ENOUGH SO YOU'D PULL THE TRIGGER.
AND NO IFS--IT WAS MILO--HE'D MADE HIS DECISION...

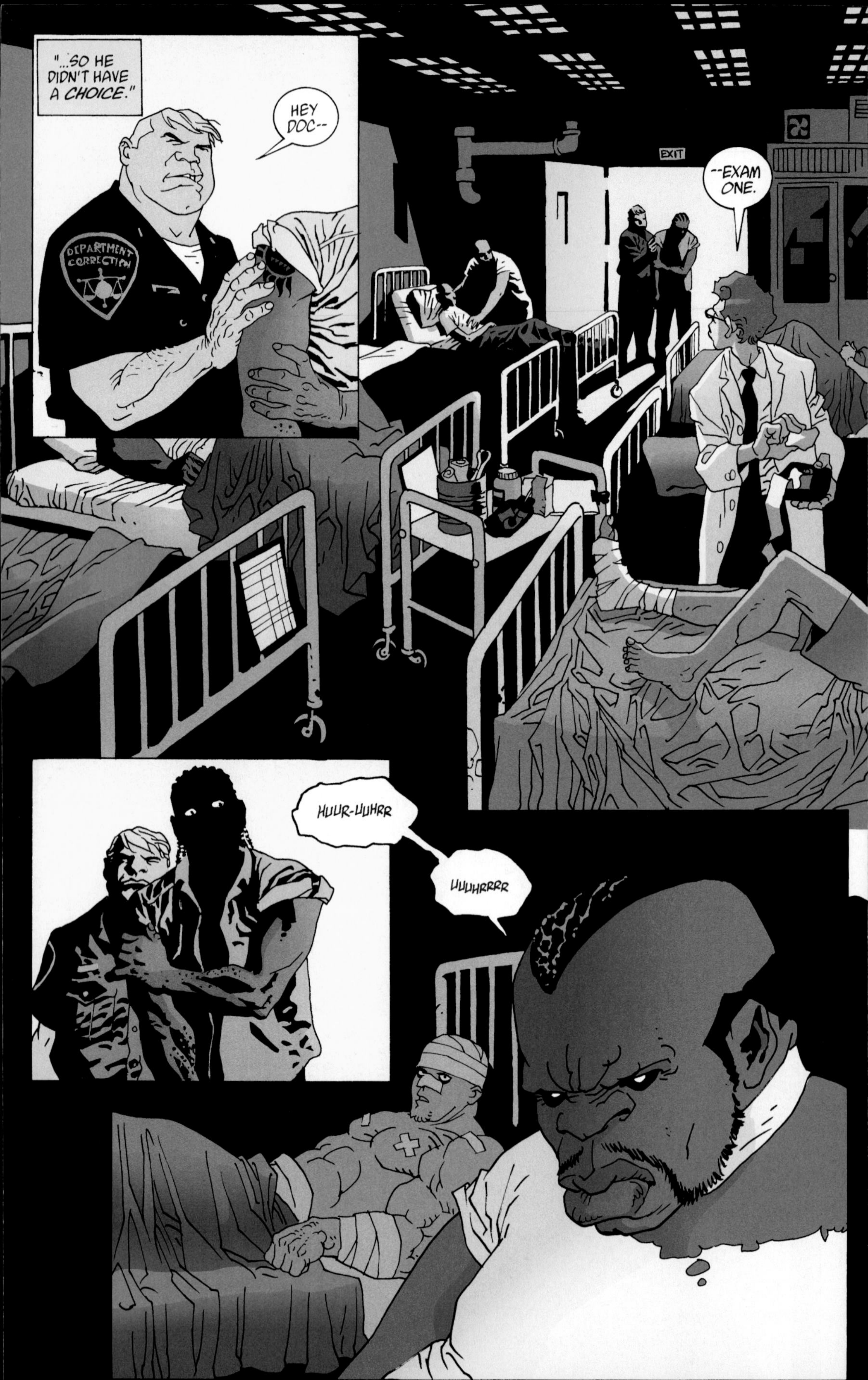
"...SO HE DIDN'T HAVE A *CHOICE*."
HEY DOC--
DEPARTMENT CORRECTION
EXIT
--EXAM ONE.
HUUR-UUHRR
UUUHRRRR

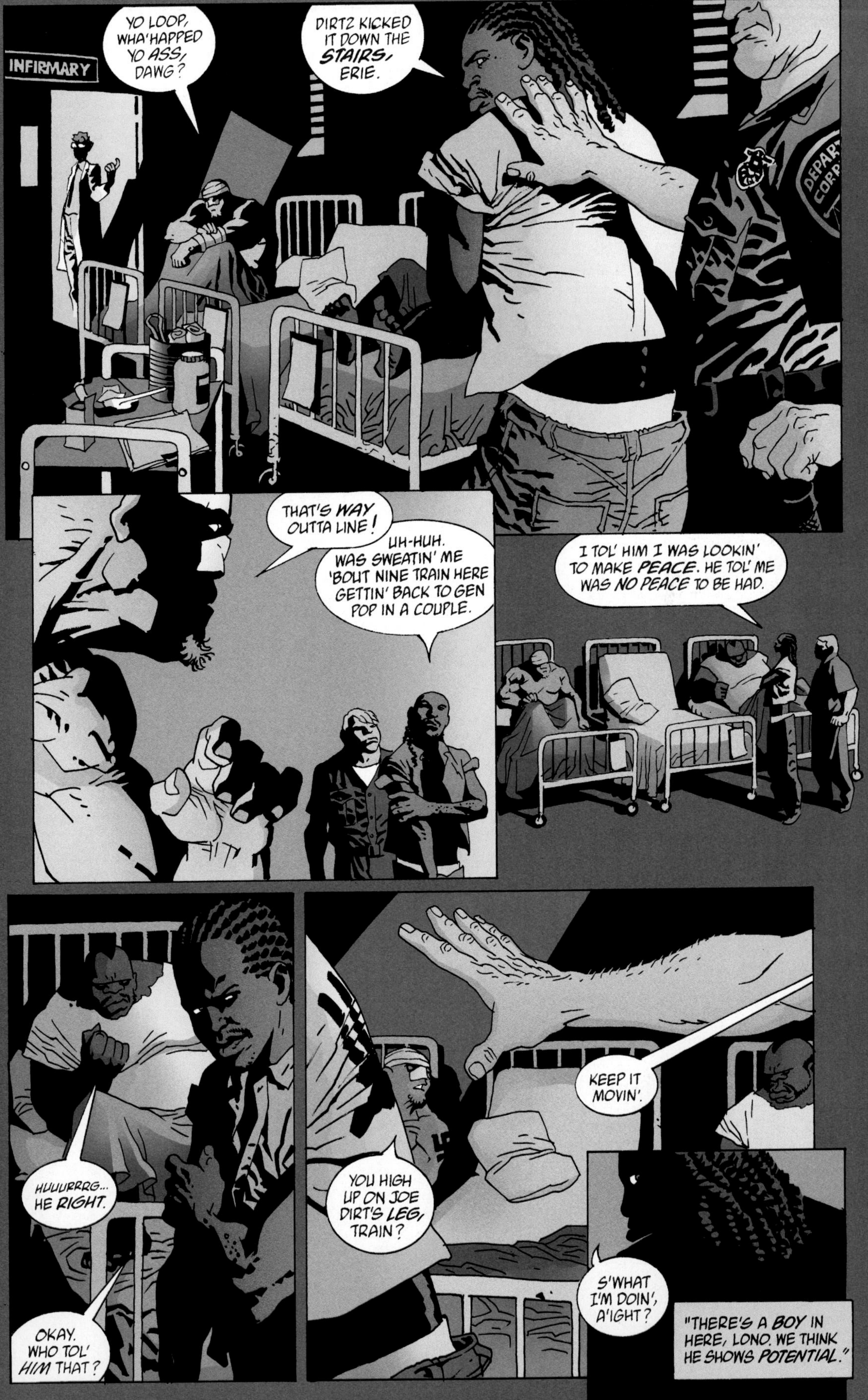

INFIRMARY
YO LOOP, WHA'HAPPED YO ASS, DAWG?
DIRTZ KICKED IT DOWN THE STAIRS, ERIE.
THAT'S WAY OUTTA LINE!
UH-HUH. WAS SWEATIN' ME 'BOUT NINE TRAIN HERE GETTIN' BACK TO GEN POP IN A COUPLE.
I TOL' HIM I WAS LOOKIN' TO MAKE PEACE. HE TOL' ME WAS NO PEACE TO BE HAD.
HUUURRRG... HE RIGHT.
OKAY. WHO TOL' HIM THAT?
KEEP IT MOVIN'.
YOU HIGH UP ON JOE DIRT'S LEG, TRAIN?
S'WHAT I'M DOIN', A'IGHT?
"THERE'S A BOY IN HERE, LONO. WE THINK HE SHOWS POTENTIAL."

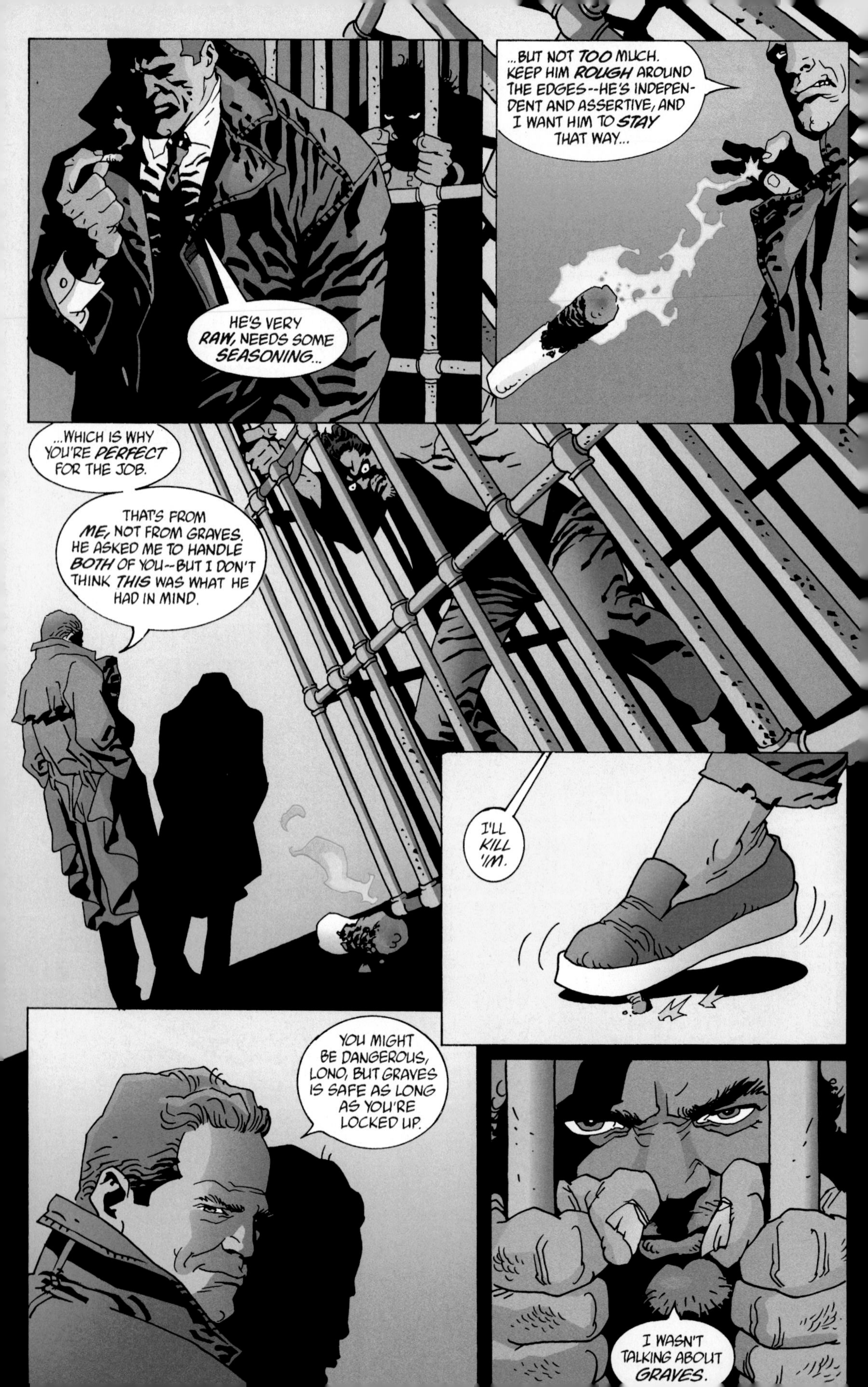
HE'S VERY RAW, NEEDS SOME SEASONING...
...BUT NOT TOO MUCH. KEEP HIM ROUGH AROUND THE EDGES--HE'S INDEPENDENT AND ASSERTIVE, AND I WANT HIM TO STAY THAT WAY...
...WHICH IS WHY YOU'RE PERFECT FOR THE JOB.
THAT'S FROM ME, NOT FROM GRAVES. HE ASKED ME TO HANDLE BOTH OF YOU--BUT I DON'T THINK THIS WAS WHAT HE HAD IN MIND.
I'LL KILL 'IM.
YOU MIGHT BE DANGEROUS, LONO, BUT GRAVES IS SAFE AS LONG AS YOU'RE LOCKED UP.
I WASN'T TALKING ABOUT GRAVES.

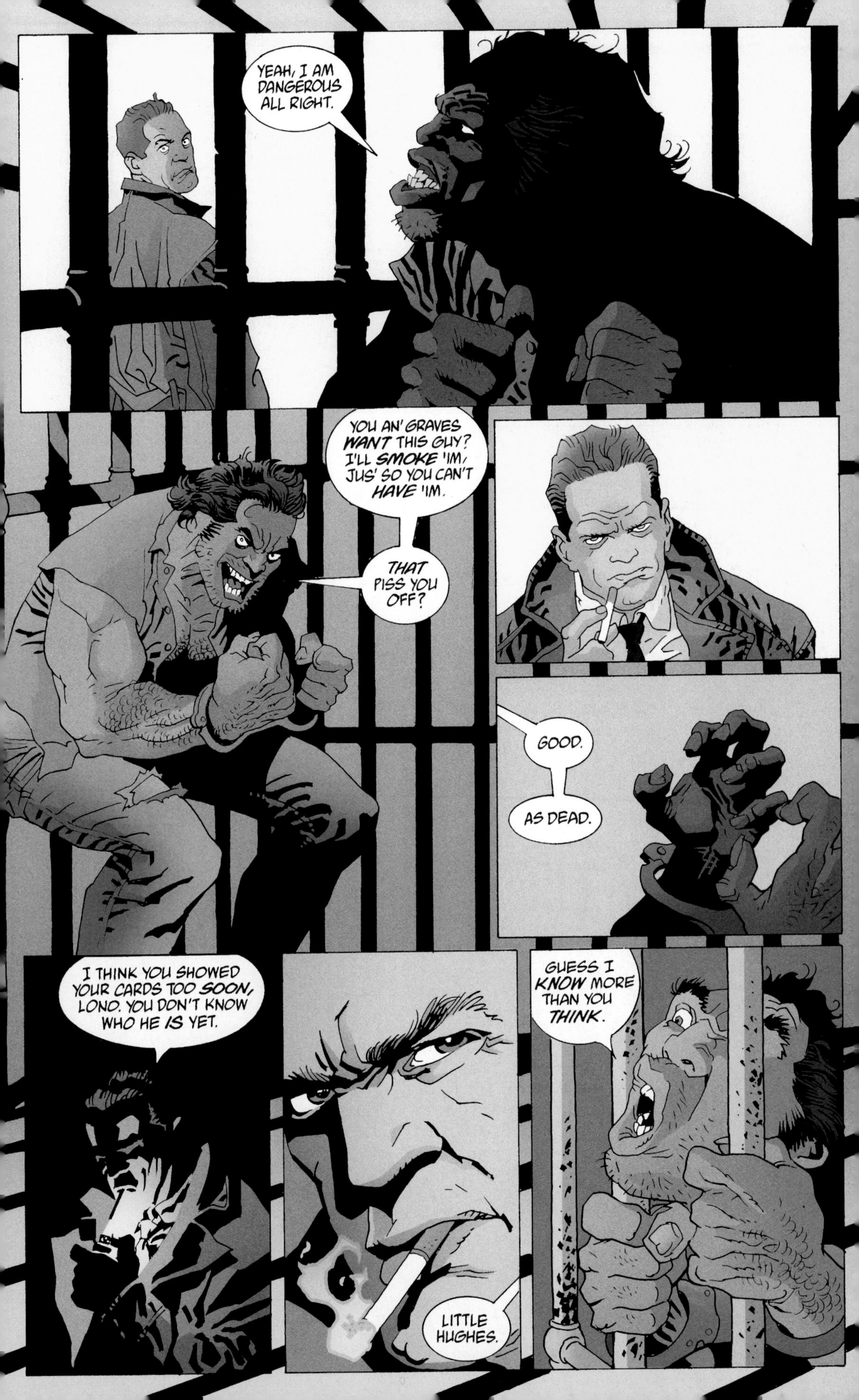
YEAH, I AM DANGEROUS ALL RIGHT.
YOU AN' GRAVES WANT THIS GUY? I'LL SMOKE 'IM, JUS' SO YOU CAN'T HAVE 'IM.
THAT PISS YOU OFF?
GOOD.
AS DEAD.
I THINK YOU SHOWED YOUR CARDS TOO SOON, LONO. YOU DON'T KNOW WHO HE IS YET.
GUESS I KNOW MORE THAN YOU THINK.
LITTLE HUGHES.

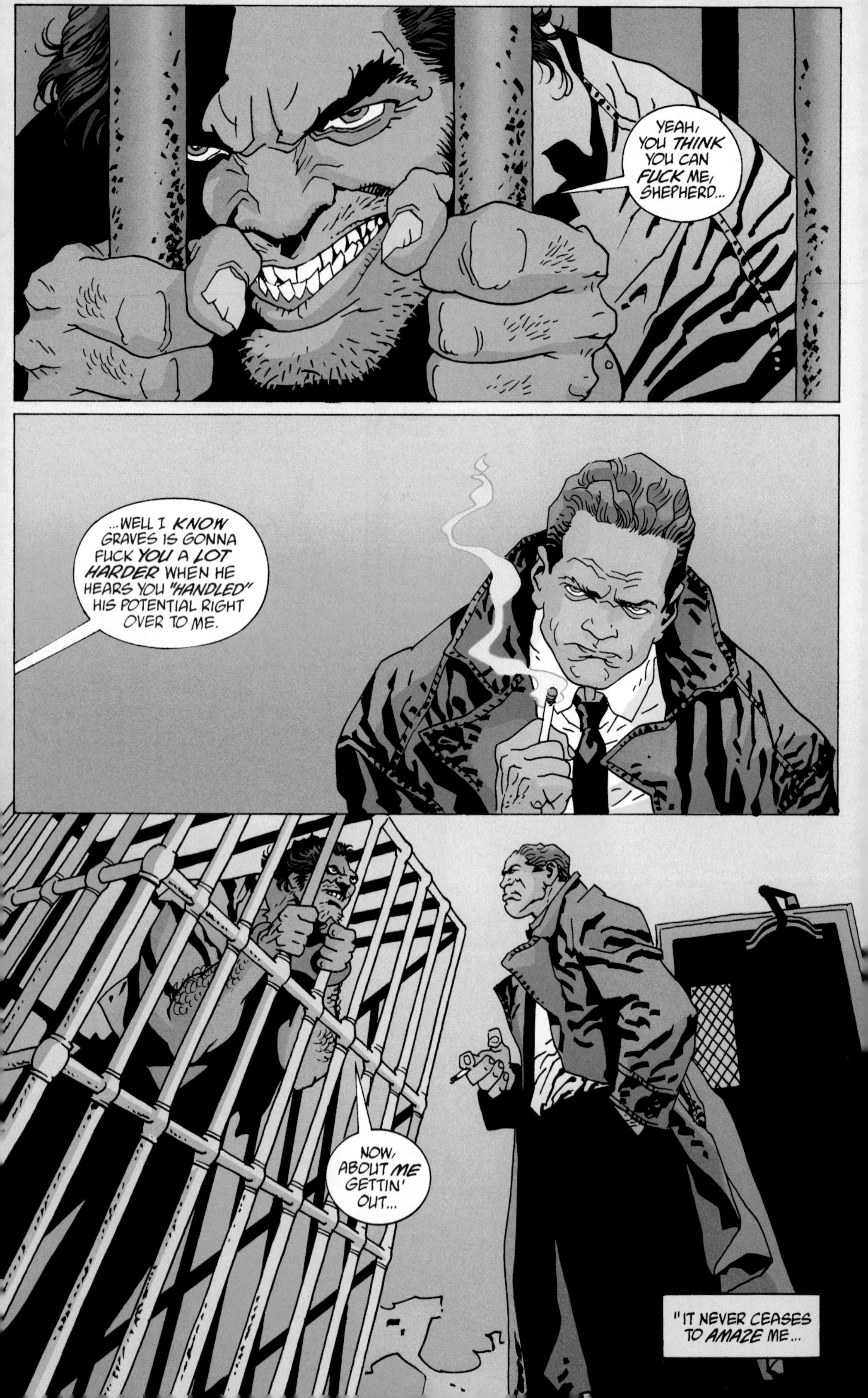
YEAH, YOU THINK YOU CAN FUCK ME, SHEPHERD...
...WELL I KNOW GRAVES IS GONNA FUCK YOU A LOT HARDER WHEN HE HEARS YOU "HANDLED" HIS POTENTIAL RIGHT OVER TO ME.
NOW, ABOUT ME GETTIN' OUT...
"IT NEVER CEASES TO AMAZE ME...

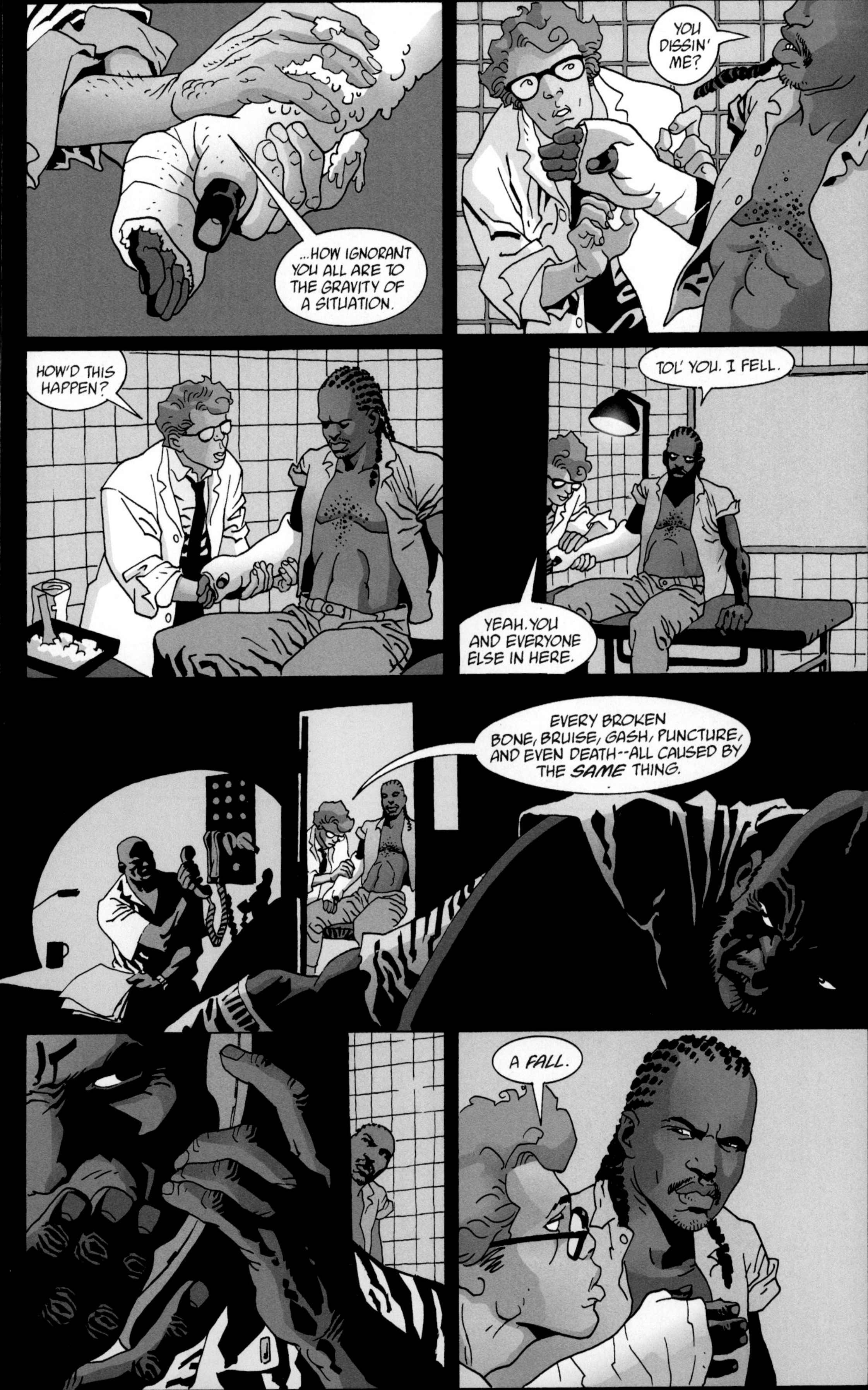
...HOW IGNORANT YOU ALL ARE TO THE GRAVITY OF A SITUATION.
YOU DISSIN' ME?
HOW'D THIS HAPPEN?
TOL' YOU. I FELL.
YEAH. YOU AND EVERYONE ELSE IN HERE.
EVERY BROKEN BONE, BRUISE, GASH, PUNCTURE, AND EVEN DEATH--ALL CAUSED BY THE SAME THING.
A FALL.

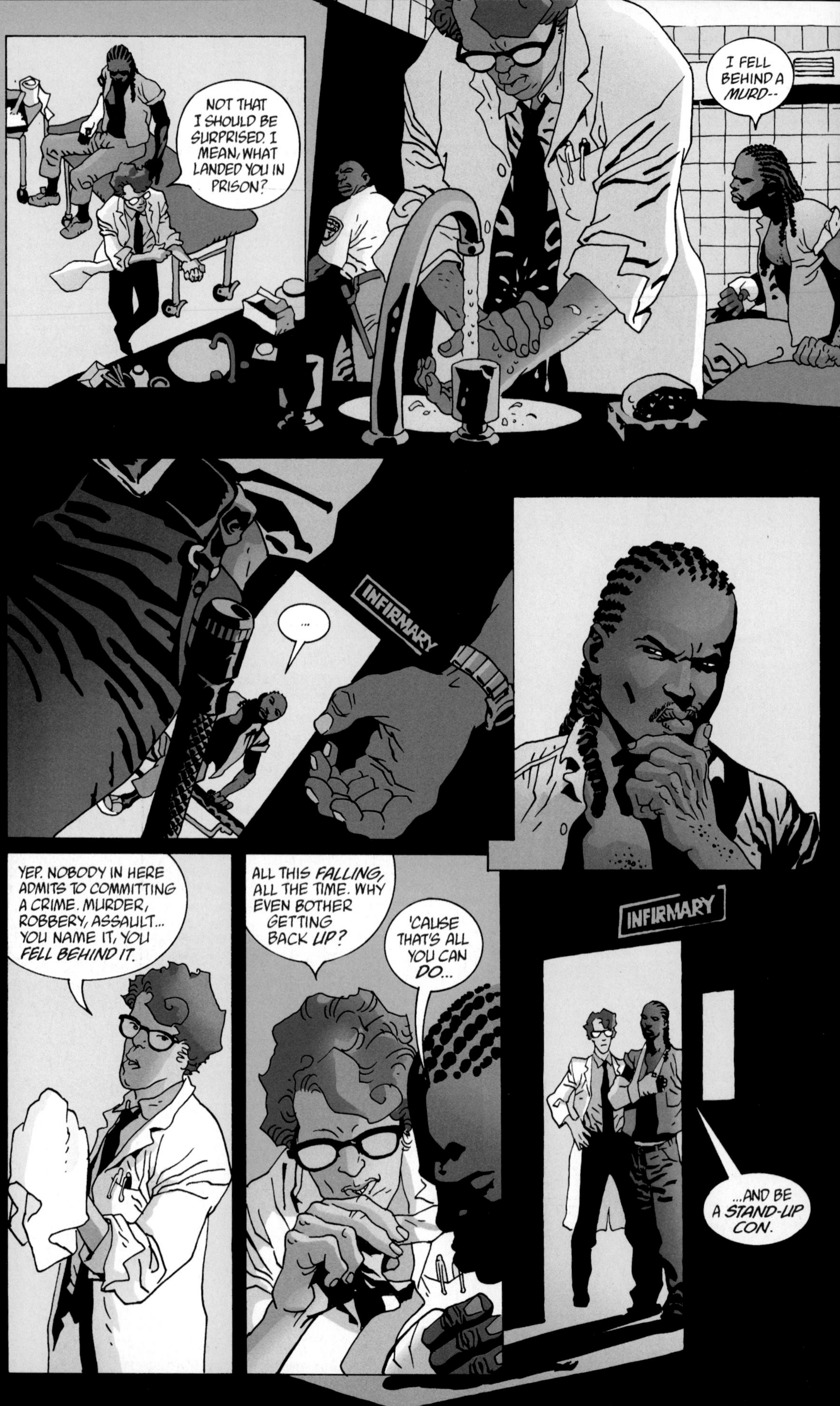
NOT THAT I SHOULD BE SURPRISED. I MEAN, WHAT LANDED YOU IN PRISON?
I FELL BEHIND A MURD--
...
INFIRMARY
YEP. NOBODY IN HERE ADMITS TO COMMITTING A CRIME. MURDER, ROBBERY, ASSAULT... YOU NAME IT, YOU FELL BEHIND IT.
ALL THIS FALLING, ALL THE TIME. WHY EVEN BOTHER GETTING BACK UP?
'CAUSE THAT'S ALL YOU CAN DO...
INFIRMARY
...AND BE A STAND-UP CON.

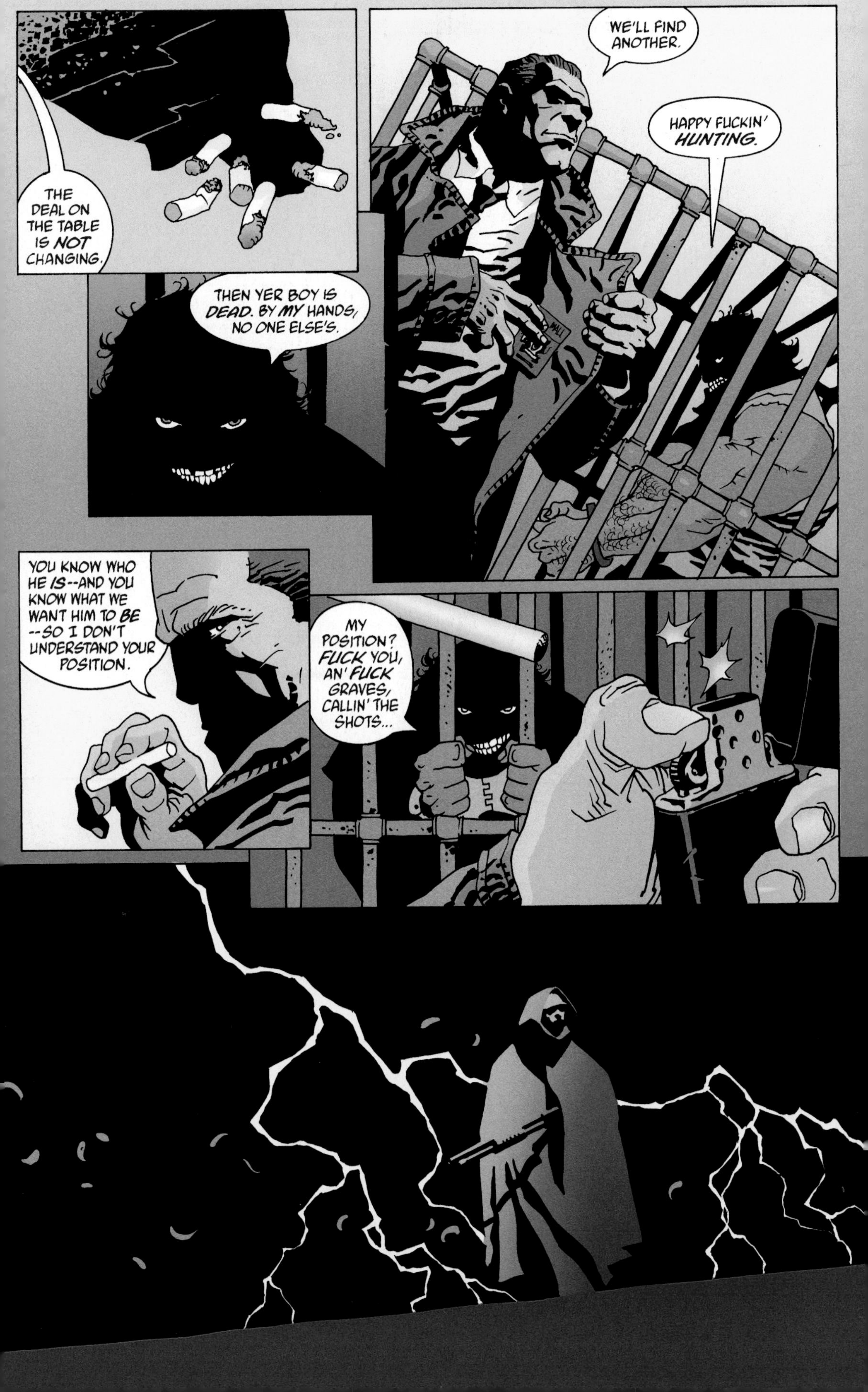
THE DEAL ON THE TABLE IS NOT CHANGING.
WE'LL FIND ANOTHER.
HAPPY FUCKIN' HUNTING.
THEN YER BOY IS DEAD. BY MY HANDS, NO ONE ELSE'S.
YOU KNOW WHO HE IS--AND YOU KNOW WHAT WE WANT HIM TO BE --SO I DON'T UNDERSTAND YOUR POSITION.
MY POSITION? FUCK YOU, AN' FUCK GRAVES, CALLIN' THE SHOTS...

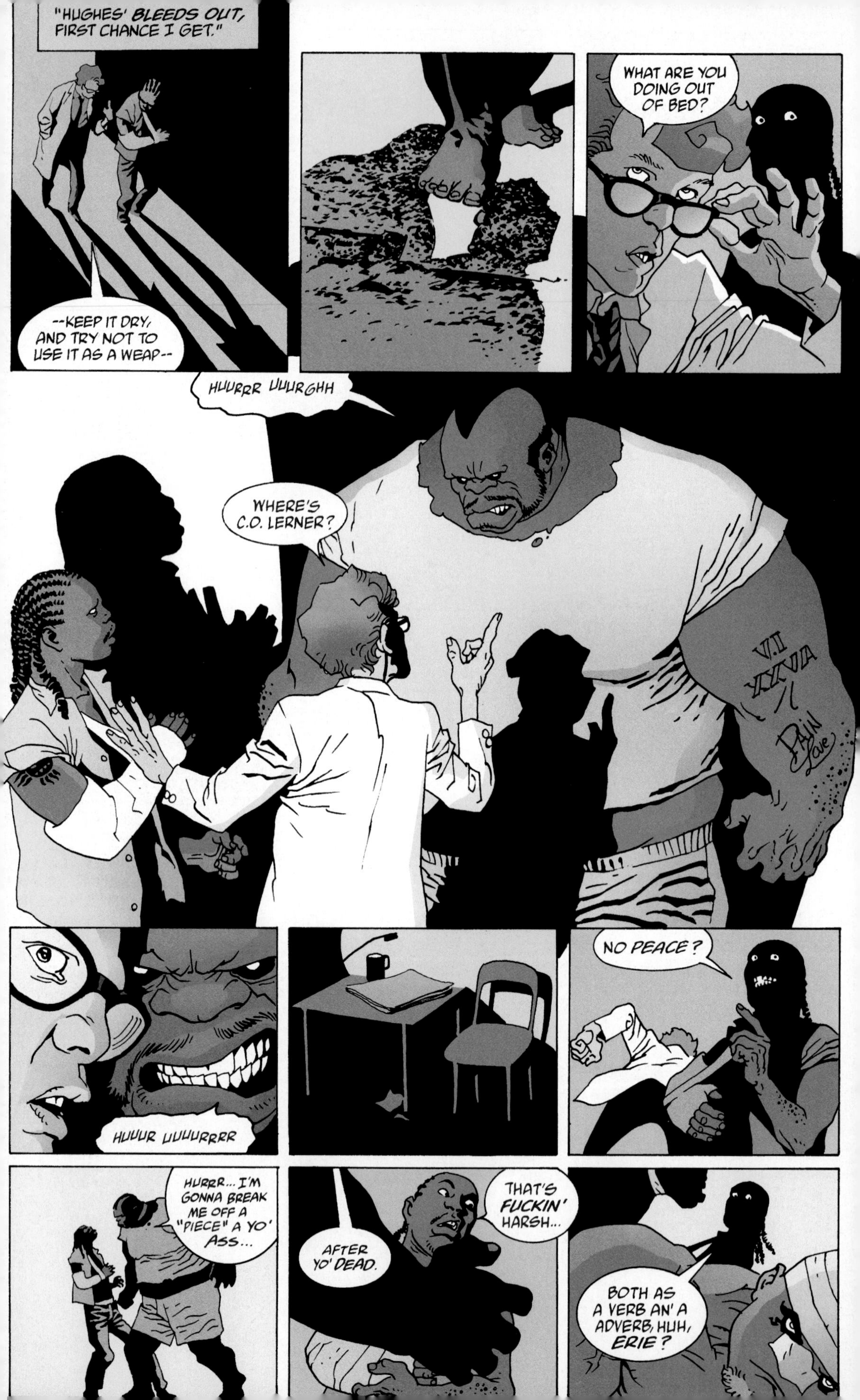
"HUGHES' BLEEDS OUT, FIRST CHANCE I GET."
--KEEP IT DRY, AND TRY NOT TO USE IT AS A WEAP--
WHAT ARE YOU DOING OUT OF BED?
HUURRR UUURGHH
WHERE'S C.O. LERNER?
HUUR UUUURRRR
NO PEACE?
HURRR... I'M GONNA BREAK ME OFF A "PIECE" A YO' ASS...
AFTER YO' DEAD.
THAT'S FUCKIN' HARSH...
BOTH AS A VERB AN' A ADVERB, HUH, ERIE?

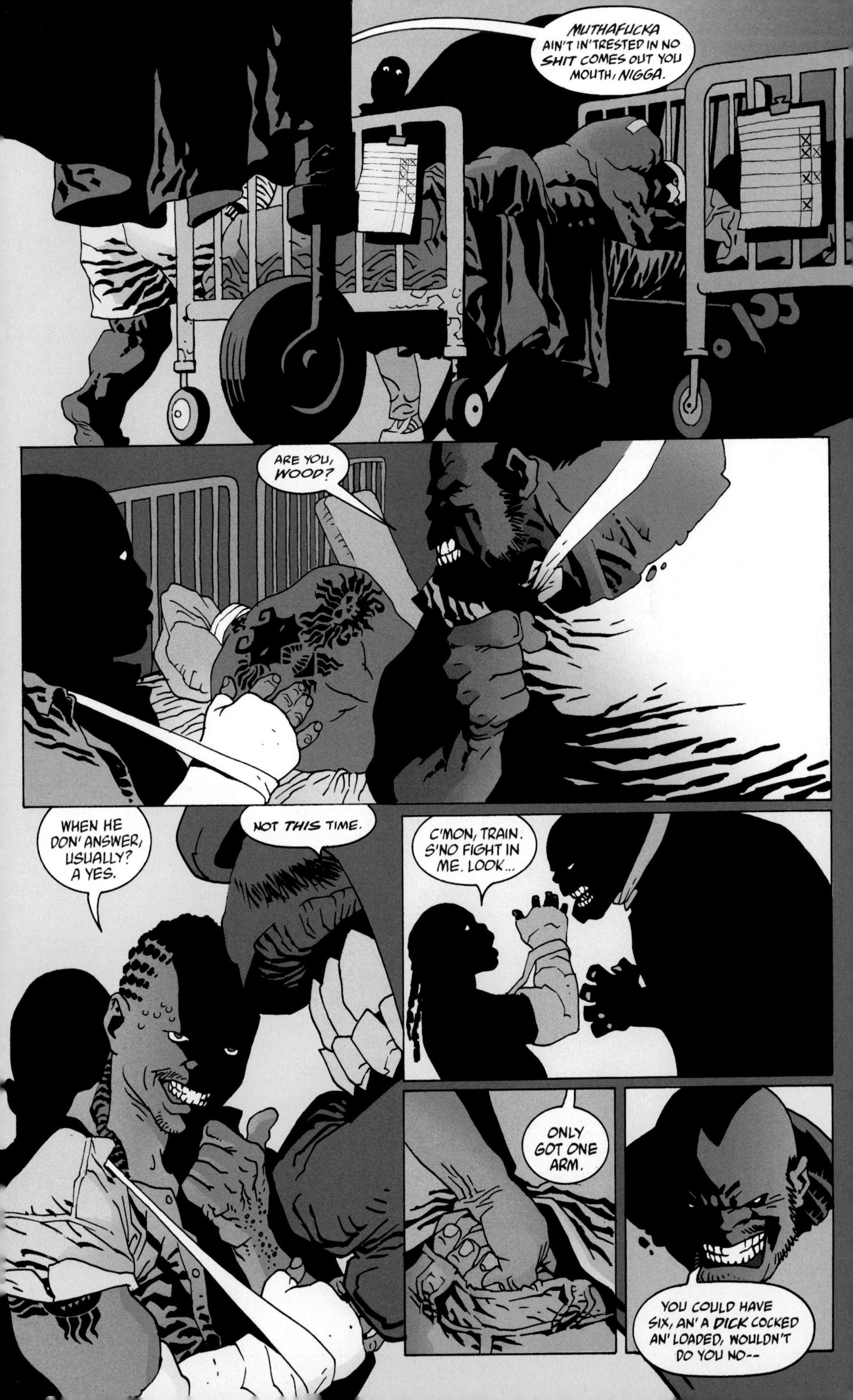
MUTHAFUCKA AIN'T IN'TRESTED IN NO SHIT COMES OUT YOU MOUTH, NIGGA.
ARE YOU, WOOD?
WHEN HE DON' ANSWER, USUALLY? A YES.
NOT THIS TIME.
C'MON, TRAIN. S'NO FIGHT IN ME. LOOK...
ONLY GOT ONE ARM.
YOU COULD HAVE SIX, AN' A DICK COCKED AN' LOADED, WOULDN'T DO YOU NO--

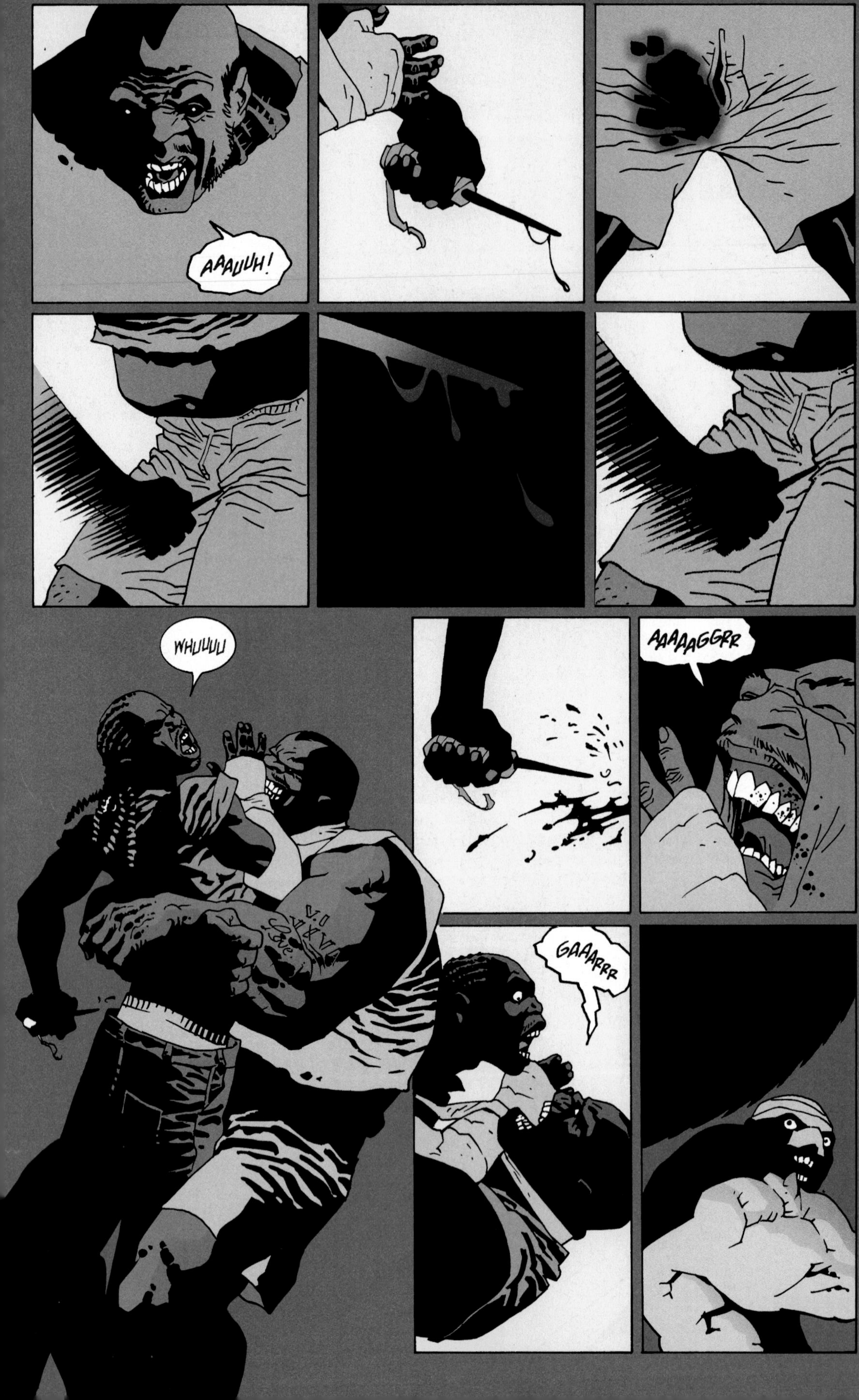
AAAUUH!
WHUUUU
AAAAAGGRR
GAAARRR

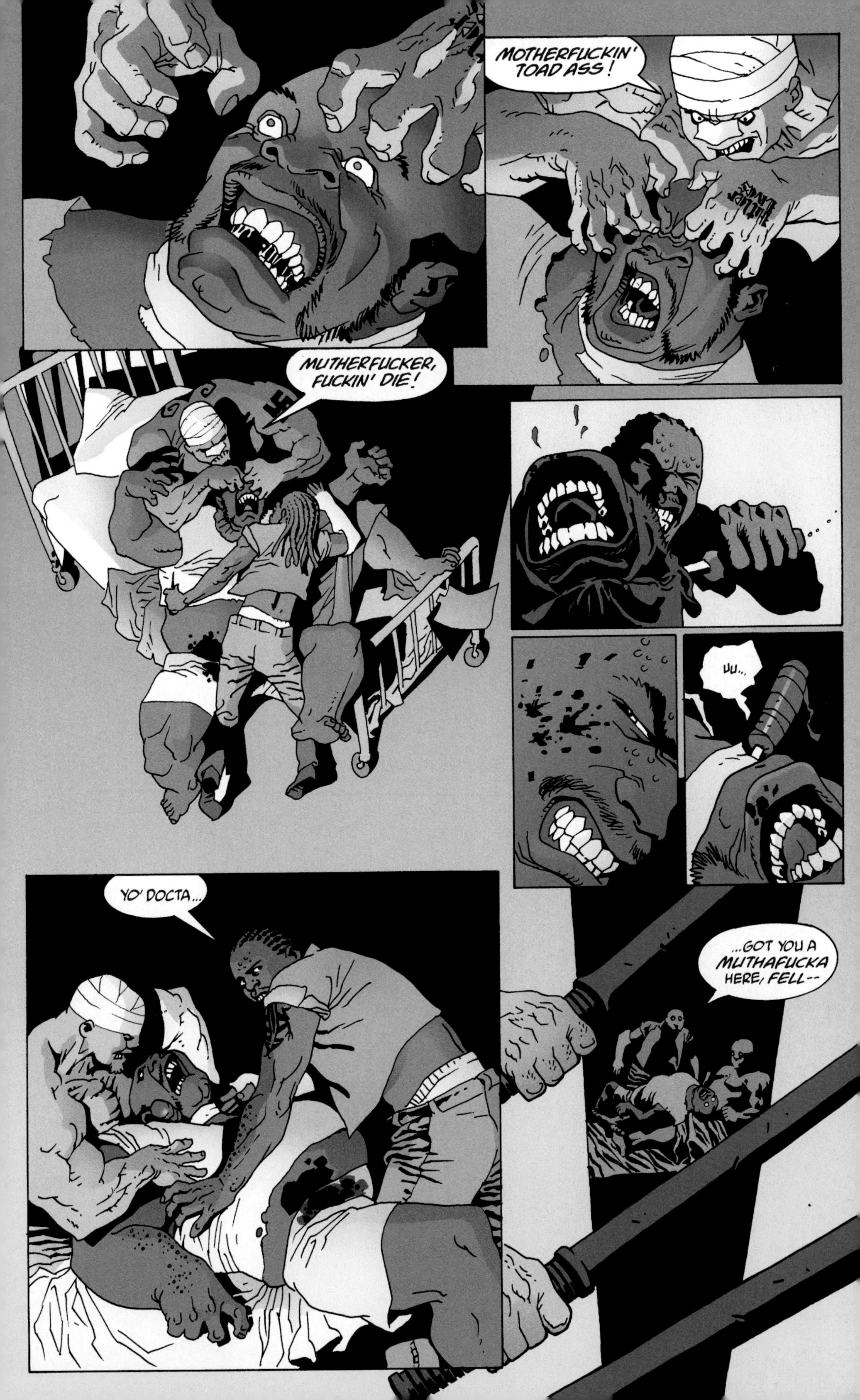
MOTHERFUCKIN' TOAD ASS!
MUTHERFUCKER, FUCKIN' DIE!
UU...
YO' DOCTA...
...GOT YOU A MUTHAFUCKA HERE, FELL--

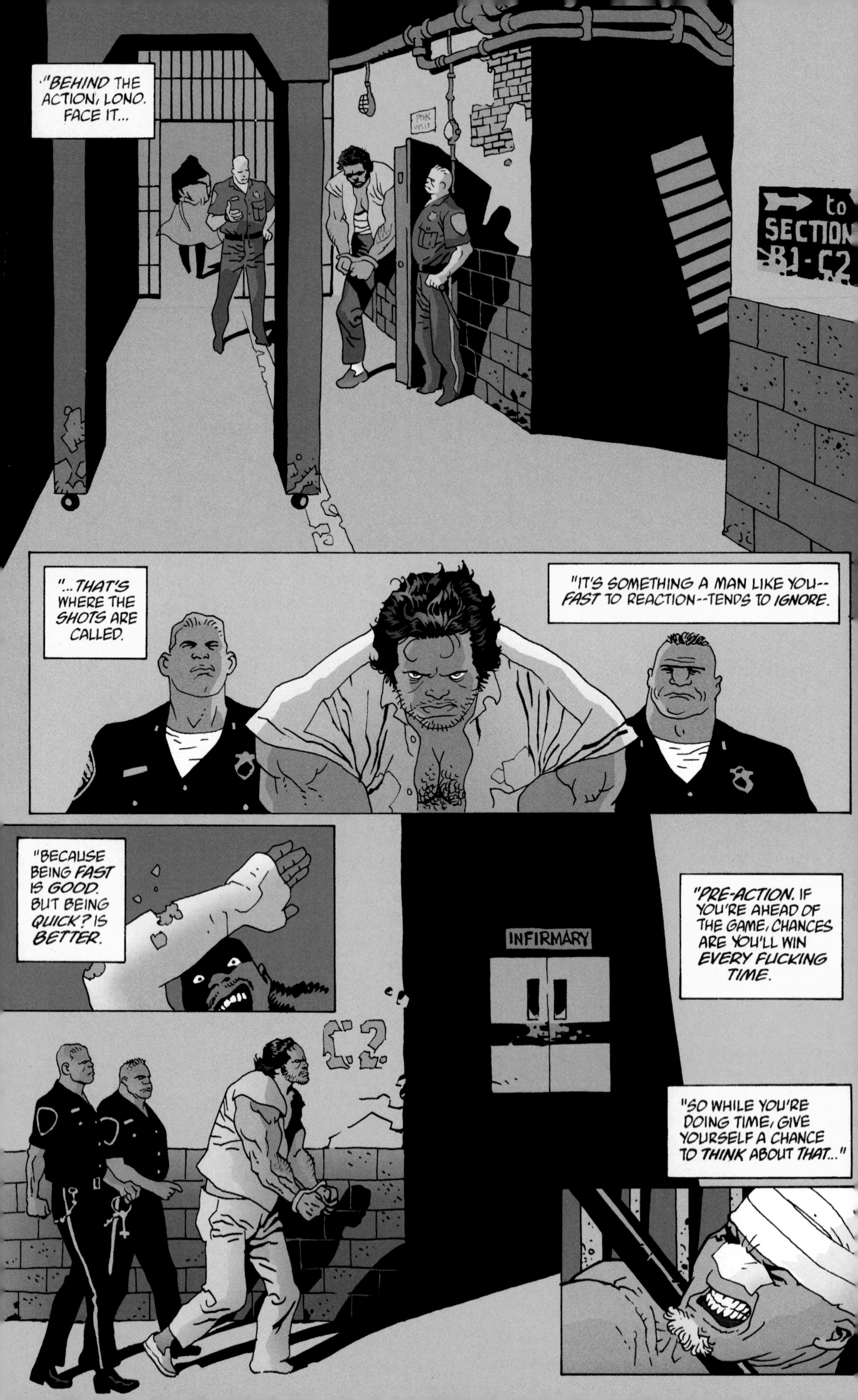
"BEHIND THE ACTION, LONO. FACE IT...
to SECTION B1-C2
"...THAT'S WHERE THE SHOTS ARE CALLED.
"IT'S SOMETHING A MAN LIKE YOU-- FAST TO REACTION--TENDS TO IGNORE.
"BECAUSE BEING FAST IS GOOD. BUT BEING QUICK? IS BETTER.
"PRE-ACTION. IF YOU'RE AHEAD OF THE GAME, CHANCES ARE YOU'LL WIN EVERY FUCKING TIME.
INFIRMARY
C2
"SO WHILE YOU'RE DOING TIME, GIVE YOURSELF A CHANCE TO THINK ABOUT THAT..."

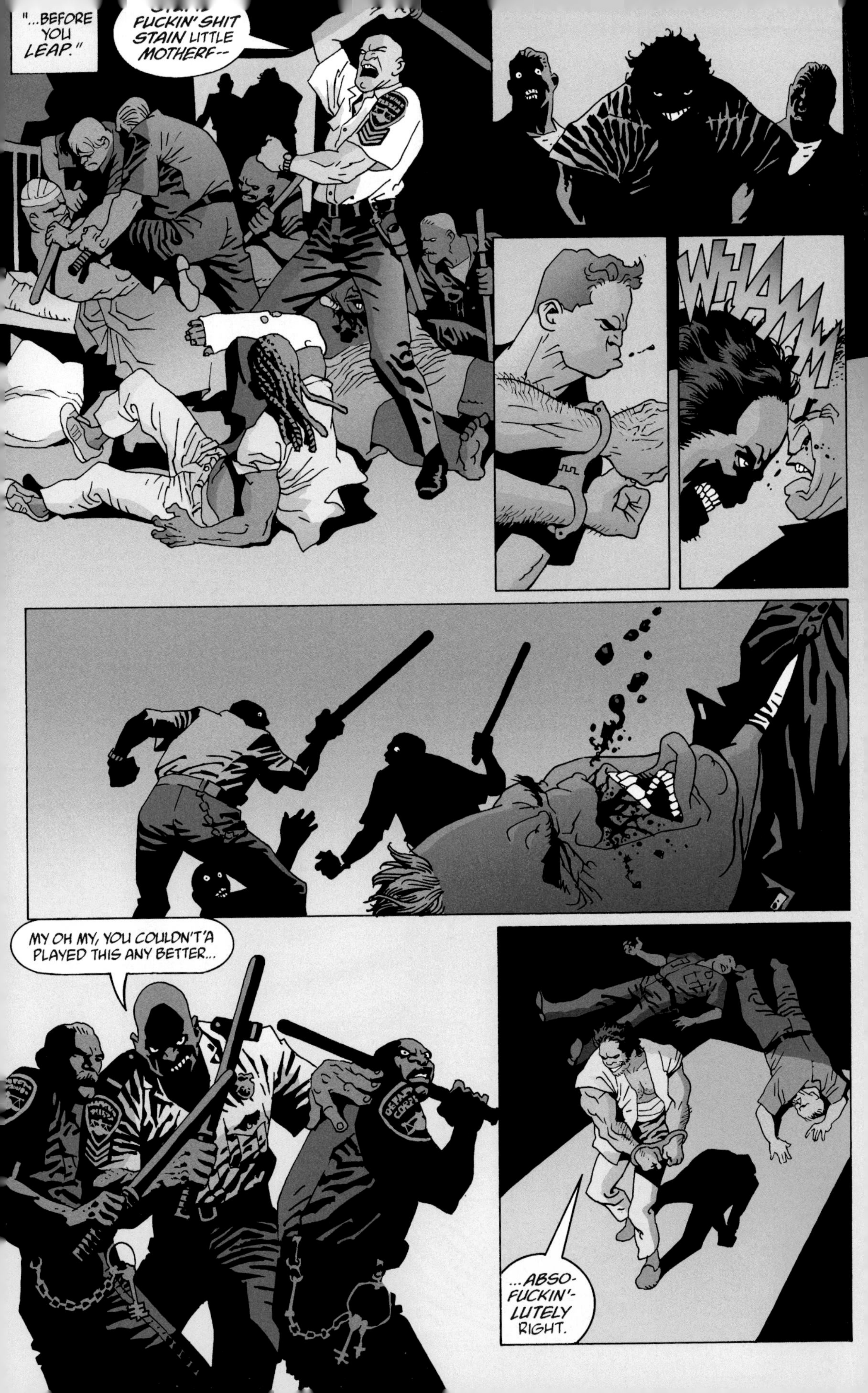
"...BEFORE YOU LEAP."
FUCKIN' SHIT STAIN LITTLE MOTHERF--
WHAM
MY OH MY, YOU COULDN'T'A PLAYED THIS ANY BETTER...
...ABSO-FUCKIN'-LUTELY RIGHT.

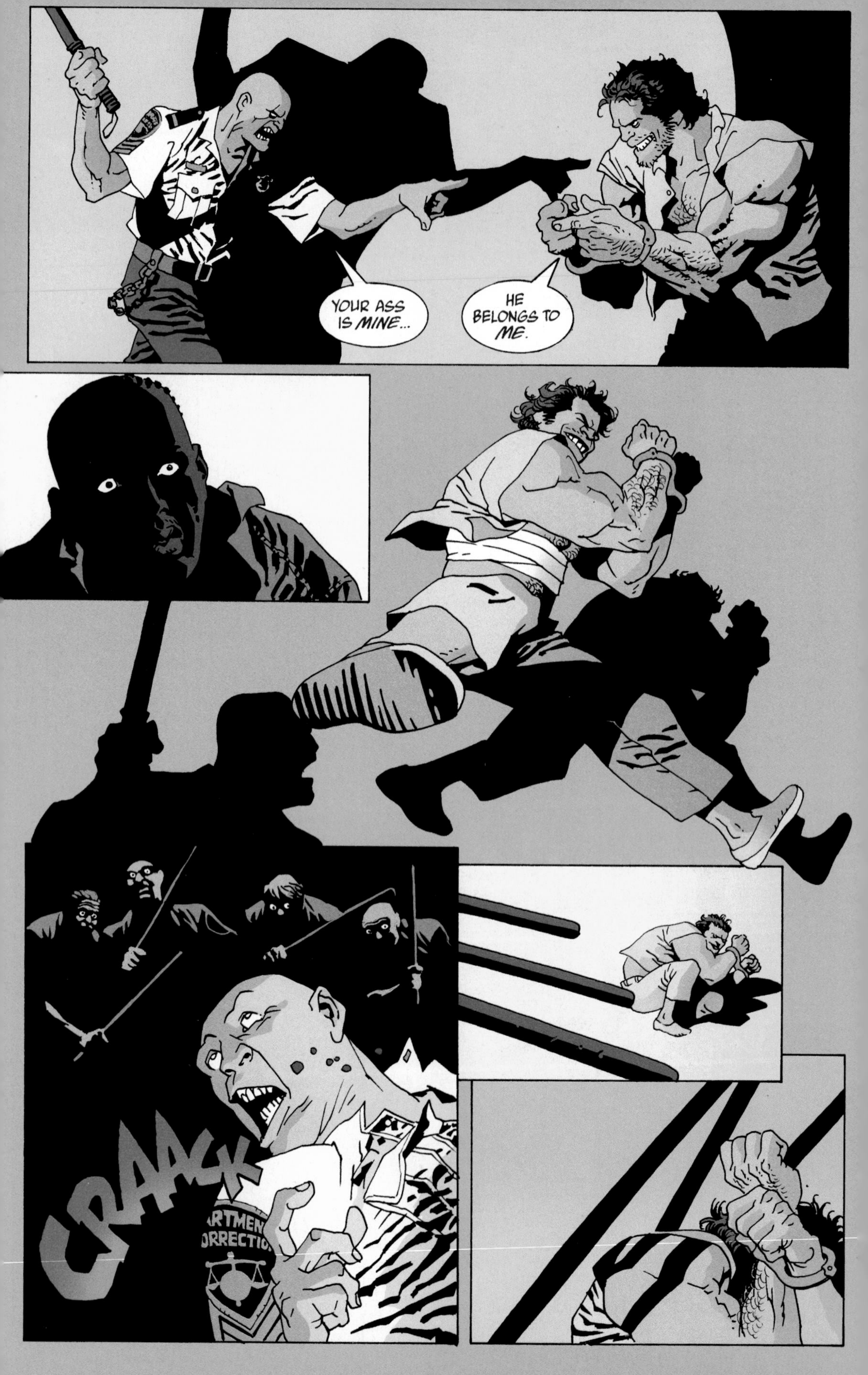
YOUR ASS IS *MINE*...
HE BELONGS TO *ME*.
CRAACK

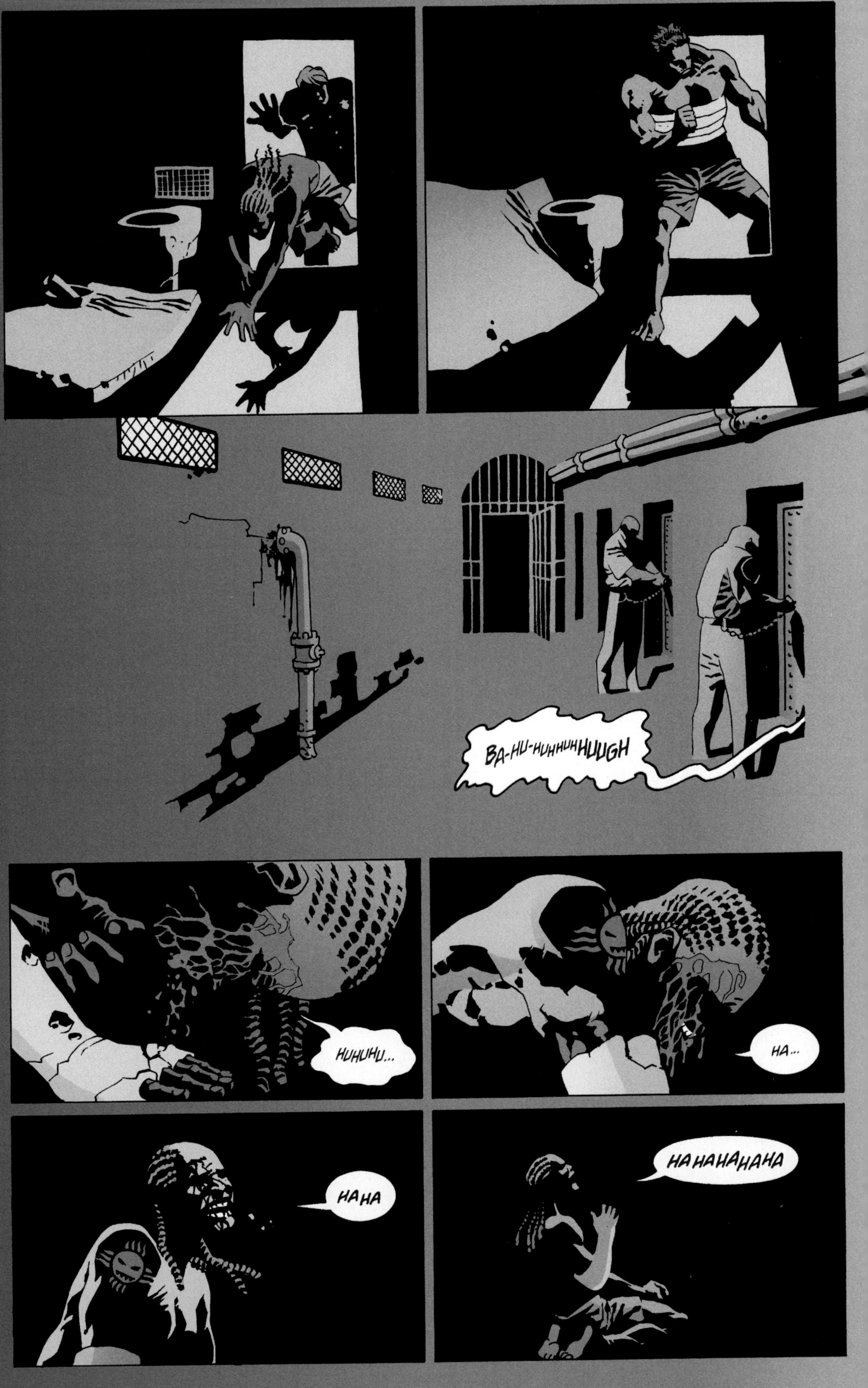
BA-HU-HUHHUHHUUGH
HUHUHU...
HA...
HAHA
HAHAHAHAHA

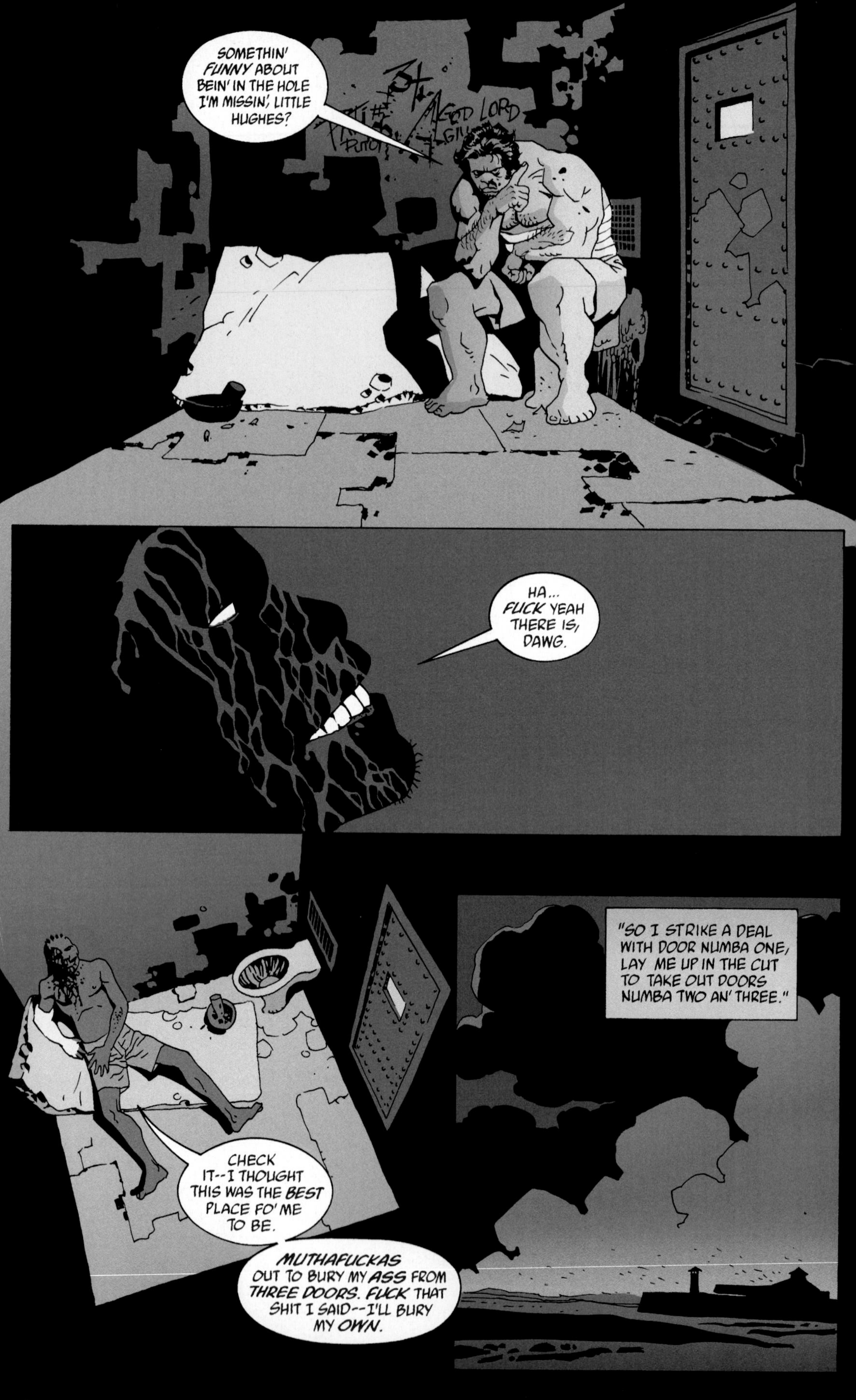

SOMETHIN' FUNNY ABOUT BEIN' IN THE HOLE I'M MISSIN', LITTLE HUGHES?
HA... FUCK YEAH THERE IS, DAWG.
CHECK IT--I THOUGHT THIS WAS THE BEST PLACE FO' ME TO BE.
MUTHAFUCKAS OUT TO BURY MY ASS FROM THREE DOORS. FUCK THAT SHIT I SAID--I'LL BURY MY OWN.
"SO I STRIKE A DEAL WITH DOOR NUMBA ONE, LAY ME UP IN THE CUT TO TAKE OUT DOORS NUMBA TWO AN' THREE."

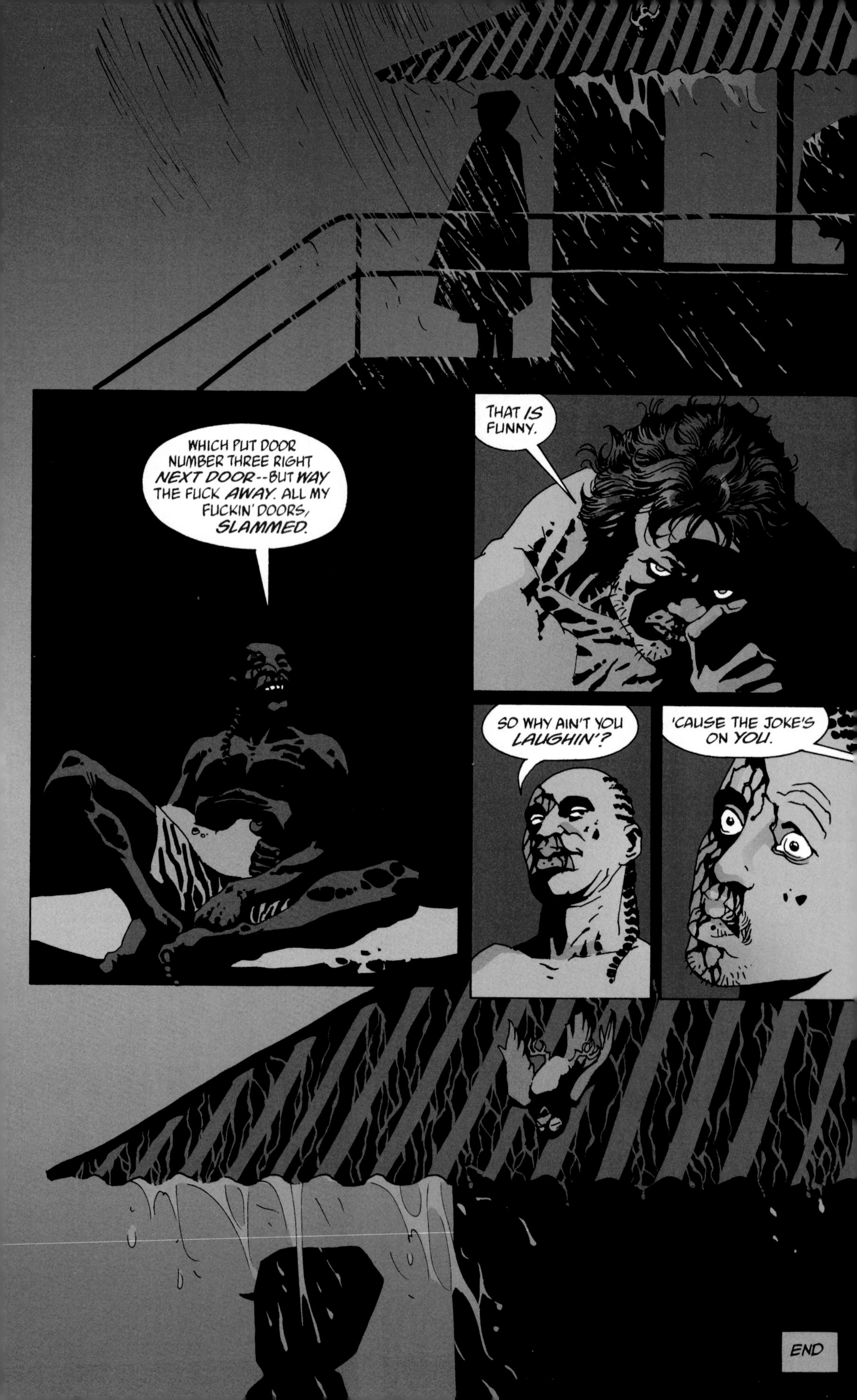
WHICH PUT DOOR NUMBER THREE RIGHT NEXT DOOR--BUT WAY THE FUCK AWAY. ALL MY FUCKIN' DOORS, SLAMMED.
THAT IS FUNNY.
SO WHY AIN'T YOU LAUGHIN'?
'CAUSE THE JOKE'S ON YOU.
END

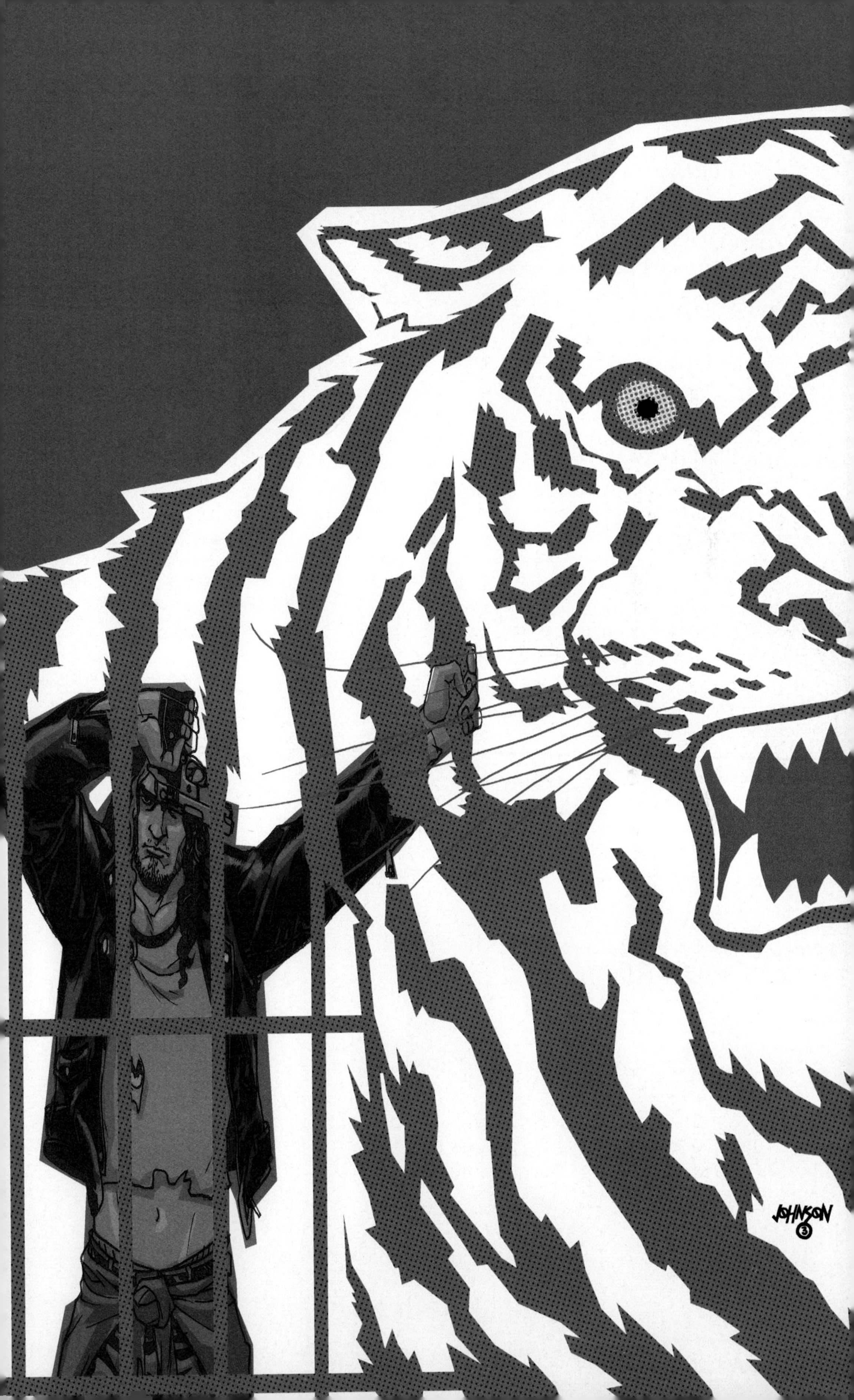
JOHNSON

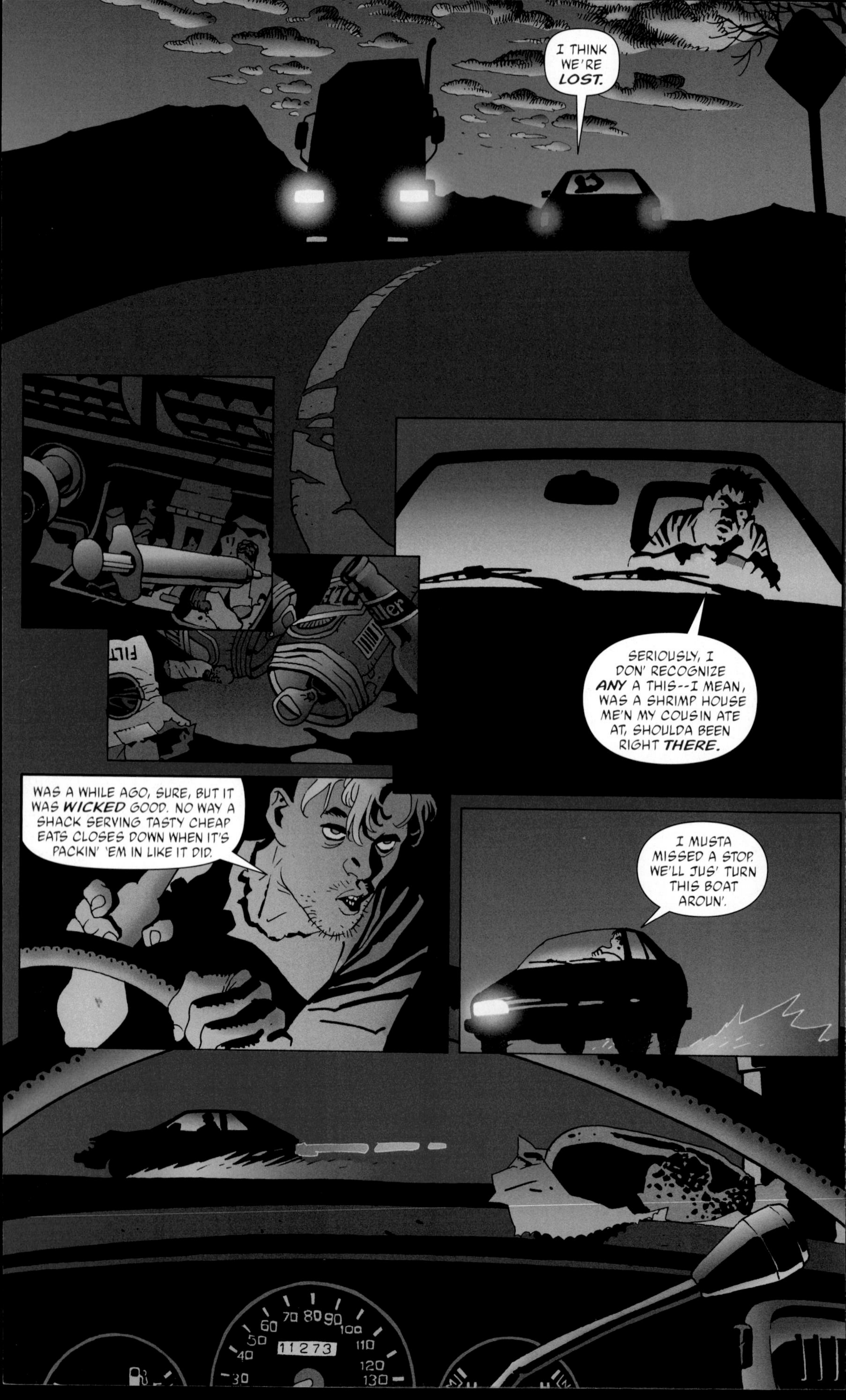
I THINK WE'RE LOST.
SERIOUSLY, I DON' RECOGNIZE ANY A THIS--I MEAN, WAS A SHRIMP HOUSE ME'N MY COUSIN ATE AT, SHOULDA BEEN RIGHT THERE.
WAS A WHILE AGO, SURE, BUT IT WAS WICKED GOOD. NO WAY A SHACK SERVING TASTY CHEAP EATS CLOSES DOWN WHEN IT'S PACKIN' 'EM IN LIKE IT DID.
I MUSTA MISSED A STOP. WE'LL JUS' TURN THIS BOAT AROUN'.
11273

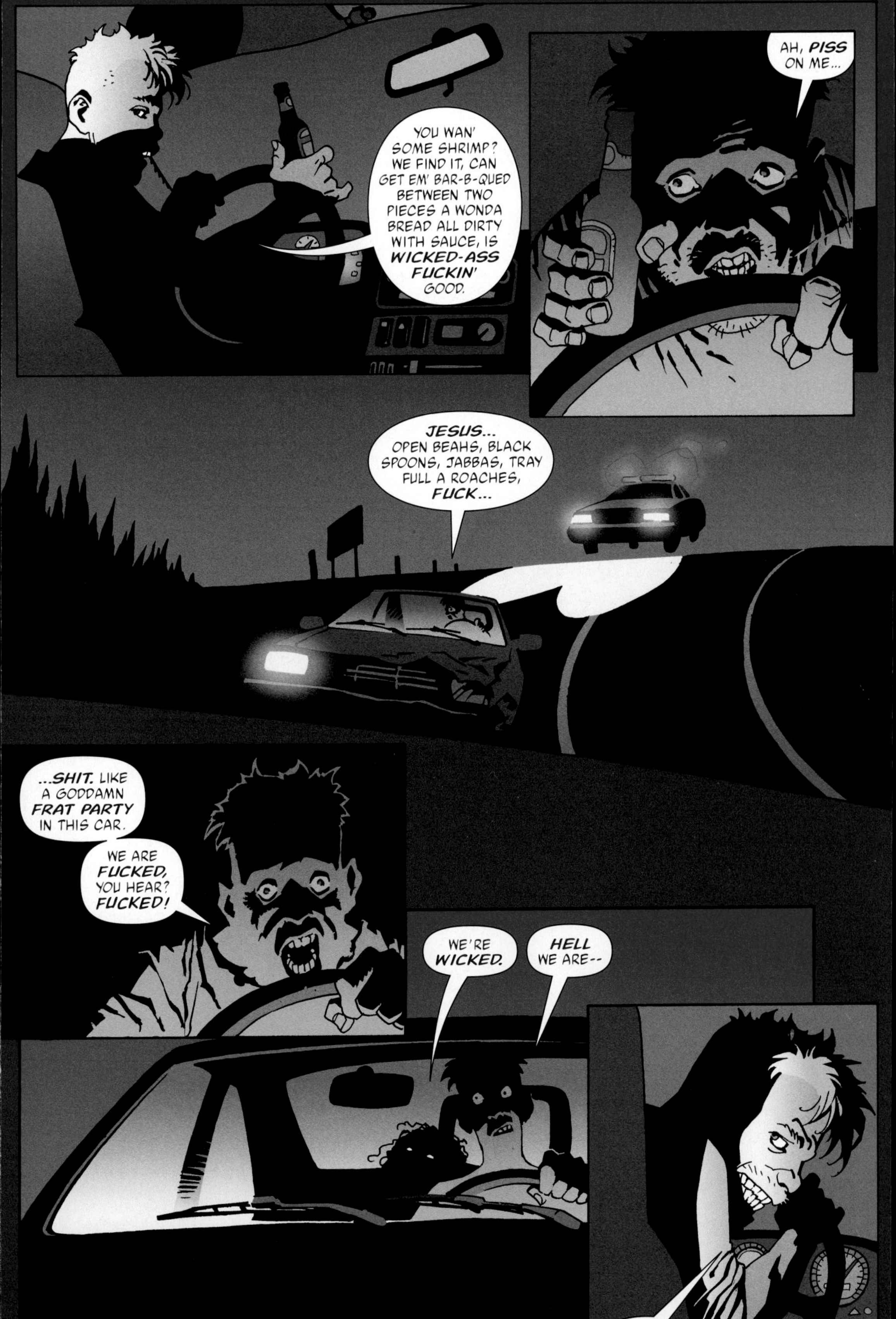
YOU WAN' SOME SHRIMP? WE FIND IT, CAN GET EM' BAR-B-QUED BETWEEN TWO PIECES A WONDA BREAD ALL DIRTY WITH SAUCE, IS **WICKED-ASS FUCKIN'** GOOD.
AH, **PISS** ON ME...
JESUS... OPEN BEAHS, BLACK SPOONS, JABBAS, TRAY FULL A ROACHES, **FUCK...**
...SHIT. LIKE A GODDAMN **FRAT PARTY** IN THIS CAR.
WE ARE **FUCKED,** YOU HEAR? **FUCKED!**
WE'RE **WICKED.**
HELL WE ARE--
RIGHT.

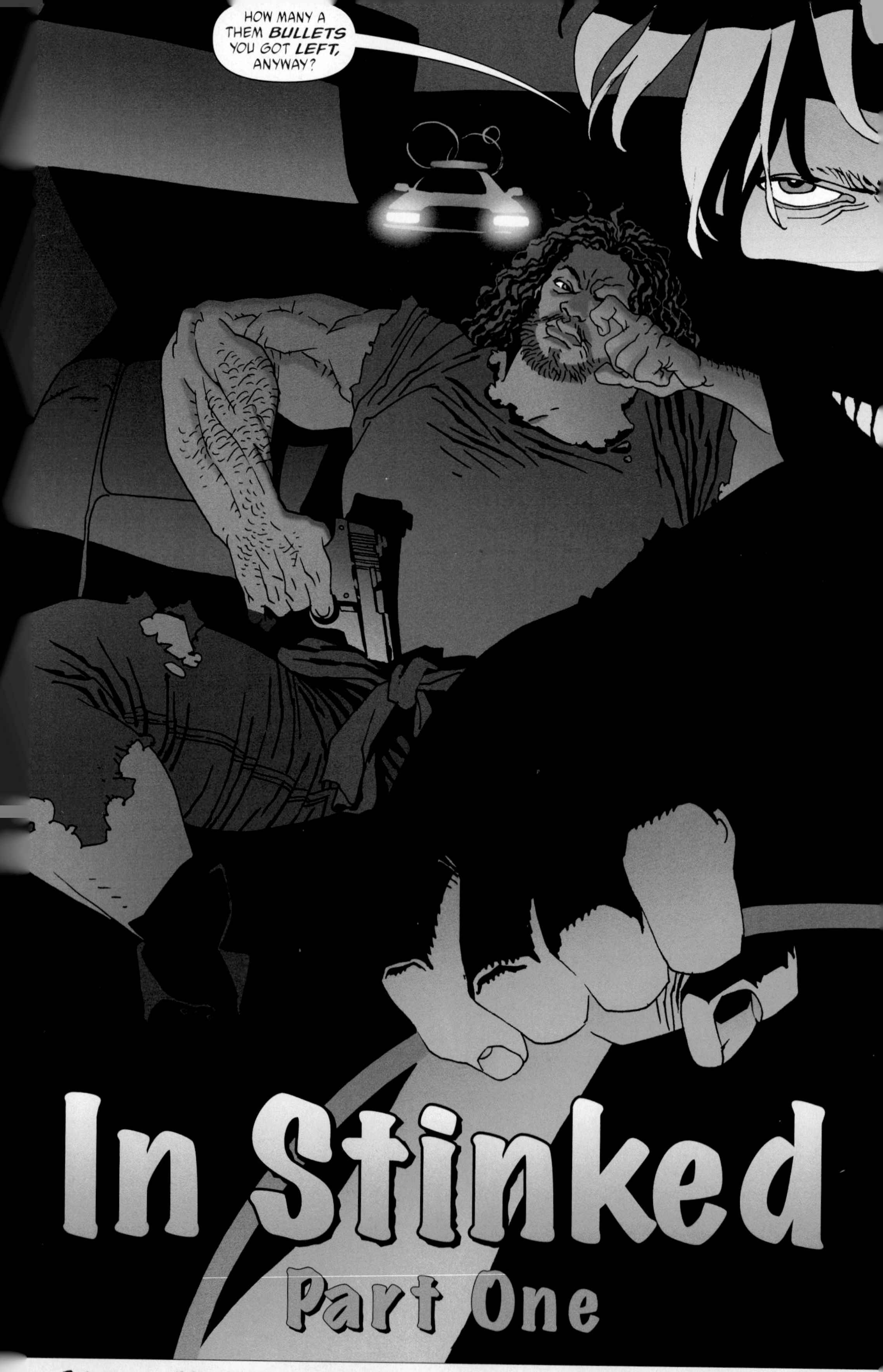
HOW MANY A THEM BULLETS YOU GOT LEFT, ANYWAY?
In Stinked
Part One

Brian **Azzarello** WRITER · Eduardo **Risso** ARTIST · Patricia **Mulvihill** COLORIST · Clem **Robins** LETTERER · Dave **Johnson** COVER · Zachary **Rau** ASS'T ED · Will **Dennis** EDITOR

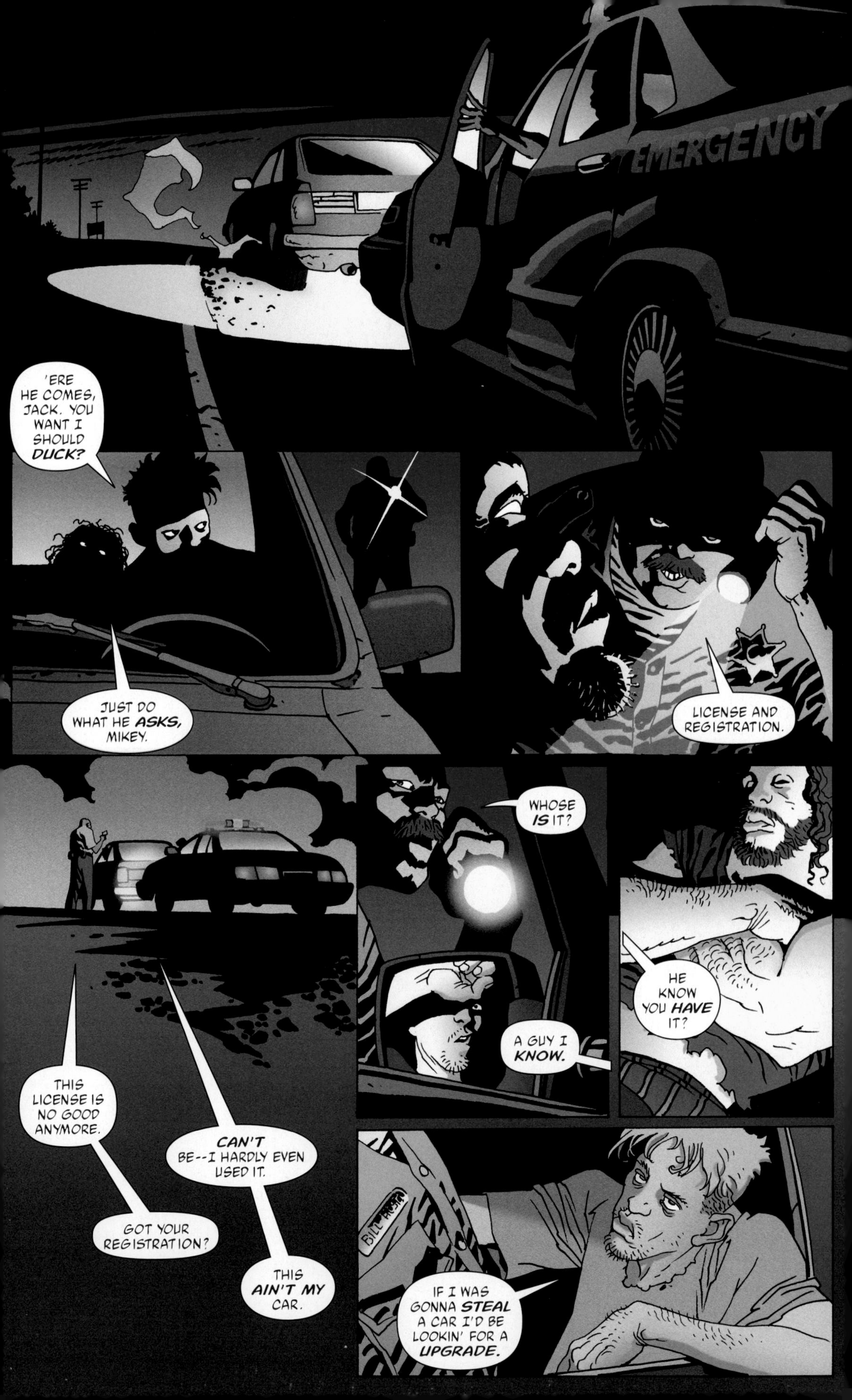
EMERGENCY
'ERE HE COMES, JACK. YOU WANT I SHOULD DUCK?
JUST DO WHAT HE ASKS, MIKEY.
LICENSE AND REGISTRATION.
THIS LICENSE IS NO GOOD ANYMORE.
CAN'T BE--I HARDLY EVEN USED IT.
GOT YOUR REGISTRATION?
THIS AIN'T MY CAR.
WHOSE IS IT?
A GUY I KNOW.
HE KNOW YOU HAVE IT?
IF I WAS GONNA STEAL A CAR I'D BE LOOKIN' FOR A UPGRADE.

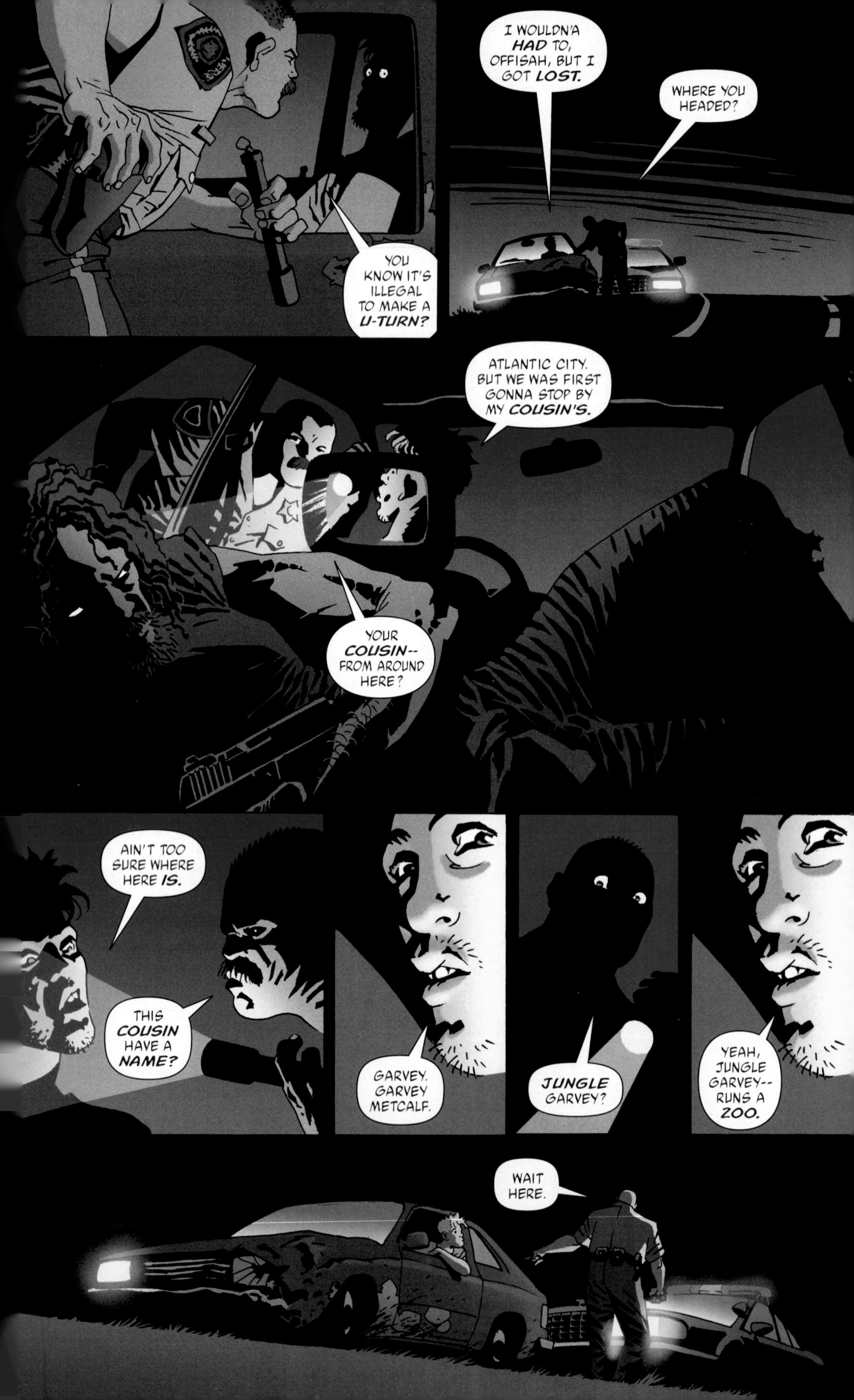
YOU KNOW IT'S ILLEGAL TO MAKE A U-TURN?
I WOULDN'A HAD TO, OFFISAH, BUT I GOT LOST.
WHERE YOU HEADED?
ATLANTIC CITY. BUT WE WAS FIRST GONNA STOP BY MY COUSIN'S.
YOUR COUSIN-- FROM AROUND HERE?
AIN'T TOO SURE WHERE HERE IS.
THIS COUSIN HAVE A NAME?
GARVEY. GARVEY METCALF.
JUNGLE GARVEY?
YEAH, JUNGLE GARVEY-- RUNS A ZOO.
WAIT HERE.

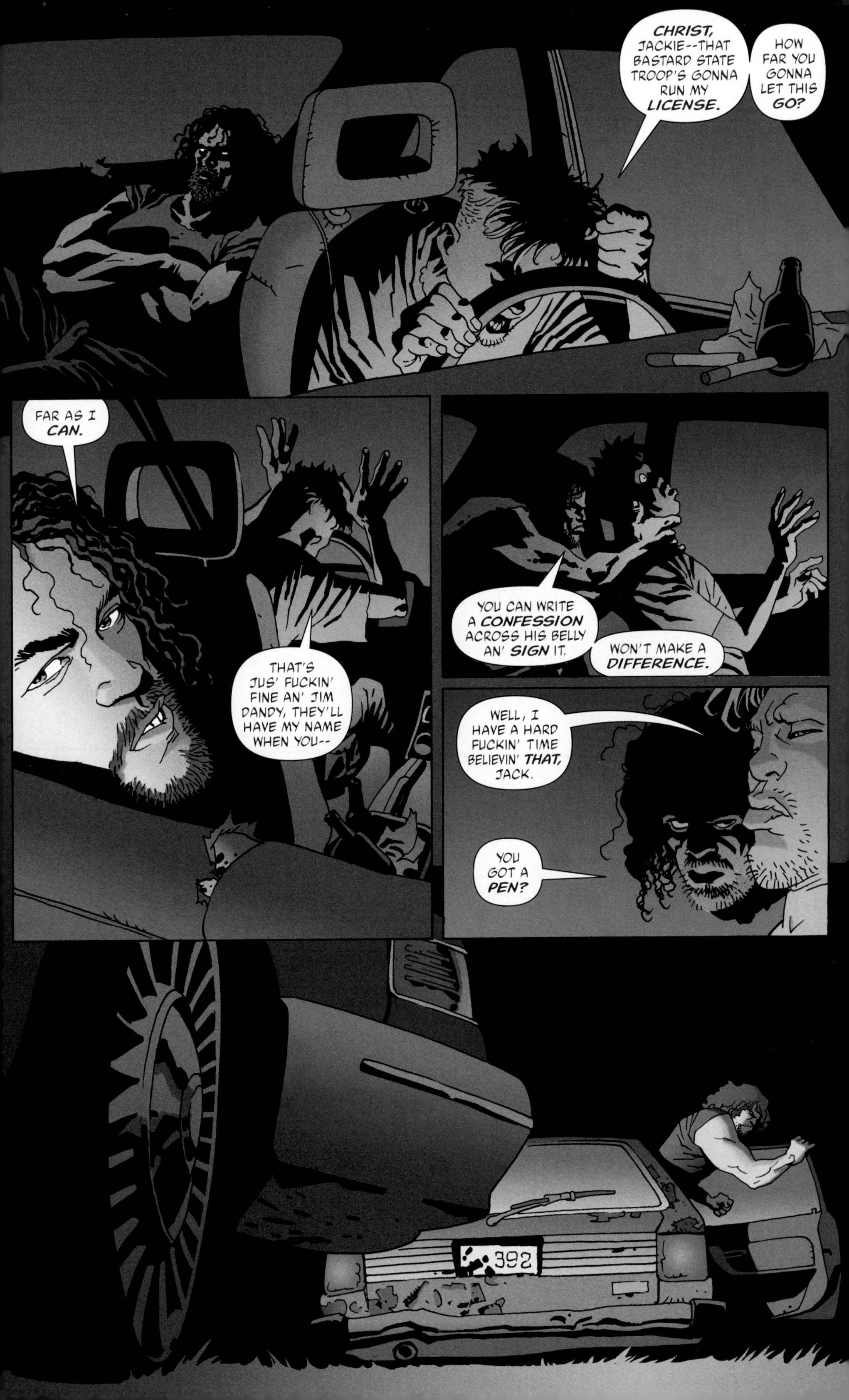
CHRIST, JACKIE--THAT BASTARD STATE TROOP'S GONNA RUN MY LICENSE.
HOW FAR YOU GONNA LET THIS GO?
FAR AS I CAN.
THAT'S JUS' FUCKIN' FINE AN' JIM DANDY, THEY'LL HAVE MY NAME WHEN YOU--
YOU CAN WRITE A CONFESSION ACROSS HIS BELLY AN' SIGN IT.
WON'T MAKE A DIFFERENCE.
WELL, I HAVE A HARD FUCKIN' TIME BELIEVIN' THAT, JACK.
YOU GOT A PEN?
392

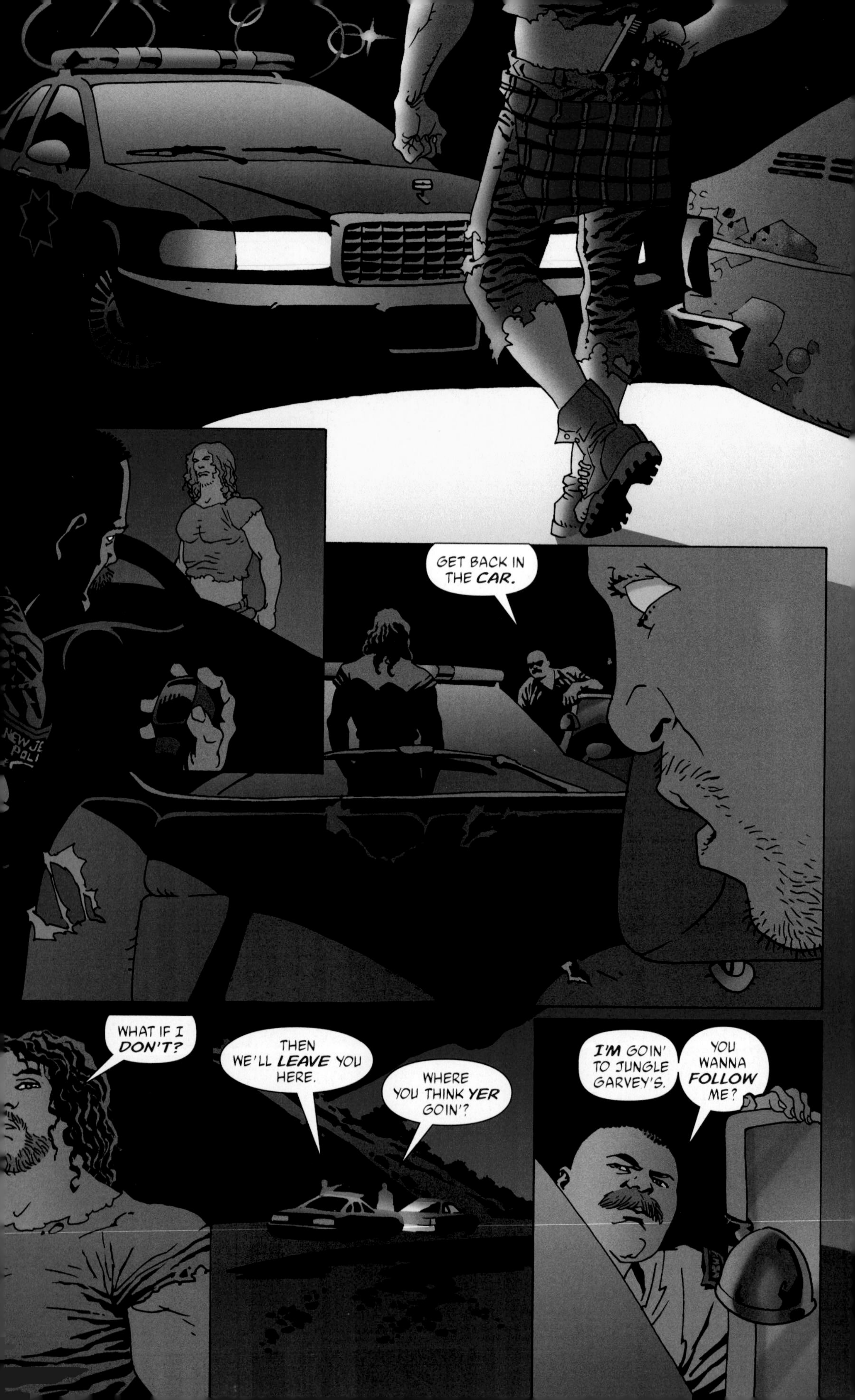
GET BACK IN THE CAR.
WHAT IF I DON'T?
THEN WE'LL LEAVE YOU HERE.
WHERE YOU THINK YER GOIN'?
I'M GOIN' TO JUNGLE GARVEY'S.
YOU WANNA FOLLOW ME?

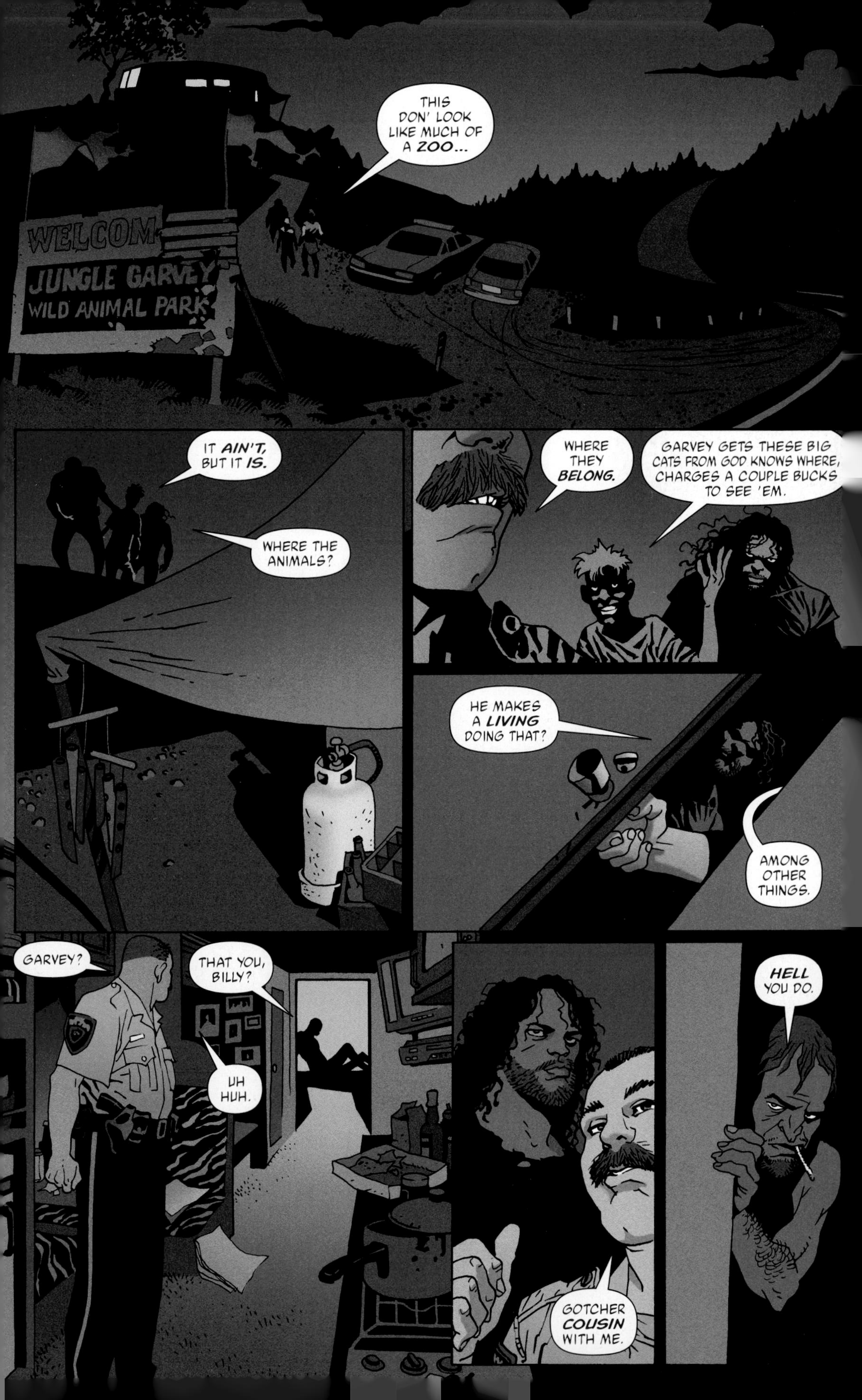
WELCOM
JUNGLE GARVEY
WILD ANIMAL PARK
THIS DON' LOOK LIKE MUCH OF A ZOO...
IT AIN'T, BUT IT IS.
WHERE THE ANIMALS?
WHERE THEY BELONG.
GARVEY GETS THESE BIG CATS FROM GOD KNOWS WHERE, CHARGES A COUPLE BUCKS TO SEE 'EM.
HE MAKES A LIVING DOING THAT?
AMONG OTHER THINGS.
GARVEY?
THAT YOU, BILLY?
UH HUH.
GOTCHER COUSIN WITH ME.
HELL YOU DO.

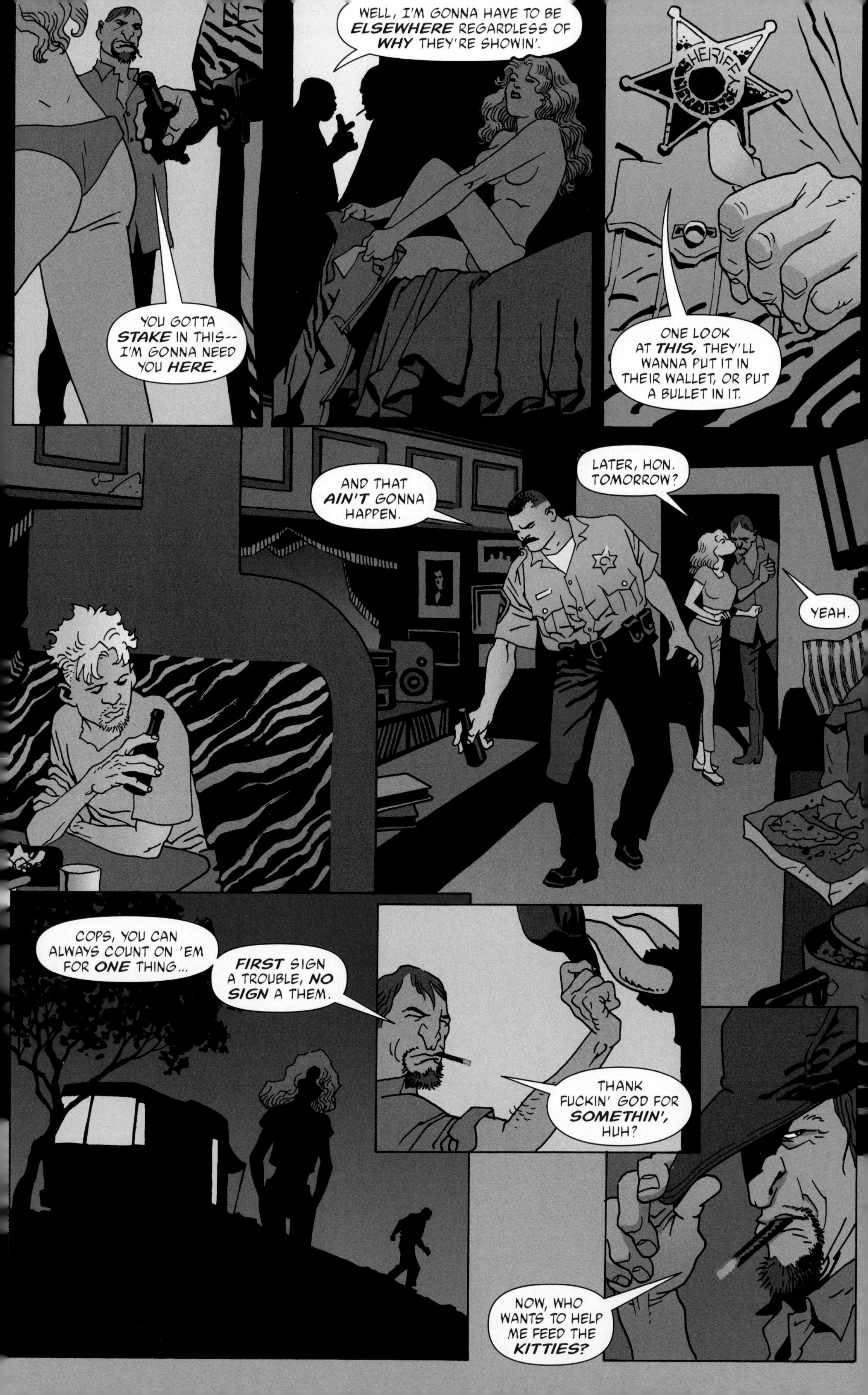

YOU GOTTA STAKE IN THIS-- I'M GONNA NEED YOU HERE.
WELL, I'M GONNA HAVE TO BE ELSEWHERE REGARDLESS OF WHY THEY'RE SHOWIN'.
SHERIFF
ONE LOOK AT THIS, THEY'LL WANNA PUT IT IN THEIR WALLET, OR PUT A BULLET IN IT.
AND THAT AIN'T GONNA HAPPEN.
LATER, HON. TOMORROW?
YEAH.
COPS, YOU CAN ALWAYS COUNT ON 'EM FOR ONE THING...
FIRST SIGN A TROUBLE, NO SIGN A THEM.
THANK FUCKIN' GOD FOR SOMETHIN', HUH?
NOW, WHO WANTS TO HELP ME FEED THE KITTIES?

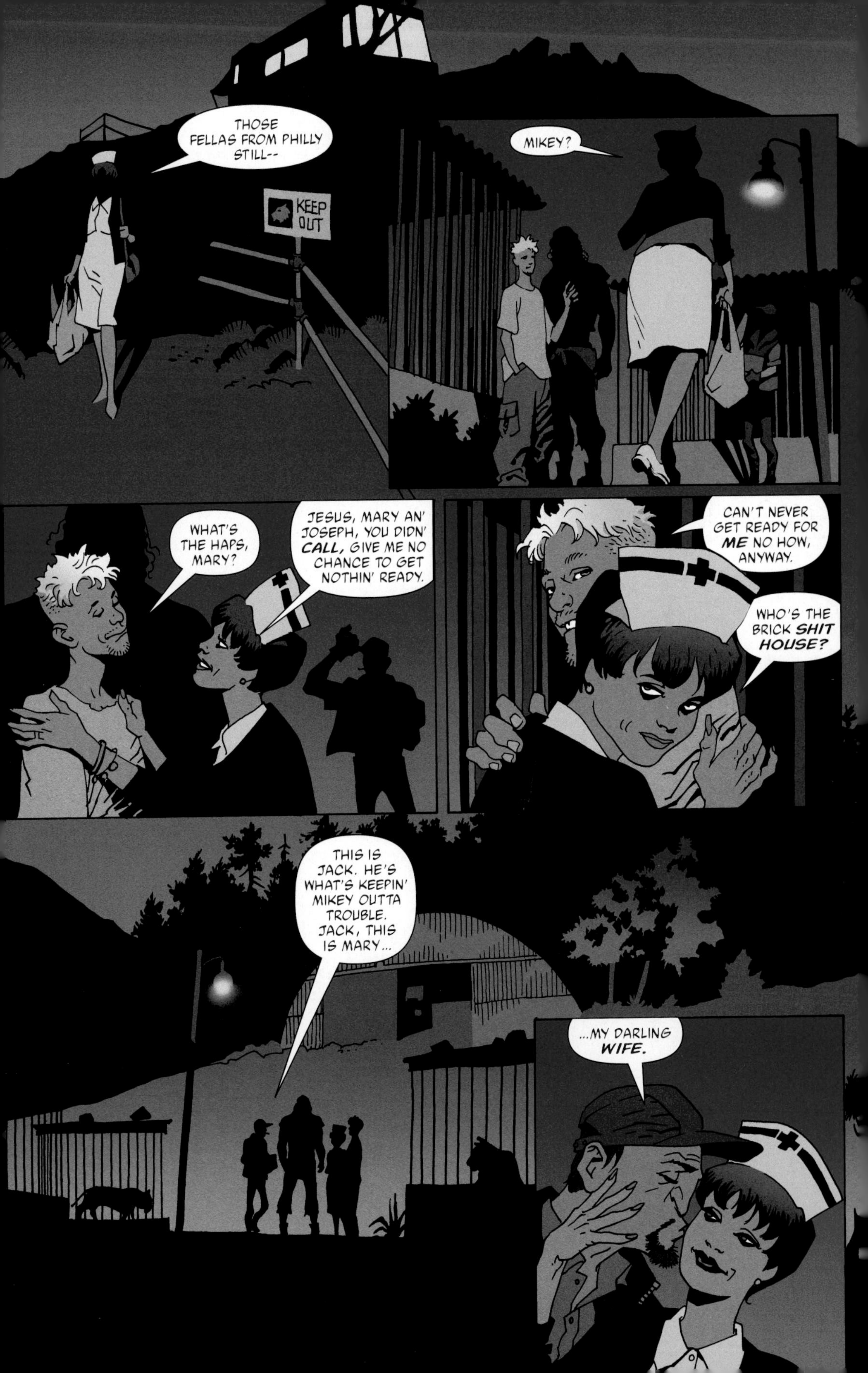
THOSE FELLAS FROM PHILLY STILL--
KEEP OUT
MIKEY?
WHAT'S THE HAPS, MARY?
JESUS, MARY AN' JOSEPH, YOU DIDN' **CALL,** GIVE ME NO CHANCE TO GET NOTHIN' READY.
CAN'T NEVER GET READY FOR **ME** NO HOW, ANYWAY.
WHO'S THE BRICK **SHIT HOUSE?**
THIS IS JACK. HE'S WHAT'S KEEPIN' MIKEY OUTTA TROUBLE. JACK, THIS IS MARY...
...MY DARLING **WIFE.**

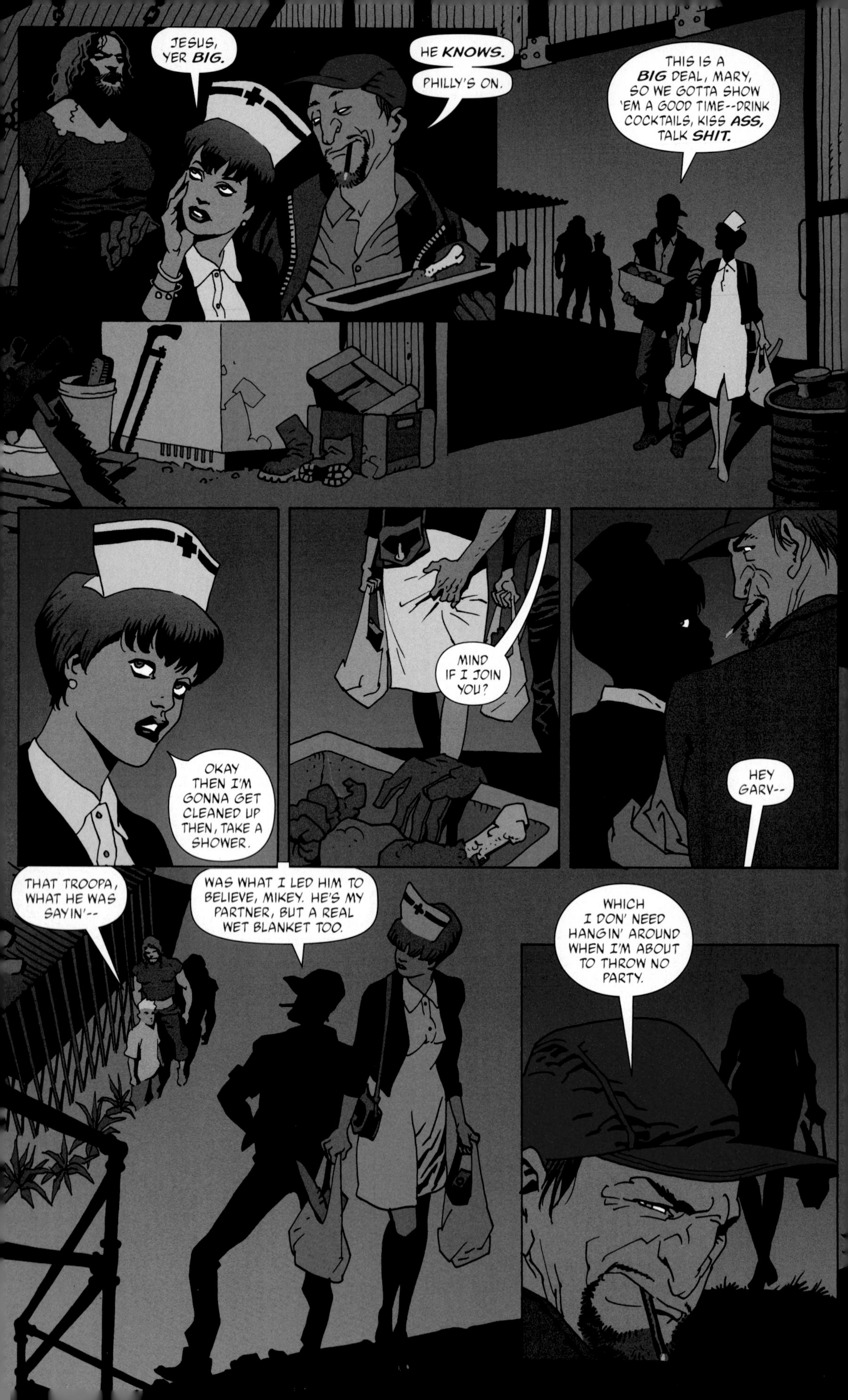
JESUS, YER BIG.
HE KNOWS.
PHILLY'S ON.
THIS IS A BIG DEAL, MARY, SO WE GOTTA SHOW 'EM A GOOD TIME--DRINK COCKTAILS, KISS ASS, TALK SHIT.
OKAY THEN I'M GONNA GET CLEANED UP THEN, TAKE A SHOWER.
MIND IF I JOIN YOU?
HEY GARV--
THAT TROOPA, WHAT HE WAS SAYIN'--
WAS WHAT I LED HIM TO BELIEVE, MIKEY. HE'S MY PARTNER, BUT A REAL WET BLANKET TOO.
WHICH I DON' NEED HANGIN' AROUND WHEN I'M ABOUT TO THROW NO PARTY.

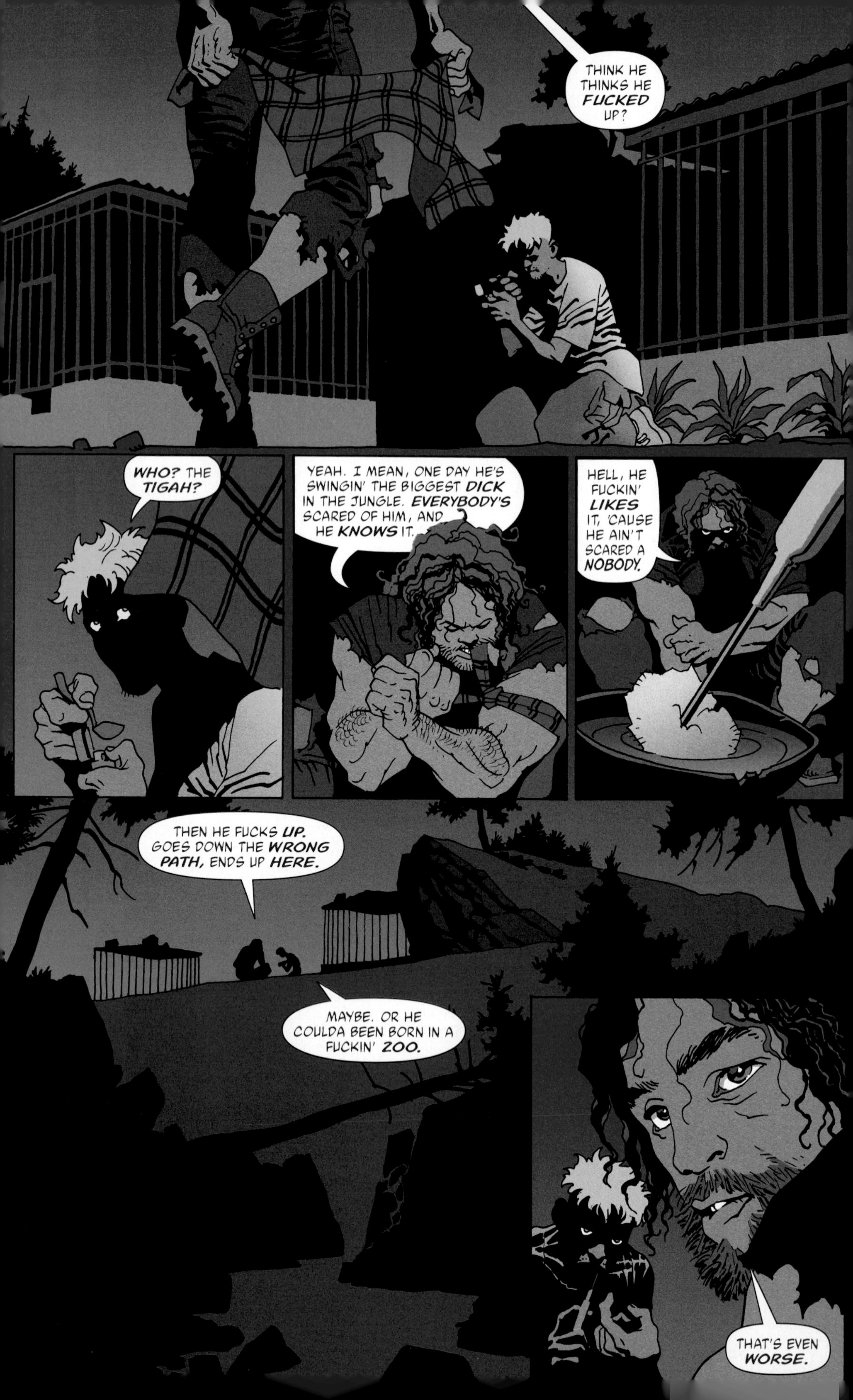
THINK HE THINKS HE FUCKED UP?
WHO? THE TIGAH?
YEAH. I MEAN, ONE DAY HE'S SWINGIN' THE BIGGEST DICK IN THE JUNGLE. EVERYBODY'S SCARED OF HIM, AND HE KNOWS IT.
HELL, HE FUCKIN' LIKES IT, 'CAUSE HE AIN'T SCARED A NOBODY.
THEN HE FUCKS UP. GOES DOWN THE WRONG PATH, ENDS UP HERE.
MAYBE. OR HE COULDA BEEN BORN IN A FUCKIN' ZOO.
THAT'S EVEN WORSE.

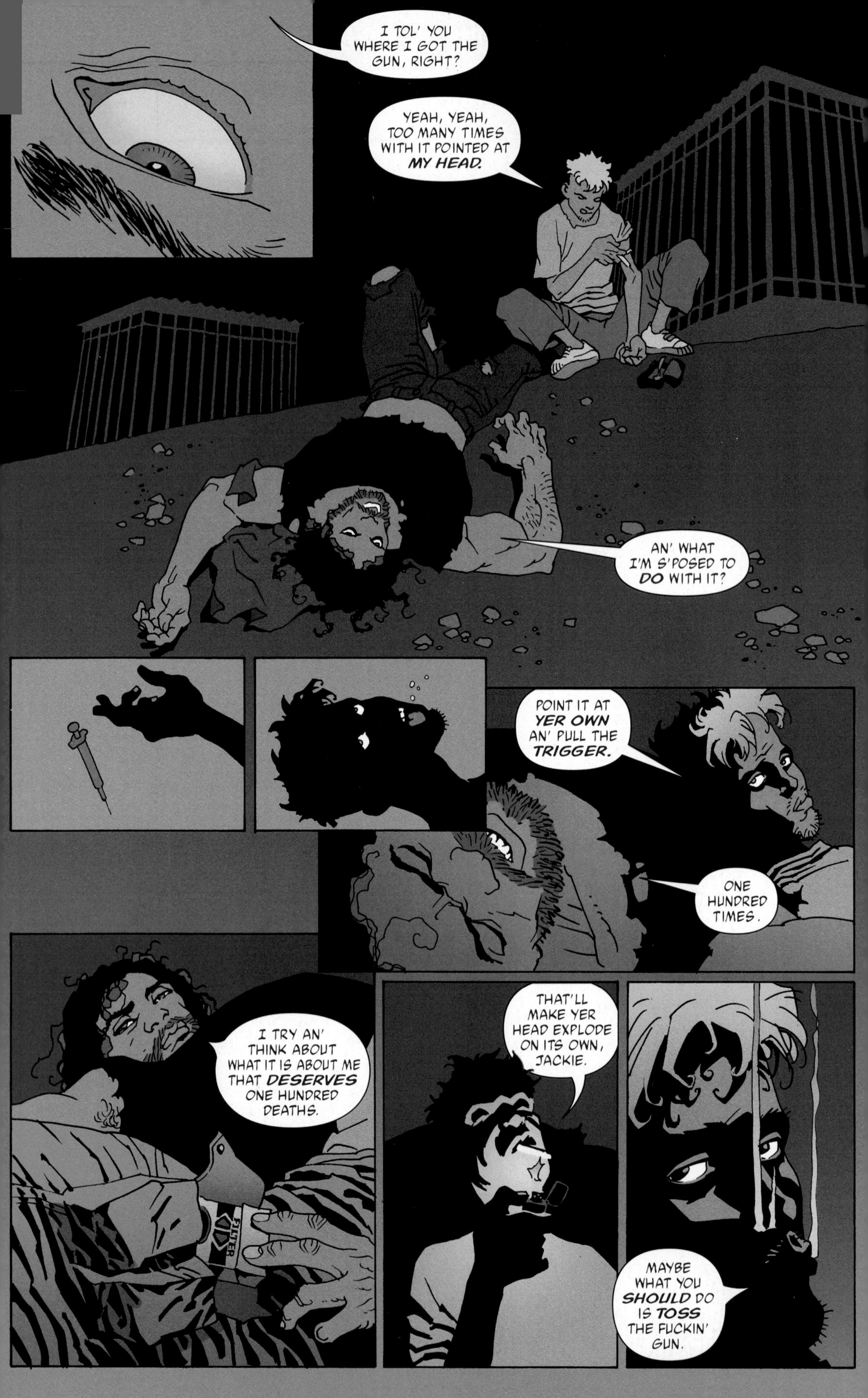
I TOL' YOU WHERE I GOT THE GUN, RIGHT?
YEAH, YEAH, TOO MANY TIMES WITH IT POINTED AT **MY HEAD.**
AN' WHAT I'M S'POSED TO **DO** WITH IT?
POINT IT AT **YER OWN** AN' PULL THE **TRIGGER.**
ONE HUNDRED TIMES.
I TRY AN' THINK ABOUT WHAT IT IS ABOUT ME THAT **DESERVES** ONE HUNDRED DEATHS.
THAT'LL MAKE YER HEAD EXPLODE ON ITS OWN, JACKIE.
MAYBE WHAT YOU **SHOULD** DO IS **TOSS** THE FUCKIN' GUN.
FILTER

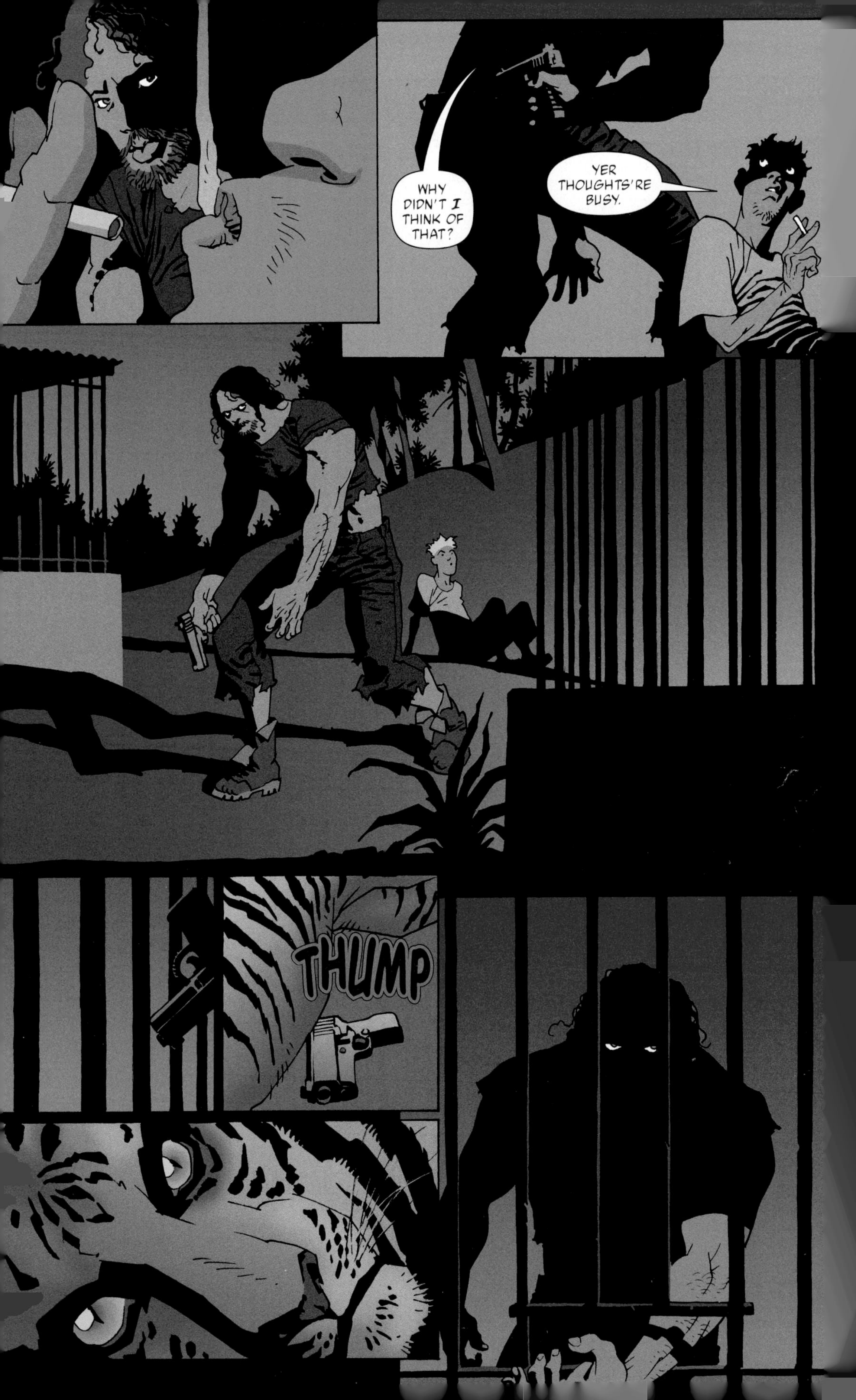
WHY DIDN'T I THINK OF THAT?
YER THOUGHTS'RE BUSY.
THUMP

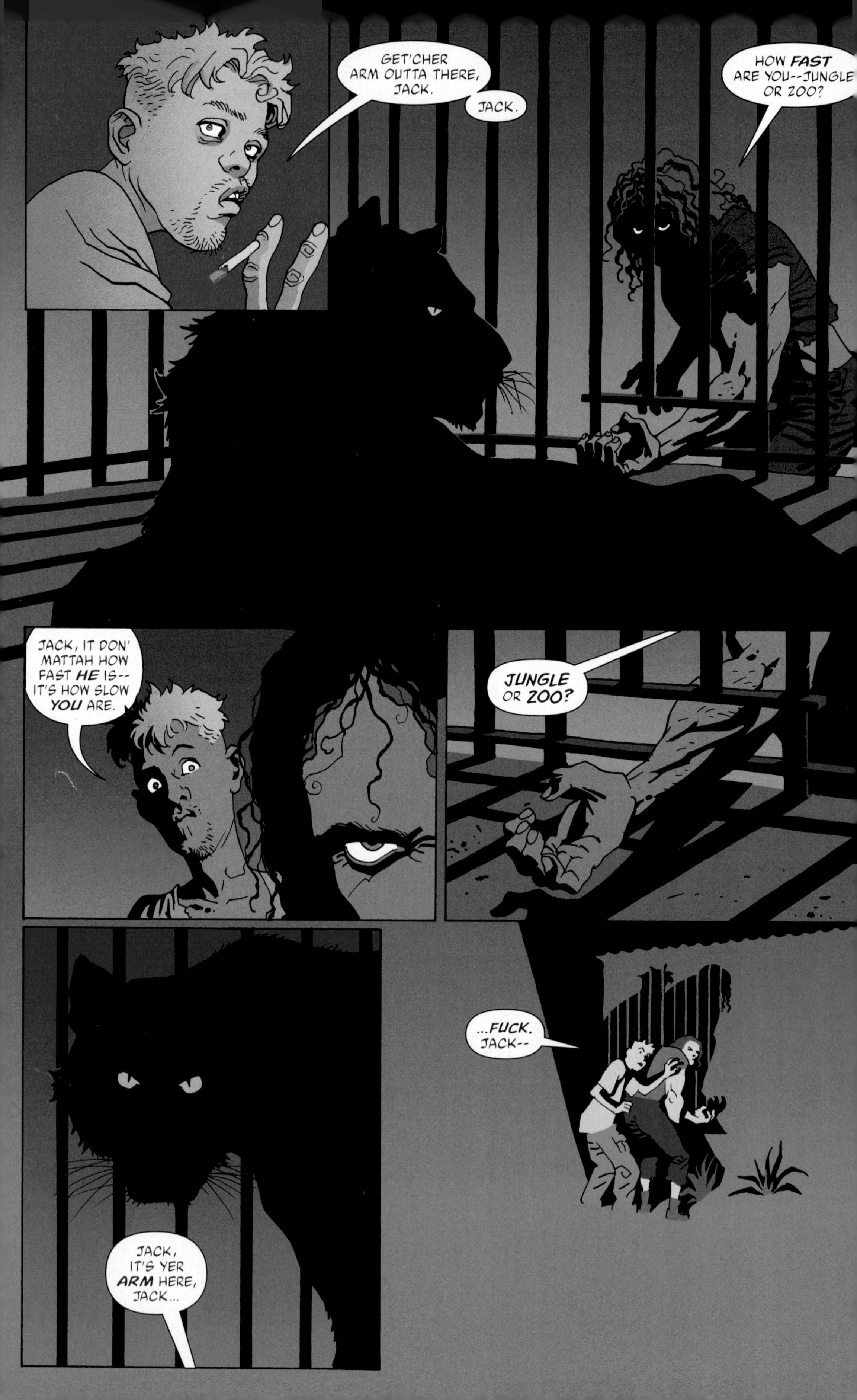
GET'CHER ARM OUTTA THERE, JACK.
JACK.
HOW FAST ARE YOU--JUNGLE OR ZOO?
JACK, IT DON' MATTAH HOW FAST HE IS-- IT'S HOW SLOW YOU ARE.
JUNGLE OR ZOO?
JACK, IT'S YER ARM HERE, JACK...
...FUCK. JACK--

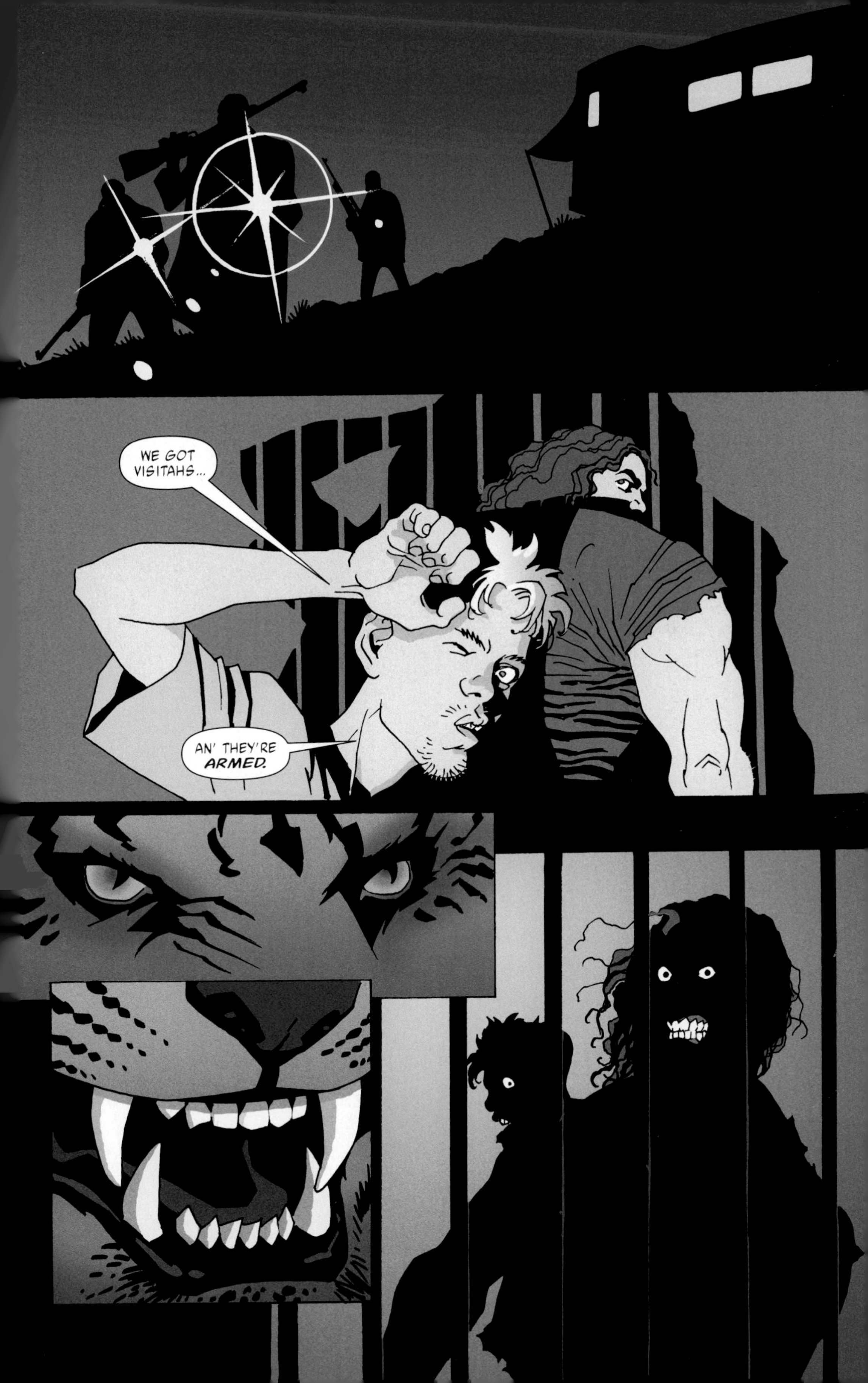
WE GOT VISITAHS...
AN' THEY'RE ARMED.

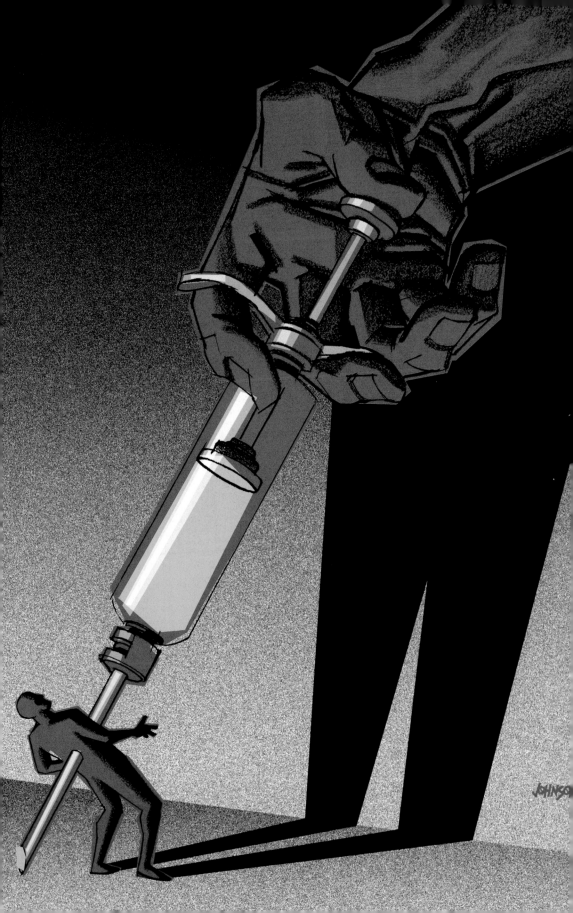

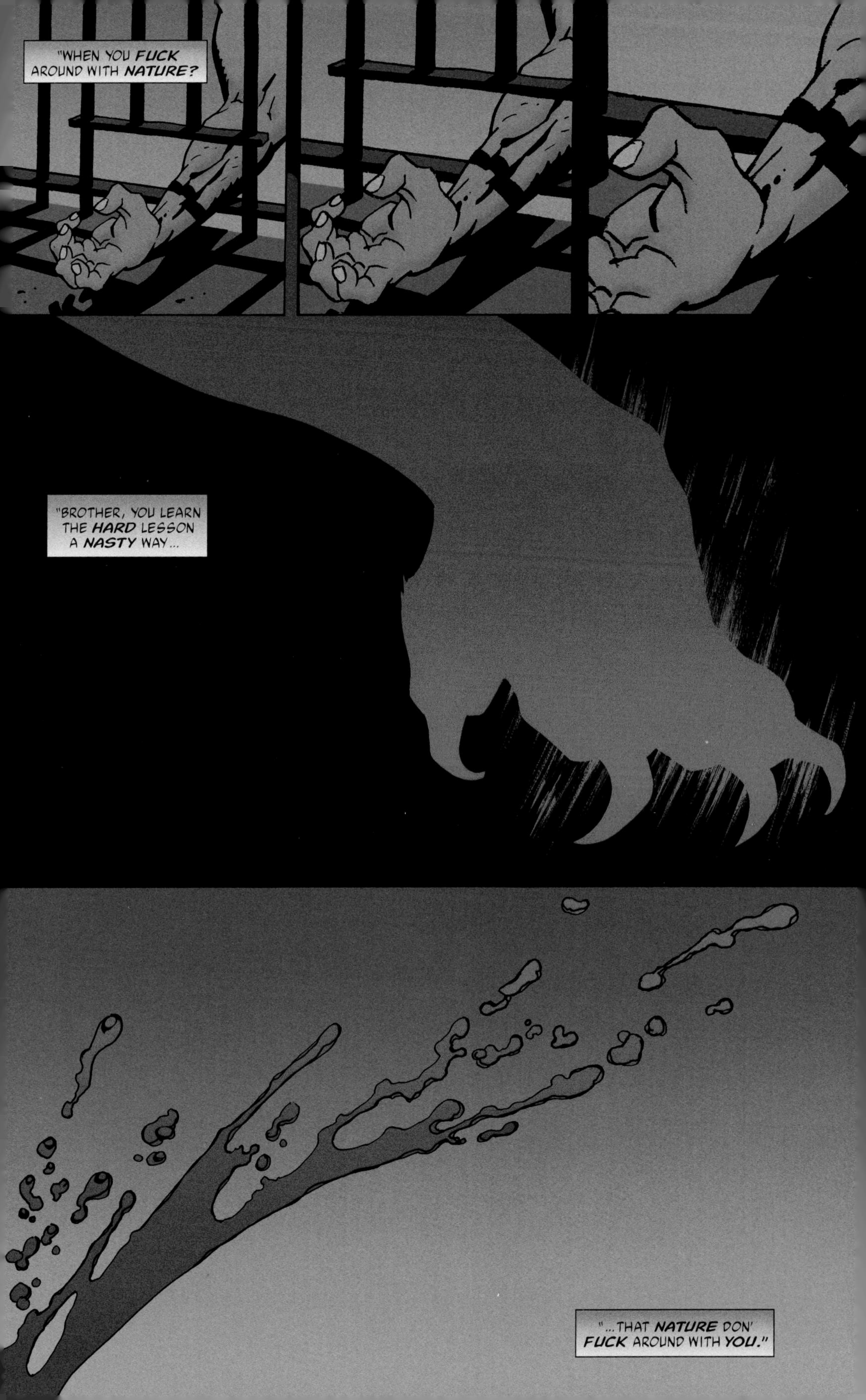
"WHEN YOU FUCK AROUND WITH NATURE?
"BROTHER, YOU LEARN THE HARD LESSON A NASTY WAY...
"...THAT NATURE DON' FUCK AROUND WITH YOU."

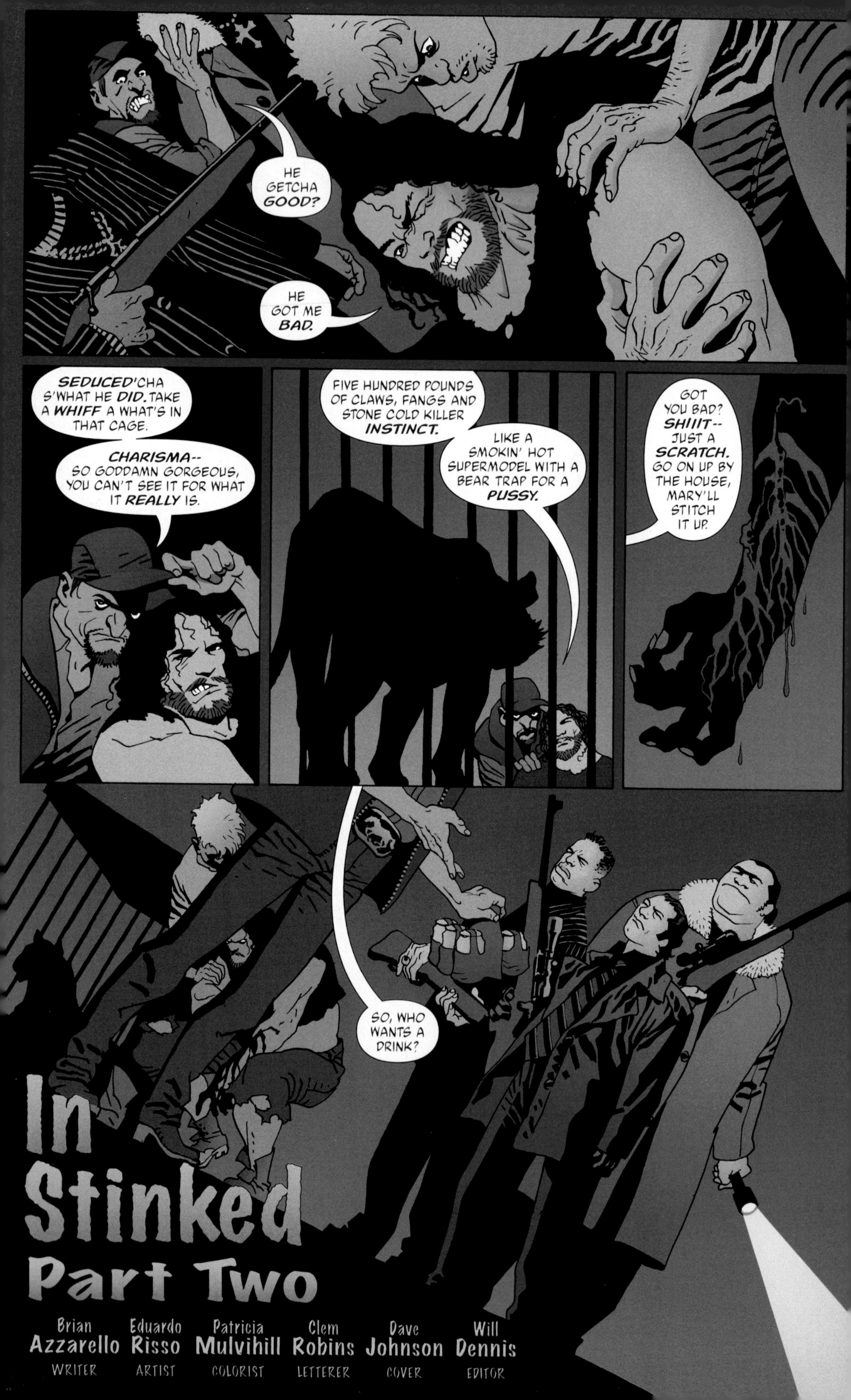
HE GETCHA GOOD?
HE GOT ME BAD.
SEDUCED'CHA S'WHAT HE DID. TAKE A WHIFF A WHAT'S IN THAT CAGE.
CHARISMA-- SO GODDAMN GORGEOUS, YOU CAN'T SEE IT FOR WHAT IT REALLY IS.
FIVE HUNDRED POUNDS OF CLAWS, FANGS AND STONE COLD KILLER INSTINCT.
LIKE A SMOKIN' HOT SUPERMODEL WITH A BEAR TRAP FOR A PUSSY.
GOT YOU BAD? SHIIIT-- JUST A SCRATCH. GO ON UP BY THE HOUSE, MARY'LL STITCH IT UP.
SO, WHO WANTS A DRINK?
In Stinked
Part Two
Brian Azzarello WRITER
Eduardo Risso ARTIST
Patricia Mulvihill COLORIST
Clem Robins LETTERER
Dave Johnson COVER
Will Dennis EDITOR

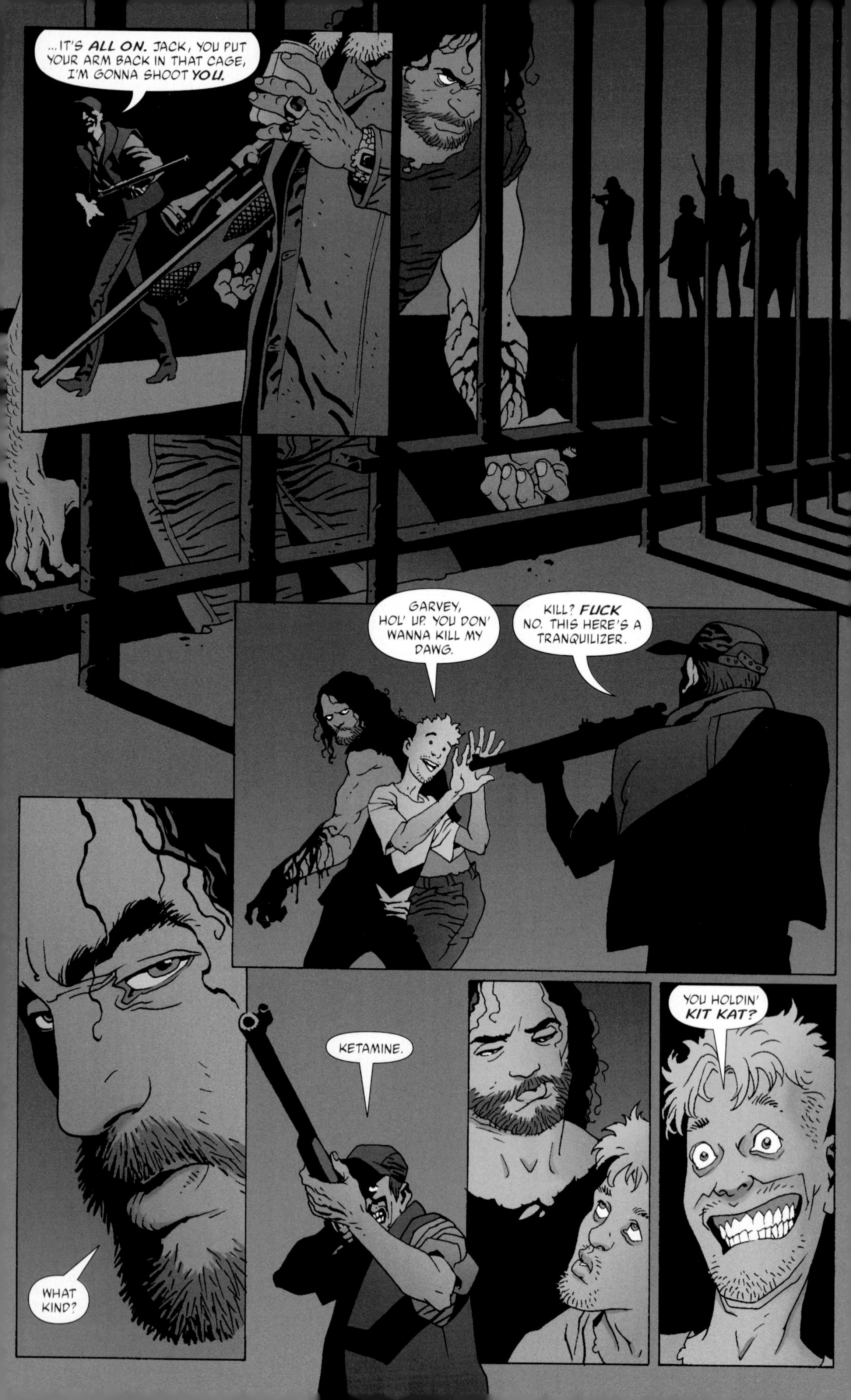
...IT'S ALL ON. JACK, YOU PUT YOUR ARM BACK IN THAT CAGE, I'M GONNA SHOOT YOU.
GARVEY, HOL' UP. YOU DON' WANNA KILL MY DAWG.
KILL? FUCK NO. THIS HERE'S A TRANQUILIZER.
WHAT KIND?
KETAMINE.
YOU HOLDIN' KIT KAT?

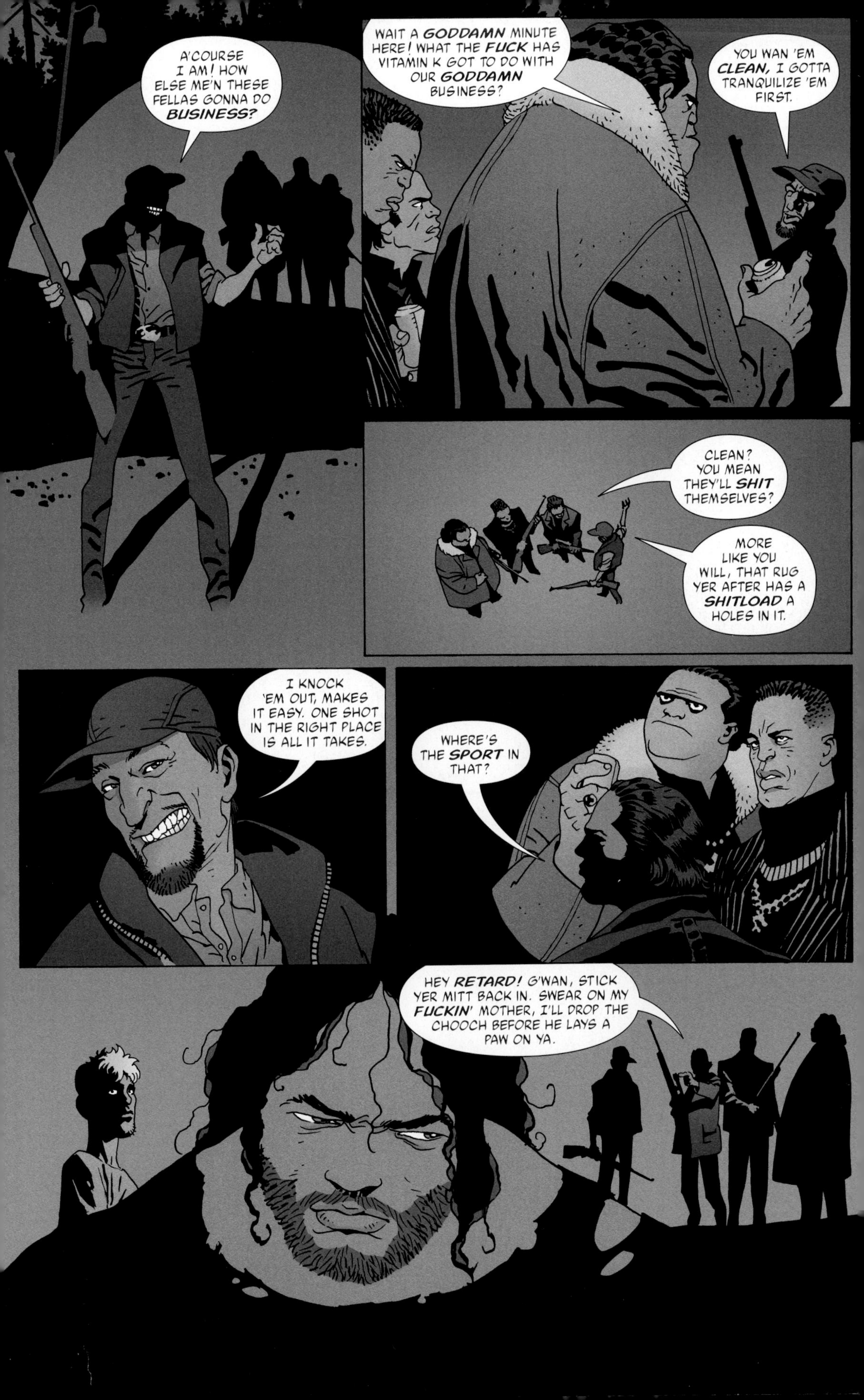
A'COURSE I AM! HOW ELSE ME'N THESE FELLAS GONNA DO **BUSINESS?**
WAIT A **GODDAMN** MINUTE HERE! WHAT THE **FUCK** HAS VITAMIN K GOT TO DO WITH OUR **GODDAMN** BUSINESS?
YOU WAN 'EM **CLEAN,** I GOTTA TRANQUILIZE 'EM FIRST.
CLEAN? YOU MEAN THEY'LL **SHIT** THEMSELVES?
MORE LIKE YOU WILL, THAT RUG YER AFTER HAS A **SHITLOAD** A HOLES IN IT.
I KNOCK 'EM OUT, MAKES IT EASY. ONE SHOT IN THE RIGHT PLACE IS ALL IT TAKES.
WHERE'S THE **SPORT** IN THAT?
HEY **RETARD!** G'WAN, STICK YER MITT BACK IN. SWEAR ON MY **FUCKIN'** MOTHER, I'LL DROP THE CHOOCH BEFORE HE LAYS A PAW ON YA.

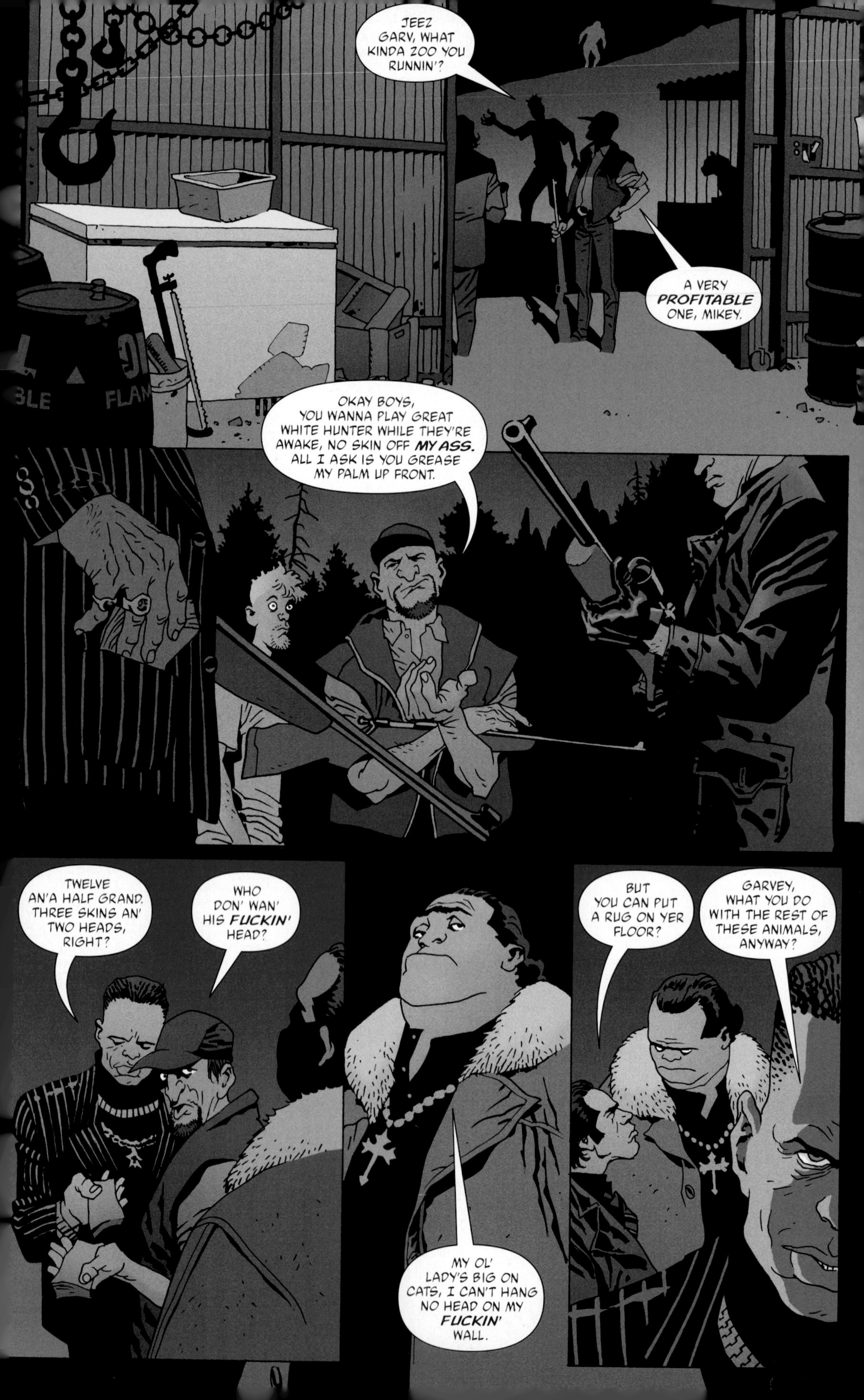

JEEZ GARV, WHAT KINDA ZOO YOU RUNNIN'?
A VERY **PROFITABLE** ONE, MIKEY.
OKAY BOYS, YOU WANNA PLAY GREAT WHITE HUNTER WHILE THEY'RE AWAKE, NO SKIN OFF **MY ASS.** ALL I ASK IS YOU GREASE MY PALM UP FRONT.
TWELVE AN'A HALF GRAND. THREE SKINS AN' TWO HEADS, RIGHT?
WHO DON' WAN' HIS **FUCKIN'** HEAD?
MY OL' LADY'S BIG ON CATS, I CAN'T HANG NO HEAD ON MY **FUCKIN'** WALL.
BUT YOU CAN PUT A RUG ON YER FLOOR?
GARVEY, WHAT YOU DO WITH THE REST OF THESE ANIMALS, ANYWAY?

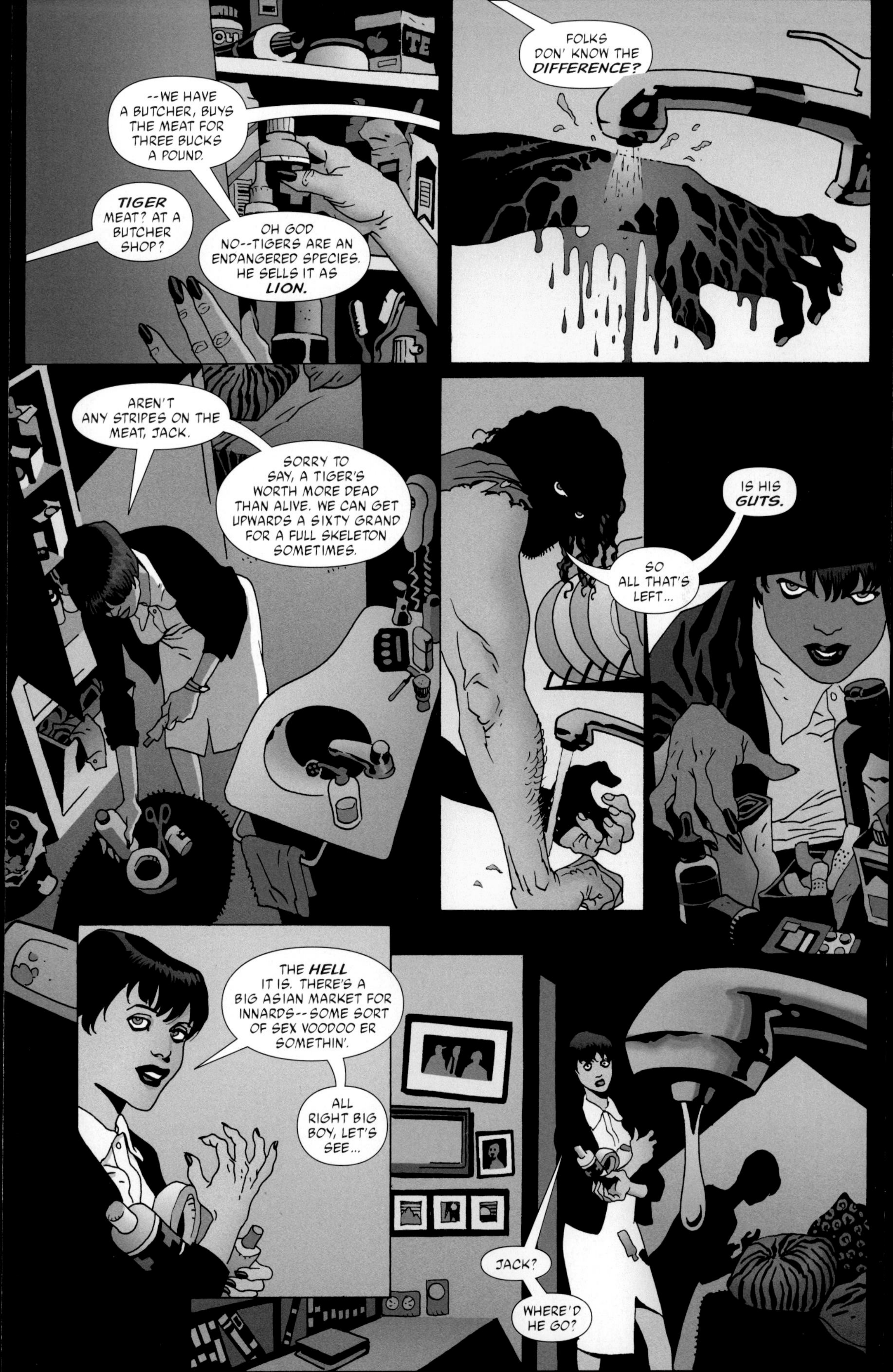
--WE HAVE A BUTCHER, BUYS THE MEAT FOR THREE BUCKS A POUND.
TIGER MEAT? AT A BUTCHER SHOP?
OH GOD NO--TIGERS ARE AN ENDANGERED SPECIES. HE SELLS IT AS LION.
FOLKS DON' KNOW THE DIFFERENCE?
AREN'T ANY STRIPES ON THE MEAT, JACK.
SORRY TO SAY, A TIGER'S WORTH MORE DEAD THAN ALIVE. WE CAN GET UPWARDS A SIXTY GRAND FOR A FULL SKELETON SOMETIMES.
SO ALL THAT'S LEFT...
IS HIS GUTS.
THE HELL IT IS. THERE'S A BIG ASIAN MARKET FOR INNARDS--SOME SORT OF SEX VOODOO ER SOMETHIN'.
ALL RIGHT BIG BOY, LET'S SEE...
JACK?
WHERE'D HE GO?

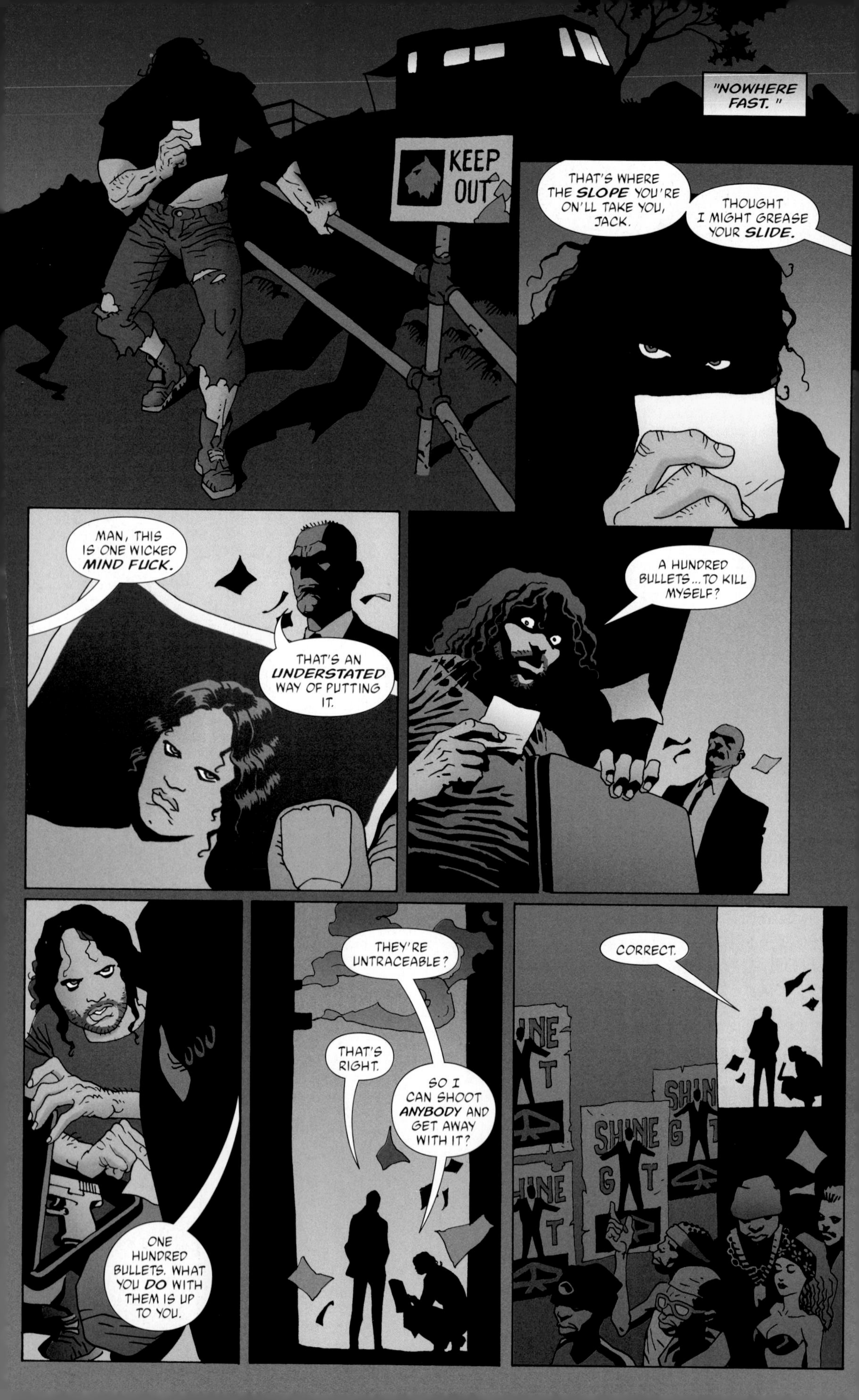
"NOWHERE FAST."
KEEP OUT
THAT'S WHERE THE SLOPE YOU'RE ON'LL TAKE YOU, JACK.
THOUGHT I MIGHT GREASE YOUR SLIDE.
MAN, THIS IS ONE WICKED MIND FUCK.
THAT'S AN UNDERSTATED WAY OF PUTTING IT.
A HUNDRED BULLETS... TO KILL MYSELF?
ONE HUNDRED BULLETS. WHAT YOU DO WITH THEM IS UP TO YOU.
THEY'RE UNTRACEABLE?
THAT'S RIGHT.
SO I CAN SHOOT ANYBODY AND GET AWAY WITH IT?
CORRECT.
SHINE
SHINE

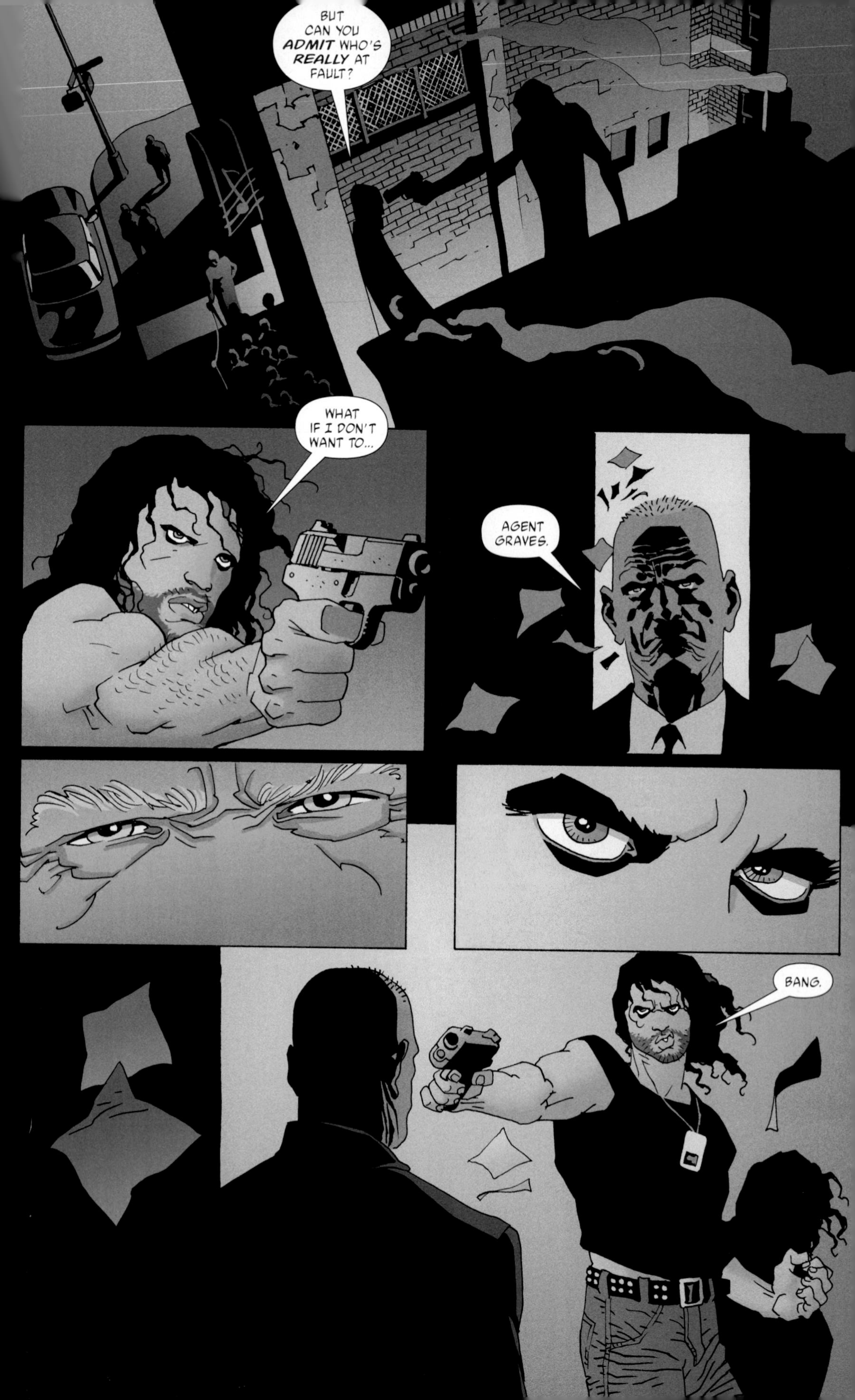
BUT CAN YOU **ADMIT** WHO'S **REALLY** AT FAULT?
WHAT IF I DON'T WANT TO...
AGENT GRAVES.
BANG.

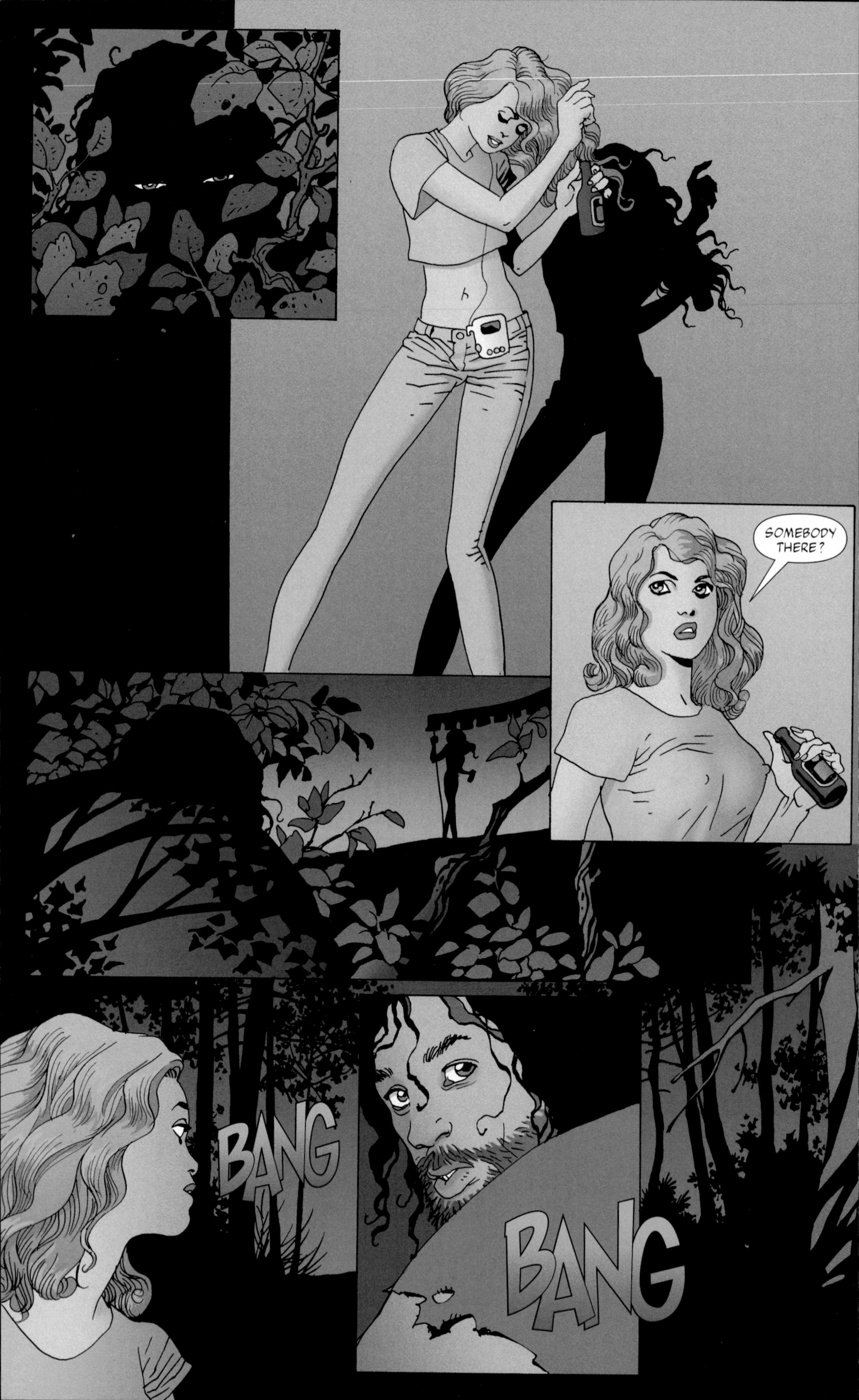
SOMEBODY THERE?
BANG
BANG

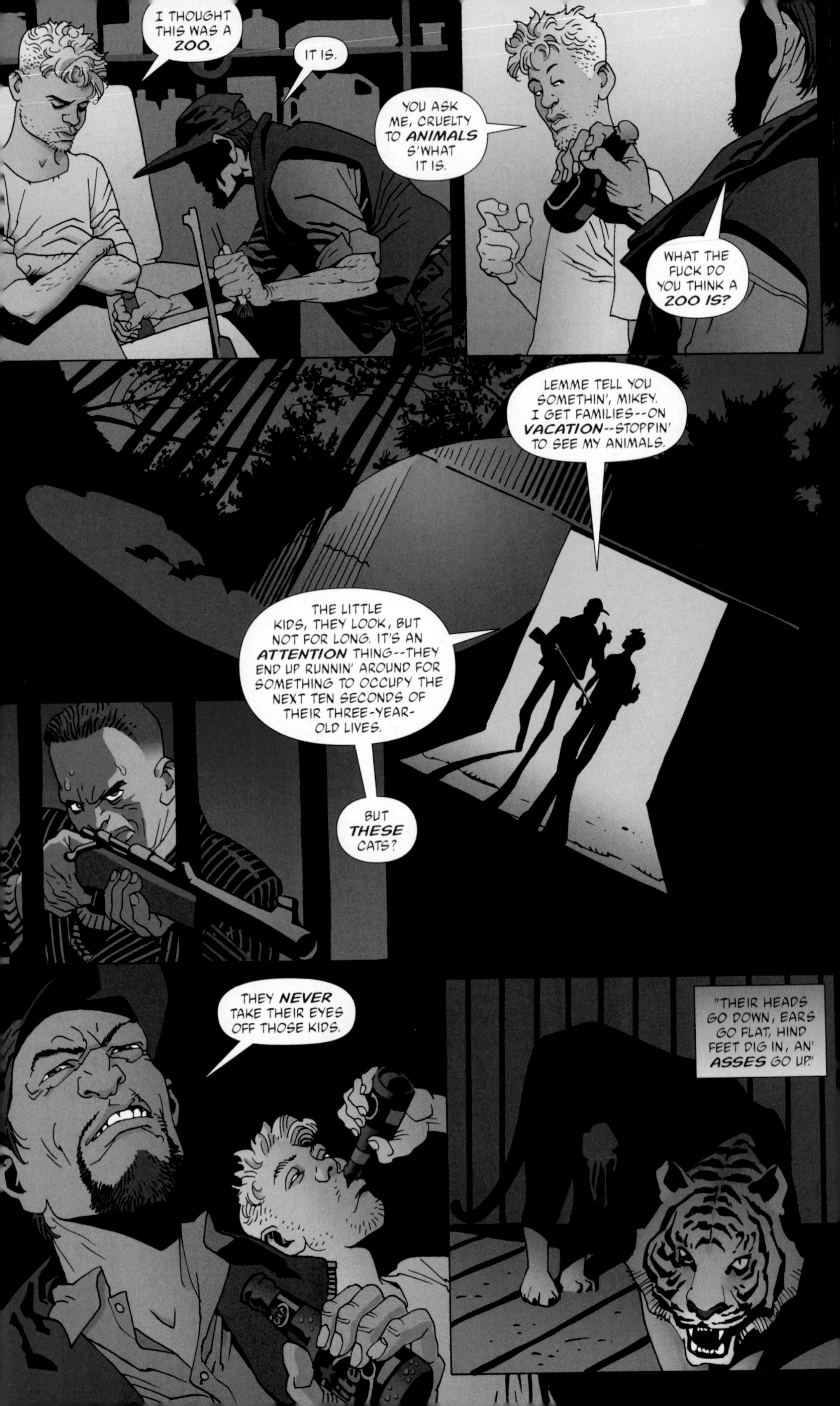

I THOUGHT THIS WAS A ZOO.
IT IS.
YOU ASK ME, CRUELTY TO ANIMALS S'WHAT IT IS.
WHAT THE FUCK DO YOU THINK A ZOO IS?
LEMME TELL YOU SOMETHIN', MIKEY. I GET FAMILIES--ON VACATION--STOPPIN' TO SEE MY ANIMALS.
THE LITTLE KIDS, THEY LOOK, BUT NOT FOR LONG. IT'S AN ATTENTION THING--THEY END UP RUNNIN' AROUND FOR SOMETHING TO OCCUPY THE NEXT TEN SECONDS OF THEIR THREE-YEAR-OLD LIVES.
BUT THESE CATS?
THEY NEVER TAKE THEIR EYES OFF THOSE KIDS.
"THEIR HEADS GO DOWN, EARS GO FLAT, HIND FEET DIG IN, AN' ASSES GO UP."

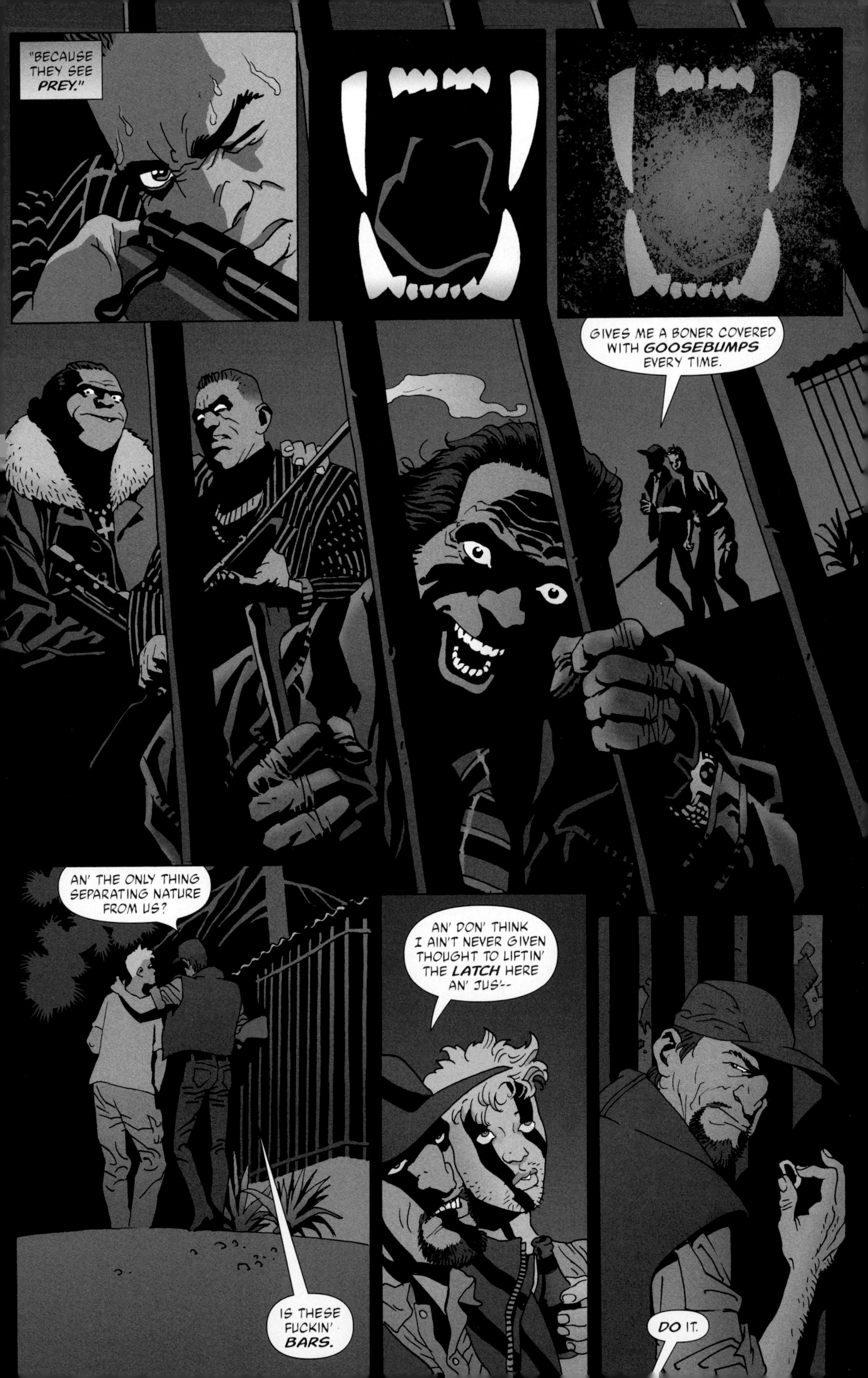
"BECAUSE THEY SEE PREY."
GIVES ME A BONER COVERED WITH GOOSEBUMPS EVERY TIME.
AN' THE ONLY THING SEPARATING NATURE FROM US?
IS THESE FUCKIN' BARS.
AN' DON' THINK I AIN'T NEVER GIVEN THOUGHT TO LIFTIN' THE LATCH HERE AN' JUS'--
DO IT.

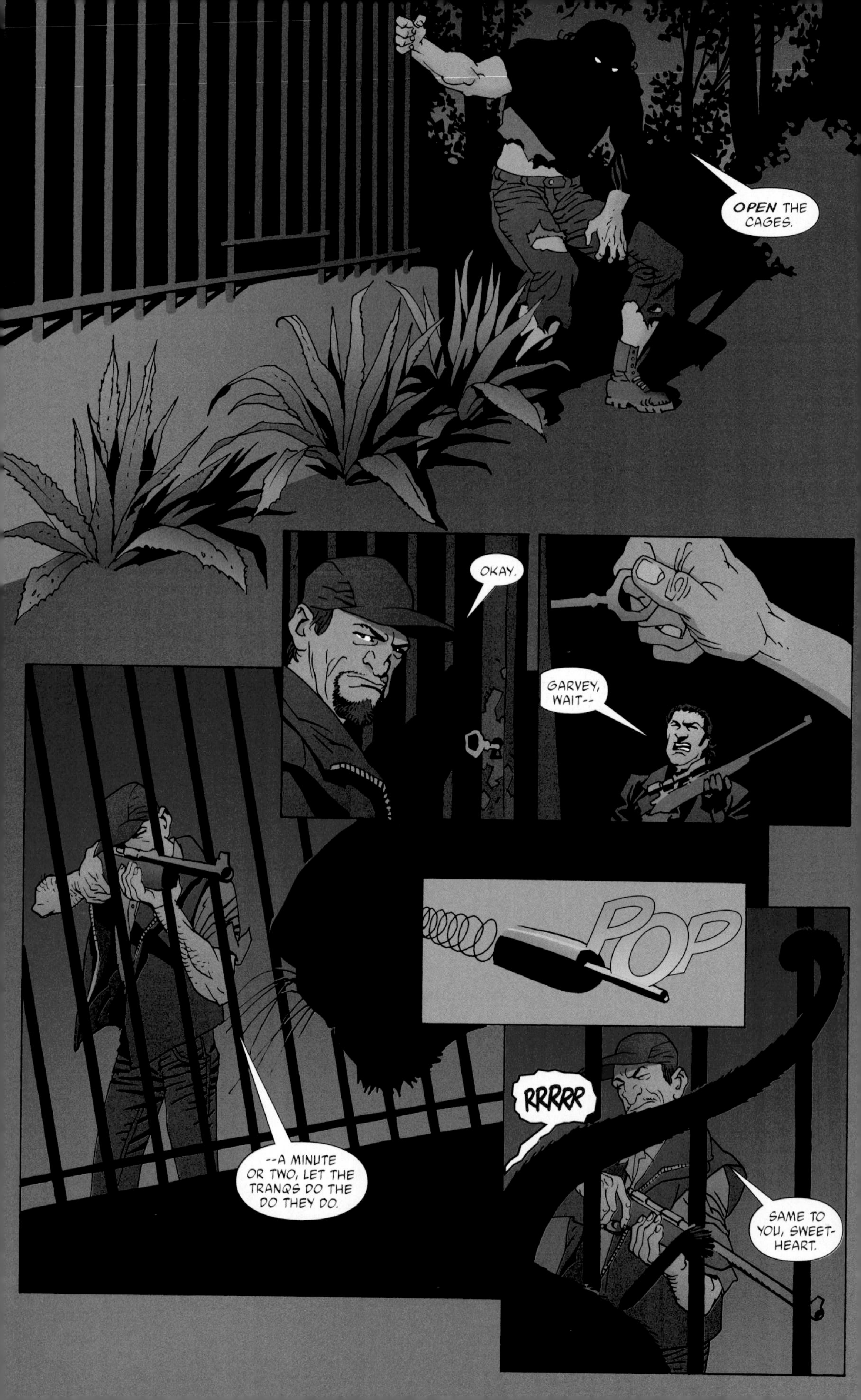
OPEN THE CAGES.
OKAY.
GARVEY, WAIT--
--A MINUTE OR TWO, LET THE TRANQS DO THE DO THEY DO.
POP
RRRRR
SAME TO YOU, SWEET-HEART.

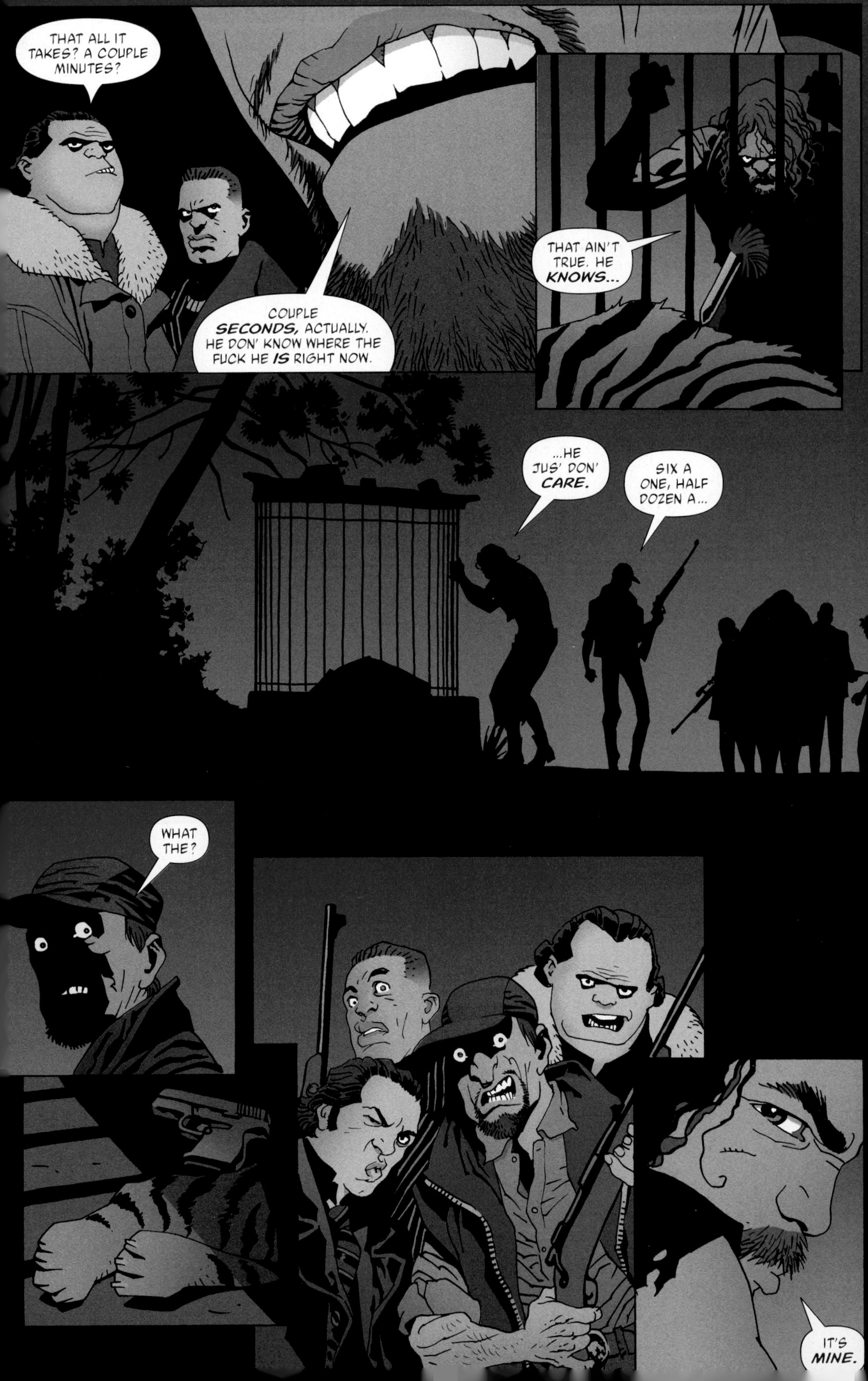
THAT ALL IT TAKES? A COUPLE MINUTES?
COUPLE SECONDS, ACTUALLY. HE DON' KNOW WHERE THE FUCK HE IS RIGHT NOW.
THAT AIN'T TRUE. HE KNOWS...
...HE JUS' DON' CARE.
SIX A ONE, HALF DOZEN A...
WHAT THE?
IT'S MINE.

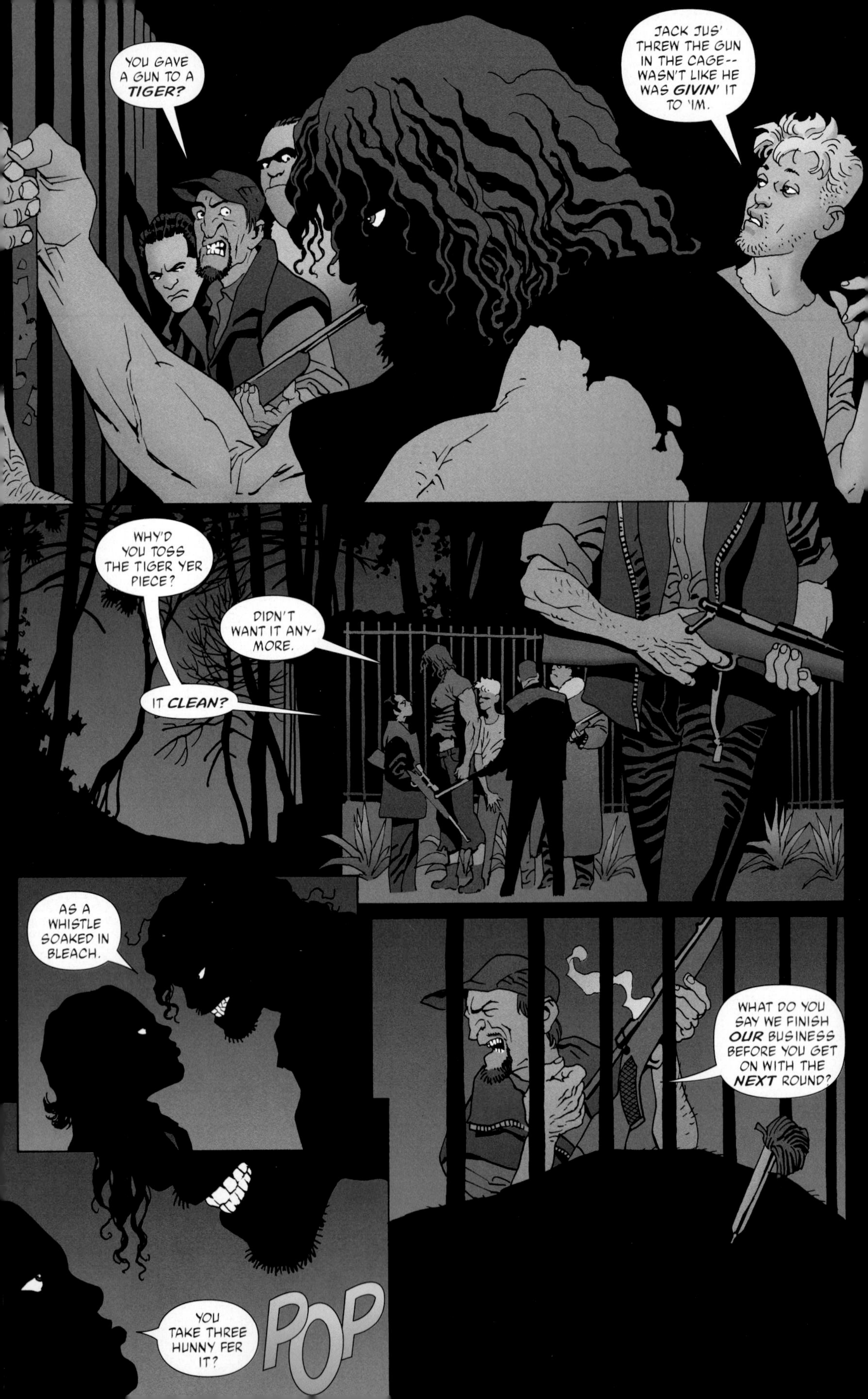
YOU GAVE A GUN TO A ***TIGER?***
JACK JUS' THREW THE GUN IN THE CAGE-- WASN'T LIKE HE WAS ***GIVIN'*** IT TO 'IM.
WHY'D YOU TOSS THE TIGER YER PIECE?
DIDN'T WANT IT ANY-MORE.
IT ***CLEAN?***
AS A WHISTLE SOAKED IN BLEACH.
WHAT DO YOU SAY WE FINISH ***OUR*** BUSINESS BEFORE YOU GET ON WITH THE ***NEXT*** ROUND?
YOU TAKE THREE HUNNY FER IT?
POP

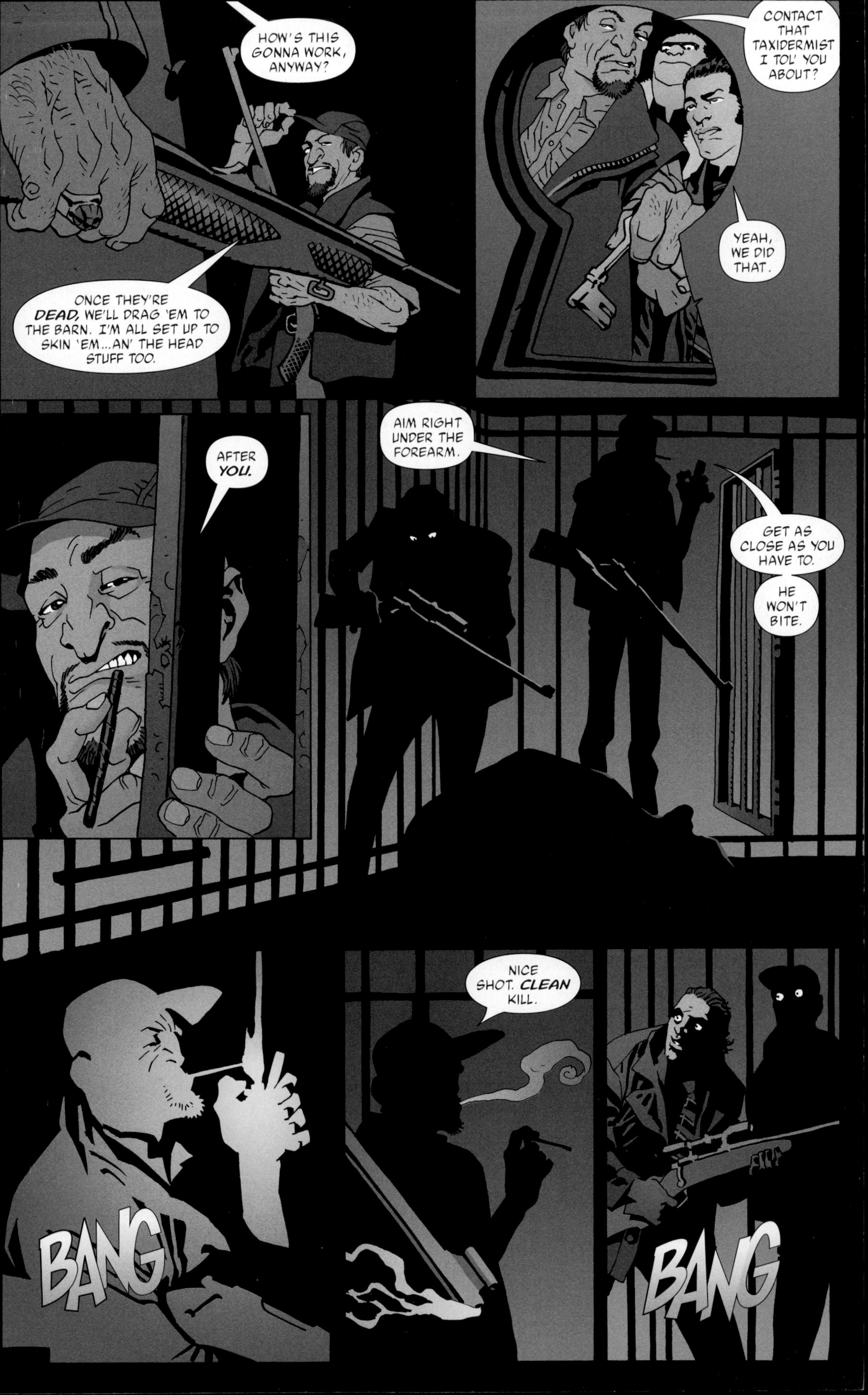
HOW'S THIS GONNA WORK, ANYWAY?
ONCE THEY'RE DEAD, WE'LL DRAG 'EM TO THE BARN. I'M ALL SET UP TO SKIN 'EM...AN' THE HEAD STUFF TOO.
CONTACT THAT TAXIDERMIST I TOL' YOU ABOUT?
YEAH, WE DID THAT.
AFTER YOU.
AIM RIGHT UNDER THE FOREARM.
GET AS CLOSE AS YOU HAVE TO.
HE WON'T BITE.
BANG
NICE SHOT. CLEAN KILL.
BANG

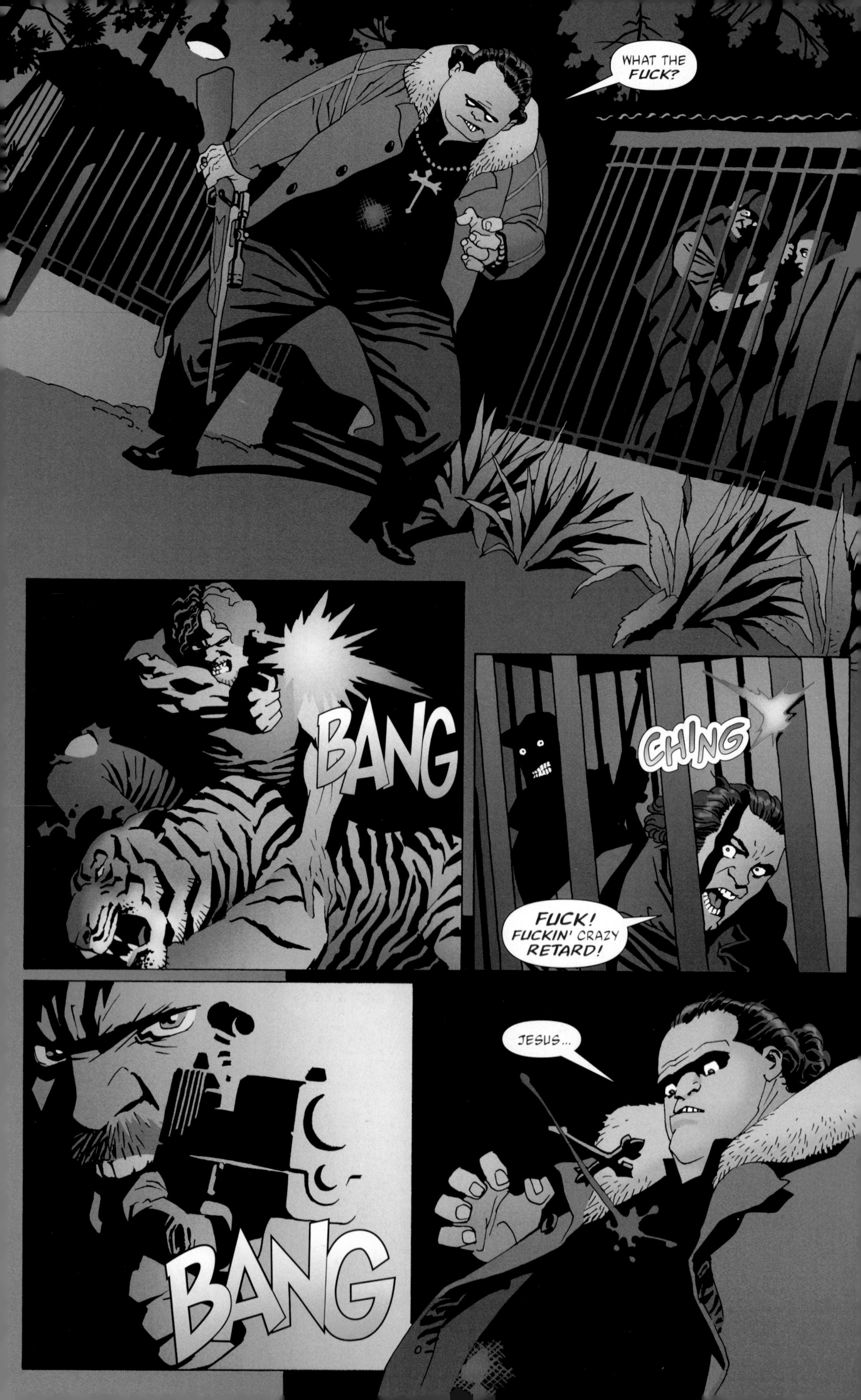
WHAT THE FUCK?
BANG
CHING
FUCK! FUCKIN' CRAZY RETARD!
BANG
JESUS...

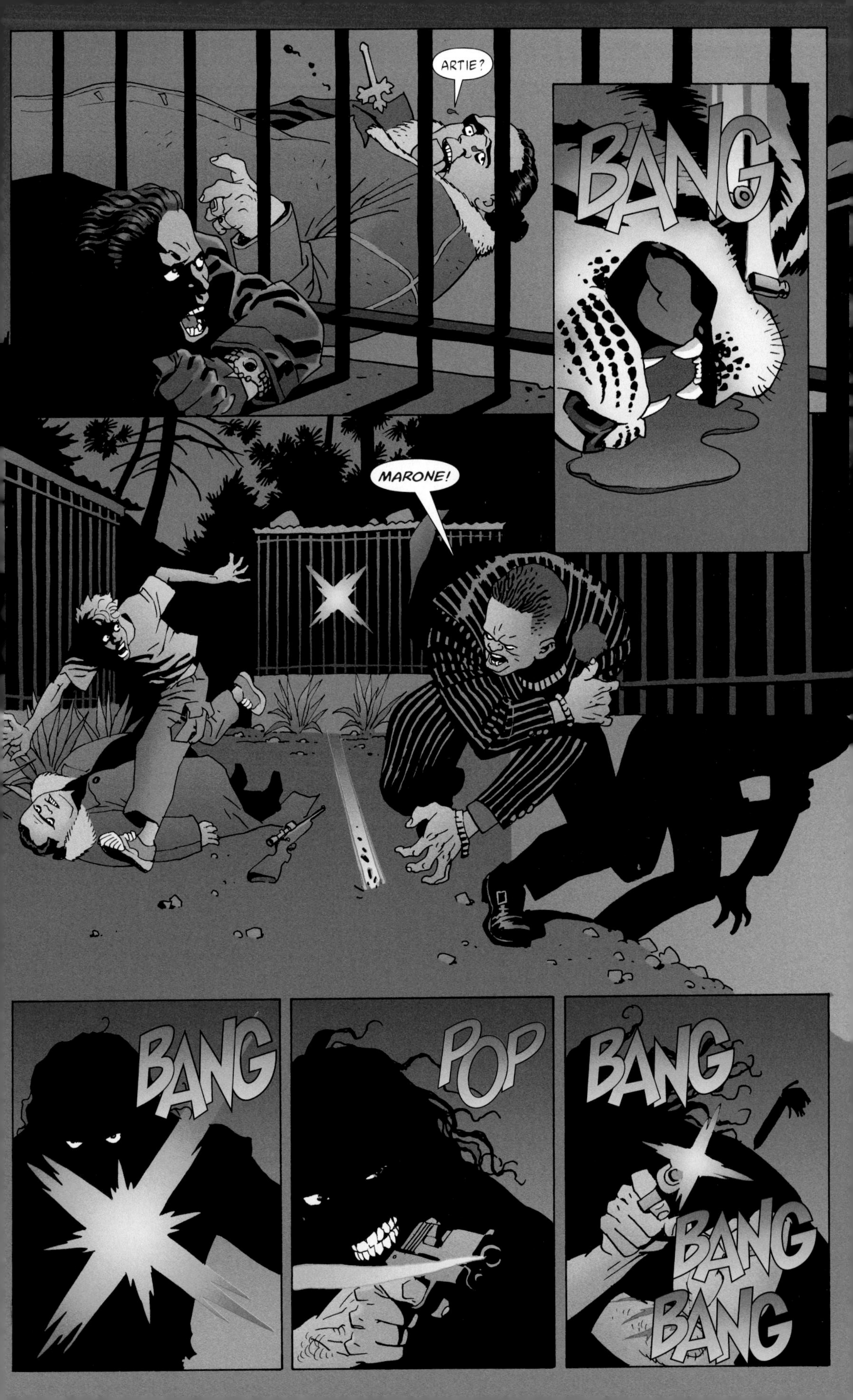
ARTIE?
BANG
MARONE!
BANG
POP
BANG
BANG
BANG

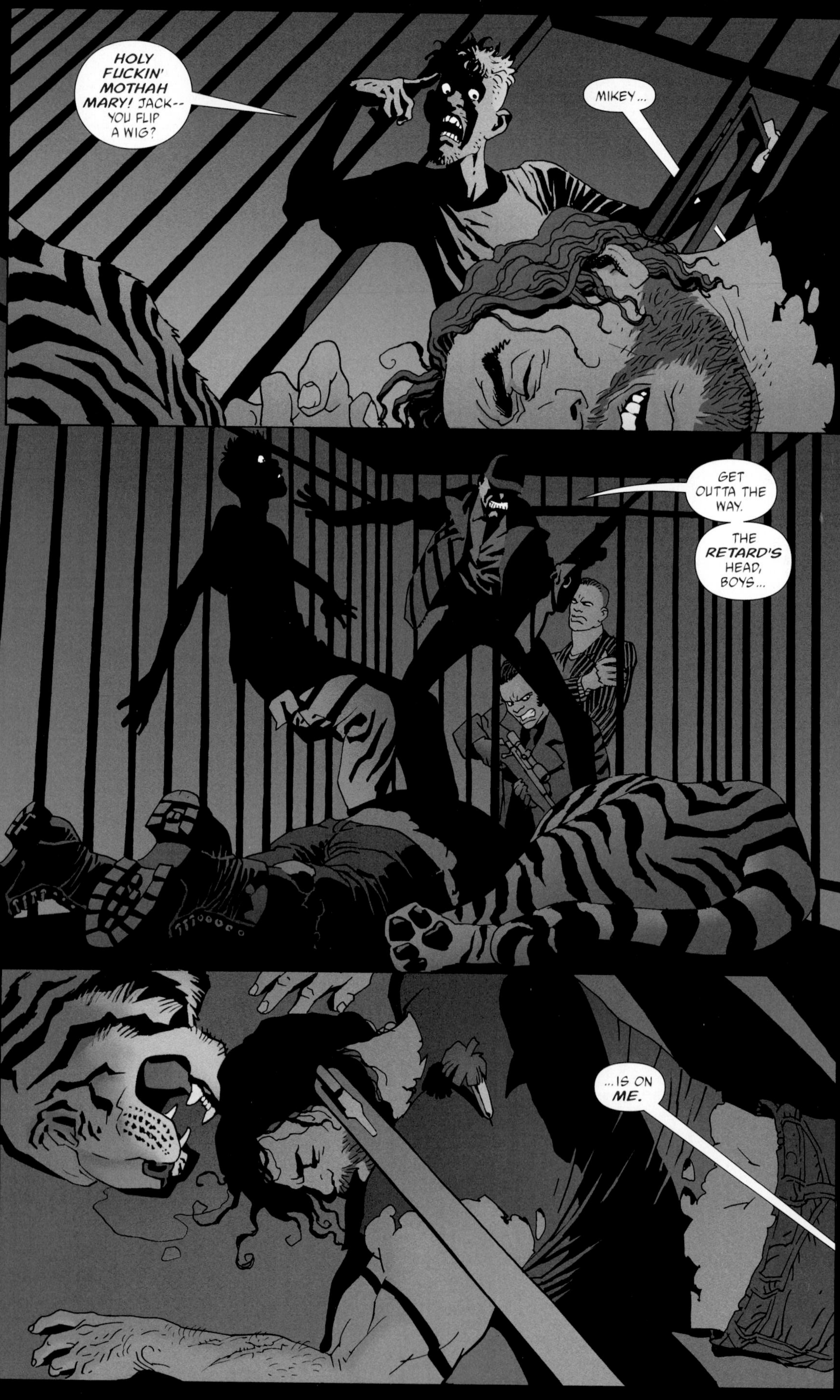
HOLY FUCKIN' MOTHAH MARY! JACK-- YOU FLIP A WIG?
MIKEY...
GET OUTTA THE WAY.
THE RETARD'S HEAD, BOYS...
...IS ON ME.

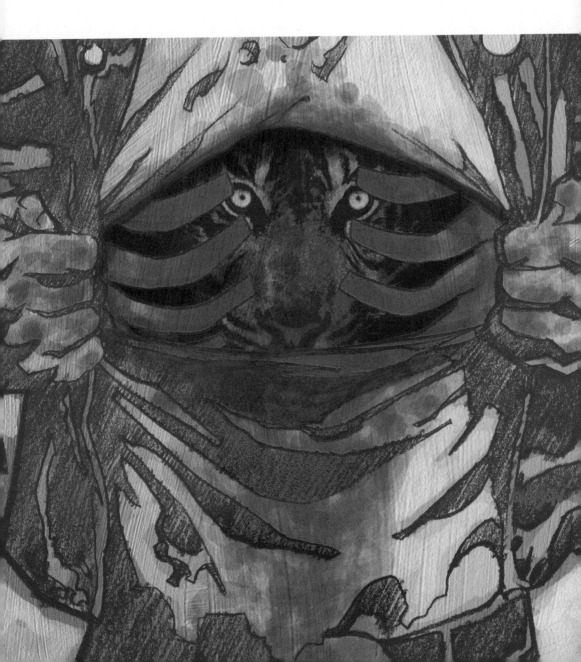

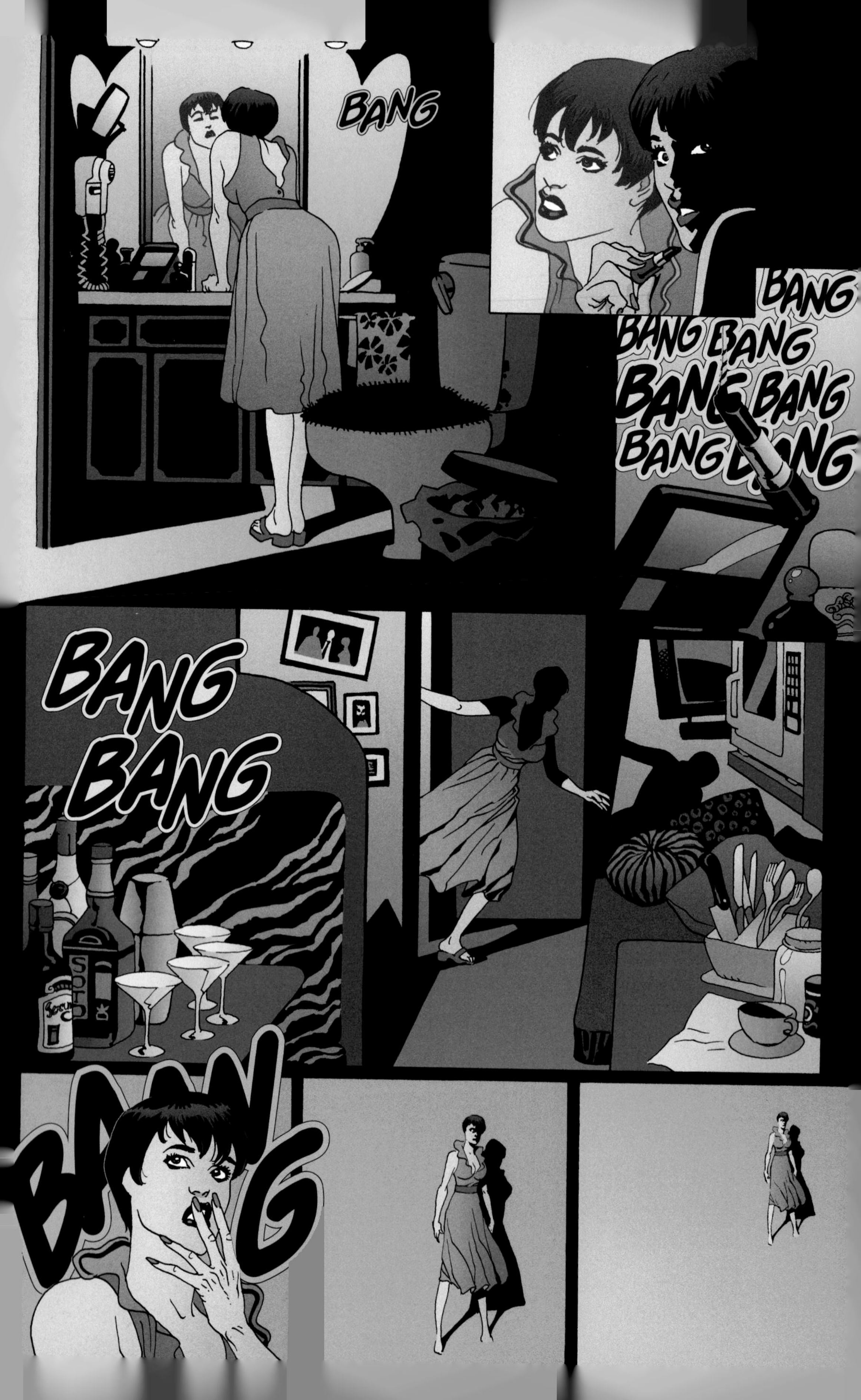
BANG
BANG
BANG BANG
BANG BANG
BANG
BANG
BANG
BANG

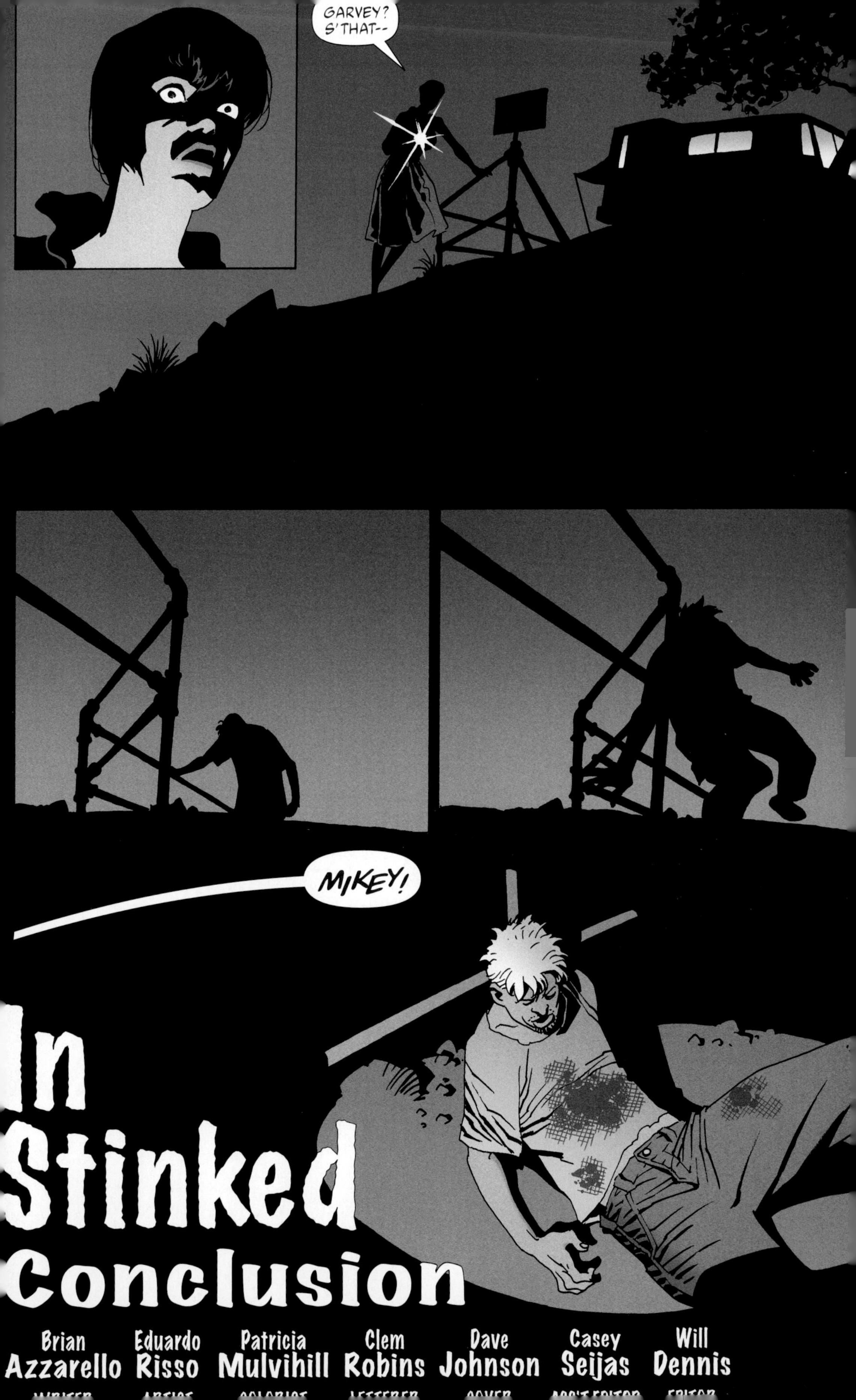
GARVEY? S'THAT--
MIKEY!
In Stinked Conclusion
Brian Azzarello
Eduardo Risso
Patricia Mulvihill
Clem Robins
Dave Johnson
Casey Seijas
Will Dennis

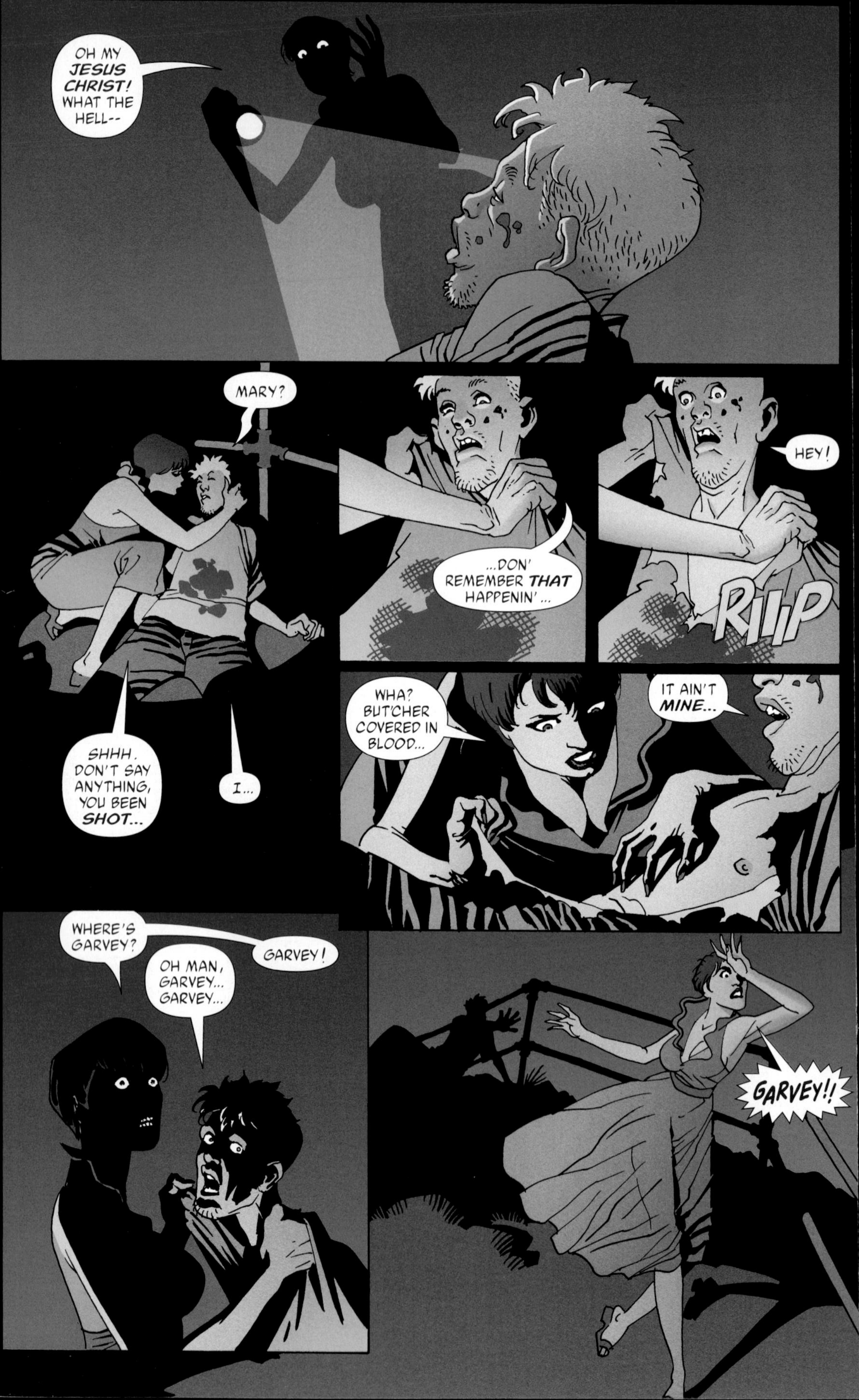
OH MY JESUS CHRIST! WHAT THE HELL--
MARY?
SHHH. DON'T SAY ANYTHING, YOU BEEN SHOT...
I...
...DON' REMEMBER THAT HAPPENIN'...
HEY!
RIIIP
WHA? BUT'CHER COVERED IN BLOOD...
IT AIN'T MINE...
WHERE'S GARVEY?
GARVEY!
OH MAN, GARVEY... GARVEY...
GARVEY!!

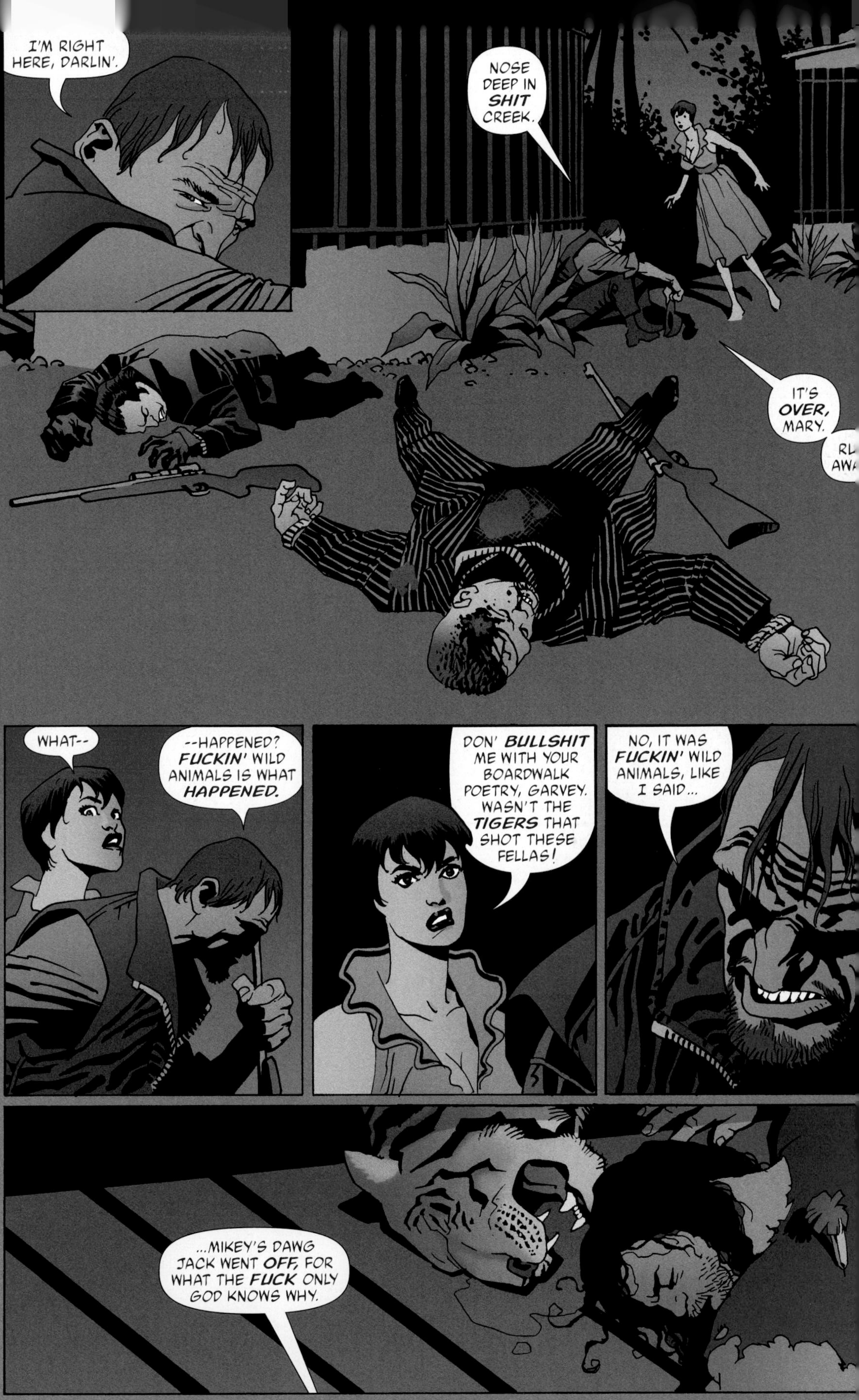
I'M RIGHT HERE, DARLIN'.
NOSE DEEP IN SHIT CREEK.
IT'S OVER, MARY.
WHAT--
--HAPPENED? FUCKIN' WILD ANIMALS IS WHAT HAPPENED.
DON' BULLSHIT ME WITH YOUR BOARDWALK POETRY, GARVEY. WASN'T THE TIGERS THAT SHOT THESE FELLAS!
NO, IT WAS FUCKIN' WILD ANIMALS, LIKE I SAID...
...MIKEY'S DAWG JACK WENT OFF, FOR WHAT THE FUCK ONLY GOD KNOWS WHY.

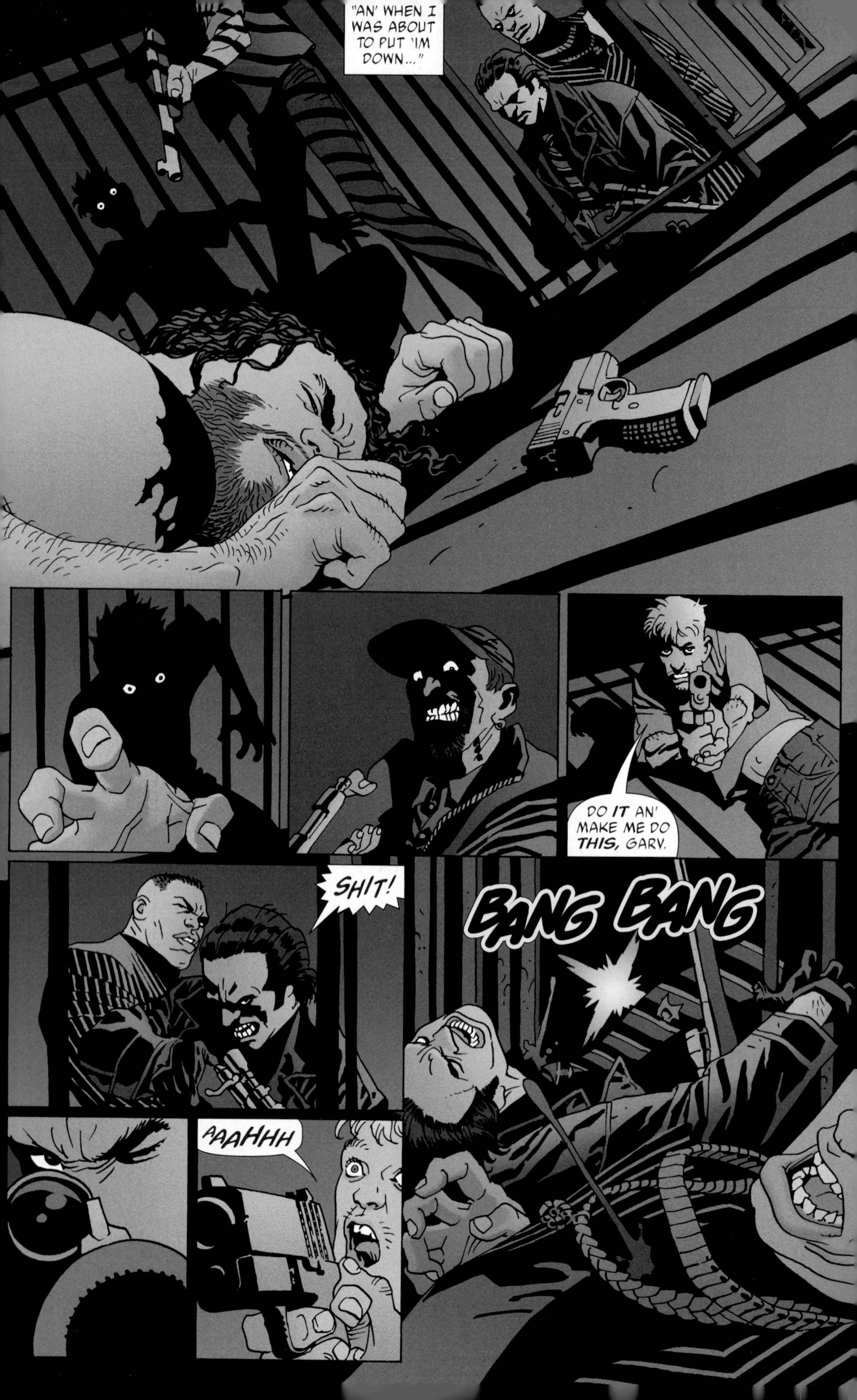
"AN' WHEN I WAS ABOUT TO PUT 'IM DOWN..."
DO IT AN' MAKE ME DO THIS, GARV.
SHIT!
BANG BANG
AAAHHH

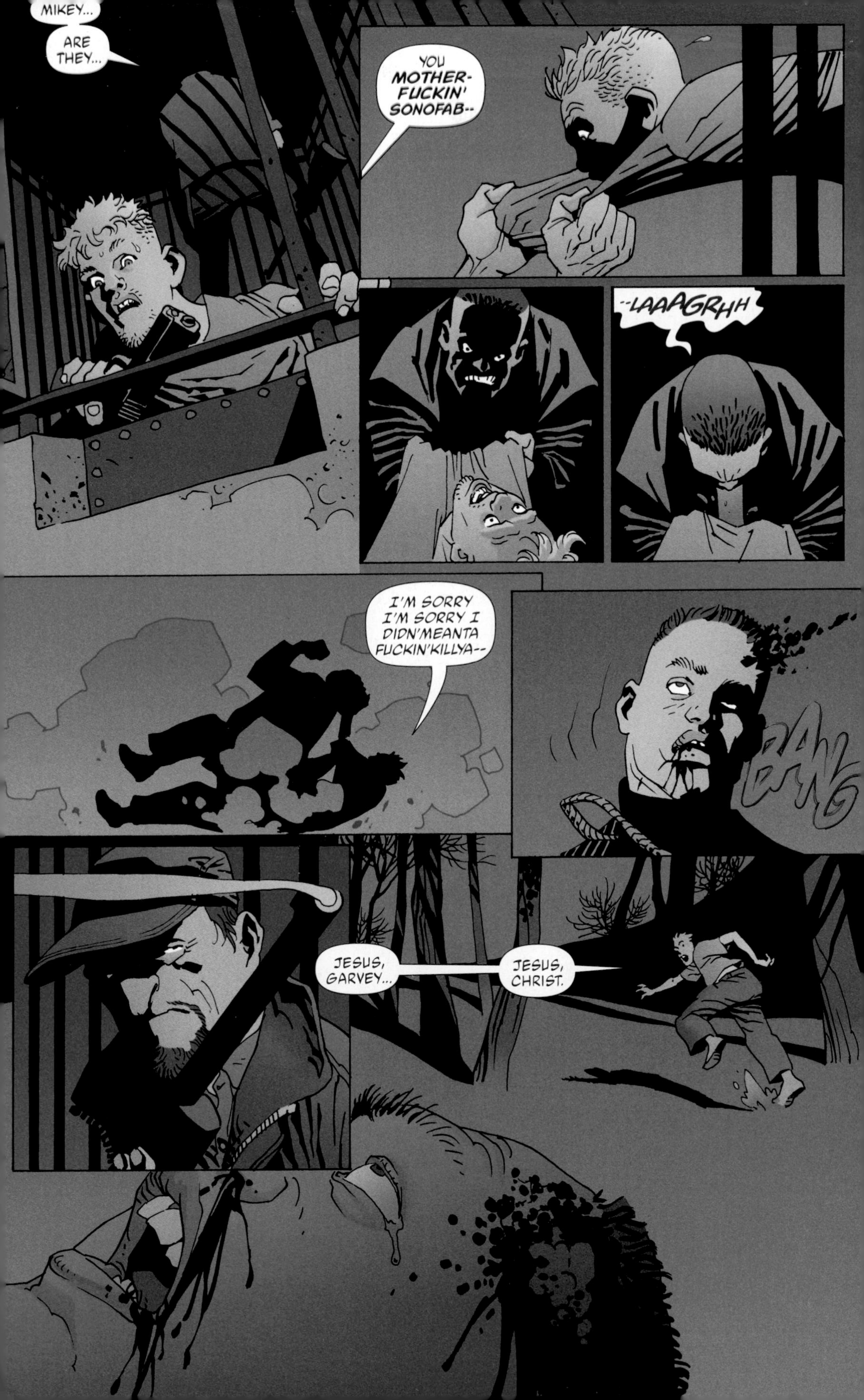
MIKEY...
ARE THEY...
YOU MOTHER-FUCKIN' SONOFAB--
--LAAAGRHH
I'M SORRY I'M SORRY I DIDN'MEANTA FUCKIN'KILLYA--
BANG
JESUS, GARVEY...
JESUS, CHRIST.

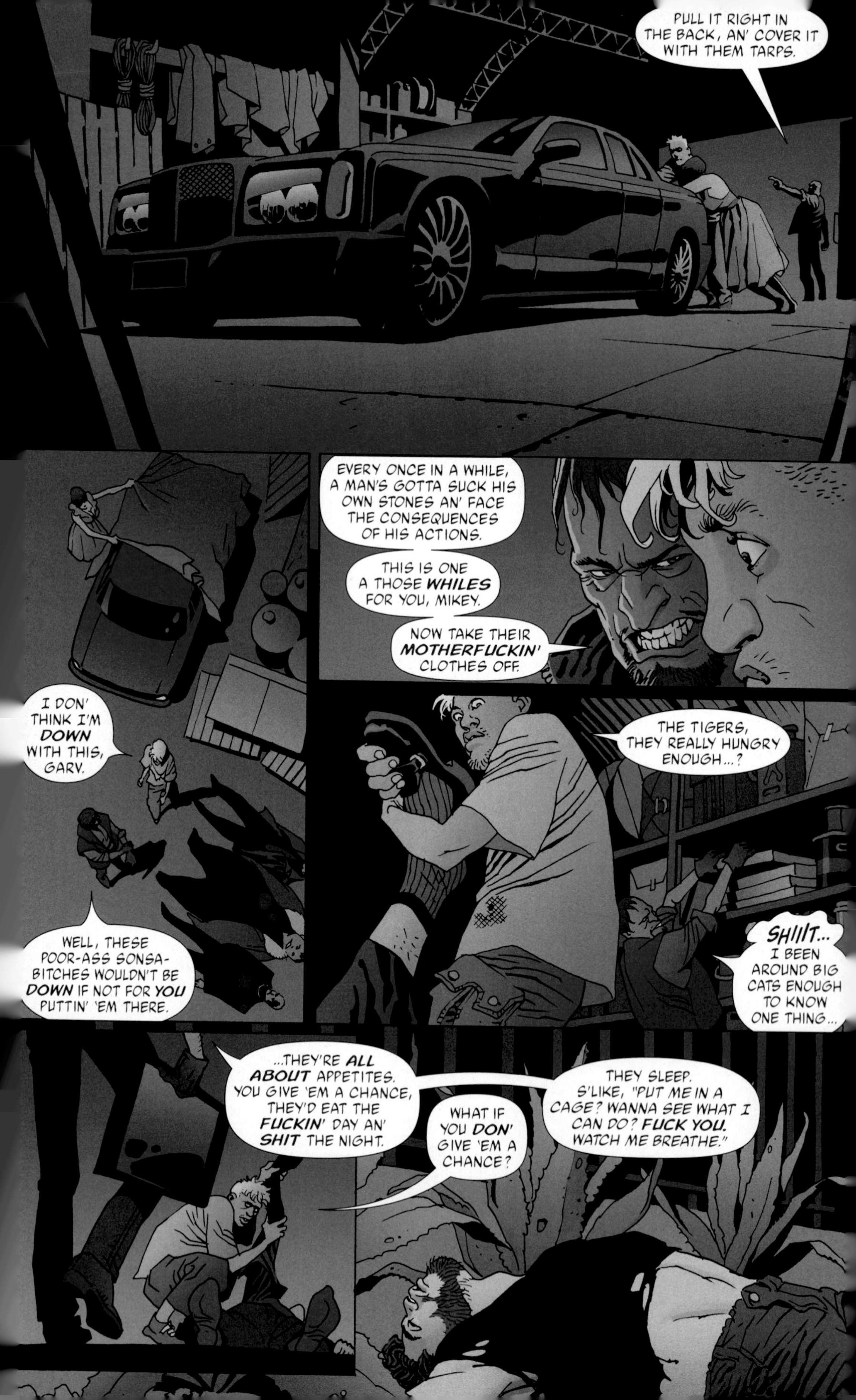
PULL IT RIGHT IN THE BACK, AN' COVER IT WITH THEM TARPS.
EVERY ONCE IN A WHILE, A MAN'S GOTTA SUCK HIS OWN STONES AN' FACE THE CONSEQUENCES OF HIS ACTIONS.
THIS IS ONE A THOSE WHILES FOR YOU, MIKEY.
NOW TAKE THEIR MOTHERFUCKIN' CLOTHES OFF.
I DON' THINK I'M DOWN WITH THIS, GARV.
WELL, THESE POOR-ASS SONSA-BITCHES WOULDN'T BE DOWN IF NOT FOR YOU PUTTIN' 'EM THERE.
THE TIGERS, THEY REALLY HUNGRY ENOUGH...?
SHIIIT... I BEEN AROUND BIG CATS ENOUGH TO KNOW ONE THING...
...THEY'RE ALL ABOUT APPETITES. YOU GIVE 'EM A CHANCE, THEY'D EAT THE FUCKIN' DAY AN' SHIT THE NIGHT.
WHAT IF YOU DON' GIVE 'EM A CHANCE?
THEY SLEEP. S'LIKE, "PUT ME IN A CAGE? WANNA SEE WHAT I CAN DO? FUCK YOU. WATCH ME BREATHE."

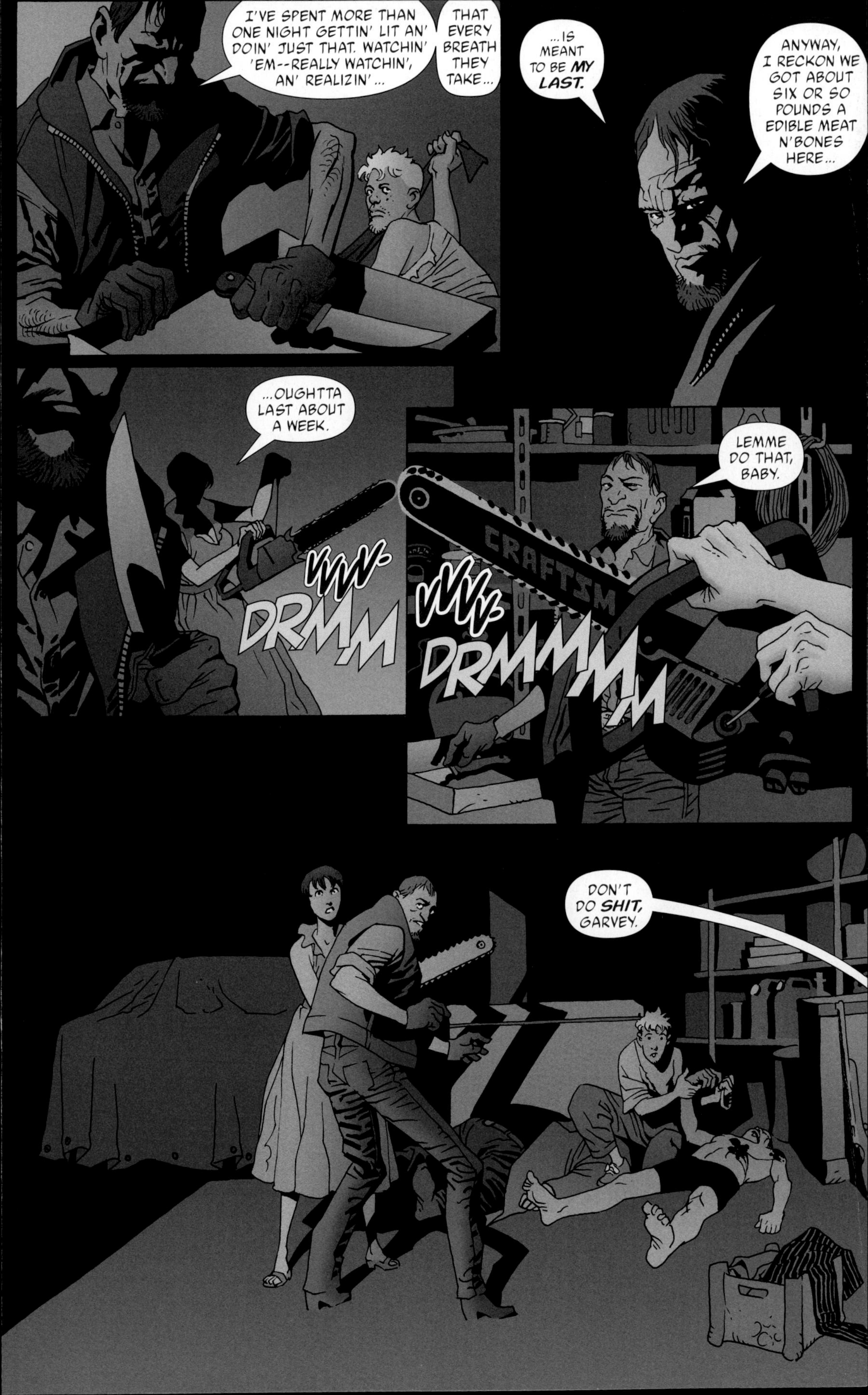
I'VE SPENT MORE THAN ONE NIGHT GETTIN' LIT AN' DOIN' JUST THAT. WATCHIN' 'EM--REALLY WATCHIN', AN' REALIZIN'...
THAT EVERY BREATH THEY TAKE...
...IS MEANT TO BE MY LAST.
ANYWAY, I RECKON WE GOT ABOUT SIX OR SO POUNDS A EDIBLE MEAT N'BONES HERE...
...OUGHTTA LAST ABOUT A WEEK.
VVV-
DRMM
LEMME DO THAT, BABY.
CRAFTSM
VVVV-
DRMMMMM
DON'T DO SHIT, GARVEY.

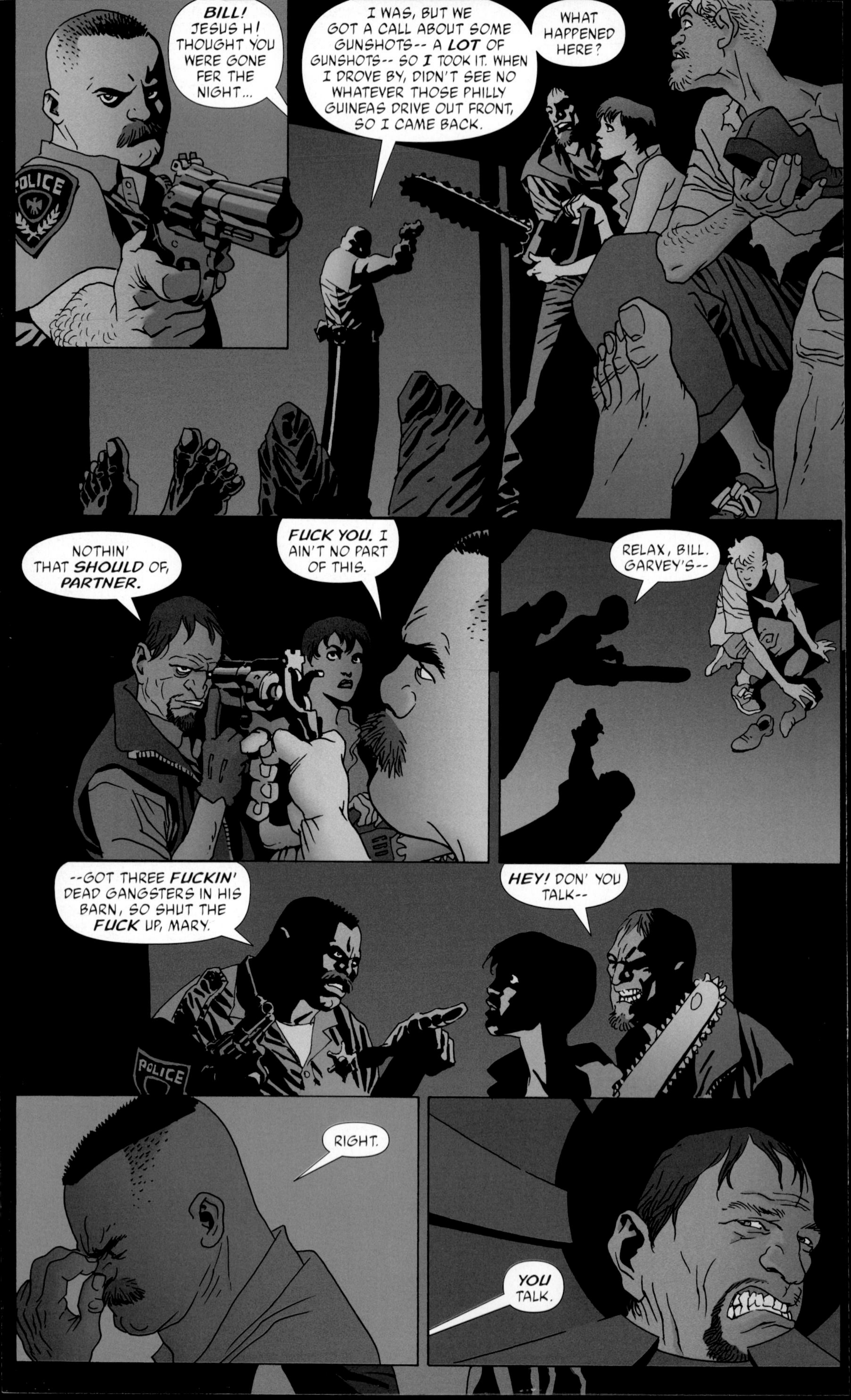
BILL! JESUS H! THOUGHT YOU WERE GONE FER THE NIGHT...
I WAS, BUT WE GOT A CALL ABOUT SOME GUNSHOTS-- A LOT OF GUNSHOTS-- SO I TOOK IT. WHEN I DROVE BY, DIDN'T SEE NO WHATEVER THOSE PHILLY GUINEAS DRIVE OUT FRONT, SO I CAME BACK.
WHAT HAPPENED HERE?
NOTHIN' THAT SHOULD OF, PARTNER.
FUCK YOU. I AIN'T NO PART OF THIS.
RELAX, BILL. GARVEY'S--
--GOT THREE FUCKIN' DEAD GANGSTERS IN HIS BARN, SO SHUT THE FUCK UP, MARY.
HEY! DON' YOU TALK--
POLICE
RIGHT.
YOU TALK.

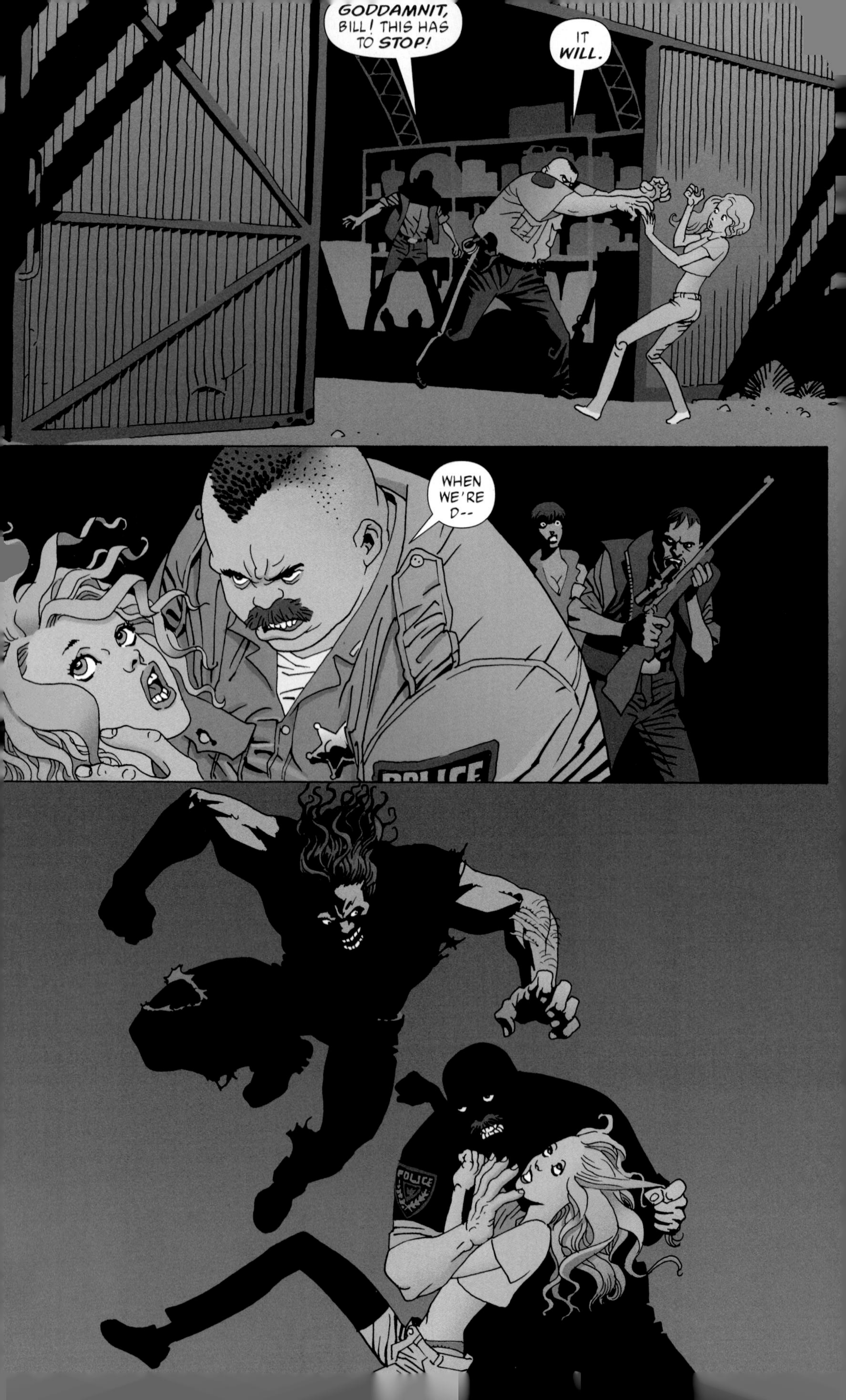
GODDAMNIT, BILL! THIS HAS TO STOP!
IT WILL.
WHEN WE'RE D--
POLICE
POLICE

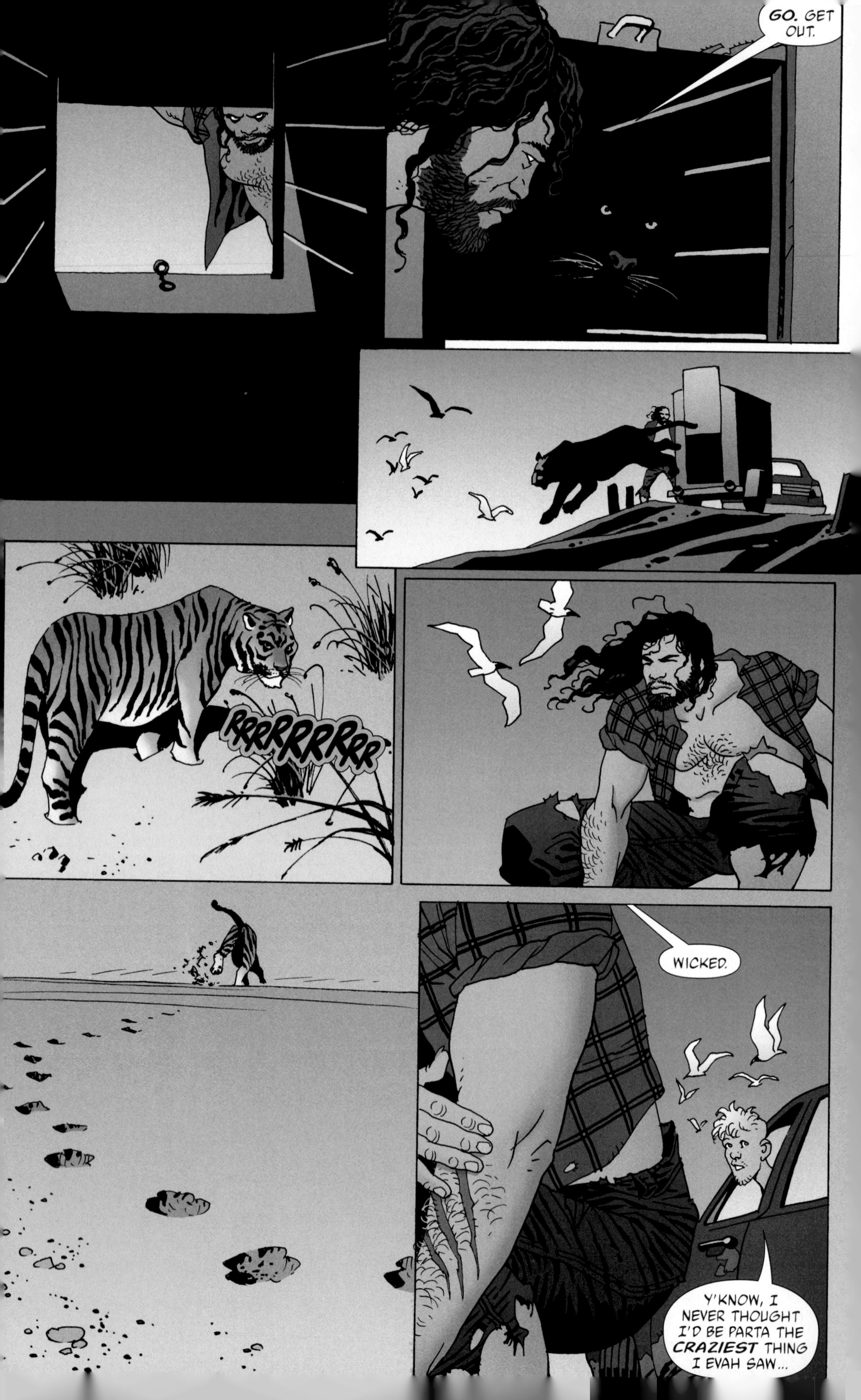
GO. GET OUT.
RRRRRRRRRR
WICKED.
Y'KNOW, I NEVER THOUGHT I'D BE PARTA THE CRAZIEST THING I EVAH SAW...

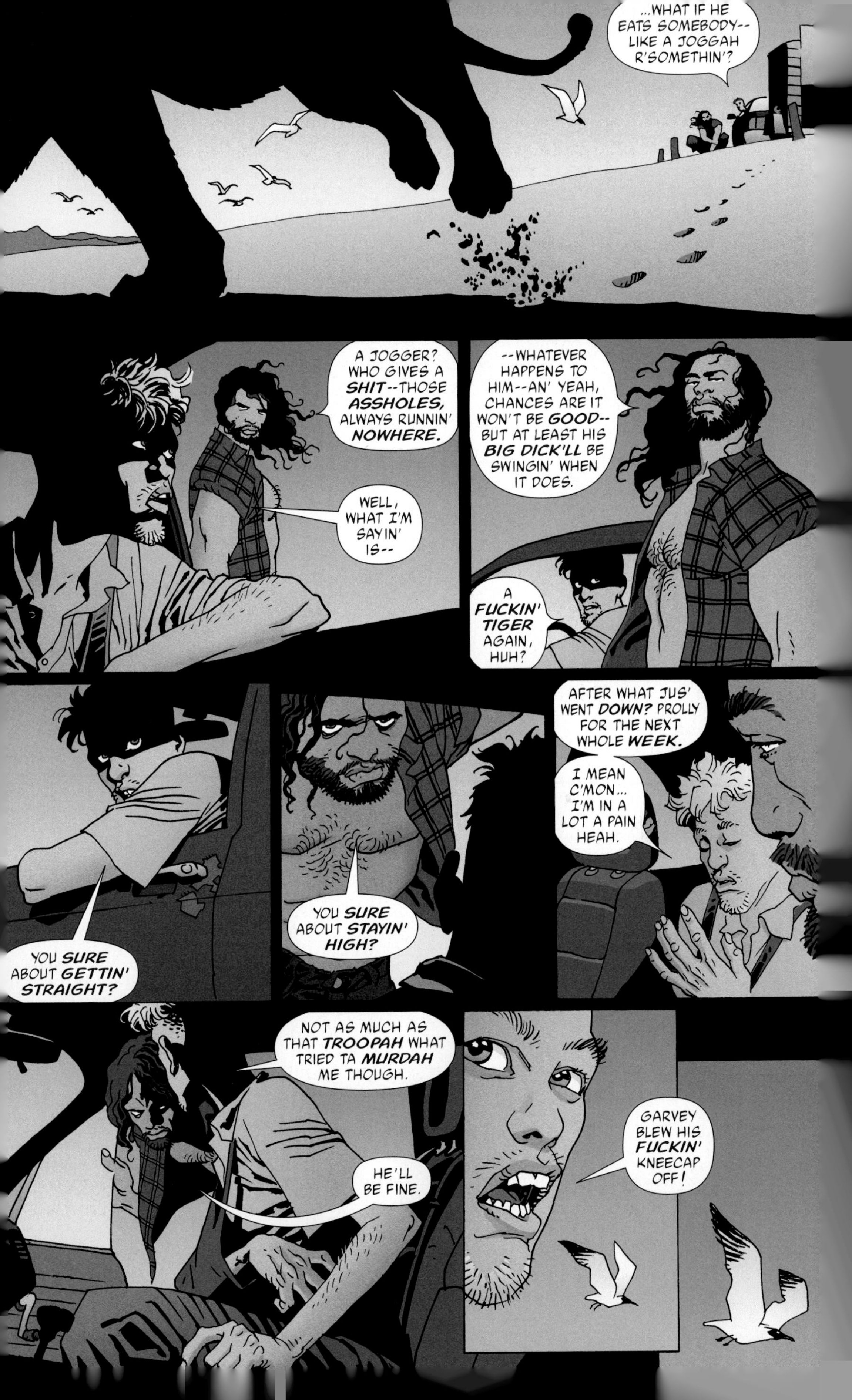
...WHAT IF HE EATS SOMEBODY-- LIKE A JOGGAH R'SOMETHIN'?
A JOGGER? WHO GIVES A SHIT--THOSE ASSHOLES, ALWAYS RUNNIN' NOWHERE.
WELL, WHAT I'M SAYIN' IS--
--WHATEVER HAPPENS TO HIM--AN' YEAH, CHANCES ARE IT WON'T BE GOOD-- BUT AT LEAST HIS BIG DICK'LL BE SWINGIN' WHEN IT DOES.
A FUCKIN' TIGER AGAIN, HUH?
YOU SURE ABOUT GETTIN' STRAIGHT?
YOU SURE ABOUT STAYIN' HIGH?
AFTER WHAT JUS' WENT DOWN? PROLLY FOR THE NEXT WHOLE WEEK.
I MEAN C'MON... I'M IN A LOT A PAIN HEAH.
NOT AS MUCH AS THAT TROOPAH WHAT TRIED TA MURDAH ME THOUGH.
HE'LL BE FINE.
GARVEY BLEW HIS FUCKIN' KNEECAP OFF!

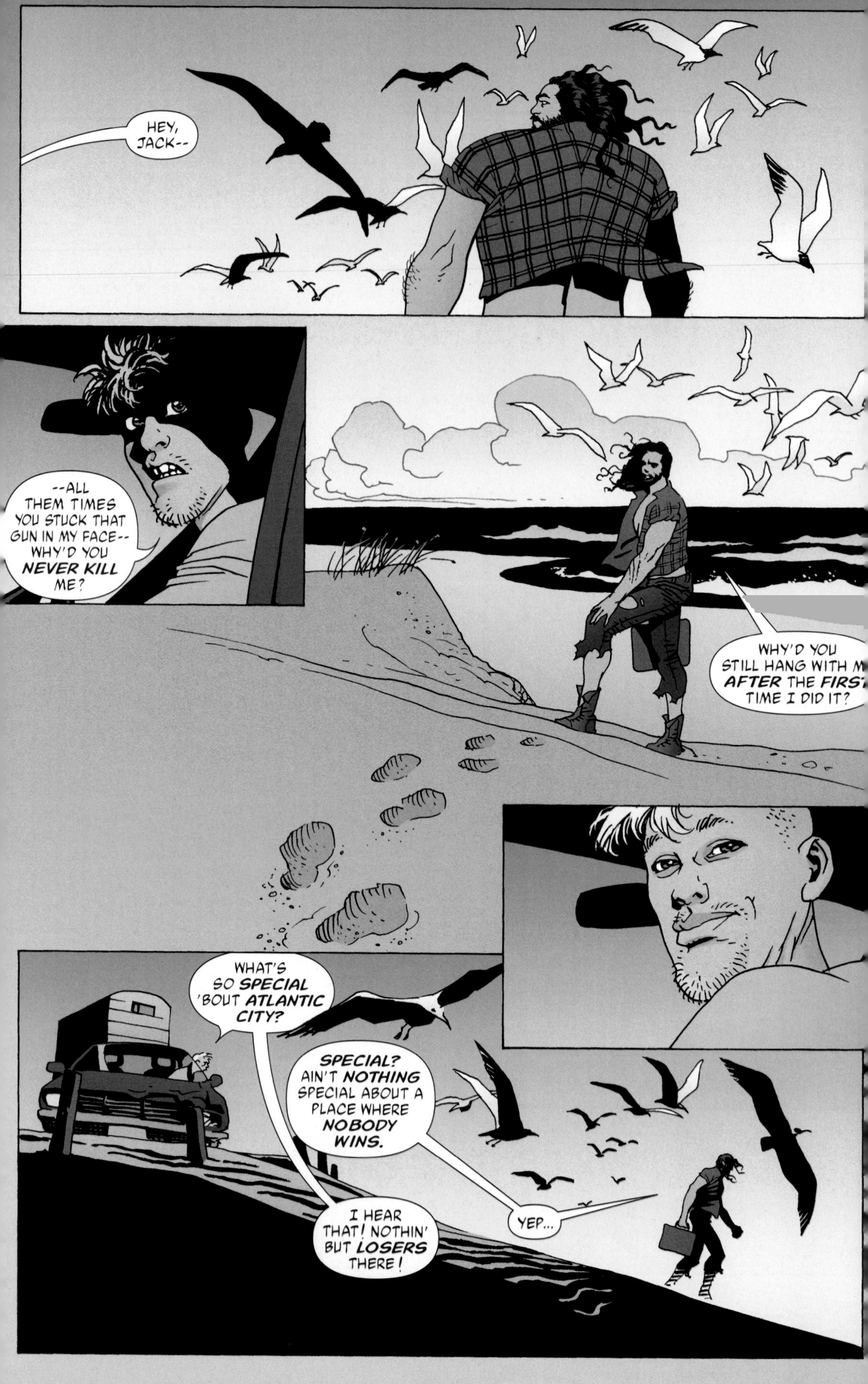
HEY, JACK--
--ALL THEM TIMES YOU STUCK THAT GUN IN MY FACE-- WHY'D YOU NEVER KILL ME?
WHY'D YOU STILL HANG WITH M AFTER THE FIRS TIME I DID IT?
WHAT'S SO SPECIAL 'BOUT ATLANTIC CITY?
SPECIAL? AIN'T NOTHING SPECIAL ABOUT A PLACE WHERE NOBODY WINS.
I HEAR THAT! NOTHIN' BUT LOSERS THERE!
YEP...

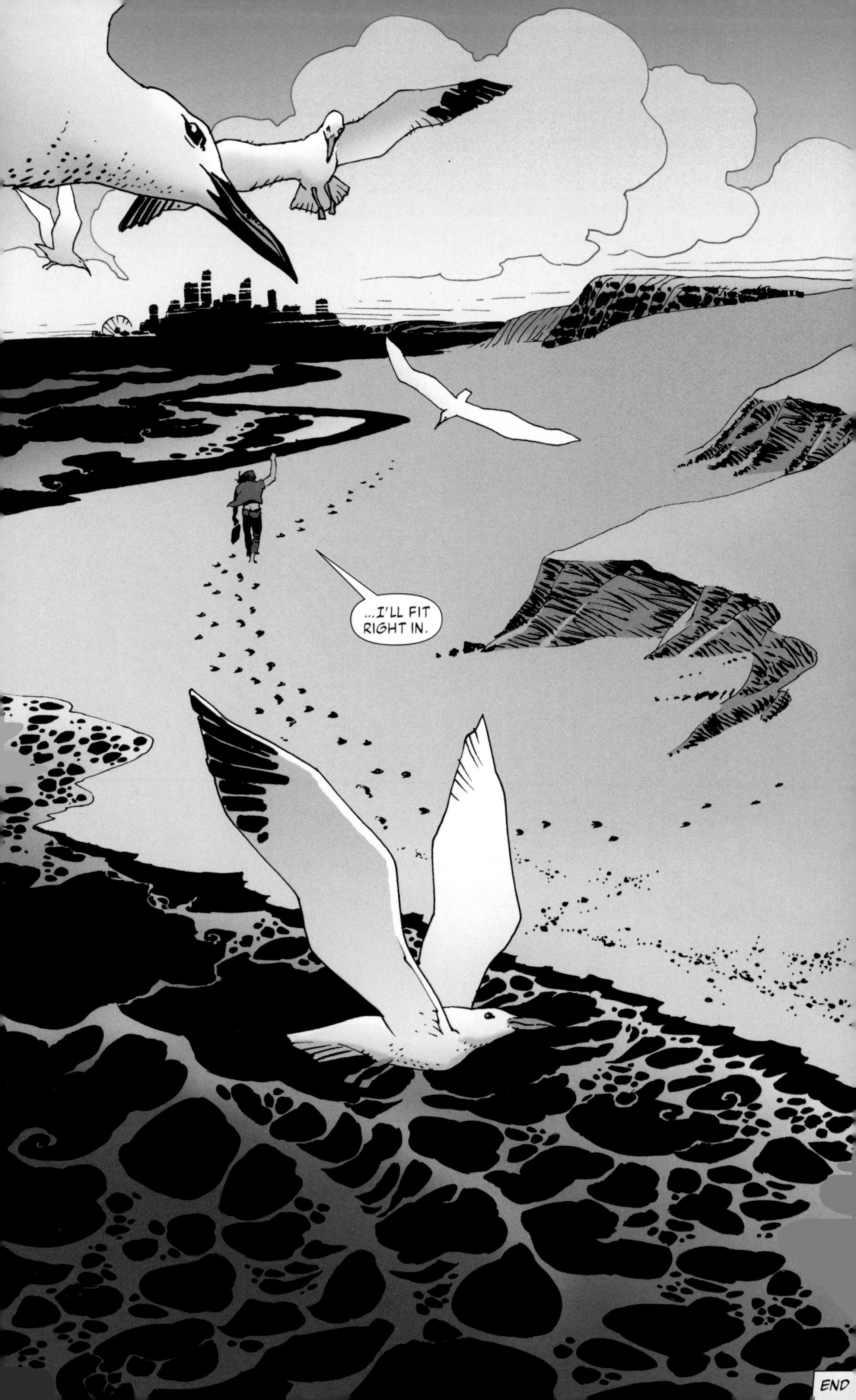
...I'LL FIT RIGHT IN.
END

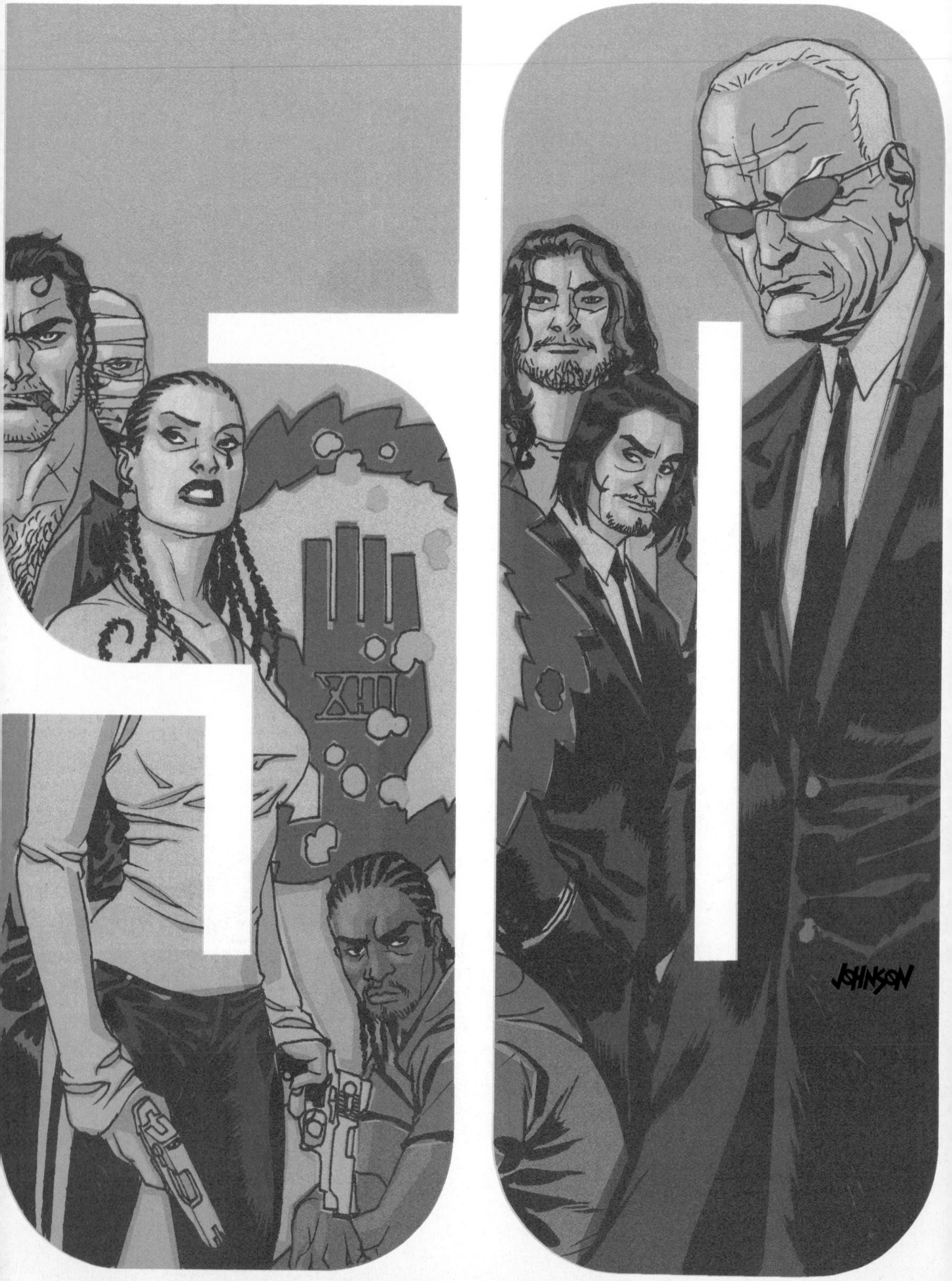
JOHNSON

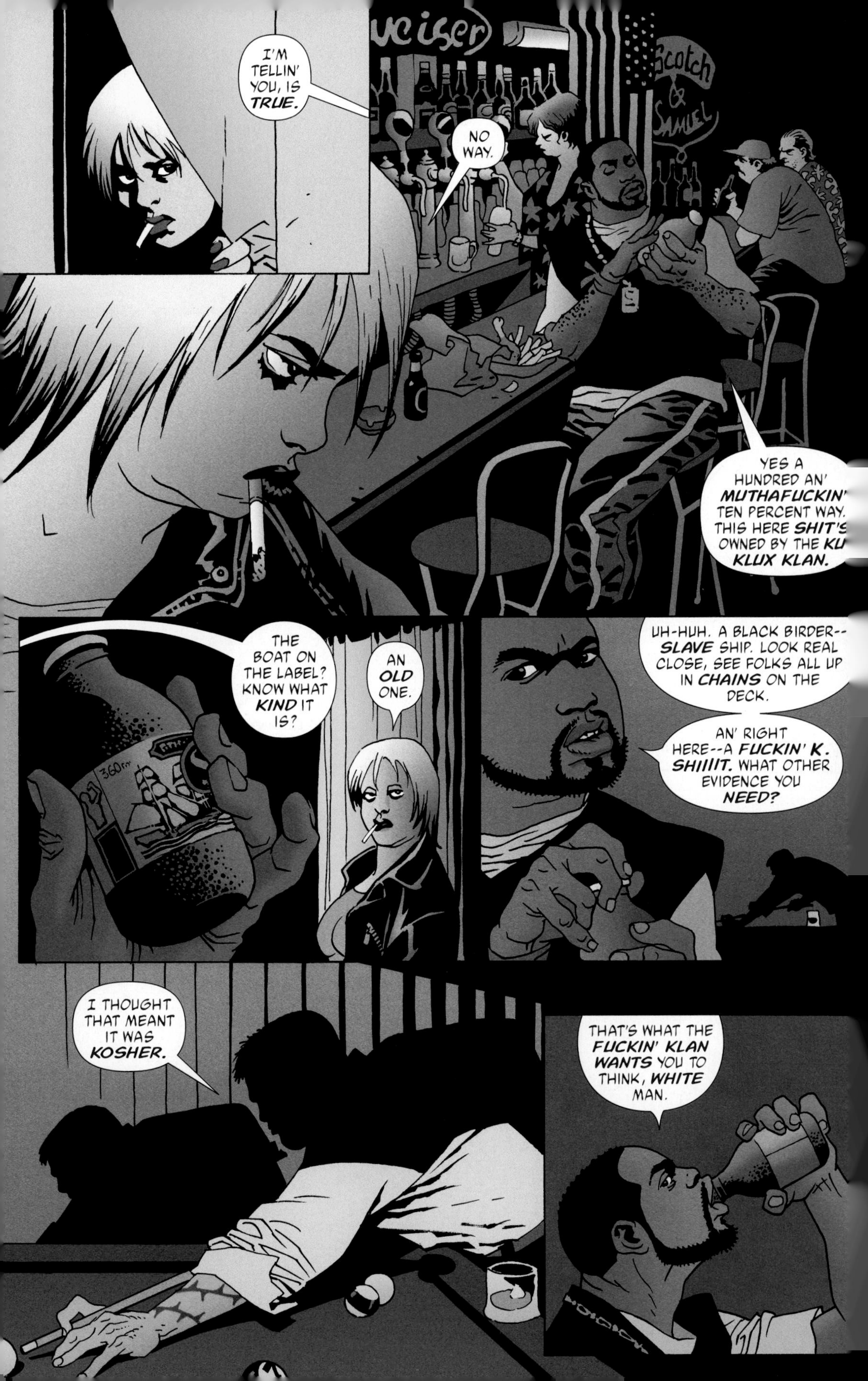
I'M TELLIN' YOU, IS TRUE.
NO WAY.
YES A HUNDRED AN' MUTHAFUCKIN' TEN PERCENT WAY. THIS HERE SHIT'S OWNED BY THE KU KLUX KLAN.
THE BOAT ON THE LABEL? KNOW WHAT KIND IT IS?
AN OLD ONE.
UH-HUH. A BLACK BIRDER--SLAVE SHIP. LOOK REAL CLOSE, SEE FOLKS ALL UP IN CHAINS ON THE DECK.
AN' RIGHT HERE--A FUCKIN' K. SHIIIIT. WHAT OTHER EVIDENCE YOU NEED?
I THOUGHT THAT MEANT IT WAS KOSHER.
THAT'S WHAT THE FUCKIN' KLAN WANTS YOU TO THINK, WHITE MAN.

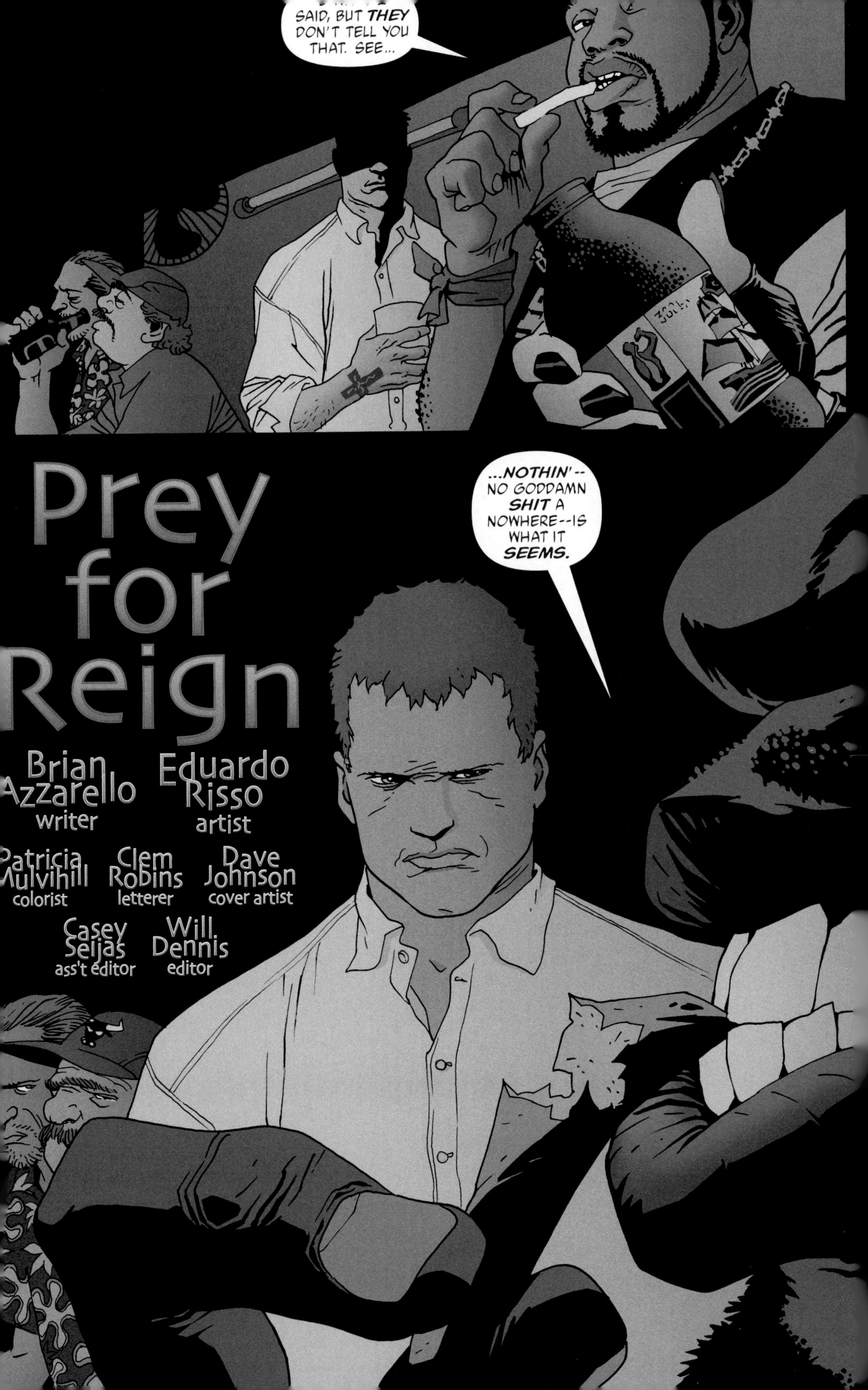
SAID, BUT THEY DON'T TELL YOU THAT. SEE...
...NOTHIN' -- NO GODDAMN SHIT A NOWHERE--IS WHAT IT SEEMS.
Prey for Reign
Brian Azzarello writer
Eduardo Risso artist
Patricia Mulvihill colorist
Clem Robins letterer
Dave Johnson cover artist
Casey Seijas ass't editor
Will Dennis editor

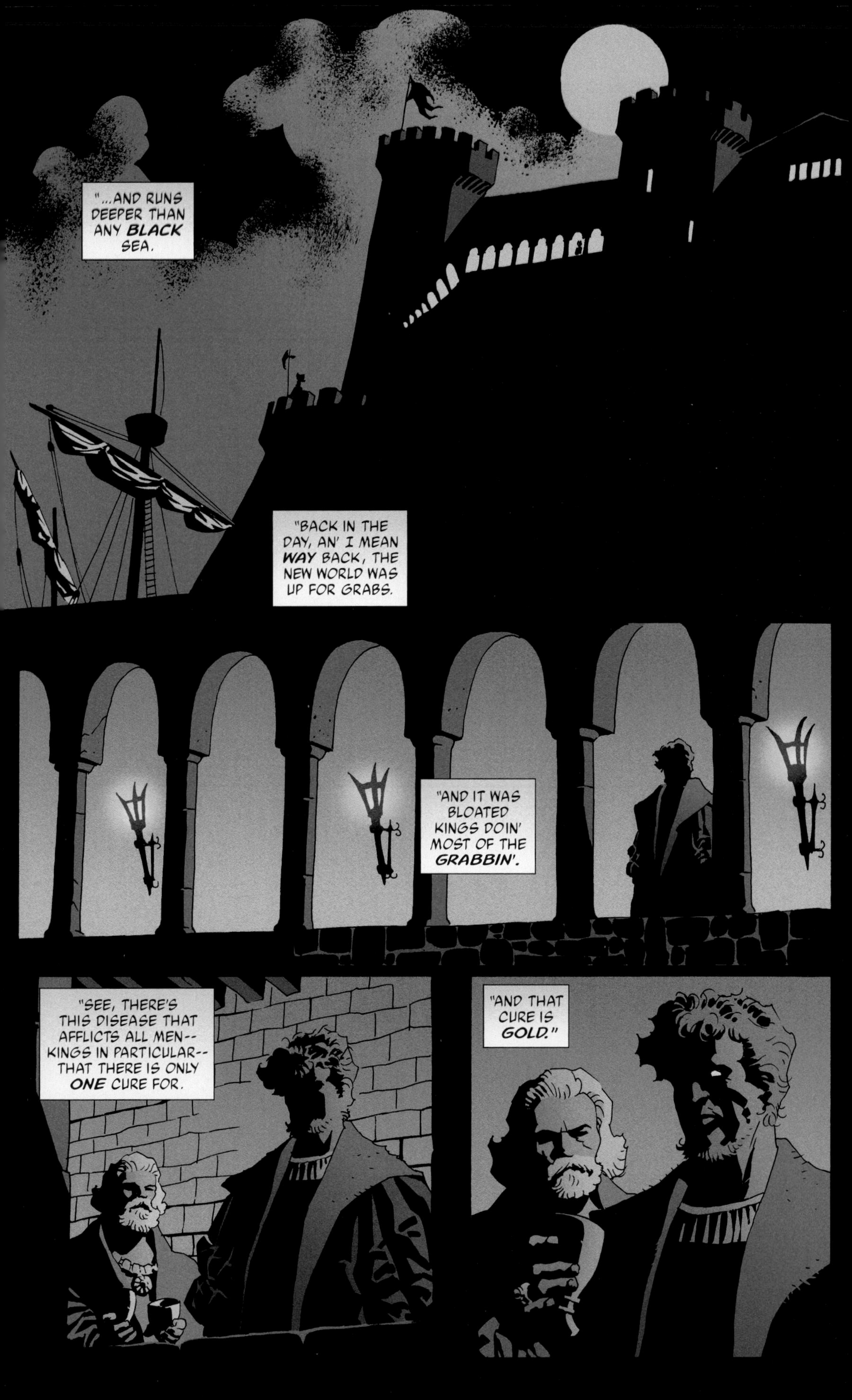
"...AND RUNS DEEPER THAN ANY **BLACK** SEA.
"BACK IN THE DAY, AN' I MEAN **WAY** BACK, THE NEW WORLD WAS UP FOR GRABS.
"AND IT WAS BLOATED KINGS DOIN' MOST OF THE **GRABBIN'**.
"SEE, THERE'S THIS DISEASE THAT AFFLICTS ALL MEN-- KINGS IN PARTICULAR-- THAT THERE IS ONLY **ONE** CURE FOR.
"AND THAT CURE IS **GOLD.**"

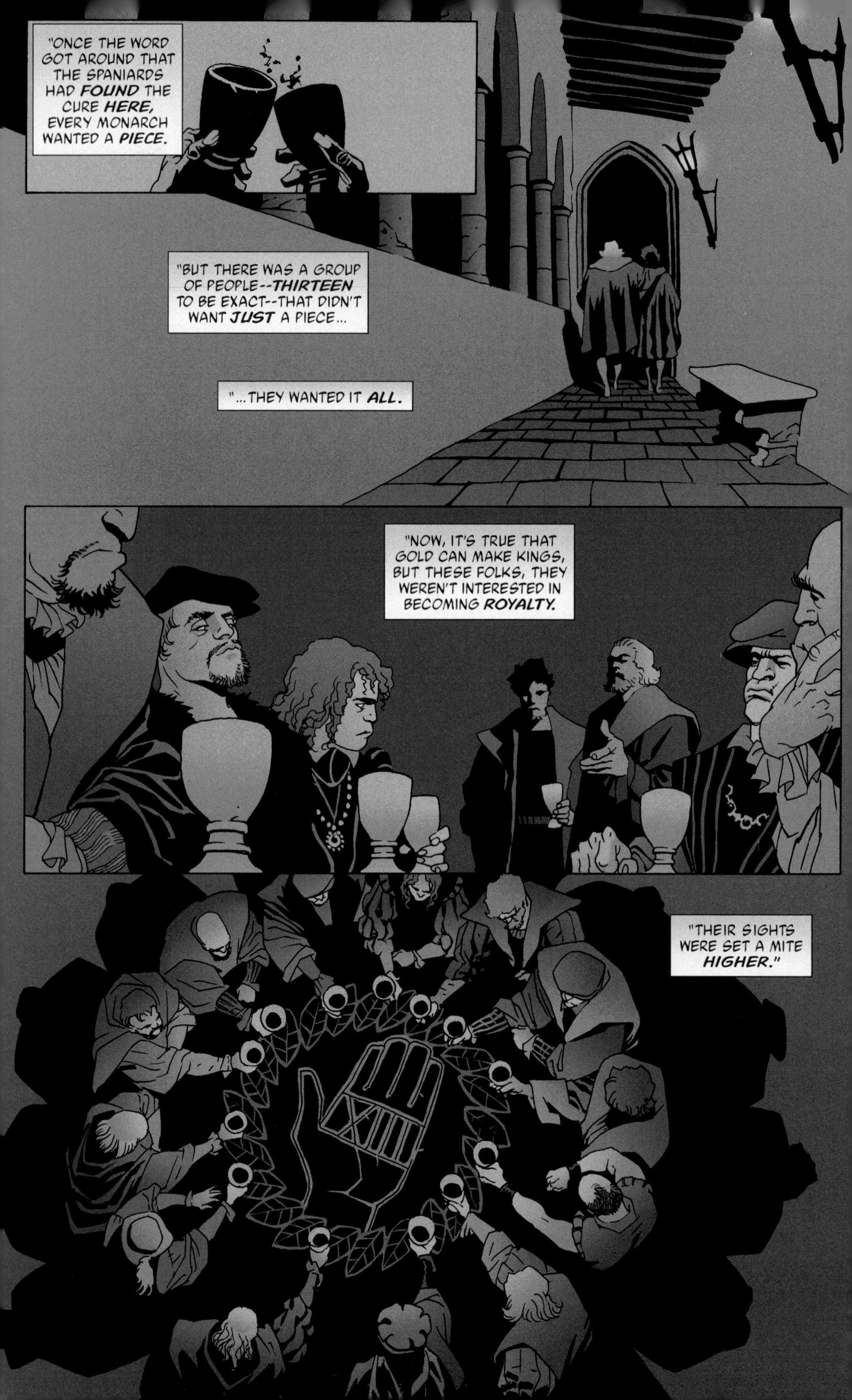
"ONCE THE WORD GOT AROUND THAT THE SPANIARDS HAD FOUND THE CURE HERE, EVERY MONARCH WANTED A PIECE.
"BUT THERE WAS A GROUP OF PEOPLE--THIRTEEN TO BE EXACT--THAT DIDN'T WANT JUST A PIECE...
"...THEY WANTED IT ALL.
"NOW, IT'S TRUE THAT GOLD CAN MAKE KINGS, BUT THESE FOLKS, THEY WEREN'T INTERESTED IN BECOMING ROYALTY.
"THEIR SIGHTS WERE SET A MITE HIGHER."

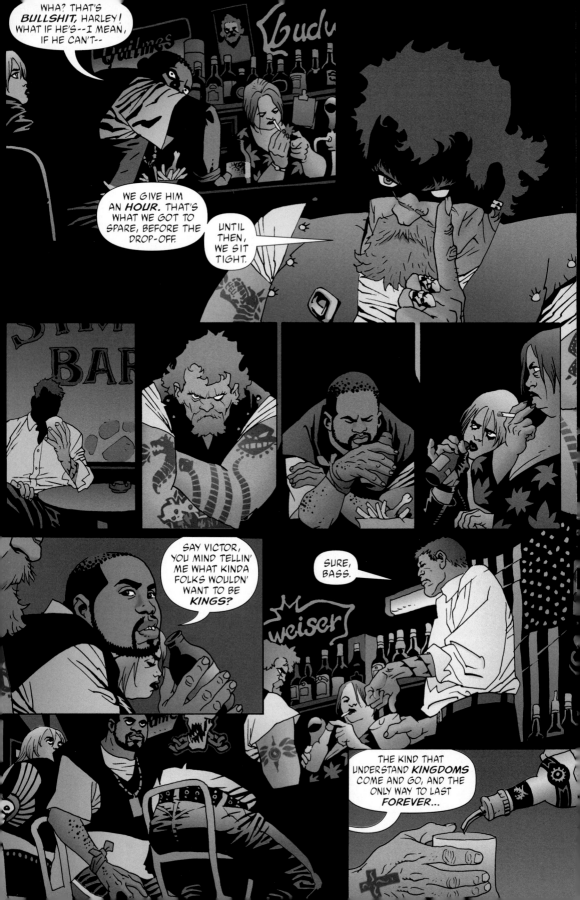

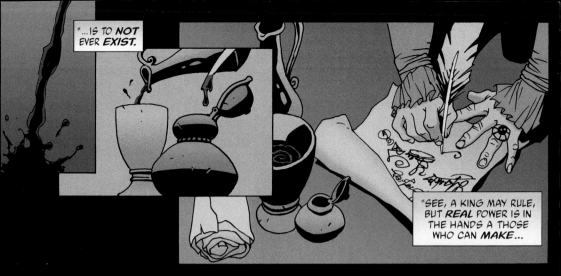

"...IS TO **NOT** EVER **EXIST**.

"SEE, A KING MAY RULE, BUT **REAL** POWER IS IN THE HANDS A THOSE WHO CAN **MAKE**...

"...OR **BREAK** 'EM. THAT'S BEEN THE WAY IT IS...

"...FOREVER.

"AND WHILE THESE FOLKS HAD BEEN AROUND JUST ABOUT AS LONG...

"...THE IDEA OF CREATING A BINDING **TRUST** WAS NEW."

"BEFORE THAT, THEY WERE *LIKE* KINGS-- ALWAYS *LOOKIN'* FOR A PIECE OF WHAT ANOTHER MIGHT HAVE.

"BUT WHEN THEY ALL REALIZED THAT ROBBIN' FROM EACH OTHER WAS A *WASTE* OF TIME...

"AN' WHAT JOINING *TOGETHER* COULD MEAN?

"THEY CAME UP WITH A PLAN, ONE THAT WOULD TAKE THEIR *THORNY SELVES* OUT OF THE KING'S SIDE...

"AND STICK IT IN A *LAND* WHERE A *KING* WOULD HAVE NO *PURCHASE.*

"WHERE THE *THIRTEEN* OF 'EM WOULD HAVE THE FREEDOM AND THE LIBERTY TO SHAPE A NATION IN THEIR *OWN* IMAGE.

"SO THEY PRESENTED THIS FAIR DEAL TO THE KINGS: YOU LEAVE WHAT'S LEFT OF THE *NEW WORLD* TO US..."

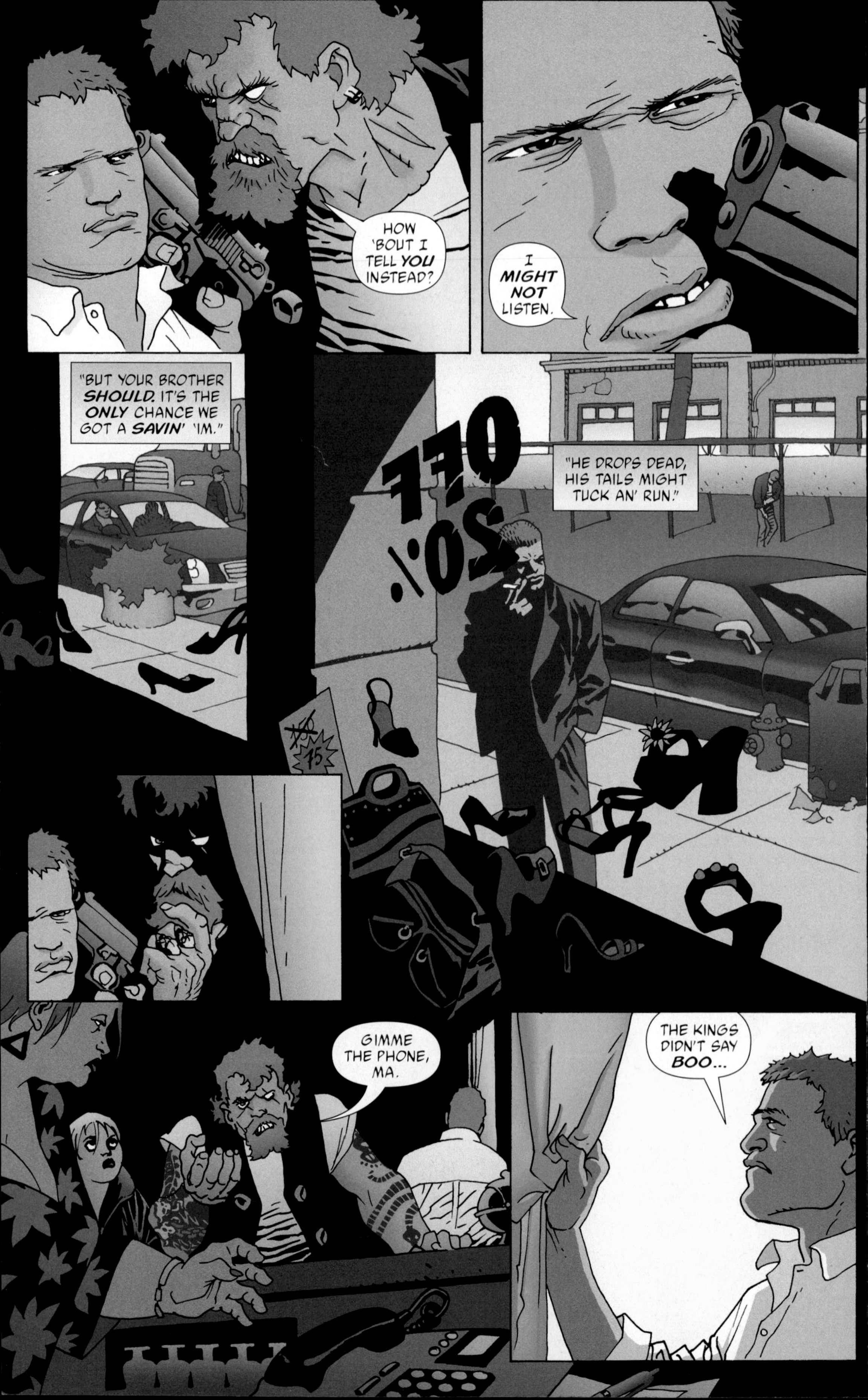
HOW 'BOUT I TELL *YOU* INSTEAD?
I *MIGHT NOT* LISTEN.
"BUT YOUR BROTHER *SHOULD.* IT'S THE *ONLY* CHANCE WE GOT A *SAVIN'* 'IM."
"HE DROPS DEAD, HIS TAILS MIGHT TUCK AN' RUN."
GIMME THE PHONE, MA.
THE KINGS DIDN'T SAY *BOO*...

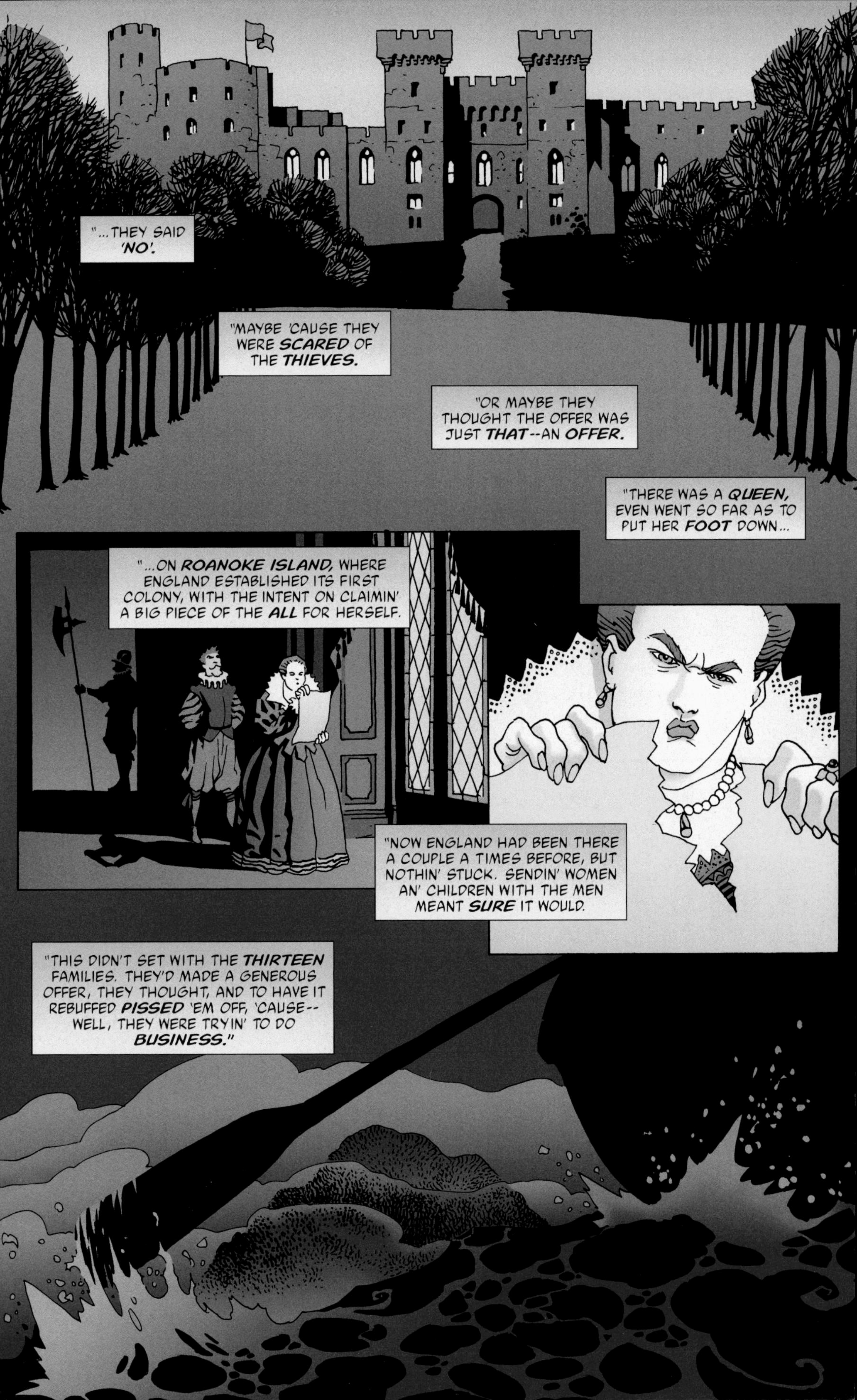
"...THEY SAID 'NO'.
"MAYBE 'CAUSE THEY WERE SCARED OF THE THIEVES.
"OR MAYBE THEY THOUGHT THE OFFER WAS JUST THAT--AN OFFER.
"THERE WAS A QUEEN, EVEN WENT SO FAR AS TO PUT HER FOOT DOWN...
"...ON ROANOKE ISLAND, WHERE ENGLAND ESTABLISHED ITS FIRST COLONY, WITH THE INTENT ON CLAIMIN' A BIG PIECE OF THE ALL FOR HERSELF.
"NOW ENGLAND HAD BEEN THERE A COUPLE A TIMES BEFORE, BUT NOTHIN' STUCK. SENDIN' WOMEN AN' CHILDREN WITH THE MEN MEANT SURE IT WOULD.
"THIS DIDN'T SET WITH THE THIRTEEN FAMILIES. THEY'D MADE A GENEROUS OFFER, THEY THOUGHT, AND TO HAVE IT REBUFFED PISSED 'EM OFF, 'CAUSE--WELL, THEY WERE TRYIN' TO DO BUSINESS."

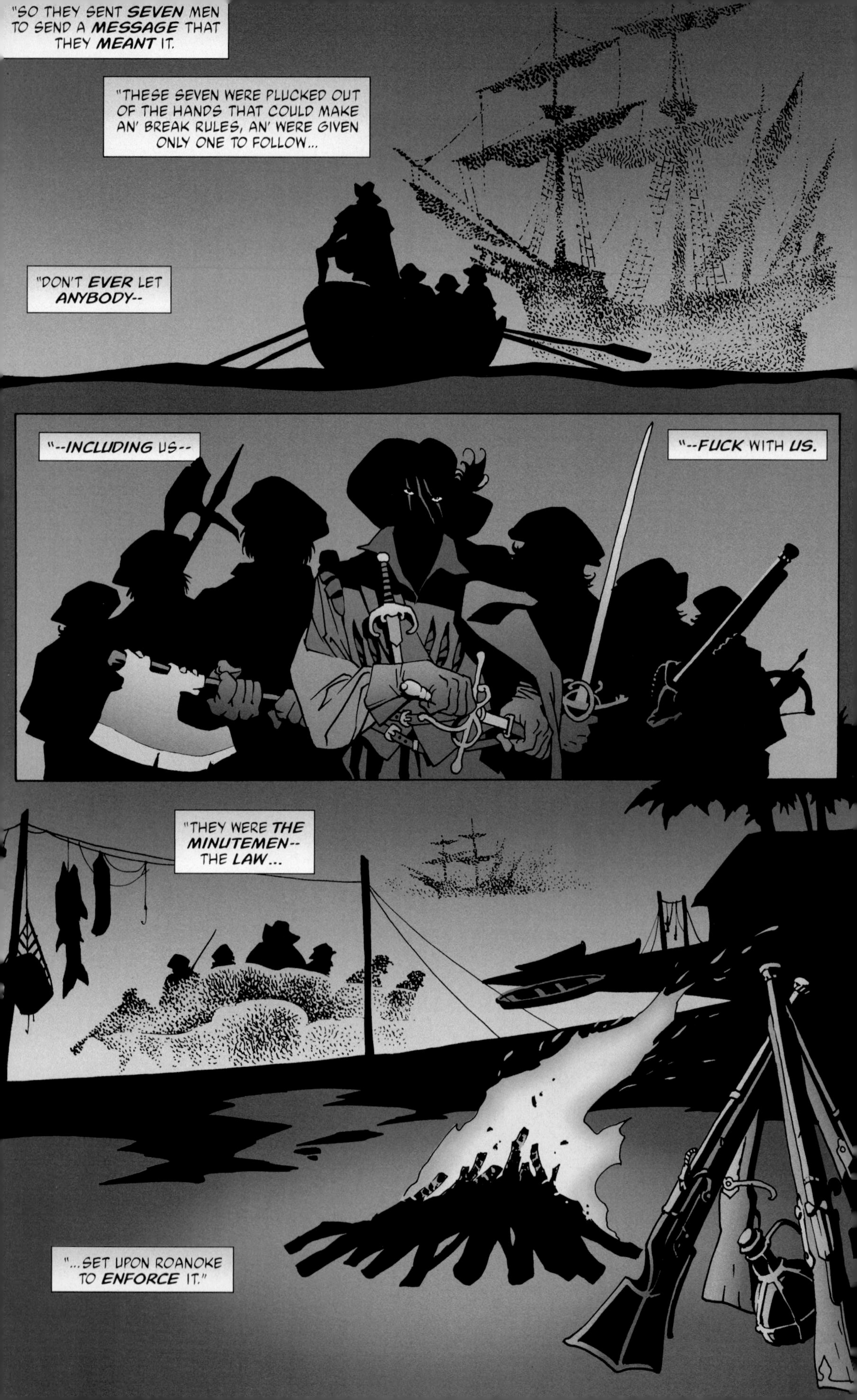
"SO THEY SENT SEVEN MEN TO SEND A MESSAGE THAT THEY MEANT IT.
"THESE SEVEN WERE PLUCKED OUT OF THE HANDS THAT COULD MAKE AN' BREAK RULES, AN' WERE GIVEN ONLY ONE TO FOLLOW...
"DON'T EVER LET ANYBODY--
"--INCLUDING US--
"--FUCK WITH US.
"THEY WERE THE MINUTEMEN-- THE LAW...
"...SET UPON ROANOKE TO ENFORCE IT."

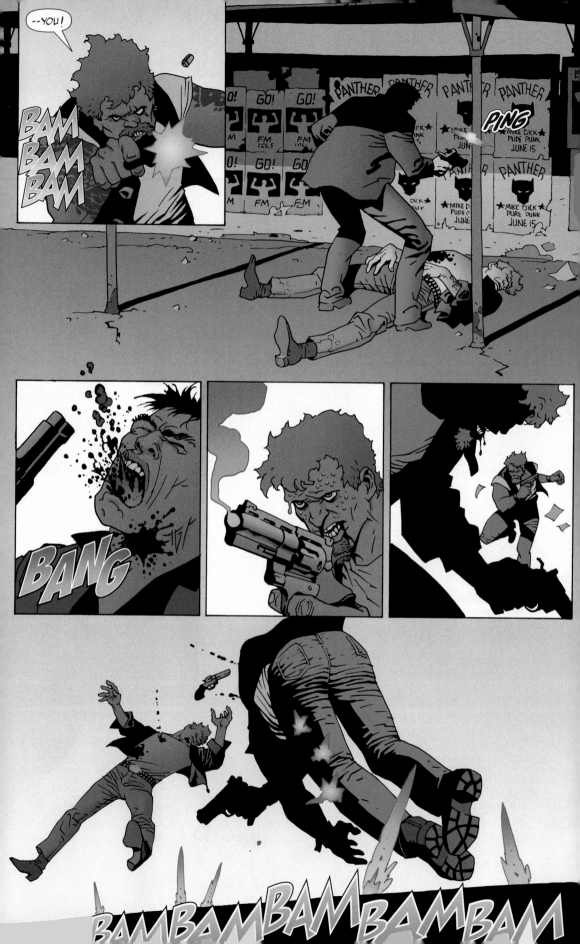

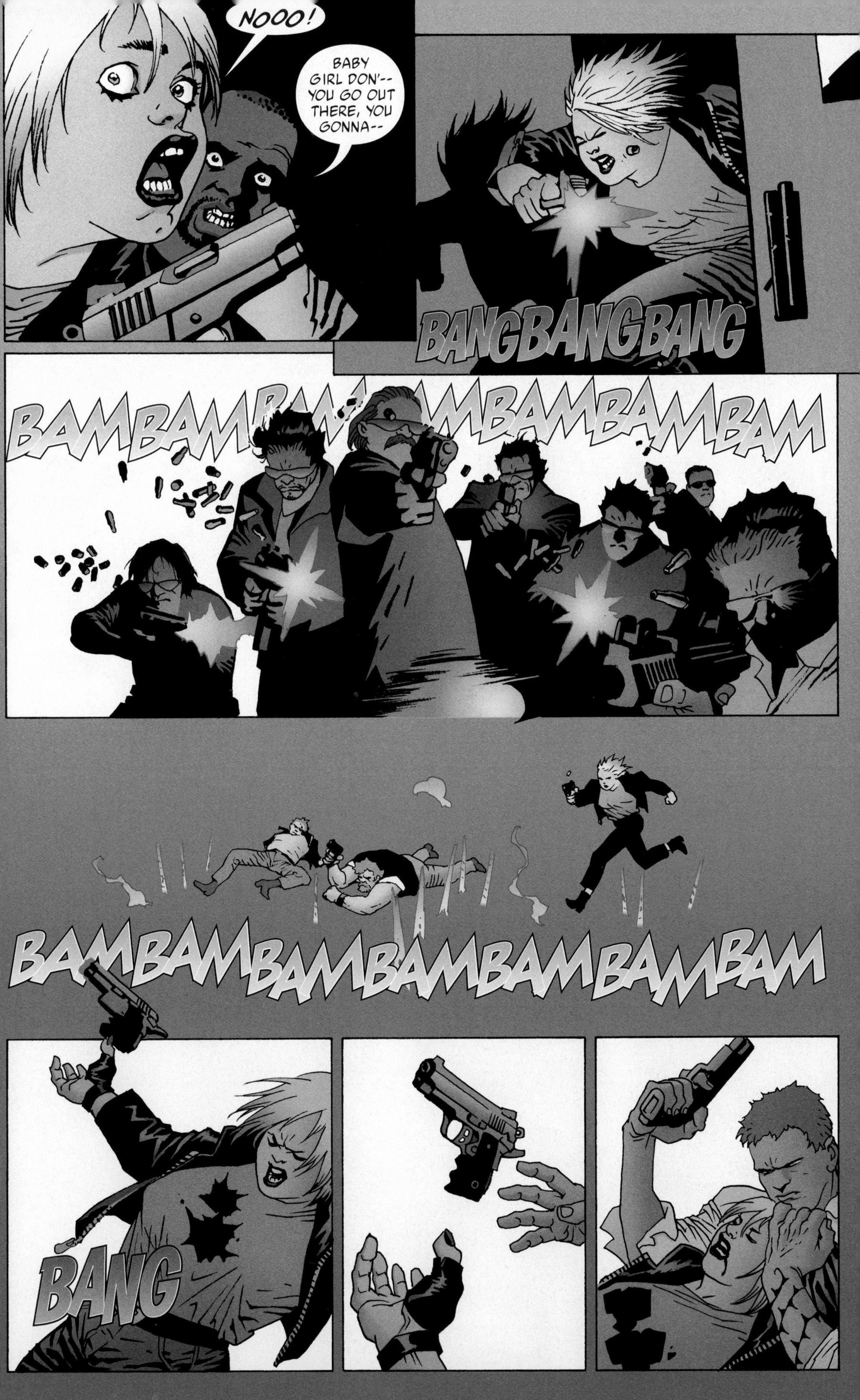
NOOO!
BABY GIRL DON'-- YOU GO OUT THERE, YOU GONNA--
BANGBANGBANG
BAMBAMBAMBAMBAMBAMBAM
BAMBAMBAMBAMBAMBAMBAM
BANG

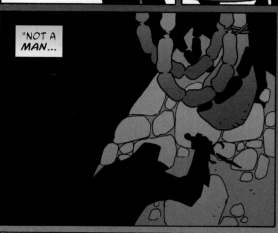

"NOT A MAN...

"A WOMAN...

"...NOR EVEN A CHILD..."

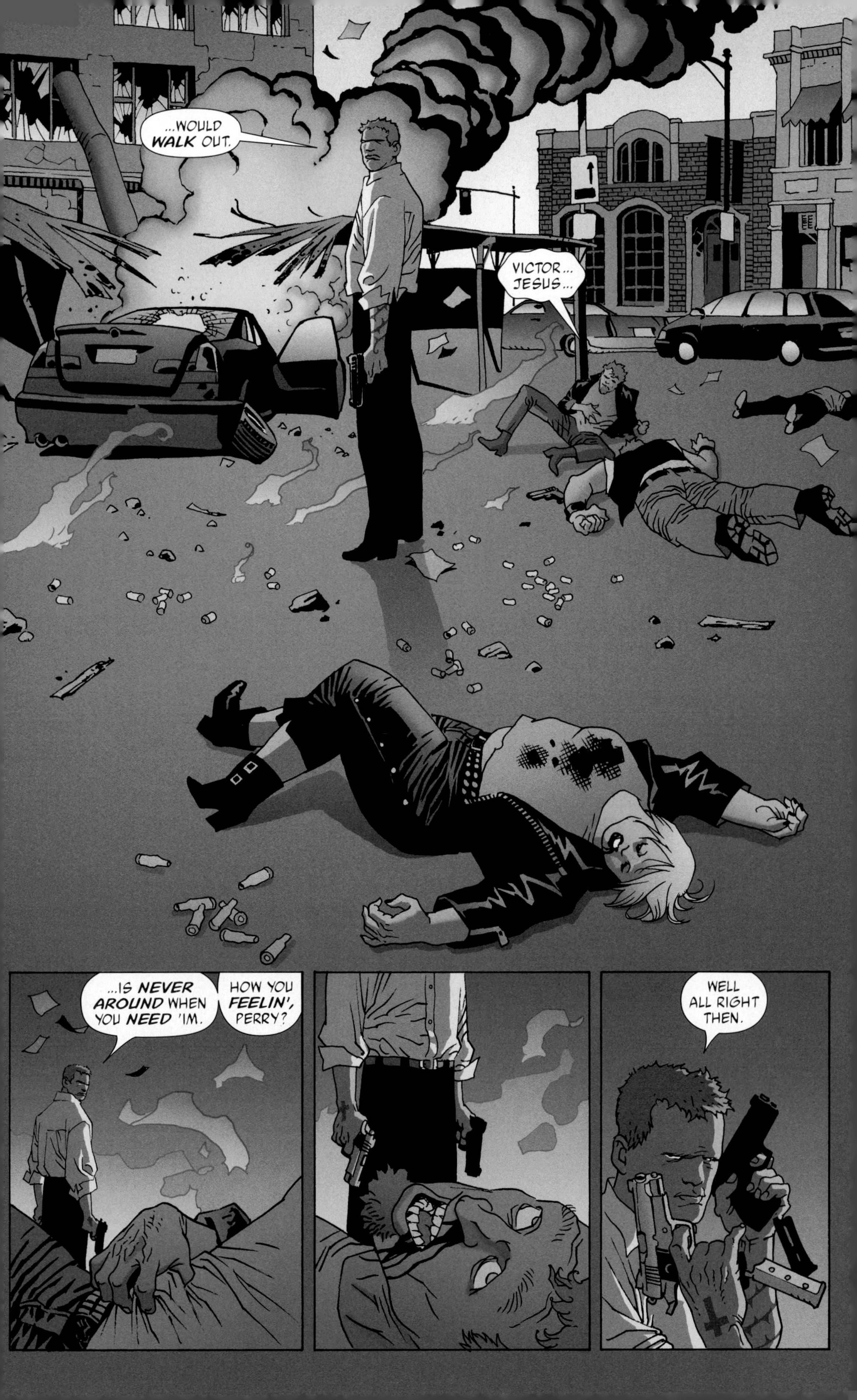
...WOULD WALK OUT.
VICTOR... JESUS...
...IS NEVER AROUND WHEN YOU NEED 'IM.
HOW YOU FEELIN', PERRY?
WELL ALL RIGHT THEN.

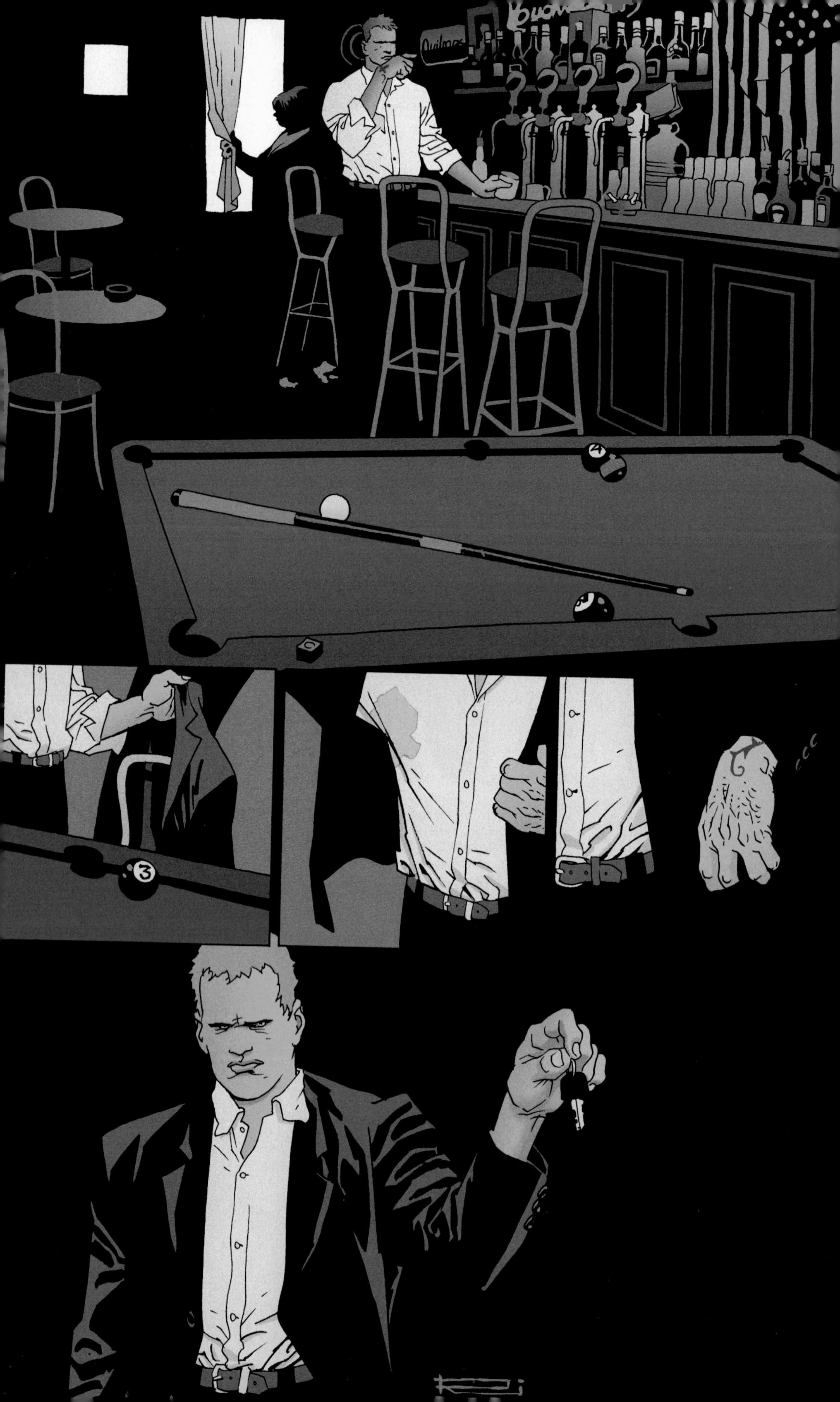

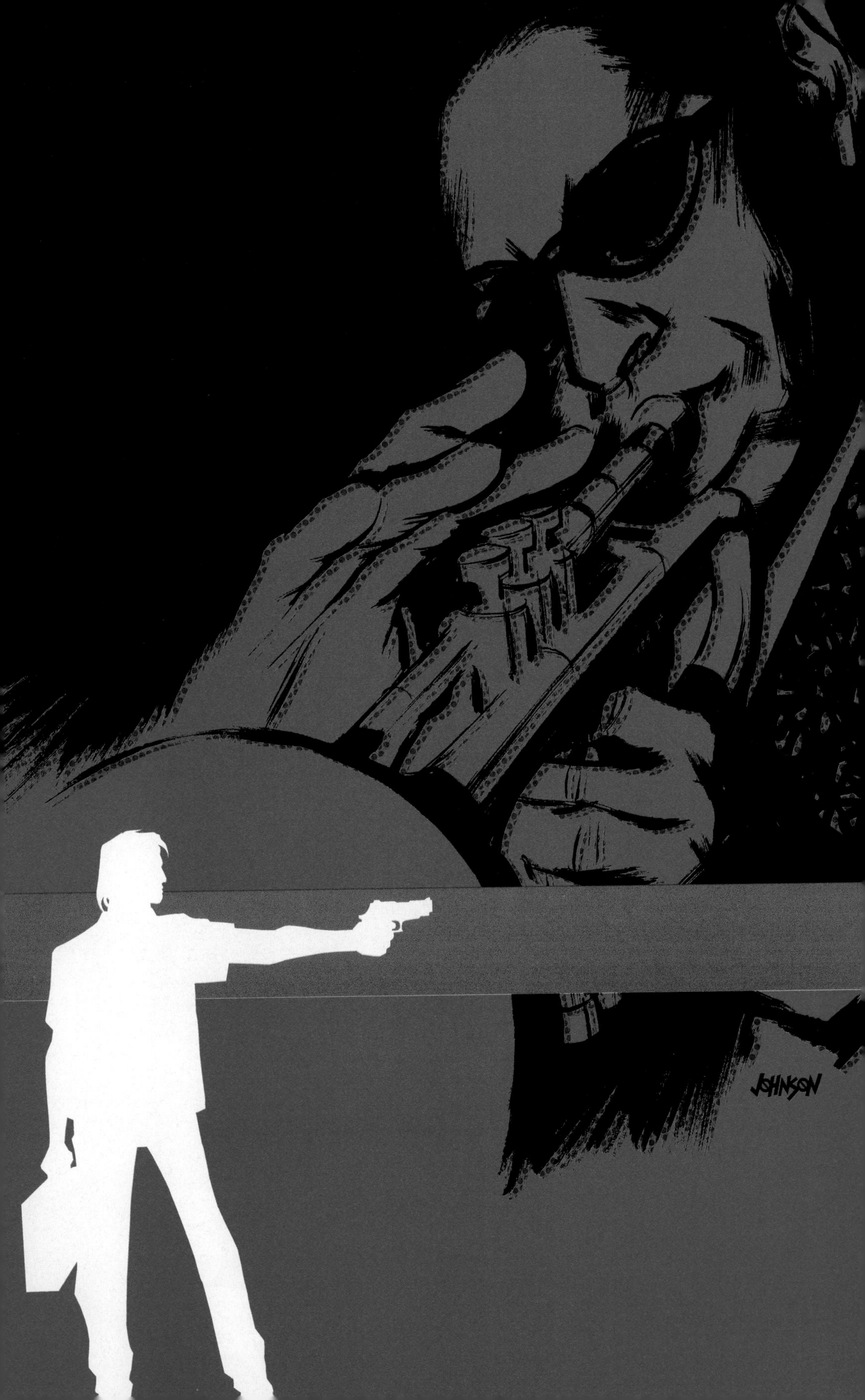
JOHNSON

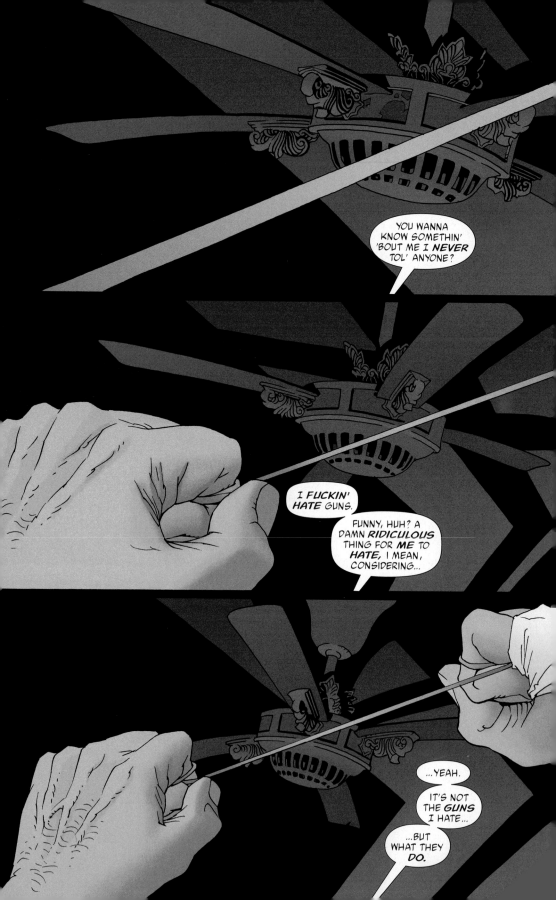

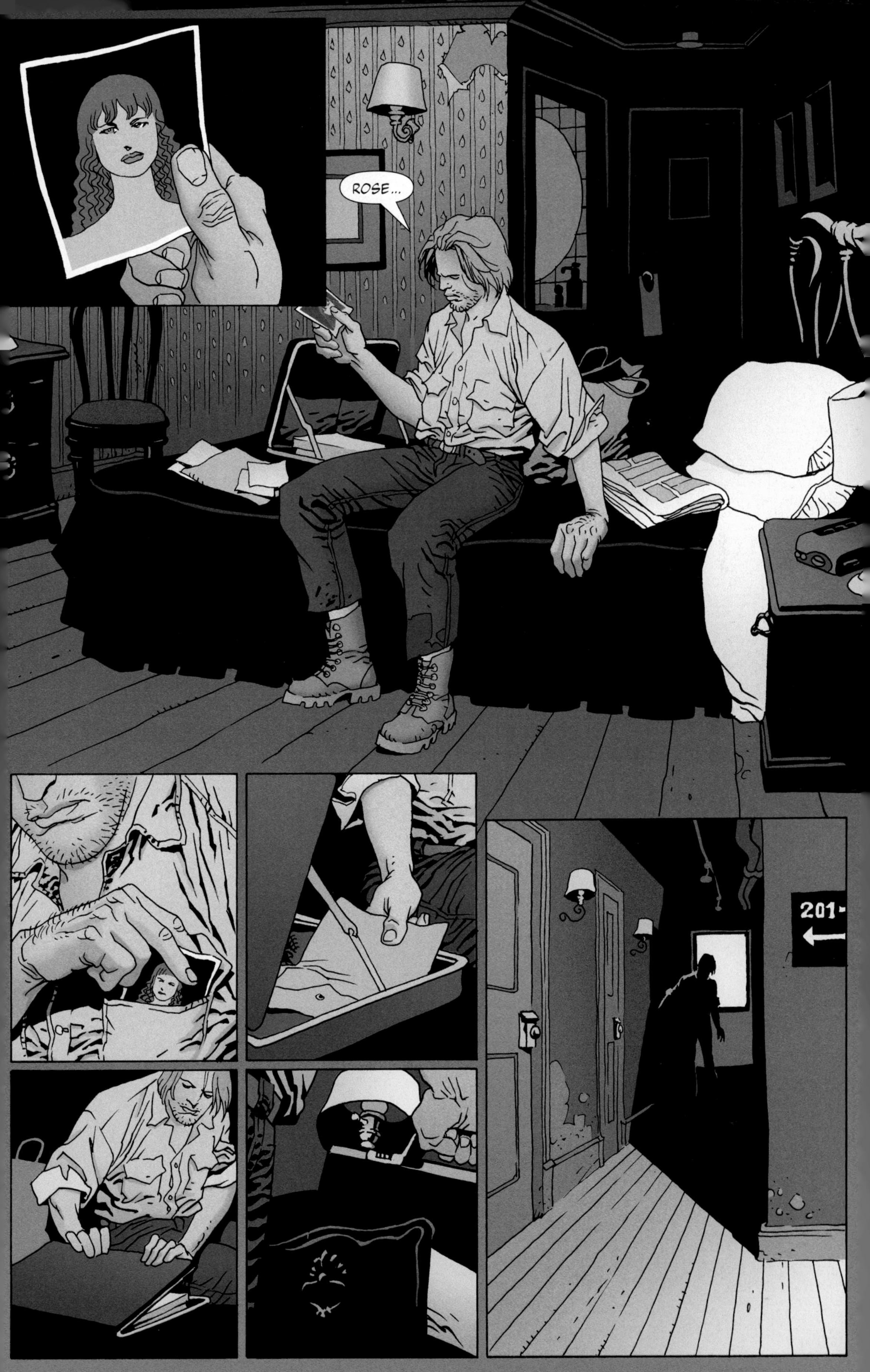
ROSE...
201-

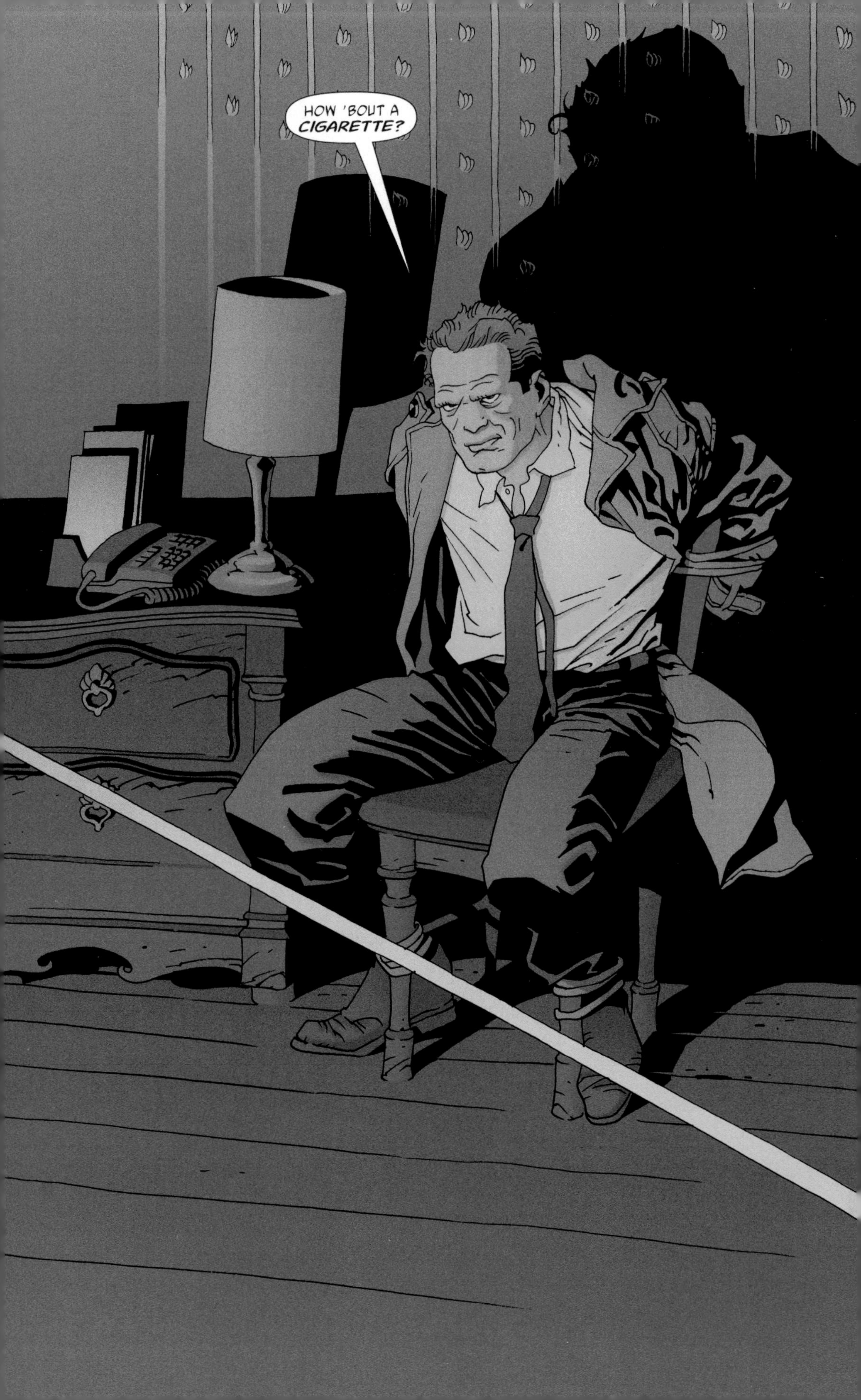
HOW 'BOUT A CIGARETTE?

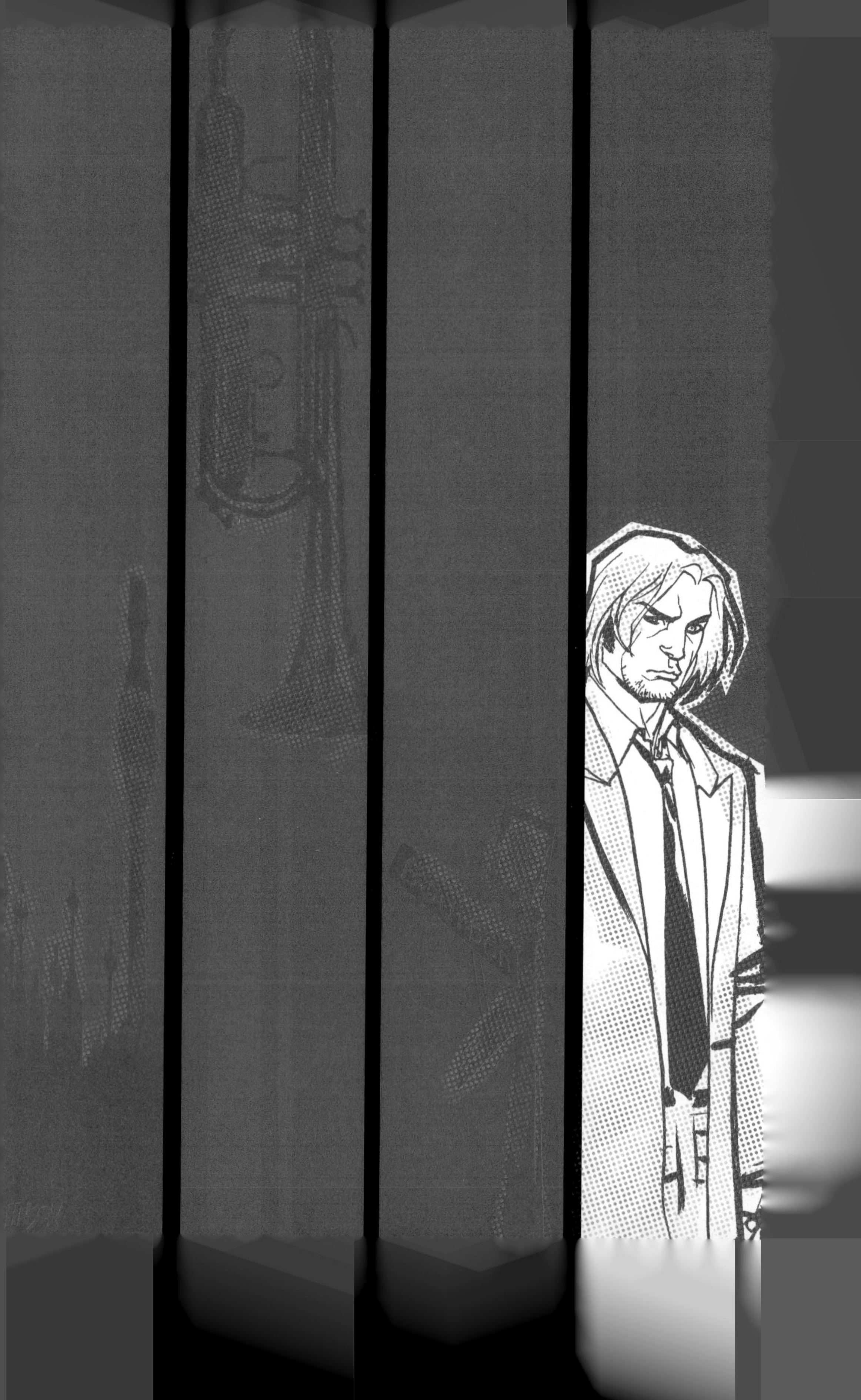

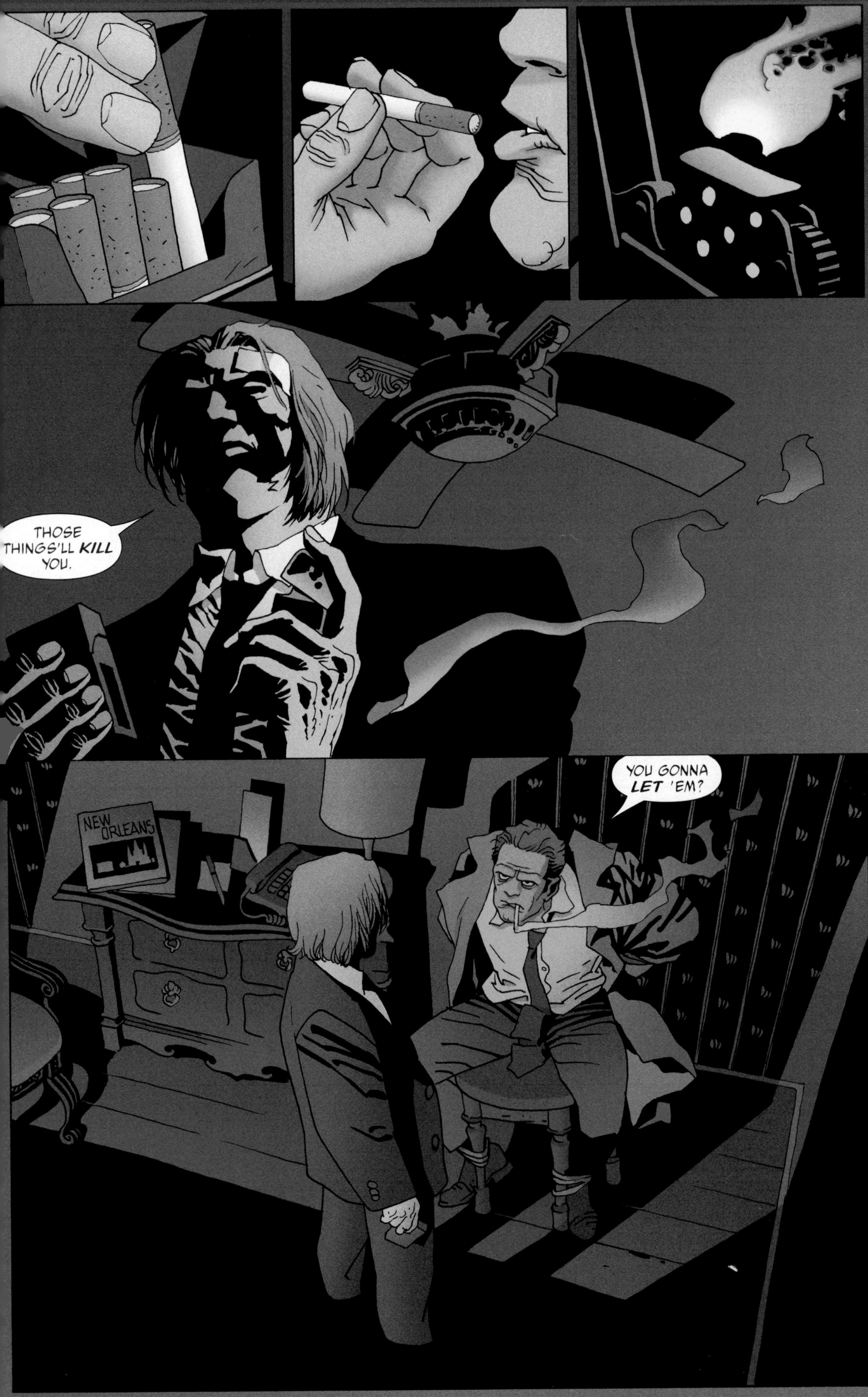
THOSE THINGS'LL KILL YOU.
NEW ORLEANS
YOU GONNA LET 'EM?

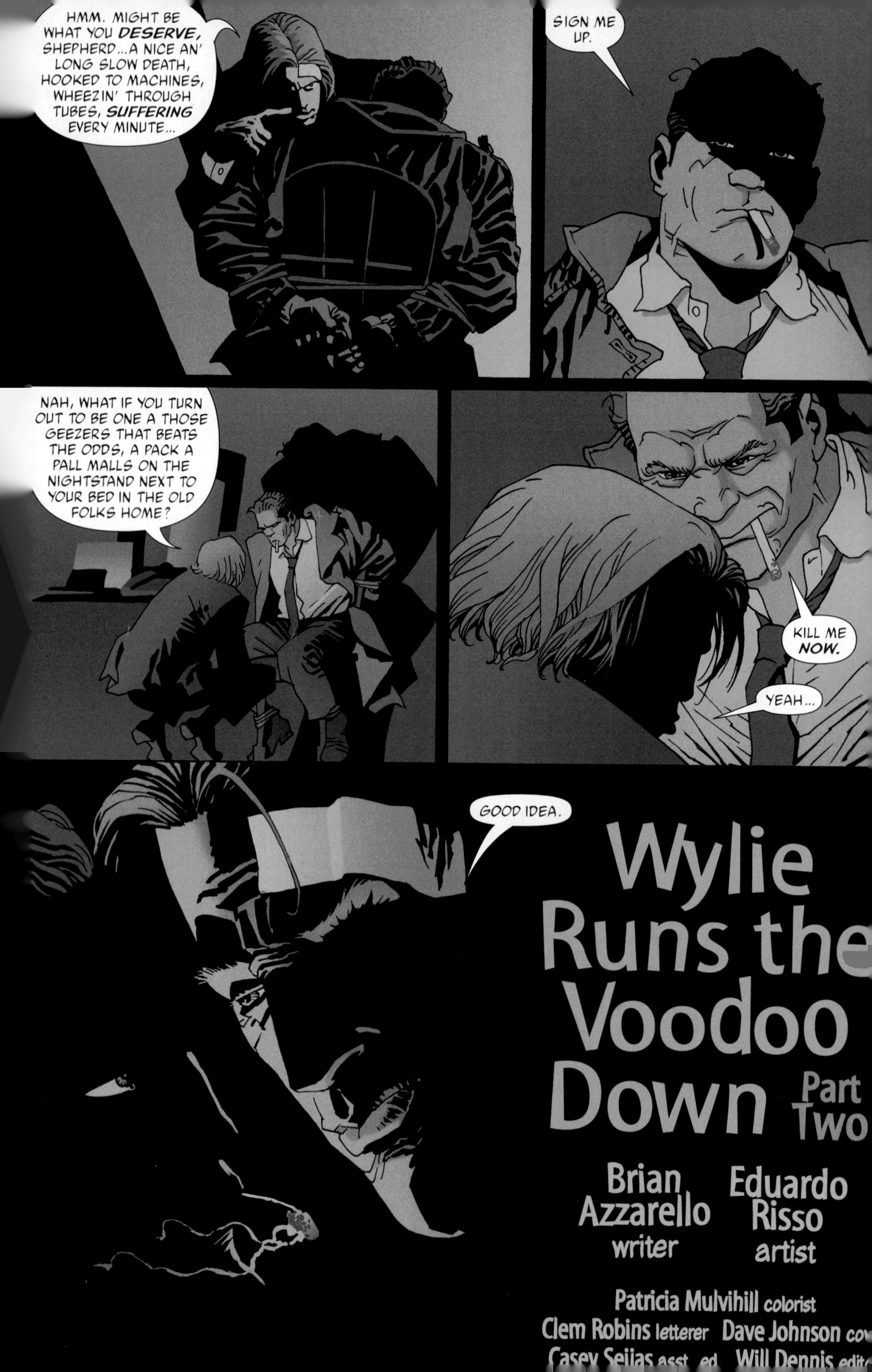
HMM. MIGHT BE WHAT YOU DESERVE, SHEPHERD...A NICE AN' LONG SLOW DEATH, HOOKED TO MACHINES, WHEEZIN' THROUGH TUBES, SUFFERING EVERY MINUTE...
SIGN ME UP.
NAH, WHAT IF YOU TURN OUT TO BE ONE A THOSE GEEZERS THAT BEATS THE ODDS, A PACK A PALL MALLS ON THE NIGHTSTAND NEXT TO YOUR BED IN THE OLD FOLKS HOME?
KILL ME NOW.
YEAH...
GOOD IDEA.
Wylie Runs the Voodoo Down Part Two
Brian Azzarello writer
Eduardo Risso artist
Patricia Mulvihill colorist
Clem Robins letterer
Dave Johnson
Casey Seijas
Will Dennis

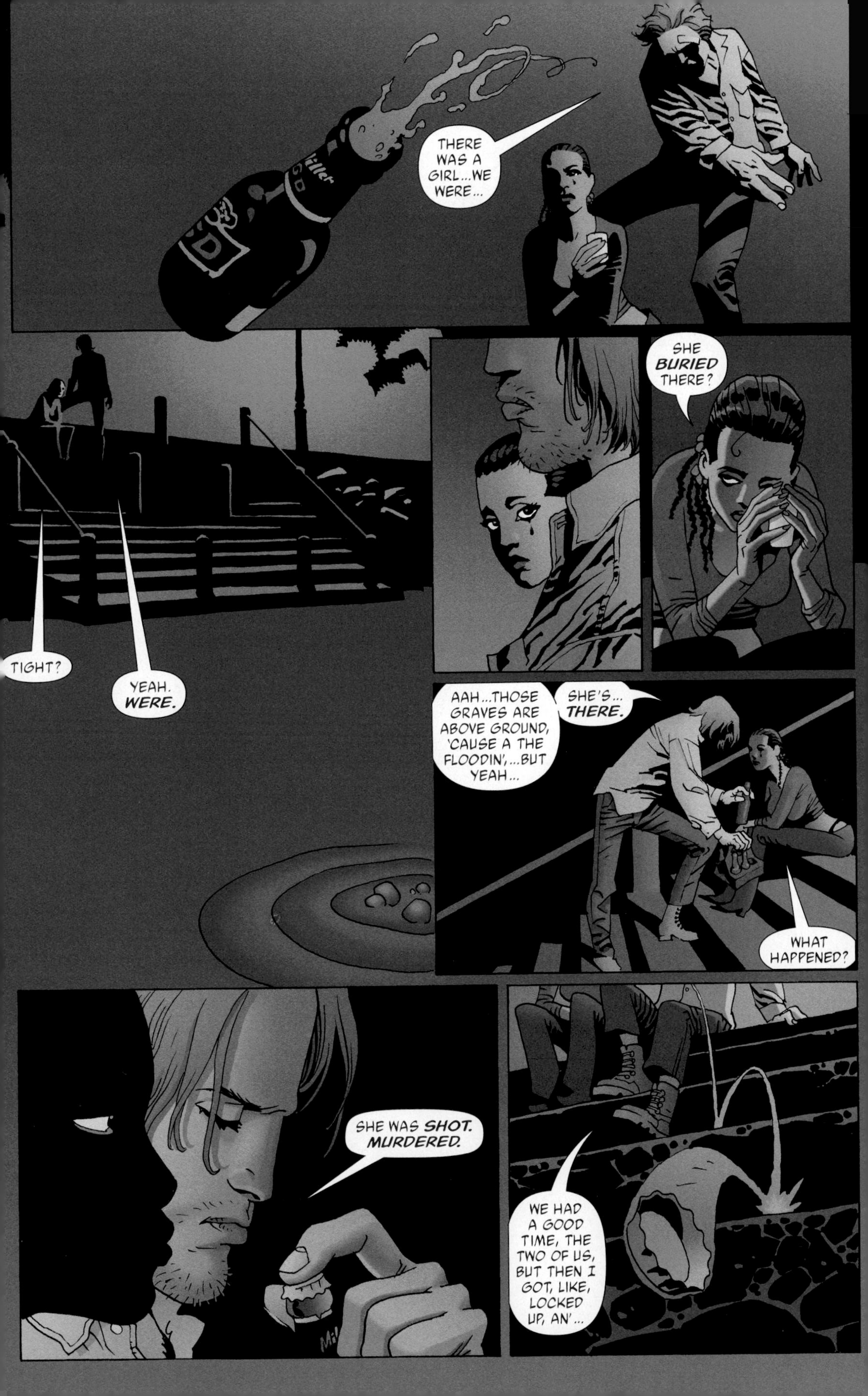
THERE WAS A GIRL...WE WERE...
TIGHT?
YEAH. WERE.
SHE BURIED THERE?
AAH...THOSE GRAVES ARE ABOVE GROUND, 'CAUSE A THE FLOODIN',...BUT YEAH...
SHE'S... THERE.
WHAT HAPPENED?
SHE WAS SHOT. MURDERED.
WE HAD A GOOD TIME, THE TWO OF US, BUT THEN I GOT, LIKE, LOCKED UP, AN'...

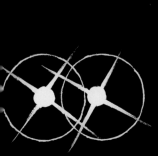

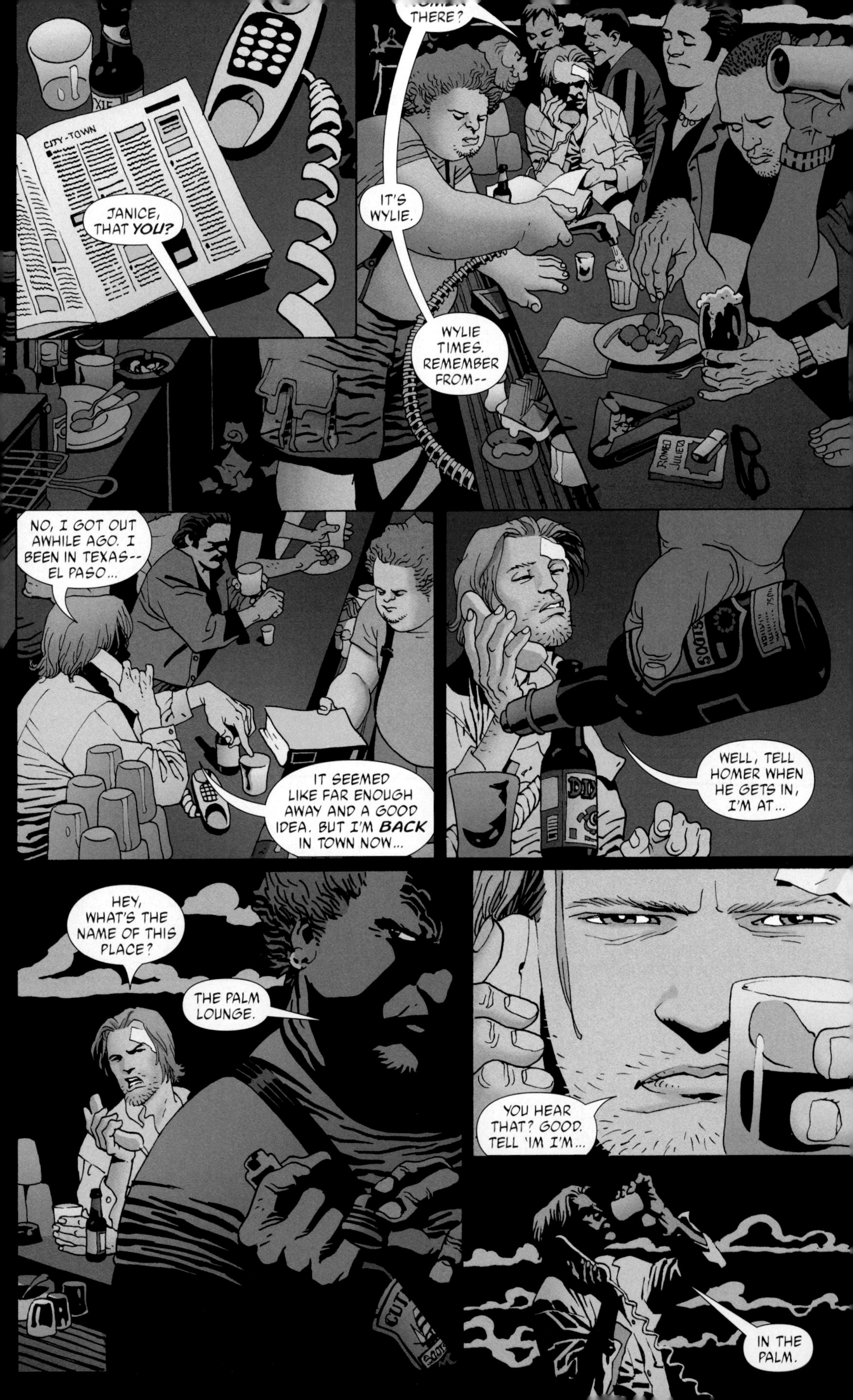
CITY-TOWN
JANICE, THAT ***YOU?***
THERE?
IT'S WYLIE.
WYLIE TIMES. REMEMBER FROM--
ROMEO JULIETA
NO, I GOT OUT AWHILE AGO. I BEEN IN TEXAS-- EL PASO...
IT SEEMED LIKE FAR ENOUGH AWAY AND A GOOD IDEA. BUT I'M ***BACK*** IN TOWN NOW...
WELL, TELL HOMER WHEN HE GETS IN, I'M AT...
HEY, WHAT'S THE NAME OF THIS PLACE?
THE PALM LOUNGE.
YOU HEAR THAT? GOOD. TELL 'IM I'M...
IN THE PALM.

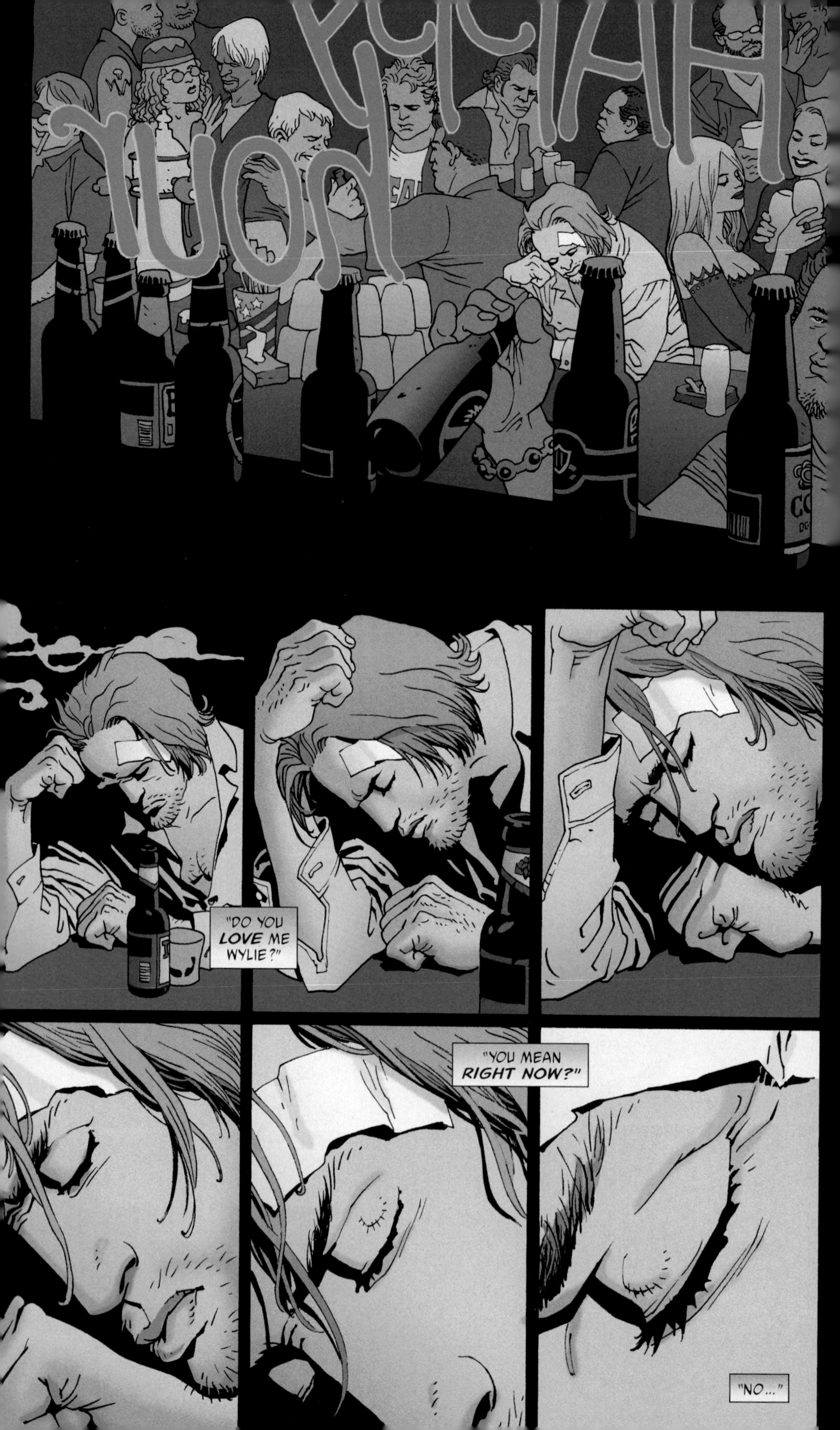
"DO YOU LOVE ME WYLIE?"
"YOU MEAN RIGHT NOW?"
"NO..."

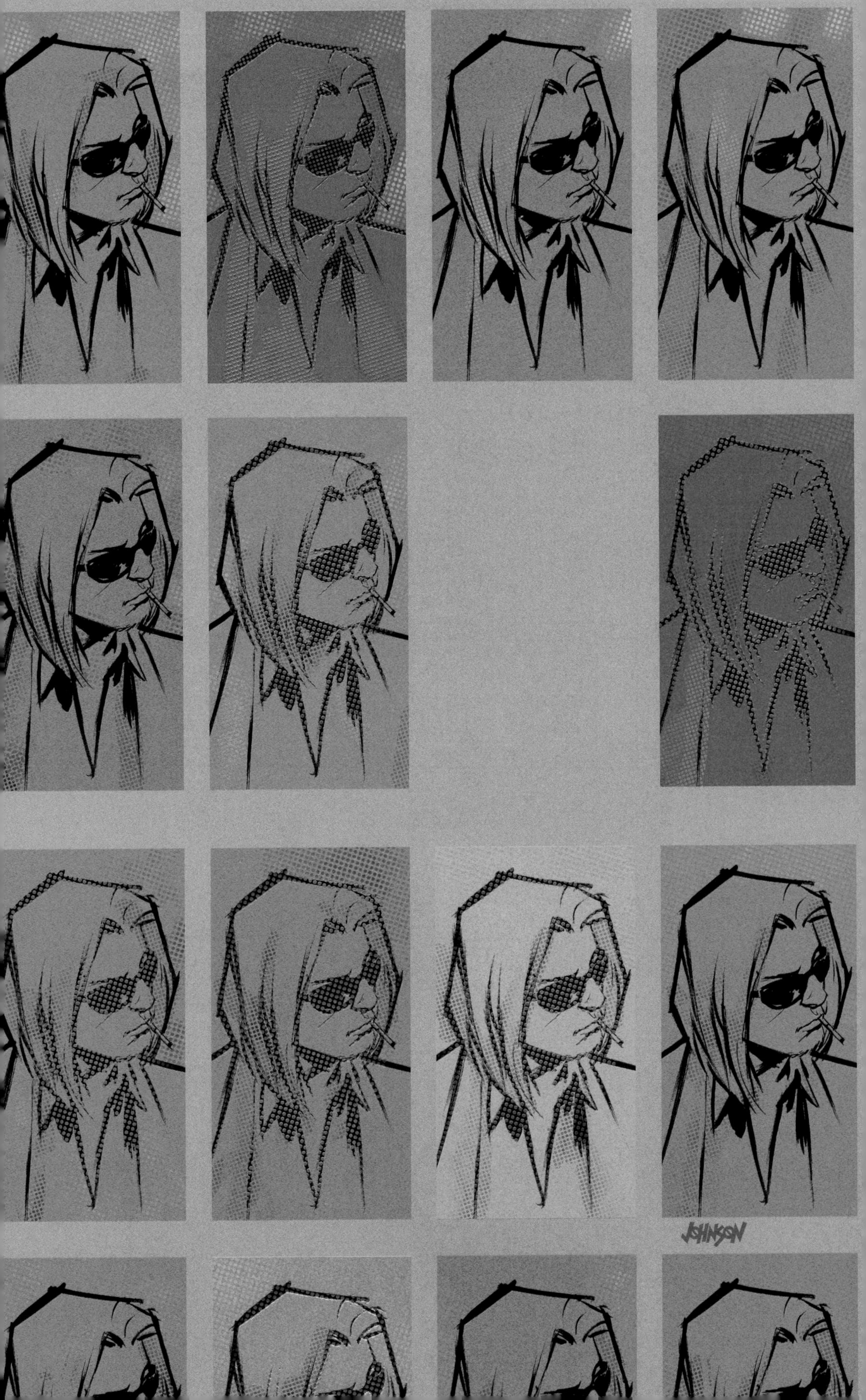
JOHNSON

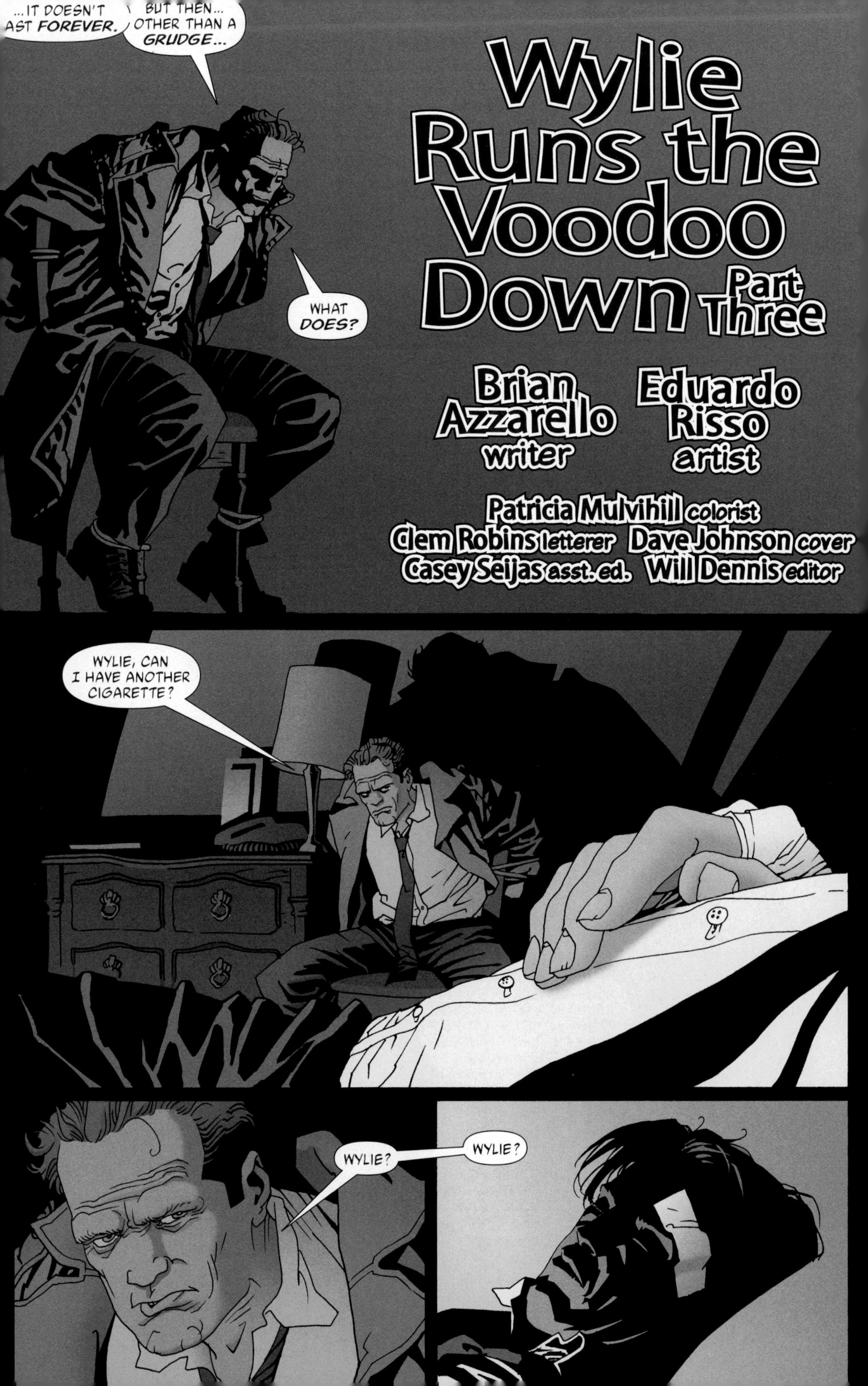
...IT DOESN'T AST FOREVER.
BUT THEN... OTHER THAN A GRUDGE...
WHAT DOES?
Wylie Runs the Voodoo Down Part Three
Brian Azzarello writer
Eduardo Risso artist
Patricia Mulvihill colorist
Clem Robins letterer
Dave Johnson cover
Casey Seijas asst. ed.
Will Dennis editor
WYLIE, CAN I HAVE ANOTHER CIGARETTE?
WYLIE?
WYLIE?

WHAT THE *HELL* YOU DOIN' STANDIN' IN THE MIDDLE OF THE STREET?

I CAN'T DECIDE WHAT I NEED *MORE*...

...A *GUN*...

...OR A *SHOT*.

HOW' BOUT A COL' BEER?

YOU *BUYIN'*?

MY IDEA... GUESS I *AM*.

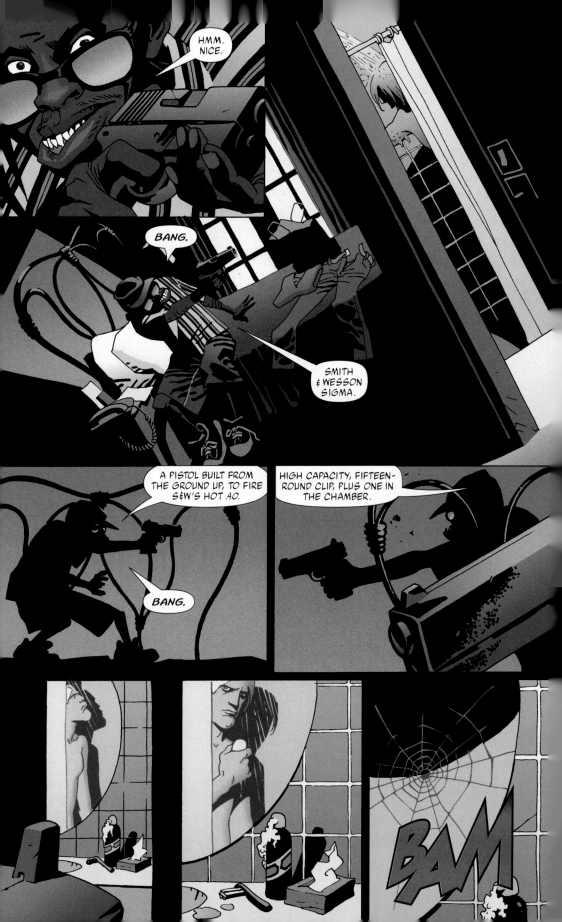

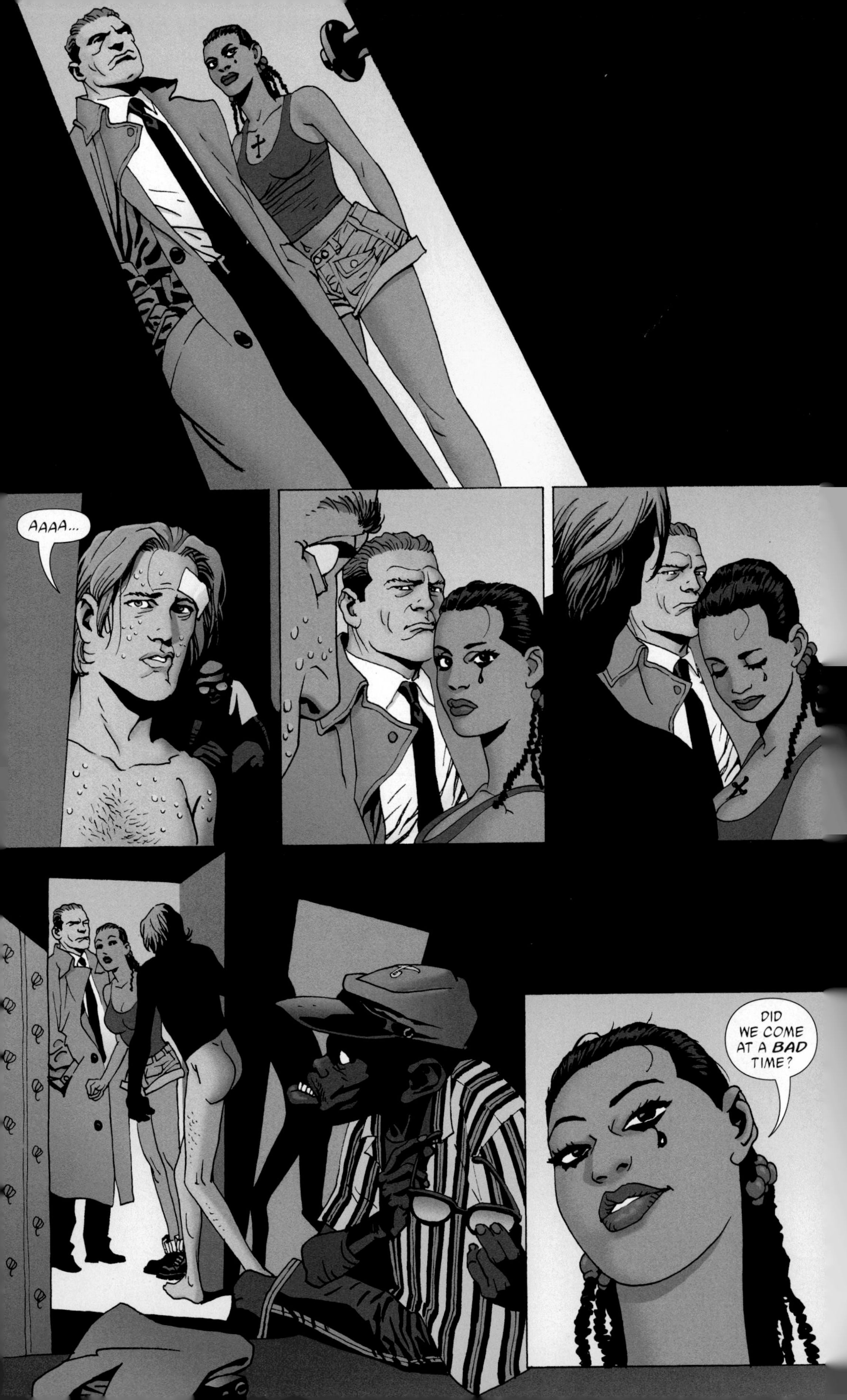
AAAA...
DID WE COME AT A BAD TIME?

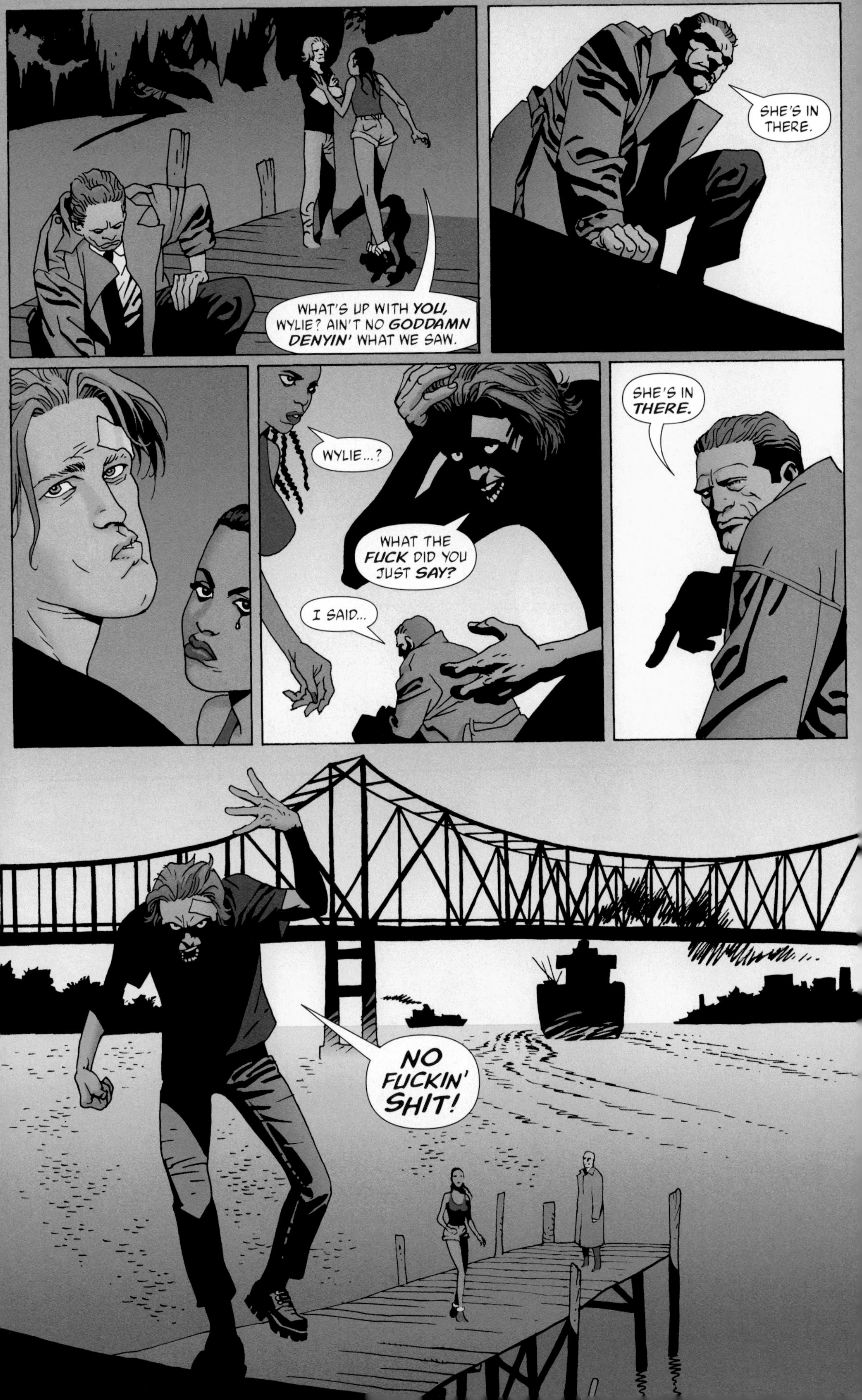
WHAT'S UP WITH YOU, WYLIE? AIN'T NO GODDAMN DENYIN' WHAT WE SAW.
SHE'S IN THERE.
WYLIE...?
WHAT THE FUCK DID YOU JUST SAY?
I SAID...
SHE'S IN THERE.
NO FUCKIN' SHIT!

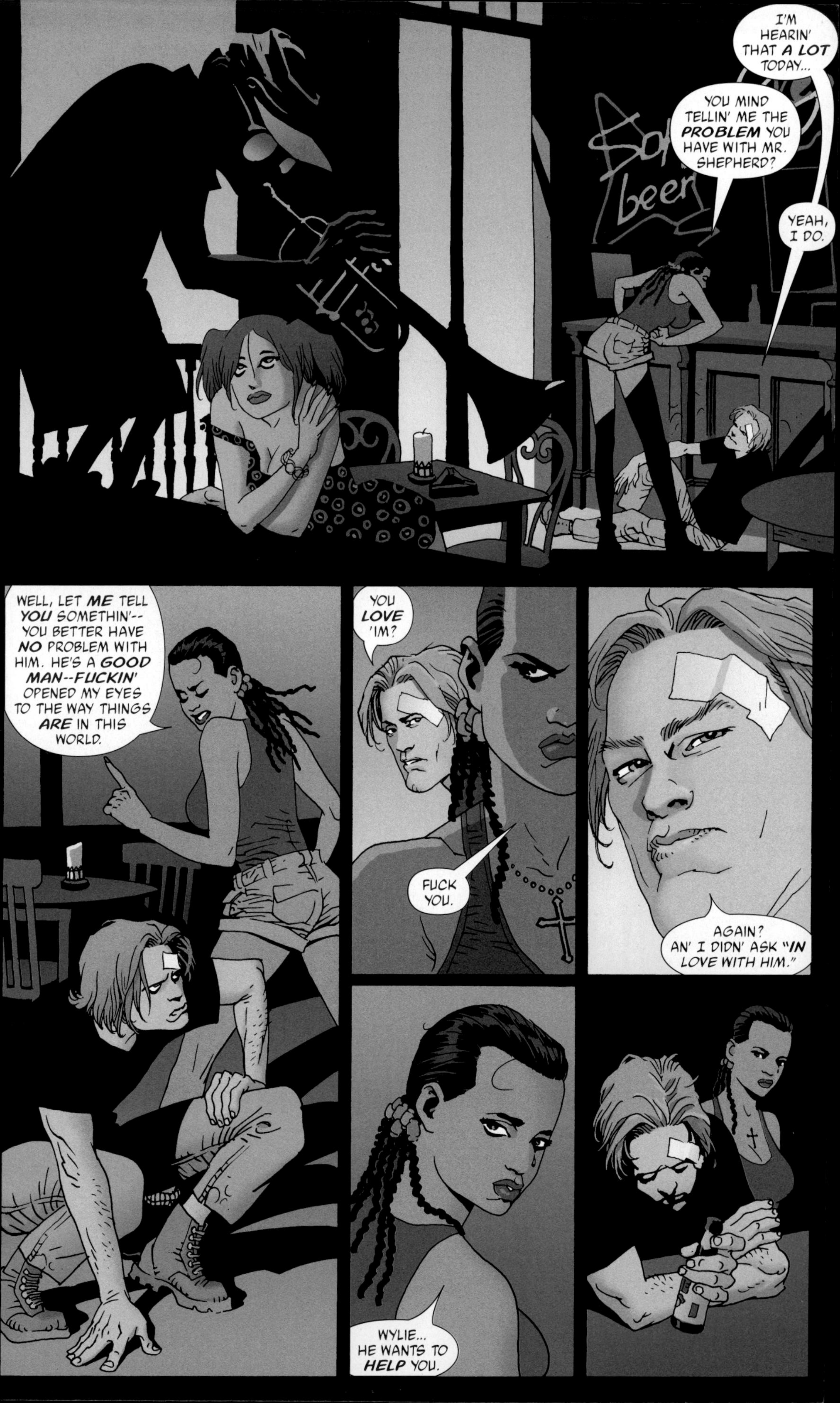
I'M HEARIN' THAT A LOT TODAY...
YOU MIND TELLIN' ME THE PROBLEM YOU HAVE WITH MR. SHEPHERD?
YEAH, I DO.
WELL, LET ME TELL YOU SOMETHIN'-- YOU BETTER HAVE NO PROBLEM WITH HIM. HE'S A GOOD MAN--FUCKIN' OPENED MY EYES TO THE WAY THINGS ARE IN THIS WORLD.
YOU LOVE 'IM?
FUCK YOU.
AGAIN? AN' I DIDN' ASK "IN LOVE WITH HIM."
WYLIE... HE WANTS TO HELP YOU.

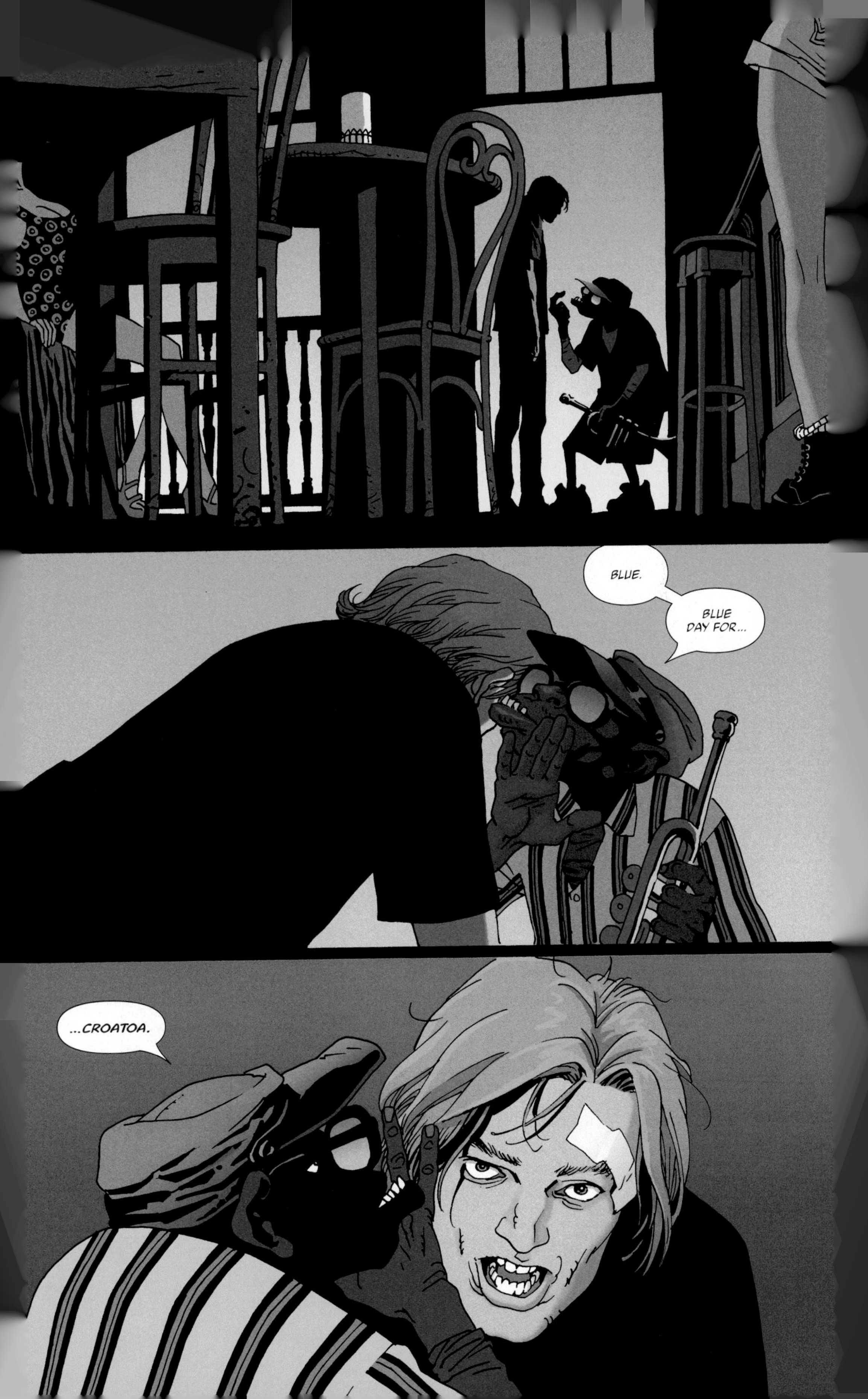
BLUE.
BLUE DAY FOR...
...CROATOA.

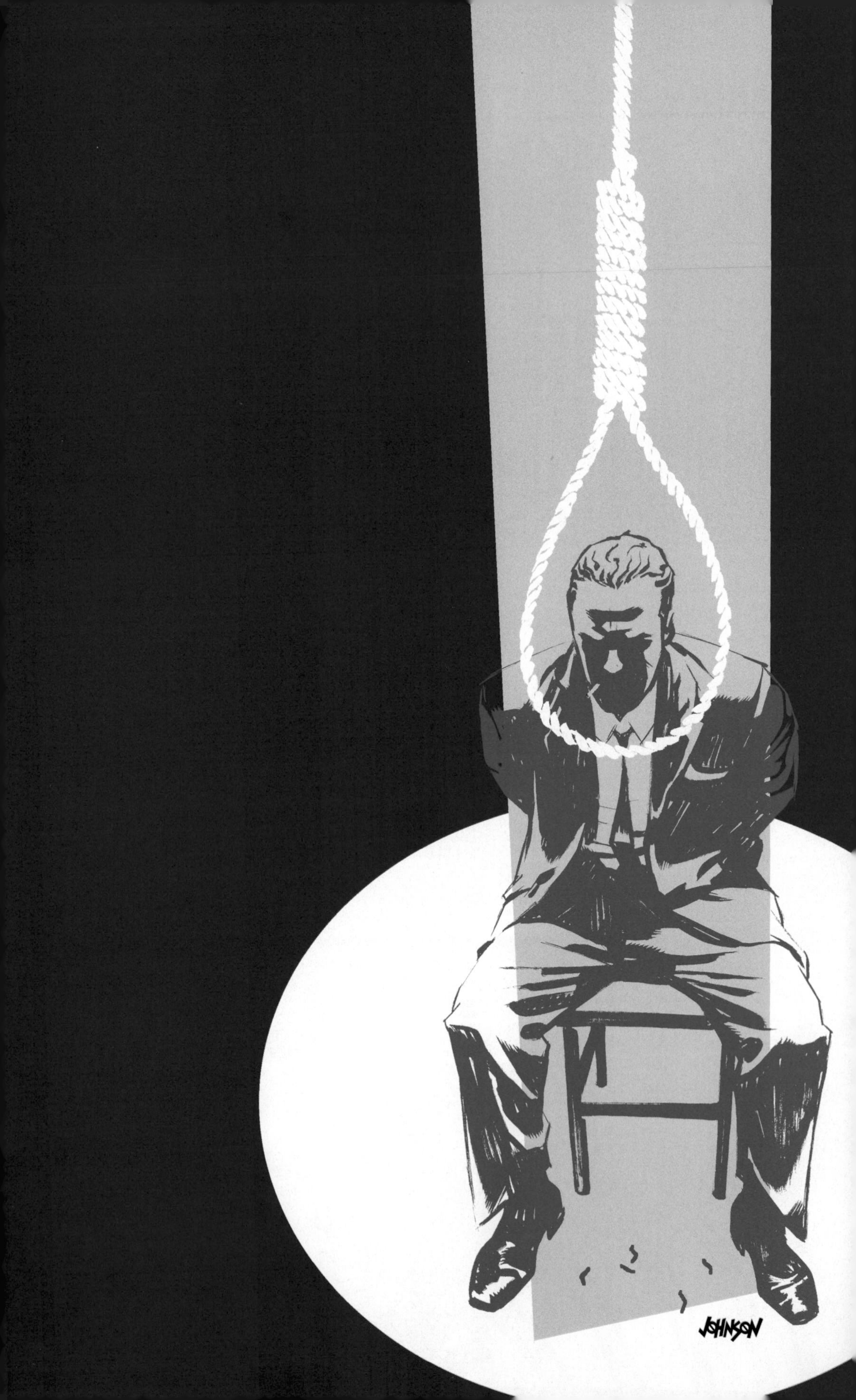
JOHNSON

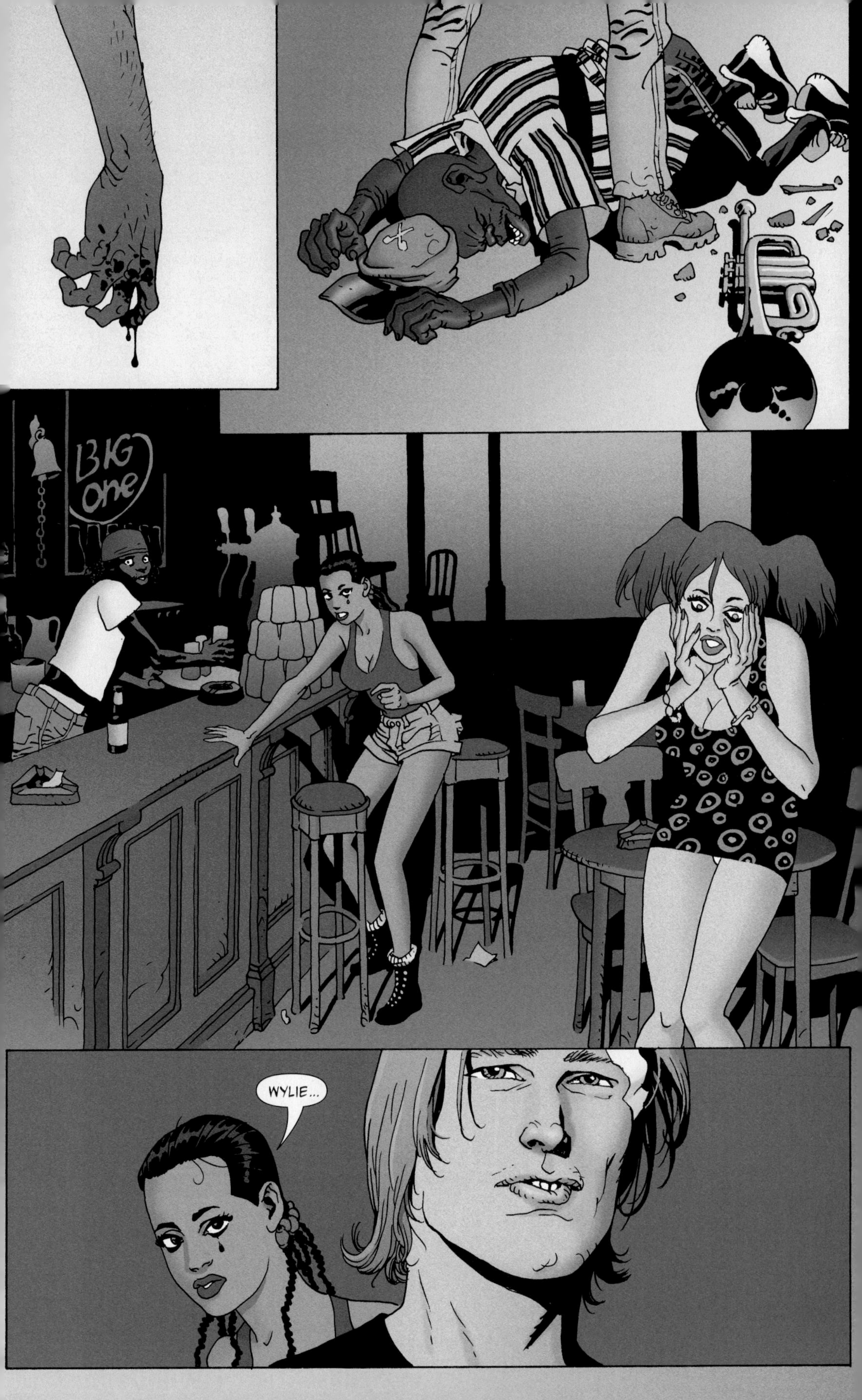
BIG one
WYLIE...

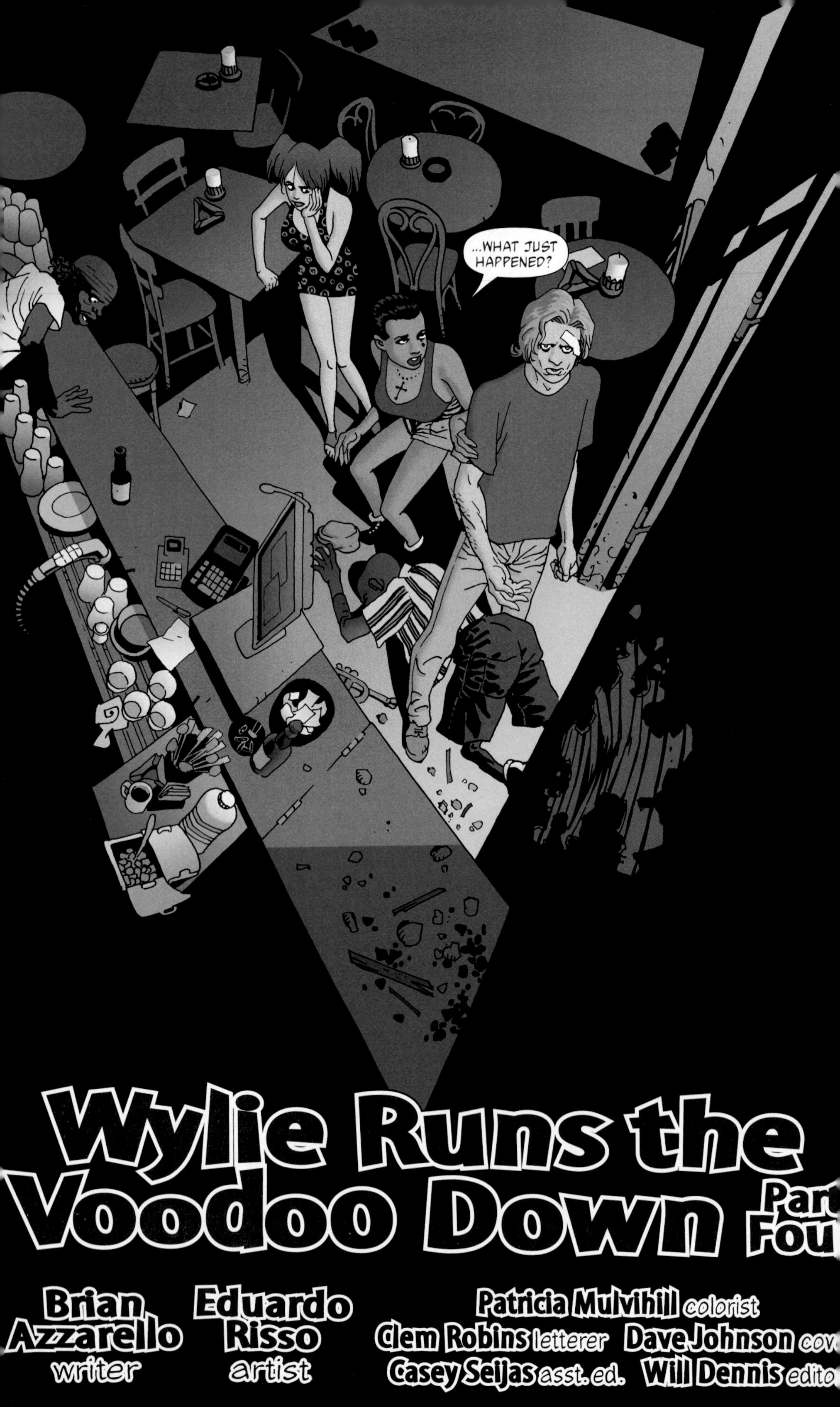

...WHAT JUST HAPPENED?

Wylie Runs the Voodoo Down Part Fou

Brian Azzarello writer
Eduardo Risso artist
Patricia Mulvihill colorist
Clem Robins letterer
Dave Johnson cov
Casey Seijas asst. ed.
Will Dennis edito

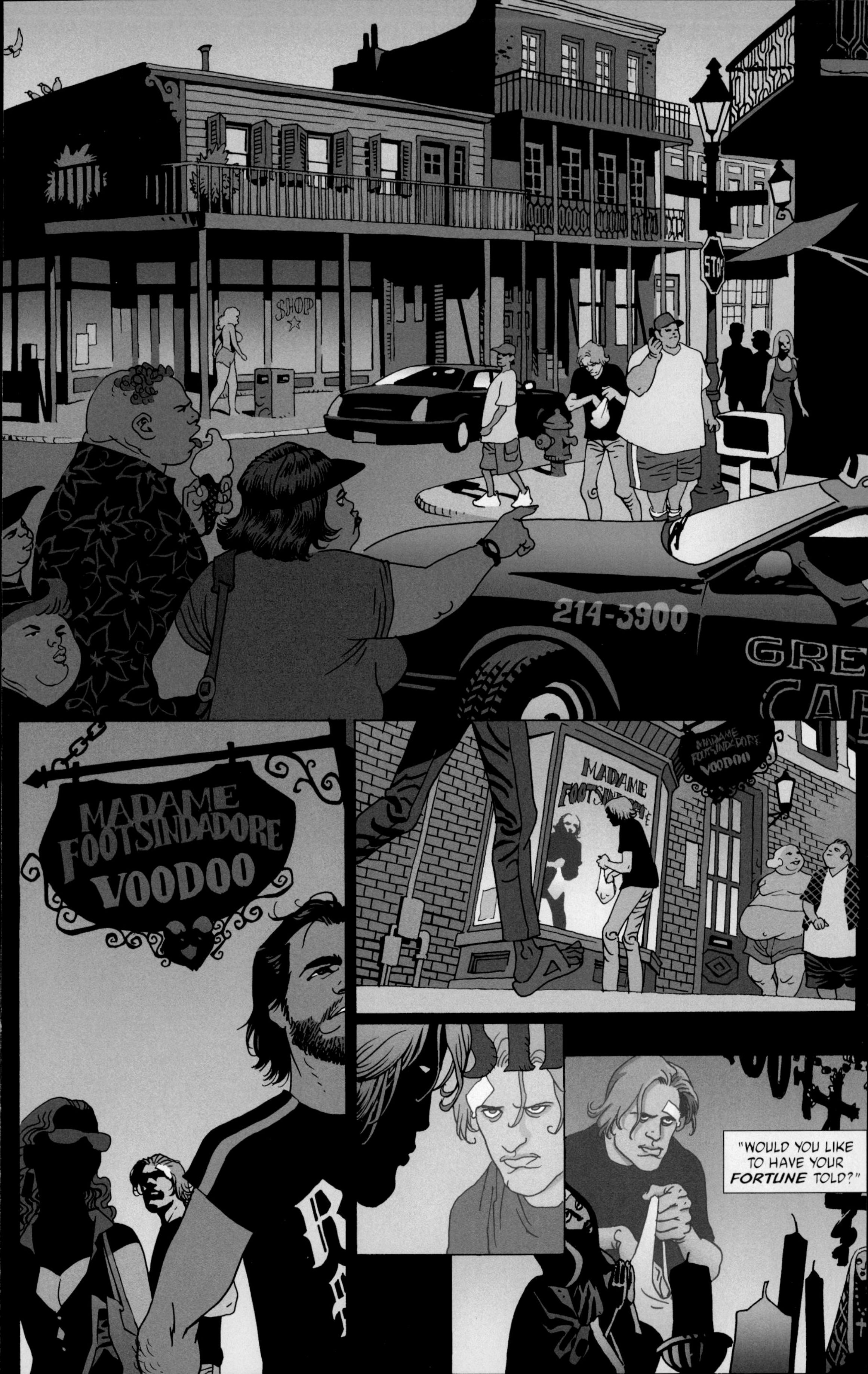
SHOP
STOP
214-3900
MADAME FOOTSINDADORE VOODOO
MADAME FOOTSINDADORE VOODOO
"WOULD YOU LIKE TO HAVE YOUR *FORTUNE* TOLD?"

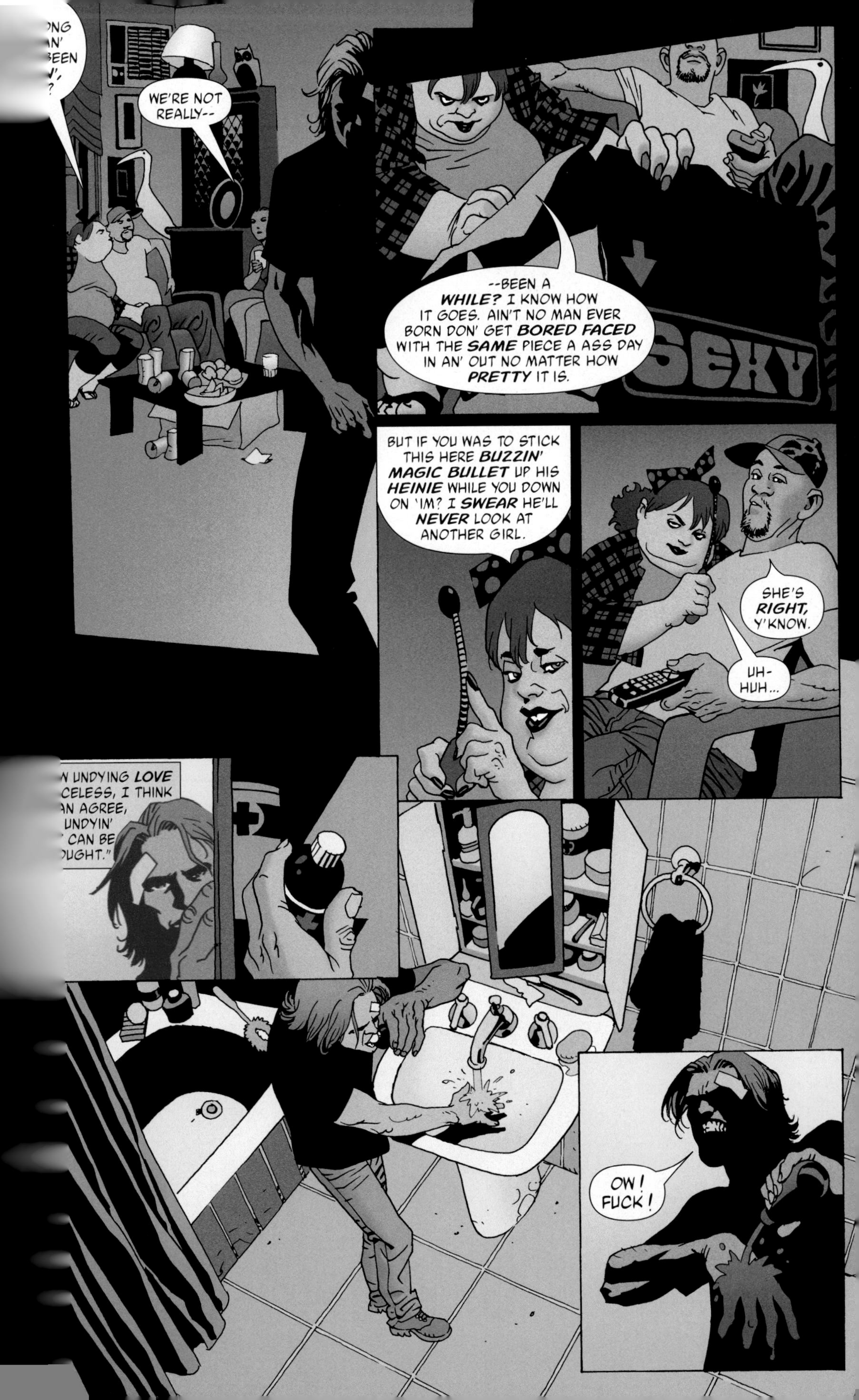

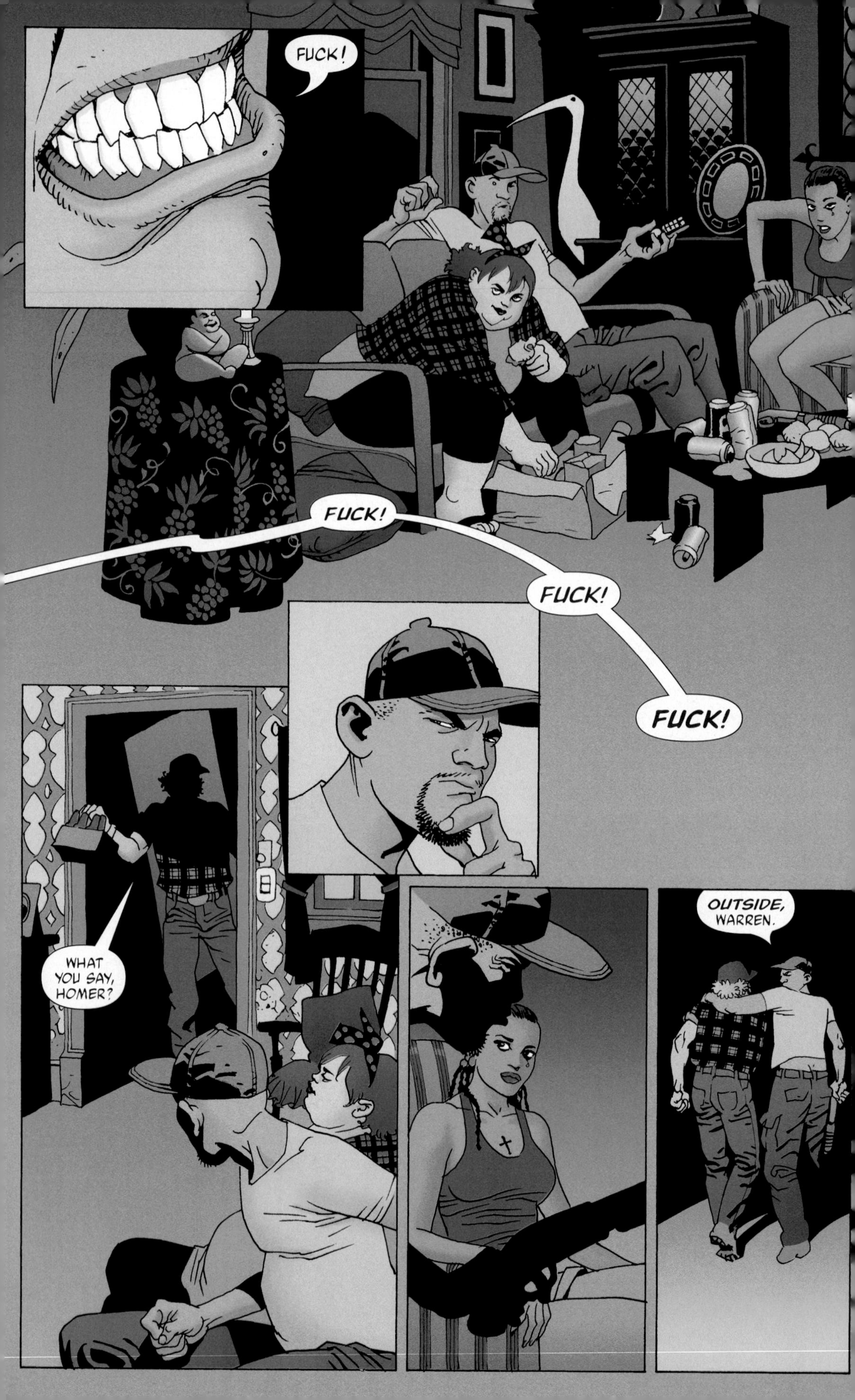
FUCK!
FUCK!
FUCK!
FUCK!
WHAT YOU SAY, HOMER?
OUTSIDE, WARREN.

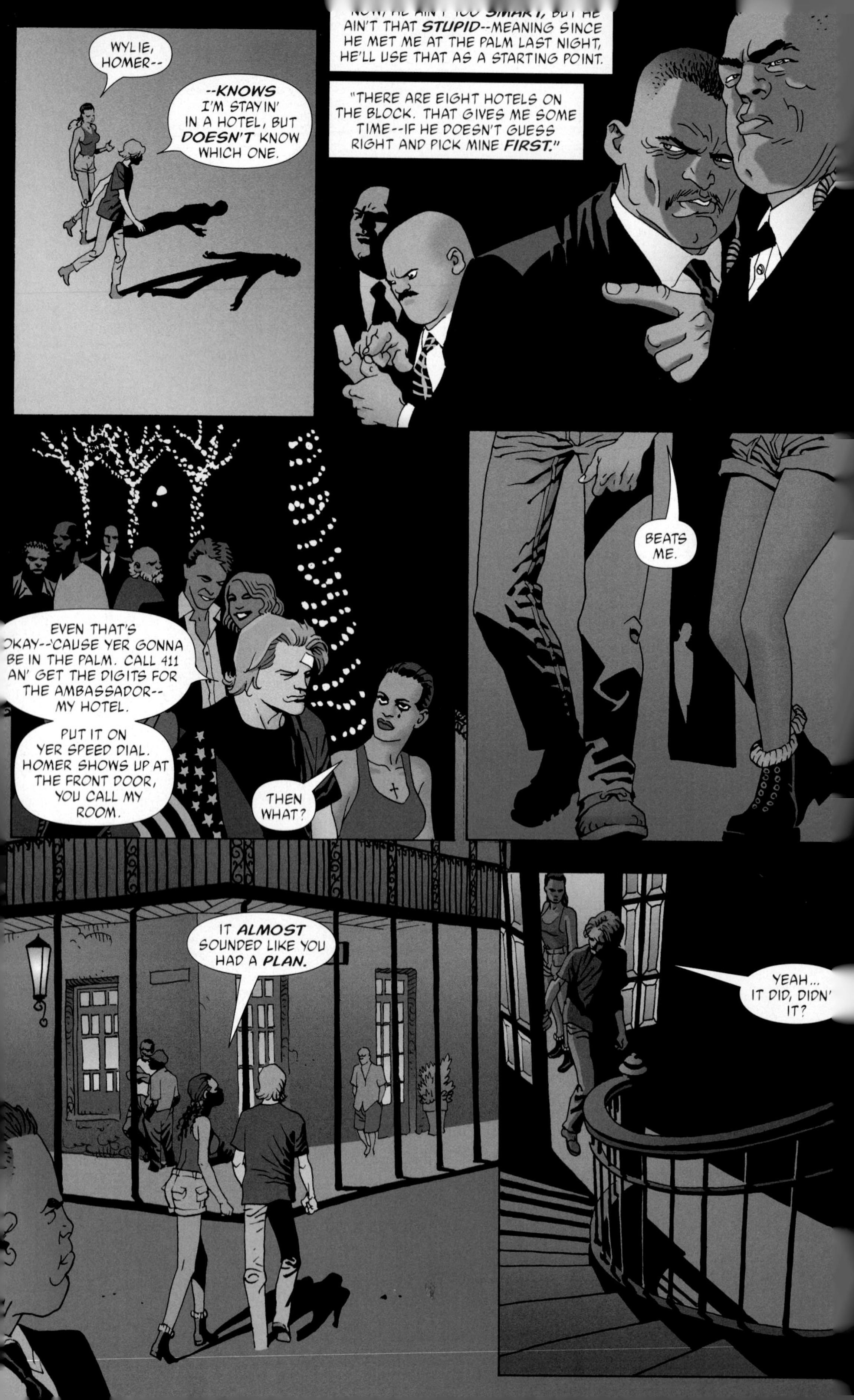
WYLIE, HOMER--
--KNOWS I'M STAYIN' IN A HOTEL, BUT DOESN'T KNOW WHICH ONE.
NOW, HE AIN'T TOO SMART, BUT HE AIN'T THAT STUPID--MEANING SINCE HE MET ME AT THE PALM LAST NIGHT, HE'LL USE THAT AS A STARTING POINT.
"THERE ARE EIGHT HOTELS ON THE BLOCK. THAT GIVES ME SOME TIME--IF HE DOESN'T GUESS RIGHT AND PICK MINE FIRST."
EVEN THAT'S OKAY--'CAUSE YER GONNA BE IN THE PALM. CALL 411 AN' GET THE DIGITS FOR THE AMBASSADOR--MY HOTEL.
PUT IT ON YER SPEED DIAL. HOMER SHOWS UP AT THE FRONT DOOR, YOU CALL MY ROOM.
THEN WHAT?
BEATS ME.
IT ALMOST SOUNDED LIKE YOU HAD A PLAN.
YEAH... IT DID, DIDN' IT?

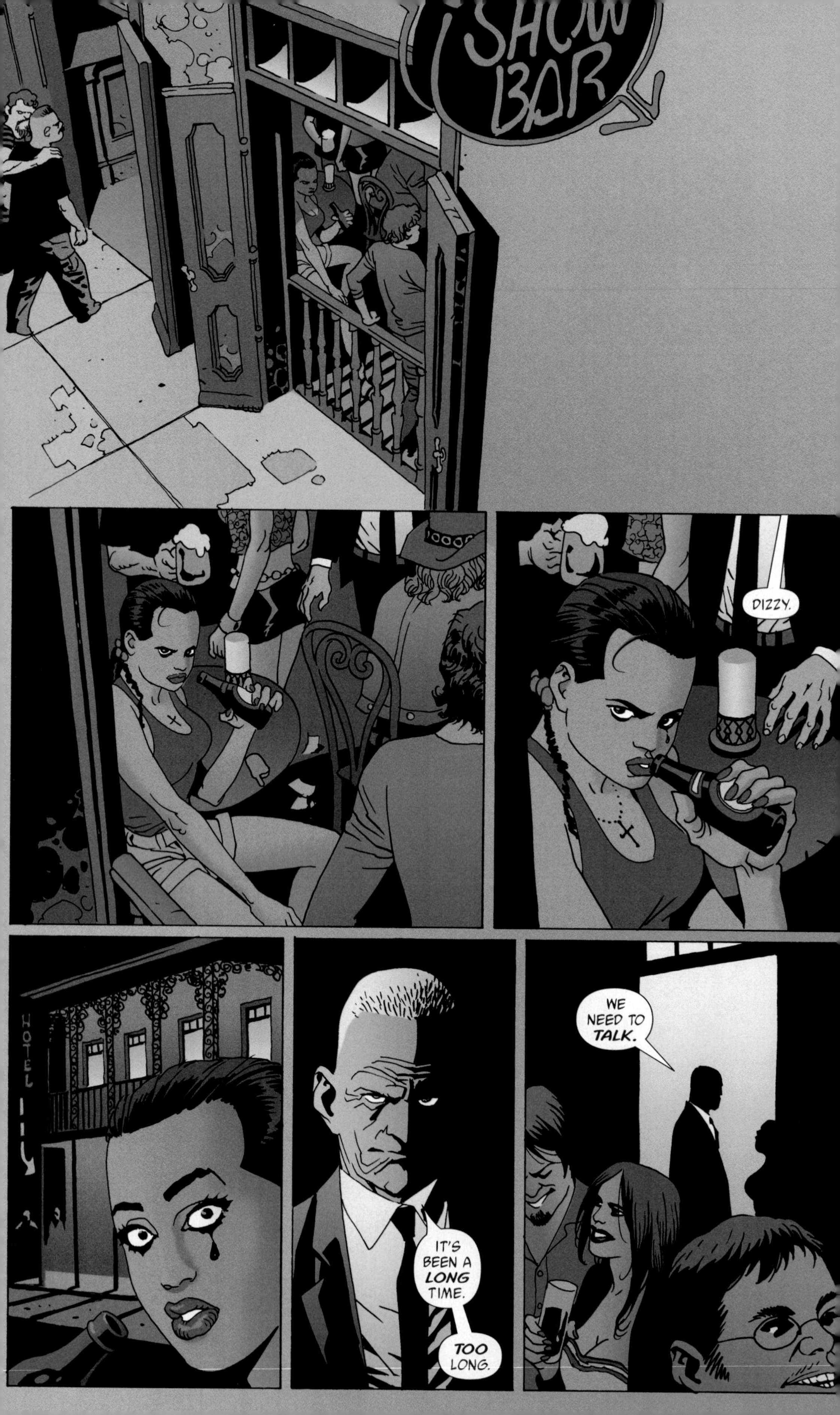
SHOW BAR
DIZZY.
HOTEL
IT'S BEEN A LONG TIME.
TOO LONG.
WE NEED TO TALK.

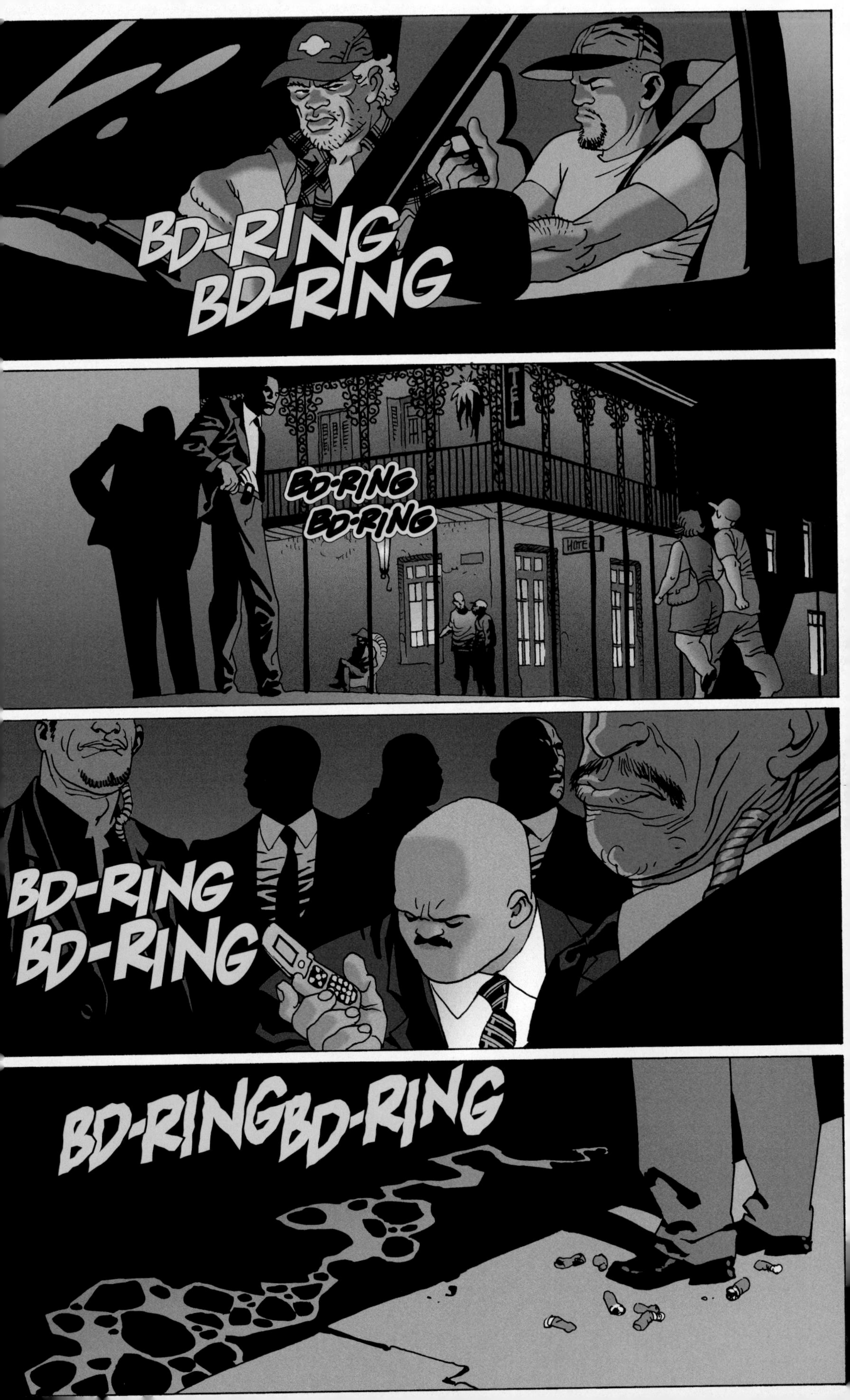
BD-RING
BD-RING
BD-RING
BD-RING
BD-RING
BD-RING
BD-RINGBD-RING

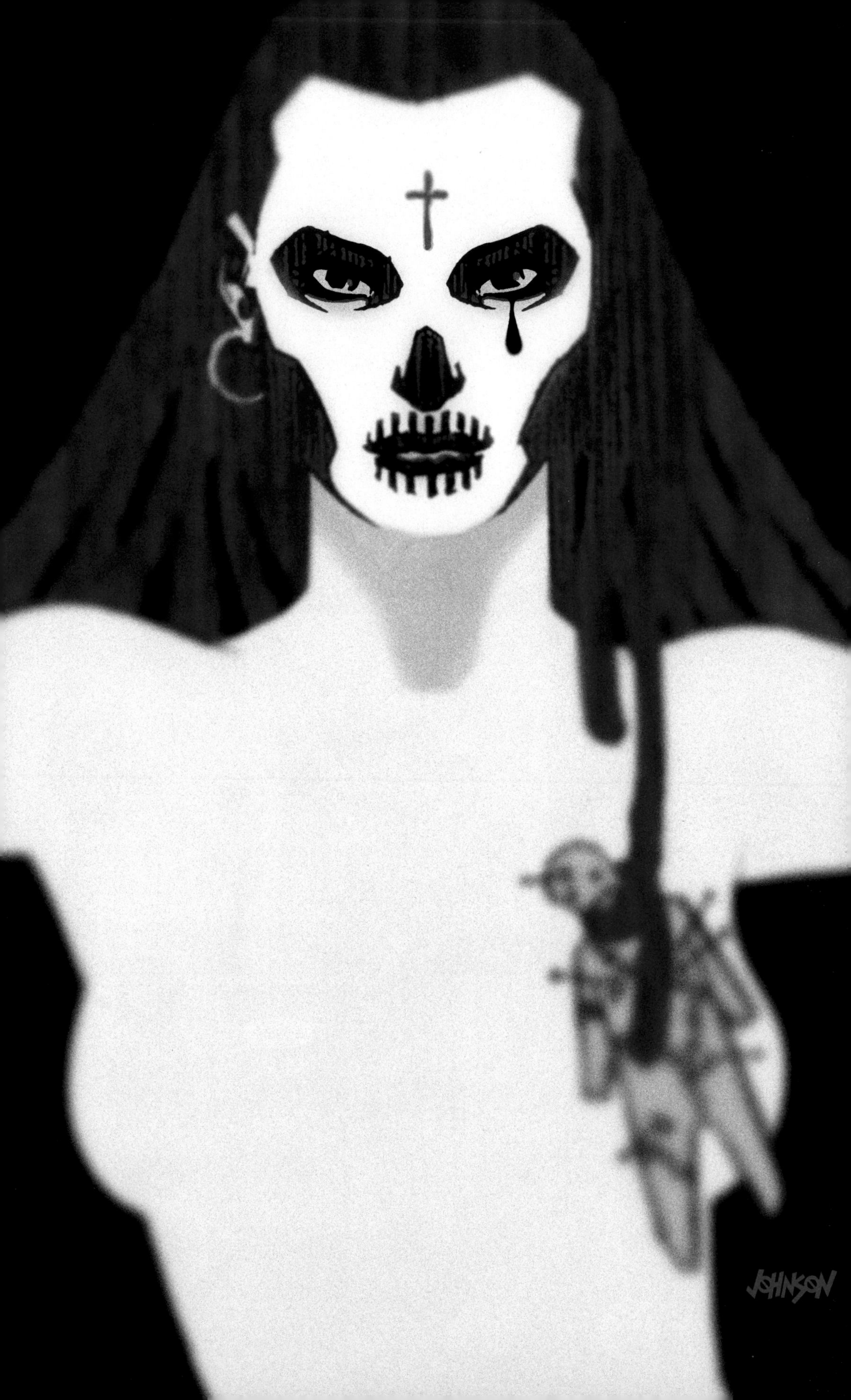
JOHNSON

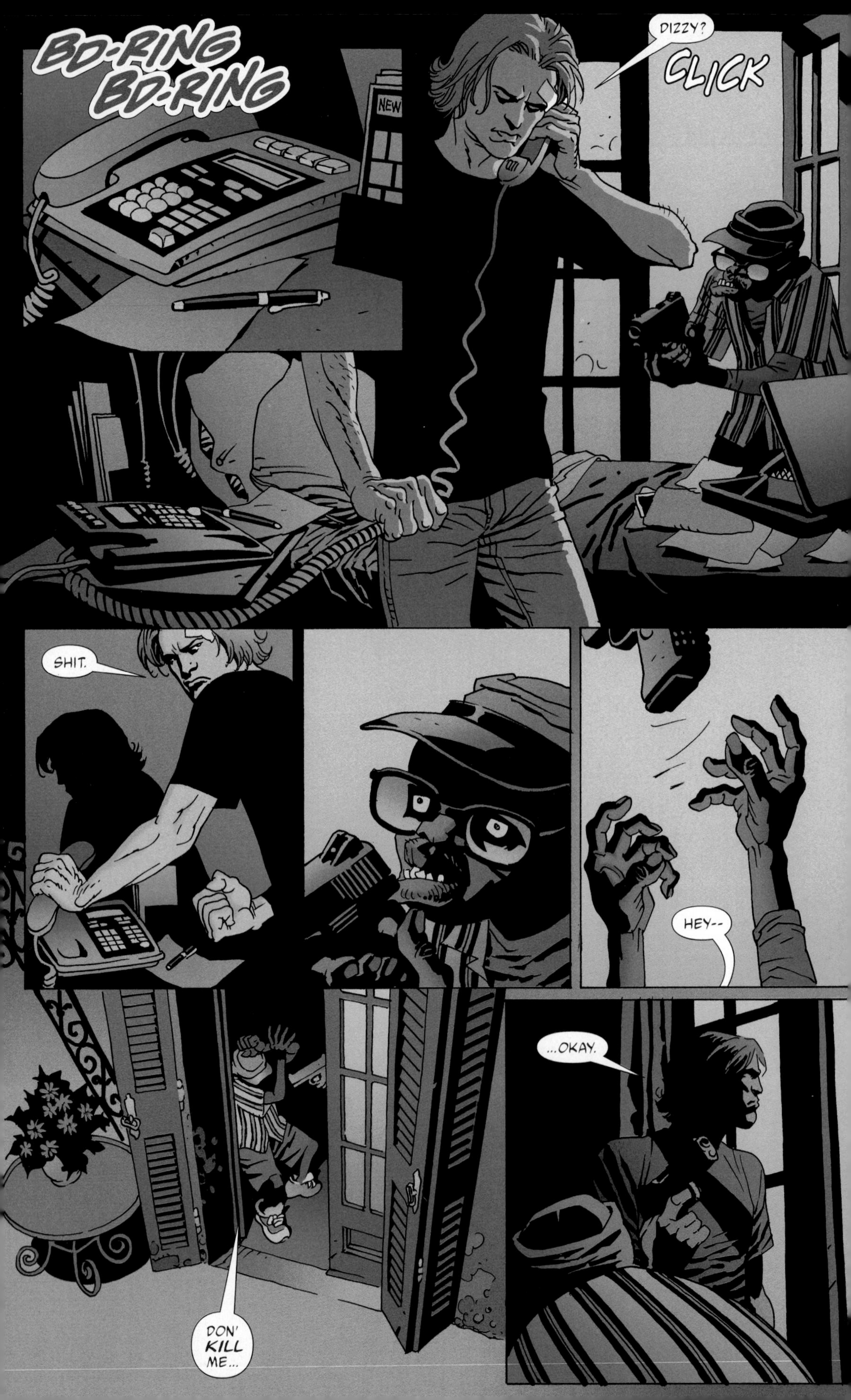

BD-RING
BD-RING
DIZZY?
CLICK
NEW
SHIT.
HEY--
DON' KILL ME...
...OKAY.

Wylie Runs the Voodoo Down

Brian Azzarello writer **Eduardo Risso** artist Patricia Mulvihill colorist Clem Robins letterer Dave Johnson cover Casey Seijas asst. ed. Will Dennis editor

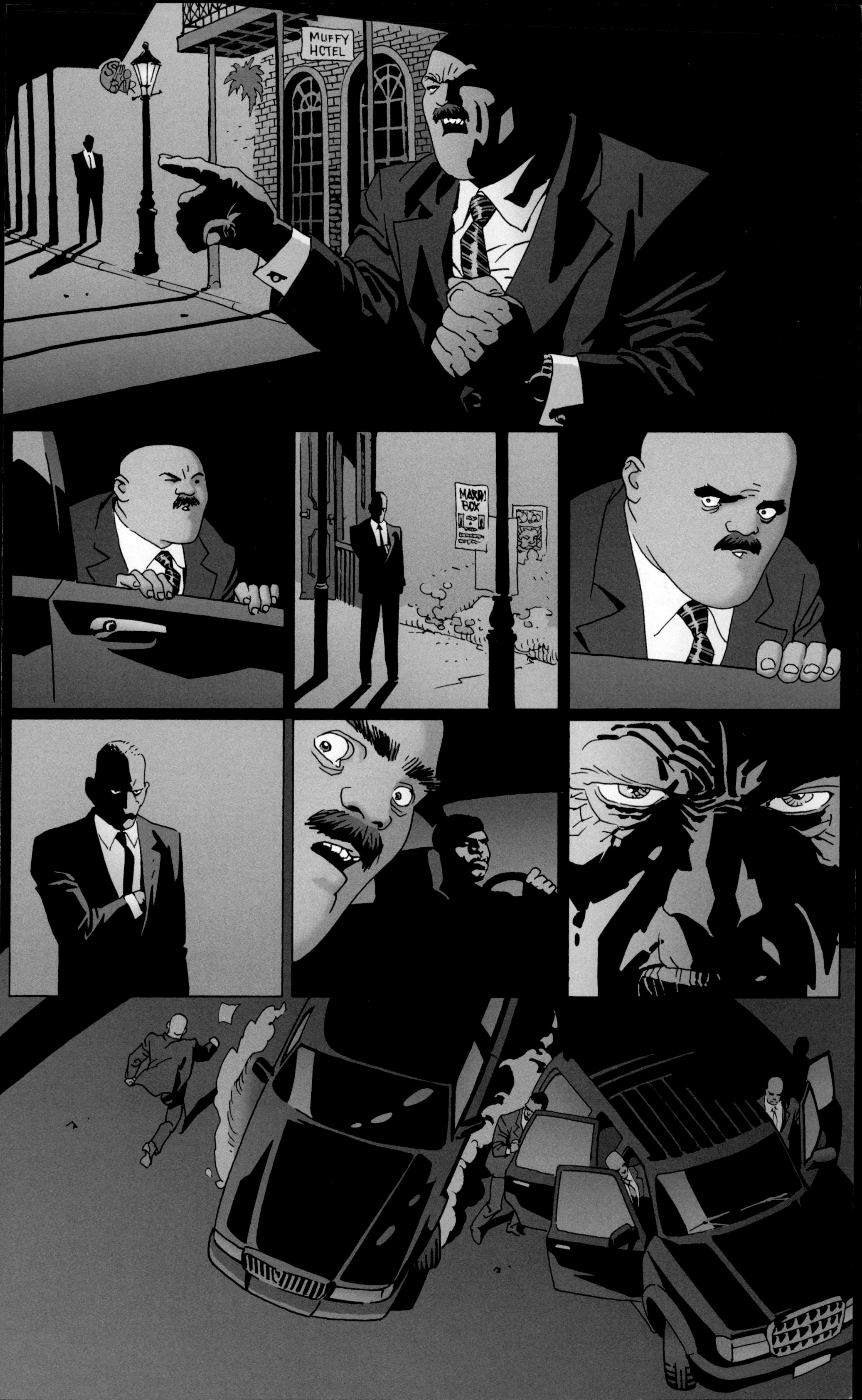
MUFFY HOTEL
BAR

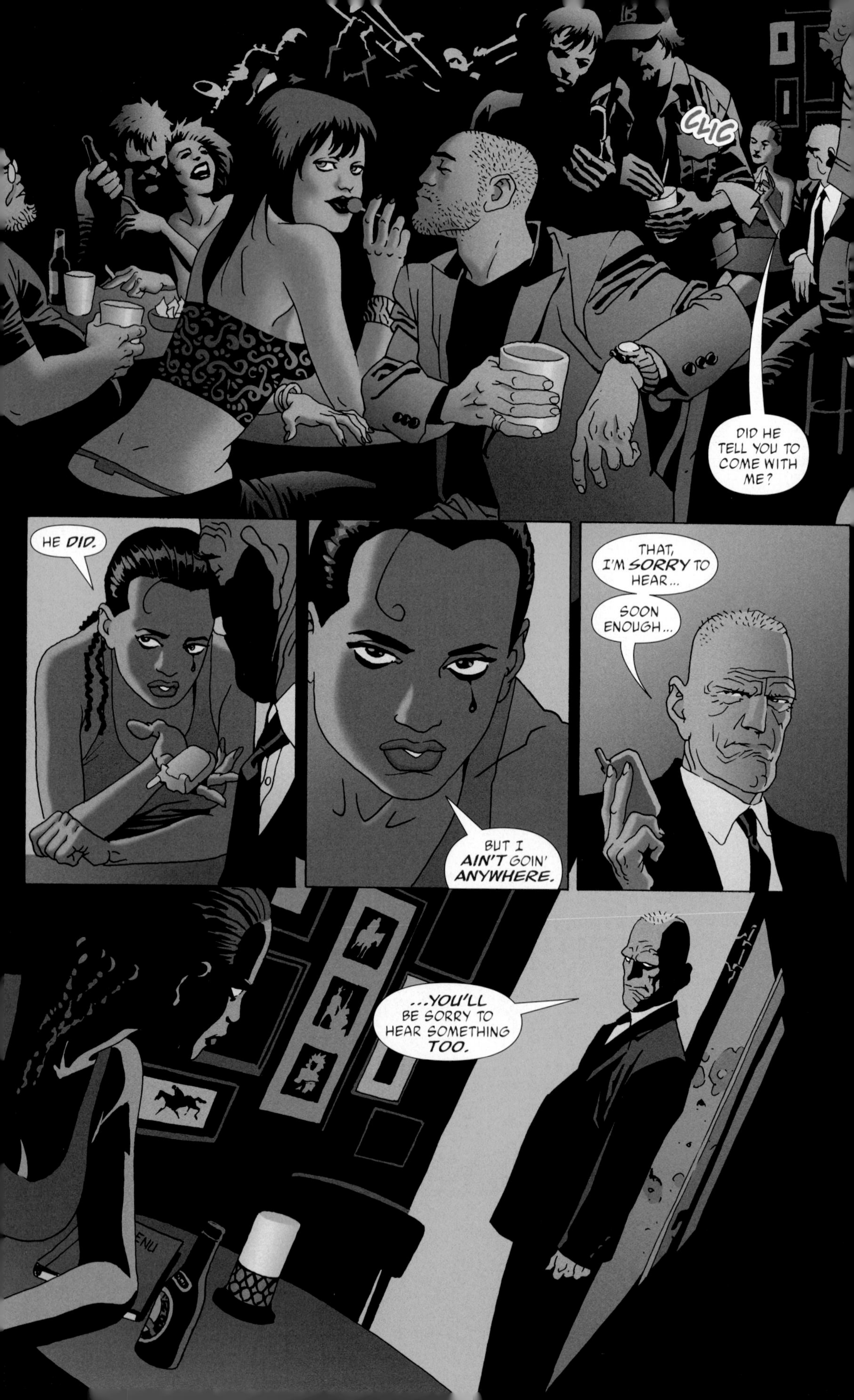
CLIC
DID HE TELL YOU TO COME WITH ME?
HE DID.
BUT I AIN'T GOIN' ANYWHERE.
THAT, I'M SORRY TO HEAR...
SOON ENOUGH...
...YOU'LL BE SORRY TO HEAR SOMETHING TOO.

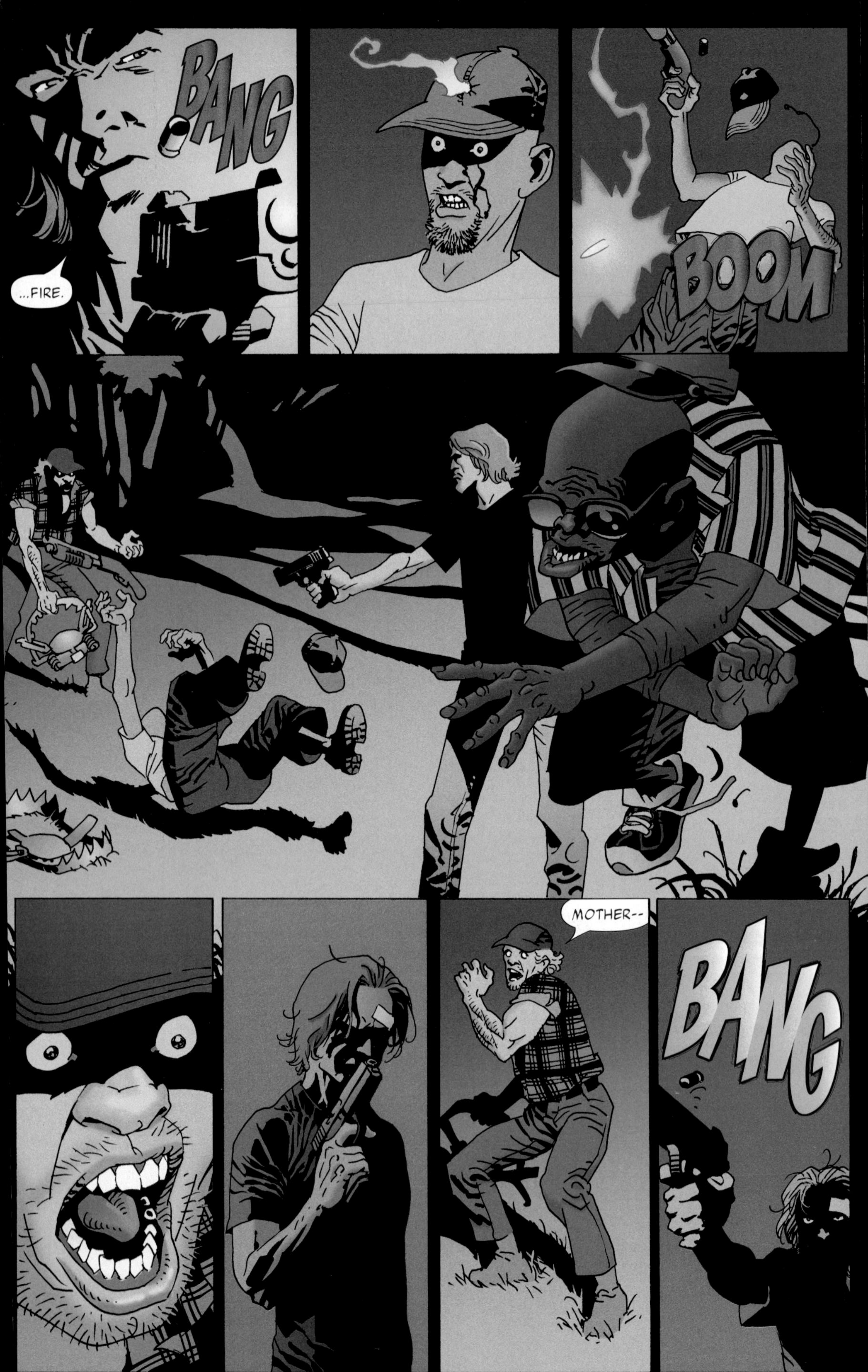
BANG
...FIRE.
BOOM
MOTHER--
BANG

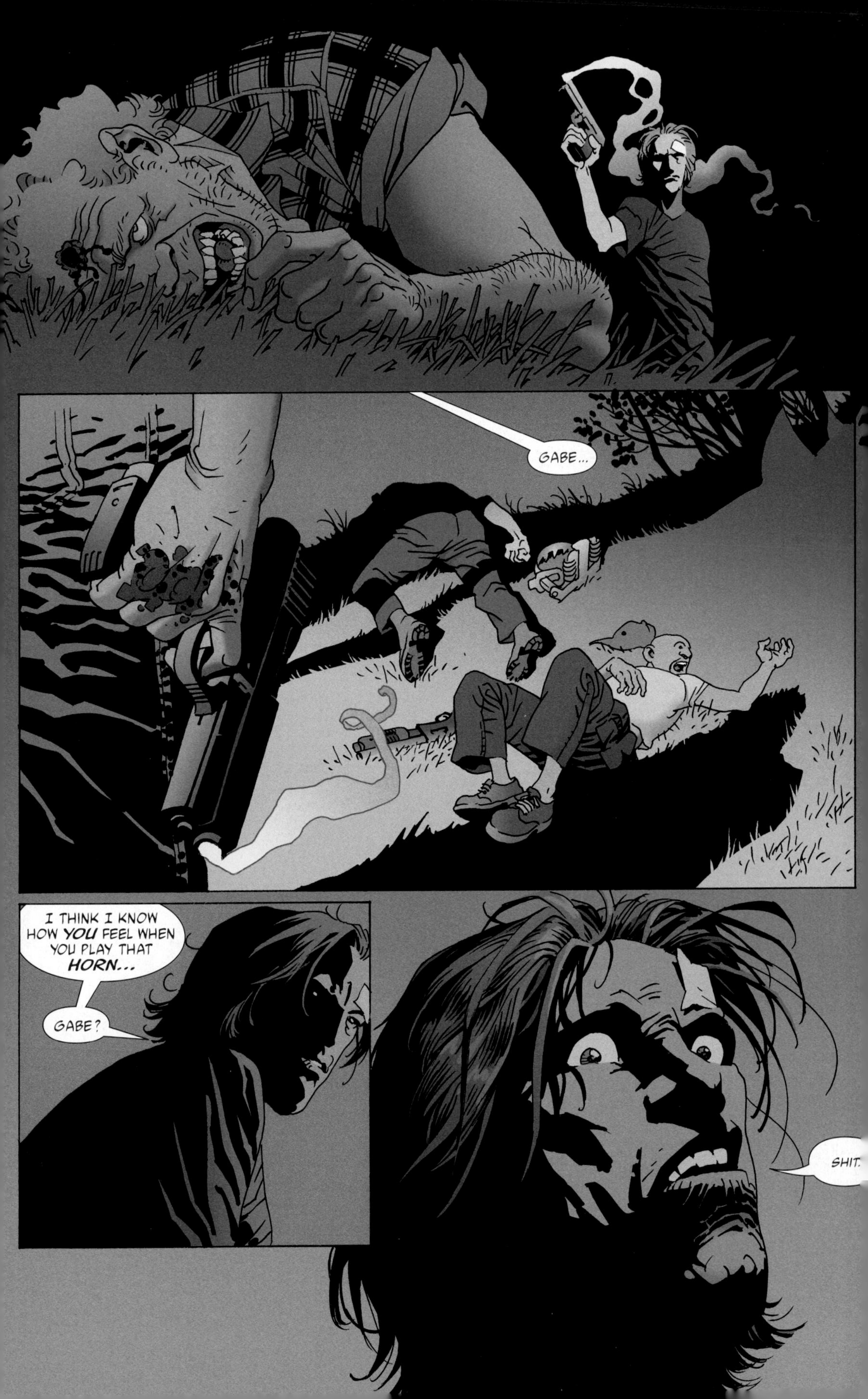
GABE...
I THINK I KNOW HOW YOU FEEL WHEN YOU PLAY THAT HORN...
GABE?
SHIT.

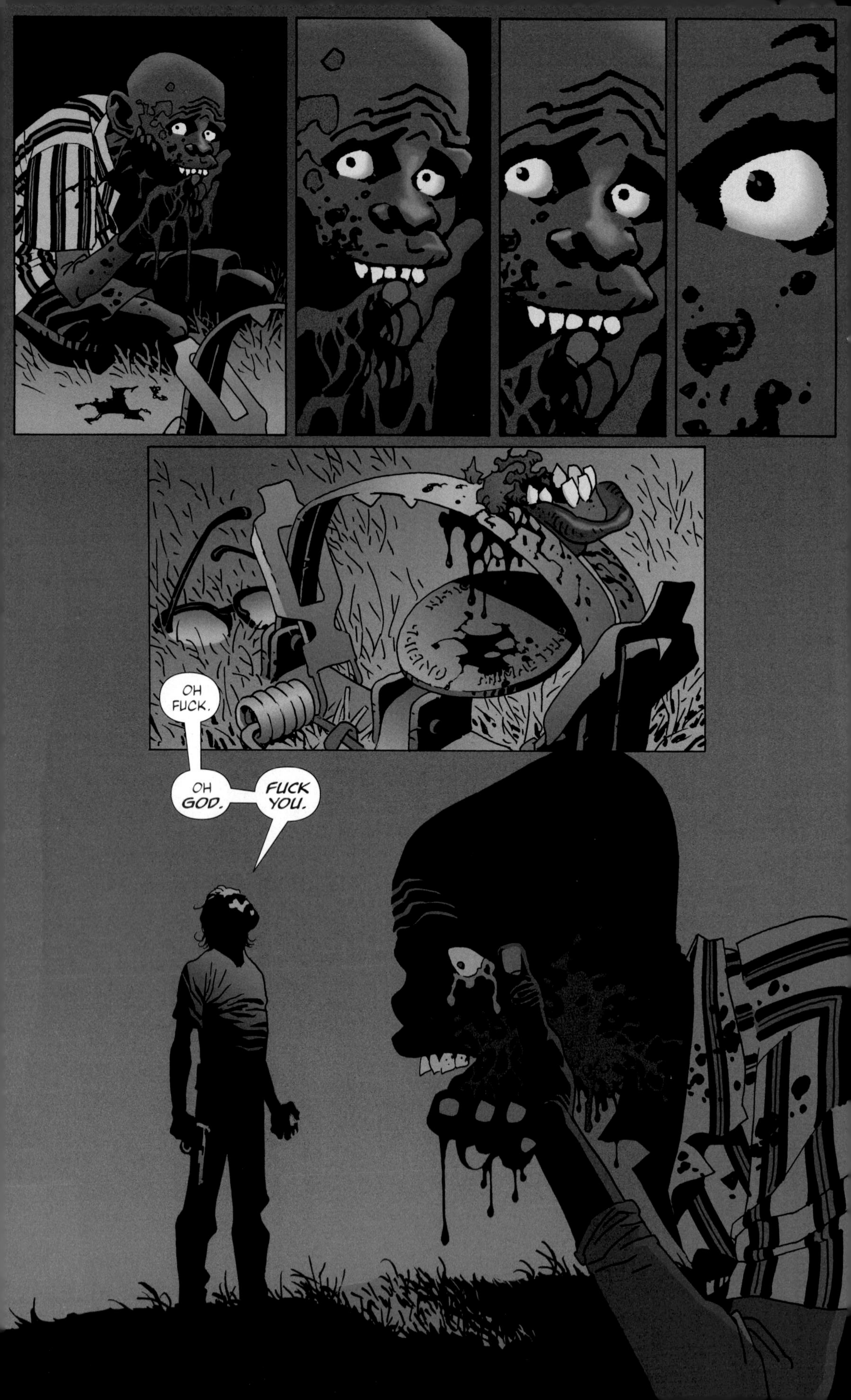
OH FUCK.
OH GOD.
FUCK YOU.

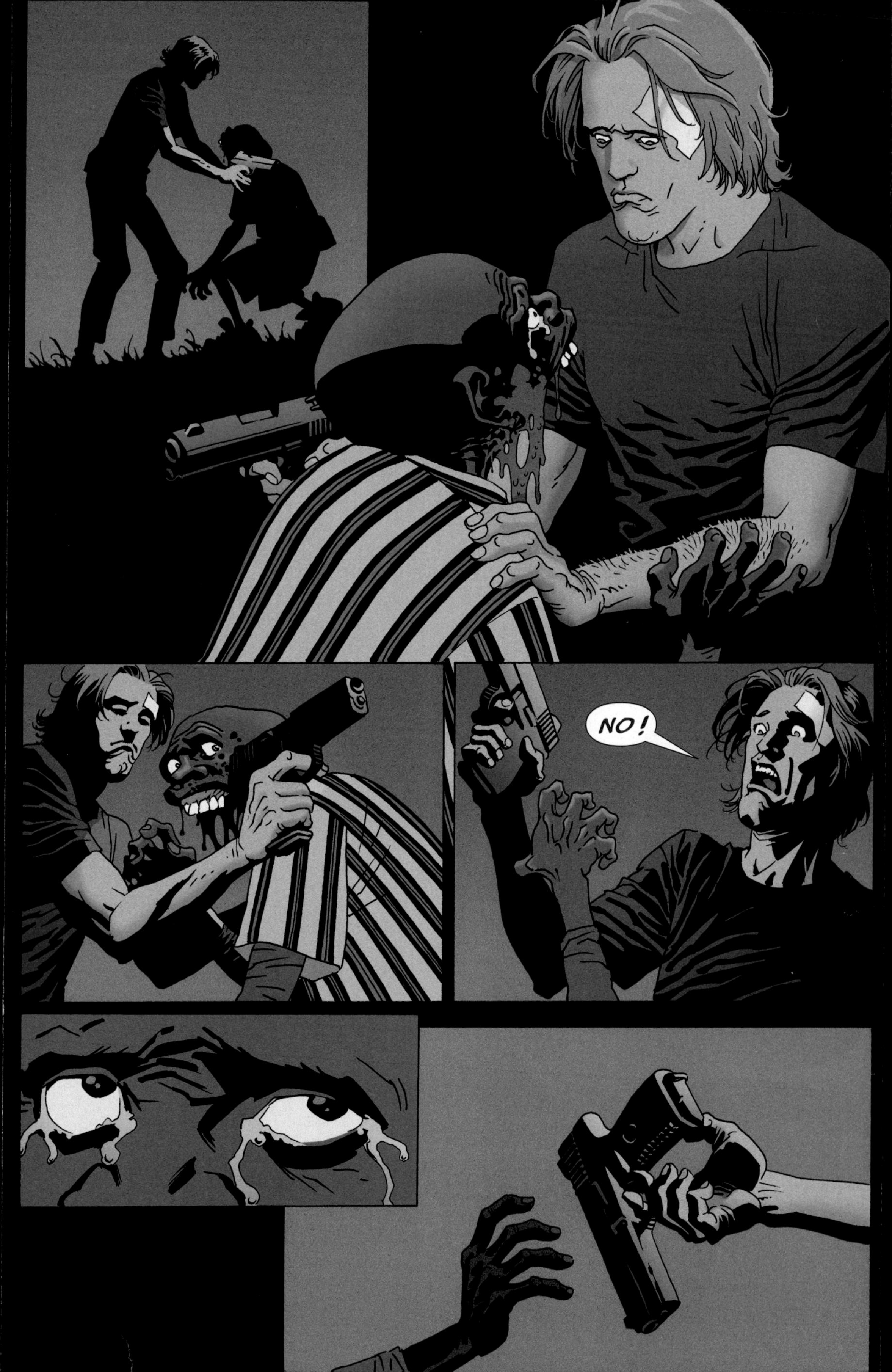
NO!

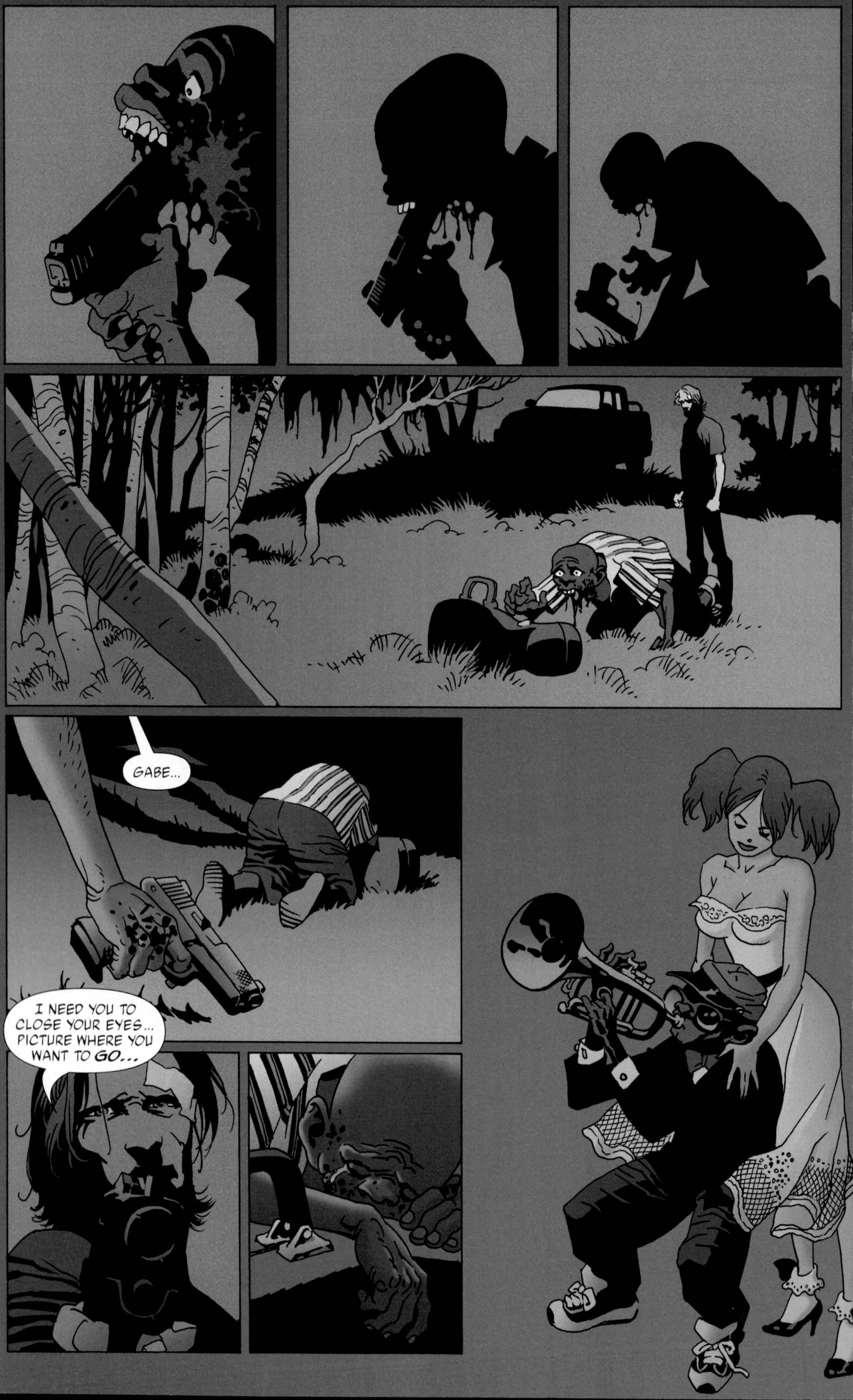
GABE...
I NEED YOU TO CLOSE YOUR EYES... PICTURE WHERE YOU WANT TO GO...

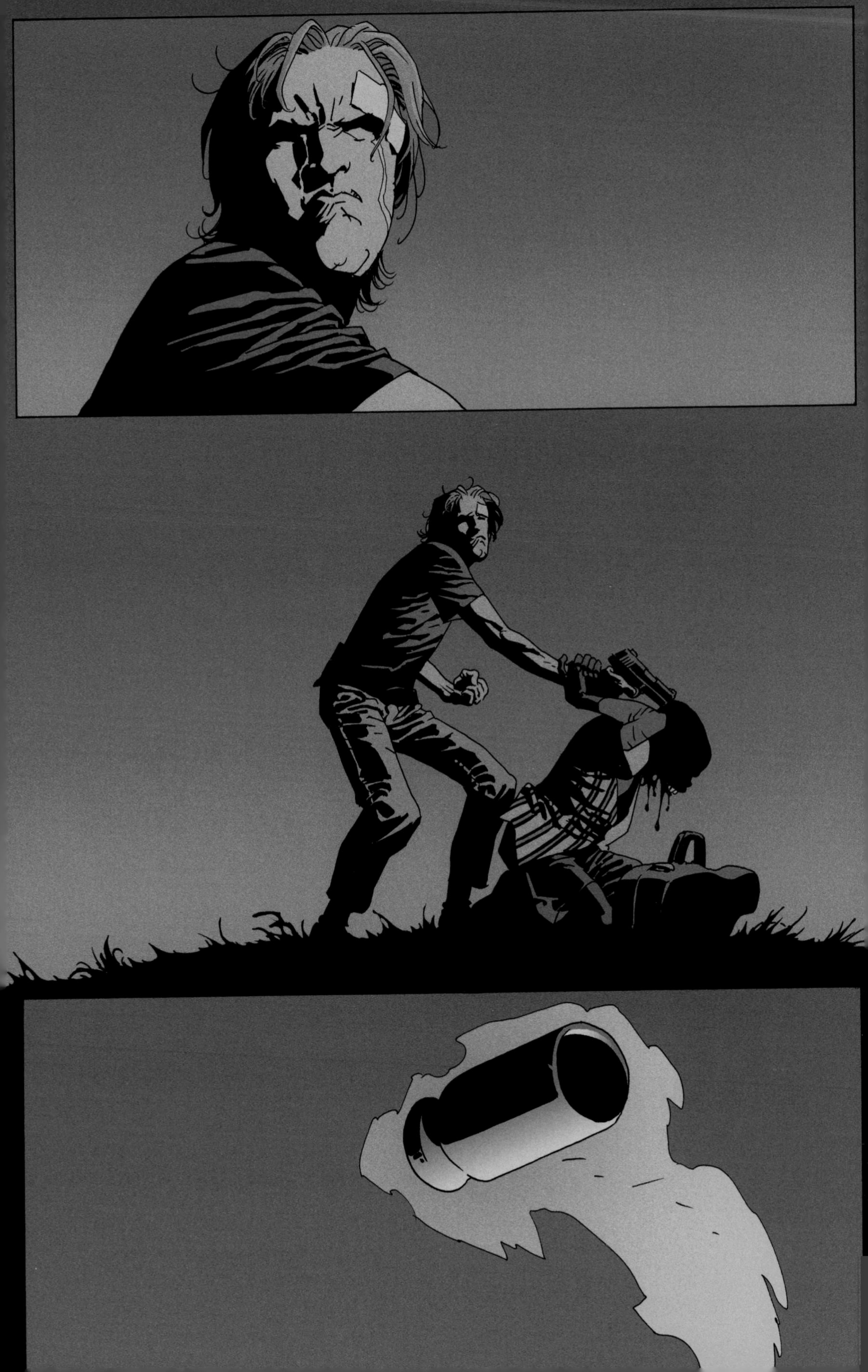

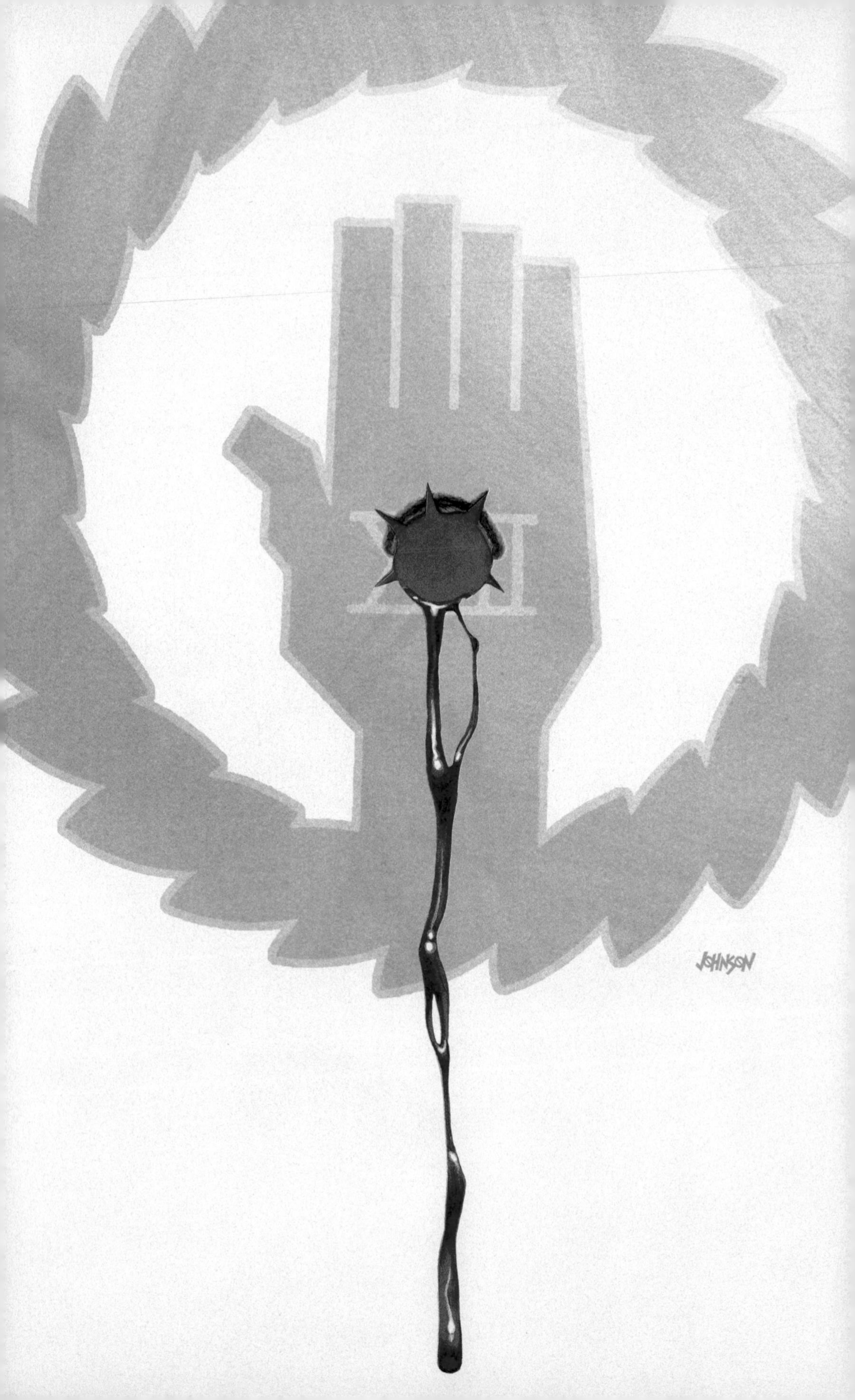
JOHNSON

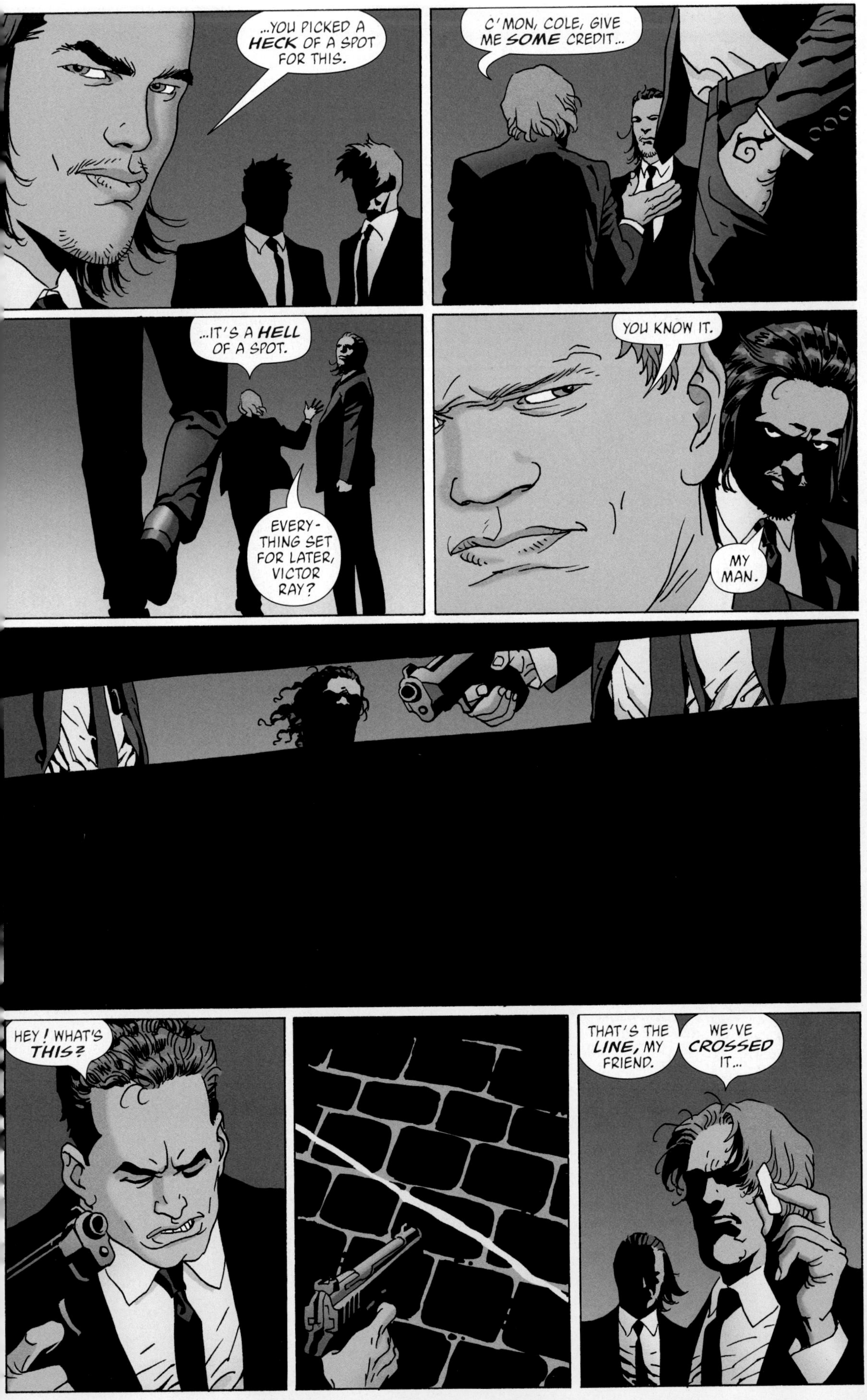
...YOU PICKED A HECK OF A SPOT FOR THIS.
C'MON, COLE, GIVE ME SOME CREDIT...
...IT'S A HELL OF A SPOT.
EVERY-THING SET FOR LATER, VICTOR RAY?
YOU KNOW IT.
MY MAN.
HEY! WHAT'S THIS?
THAT'S THE LINE, MY FRIEND.
WE'VE CROSSED IT...

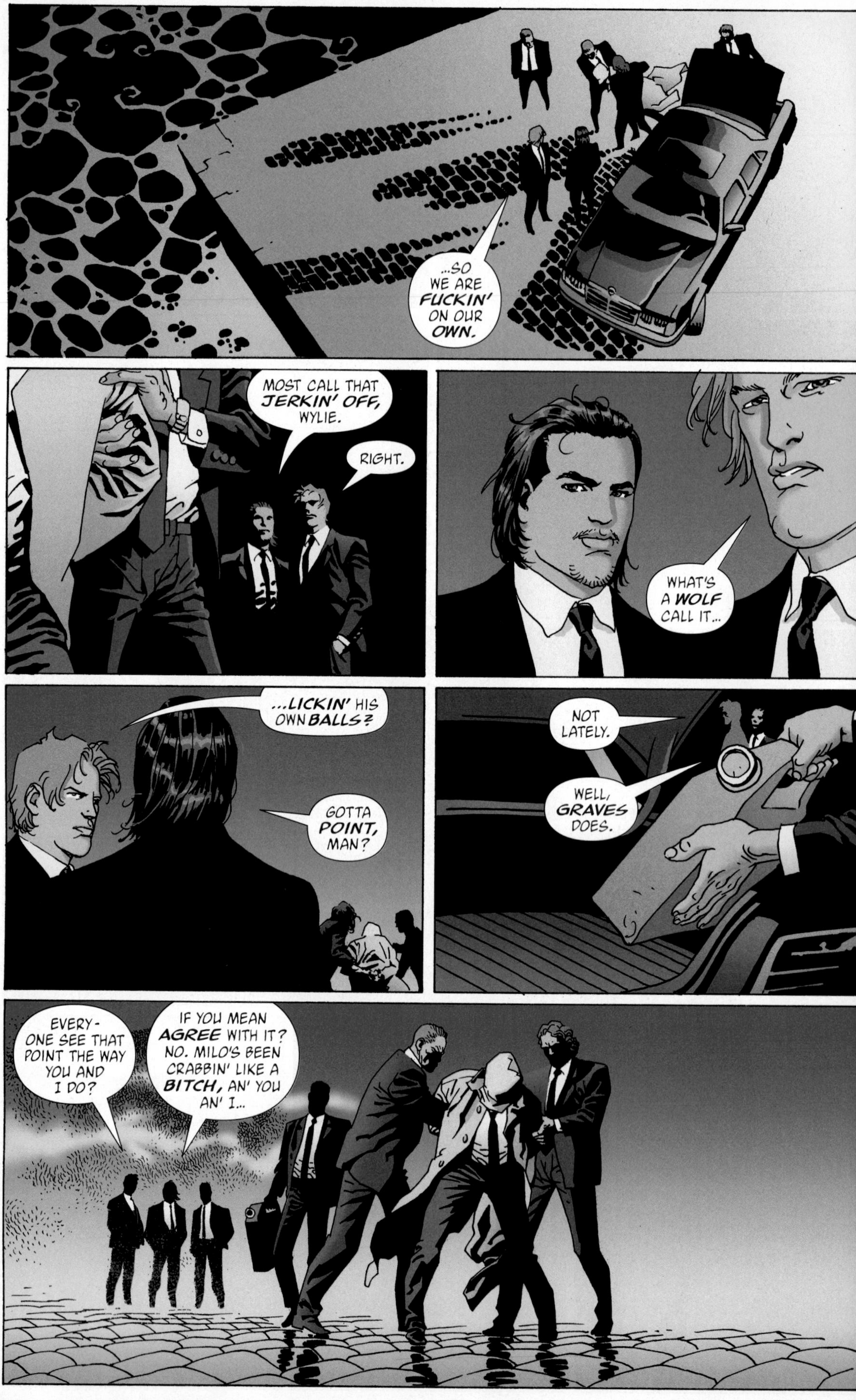
...SO WE ARE FUCKIN' ON OUR OWN.
MOST CALL THAT JERKIN' OFF, WYLIE.
RIGHT.
WHAT'S A WOLF CALL IT...
...LICKIN' HIS OWN BALLS?
GOTTA POINT, MAN?
NOT LATELY.
WELL, GRAVES DOES.
EVERY-ONE SEE THAT POINT THE WAY YOU AND I DO?
IF YOU MEAN AGREE WITH IT? NO. MILO'S BEEN CRABBIN' LIKE A BITCH, AN' YOU AN' I...

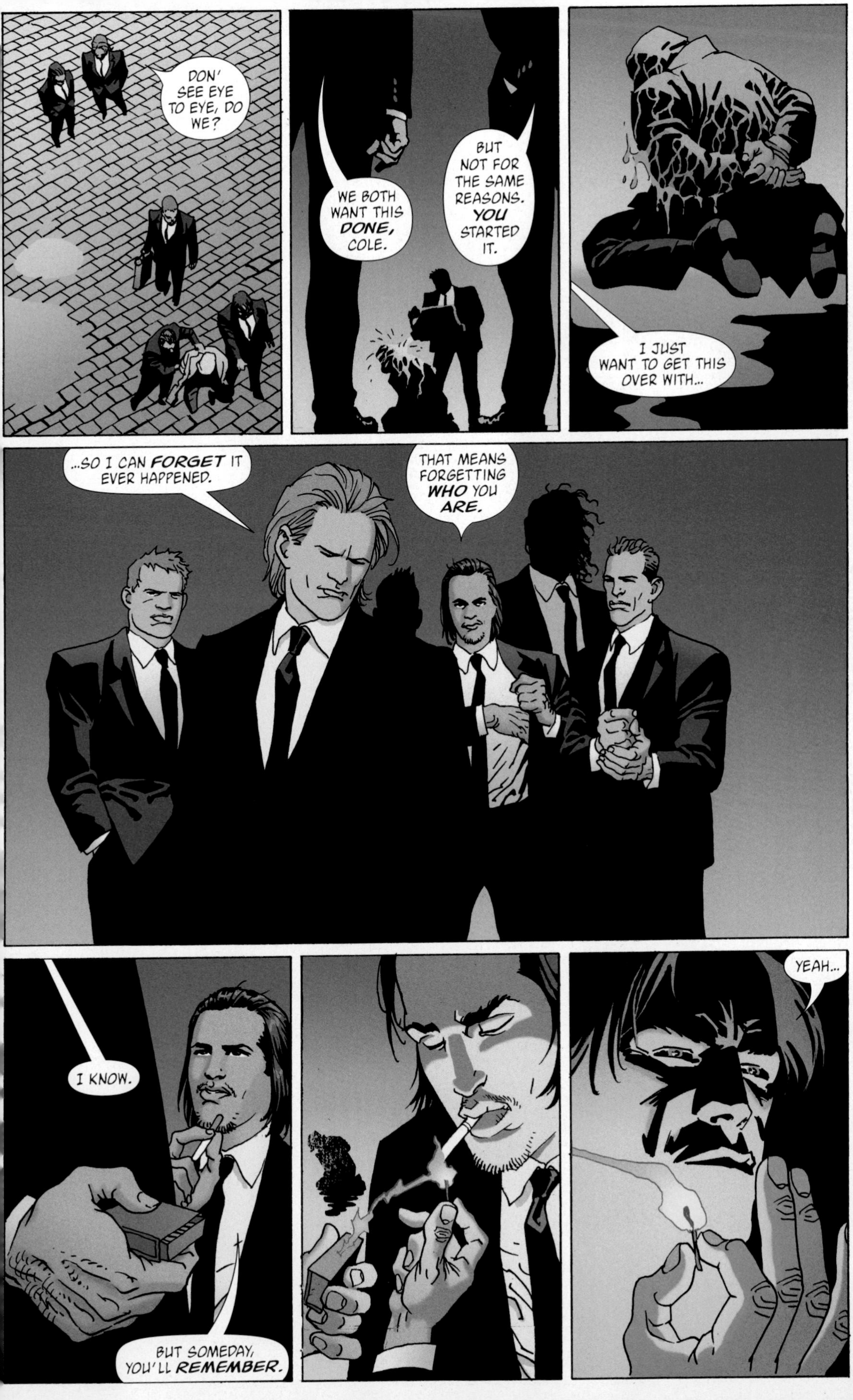
DON' SEE EYE TO EYE, DO WE?
WE BOTH WANT THIS DONE, COLE.
BUT NOT FOR THE SAME REASONS. YOU STARTED IT.
I JUST WANT TO GET THIS OVER WITH...
...SO I CAN FORGET IT EVER HAPPENED.
THAT MEANS FORGETTING WHO YOU ARE.
I KNOW.
BUT SOMEDAY, YOU'LL REMEMBER.
YEAH...

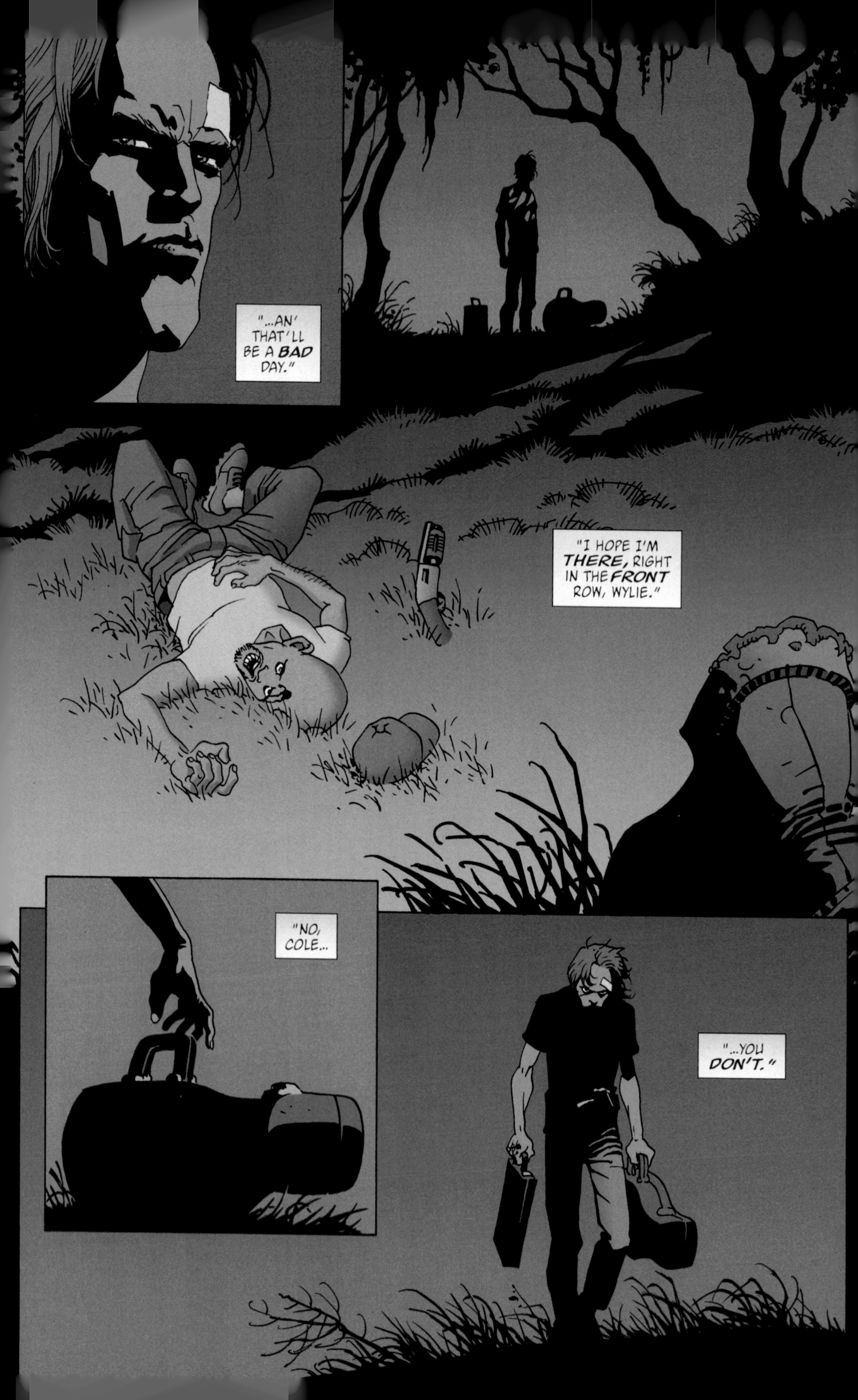
"...AN' THAT'LL BE A BAD DAY."
"I HOPE I'M THERE, RIGHT IN THE FRONT ROW, WYLIE."
"NO, COLE...
"...YOU DON'T."

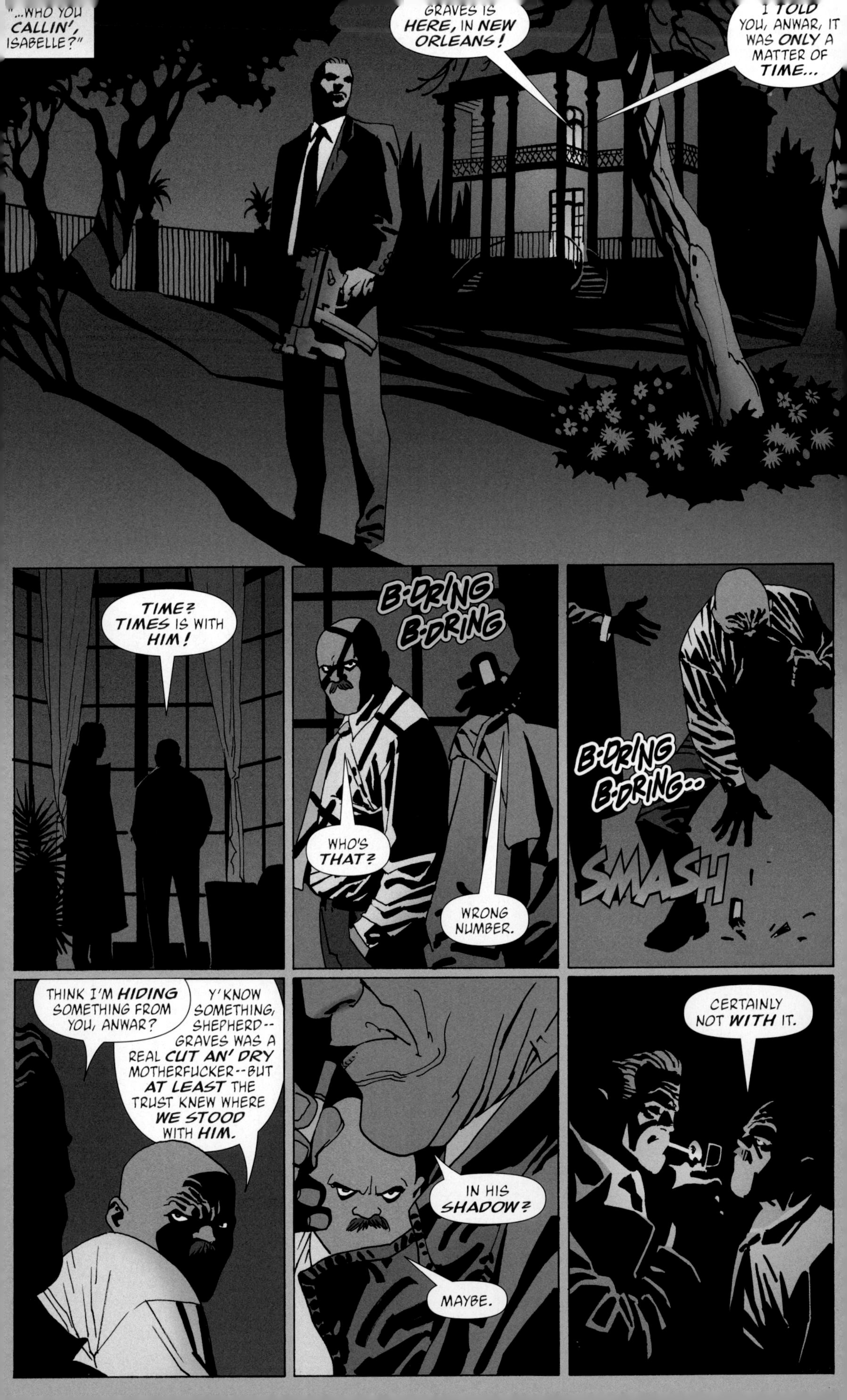
"...WHO YOU CALLIN', ISABELLE?"
GRAVES IS HERE, IN NEW ORLEANS!
I TOLD YOU, ANWAR, IT WAS ONLY A MATTER OF TIME...
TIME? TIMES IS WITH HIM!
B-DRING B-DRING
WHO'S THAT?
WRONG NUMBER.
B-DRING B-DRING..
SMASH
THINK I'M HIDING SOMETHING FROM YOU, ANWAR?
Y'KNOW SOMETHING, SHEPHERD-- GRAVES WAS A REAL CUT AN' DRY MOTHERFUCKER--BUT AT LEAST THE TRUST KNEW WHERE WE STOOD WITH HIM.
IN HIS SHADOW?
MAYBE.
CERTAINLY NOT WITH IT.

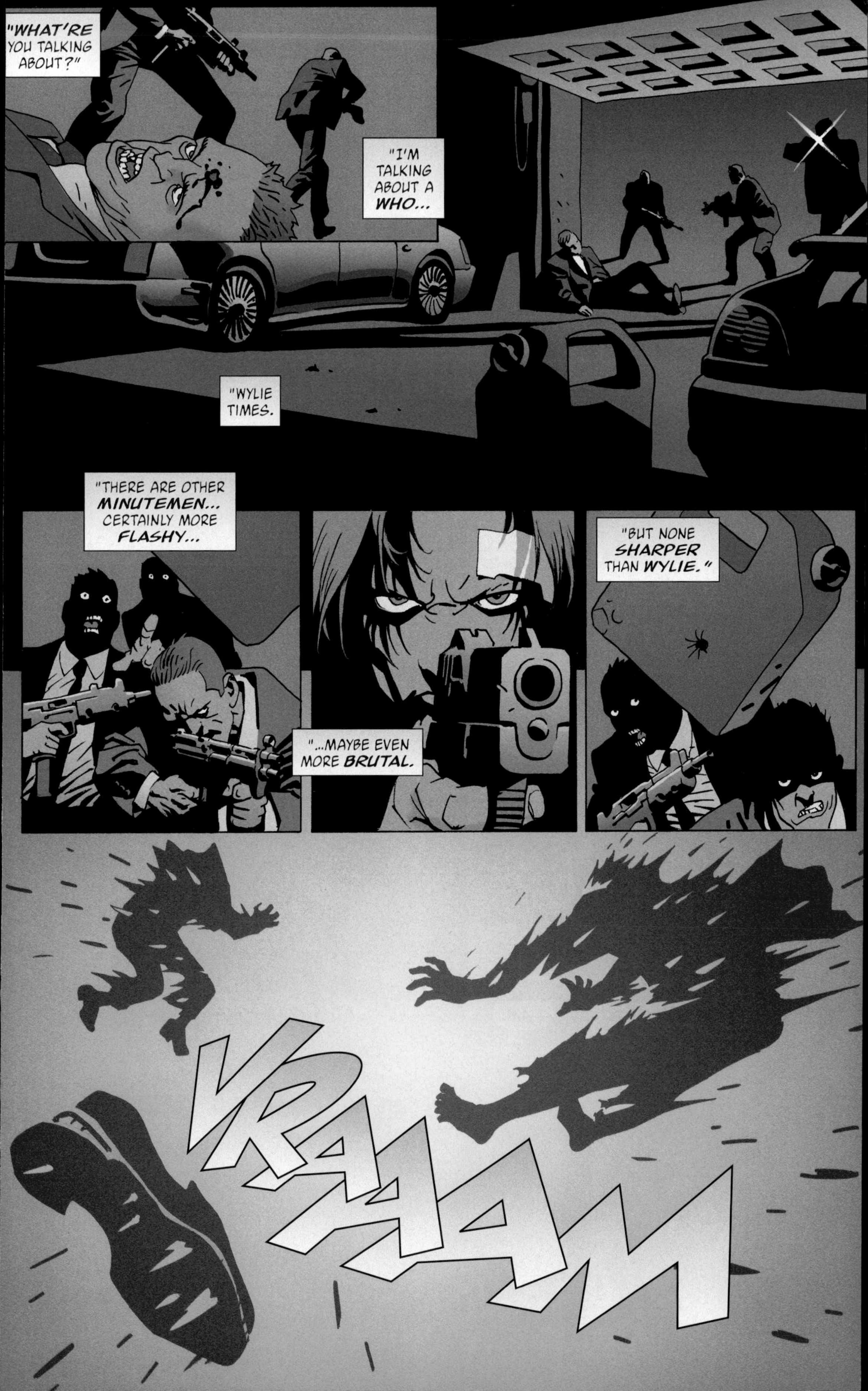
"WHAT'RE YOU TALKING ABOUT?"
"I'M TALKING ABOUT A WHO...
"WYLIE TIMES.
"THERE ARE OTHER MINUTEMEN... CERTAINLY MORE FLASHY...
"...MAYBE EVEN MORE BRUTAL.
"BUT NONE SHARPER THAN WYLIE."
VRAAAM

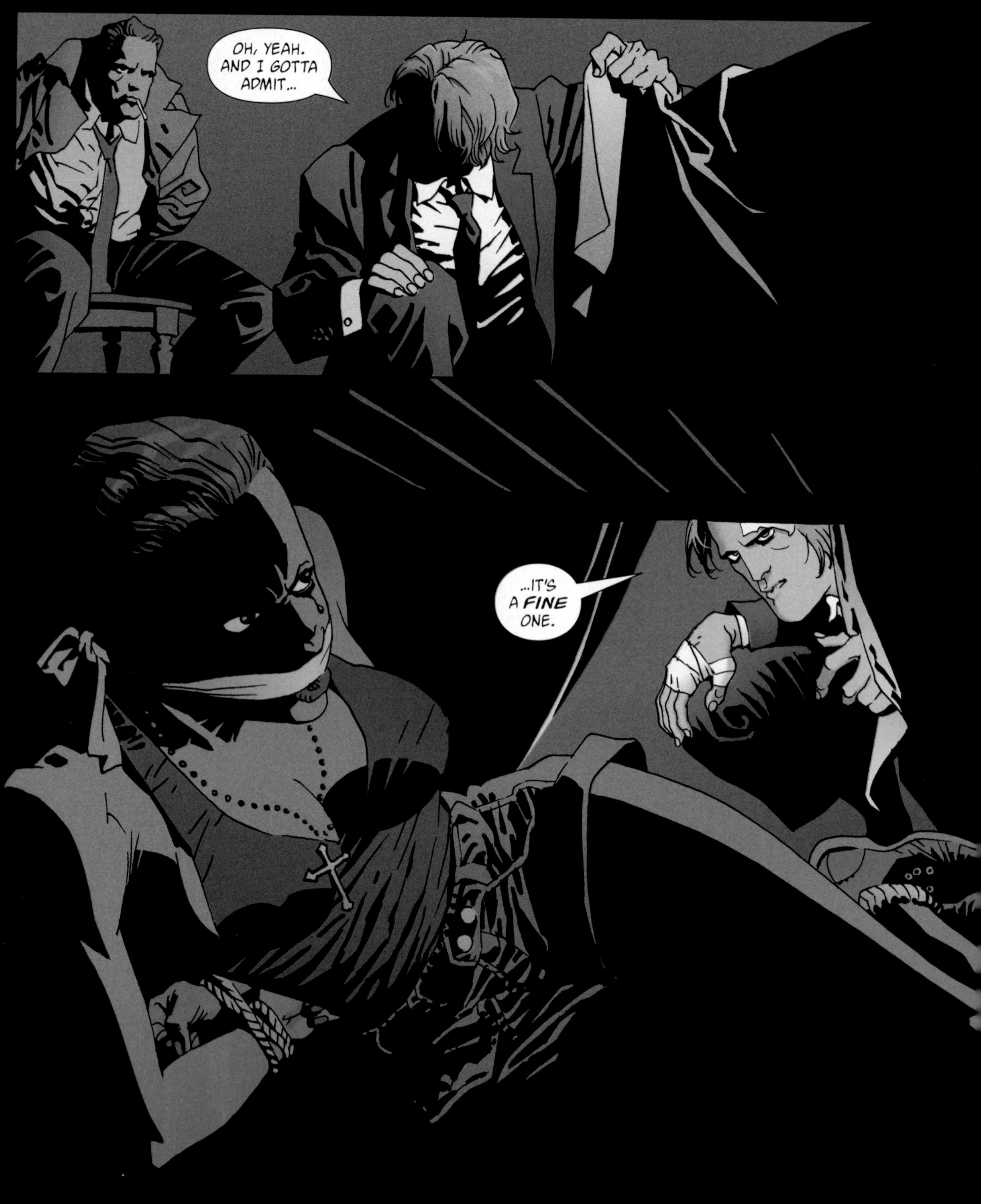
OH, YEAH. AND I GOTTA ADMIT...
...IT'S A FINE ONE.

Wylie Runs the Voodoo Down Part Six

Brian Azzarello writer
Eduardo Risso artist
Patricia Mulvihill colorist
Clem Robins letterer **Dave Johnson** cover
Casey Seijas asst. ed. **Will Dennis** editor

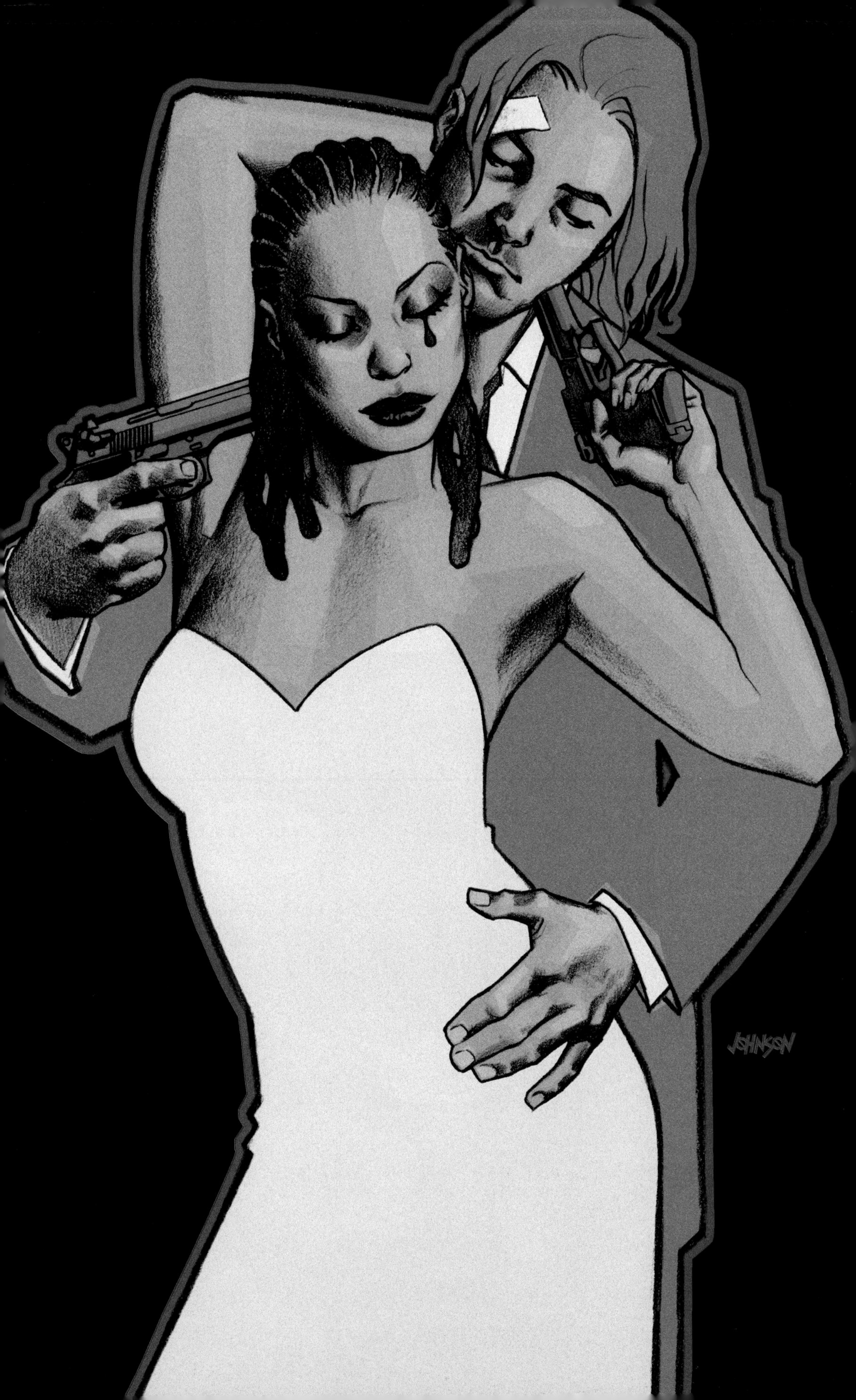
JOHNSON

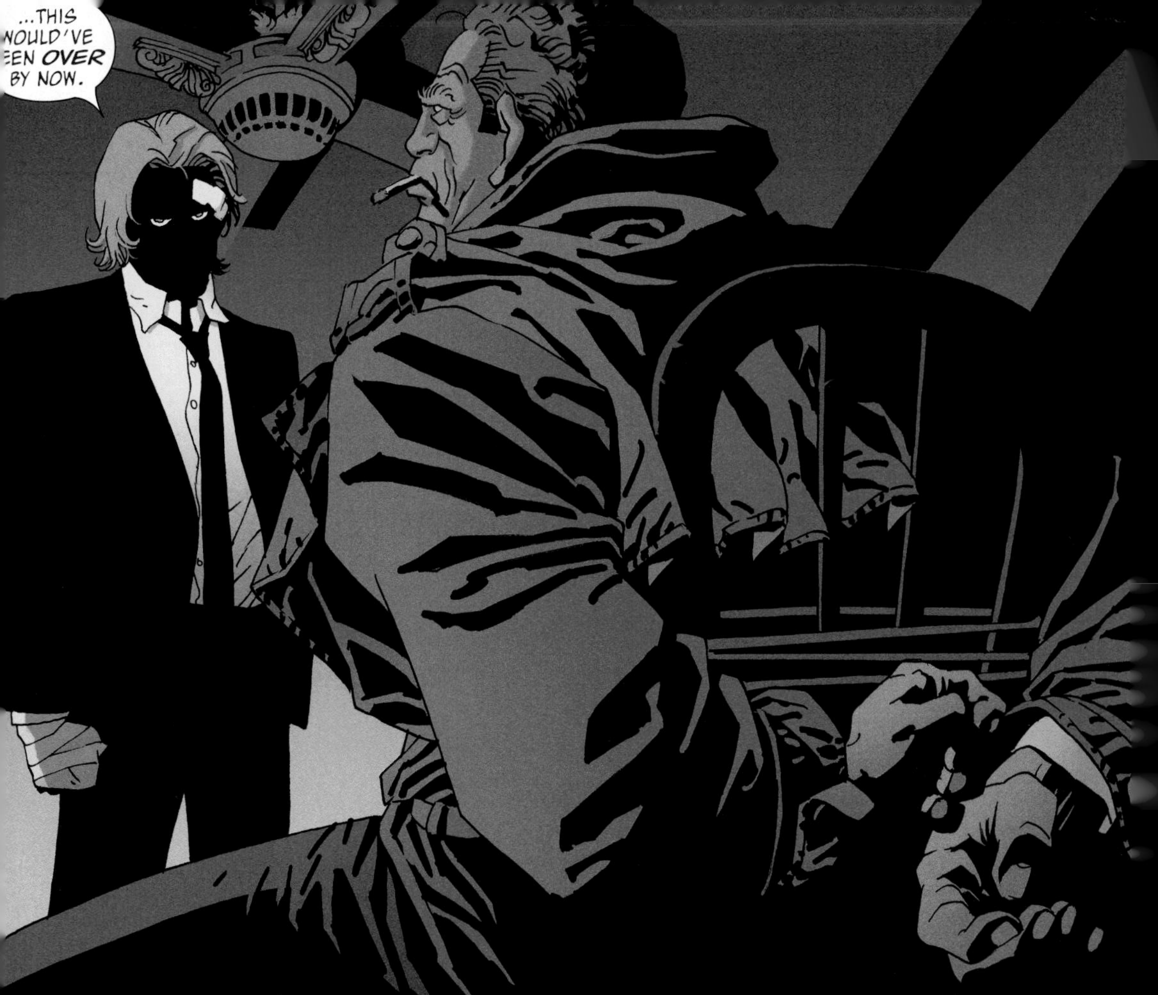
...THIS WOULD'VE EEN OVER BY NOW.

Wylie Runs the Voodoo Down

Conclusion

Brian Azzarello writer

Eduardo Risso artist

Patricia Mulvihill colorist

Clem Robins letterer

Dave Johnson cove

Casey Seijas asst. ed.

Will Dennis editor

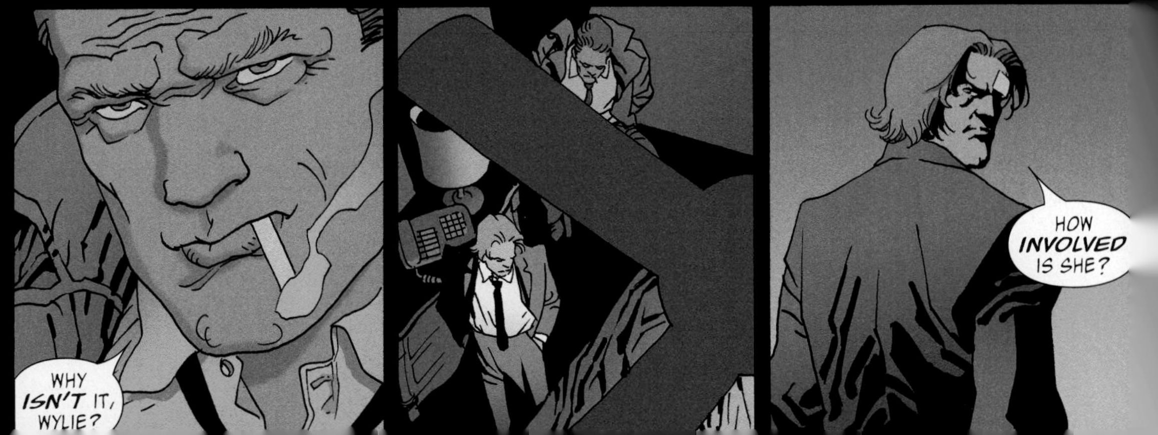
WHY ISN'T IT, WYLIE?
HOW INVOLVED IS SHE?

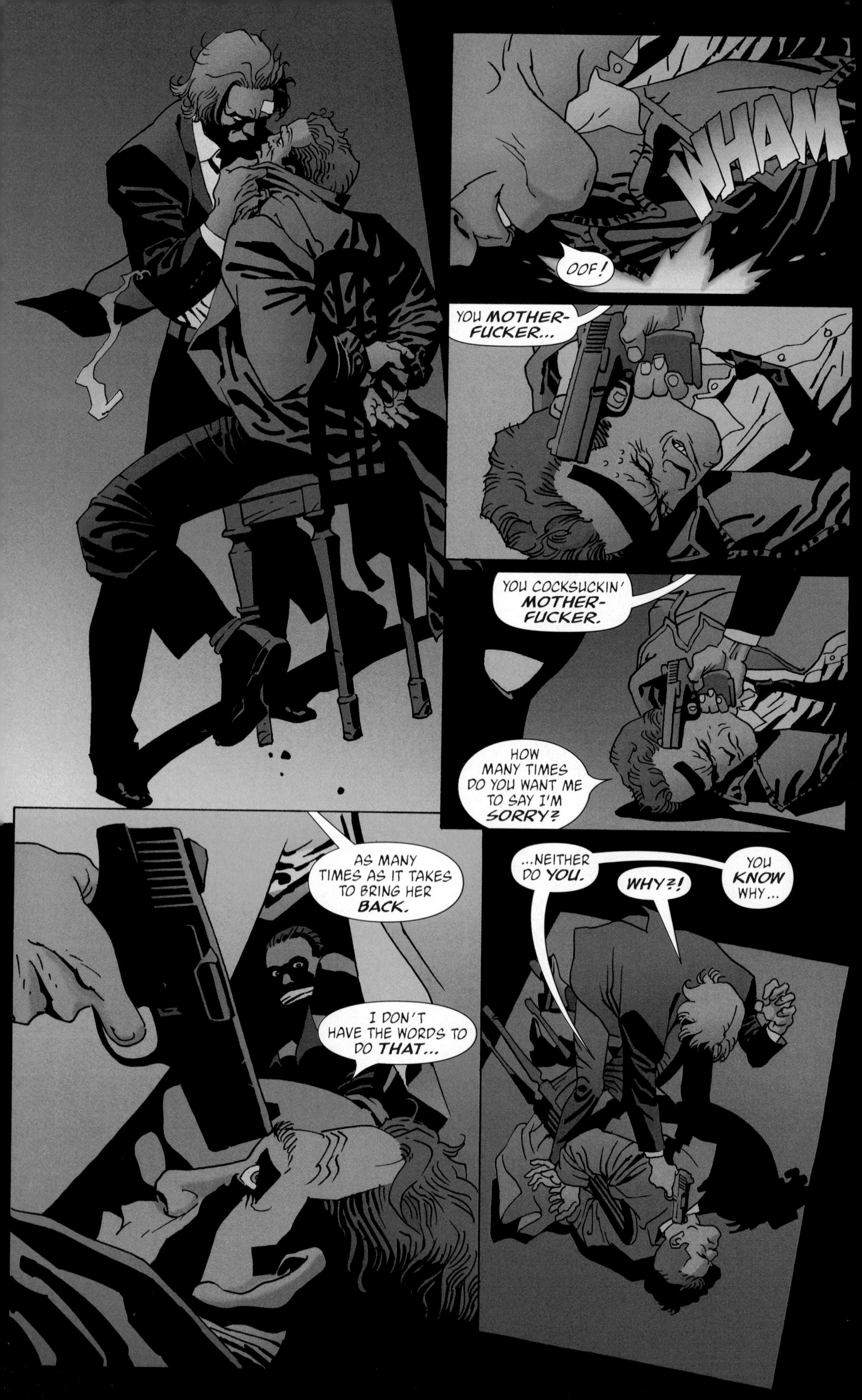
WHAM
OOF!
YOU MOTHER-FUCKER...
YOU COCKSUCKIN' MOTHER-FUCKER.
HOW MANY TIMES DO YOU WANT ME TO SAY I'M SORRY?
AS MANY TIMES AS IT TAKES TO BRING HER BACK.
I DON'T HAVE THE WORDS TO DO THAT...
...NEITHER DO YOU.
WHY?!
YOU KNOW WHY...

THAT WAS ONE OF THE FIRST THINGS YOU TAUGHT ME. AND RIGHT NOW...

...I FEEL *FUCKED* FOR EVER GOING TO YOUR *SCHOOL.*

ORLEAN HOTEL

SO THIS IS IT, HUH?

WHAT?

GRADUATION DAY.

ORLEANS HOTEL

"WHEN YOU WALKED OUT OF THE CAR, I *WAS* SORRY..."

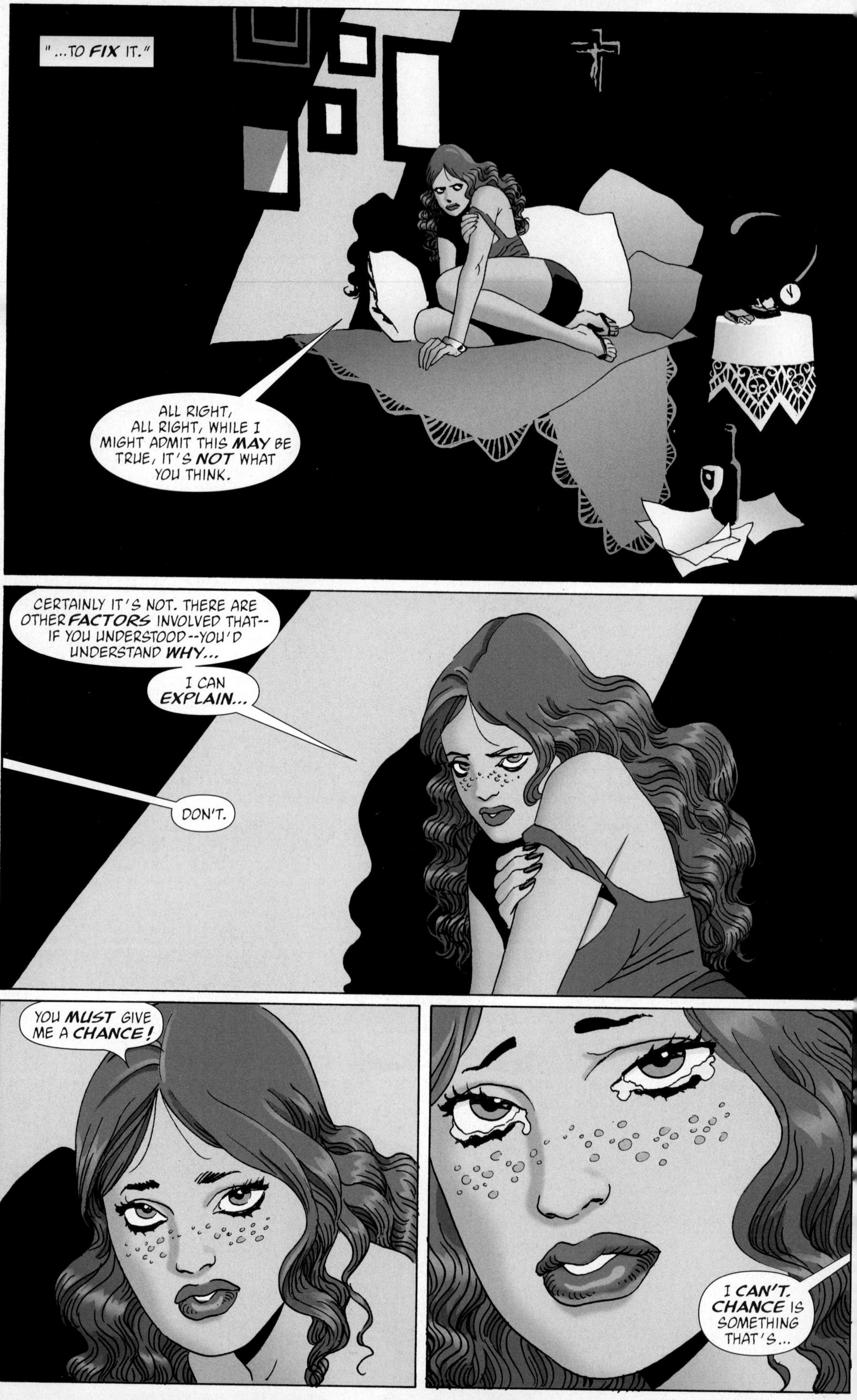
"...TO FIX IT."
ALL RIGHT, ALL RIGHT, WHILE I MIGHT ADMIT THIS MAY BE TRUE, IT'S NOT WHAT YOU THINK.
CERTAINLY IT'S NOT. THERE ARE OTHER FACTORS INVOLVED THAT-- IF YOU UNDERSTOOD--YOU'D UNDERSTAND WHY...
I CAN EXPLAIN...
DON'T.
YOU MUST GIVE ME A CHANCE!
I CAN'T. CHANCE IS SOMETHING THAT'S...

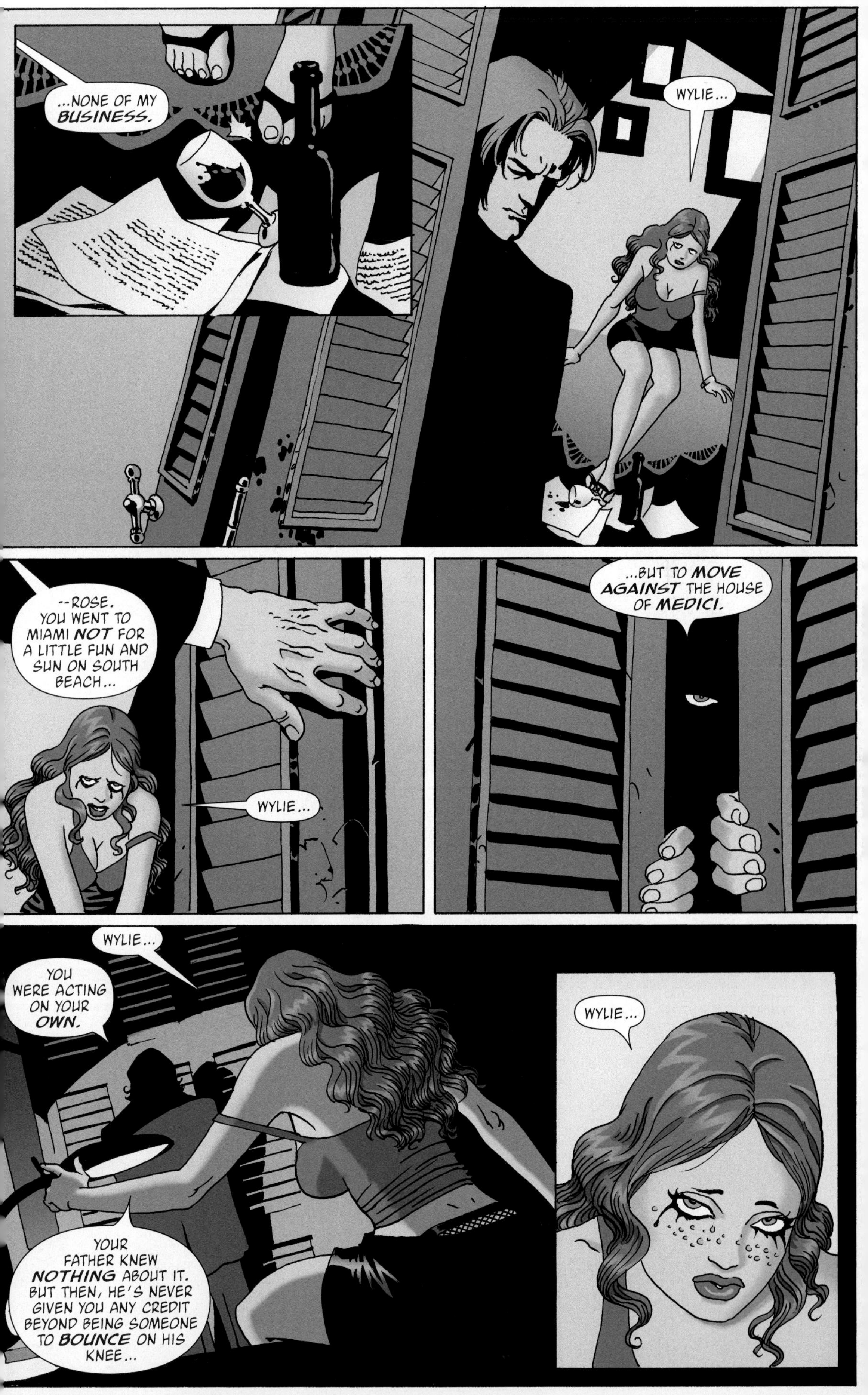
...NONE OF MY BUSINESS.
WYLIE...
--ROSE. YOU WENT TO MIAMI NOT FOR A LITTLE FUN AND SUN ON SOUTH BEACH...
WYLIE...
...BUT TO MOVE AGAINST THE HOUSE OF MEDICI.
WYLIE...
YOU WERE ACTING ON YOUR OWN.
YOUR FATHER KNEW NOTHING ABOUT IT. BUT THEN, HE'S NEVER GIVEN YOU ANY CREDIT BEYOND BEING SOMEONE TO BOUNCE ON HIS KNEE...
WYLIE...

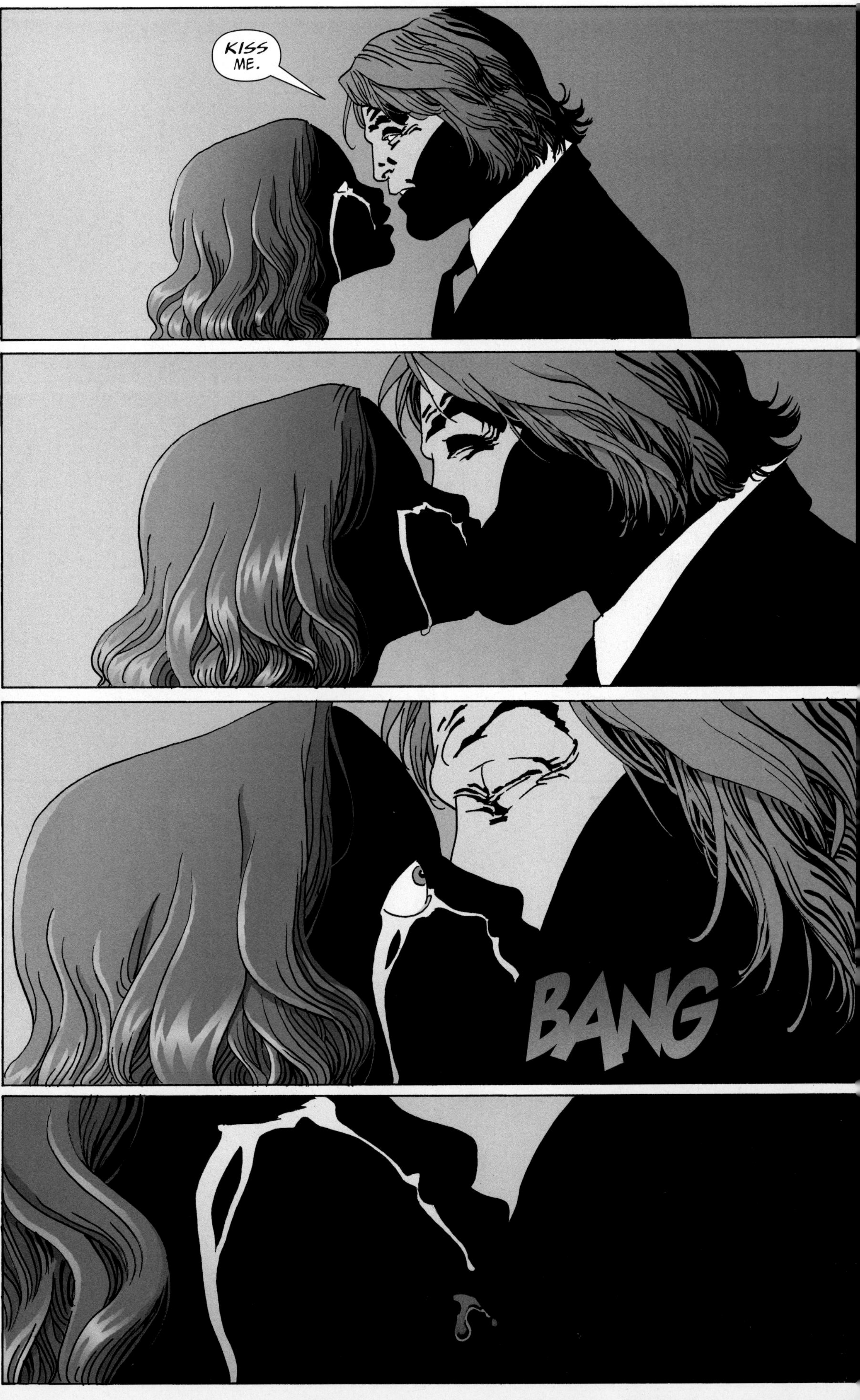
KISS ME.
BANG

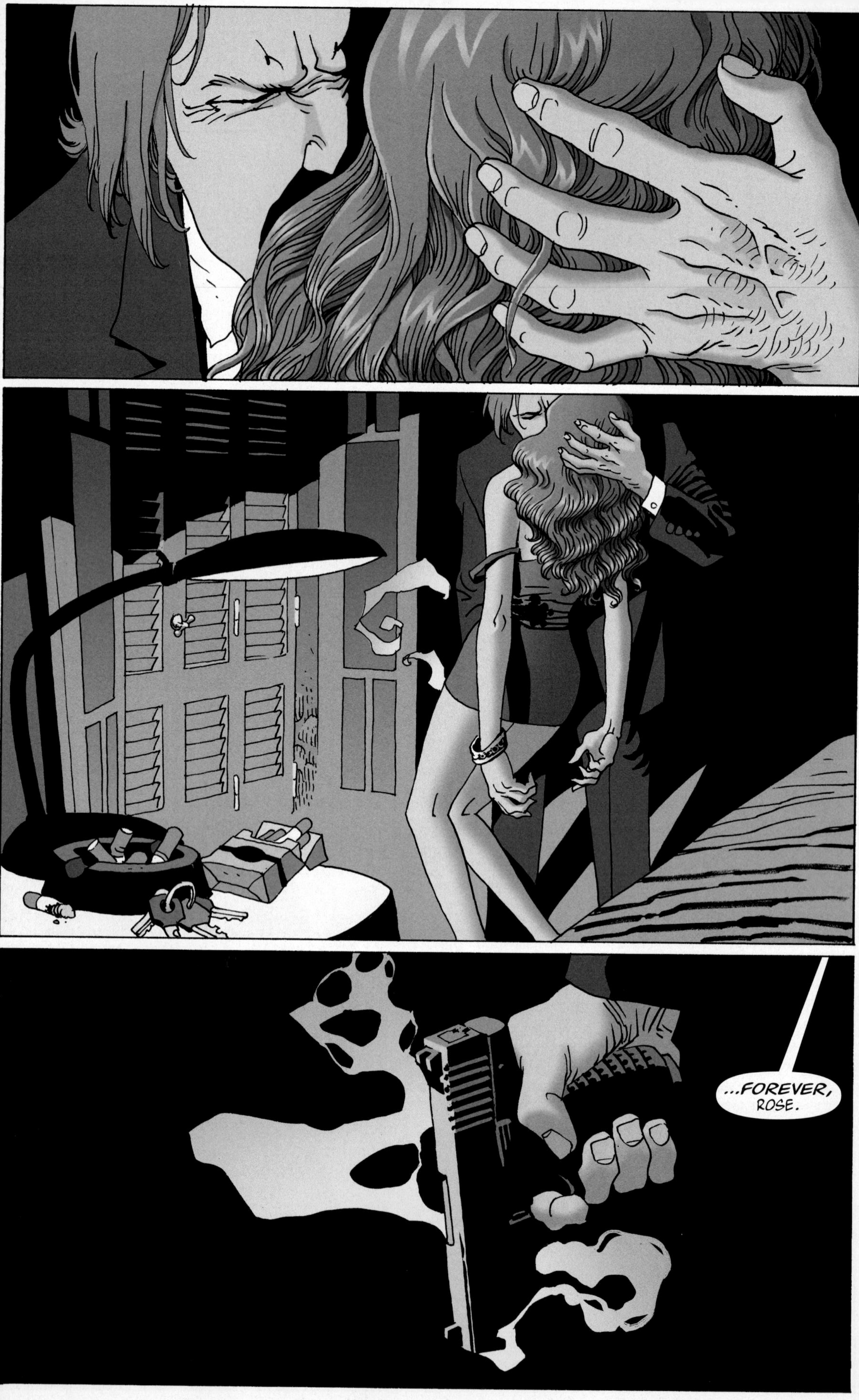
...FOREVER,
ROSE.

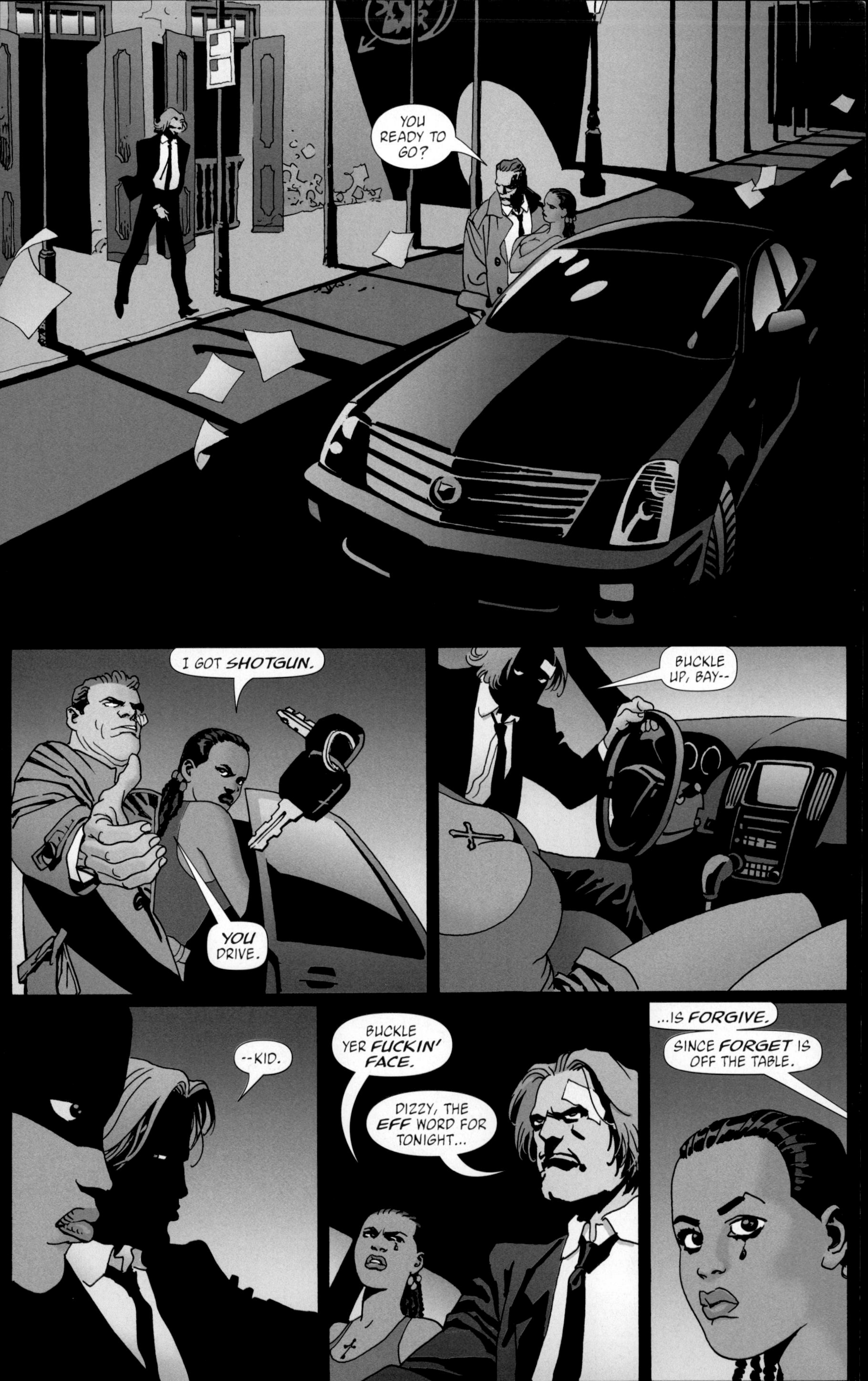
YOU READY TO GO?
I GOT SHOTGUN.
YOU DRIVE.
BUCKLE UP, BAY--
--KID.
BUCKLE YER FUCKIN' FACE.
DIZZY, THE EFF WORD FOR TONIGHT...
...IS FORGIVE.
SINCE FORGET IS OFF THE TABLE.

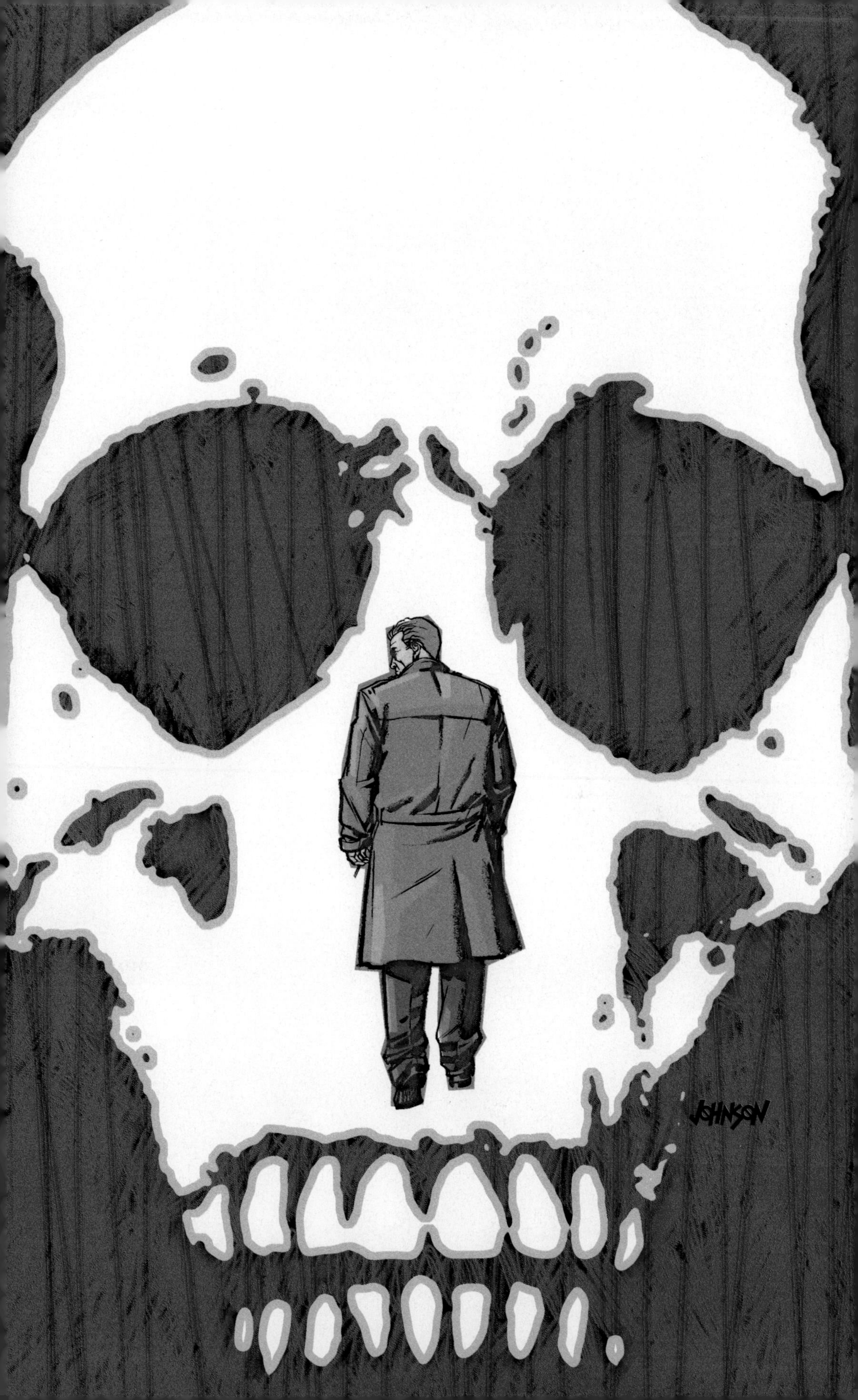
JOHNSON

Coda Smoke

Written by **Brian Azzarello**   Illustrated by **Eduardo Risso**

Colored by   Lettered by   Cover by   Assistant Editor   Editor
Patricia Mulvihill   Clem Robins   Dave Johnson   Casey Seijas   Will Dennis

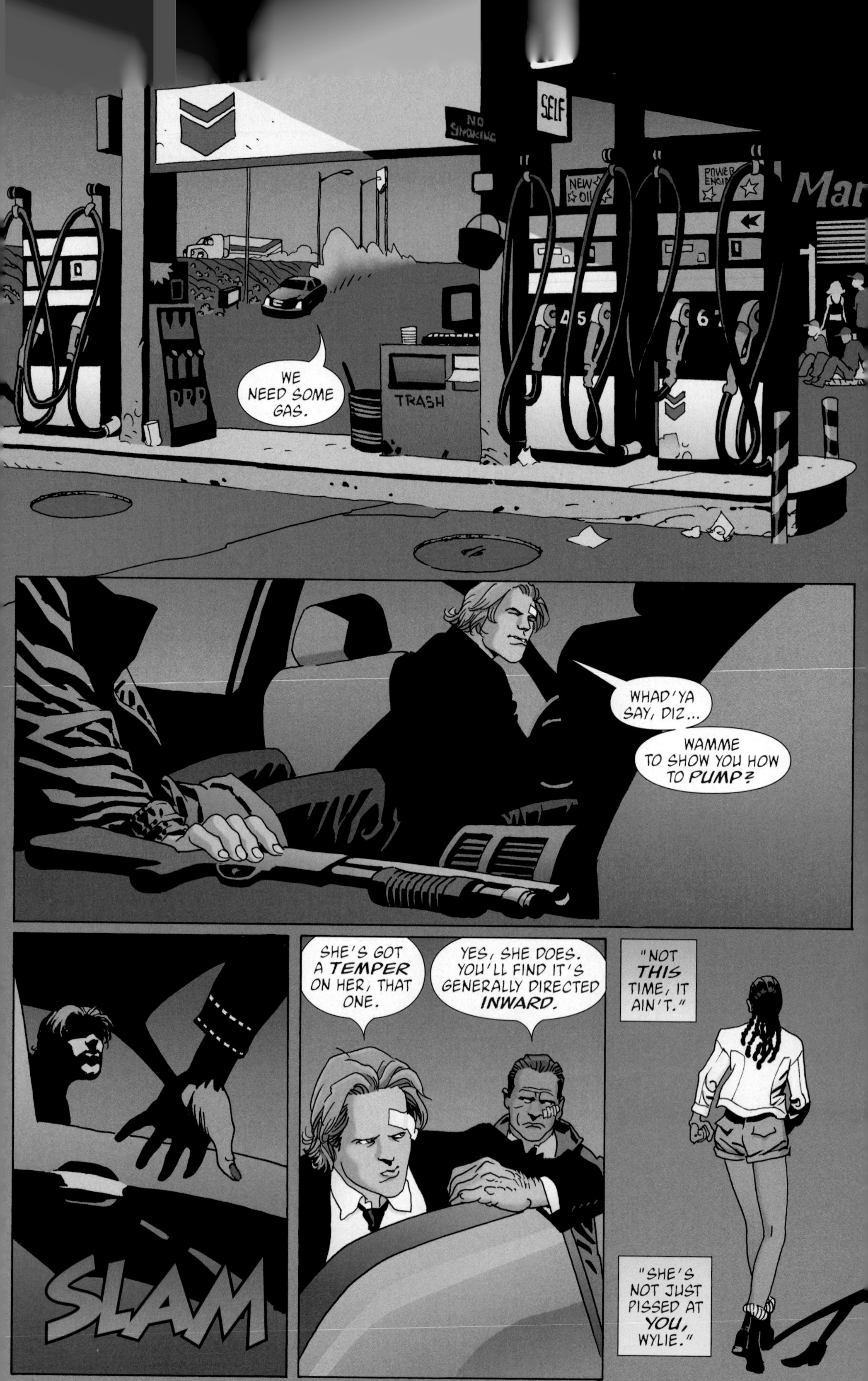

SELF
NO SMOKING
NEW OIL
TRASH
WE NEED SOME GAS.
WHAD'YA SAY, DIZ...
WAMME TO SHOW YOU HOW TO PUMP?
SLAM
SHE'S GOT A TEMPER ON HER, THAT ONE.
YES, SHE DOES. YOU'LL FIND IT'S GENERALLY DIRECTED INWARD.
"NOT THIS TIME, IT AIN'T."
"SHE'S NOT JUST PISSED AT YOU, WYLIE."

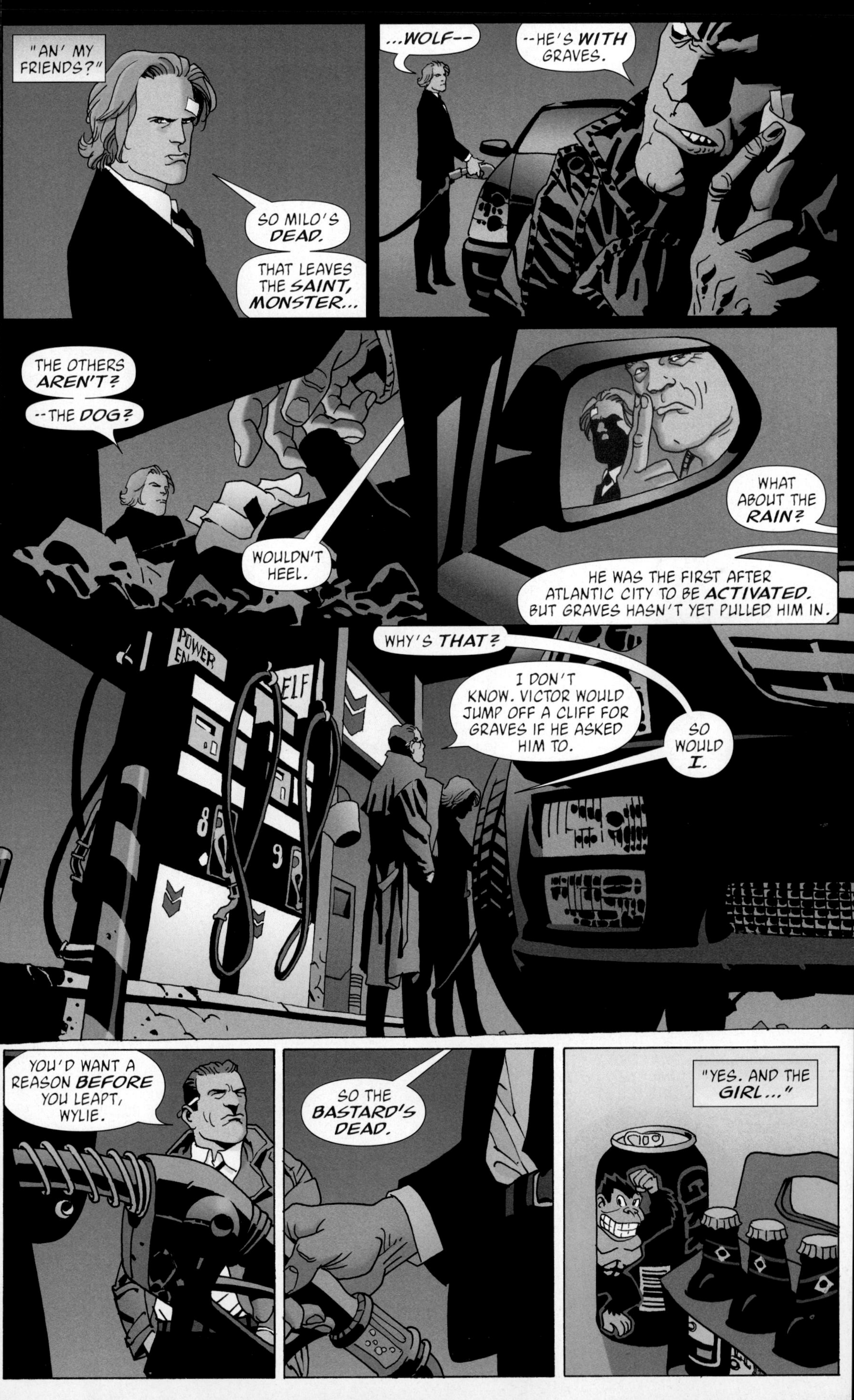
"AN' MY FRIENDS?"
SO MILO'S DEAD.
THAT LEAVES THE SAINT, MONSTER...
...WOLF--
--HE'S WITH GRAVES.
THE OTHERS AREN'T?
--THE DOG?
WOULDN'T HEEL.
WHAT ABOUT THE RAIN?
HE WAS THE FIRST AFTER ATLANTIC CITY TO BE ACTIVATED. BUT GRAVES HASN'T YET PULLED HIM IN.
WHY'S THAT?
I DON'T KNOW. VICTOR WOULD JUMP OFF A CLIFF FOR GRAVES IF HE ASKED HIM TO.
SO WOULD I.
YOU'D WANT A REASON BEFORE YOU LEAPT, WYLIE.
SO THE BASTARD'S DEAD.
"YES. AND THE GIRL..."

"...JUST SAY THE *WORD*."

AFTER ATLANTIC CITY, GRAVES HAD ME *HIDE* THE MINUTEMEN IN YOUR NEW LIVES.

WELL, ALL OF YOU EXCEPT THE *SAINT.* GRAVES WANTED TO HANDLE THAT ONE *HIMSELF.*

WHY'S THAT?

HE *NEVER* TOLD ME.

SOME THINGS GRAVES LIKES TO KEEP TO HIMSELF.

MORE LIKE THERE ARE *FEW* THINGS GRAVES *SHARES* WITH ANYBODY.

TRUE ENOUGH. LIKE THE WORD TO ACTIVATE YOU...IF ANYTHING...*UNFORTUNATE* HAD HAPPENED TO HIM, YOU'D *STILL* BE BURIED.

GRAVES HAD HIS REASONS.

SO WHAT'S THE *PLAN?*

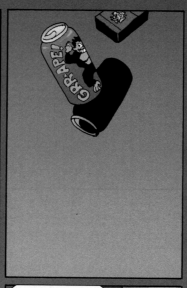

IN MY OPINION? FLAWED.

MAYBE EVEN BY *DESIGN.*

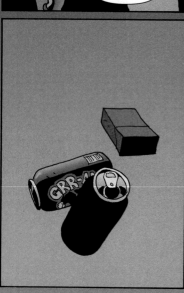

YOU BETTER THINK ABOUT WHAT YER SAYING, SHEPHERD.

GRAVES' PLAN IS TO PREVENT AUGUSTUS MEDICI FROM GRABBING *SOLE* CONTROL OF THE TRUST.

WHY THEN DOES EVERY MOVE WE MAKE HAND MEDICI *MORE* CONTROL?

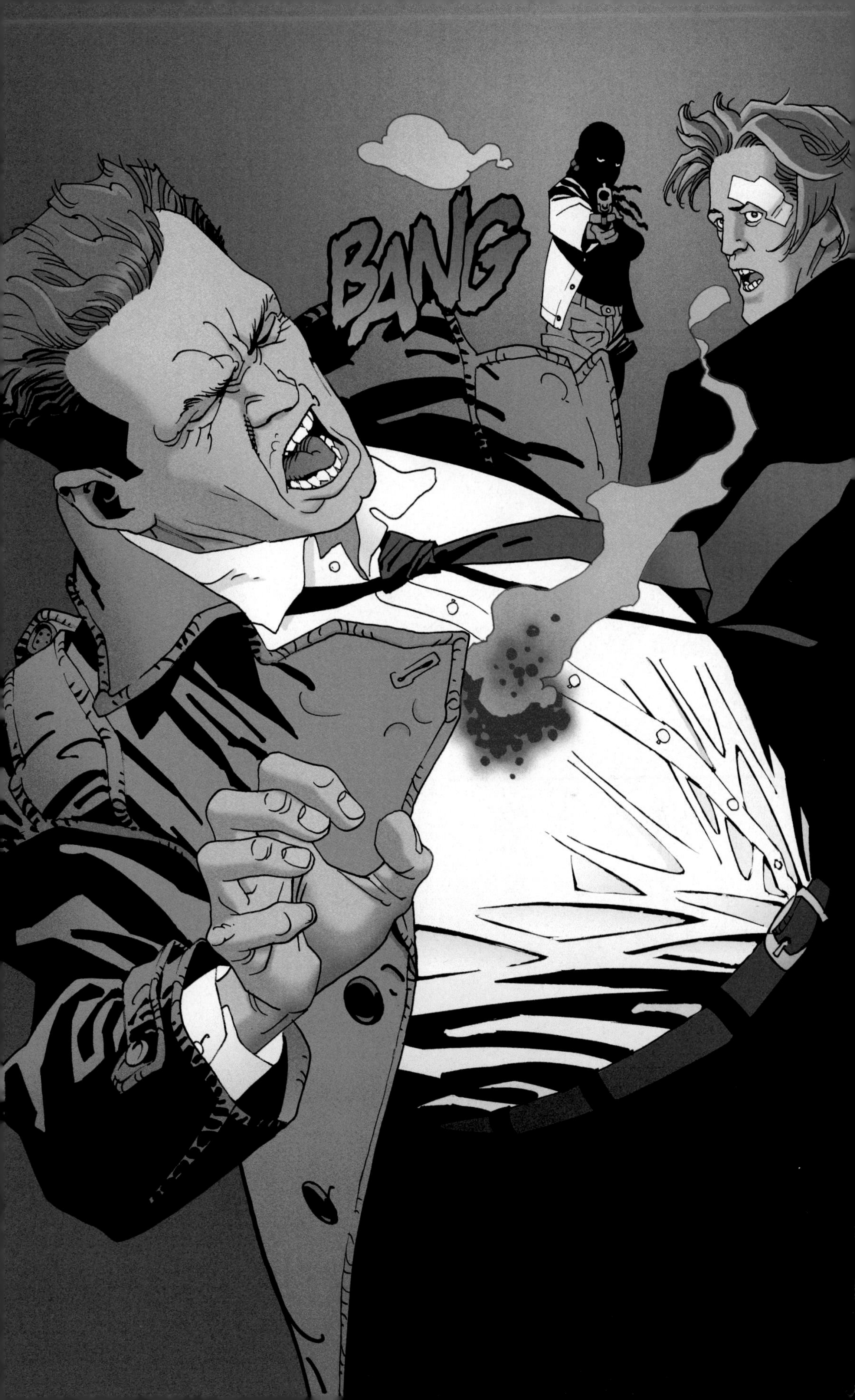
BANG

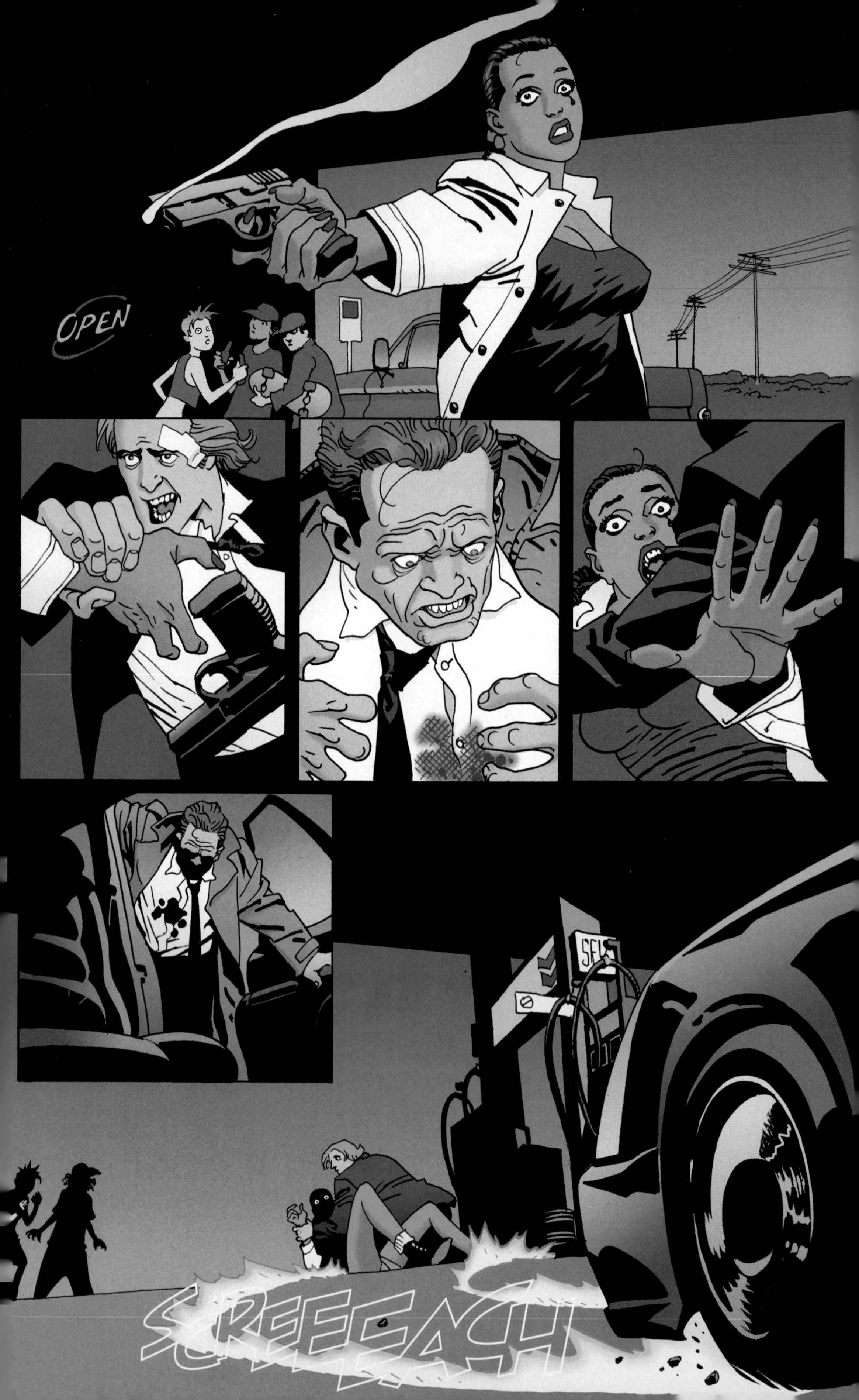
OPEN
SCREEEACH

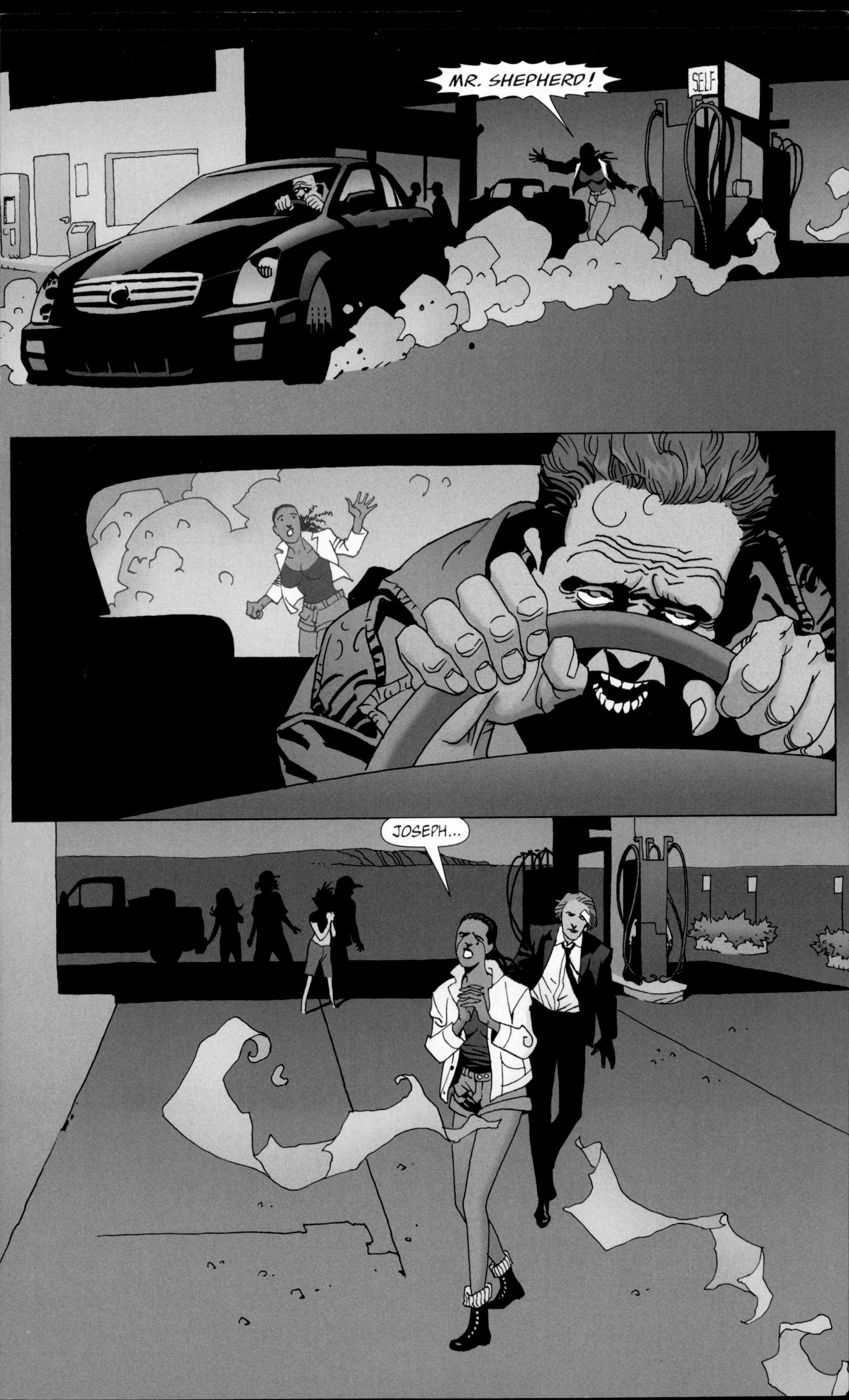
MR. SHEPHERD!
SELF
JOSEPH...

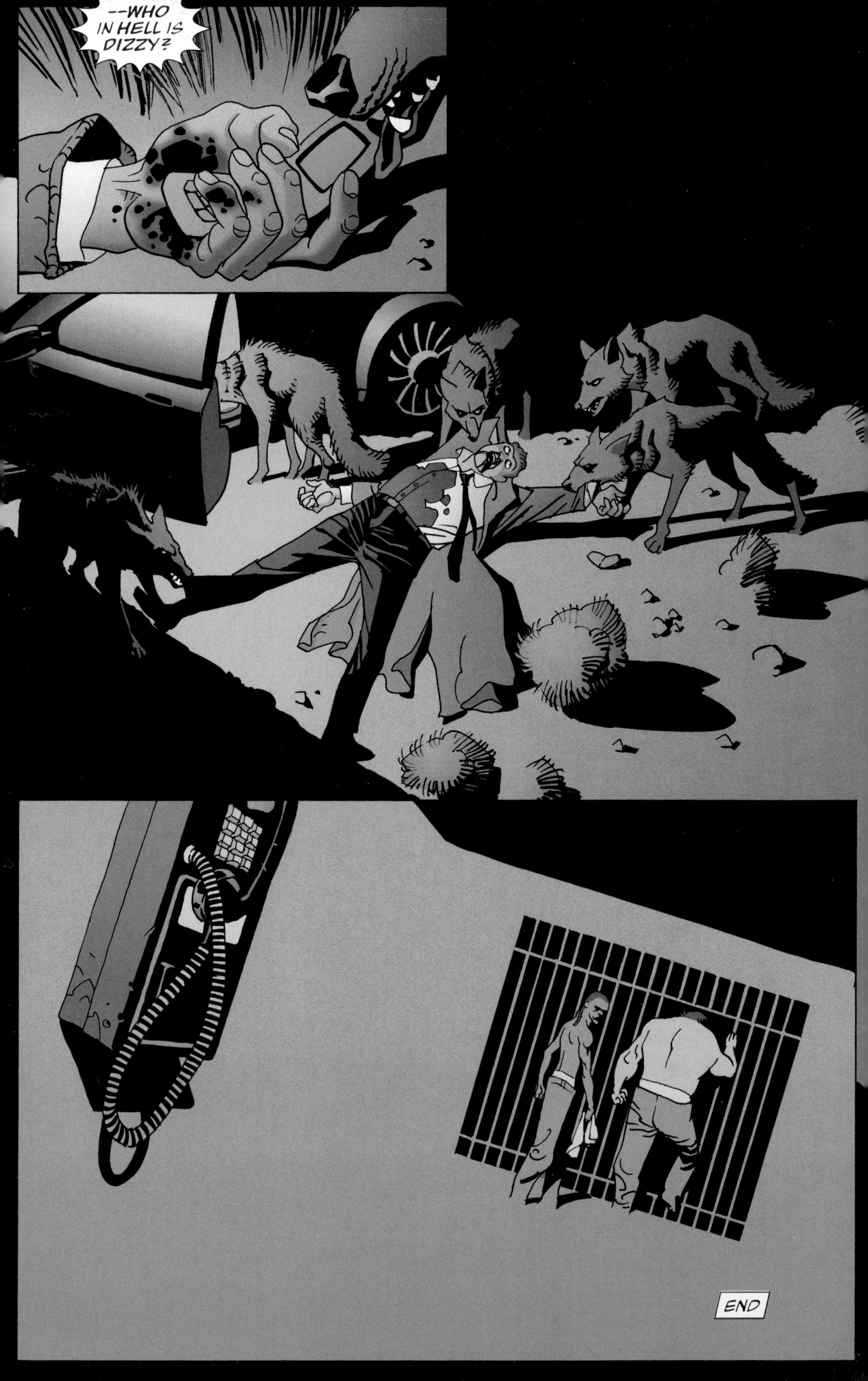
--WHO IN HELL IS DIZZY?
END

AVATARS

The Lost 100 BULLETS Video Game

During the original publication of 100 BULLETS, numerous offers for licensed products related to the series were considered by its creators and the Vertigo editorial team. One such proposal was a video game that would have featured new characters in its content. Though development on the project eventually stalled, Eduardo Risso did produce a series of model sheets for the characters, which are reproduced for the first time on the following pages.

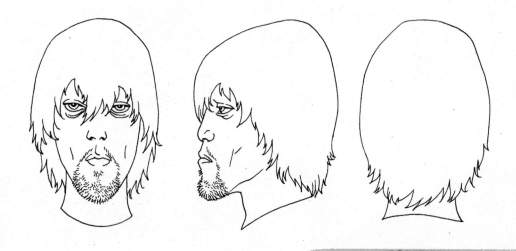

JONNY

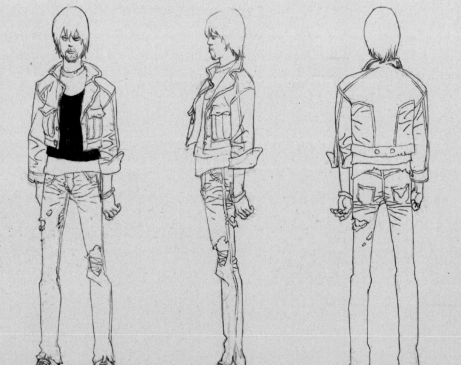

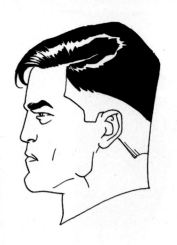

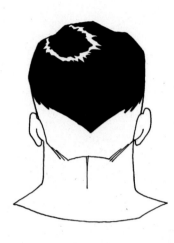

MARCUS

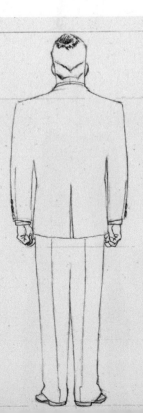

 WINTER

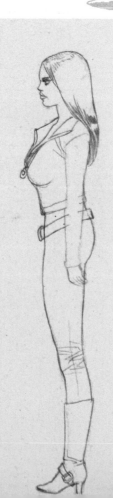
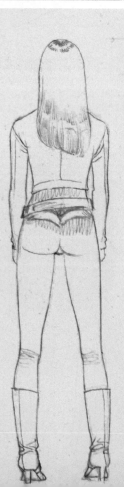

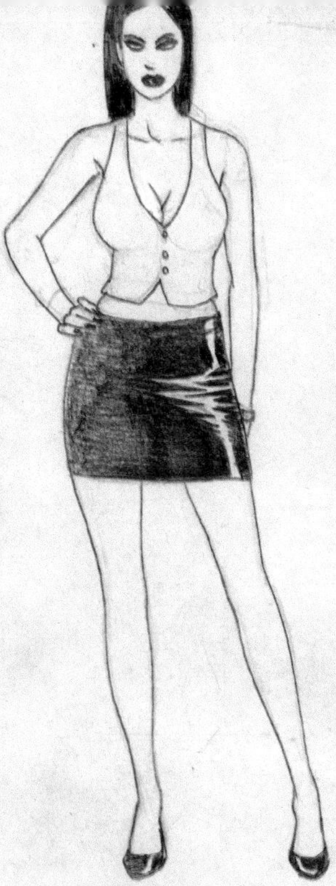

WINTER 1

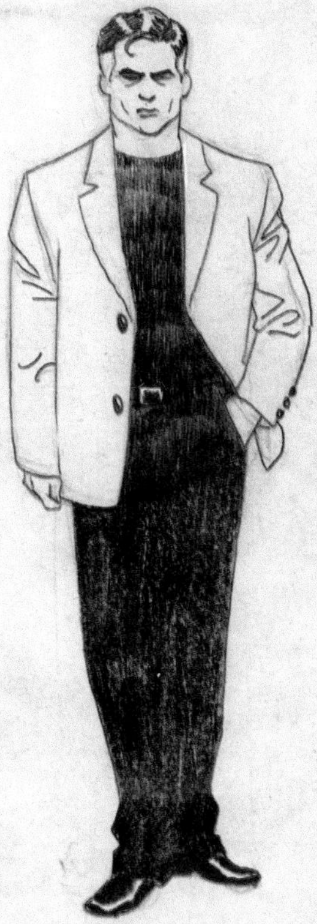

MARCUS 1

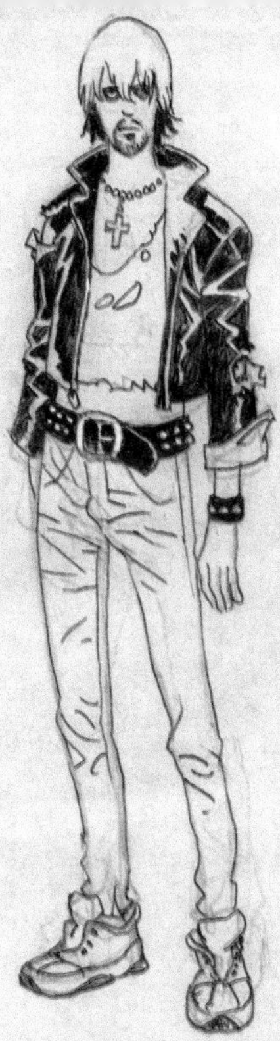

JONNY 1

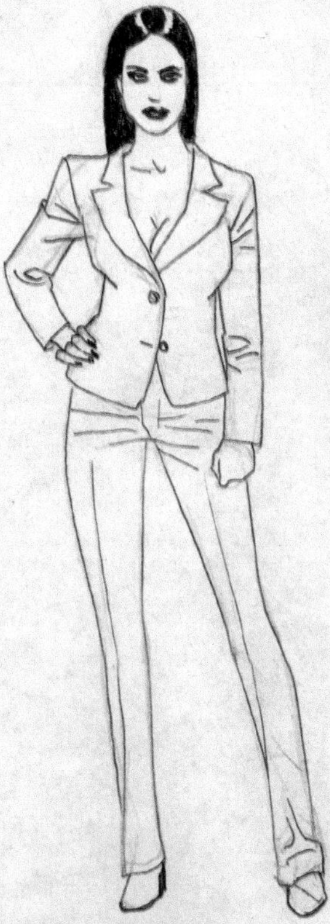

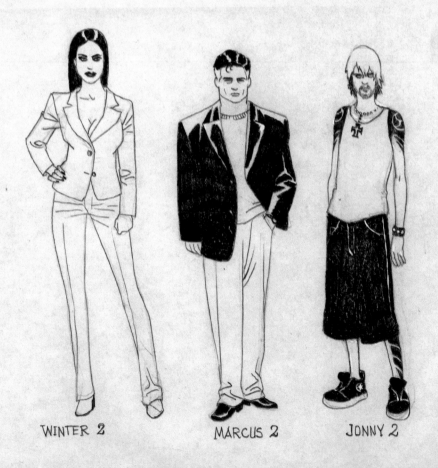

WINTER 2

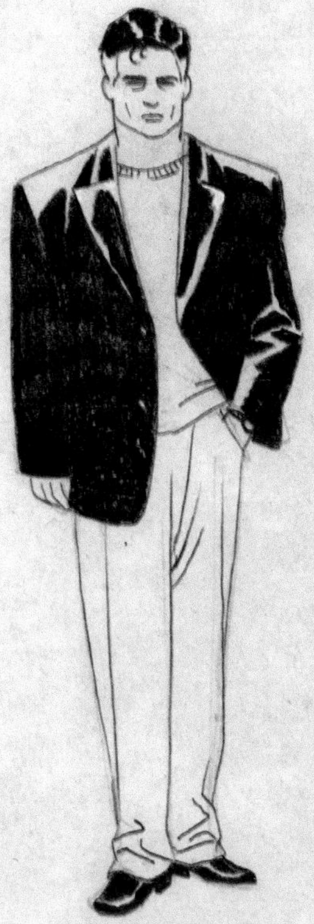

MARCUS 2

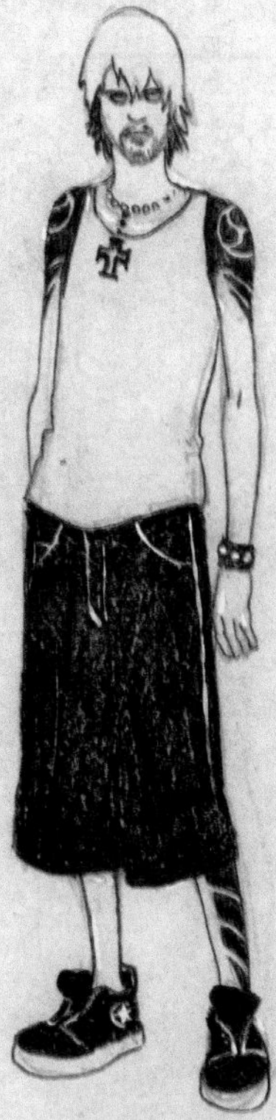

JONNY 2

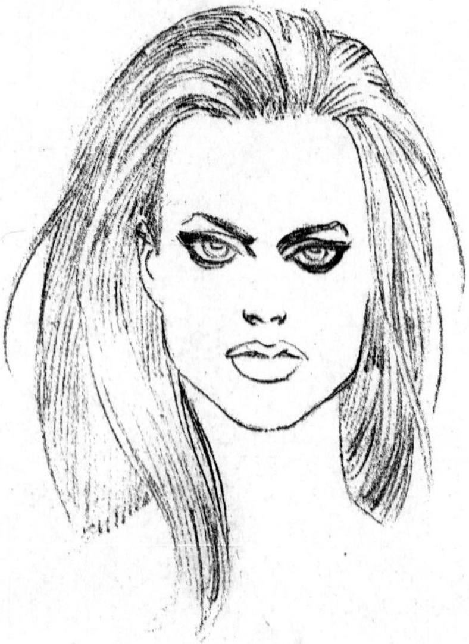
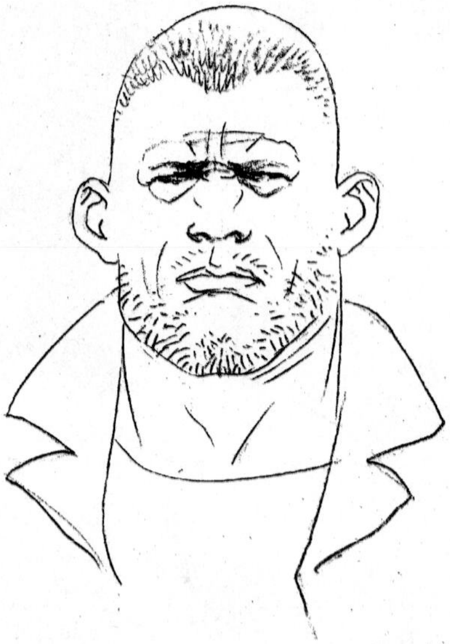
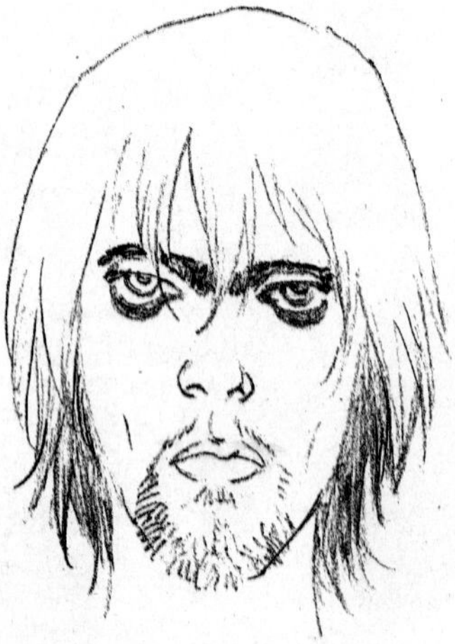